# LEONARD BERNSTEIN

*In full Mahlerian embrace, with the Vienna Philharmonic Orchestra in 1974.*
*"They had become the vessel for something holy."*

# LEONARD
# BERNSTEIN

# HUMPHREY
# BURTON

ff

*faber and faber*

LONDON · BOSTON

First published in 1994
by Faber and Faber Limited
3 Queen Square, London, WC1N 3AU

Printed in the USA
Book design by Marysarah Quinn

Humphrey Burton is hereby identified as author of this work
in accordance with Section 77 of the Copyright, Designs and
Patents Act 1988

A CIP record for this book is available from
the British Library

ISBN 0–571–16690–3

This book is dedicated to the memory of

# HUW WHELDON (1916–1986)

my mentor and friend at BBC Television for twenty years.
It was in his ebullient company that
I first met Leonard Bernstein.

# TABLE OF CONTENTS

22   Return to Show Business                                          219
23   Diversionary Tactics                                             228
24   From La Scala to Broadway                                        243
25   *Candide*                                                        257
26   *West Side Story*                                                265

PART FOUR—THE NEW YORK PHILHARMONIC ERA: 1957–1969
27   The Heir Apparent Takes Command                                  281
28   Music Director at the New York Philharmonic                      290
29   To Russia with Love                                              298
30   Last Years at Carnegie Hall                                      313
31   A Kaddish for a President                                        332
32   The Conquest of Vienna                                           352
33   End of an Era                                                    363

PART FIVE—COMING APART: 1969–1978
34   Radical Chic                                                     385
35   Professor Bernstein                                              410
36   Crises and Catastrophe                                           426

PART SIX—ANYTHING BUT TWILIGHT: 1978–1990
37   Toward *A Quiet Place*                                           451
38   Royal Progress                                                   471
39   The Living Legend                                                499
40   Final Days: August–October 1990                                 523

     *Principal Events in the Life of Leonard Bernstein*             535
     *Principal Compositions of Leonard Bernstein*                   539
     *Notes to Sources*                                              542
     *Selected Bibliography*                                         573
     *Author's Note*                                                 579
     *Permissions*                                                   582
     *Index*                                                         585

# FOREWORD

As I write it is three years to the day since Leonard Bernstein died. He was a man for whom music was a permanent, obsessional necessity, whether as composer, conductor, teacher, pianist or writer. On his passport under the heading "profession" he described himself in one word: "musician." His was a rich, full-blooded and sometimes tortured personal life, with music always at its heart. But a book for the general public cannot supply the music. I can only urge you to take time out to listen to the appropriate recordings or videos.

This biography, commenced in September of 1991, could easily have been twice the length of the present volume. I know, because my first draft ran even longer, to eighteen hundred and fifty typescript pages. To my incisive editors I make the appropriate acknowledgments at the end of the story, together with a chronology, a list of Bernstein's principal compositions and the names of several hundred people and organizations who have helped me with their recollections and researches. The source of each anecdote, letter, newspaper quotation, program note, magazine interview and television script is provided at the end of the book, together with a Selected Bibliography.

While I have had a great deal of help from members of Leonard Bernstein's family and former colleagues, I would like to emphasize that this is not an "authorized" biography. Nobody has told me what to say or prevented me from saying what I wanted. I must add that I am personally responsible for any error that may have passed through undetected.

My special thanks to the Leonard Bernstein Estate, who afforded me exclusive access to the Bernstein Archive, and permission to quote extensively from Bernstein's correspondence and other musical writings of which they are the copyright owners.

HUMPHREY BURTON
*New York, October 14, 1993*

# PROLOGUE
# THE FUNERAL

THE funeral was announced for 11 A.M., Tuesday, October 16, 1990, and when my wife and I arrived, ten minutes early, the room was already full.

The Bernstein apartment, Number 23, occupies the second floor of the northeast corner of the Dakota, the historic building on Central Park West where Leonard Bernstein had lived for nearly twenty years. For the occasion, the living room and the library had been transformed into a funeral parlor, and there was an overwhelming sense of heaviness in the air, for it was less than two days since Bernstein had died at the age of seventy-two. On the drinks bar in the hall, I saw a bowl full of yarmulkes. I put one on, feeling a bit of an impostor since I am not Jewish, and glanced nervously at the impassive looking Puritan housemaid, a painted, life-sized cutout which had been part of the entrance hall furniture since Felicia Bernstein, Lenny's wife, had bought it in a London shop. I could still remember transporting it back to America for her, wrapped up in brown paper, on a jumbo jet nearly twenty years ago.

In the living room the two grand pianos with their crowd of silver-framed photographs had been pushed against the wall and a huge coffin stood in state under the window looking out onto Seventy-third Street, with forty or fifty chairs laid out in a shallow curve around it. This was the room where in 1984 Bernstein had held the first piano rehearsal for his new recording of *West Side Story*—when I closed my eyes I could see Kiri Te Kanawa and Tatiana Troyanos singing "America," with Bernstein applauding them madly. Now he was gone, "cut down in the prime of his youth," as he had joked with his friend Mendy Wager the day before his death. Wager, who had known Bernstein since the forties, was seated near us, still reeling from the shock of having his friend die in his arms.

The lyricist and writer Adolph Green sat close by with his wife, Phyllis Newman. Green and his writing partner, Betty Comden, who was also present, had not written much together with Leonard since their hit musical *Wonderful*

*Town* back in the fifties, but they had remained very close friends and lived only a few blocks apart. Leonard, Betty said, remembered the words of their lyrics better than they did themselves. Another mourner, Sid Ramin, one of the orchestrators of *West Side Story,* had known Bernstein even longer—they had gone to the same school together in Roxbury, Massachusetts. Among other *West Side Story* collaborators present were Arthur Laurents, who wrote the book; Stephen Sondheim, who wrote the lyrics; Oliver Smith, the designer; Harold Prince and Roger Stevens, two of its producers; and Jerome Robbins, the choreographer who conceived and directed the show. They had all been through the fire with Bernstein.

Another strand in Bernstein's life was represented by Dan Gustin, the manager of the Berkshire Music Center at Tanglewood, the summer home of the Boston Symphony Orchestra. Tanglewood had been founded by the most important of Bernstein's mentors, the Russian-born conductor Serge Koussevitzky, and had always been an inspirational place for Bernstein. He'd conducted his very first concert there, in 1940, and the last, less than two months before his death. Gustin had watched him struggle through Beethoven's Seventh so short of breath that he could hardly make it off the stage.

Another of Bernstein's mentors, the composer Aaron Copland, almost ninety, was too old and frail to attend the funeral, but several composer friends were in attendance, among them Lukas Foss, who had shared the same professors with Bernstein at the Curtis Institute in Philadelphia. Both had risen from the ranks at Tanglewood to become associates to Koussevitzky and both had become professional conductors, pianists and composers. Foss had even been mentioned twenty years earlier as a possible successor to Bernstein as music director of the New York Philharmonic.

Hurrying from a rehearsal the violinist Isaac Stern squeezed in at the last moment. He had premiered Bernstein's *Serenade* half a lifetime previously, and they had fought many fights together on behalf of their beloved Israel. Other musical figures included Michael Tilson Thomas—of all Bernstein's conducting protégés perhaps the closest in spirit to Bernstein himself; John Mauceri, who had labored long to reestablish *Candide;* and the opera director and librettist Stephen Wadsworth, with whom Bernstein had written *A Quiet Place,* his only full-length opera. The room was crowded with other significant players in the drama of Bernstein's life: his lawyers and agents, orchestra managers and record producers, publishers and administrators—all friends who had devoted much of their professional lives to him.

Standing at the back were his last companion, a tall thirty-year-old Southerner named Mark Adams Taylor, and Aaron Stern, the educational theorist who had read mystic Persian poetry to Bernstein over dinner the night before his death.

Finally there were the members of Bernstein's family. Jennie, his mother, had flown from Boston, where she had lived for over seventy years. She was ninety-two, and in a wheelchair; her husband, Sam, like her a Russian immigrant, died in 1969. She was taking her son's death very hard. Her daughter Shirley was with her. Five years younger than Leonard, she had shared many of his successes in the 1940s. Burton Bernstein, Leonard's younger brother, and a staff writer at *The New Yorker,* was there, too, greeting well-wishers and murmuring to members of the family; his second wife, Jane, and his two grown-up children, Karen and Michael, were joined by Bernstein's three children: Nina, twenty-eight; Alexander, thirty-five; and Jamie, thirty-eight, supported by her husband, David Thomas, with their three-year-old daughter, Frankie, beside them.

Everything was orderly and quiet. It made a startling contrast with the jagged tensions of the funeral parlor scene Bernstein had imagined for the opening of his opera *A Quiet Place.* Rabbi Marshall Meyer led the prayers, his rich baritone voice throbbing with emotion. *"Eicha yashva vadad ha'ir . . ."* he began—"How desolate lay the city"—the opening lines of the Lamentations of Jeremiah, which Bernstein set for female voice in his first symphony.

After the prayers the family took turns testifying. Bernstein's mother and sister were too overwrought to speak before the gathering. In the end it was Burton who spoke first, describing how hard it was to accept that his brother, who had "always been larger than life, turned out to be smaller than death. Amazingly—just like that—he is no more." His sense of pained surprise seemed to put into words the sentiment so many had been groping for since the shocking news had been announced.

"Daddy swore to me once that he would never get cancer, and I believed him," Jamie said when it was her turn to speak. "It made sense; look at the guy's luck over the years. This is the luckiest man on the planet. Look at the way he drove. Did he ever have an accident? No. Look at the way he caroused, stayed up all night. Sure he got sick sometimes, and sometimes he got very, very depressed. But nothing a little Viennese adulation couldn't turn around. Nothing a little celestial Brahms couldn't patch up. What do you mean he's not going to snap out of it this time? Impossible!"

Alexander read a short poem by a Czech poet that his father, in his enthusiasm, had translated from the German version. Then Nina tried in vain to say something cogent through her tears. After final prayers and a last "Amen" there followed the touching of sleeves and the murmuring of condolences over coffee and cake. In the empty library the burnished mahogany coffin acted like a magnet, pulling back the mourners one by one to make silent farewells.

Twenty black stretch limousines were parked in the sunlit street waiting to take the mourners across the Brooklyn Bridge to the Green Wood Cemetery in Brooklyn. When the coffin emerged from the Dakota, the crowd that had gathered on the sidewalk opposite the apartment applauded it all the way to the waiting hearse. Even in death Bernstein was crowned with ovations. As it made its way across town, the funeral procession was given the kind of police escort—blaring sirens, blocked traffic, processional motorcade—that is normally accorded to heads of state: New York City was keenly aware that one of its princes had passed on. At a highway construction site in Brooklyn some of the workers looking down on the somber motorcade took off their yellow hard hats and called out, "Good-bye, Lenny."

From the cemetery one could see the Statue of Liberty through the trees and across the blue water. It was a brilliant autumn day. The mourners, adherents of different faiths and of none, united in the reciting of the Kaddish and in the symbolic shoveling of earth onto the coffin. Leonard Bernstein had been laid to his final rest deep on a green hillside next to his wife, Felicia, who had died twelve years before. And so ended the last chapter in the life of one of the most remarkable and flamboyant artists and towering musical presences of the twentieth century. In his music he had expressed the spirit of a restless, yearning, anxious age. Through his teaching, conducting and cultural leadership he had given inspiration to entire generations of musicians and music lovers. Early in his life he became America's best-known classical musician: by the time of his death, he truly belonged to the world.

# PART ONE

*The Little Old Man—aged two.*

# 1918–1943

# THE EDUCATION
# OF AN
# AMERICAN MUSICIAN

# 1.

# BEGINNINGS

*Sam Bernstein and Jennie Resnick.*
*Engagement photograph, 1917.*
COURTESY OF THE ESTATE OF LEONARD BERNSTEIN

*How could I know my son was going to grow up to*
*be Leonard Bernstein?*

—SAMUEL BERNSTEIN

H E was almost born on the kitchen floor. Jennie Bernstein, age twenty, had gone back to her parents' house in Lawrence, Massachusetts, for the final days of her pregnancy so that her mother could look after her. When she awoke with her labor pains at three in the morning on August 25, 1918, her mother telephoned the family doctor; before he could arrive, her water broke. Her mother slipped old newspapers under Jennie's straining body to help soak up the birthing fluids. Shortly afterward the doctor arrived and drove Jennie in the throes of labor to the Lawrence General Hospital, where around one in the afternoon (she remembered the clock on the delivery ward wall) she gave birth to a rather sickly baby boy.

He was registered as Louis Bernstein. The name Louis was a potentially confusing choice, since Jennie's recently deceased *zayde*—or grandfather—had been named Louis, as was her twelve-year-old brother. But Louis was the name

Pearl and Samuel Resnick, Jennie's parents, wanted, and so Louis he became, at least on the register. Jennie and her husband, Sam, preferred the name Leonard for a boy, and to avoid confusion with Jennie's brother they called him Leonard from the beginning—Leonard, Len, or Lenny. (It was not until sixteen years later that Bernstein, upon obtaining his driver's license, borrowed his mother's car and drove back to Lawrence from Boston to have his name officially changed to Leonard in the town registry.)

The origins of the name "Bernstein" are sometimes linked with the German noun *Bernstein,* which means "amber"—a translucent yellowish fossilized resin, used for ornaments and thought to possess magical properties. Leonard Bernstein would later call himself "Lenny Amber" when he needed a pseudonym for the popular piano transcriptions he published in his mid-twenties, and his business affairs would be organized within a company called Amberson Enterprises. There are several towns and villages named Bernstein in Germany and Austria (where the pronunciation is BernSTINE), but Bernstein's parents came from Jewish ghettos in northwestern Ukraine, where the last syllable is usually pronounced BernSTEEN. Sam insisted, however, on the mid-European style employed by the earlier immigrants.

Leonard Bernstein's mother was the first of his parents to immigrate to America. Born in 1898, she was only seven when her mother, Pearl Resnick, took her (with a brother, a sister, and a cousin) on the terrifying month-long journey from the town of Shepetovka through Poland and on to join her husband, Samuel, in America, to which he had immigrated three years before, saving money for his family to join him from his five-dollar-a-week wages. Traveling steerage in rough seas, Charna, as she was then known, broke her wrist on the nightmare voyage from Riga to New York. The immigration officer at Ellis Island gave her the name Jennie.

The Resnicks set up house in Lawrence, Massachusetts. A bright student, Jennie was quick at English, and impressed her teachers. Her father worked for the American Woolen Company, whose huge mills dominated a stretch of the Merrimack River. He was experienced in the craft of dyeing wool, but it was his wife who was the more skillful in business; when Jennie was a teenager her mother set up a provisions store in the first-floor front room of the Pine Street house to which the family moved. Money was short, however, and Jennie's schoolgirl hopes of studying to become a teacher were dashed; instead she was sent out to earn money at the mills, lying about her age by a couple of years to obtain employment. Working conditions were dreadful and poverty was endemic—and yet the Resnick household was in many ways a happy one. There were always good things to eat at the Passover *seders,* when Jennie's father would read from the Haggadah, and her sisters would dance and sing, and the house was filled with laughter. Although there were no professional musicians in the family, Jennie loved the sound of music. "There was always music in my mind, my ears. I used to wake up in the night and hear music."

Jennie's future husband, Samuel, born Shmuel Yosef in 1892, arrived in

America five years later. Like Jennie a firstborn child, he had grown up in an Orthodox (Hasidic) family in the village of Beresdiv, near Korets, a market town on the banks of the river Kovihyk halfway between Kiev and Rovno and only a few miles north of Shepetovka. The Bernstein family may well have been known to the Resnicks as a result of the exploits of Samuel's grandfather, Bezalel. Bezalel was a blacksmith of considerable renown among both Jews and Gentiles in that part of Russia. His strength was such that he could lift a carriage or *droshky* off the ground unaided, and remove one of its wheels before setting it down again. He was famed far and wide as a God-fearing, vodka-swigging craftsman. The father of four children, his tragic early death created a legend. He was awakened one night when his blacksmith's shop caught fire. Clothed only in a blanket, according to Burton Bernstein's account in *Family Matters,* he "raced out into the winter night, doused himself with a pail of water, and walked into the flaming shop." The crazed blacksmith emerged several minutes later "dragging his most prized possession—an iron tool chest, glowing red from the fire." Moments later he collapsed over the chest, dead from his efforts.

Perhaps in reaction to this gesture of recklessness, Samuel's father, Yudel, chose the narrow contemplative religious life of a scholar-rabbi, spending his days reading, praying, and discussing the Talmud. Samuel's mother, Dinah, born a Malamud, became an industrious small farmer, working the fields while her devout husband stayed at home or worshiped in the synagogue. Life in the Jewish pale of the Ukraine was hard and monotonous, and was taken up chiefly with plowing and cooking, milking and Sabbath candle-making, baking bread, collecting chickens' eggs, and raising a large family. Soon after his Bar Mitzvah, young Sam resolved to emigrate. The *shtetl* life was oppressive, anti-Semitism was rife, and there was a real danger that he would be conscripted into the Czar's army. In 1908, when he was sixteen, he walked out one night, dodging frontier guards as he hiked all the way across Poland to Danzig, where he took a ship first to Liverpool, and then to New York. He left against his parents' wishes, but with the active help of his recently emigrated uncle Herschel Malamud, who sent him cash from his new home in Hartford, Connecticut.

At the turn of the century fifty thousand Jews came to America from Russia each year. Samuel Bernstein began life in America at the bottom of the Jewish immigrant ladder, earning five dollars a week cleaning fish in New York's Fulton Street Market. After three years, in which he studied English (with less than complete success) and dreamed of a job as a post office worker, his uncle, who had changed his name to Harry Levy, rescued him from the squalor and the stench with the offer of a job in what was by now a full-fledged barbershop. Samuel did well, eventually accepting a position with better prospects at Frankel & Smith, suppliers of hair and beauty products to hairdressers in the Boston area.

By 1916, at the age of twenty-four, Samuel had enough put aside to think of starting a family. He had become an American citizen and the conventional stiff white collar he wore, as well as his three-piece suits and slicked down curly black hair, gave him the air of a young man on the way up: he was soon made assistant manager. When Samuel first met Jennie, a distant cousin of his Boston roommate, she was a good-looking young woman of eighteen and her mother was eager to get her married; marriage, in Pearl's eyes, was the duty of every good Jewish girl and would be an escape from the mill and the overcrowded living quarters at home. Sam had never entirely lost his thick accent, and that, combined with a dismally unfashionable sense of dress and his cheap dimestore glasses, made him a somewhat comical figure in Jennie's eyes. When he took the Sunday train out to Lawrence to court her he brought her gifts, which for months she steadfastly ignored. But the earnest Samuel persisted in his court-ship; what won Jennie over, she remembered, was his sense of humor. "He always had a good story to tell and he always knew a joke."

How romantic their meetings were is a matter of some debate in the Bernstein family. When Sam visited the Resnicks in their new house on Juniper Street (bought for a hundred dollars down, following an astute property sale by Pearl), Jennie's sister Dorothy would spy on the young couple by peeping down through the fire grate of the upstairs sitting room. She later intimated that Sam and Jennie were caught in a compromising position and hustled into marriage. A different family legend has it that another of Jennie's sisters agreed to slip a diamond engagement ring supplied by Sam onto Jennie's finger while she slept. Supposedly Jennie awoke believing she was officially engaged, and was im-pressed by Sam's stratagem. In any case, the couple were engaged to be married.

In the spring of 1917 America went to war and Sam Bernstein was drafted into the Army. The expected interruption to his wedding plans was forestalled when his nearsightedness led to an honorable discharge. A few months later, on Sunday October 28, Sam and Jennie were married. Jennie later claimed that her mother had organized an engagement party and set the wedding date before she herself knew what was happening. A small synagogue service was followed by a lavish feast at home.

Their honeymoon consisted of a single restless night at the Essex Hotel in downtown Boston. The noise of the trains at the nearby South Street Station kept them awake, and Jennie's mother had made her promise not to consum-mate the marriage because in the rush of preparations for the wedding, Pearl had forgotten to take her to the *mikvah,* the monthly ritual cleaning bath observed by Orthodox Jewish women. Next day the newlyweds moved into a tiny apartment in the Jewish working class district of Mattapan, where the marriage was consummated; ten months later, the first child was born.

Only just twenty, Jennie Bernstein was by her own account a nervous and inexperienced mother. She was frequently on the phone to the doctor for advice because Leonard as a baby was troubled, like his father, by asthma and a weak chest. He also inherited a vulnerable stomach and frequently suffered from colic. When the baby was strong enough to travel, Sam took his family back from Lawrence to Mattapan. In 1920 Sam was promoted to manager, permitting the young family to move to a more spacious apartment in Allston, near Cambridge. It was to be the first in a series of relocations, each testifying to Sam's swift upward mobility, even as the moves created an extra strain in their marriage. As Samuel Bernstein prospered, he deliberately separated himself, and his family, from his less successful in-laws. They were not invited to the Bernstein home, nor did they share Friday evenings together, even when the Resnicks moved to nearby Dorchester. Visits were discouraged. Perhaps it was the less rigorous orthodoxy of the easygoing Resnicks' faith that riled Sam Bernstein. Perhaps he was impatient with their passive acceptance of their relative poverty, in contrast to his own fierce determination to pull himself up to middle-class prosperity. In addition, he may have resented their relaxed lifestyle, in which food and song and dance played such an important role. When attending Hasidic celebrations, Sam would occasionally let himself go after a few glasses of schnapps, but he had inherited from his father a bookish frame of mind. In later years, his humor often became malapropian: he referred to "psychosemitic" illnesses, and insisted on cleaning out "cowwebs." His favorite line for wishing good luck was the injunction "keep your finger crossed."

As a relatively affluent young Jewish wife, Jennie, despite her schooling, did not work outside the home. Her life was centered on her family. As a consequence she did not meet many people or have many friends, and her innate high spirits were sadly dampened by her circumstances. Twice in Leonard's infancy Jennie left Sam to return to her mother in Lawrence. The causes remain obscure; they were possibly connected with the household budget—Sam was tight-fisted—or, just as possibly, with Sam's black moods and his growing dislike of the Resnicks. But Jennie's mother eventually persuaded her to return to the marriage fold, the first time bearing a new set of bed linens as a peace offering. Perhaps the craving to be loved that Leonard exhibited throughout his life had its origins in his separation from his father as an infant. Yet Leonard was "spoiled rotten"; according to Jennie everybody loved him. When the Bernsteins spent time in the house of friends at Revere Beach, two daughters of the family enjoyed pushing Leonard's baby carriage around on Sundays. They called him the Little Old Man, because he was able to talk so fluently when he was only a year and a half old.

Even as a toddler Leonard was tremendously drawn to music. The friends in Revere had a piano in the living room, and Leonard is still remembered for banging away on the door outside, shouting "Moynik, moynik"—music, music. The Bernstein household was without a piano, but the Victrola inherited from Jennie's father was a regular source of delight for Leonard. "He was too short to reach for the wind-up," Jennie recalled. "He'd cry a lot, the tears streaming down his face. Then he'd say 'moynik, moynik!' and I'd turn on the Victrola and play him a record and he would stop crying, like on a dime." Their seventy-eights included recordings of Jewish cantors and pop songs like "Oh by Jingo" (adored by Bernstein), as well as a much-requested record featuring Galli-Curci, one of the great lyric coloratura voices of the 1920s and 1930s.

Jennie called her son her "windowsill pianist" because he would sit in the front room listening to the Victrola and rhythmically tapping music as he watched the passers-by. But neither the family nor his kindergarten teachers noticed any special talent in him, and nothing was done to introduce him to the world of serious music. It remained an exciting mystery unconnected with daily life. Nor did the teachers in his first school, the William Lloyd Garrison School in Roxbury, which he attended from age six to eleven, spot the potential genius in him. Bernstein would later remember only that he was taught—"by a glorious teacher named Miss Donnelly, with whom I was deeply in love"—a simple way to read music, using a rudimentary system of movable "doh" known as solfège, at which he was the "best in the class." Bernstein recalled his teachers at the William Lloyd Garrison School with great affection. "Everything they taught me was fun to learn, whether history or spelling, whether such fun things as drawing with crayons or such boring things as penmanship. They simply loved to teach and we responded in kind. For me, of course, the most shining hours were the *singing* hours; Mrs. Fitzgerald, my fifth-grade home room teacher, taught us many dozens of songs . . . God bless those lovely ladies; there was something special about them, maybe their being good old-fashioned Boston Catholics."

Radio proved to be the prime instrument of young Bernstein's awakening musicality. Bernstein's childhood coincided with the rise of the age of broadcasting. Even in old age he could fondly describe the tuning of the three dials of an Atwater Kent heterodyne receiver for an afternoon of listening. "With any luck you finally got the broadcast. There was a lot of static and a lot of dirty noise, but you could sort of hear Rudy Vallee (in the late twenties) and Jack Benny (in the early thirties)." With the quality of radio reception improving year by year, Leonard spent countless hours polishing his renditions of popular songs. All his life he could rattle off the names and sing the commercial jingles of a dozen radio musical programs he had followed in his childhood.

Bernstein grew up on a rich diet of popular music, seasoned on the weekends by music heard at the synagogue. He later cited religious music as the biggest influence on him in childhood. The family attended Temple Mishkan Tefila (the Dwelling of Prayer) for Friday evening Sabbath services where the rabbi was H. H. Rubenovitz. Like many other aspiring middle-class Jewish families, Samuel Bernstein had decided that the Orthodox form of worship was too confining. "We were of the Conservative persuasion," Leonard would later remember, "which allowed for an organ and a choir in a hidden choir loft, and when they let rip I used to go mad! We had a fabulous cantor [Isadore Glickstein] who was a great musician and a beautiful man, very tall, very majestic. He would begin to sing the ancient tunes—they are not exactly melodies, because they are not really written down; they're traditional, handed down orally—and he had a tenor voice of such sweetness and such richness—with a dark baritonal quality, I now realize; I didn't know a tenor from a baritone in those days—and then the organ would start and then the choir would begin with its colors, and I just began to get crazed with the sound of choral music."

The man responsible for the music at Temple Mishkan Tefila was Solomon G. Braslavsky, who was both organist and choirmaster. Born in Russia and trained in Vienna, he was much beloved by his Boston congregation. He was a composer himself, but the music performed was mostly that of classical composers such as Schubert, Mendelssohn and Verdi, to which Braslavsky fitted appropriate Hebrew texts. Braslavsky also created a festive arrangement of the hymn "Adon Olom" ("Lord of the World"), which was sung on important Jewish occasions such as the Day of Atonement. According to Bernstein, it was of a complexity "not to be believed. Each stanza was a setting with organ interlude and great introductions. The basses would enter alone and then the sopranos— this is when I discovered that there was such a thing as counterpoint: great obbligatos floating from on high. 'Arrangement' is too small a word. It was a great composition. I knew every note of it because I heard it every year: it was like an opera."

As Sam's career flourished at Frankel & Smith's, he moved his family from Allston to Revere, a suburb farther north of Boston. It was here that arguments led to the family's second separation. Eventually a reconciliation was effected, and shortly afterward the family moved to Mattapan, where, on October 3, 1923, Jennie gave birth to a baby girl, whom the couple named Shirley Anne (after the heroine of Jennie's favorite book, *Anne of Green Gables*). Shirley's birth coincided with what proved to be the major career decision in Sam Bernstein's professional life. He gave in his notice and set up his own beauty supply business. At the age of thirty, with a wife and two children to support, his decision required both courage and vision, but he was lucky with his timing: the popularity of the silent film star Irene Castle had inspired women all over America to bob their hair in imitation. In the beginning, much of his business came from the making and selling of wigs to Orthodox Jewish women, who were required to wear a *shaytl*—a wig endowed with religious significance. (Jennie's youngest sister, Dorothy, was said to have been an exceptionally skilled wig-maker. Another sister, Bertha, also worked at the warehouse; it was a way for Sam to help the Resnicks.) But Sam's subsequent success—his firm became the largest supplier of beauty parlor goods in New England—was largely due to his astute acquisition, in 1927, of the franchise for the Frederics permanent wave machine, which proved exceptionally popular.

As the Samuel Bernstein Hair Company expanded, the pace at which the family rented homes grew faster. From Mattapan they moved to the pleasant suburb of Roxbury, where they changed residences five times in as many years. One Roxbury apartment, in Crawford Street, was never actually slept in by the Bernsteins. The move had taken place during the day; when Sam came home from his office he saw a cockroach on the wall and promptly walked out, never to return. Sam's pathological dislike of dirt can be traced back to the squalor of his Atlantic crossing in steerage. He was not an easy man to live with. Nor, Jennie claimed, would he lift a finger to do anything around the house himself. "It all had to be ticketyboo, 100 percent."

There is little information on Leonard's early childhood. In a photograph of him in an attractive sailor suit at age four or five, he looks handsome and demure in a Buster Brown haircut, with a center parting and a fringe. But he was chronically wheezy from asthma. "Every time he had an attack we thought he was going to die. I would be up all night with steam kettles and hot towels helping him to breathe," his mother recalled. He developed a lifelong allergy to dust, too. Shirley traces it back to an incident that occurred when Leonard was about nine. "He wanted to see how you do things, genitally. So who better to try it out on than me? And evidently I went screaming to my mother that 'Lenny tried to put his jibbick in my wo-wo' and my mother went after him with a broom and he scuttled under a bed—a high kind of iron bed—way into a corner where she couldn't get at him with the broom. And he sat under that bed for hours having all these dust whorls roll around him and he always said that's where he got his dust allergy: it was so traumatic inhaling all that dust." Nonetheless, it is as likely that Bernstein's allergy was congenital, given his asthma and chronic illness.

Among the personalities in the Bernstein family, none was more eccentric than Sam's younger sister Clara—"Crazy Clara" as the family called her—who followed Sam to America in 1911. In later years she would descend on the family's summer house loaded down with all the apparatus of a vegetarian food faddist. She was also a nudist sun-worshiper, a fervent believer in exercise, and —most importantly—a great music lover. She had a piercing voice; with proper training, Bernstein later claimed, she might have become a Wagnerian soprano. Clara owned a bridal shop in Brooklyn. Her first husband died in the flu epidemic of 1918. Her second husband, who ran a chicken farm outside Boston, literally drove her mad. For a while she became virtually blind, consumptive, and diabetic—hence the preoccupation with nutrition after her miraculous recovery. She divorced her husband and returned to Brooklyn, where she eventually married a third time and reestablished her bridal business. When she moved, Clara gave a sofa and an upright piano to Leonard's parents. "The piano, a handsome mahogany affair, with a third pedal for the mandoline effect, was in the hall for ages because no one knew where to put it and we had to make room for the sofa, which my parents believed they needed more desperately than an upright piano. I remember touching this thing the day it arrived, just stroking it and going mad. I knew, from that moment to this, that music was 'it.' There was no question in my mind that my life was to be about music."

With the arrival of Aunt Clara's piano, ten-year-old Leonard's general health improved, he became self-confident, and almost overnight he shot up to become the tallest boy on the block. His first step in learning to play the piano was to imitate the sounds he had been hearing on the radio. The first tune he played was "Goodnight Sweetheart." "I picked it out on the piano—that was easy. I knew it had to have a fox-trot accompaniment. But I didn't know what notes to play in the left hand so I would just play anything . . . loudly and triumphantly, to the point where my father would scream from the bedroom, 'Stop that noise, I can't sleep.' But I was in heaven!"

Leonard quickly asked for piano lessons. His first teacher, a local girl, was "the dark, unbelievably beautiful and exotic-looking Frieda Karp," who came to the house once a week and gave him a lesson for a dollar. "After a couple of weeks," Bernstein remembered, "I had learned to read so quickly—I was very fast—that Frieda Karp had to bring me harder stuff. The first memorable piece I played with her was 'Mountain Belle Schottische.' . . . After less than a year she was forced to bring Chopin and Bach preludes and Chopin nocturnes. . . . With the E flat Nocturne I went mad and my mother used to stand there crying." One of the books from which Leonard studied was a green-covered miscellany entitled *100 Pieces the Whole World Loves,* which included piano works by Bach, Chopin and Tchaikovsky, as well as arrangements of the grand march from *Norma,* the triumphal march from *Aida,* the "Ave Maria" of Schubert, Mendelssohn's "Spring Song" and Elgar's "Salut d'Amour." It also introduced Bernstein to the joys of Spanish music, through the "Aragonaise" from *Le Cid.* The "green book" would always remain a part of his musical life. In his final years a much-thumbed copy stood on his piano wherever he traveled.

Bernstein was swift to grasp how harmony worked so that he could supply the correct chords for Rudy Vallee's "Goodnight Sweetheart," "Blue Skies" and the other favorites he had learned from the radio. From a piece called "Phantasie Orientale" he discovered how to bend notes and add grace note embellishments. The Chopin mazurkas he began to explore inspired him to improvise in ever more imaginative ways. By the age of eleven he had learned the rudiments of form, melody and harmony, "but I hadn't yet discovered the wonders of counterpoint because Miss Karp bought me Bach preludes, but not the fugues; they were considered too difficult."

Among the happiest events of Leonard's childhood were the visits the family made to his great-uncle Harry and great-aunt Polly in Hartford, Connecticut. By the late twenties Sam had bought his first motor car, a Ford. His driving skills were mediocre—a trait his son inherited—and when he was lost he developed a disconcerting inability to make turns in any direction except right. But the visits to Hartford were well worth the day-long drive because of the warm reception the family was given. "They'd always have a big table of food," Jennie remembered, "and they'd invite all the family cousins by the dozens, nieces and nephews, too." The family get-togethers provided Leonard with a vision of what home life could be like, echoing the intimate Jewish life of his maternal grandparents in Russia. They became a model for the family parties he would organize at Thanksgiving and Passover once he became a father. His Hartford relatives seemed to him to be the healthiest, least neurotic people he knew; the tensions of home life in Roxbury were replaced by warmth and laughter, food, music and affection. Thanks to Harry Levy's expensive wind-up Victrola phonograph, Leonard fell in love with the voice of Rosa Ponselle singing the "Suicidio" aria from *La Gioconda,* as well as Billy Rose's comedy song—" 'Barney Google' with the Goo, Goo, Googly Eyes," as Bernstein called it. He made no distinction between serious classical and low-brow popular music: "I loved all music," he said, "and I liked to dance." This was the era of novelty numbers like "Kitten on the Keys" by Zez Confrey. "Dancing Tambourine" was another. "I heard it on a record and I went crazy. All the way home in the car back to Boston I remember being obsessed by this number, and I went over and over it in my mind and I couldn't wait until we got back to run to the piano to try it out. But it was in the car that I figured it out; I realized that 'Dancing Tambourine' was nothing more or less than a Sousa march made into a novelty piece." His understanding of the mechanics of musical composition already marked him out from other talented child performers.

Soon Bernstein needed a better teacher. "This boy is gifted," Frieda Karp told Jennie. "I can't keep up with him anymore."

"I was reading a Chopin ballade which she could barely play herself," Bernstein recalled. "I not only read it and played it—badly, with the pedal down the whole time and really banging on the keys—but I was having the best time of my life." Frieda Karp recommended to Leonard's parents that they find a replacement at the New England Conservatory of Music in Boston. There, Leonard himself chose as his instructor a teacher named Susan Williams. "I was now thirteen, I recall, and I began to study Liszt's Hungarian Rhapsodies. I had no idea one could play things like that—beyond my wildest dreams of complexity! It came to me like drinking water." There was only one snag. Miss Williams charged three dollars an hour. "All hell broke loose between Sam and me. He saw that things were getting serious and he was not going to spend three dollars a lesson. So the fights began."

# FAMILY LIFE

*The young Leonard Bernstein and his sister Shirley*
*with their parents, 1933.*
COURTESY OF THE ESTATE OF LEONARD BERNSTEIN

*Every happy family is alike; every unhappy family is*
*unhappy in its own way.*

— LEO TOLSTOY, *Anna Karenina*

I N 1929, at the end of his sixth-grade year, Leonard won admission to the prestigious three-hundred-year-old Boston Latin School. Entrance was based strictly on merit, and was open to students from all backgrounds. Bernstein recalled vividly how he and his friend Sammy Kostic learned of their acceptance to the school. "It was the biggest trip I had ever taken by myself. . . . We stood in a long, long line of applicants with our hearts pounding and finally showed our report cards to the person at the desk, who stamped them 'exempt.' We didn't know what to make of that word: we thought it meant 'out' because exempt has a sort of 'ex'-out quality about it (and as I was to learn shortly thereafter the 'ex' prefix in Latin means outward-going) but what it actually did mean was 'exempt from further testing.' In other words it meant admitted, and when we found that out we just jumped up and down and danced."

Boston Latin was founded in 1635, a year before Harvard University. Distinguished pupils over the centuries have included Samuel Adams, Ralph Waldo Emerson, George Santayana, Bernard Berenson and Theodore H. White. The school was to have a profound influence on Bernstein, introducing him to a broad range of subjects. In addition to six years of Latin, the school required four years of French, as well as either Greek or German. Bernstein chose German and ever afterward lamented his lack of Greek; he was also introduced to physics and history. One of his teachers, Philip Marson, became the first of several father figures whom Bernstein adopted as counterweights to his influential but much-feared real father. Marson awakened in him a love for the English language, and more. "He taught me something unique, incomparable, invaluable in education, far beyond the teaching of tetrameter or dangling participles or even the glories of English verse: he taught me how to learn." Marson remembered Bernstein "lapping up everything I could dish out in drama and poetry as [he] sat, all attention, in the first seat of the second row of Room 235."

The Bernsteins' Roxbury home was located many miles from the school. "I had to get up very early in the morning and take a series of elevated trains and street cars that went 'clang, clang, clang' on tracks in the street." In the evenings of his first two years at Boston Latin he hurried back to Roxbury to attend the Hebrew school associated with his synagogue; he "graduated" as an honor student after five years of study in 1931. Around 5 P.M., Bernstein recalled, "one could play a game of baseball on the back lot." He was considered a good first baseman. "But at five-thirty I would say, 'I'm sorry, kids, I have to go!' I would be assailed by cries, derisive hoots, taunting 'fruit, fruit, sissy!'—unbelievable torture—and I would go home and sit at the piano. I had my homework, and my Hebrew homework. . . ."

At the age of twelve, Bernstein met Sid Ramin, a boy from the neighborhood who would become a lifelong friend. Five months younger than Leonard, Sid had been a grade behind at the Garrison Grammar School and they experienced some of the peculiar rites of passage of adolescence together: Ramin remembers roaming around Franklin Park, across the road from the Mishkan Tefila Temple, on the lookout for discarded contraceptives. The boys had first met at the Schuyler Street house of Eddie Ryack, a mutual friend. Leonard was in the Ryack parlor one afternoon vainly trying to teach Eddie to play "Goodnight Sweetheart" on the piano. After watching for a few minutes Sid interrupted. "Mind if I try?" He proceeded to play the piece perfectly. "Well, you're the fellow I should be teaching!" exclaimed Leonard. Bernstein had invented his own method for the teaching of harmony and Ramin was prepared to pay a dollar an hour to take lessons from him. He became Bernstein's first music student.

It was not only music that Sid and Lenny explored: they also conducted perilous chemical experiments in the loft of the Bernstein apartment on Pleasanton Street. Bernstein's restless curiosity manifested itself in many ways. All his life he loved taking things apart—clocks, cigarette lighters, fountain pens, and gramophones—trying to figure out how they worked and fitted together. It was not unlike his fascination with the structure of "Dancing Tambourine." With mechanical objects, however, he had more success taking them apart than in reassembling them.

LEONARD'S vivid imagination and love of words led him to invent, with Eddie Ryack, an imaginary language called "Rybernian," named after the imaginary state called Rybernia (a composite of the two boys' last names). The language itself was originally based on a cruel mimicry of the speech defects of Sonny, a neighborhood kid, who had a harelip. Rybernian depended for its vocabulary on "anybody who talked funny." One source was the Polish-born wife of Sam Bernstein's cousin Abraham Miller. She referred to her husband, Abe, as "Ape." "Ape" became an important Rybernianism, whether used as proper, common or adjectival noun, and "Dear Ape" can be found throughout the family correspondence. The very approximate English of East European immigrants was often incorporated. When telling the time, "almost half-past seven" might come out as "smose snapas seven" and the prefix "smose snapas" was used to indicate RST, or Rybernian Standard Time. Another problem for newcomers to English was the past tense. "How you gonna *did* it?" was a familiar Rybernian question. Yiddish influences abound, together with odd, German-looking umlauts such as "Laudü" for Lenny. Laudü degenerated into the more obvious "Lennuhtt," which is "Leonard" as it might be spoken by someone with a harelip or a major sinus problem. Shirley Bernstein, a Rybernian mascot from the age of five onward, was originally known as "Mascodü," which evolved into the incomprehensible "Suyanmü" before settling down, again more obviously, as "Hilee." Burton Bernstein's name, "Baudümü," was never altered. A reflection of the unusual closeness of the three Bernstein children, this private language flourished long past childhood and is spoken at family gatherings to this day by Shirley and Burton, as well as by Leonard's and Burton's children and their close friends.

SAM Bernstein's income reached its peak in the early 1930s. Since he owned no stocks, he was one of the few businessmen who did not suffer from the Wall Street crash of 1929 and, fortunately for him, New England women continued to demand permanent waves despite the Depression. He eventually ran a staff of fifty at the Samuel Bernstein Hair Company: his sales representatives covered all of New England. He was generous to less fortunate business customers, extending credit in hard times, but he had enough cash to buy a new car, and in 1931 he hired an architect to design a big new family house.

Despite their financial security, anger and bitter arguments often poisoned the family atmosphere, leaving a permanent scar on Leonard's psyche. One dramatic incident occurred in the late fall of 1931, on a Tuesday morning—

banking day at Shirley's school. "We were all having breakfast around the breakfast table," Shirley remembered, "and I asked my mother for a quarter for banking day. . . . She was in her dressing gown and she turned to my father and said, 'Sam, give her a quarter.' A perfectly normal thing to say. He was in his business suit ready to go. God knows what went on the night before, but he flew into a rage for no apparent reason. She was asking for money again; I guess that was at the base of it. . . . [Jennie regularly remitted Sam's dollars to her less fortunate family.] On the surface it was nothing. And he flew into such a rage, the only time I saw him get almost physical. In those days we had bottles of milk, not cartons . . . and he picked up the bottle as if to hit her. . . . She was very pregnant [with her son Burton, born in January 1932] . . . and she flew into what was to be Burtie's room and slammed the door and Lenny ran and spread-eagled himself against the door, against his father, and I ran scream- ing to the other end of the house, with my hands over my ears. It was horrible . . . the worst scene I remember.

"My mother and father were mismated, mismatched, both interesting and good people who should never have been married. . . . They were never in love with each other, unfortunately. And my father was a basically melancholic man who needed a lot of love and wasn't getting it from his marriage. If he was feeling loved he was the most generous, good-hearted, sweetest man in the world. If he was feeling unloved, he got very mean—to my mother, not to the kids. . . . He was a manic-depressive type, so when he was with his rabbis celebrating the Sabbath, dancing and singing, he was an ecstatic Hasid. But he could also be pacing the floor for no apparent reason in a terrible melancholy. And Lenny caught that, and so did I, in our personalities." Meanwhile, Jennie poured all her frustrated love into her feelings for her eldest child.

Concerts, excursions to the theater or the movies rarely played a part in the everyday life of the Bernsteins. Sam's idea of an evening's entertainment after the family supper, which coincided with Lowell Thomas hosting the radio news from 6:45 to 7 P.M., was to spend a couple of hours reading in his favorite chair in the living room. Although he had shelves of books, his scholarship was confined to the Talmud, the learned commentary on the five books of Moses known as the Torah. For Jews this can be a lifetime study. In later years Leonard paid graceful homage to his father, publicly calling him a lovely man and a great Hebrew scholar with an incredible respect for the love of learning. "He has one fault only: whenever he has to make a speech . . . he always resorts for his text to the Bible or the Talmud. At his knee I learned my lesson well—I'm a chip off the old Tanach." But at age twelve and thirteen, Bernstein had a darker view of his father. He confessed to Sid Ramin how much he envied the happy family atmosphere at Sid's home and claimed to hate his father, both because he treated his mother so badly (an accusation that Jennie herself stoutly denied) and because for a time he actively tried to stop Leonard from pursuing his musical training.

The trouble between Leonard and his father came to a head when Leonard switched music teachers to Miss Susan Williams. Since Sam was making a handsome income, his objection to paying three dollars a lesson was a matter of principle rather than cash flow: he did not want his son to take music seriously. Later in life Bernstein recognized that his father had been trying to protect him, but it was difficult to see the love behind his father's attitude when at the time his very happiness seemed to be at stake. "His concept of a professional musician, which he'd brought with him from the Russian ghetto, was of a *klezmer,* which is little better than a beggar, a guy with a clarinet or a violin going from town to town to play for a few kopecks at weddings and bar mitzvahs. He saw my future playing piano in a palm court trio."

Leonard, stubborn as his father and crazy about music, was determined to raise the money he needed on his own initiative. He had no time to deliver newspapers, so he turned to the piano as a source of income instead. "I began giving lessons to the kids, tiny tots, seven or eight years old, children of friends and neighbors. I charged them a dollar a lesson." He made more money on the weekends. "Some friends of mine, a saxophonist and a drummer, had some stock arrangements and we formed a little jazz band. We would play at weddings and I would come home with two bucks—bleeding fingers and two bucks. . . . The piano really had to make up for the lack of clarinets, trumpets, and trombones—we didn't have any of that kind of stuff. . . . Sometimes I played pianos you wouldn't believe, without ivories on the keys, where your fingers would just get stuck and bleed and get very painful. . . . I played tremolos to imitate strings and blue notes to imitate trumpets or whatever. . . . Playing in jazz bands filled me with a new kind of knowledge of popular music and black music that was far beyond anything I knew from the radio . . . and it became part of my musical bloodstream as had Chopin and Tchaikovsky. It was a big hardship but such fun because it made me independent of my father."

During his two years of study with Susan Williams, Leonard gave his first public performance, playing at one of her pupils' concerts on March 30, 1932. He was something of a star already, playing last in the program of eleven students; he performed "Cracovienne Fantastique" by Paderewski, "Tendre Aveu" by Schuett and the Brahms G Minor Rhapsody. But the piano technique instilled by Miss Williams was a mixed blessing. Her "method" involved curling the fingers into a ball so that the knuckles nearest the fingertips were invisible from above—a recipe for long-term technical disaster. Neither did she do anything to open up the larger world of music to Leonard—even though her studio was across the road from Symphony Hall. After three years of piano study Bernstein had developed plenty of musical panache but he had still never heard a live symphony orchestra performance. He had already begun to compose, however. His studies of Beethoven's *Tempest* Sonata, op. 31, No. 2, and of Liszt's Hungarian Rhapsodies influenced the style of his first effort, a fullblown piano concerto in C minor which had the subtitle "The War of the Gypsies and the Russians." "I guess I had fallen in love with gypsy music," Bernstein recalled. (The concerto was never finished.)

Leonard also played four-hand duets with Sid Ramin, with Sid playing the *secondo* part. Together they discovered and fell in love with Gershwin's *Rhapsody in Blue*. "We bought the sheet music of the piano solo arrangement," Bernstein remembered, "and we went home and played it with tears till dawn. The excitement! We made our own sort of arrangement so we could do it four hands and try to sound like an orchestra." Their best piece, Sid remembers, was "St. Louis Blues"; their repertoire also included a flashy arrangement of "The Carioca" and various numbers by Jerome Kern, including "Music in the Air" and "I Hear Music When I Look at You." "I had a lot of energy," Bernstein said fondly of this period. And because he could play the piano, he became the life and soul of the various parties to which he was invited, with girls constantly flocking round him.

Leonard's Bar Mitzvah ceremony provided yet another opportunity for taking center stage, a role he willingly embraced, delivering a speech he had written himself in both English and Hebrew. Samuel Bernstein was so proud of his son that he presented him with a baby grand piano to replace Aunt Clara's by now battered upright. At the age of thirteen, on the verge of manhood, Leonard was already an impressive figure, cocky, dashing and glamorous. He was also a good athlete. At summer camp that year he won the high-jump prize. When he also won the award for best all-around camper he was, he remembered, proud to a degree he had so far never experienced in music.

# 3.

# THE PROVINCIAL BOY
# GROWS UP
# 1932–1935

*On the waterfront with his father, 1935.*
COURTESY OF THE ESTATE OF LEONARD BERNSTEIN

*1932 was the year I began to smoke in secret, the year
the conflicting torments of the flesh and the spirit
awakened me to the problems and challenges of life.*

—Speech in honor of his father (1962)

MUSIC became a means of rapprochement between Bernstein and his
father in May 1932 when they attended a symphony concert together, a
first for both father and son. Arthur Fiedler was conducting the Boston
Pops for the benefit of Histadrut, the Palestine trade union movement, and
Temple Mishkan Tefila had taken a number of tables. For the Pops season the
downstairs audience seating in Symphony Hall is removed and the area is
transformed into a vast arena of cocktail tables where people drink and nibble
on appetizers before settling into an evening of listening to well-known classics.

Fiedler's programs generally contained popular overtures interspersed with movements from a Beethoven symphony or a short concerto such as the *Rhapsody in Blue*. On the night Sam and Leonard attended, the final work was a novelty piece whose popularity was sweeping the world—Ravel's *Boléro*. "I had never experienced anything like this in my life! That piece of orchestration is like the bible of orchestrators. And it was important for another reason: my father liked it! He thought it was the most wonderful thing he had ever heard. The tune reminded him of Hebrew chants and Arabic melisma. That shed a ray of light into my otherwise dark, despairing life because I was in a state of rebellion against him. . . . He once said to me 'Why don't you become a rabbi if you won't go into my business?' He was convinced that I would never be able to support myself or a family as a musician. He didn't know about composers, he had never heard of Beethoven. How did you hear of Beethoven in the Ukraine, where he came from?"

Soon Sam got tickets for another concert at Symphony Hall, this time for a piano recital by Serge Rachmaninov. Sam's new interest in classical music prompted an invitation to Leonard to give a recital at a meeting of the Brotherhood of the temple, where Sam was an active member. As an expression of his gratitude, Leonard included in his program a set of variations, improvised in the style of Bach, Chopin and Gershwin, based on a Hasidic meditation he had heard his father sing while taking a shower. Whatever his reservations about his career prospects as a musician, Sam was proud of his son's abilities. That winter he took him down to Miami for a Caribbean cruise and after dinner Leonard would perform the same trick at the ballroom piano, adding other composers upon popular request. Sam never offered to take Jennie on these cruises; it was an occasion for father and son to be together on their own.

When he was fourteen Bernstein met a sixteen-year-old piano student named Mildred Spiegel. Sixty years later she could recall the occasion with cinematic precision. "He came after school hours from Boy's Latin to my school, Roxbury Memorial High School for Girls. I found him playing the 'Malagueña' by Lecuona on the Steinway grand in a large empty auditorium surrounded by a small group of admiring students. I was astonished at his sense of drama, verve, authority, [and] stupendous enthusiasm. . . . He sounded like an orchestra. It was love at first sight. We fast became musical friends, playing lots of duets and two pianos almost every Tuesday afternoon, alternating between the Harvard Musical Society and the New England Conservatory of Music, where we would meet under the heroic bronze statue of Beethoven. . . ."

Bernstein took to visiting Mildred at home, usually without advance notice. He would bounce up the stairs, give her mother a bear hug in the kitchen, and lift up the pot covers to see what was cooking. He made himself at home wherever he went. He often practiced on the Spiegels' new Baldwin grand piano; a few times he played so hard that he broke a string. Leonard and Mildred became a popular couple in Roxbury and were often invited to perform at parties. Their musical partnership coincided with the flowering of his sister's musical talents at home. Shirley Bernstein had begun learning five-finger exercises on Aunt Clara's piano when she was eight or nine, but she was very conscious of the fact that she did not play as well as her brother, who was often upstairs at the same time practicing on his new grand. Eventually Shirley informed her mother she wanted to stop. Jennie, surprisingly, was delighted: "There's enough noise in this house," she told her. But neither had reckoned on Leonard's enthusiasm for teaching, or his passion for playing four-hand music and singing. He would borrow duet versions of symphonies and tone poems from the public library and urge his sister on in her playing, slapping her hand if she did something wrong. Shirley persevered, and eventually they moved on to operas such as *Aida, La Traviata* and *Carmen.* "He'd be all the guys, I'd be all the girls, and we'd both be all the chorus. I was a pretty little soprano voice then. That's how my voice got so low, from screaming. I got nodes on my vocal cords. I didn't know what I was doing: I had no training and I was screaming high Cs! But oh it was fun! . . . And that really began our bonding." These impromptu opera sessions at home eventually inspired Leonard to put on an opera with his friends at the lakeside community of Sharon, where the Bernstein family began spending their summers.

Twenty miles south of Boston, Sharon served as second home for some two dozen affluent Jewish families. After renting a house there in 1931, Sam liked the community so much that he decided to put down roots: he became treasurer of the Congregation Adath Sharon and built a pleasant summer cottage just across the road from Lake Massapoag at 17 Lake Avenue. Sharon became the center of the Bernstein family life from June through September. Many Boston parents packed their children off to summer camps but having a summer house was infinitely preferable, particularly when you could go swimming in the Sharon lake every day. While Sam commuted into the city, the rest of the family enjoyed the country air, which was especially beneficial for Leonard's asthma. Helped by a succession of maids, Jennie spent much of her time fussing over her youngest child, Burton.

On the weekends in Sharon, Burton recalls, the entire family went to a temple service and afterward to the tasty feast—the *Kiddush*—which was prepared by a different resident in the community each weekend of the summer. The rest of the week the kids were on their own. Leonard's letters to Sid Ramin in the summer of 1933 give a sense of his teenage enthusiasms, and his continuing passion for music:

"I bought Bolero!!! Well, well! You see, I didn't know it was arranged for one piano. . . . Of course, dad gave me the necessary eighty cents as he is so enthused about the piece. So for the past week it's been nothing but Bolero. My mother says I'm boleroing her head off. But I am in heaven! It's all written in French and it's all repeats. In the original orchestral score they repeat four times but I repeat only once—which is enough because it gets boresome on the same instrument all the time. . . . And the ending! Speaking of cacophony!! Boom!

Crash! Discord! Sock! Brr-rrr!! P.S. I'm starting to teach my mother jazz. Heh! heh!"

A month later he wrote: "Little Lenny has turned chauffeur! In the past week I have driven (in my mother's old Chrysler) some 90 miles [at] 60 an hour to and from Newton on the new road. What a life! My mother calls me 'a good driver but a little reckless.' "

A few days later he informed Ramin that he was earning a dollar a day from his father. He worked in the company shipping room for two weeks and found he couldn't bear it. He was also, at the age of fourteen, a confirmed cigarette smoker, a habit he would try to break all his life. "I'm on a 'no cigarette' campaign. I'm trying my darndest not to smoke. But you know the old psychology, 'If you want to break one habit you must substitute something else for it.' So I'm trying the old pipe. And it seems to be working OK. You know, a pipe is a much healthier smoke than a cigarette.

". . . You're not the only one who's met a nice girl. . . . Last night a crowd of us went for a moonlight swim (it was wonderful till it began to thunder and lightning) and I met her—and—well, we're kinda interested in each other."

Ramin has no memory of the fourteen-year-old Bernstein having a regular girlfriend. Girls liked his debonair and studiedly gracious ways: he would always kiss hands and bow deferentially to them. But it went no further, it seems. He taught Sid Ramin about the mysteries of sex as well as the rules of harmonic progression, but he held back from committing himself physically with either sex.

In June 1933 Leonard acquired an "inexpensive but rather satisfying" up-right piano on which he studied the Grieg concerto at Sharon. But by September he was bemoaning the fact that the instrument had become unbearable: "Now even the pedal fails to give results," he wrote to his teacher. "It is completely gone, as is the action. At the slightest hint of damp weather (of which we have had an unusual frequency this year at Sharon) the keys stick and are silent." Nevertheless the presence of a piano, presumably replaced or re-stored by the following summer, encouraged Leonard to mount a spoof produc-tion of *Carmen* in 1934. The fifteen-year-old director joined forces with a Boston Latin schoolmate named Dana Schnittken, a "thick-set, dark, heavy-bearded boy, very intense, with a brilliant literary mind. Together we wrote a highly localized joke version of a highly abbreviated *Carmen* in drag, using just the hit tunes. Dana played Micaela in a wig supplied by my father's Hair Company—I'll never forget his blonde tresses—and I sang Carmen in a red wig and a black mantilla and in a series of chiffon dresses borrowed from various neighbors on Lake Avenue, through which my underwear was show-ing. Don José was played by the love of my life, Beatrice Gordon. The bull-fighter [a prizefighter in this version, which predates *Carmen Jones* by a decade] was played by a lady called Rose Schwartz. For my little sister, I wrote a prologue in verse in which she explained the story because otherwise nobody would have gotten it."

The sex changes might have given a darker subtext to the seduction of Don José, but the Bernstein-Schnittken dialogue was surely written more for laughter than for sexual significance. "It all took place at the local hotel called Singer's Inn," Bernstein recalled. "They had made the dining room available to us after dinner for this presentation." [Actually it was an annex in the beer garden.] "We hung up enormous white sheets to make a curtain and charged twenty-five cents." Shirley, with two front teeth missing, spoke her prologue with a lisp. Another young musician from Boston, Victor Alpert (later to be the librarian of the Boston Symphony), played the referee at the prizefight. The chorus consisted of girls dressed like old Jewish men, complete with long black beards and yarmulkes. The accompanist was another neighbor, Ruth Potash; reportedly Bernstein took over at the keyboard whenever he was not performing on stage. Many of the Jewish families vacationing in Sharon had somebody working on the show, and according to Alpert they collected about fifty dollars for charity that evening, which suggests an audience of at least two hundred people.

Leonard was in charge of staging and choreography as well as the music. That he could cope without help from an experienced guiding hand, such as a drama teacher or music teacher, illustrates an early ability to organize and lead a large group of performers. His innate sense of theater was already beginning to assert itself.

In July 1935 Bernstein began to think of mounting a second opera. "My summer has so far been so full I haven't had time to waste. . . . I'm in perfect health, have gained weight, and grown bodily and mentally. But there's more than that. I intend to offer the public another Bernstein operatic production such as *Carmen* last year. We intend to use *Rigoletto* or possibly *Faust*." But ambition had to be tempered by practicality: in the end he chose *The Mikado*.

Bernstein produced it in only four weeks. He had studied the music during the winter, teaching the part of Yum-Yum to his sister Shirley. At Sharon he simplified the story, cast it, organized the props and scenery, directed the staging and sang Nanki-Poo, one of the leading roles. Victor Alpert remembered Bernstein as "always center of the crowd. [His] personality was so strong that there was no question who was the leader of the gang." Rehearsals took place at 17 Lake Avenue. "Strewn around our living room were thirty-odd young performers," Shirley recollected in her biography, "draped carelessly over the furniture and sprawled on the floor, singing away at the top of their voices to Lenny's direction . . ." Eleven years old, Shirley was young to sing a lead role, but she was as precocious as her brother. For the role of Yum-Yum she wore big red knitting needles in her hair, borrowed an embroidered jacket from neighbors, and made up her eyes to give them an oriental look.

"They all laughed and had fun," his mother remembered. "When Lenny was around they all followed him. . . . They were practicing and along came the Good Humor man with the ice cream. . . . Everybody ran out *en masse*. . . . My husband didn't like it. It was in his way, he couldn't read the Talmud. . . . There was too much noise and excitement. The doors were slamming, in and out, in and out. Sam liked quiet, relaxing. 'This is *Shabbas,* he used to say; get to the *shul.*'"

The Sharon Players were sufficiently confident to switch venues for *The Mikado* to the more prestigious Town Hall. Admission was again twenty-five cents, and each performer received a seventy-five-cent honorarium. "For that seventy-five cents," Shirley remembers, "you could buy a hot-dog, a royal banana split, a double-thick frosted and a big bag of pop-corn."

The Sharon productions continued the next year, 1936, with Gilbert and Sullivan's *H.M.S. Pinafore.* Leonard once again divided his time between performing and producing. The cast was larger than ever with a chorus of forty, made up of fifteen sailors and twenty-five of Sir Joseph Porter's sisters cousins and aunts. Bernstein requisitioned the family's maid, who had a strong soprano voice, for the female lead in the production, driving her off to rehearsals every morning in his mother's Plymouth roadster. In doing so he risked antagonizing both his mother and his sister: Jennie was left at home without a car and with dirty dishes in the kitchen, while Shirley, despite her evident singing ability, was unceremoniously dropped in favor of an outsider with a better voice. Burton Bernstein describes the episode hilariously in *The Grove,* his lightly fictionalized account of summer days in Sharon.

Shirley was mollified by the offer of a star dancing role, which saved her from the humiliation of being relegated to the chorus. "He had to find something to make me feel better . . . so he interpolated a dance, when Sir Joseph Porter KCB comes aboard HMS *Pinafore,* to the cry of 'Bring on the dancing girls'—which is not in it at all. And out I came with my girlfriends, the twins Kaplan, in cheese cloth, to the tune of the *Aida* ballet. We could do that choreography till the day he died. Somewhere we saw a production of *Aida* together and when it came [to the ballet] we turned to each other and said, 'You did it better.'"

Bernstein would reminisce affectionately about his Sharon operatic days ever after. The experience of writing and directing stage shows proved invaluable when he began composing and directing at Harvard. He seemed destined for a career in the musical theater, not unlike Cole Porter twenty-five years earlier. His piano playing, too, was largely popular in its repertoire—at Sharon he was often called upon to entertain his father's friends at weekend gatherings. "Play the Hungarian," they would call out from their game of pinochle, and Leonard would happily oblige with the "Hora Staccato," which in fact was not Hungarian at all but a novelty number by the Romanian composer Grigoras Dinicu.

∾

MUSIC at Boston Latin was much less fun. Bernstein played the piano in the school orchestra for three years, substituting for the harp and other missing instruments, and he gave brief recitals at school assemblies. But although the head of the music staff, Joseph Wagner, had studied conducting with Felix Weingartner and composition with Nadia Boulanger, Bernstein's abilities were not noticeably encouraged. It was his new piano teacher who did the most to develop Bernstein's innate musical talent.

In the fall of 1932 Mildred Spiegel suggested that Leonard audition with Boston's best-known piano teacher, Heinrich Gebhard. Gebhard was encouraging and promised to give him occasional lessons; for regular sessions, however, he referred Bernstein to his associate, Helen Coates, who charged a relatively modest six dollars an hour, compared with Gebhard's fee of fifteen. Shamed by gossip among the neighbors, Sam agreed to resume paying for Leonard's piano tuition. Bernstein wrote to Helen Coates on October 15, 1932: "Having talked the matter over at home, I have decided to study with you, taking one lesson every two weeks. Would you please let me know by mail or 'phone when it would be convenient for you to give me my first lesson?"

He took that first lesson the following Saturday, and thus began a relationship that would span more than fifty years. In Miss Coates, Bernstein found someone who would help to refine his piano technique and broaden his musical horizons. Before long she began scheduling Leonard's lessons for the end of the day, in order to allow them to stretch beyond the allotted hour to something closer to three. They would sit side by side at two keyboards, working through technical studies as well as a wide-ranging sweep of the piano repertoire, as she instilled the discipline and the polish that was missing from his playing. "She taught me how not to 'bang,' how to use the pedal discreetly, how to discipline my crazed and raging fingers." She described Bernstein as the "quickest learner" she ever had: each year he was one of the top performers in her annual pupils' concerts. He later described his lessons with her as an "experiential learning process," a complement to the stringent teaching approach at Boston Latin.

Only a year younger than Bernstein's mother, Helen Coates was the first person fully to comprehend Leonard's talent. Miss Coates (the formal address was part of her personality) had spent ten years teaching at a girls' school before she launched her own teaching practice in Boston, where she lived with her mother in a pleasant house on The Fenway. A tall, and in later life rather gaunt woman, she never married. Well educated, if somewhat prim and prissy, she developed a strong maternal devotion for her gifted young pupil. For his part, Leonard reveled in her attention. His affection toward her may have been the attraction of opposites, since her straitlaced reticence was diametrically opposed to Bernstein's flamboyance. Perhaps he himself intuitively recognized his need for her disciplined approach.

After a year studying with Helen Coates, Leonard appeared to have won over his father to his musical ambitions. "I certainly do appreciate the faith and confidence you feel in my son, Leonard, and I am quite sure that a great deal is to be attributed to the excellent co-operation which you, as well as Mr. Gebhard, have given him," Sam wrote to her.

"While I must confess that my hopes of Leonard's becoming a business man are rapidly vanishing, I do realize that there are even greater achievements to be made in the musical field, and I trust that Leonard will eventually become one of the talented pianists."

Leonard wrote that summer to his teacher to describe his response to learning the Grieg concerto: "I can't seem to practice it enough. It is truly the most fascinating study I have ever entertained. Of course, having made my usual 'first readings' in impromptu style, I have settled down to work vigorously at it. It is falling to my fingers surprisingly easily. I am confident that I shall have probably mastered it by the coming fall. . . . At times, my impatience for our two-piano rehearsals next fall drives me to such desperation that I endeavor to teach my younger sister the second-piano part in the bass. A hopeless failure, of course. My father cheers me with hopes of playing over the radio next fall, however. So, as you see, I have a great deal to look forward to." (Samuel Bernstein eventually kept his word about the radio. In 1935 he paid three hundred dollars to Station WBZ in Boston to broadcast a series of fifteen-minute piano recitals sponsored by AVOL Laboratories beauty products— Sam's own-brand cosmetics. These were Leonard Bernstein's first broadcasts.)

When the Bernsteins returned from Sharon in the fall of 1933, the family moved into their spacious new red brick home in Newton. Jennie called it an ark of a house. It was, as Bernstein himself put it nearly sixty years later, "very upper class indeed." For Sam, the move underscored his enhanced social status, but it also meant additional expenses for Leonard's school fees, since students who did not reside in Boston proper had to pay one hundred dollars a term. (Sam would later balk at paying the equivalent amount for his daughter Shirley to attend the Boston Latin Girls School; although she passed the entrance exams she was enrolled instead in nearby Newton High School.)

Newton in the thirties, with its meadows and unpaved roads, has been characterized by Burton Bernstein as both genteel and Gentile, and the older parts of the town boasted gaslit streets lined with old and gracious mansions. The Bernstein house at 85 Park Avenue was built on a plot of land adjacent to a house owned by the Marcus family, who also worshiped at Mishkan Tefila synagogue. The properties shared a driveway, which became the cause of endless disputes concerning rights of way, felled trees, shifting gravel and snowdrifts. The parents of the two families were at each others' throats for a decade. For the children it was another story—Burton remembers admiring young Sumner Marcus for his skill at constructing crystal radio sets and battery-operated intercoms, while his brother was infatuated with Grace, the eldest Marcus daughter, who was a poet, painter and Oscar Wilde–loving intellectual.

Leonard started attending Boston Symphony Orchestra concerts in the fall of 1933. He and Mildred Spiegel bought Saturday night subscriptions which entitled them to attend twenty-four concerts for twenty-five dollars. They sat, she remembers, in the second balcony "under one of the male Greek nude statues." One evening, during a standing ovation for the orchestra's music director, Serge Koussevitzky, Lenny "just sat there" clapping very softly. " 'What's the matter,' I asked, 'didn't you like it?' 'Not like it? I loved it! That's the trouble. I'm just jealous of any man who can make music like that.' " But Bernstein expressed no ambition to conduct or direct anything grander than the amateur opera productions at Sharon. He told interviewers later in life that as a boy he felt conducting to be something rare and exotic, done exclusively by foreigners like Toscanini, Stokowski or Koussevitzky. From the second balcony of Symphony Hall, the conductor was an unreal miniature figure on the platform; it was the music itself that made the most impact on Bernstein. Mildred Spiegel remembers him being so exuberant after a piano recital given by Jan Smeterlin that "we left Jordan Hall dancing mazurkas on Huntington Avenue in front of the Claw Restaurant."

Bernstein's mother encouraged him constantly. "The neighbors used to call me on the phone," she recalled. " 'Will you tell your son to stop banging on the piano. We can't sleep.' . . . So you know what I said to them? 'Some day you're going to pay to hear him!' And they did."

Leonard, who could be perfectly bourgeois when he wanted to, enjoyed acting the artist and enraging his father with his Bohemian conduct. But the relationship was rarely strained to the degree he later claimed. On the contrary, Samuel took Leonard with him to Miami again a few days after Leonard won second prize in a 1933 *Boston Traveler* musical quiz, and had his photograph published in the paper. (He sent a not noticeably modest postcard of the Florida Everglades swamp back to Miss Coates with the report, "This place is beyond description. It has fulfilled all my expectations. I have created quite a stir with the piano and am even giving musicales.")

In May 1934 Sam failed to attend Leonard's performance of the first movement of Grieg's piano concerto with the Boston Public School Orchestra—his debut as a soloist and therefore a landmark occasion for a promising concert pianist. Miss Coates must have sensed her pupil's disappointment: she wrote to Samuel regretting his absence. Sam's reply revealed renewed opposition to a musical career: "Your letter of July 16th affords me this opportunity of expressing my gratitude for your kind efforts exercised in the interests of Leonard's musical career.

"I, too, deeply regret that I was unable to attend the concert to which you refer; you can believe me that I was unavoidably detained that evening from making an appearance. . . . While I am confident of his progress in his musical education, I shall want him to continue to treasure his accomplishments in this connection solely from an idealistic viewpoint. Notwithstanding my respect for a professional career in the musical world, from a practical standpoint, I prefer that he does not regard his music as a future means of maintenance."

Leonard took stock of his position in a school essay he wrote for Philip Marson in the fall of 1934, his final year at Boston Latin. "There stands ready for my claiming a fairly stable business, over a decade old and offering excellent means for development and improvement. On the other hand, I care nothing for it, but am exceedingly interested in music. In fact there is never a time when I do not prefer playing my piano to any other sort of work or recreation. It is inexplicably true that because of rather than in spite of home discouragement, I am filled all the more with the desire for a musical life." The essay went on to argue that whether he opted for a business career or a musical one, his next step should be a college education. "I would probably attempt a Harvard training because of the superb musical department there. Several German professors, such as [Dr. Hugo] Leichtentritt, who have left their native land for obvious reasons, are now giving instruction there. At the same time I would not omit the liberal arts training, as a general knowledge is essential to success in any field." Leonard was one of the brightest students in his class, but even with grants and scholarships (and Bernstein was later awarded them every year) attending Harvard as an undergraduate would be expensive. To Leonard's relief, his father accepted the plan.

In his conversations looking back on his days at Boston Latin, Bernstein constantly used the word "fun." It was fun to him to discover the beauty of Ovid and Keats, to untangle the connections between Shakespeare's history plays and the real-life history of Plantagenet and Tudor England. A scribbled list of titles on the opposite page of his 1934–35 exercise book gives a hint of the breadth of Leonard's required reading in his final year: *The Story of Philosophy, The Mind in the Making, Why Men Fight, Roads to Freedom, The Arts* and *The Meaning of Liberal Education*. This is not the conventional reading of a conductor or a composer. But Bernstein was fortunate, first in having a father who was a scholar himself, and second in the choice of his school. Boston Latin School was passionately dedicated to learning, and to amassing a body of knowledge, with a rigor that was possibly French-derived in its classical severity, yet decidedly English in its reverence for language and literature. Both elements found a place in Bernstein's makeup.

In another of the essays Bernstein wrote in his last year at Boston Latin he discussed a subject with which he was fascinated all his life: friendship and love between members of the same sex. The essay was to be based on the theme of "Friends and Freud" coupled with a quotation from Proverbs 17.17, "A friend loveth at all times." It read in part:

> Most people have experienced, at some time during their adolescence, the psychological sublimation of consuming friendship. Those who have read Rolland's "Jean-Christophe" and have sympathy with the relations of the hero and Otto will readily understand the type of friendship to which

I am referring. It is that companionship which has been so exaggeratively theorized by the doctrinaire Freud as love between two members of one sex.

. . . It seems to me that Freud has unnecessarily placed the subject in a decidedly unclear light which tends to affect destructively the relations of youth. Friendship, on the contrary, can be constructive. "G," for example, has had a veritable course in music in my company, and I one of philosophy in his. "A" has helped me to keep my feet on the ground when they were on the verge of carrying me into the clouds. So I could enumerate a list of friends who have formed an integral part of my life, and I, to some extent, of theirs. Why should beautiful relationships like these be smutted with talk of abnormality?

The tragedy of these intimate friendships is that they rarely last any mentionable length of time. I can cite three cases of this type that, to my knowledge, have failed in the past few years. Unfortunately the law of compatibility in most cases is "Give and take—and give!" One party will eventually cause the eruption.

It seems to me that Fate is distinctly Machiavellian to allow these most holy bonds to be broken by mere differences; much more so by intervention in the name of Freud. Was it Walter Winchell who said recently "If the bandage were removed from Justice's eyes, she would be found winking?"

Philip Marson scribbled over the opening of the essay: "You quote and allude and consequently give too little of yourself." But Bernstein was revealing more of his doubts concerning his sexual orientation than his teacher allowed. Among his peers, however, Bernstein kept his feelings to himself. Any young man concerned with artistic matters risked the label "sissy" in those unforgiving, uncomprehending days. Robert Lubell, who was in the same class at Boston Latin, remembers nothing unusual about the sexual preferences of his friend Leonard: "There were a couple of people that he was friendly with whom I suspected might be homosexuals, but they were all in the closet in those days. I was awfully close to Lenny and I saw no evidence of it."

Whether he slept with a girl in his school days is unknown but Leonard certainly had girlfriends, as well as girls who were friends. His attachment to Beatrice Gordon, who sang Don José in matador pants at Sharon, went well beyond music. They were both romantics, enamored of poetry and words. He called her "Tiger on Brocade" (an early example of his obsession with anagrams) and "Rosebeam." In the weeks leading up to *Carmen,* Bernstein scribbled four nocturnal poems for her in the space of eight days. The first, called "Thoughts on People Like Myself," included the lines:

> *I wondered if their souls were escapading;*
> *While in their hearts, their passion ne'er abating,*
> *They scorned to tell the secret of their fire. . . .*

There is probably more genuine Bernstein in his translation of the *Carmen* lyrics. Leonard's handwritten sketch for the "Habanera" was found among Beatrice's papers when she died in 1983.

> *Oh my lover—my big strong hero—*
> *Oh my lover, where have you been?*
> *Come on up and pay me a visit,*
> *I'll be dancing at Singer's Inn.*

In 1935, Leonard's favorite girlfriend was the petite and high-spirited Elaine Newman, whom his sister Shirley remembers as "a dream of a girl, dark hair and glorious dark blue eyes. She looked like Loretta Young. . . . Lenny was crazy about her." He called Elaine his first love, a "little girl in a top hat gown," and years later could remember her eau de cologne and the violet notepaper upon which she wrote to him. One of the routines they did together at parties was a parody of Noël Coward and Gertrude Lawrence playing a scene from *Private Lives.* He introduced her to Bob Lubell, and Elaine began dating Bob, too, when Leonard was away in Sharon for the summer. (She eventually married Bob in 1942.)

Yet for all the high spirits of his friendships with girls, one feels Bernstein to be writing closer to his heart in the following passage from a letter to Miss Coates dispatched from Sharon in 1935. "I know how interested you are in my friends and associations; and so I must tell you what a wonderful friend I have just made. . . . His name is Laurie Bearson, and he is the epitome of intelligence and artistic sympathy. We became very close friends in this past week. It is as though we were soul-mates; there is a perfect understanding between us. He is intensely interested in dramatic work and has been doing Sunday night broadcasts for some time. He is four years older than I, but that seems such an insignificant factor when we talk together. Of course there is always an interference, and in this case it is that he is going to New York to work. He left this morning and it feels as though a mountain has collapsed. But we shall correspond regularly."

Another letter from Sharon, this time to Mildred Spiegel, suggests that what mattered most to Bernstein was friendship, friendship from either sex. When he found himself alone, as he was on this occasion, he became desperately depressed. "Great God, do I have to be *sick* to expect a visit?"

Bernstein's school days concluded in June 1935 in a burst of glory. Boston Latin produced an especially handsome yearbook for its tercentenary celebrations. Bernstein's list of school achievements shows how his memory played tricks when in later years he claimed that "musical life was practically nil" at Boston Latin and that there was no glee club at the school: "Modern Prize, 1929–30; Special Reading Prize, 1929–30; Classical Prize, 1932–33; French Club, 1934–35; Physics Club, 1934–35; Glee Club, 1929–30–31–33–34–35; School Orchestra, 1931–32–33; Soloist with the School Orchestra, 1933–34–35; co-author of the 1935 Class Song, 1935." The class song, according to Bernstein, "was the first completed work that I ever wrote down and drew a double bar. . . . It was a valedictory song for the graduating class to sing . . . called 'All for one and one for all.' How's that for an original title? . . . The song indicates a great talent for mimicry—in this case to absorb the feeling and style of Sir Arthur Sullivan."

At the Class Day Exercise, Leonard performed a piano duet with Edward Goldman (who had recently beaten him in a piano competition) and accompanied the violist Jerome Lipson (later a member of the Boston Symphony Orchestra). The visiting dignitary for the graduation ceremony was Joseph P. Kennedy.

Six weeks later he received his examination results. He was top of the school in English. A poor mark in history, 60 percent, pulled him down a little, but his overall average was 82 percent. "With the fine recommendations I have received," he told Helen Coates, "I should be accepted into Harvard."

# 4 .

# HARVARD

*Practicing on the grand piano given to
him by his father.*

*In his late teens he said that some day he wanted love,
marriage and children. Also that he was going to try
everything in his lifetime.*

—MILDRED SPIEGEL ZUCKER,
childhood friend of Leonard Bernstein

On the brink of manhood, Leonard Bernstein knew he wanted to be a
musician, yet paradoxically he was not an obvious candidate for the
music profession. Playing the piano was a passion and a concert pianist's career remained a possibility, but he was well below the level which most
successful performers have achieved by the time they are seventeen: he had only
two concerto movements in his repertoire and a handful of romantic recital
warhorses. He played no other instrument, nor was he any kind of youthful
prodigy as a composer in the manner of Mozart or Mendelssohn; indeed he was
a surprisingly late starter. He never completed his teenage piano concerto, and a
modest four-minute setting of Psalm 148 for voice and piano, composed in 1935,

is his only surviving schoolboy composition which possesses a hint of poetic imagination buried within its Gounod-esque harmonies.

Teaching and music criticism were other musical avenues to explore, but Samuel Bernstein was right to be concerned about his son's career prospects as a musician. In the long run, becoming a music major at Harvard was the best way forward. The specialized conservatories dedicated to the training of musical performers, such as Juilliard in New York and the Curtis Institute in Philadelphia, could never have provided the intellectual stimulus he received when he took up residence at Wigglesworth, one of the freshmen residence halls, in the fall of 1935. Yet for prospective musicians the syllabus was astonishingly restricted. "You could not study composition at Harvard," Bernstein recalled, "and you could not study applied music of any sort, although there was an orchestra named the Pierian Sodality of 1808 and the famous Harvard Glee Club, which sang Gilbert and Sullivan and everything in the choral tradition. . . . One could walk through the Music Building for two hours and never hear a note because it was all on a blackboard or being discussed in hushed whispers. We tried to rectify that by organizing a music club under the tutelage of a wonderful freshman adviser named Edward Ballantine. . . . We met in his attic. Mrs. Ballantine brought us tea. We could exchange views and our own music and hear new music—we played Stravinsky's *Sacre du Printemps* arranged for four hands. . . . Somebody came with a record of Alban Berg's *Lyric Suite* and we all listened to this amazing new thing like a cabalistic society. All of a sudden, new worlds were open to me."

Higher education was a privilege in 1935. Despite President Roosevelt's New Deal, unemployment was still endemic. A mere 20 percent of America's families could afford to send their children to college, and of those families many had a hard time paying their way. Bernstein was intellectually privileged, too. His Boston Latin education had prepared him well for Harvard, giving him a sense of history and the ability to interpret facts intelligently. At Harvard, which was celebrating its tercentenary, he became active in politics, attending meetings, signing manifestos and playing the piano at fund-raising concerts for good causes in China, Spain and Czechoslovakia, sometimes defying the expressed wishes of the college authorities.

Boston Latin had been a racial melting pot, its pupils selected strictly on academic merit. The sons of affluent white Anglo-Saxon Protestant families in the Eastern states were educated elsewhere, at expensive private schools. At Harvard, Bernstein encountered for the first time the power and prejudices of these privileged classes. In the 1930s Harvard had a racial quota—Jews were restricted to 10 percent of the student population. And prejudice at Harvard went further than mere numbers. Because he was Jewish, Bernstein was not elected to the Signet Society, a campus group for those interested in the arts. And despite his gifts as an entertainer he was never invited to perform with the Hasty Pudding Show, a Harvard revue that put on amusing musicals, akin to the Footlights Club in Cambridge, England. But if Bernstein was angered by the anti-Semitic attitudes he encountered, he did not dwell on them. In later years he preferred to rhapsodize about Harvard's special pleasures: the joys of rowing a one-man skiff on the Charles River, of playing squash, of singing at the piano after supper in the Junior Dining Room, and of accompanying Gilbert and Sullivan with the Glee Club, a post from which he was eventually banished for arriving late to rehearsals.

Bernstein also continued a busy musical and social life in Boston. He often went home to attend synagogue with his family, to practice on his own piano, to get his laundry done, to give piano lessons, and of course to see his beloved mother, his sister Shirley and his younger brother Burton. He continued his friendships with several of his friends from high school days. Mildred Spiegel remembers visiting his dormitory at Wigglesworth and playing duets of *Fingal's Cave* and a Schubert symphony, while Sid Ramin went to Bernstein for lessons in jazz. (Bernstein confided to him that he intended to develop a Harvard accent.)

In their first year, students could select courses from a variety of disciplines; already fluent in French, Bernstein took courses in English literature and Italian, as well as single semester half courses in Fine Arts and German. "I wanted to read *Faust* in German and I wanted to read Dante in Italian." In music he took only a general course, but outside the university he was heavily involved in his piano studies, having been promoted to the regular piano classes of Heinrich Gebhard, the doyen of Boston's teachers. He studied with him for the next four years. Gebhard had made his debut with the Boston Symphony in 1899: German-born, he had been a pupil of Leschetizky. Each lesson in his studio, Bernstein wrote many years later, felt like a major event. "We would sit at two fine old Mason and Hamlins, abreast: I would play, he would play: he would leap up, with that light, deer-like energy, and over my shoulder coax my piano to sing like his. Anything that I did that pleased him was magnified into a miracle by his enthusiasms: my failures were minimized and lovingly corrected. All was bathed in the glow of wonder, of constant astonishment at the golden streams of Chopin, the subtle might of Beethoven, the fevered imaginings of Schumann, and the cooler images of Debussy. But nothing ever became really cool. Sound, in itself, was passion; the disposition of sound into constellations for the piano was life itself. I never once left that studio on my own two feet: I floated out."

At Harvard, his musical education was guided by Professor Arthur Tillman Merritt, who introduced him to the music of Monteverdi, then being championed by Nadia Boulanger. "We would sit and play and sing and cry with joy. . . . My God, I will never forget the first time we sang *Orfeo* and played it four hands together!"

The seventeen-year-old Leonard Bernstein was a good-looking, debonair young man, five feet eight and slim, with a thick shock of wavy dark hair; he dressed smartly, usually sporting a bow tie and a cigarette in an elegant holder. "Lenny had a natural inclination for the spotlight; he never hid his light under a bushel," recalled Mildred Spiegel. "He was magnetic, outgoing, fun-loving, surrounded himself with many friends and had an abundance of acquaintances from all walks of life." Perhaps because of a subconscious feeling of inadequacy, he was also endlessly energetic, and exuded a kind of contagious enthusiasm to which both friends and teachers responded. He also needed constant variety. "He became bored if made to have a regimental existence. He had a fascination with unique people and artistic projects, and needed to have many projects going on at once."

The summer of 1936 saw Bernstein supervising *H.M.S. Pinafore,* the last of his hilarious Sharon productions. In September as Mildred Spiegel noted in her diary, he took a short vacation at Elm Tap Farm in Alfred, Maine. "He borrowed the farmer's truck and drove to the Emerson House at York Harbor where I was playing with my trio. I was delightfully surprised." Bernstein must have been impressed, since he later wrote a piano trio for Mildred and her friends; it was performed at Harvard in 1937.

Bernstein chose to spend his remaining Harvard years in Eliot House, a handsome building, in Georgian style, accommodating some three hundred students; it had opened only five years before, in 1931. Professor Tillman Merritt remembers it as an "artistic house." Every Christmas a Shakespeare play was put on in the dining hall. Bernstein shared a small suite, consisting of a sitting room, two bedroom cubicles and a bathroom, with Norman Brisson, who had been a fellow pupil at Boston Latin School. The roommates did not get along. Bernstein admired Brisson's practical nature, describing him as somebody who "does everything by system and budget. . . . [In his company] I shall perhaps prosper," but Brisson complained later that Bernstein had called him a reactionary and a fascist.

His sophomore classes included the study of Socrates and Plato. "This is where the relationship with my father comes in, because his Talmudic study had all been philosophically oriented," he remarked. He also studied English literature, and claimed to have read all the plays of Shakespeare, as well as hearing the Shakespeare scholar George Lyman Kittredge giving his last lectures. Bernstein's marks—an A and two Bs—reflected his interest in philosophy and literature; he did equally well in his two music courses, studying advanced harmony and fugue under the composer Walter Piston, then Harvard's senior music professor. Piston had been a pupil of Nadia Boulanger and wrote standard textbooks on harmony and orchestration. But Bernstein's favorite course was the aesthetics class taught by David Prall, one of Harvard's star lecturers and the author of two books on the subject. A committed music lover, Prall became a strong supporter of Bernstein.

Another important friendship, one that would endure for nearly a quarter of a century, began in January 1937. "It's the most fascinating, occult, hair-raising fairy story you could conceive of," Bernstein wrote to his friend Beatrice Gordon, investing his meeting with Dimitri Mitropoulos with almost mythical significance. The famous Greek conductor had just turned forty. He was a tall, commanding figure, with piercing blue eyes. His huge head was totally bald. His American debut with the Boston Symphony Orchestra the previous season had caused a big stir and he was one of the few distinguished conductors to have been invited back; Koussevitzky conducted nearly all the concerts himself. Bernstein attended his Saturday night concert and, in his own phrase, "had gone bananas" with excitement.

Next day the Greek students of Harvard's Helicon Society had arranged a reception for Mitropoulos. By what he termed "great celestial luck" Bernstein had been invited to attend and play for the maestro, who was so impressed by Bernstein's passion and compositional gifts (Bernstein included the sonata he had just written for Heinrich Gebhard in his impromptu recital) that he urged him to attend the orchestral rehearsals he was to commence the next morning. "If they will not allow you in, ask for to see me," he added, in what Bernstein described in a thinly disguised fictional account of the meeting, titled *The Occult,* as a "strange, cosmopolitan language."

Although mid-year exams were upon him, Bernstein virtually abandoned Harvard for a week, in order to attend Mitropoulos's rehearsals and performances. The first of the conductor's two programs—each was repeated several times—had consisted of Ravel's *Rapsodie Espagnole,* the *Toccata* for piano and orchestra by Resphigi, in which Mitropoulos was the soloist as well as the conductor, and Mitropoulos's arrangement of Beethoven's C sharp minor String Quartet, op. 131. The second program included the Second Symphony of Robert Schumann, a work with which Bernstein was to feel a passionate identification for the remainder of his life.

Dimitri Mitropoulos was born on February 18, 1896. Fluent in five languages, he had been educated to become a priest before choosing music as a career. He was an excellent pianist, having studied with Ferruccio Busoni in Berlin in the early 1920s, and he sometimes conducted piano concertos from the keyboard. Bernstein was to emulate him, notably in performances of *Rhapsody in Blue* and the Beethoven C major Piano Concerto. After serving as an assistant to the great Erich Kleiber, Mitropoulos had become one of the most mesmeric of the world's conductors. He had appeared throughout Europe in the 1920s and 1930s, often donating his fees to his own Greek orchestra to help purchase musical instruments. His 1936 Boston concerts had been the talk of the town; his subsequent visits to Minneapolis—a German-populated city— were so successful that in 1938 he was invited to become that orchestra's chief conductor.

On the podium Mitropoulos was a flamboyant personality. He achieved his musical effects without a baton but with immensely expressive body language. Like Koussevitzky, he was a passionate advocate of contemporary music, favoring Central European composers rather than the Americans whom Koussevitzky was championing alongside Stravinsky and Prokofiev. He was a man of great magnetism and physical power—he was an enthusiastic mountain climber

—who lived his life with intense dedication to his art. Bernstein was overwhelmed by the experience of meeting him. "I learned for the first time what a conductor does and how he has to study. His memory was incredible: he even rehearsed without a score. . . . He had a passion that at times in rehearsal made him rush into the viola section and grab them by the shoulders and shake them to make them play the way he wanted."

In *The Occult,* Bernstein called himself Carl and described the rehearsals as the most memorable and confused in his life: "Monday morning [Carl] was . . . awaiting with the orchestra the arrival of Eros Mavro [Mitropoulos]. When he came upon the stage, on the dot of ten o'clock, there was much applause from the members of the orchestra. . . . The music was glorious. Mavro, in his never-ceasing excitement, broke two chairs by dropping down on them with all the force of his wiry body, in order to signify a sudden *diminuendo* to the orchestra. The first time, he went right through the cane seat. The concertmaster rushed to the rescue. The second time, the orchestra tittered. Mavro pulled himself up still conducting, too full of the music to stop even for an instant. Carl began to feel a great and awful love for the man."

Mildred Spiegel attended one of the rehearsals with Bernstein and remembers that Mitropoulos afterward treated them to lunch at the nearby Café Amalfi. Mitropoulos, in a seductive gesture, put an oyster on the end of his fork and gave it to Leonard to eat. Bernstein's own choice of food was more prosaic: spaghetti with tomato sauce. Mildred recalls Mitropoulos sprinkling Parmesan cheese on it.

In his short story Bernstein wrote that at the concert he was overwhelmed "with a strange mixture of pride and despondency"—evidently experiencing some of the same jealousy he once expressed to Mildred Spiegel at the end of a Koussevitzky concert. But the emotional importance of his meeting with Mitropoulos was not so much the revelation of the conductor's métier as the fact that for the first time in Bernstein's life, as renowned a figure as Mitropoulos had recognized him as a creative spirit. " 'The moment I set eyes on this boy [Mavro says in *The Occult*], I felt a—something'—he struggled for expression—'a feeling of the presence of—of greatness; of something—genius.' "

Mitropoulos was probably responding to Bernstein's personality rather than to his compositional gifts. But if Bernstein's fictional account is accurate, Mitropoulos took Bernstein to one side in his crowded dressing room and told him he had the talent and ability to be a successful composer. "You are sensitive in an ideal way—I know, do not say a word. You must work, work very hard. You must devote all your time to your art. You must keep yourself pure. Do not let friends spoil you with flattery. You have everything to make you great; it is up to you only to fulfill your mission."

Two and a half years later, in September 1939, Mitropoulos would repeat that advice, with the crucial difference that he now suggested that it was as a conductor rather than as a composer that Bernstein should dedicate his life. Even as a boy, Bernstein was eager for fame. But it may have been Mitropoulos who inspired him to believe that he had the potential for greatness.

I N previous summers Leonard had stayed with his family at Sharon, relaxing and producing his Gilbert and Sullivan operettas. In 1937 he took a summer job for the first time, working as the music counselor at Camp Onota, just outside Pittsfield in northwest Massachusetts. Among his duties were teaching camp-fire songs, performing two- and three-part rounds before meals, recruiting and rehearsing a swing band (using washtub lids for percussion), and putting on modest entertainments for the camp once a week. By his own account his bunkhouse was filled with the New York Jewish kids who were his special care.

On July 11, the Sunday of a Parents' Weekend, Bernstein was informed by the camp director that he would have to entertain at the piano during lunch. He refused at first, knowing how difficult it would be to be heard in the mess hall, but then news came through on the radio of the sudden death in Los Angeles of George Gershwin. In the midst of the meal, Bernstein struck a loud chord to get his audience's attention: when the clatter of cutlery and crockery had ceased, he announced that America's greatest Jewish composer had passed away. He then played Gershwin's Prelude No. 2, requesting in advance that there should be no applause afterward. When it was over there was a heavy silence in the hall. "As I walked off I felt I *was* Gershwin."

When he had a night off, Bernstein used to visit Camp Allegro for girls, across the lake from Camp Onota. There, too, he would entertain at the keyboard. When the director of Camp Allegro asked Bernstein to recommend a music counselor, he sent a telegram to Mildred, who got the job. "We had a great time visiting at each other's camps," she remembers, adding that Leonard told her he was "in the clutches of a million women."

The highlight of the summer was Camp Onota's production of *The Pirates of Penzance*. Bernstein was the music director and the role of the Pirate King was assigned to a young man named Adolph Green. Born of Hungarian parents, Green had grown up in the Bronx. He left the De Witt Clinton High School at seventeen and did not have the grades to get into college. But he was clever with words and had a phenomenal musical memory; he sang complete symphonies and Frank Crumit songs with equal skill. He had been good at amateur dramatics as a boy and he loved the theater; as a teenage camper he had done recitations of "Gunga Din" and imitations of Al Jolson, but he had not yet broken into the professional entertainment business. Green described his meeting with Bernstein as a lifetime landmark. "A sallow, bloated (185 lb.) unemployed Hungarian-American Pirate-King-to-be disembarked on the steps of the Mess Hall of Camp Onota to be greeted by my mentor—Monitor R. Weil, counselor of Dramatics, who had . . . self-effacingly plotted my engagement extraordinaire at Uncle Len's Heavenly Haven for healthily well-fed young Hebrews." Green had already heard about the prowess of Leonard Bernstein, and was convinced he was too good to be true; he must be a faker. Similarly suspicious about Green, Bernstein bounded down the steps to greet him and whisked him indoors for a music quiz. He sat down at the mess hall piano and asked Green to give the title of a piece by Shostakovich he was playing. Green said he'd never heard it, at which point Bernstein jumped up and threw his arms around him: the music was actually Bernstein's latest composition, the *Music for the Dance,* which he had just dedicated to Mildred Spiegel on her twenty-first birthday. Then it was Green's turn to ask a question; he requested a piece by Debussy, *Puck.* Bernstein, who had claimed he could play anything, admitted he didn't know it. Nor had he heard one of Green's symphonic favorites, Sibelius's Fifth. Bernstein had met his match and he loved it. His exuberant reaction prompted an equally vivid response in Green: "I felt the fresh air of 1,000,000 windows opening simultaneously and a sense that my life had been building towards a turning point and that it had happened, now. . . . We tramped the Onota Hills that night, for hours and hours up and down, to the clock and back to the camp gate and up and around the bunks and back and forth and every moment was a new miracle. I knew I had been listening to music all these years and making my funny and odd full-orchestra phonographic sounds, with soloists thrown in simultaneously, in preparation for this meeting, and I had been carefully rehearsing Sibelius 5th Symphony to give you its definitive performance that night."

Evoking their meeting thirty years later, Green listed some of their shared joys: "Borneo," as sung by Frank Crumit, T. S. Eliot, *Alice in Wonderland, L'Histoire du Soldat,* W. H. Auden and Stephen Spender (as early as 1937!), Gilbert and Sullivan, old, old movies—"I knew as we walked and sang and talked, that you, the boy LB, were nothing less than a genius, but this knowledge was only another comfortable fact to me by now—part of the magic of our continuing dialogue."

That same summer Camp Onota put on Gershwin's *Of Thee I Sing,* the zany musical about a presidential election; it was a topical choice since Roosevelt had won a landslide second term the previous fall. Then Bernstein took Adolph home to meet his family. "When Lenny invited Green to Sharon," Burton Bernstein wrote later, "they would sit around the house for hours, quizzing each other on, say, Beethoven scherzi and inventing brilliant musical parodies while Sam stewed and paced. 'Who is that nut?' he'd say to the equally bemused Jennie. 'I want him out of my house!' "

Bernstein's friendship with Green was high-octane fun. There had been no laughs in his *coup de foudre* encounter with Mitropoulos, indeed his two new friends could hardly have been more different, but they had one thing in common: both made it clear they felt Bernstein was a genius, and that was something he very much needed to hear.

# BROADER HORIZONS

*The Harvard undergraduate.*
COURTESY OF THE ESTATE OF LEONARD BERNSTEIN

*I envisaged the composer as patriarch, perhaps bearded
like Whitman, certainly Mosaic. Some time later I met
the patriarch, cleanly shaven, broadly smiling, a young
thirty-seven.*
—Bernstein on Copland, after hearing the *Piano Variations*

WHEN Bernstein began his junior year at Harvard in the fall of 1937, his
life was dominated by what for all practical purposes was his professional debut. On October 31 he performed Ravel's piano concerto with
the federally funded State Symphony Orchestra at the Sanders Theatre in
Cambridge. Although as a freshman he had played a few recital pieces with the
quaintly named Pierian Sodality of 1808—the organizer of the Harvard-
Radcliffe Orchestra—and performed music by Joseph Wagner at concerts in
Boston, nothing thus far could compare in importance with the Ravel concerto.

First heard in 1932, Ravel's concerto was commissioned for the Boston
Symphony's fiftieth birthday. Bernstein's performance was billed as only the
second in the Boston area, and it attracted several newspaper critics. The *Christian Science Monitor* wrote that although Bernstein was still in his teens, he

played "with an authority and ease which betoken an unusual talent. His tone is crisp and his fingerwork clean and clear-cut. . . ." The *Boston Herald* wrote that he possessed "assurance and a considerable technique to clothe his genuine talent." At the end of the concert he was accorded an ovation. Such positive reactions must have convinced Bernstein that a pianist's career was not closed to him, despite his late start, and it was as a pianist that he continued to make his musical mark at Harvard. He entertained in the Common Room at Eliot House and at the end-of-semester entertainments, and was a stalwart of the Music Club. Although he was dropped from the Glee Club, he was in demand to accompany ad hoc choral groups. On occasion he also played the piano for the Harvard Film Society's screenings of great silent movies. *"Battleship Potemkin* rode at anchor," the composer Irving Fine remembered, "to the accompaniment of Copland's *Piano Variations,* extracts from *Petrouchka,* and Bernstein's own paraphrases of Russian folk songs."

Aaron Copland's *Piano Variations,* a tough, sinewy composition lasting less than a quarter of an hour, became a key work for Bernstein. David Prall gave Bernstein the sheet music of *Variations*—"because I couldn't afford it," Bernstein recalled—and Bernstein wrote a paper about them for the aesthetics course given by Prall. "A new world of music had opened to me in this work—extreme, prophetic, clangorous, fiercely dissonant, intoxicating." Once he had learned it, Bernstein spoiled many a Harvard party, he remembered, by playing it when people asked him to perform. "I could empty a room, guaranteed, in two minutes."

Later in the fall of 1937 Bernstein actually met Aaron Copland. In the company of a graduate student friend named I. Bernard Cohen, who later became head of Harvard's History of Science Department, Bernstein had attended the Boston debut of Anna Sokolow, a member of Martha Graham's company who was branching out on her own. When the two dance buffs went backstage for autographs, Sokolow invited them to her November 14 debut in New York. Cohen called his poet friend, Muriel Rukeyser, to get them tickets. "We found ourselves sitting in the first row of the first balcony at the Guild Theater," remembered Bernstein. "We were old hands, we had seen this in Boston. . . . For everybody else in the front row it was news, and so I guess we were looked at with some sort of bemused interest because we seemed to know so much about Anna's repertoire. . . . On my right sat this unknown person . . . an odd-looking man in his thirties, a pair of glasses resting on his great hooked nose and a mouth filled with teeth flashing a wide grin at Muriel. She leaned across to greet him, then introduced us: 'Aaron Copland. . . . Leonard Bernstein.' I almost fell out of the balcony." Prompted by the music he knew, Bernstein had pictured Copland as a bearded Old Testament prophet. "I was shocked to meet this young-looking, smiling, giggling fellow whose birthday it happened to be."

After the recital Copland invited everyone in the front row to a birthday party at his New York loft on West Sixty-third Street (where the State Theater at Lincoln Center now stands). The provincial Jewish boy was entering one of the salons of the New York intellectual elite, in the company of poets, photographers, filmmakers, writers and composers, among them Virgil Thomson and Paul Bowles. Bernstein's talents did not remain undiscovered for long that evening. When he informed Copland that he was a great fan and that he knew the *Piano Variations,* Copland dared him to play it. Bernstein replied, " 'Well, it'll ruin your party. . . .'

"He said, 'Not *this* party.'

"So I played it, and they were all—he particularly—drop-jawed. And it did not empty the room." Then he played part of the Ravel concerto. "I remember distinctly Paul Bowles, spread out on some sort of studio bed that everybody was sitting on, saying, in that rather perfumed drawl of his, 'Oh, Lenny, *ne Ravelons plus!'* [Let's not Ravel any more!] He was very witty."

It is impossible to exaggerate the culture shock this party gave the nineteen-year-old Harvard undergraduate. Bernstein was meeting some of the giants of American music. The composer Virgil Thomson, for example, had lived for years in Paris and was not just a former student but also a firm friend of the legendary teacher Nadia Boulanger. He had collaborated with Gertrude Stein on the opera *Four Saints in Three Acts;* at the time of the party he had worked with John Houseman and Orson Welles on several Theater Guild projects, and he had recently written a ballet score and two movie sound tracks.

Paul Bowles was another deeply intriguing personality. Then known only as a composer, he had studied with both Thomson and Copland and had met Christopher Isherwood, W. H. Auden and Stephen Spender in Berlin, where he had traveled with Copland in 1930. (Isherwood's *Cabaret* heroine, Sally Bowles, is named after him.) His chief source of composing income was as a writer of incidental music for the theater—among his commissions were Lillian Hellman's *Watch on the Rhine* and Tennessee Williams's *The Glass Menagerie* and *Sweet Bird of Youth.*

Bowles liked Bernstein immediately and a few days later sent him a post-card at Eliot House promising to send some of his songs. Bernstein always admired Bowles's cool, understated music and his eccentricity, but it was his host, Aaron Copland, who attracted Bernstein the most powerfully, as teacher, father-figure, and friend. Outwardly, Copland was the antithesis of the already flamboyant Bernstein: he was sober in demeanor, considerate, direct and at the same time tactful. According to Virgil Thomson, Copland's physical appearance did not radically change after 1921, and neither did his loose-hung suits and unpressed neckties, nor his abstemious habits and seemly ways—which, concluded Thomson in a splendid phrase, "by their very simplicity add up to a princely grace."

Copland studied from 1921 to 1924 with Nadia Boulanger and through her met Serge Koussevitzky in 1924. When the great Russian conductor took over the Boston Symphony Orchestra, his self-appointed task was to develop an American school of composers and Copland was given regular encouragement starting with his 1925 *Organ Symphony.* He had just completed a children's opera, *The Second Hurricane,* and his first major ballet, *Billy the Kid,* was on the way. At the age of thirty-seven Copland was already talked of as America's leading composer. He was active as an organizer of composers' leagues and contemporary music concerts, and his generosity and practical help to colleagues were well known.

Yet Aaron Copland's personality remains something of an enigma. He never flaunted his homosexuality in the way certain of his friends did. (So many of the leading musical figures in the New York left-leaning musical intelligentsia were homosexual that the American Composers League was once dubbed the Homintern.) He managed his emotional affairs with discretion, enjoying throughout his life a sometimes bewildering series of personal relationships with younger men; the longest was with Victor Kraft, whom he described in 1932 as "a young violinist who is a pupil, companion, secretary and friend."

Did Bernstein temporarily displace Kraft in Copland's affections? Nobody can say for certain whether they were lovers but Copland certainly recognized a kindred spirit in Bernstein from the tremendous conviction with which he performed the *Piano Variations* at their first meeting. For the next six years they would see each other frequently and write to each other regularly. Bernstein derived enormous support from his friendship with Copland and learned much from him about the practicalities of professional musical life. Copland became Bernstein's composition adviser and critic. "I remember I was writing a violin sonata during those Harvard days [actually in 1940] and a two-piano piece, and a four-hand piece and a string quartet. I even completed a trio. I would show Aaron the bits and pieces and he would say, 'All that has got to go. . . . This is just pure Scriabin. You've got to get that out of your head and start fresh. . . . These two bars are good. Take these two bars and start from there. . . .' He taught me a tremendous amount about taste, style and consistency in music."


A few weeks after meeting Copland, Bernstein encountered another American composer of distinction, William Schuman. At Copland's prompting, Koussevitzky had decided to conduct Schuman's Second Symphony and the composer, then twenty-seven, was invited to stay in the Alumni Suite at Eliot House for the rehearsal period. "I.B." Cohen and Bernstein were appointed to meet him at the station and look after him. "I remember we went back and had some beer at Eliot House," recalled Schuman in 1992, "and we talked about music and the Bible and baseball, everything you can imagine." Bernstein asked if he might study the score of the new symphony overnight. Schuman woke early, his score nowhere to be found and a ten o'clock rehearsal imminent. Bernstein was asleep in his room, dead to the world. When Schuman entered to retrieve his manuscript Bernstein opened his eyes, said, "You like Sibelius," and promptly went back to sleep. At the concert the symphony was roundly hissed by many in the audience, while Bernstein and a handful of friends loyally shouted "Bravo" from the second balcony. Notwithstanding the Sibelius remark, the two men became firm friends and remained so for half a century.

In 1938 Bernstein became music editor for the *Harvard Advocate* and was informally appointed the Boston correspondent for the New York magazine *Modern Music,* edited by Minna Lederman. His writing style, like his personality, was energetic, his criticism refreshingly direct. A Prokofiev concert, conducted by the composer "opened brilliantly" he wrote, "with a suite from his ballet *Chout* which strains the word 'cleverness' to a snapping point . . . One is very thankful these days for a concert piece that has a finale one can whistle while leaving the hall." Prokofiev's First Piano Concerto made a less favorable impression. "Truthfully it is not a good piece. . . . its one real tune is worked to death . . . it lacks continuity, and it sounded like the student work that it is"—cheeky stuff coming from a Harvard student whose own concerto lay unfinished in his bottom drawer. But Bernstein was already well known for his *chutzpah.*

His attention was not focused exclusively on music, however, as a letter he dashed off to Aaron Copland in a white fury on March 22 attests. Hitler had just marched into Vienna, welcomed by cheering crowds celebrating the *Anschluss* of greater Germany. "The week has made me so sick, Aaron, that I can't breathe any more. The whole superfluousness of art shows up at a time like this, and the whole futility of spending your life in it. I take it seriously— seriously enough to want to be with it constantly till the day I die. But why? With millions of people going mad—madder every day because of a most mad man strutting across borders—with every element that we thought had refined human living and made what we called civilization being actively forgotten, deliberately thrown back, like railroad tracks when you look hard enough at them—what chance is there?"

This outburst had been prompted by a recital in Boston at which a pianist named Cara Verson had attempted, among other works, the Copland *Variations.* "I don't know whether you knew it was going to be played here, but if you did, how did you allow it? In short, she gave really no performance at all: I can stand a bad performance, but not *no* performance. She began the thing wrong, played about two measures, skipped some variations, got lost again, skipped about 5 pages, played a few measures out of tempo—entirely without any discernment, without any idea of rhythm—and kept this up (playing little measures from choice variations) until she reached the coda. Then she played about half of it and called it a day. I was purple—I wish I could let you know how incredibly bad it was: it was the work of an imbecile. I left then and broke dishes in the Georgian cafeteria. . . . Excuse this outburst, Aaron, but the whole concatenation of rotten, destructive things has made me very angry and disappointed. At Harvard the situation is aggravated by these horrible musical dolls who infest the place. I find it almost impossible to stand. Thank God for you. Our last hope is in the work you are doing."

From his little bedroom at the Empire Hotel, Copland replied immediately with sympathy and encouragement:

Dear Leonard,

What a letter! What an "outburst"! Hwat [*sic*] a boy! . . . I had reports of [Cara Verson] at a time when she played the Variations here, which I studiously avoided attending. I see that did no good, since she continues to "play" them. But what can a poor composer do? I know of no way of stopping her once the piece is published, do you? Think what people do to the three B's etc. and nothing can be done about *that*. As for your general "disappointment" in Art, Man and Life I can only advise perspective, perspective and yet more perspective. This is only 1938. Man has a long time to go. Art is quite young. Life has its own dialectic. Aren't you always curious to see what tomorrow will bring?

Bernstein wrote to Dimitri Mitropoulos again soon after the anniversary of their first encounter. In *The Occult*, he described the experience with melodramatic fever: "He recalled sadly that Mavro had promised to write him and even to send him some of his compositions. Yet he had had no word from him. He had made sufficient excuses for this to himself, but he could not help feeling that perhaps his relationship . . . had been only the result of the great man's need to give his love to every human . . . [but] when he began to write, the whole experience was magnificently re-created in him, and his letter proved to be, after the fourth draft, a series of declarations of faith."

The facts are more interesting than the fiction of Bernstein's undergraduate prose. Dimitri Mitropoulos's actual response from Minneapolis to his young Harvard disciple was heartfelt but less passionate and less overtly sexual than Bernstein made it out to seem: "My dear, dear boy, believe me your letter touched me very deeply. I never forgot you. I was only really very busy this past year and now just the same. But now I feel you more near and that gives me more courage to write you.

"Then, dear friend, is that so, is that true, that you believe so much in me? Have I really failed you, have I really left you a void after our last meeting? This thought makes me crazy, and so happy that I dare not believe it. Nobody else has ever written such a thing!"

Mitropoulos suffered alarming bouts of loneliness. Whether he was in love with Bernstein is open to question. Six months later he would write to his fellow Greek Katy Katsoyanis: "I've always felt this abyss isolating me from the whole world, so that I am and will remain *always* always alone, even when I am near those who love me." His loneliness and desire for a partner is a theme in most of his letters to Bernstein. "All my life is a devotion to my art. Beyond this I am living like an ascetic. There are many people who love me and are my friends but it fails me [i.e., I cannot find] this unique one to whom I can believe with the necessity to give my love. I am so full of love, that I am always spending it to every human being. Your letter was really a great gift to me. . . ." That he could have elicited this kind of response from one of the world's greatest conductors, only a few weeks after he had taken Aaron Copland and his friends by storm, must have given Bernstein an enormous sense of power.

Mitropoulos urged Bernstein to join him in late April when he would be conducting an all-Wagner program with soloists from the Metropolitan Opera. Mitropoulos dispatched a telegram ten days later, announcing that a free ticket was waiting for him for pick up at a Boston train station. Soon Bernstein was headed west to Minneapolis. It was the farthest he had traveled from home—in more senses than the merely geographical.

The week the two spent together provided Mitropoulos with an opportunity to assess his protégé's musical abilities during long sessions in the conductor's greenroom at which Bernstein sight-read orchestral scores such as *Le Sacre du Printemps,* and played the Ravel piano concerto. There are no clues regarding the nature of their friendship other than the letter Bernstein received when he got back to Harvard: "Yes, you are right to be worried about me. I couldn't answer your first letter; you were asking me too much. If you remember, you wished to know more about me, but I think it is better that you look at me as you wish to. . . . Who knows?—otherwise you would be disappointed. And, dear boy, I need your appreciation, your respect, your love!" The developing relationship was based on mutual affection. Mitropoulos was a homosexual, but Bernstein was not his type: theirs was essentially a spiritual friendship.

Mitropoulos asked Bernstein for a small photograph to carry with him on his forthcoming European tour. "Your picture is so good," he wrote when he received the portrait; "can you imagine, for a moment I thought I lost your love and then I was asking myself perhaps I am not right to expect anything from anybody, that my destiny is to be alone with myself and my art. But you, my dear friend, tell me it is not so, I am something for you, yes, . . . don't forget me."

Mitropoulos's letters helped to instill in Bernstein a sense of the performing artist's spiritual mission. On the subject of the artistic temperament he wrote: "There is, behind the soul and the whole life of the artist, perhaps a suffering soul. . . . The moment one day will come in which perhaps yourself—if you possess a soul as I wish to believe—you will be able to see through feeling without any explanation." From his earliest days as a conductor Bernstein's interpretations were as remarkable for their depth of feeling as for their technical prowess.

By the following year, however, there seemed to be a certain cooling off on the part of Mitropoulos in his feelings for the "boy genius." "I am very happy to hear that you are working hard," Mitropoulos wrote in February of 1939, "but I am sorry to see that you neglect your piano, that could be a great help to your career. I see you too come to the position now to have problems: musical, artistic, social and spiritual—and the worst of all, sexual. Unfortunately I am too far away to help—to give you good advice. But I hope you are a clever boy and that you realize the great responsibility to yourself, its importance. . . . I look forward to have some moments again in your inspiring and friendly company."

The reference to Bernstein's sexual problems underscored the confusion he felt about his sexuality, a confusion which he would continue to confront in his final year at Harvard.

BERNSTEIN'S friendships with Mitropoulos and Copland, and his exposure to the latest ideas in composition and performance, had a more profound effect on him than anything learned in the lecture halls and tutorials of the university. In later life he paid lip service to the spirit of cross-disciplines he imbibed at Harvard. But in going through his carelessly scribbled university exercise books, one is struck by the ordinariness of Bernstein's writing. His tutors were not impressed either. "You use the personal pronoun too freely . . . verbosity and laziness . . . you have talents that are shamed by this kind of thing." Bernstein's intellectual gifts were undisciplined until they were applied to music. The music criticisms he published in the *Advocate* are infinitely livelier than his labored essays on aesthetics and Shakespeare, which prompted one examiner to note that while he admired Bernstein's forceful language he couldn't understand the point he was trying to make.

Overall, his academic record in his junior year was not impressive—he earned a solitary A, in English, and a B in comparative literature. He received a B in one music course and a disappointing C in the other, awarded by Arthur Tillman Merritt. "I never graded students on their talent," Professor Merritt recalled much later. "If he didn't do the work why should I give him an 'A'? That was my theory and I did it with all my students. So I did give him a 'C' and he became famous. It was even in *Time* magazine."

The composer Harold Shapero, who lived a few doors away from Bernstein in Newton and was a year behind him at Harvard, also noted Bernstein's cavalier approach to counterpoint studies. "Lenny didn't come to class at all. I was a dutiful little student. I did my Palestrina stuff and I got an 'A'. . . . Lenny showed up around the end of the first term and put a piece up on the piano. It was some kind of wild chorus, rather ugly and painful. . . . It had nothing to do with sixteenth-century counterpoint. In typical stentorian Harvard style, Merritt said, 'Well, Leonard, this is not exactly what we're doing in this class,' and Lenny took his fist and smashed it down and said, 'I like it!' I was astonished. . . . It showed the power of conviction that he had about his own music."

Bernstein's inner time clock was already gravitating toward the night hours. Attendance at 9 A.M. lectures grew ever more onerous; long talks into the small hours of the night became the norm. A new friendship had encouraged Bernstein's nocturnal trend. Early in 1938 Leonard and his roommate Norman

Brisson moved to another suite in Eliot House, which would accommodate a third roommate and thus cut costs. Although Bernstein claimed he needed to make economies because his father was in financial difficulties, he was probably being tactful about his need for a more sympathetic companion. The new man was Alfred Eisner, the editor of the *Harvard Advocate*. A New York–born intellectual and an active member of Harvard's Communist party cell, he and Bernstein would sit up late endlessly discussing T. S. Eliot, proletarian literature, and the relative merits of music and language as expressive tools. Brisson meanwhile had discovered "a morose but willing widow in a street near Harvard Square."

In the summer of 1938 Bernstein concentrated on his piano playing. His brother remembers as a six-year-old being forced to go to the swanky Scituate Yacht Club between Boston and Plymouth for Leonard's first full-length piano recital on August 1. The program included Hindemith's Second Piano Sonata (played twice) and Bernstein's own *Music for the Dance No. 1,* which had been inspired by Anna Sokolow, as well as some familiar nineteenth-century fare: a Schumann novelette, two of Liszt's Hungarian Rhapsodies and a handful of mazurkas by Chopin.

Bernstein also joined forces with the New England String Quartet for three concerts at the Scituate Yacht Club and played Gershwin's *Rhapsody in Blue* with the State Symphony in Lynn and Brookline. He made $150, most of which he spent on a trip to California to visit Ken Ehrman, a friend from Eliot House who graduated in 1938. Ehrman lived in Atherton near San Francisco, and Bernstein fell in love with the area and its food. Ehrman sent him artichokes for Christmas for many years after that. "California is all and more than the most ardent western patriot could boast," he wrote to Helen Coates. "I am completely in love with it—the gorgeous brown hills—the mighty fog—the particular blue of the sky—the rows of eucalyptus with their dramatic bark—the friendly people—the earnest atmosphere. I am reborn with each crossing of the Bay Bridge."

Ehrman and Bernstein toured California for several weeks, including a visit to David Prall, who was staying in Berkeley with his sister, a music professor at Mills College, Oakland. At one friend's home a younger brother was discovered weeping tears of frustration over his forthcoming music lesson. "Lenny told the kid to slide over on the piano bench, and within five minutes had him convinced that piano was more fun than Little League," Ehrman remembers. The one thing Bernstein did not do that summer was compose, despite encouragement from Aaron Copland, who tried unsuccessfully to get him a cottage at the creative haven of the MacDowell Colony. He could have concentrated on composition for a few weeks, but old Mrs. MacDowell (Edward's widow) was suspicious of teenage composers.

When Bernstein got back to the East to commence his senior year at Harvard he faced many challenges connected with his future, not the least being his own sexuality. In the past year the world of New York homosexual society had been revealed to him. For the first time he discovered that it was possible for emancipated spirits to lead a gay life without a constant feeling of guilt. But his was not an emancipated spirit. Neither had he committed himself, at least exclusively, to being gay. In April 1939 he told Kenneth Ehrman that he had "met a wonderful girl. I'm about to have a sex life again. That's encouraging." To Mildred Spiegel he admitted that he didn't know what sex he would choose—"the pendulum was swinging back and forth."

At heart Bernstein was still a good Jewish boy, anxious to do well by the family, by his piano teachers, by David Prall, whom according to Kenneth Ehrman he idolized, and by his music professors. Undoubtedly the thought of declaring himself gay must have terrified him, and so he shied away from confronting his inclinations. He felt uncomfortable giving up on school, as well, despite his divided interests. To Copland he described Harvard as a "great waste," but he was not prepared to abandon respectability and drop out, however "prim" and "high schoolish" the university now seemed to him. He still did not have the necessary technical facility or motivation to become a concert pianist and neither did he have the inspiration (nor the application) to stay at home and compose a substantial concert work. At least Harvard provided the stimulus to compose *something*: he had been asked by the Harvard Greek Society to write music for a production of Aristophanes's *The Birds,* and then to conduct the score at the end of the school year.

In October of 1938 Aaron Copland visited Boston to supervise the American public premiere of *El Salón México,* which was being performed by Koussevitzky and the Boston Symphony Orchestra. Copland and Bernstein spent a delightful evening at Harvard, and Bernstein fell in love with Copland's new piece, which his publisher described as an American *Boléro.* "It's getting to be hard to keep this from being a fan letter," he wrote after the performance. "I still don't sleep much from the pounding of [the opening theme] in my head. In any event, it's a secure feeling to know we have a master in America. I mean that too (don't pooh-pooh). I sat aghast at the solid sureness of that construction of yours. Timed to perfection. Not an extra beat. Just long enough for its material. Orchestral handling plus. Invention superb. And yet, with all that technique, it was a perfect rollercoaster ride. And it's not the exhaustible kind of cleverness (like [Jean] Françaix, or his ilk).

"I want seriously to have the chance to study with you soon. My heart's in it. Never have I come across anyone capable of such immediate absorption of musical material, possessing at the same time a fine critical sense *with* the ability to put that criticism into words—successfully. This is not rot. The little demonstration you gave with those early things of mine proved it for me conclusively. . . . I tremble when I think of producing something like the Saloon."

Bernstein's enthusiastic appraisal has to be kept in perspective: *El Salón México* is only twelve minutes long. Copland responded with enthusiasm to his friend's critical fervor. "Of course come to N.Y. and of course I'll be delighted to tell you all I know. But be sure to learn a lot about counterpoint first. No-one can beat Piston at that. . . . I had *such* a nice time in Boston. Partly your fault." Bernstein was no longer studying with Professor Piston, but his senior year courses included a class on orchestration given by another of Nadia Boulanger's pupils, Edward Burlingame Hill, "not a first-rate genius but a master of orchestration, a salty New Englander who loved Debussy."

With all his extracurricular activities, Bernstein neglected some of his other studies. His sister Shirley remembered a final in political science for which he had to cram madly the night before, having skipped most of the classes. Flunking a course at the end of his senior year would put his graduation in jeopardy. The major question on the two-hour test was "Compare Europe before and after 1848." "Faced with the impossibility of answering the question in any expected style," wrote Shirley with sisterly pride, "he was able to fill several blue books with poetry quotations, drawings, snatches of music, and other thoroughly unorthodox material. Somehow all of it turned out to be pertinent and impressive. The result was a grade of A-plus on the examination, with a comment from the professor that Lenny's was one of the most brilliant examination papers he had ever read."

Much more significant, however, was Bernstein's senior thesis, more than thirty thousand words long, on "The Absorption of Race Elements into American Music," a lively account of the way American composers, notably two of his favorites, Gershwin and Copland, had responded creatively to jazz and Latin-American influences to create a national musical style. The thesis occupied him from December 1938 through March 1939. Early on he wrote to Aaron Copland for advice:

> The thesis tries to show how the stuff that the old boys turned out (Chadwick—Converse—Shepherd—Gilbert—MacDowell—Cadman (!) etc.) failed utterly to develop an American style or school or music at all, because their material (Negro, American Indian, etc.) was not common—the old problem of America the melting pot. Having ruthlessly revealed the invalidity of an Indian tune surrounded by Teutonic development, etc., I will try to show that there is something American in the newer music, which relies not on folk material but on a native spirit, (like your music, and maybe Harris' and Sessions'—I don't know), or which relies on a new American form, like Blitzstein's. Whether this is tenable or not, it is my thesis, and I'm sticking to it.
>
> Now how to go about it? It means going through recent American things, finding those that sound, for some reason, American, and translate that American sound into musical terms. I feel convinced that there is such a thing, or else why is it that the Variations [Copland's *Piano Variations*] sound fresh and vital and not stale and European and dry?
>
> This is where you can help, if you would—what music of what other composers in America would support my point, and where can I get hold of it? Would the music of Harris? or Ives? or Schuman? or Piston? or

Berezowsky? You see, I know and hear so little American stuff. This is my great opportunity to get to know it well, and find out something about it. I feel more and more that there's something to all this, and that it can be told in terms. I'll be infinitely thankful for any suggestions.

Copland replied with his customary wisdom:

You sound as if you were very much on the right track . . . both as to ideas and composers' names. Don't make the mistake of thinking that *just* because a Gilbert used Negro material, there was therefore nothing American about it. There's always the chance it might have an "American" quality despite its material. Also, don't try to prove too much. Composing in this country is still pretty young no matter how you look at it.

In the introduction to the finished thesis, Bernstein thanked Professors Prall and Merritt for "invaluable assistance" and acknowledged stylistic suggestions from his friend "I.B." Cohen. He made no reference to Aaron Copland, perhaps because Copland's music features extensively in the examples quoted in the thesis. Bernstein wrote with vigor, supplying copious handwritten music examples to illustrate his argument that a specifically and genuinely American music style emerged in the 1920s and 1930s. It was brilliantly insightful (if somewhat disparaging about the composers of the generation preceding Copland). Apart from the Norton Lectures of 1973, it is the most substantial essay he ever wrote.

Surprisingly, Bernstein graduated *cum laude* rather than *magna cum laude*. It was a respectable, better-than-average grade point and considering all his other Harvard activities it must have given him and his family a tolerable sense of achievement. One reason he did not do better is the dissenting opinion Dr. Hugo Leichtentritt, one of Harvard's émigré German musicologists, attached to the thesis. "I thoroughly disapprove of Mr. Bernstein's arrogant attitude and the air of superiority assumed by him. His otherwise interesting analysis of the modernistic idiom would have gained much without this display of immature, juvenile and unjust criticism. With this reservation I accept his thesis for honors, but would like to see that my objections are made known to him."

Despite his success at Harvard, Bernstein was in a black mood when he reviewed his future prospects a few weeks before graduation. There was, he reported to Ken Ehrman, no chance of a fellowship for graduate studies. A summer job at Mills College fell through. "Maybe a job with a dancer next year. May be a [writing] job on *Modern Music*. Maybe Sharon (God forbid!) . . . It's a dull and wretched state I'm in. No money, no practicing, no ideas."

The Greek Society production of *The Birds* helped to buoy his spirits. Performances took place on April 21 and April 22 at the Sanders Theatre, and tickets were at a premium. Bernstein sent a couple to Helen Coates with the apologetic request that she bring Heinrich Gebhard as her guest because there was no way he could lay his hands on any more. The president of Harvard headed the list of patrons, supported by Dean Chase and thirteen professors.

In the Aristophanes satire the birds have turned themselves into gods and are seeking to starve the real gods into submission. They have built a city between heaven and earth called Nephelococcygia (Cloudcuckootown). There are twenty speaking parts (it was performed in Greek) and a chorus of thirteen. Bernstein composed for a small orchestra consisting of a string quartet (two violins, viola and cello), a wind quartet (flute, oboe, clarinet and bassoon), a harp and percussion (three players). The music—about forty minutes in all—consists of eighteen numbers, ranging from brief flourishes and fanfares to substantial movements such as the "Prelude" and "Hoopoe's Serenade," marked *romanticissimente,* which incorporates the song "Me and My Shadow," later whistled by the entire cast.

Helen Coates and Aaron Copland were among those who witnessed Bernstein's impressive conducting debut. But his success with *The Birds* was to be overshadowed—at least in terms of public attention—by his final Harvard venture: a student production a month later of Marc Blitzstein's *The Cradle Will Rock.* Bernstein later referred to Blitzstein, who was thirty-four when they met, as the man who "seduced my soul."


AFTER Aaron Copland, Blitzstein was the American composer who had the greatest influence on Bernstein's development as a composer and personality. *The Cradle Will Rock* is set in the mythical Steeltown, U.S.A., and tells of a bitter fight between the bosses and the workers struggling to form a union. Produced by John Houseman and directed by Orson Welles, the show ran in New York for 108 performances, with Blitzstein himself playing the piano. The story of how on opening night in June 1937 the entire company, led by Houseman, Welles and Blitzstein, had outwitted a U.S. Government ban, imposed for political reasons, by marching twenty blocks from their padlocked theater to a different venue, had passed into theatrical history. Instead of being muzzled, *Cradle* had become front-page news and Blitzstein a national figure, America's leading exponent of music theater.

Bernstein saw a performance on Broadway in 1938 and was attracted by the responsive way Blitzstein set the American language, sometimes as simple and direct song, sometimes as metrically noted speech. Bernstein also liked *Cradle*'s parodies of Mussorgsky, Offenbach and Mozart, its sly reference to Beethoven's *Egmont* Overture—Beethoven's theme was played on car horns à la *American in Paris*—its audacity, energy and wit. Orson Welles's production style was another attraction. Seated in rows of chairs placed mid- and upstage, the actor-singers moved to the front when their turn came to perform. Blitzstein played the piano each night with his back to the audience, turning to call out the titles of the scenes as the show unfolded. Alistair Cooke reviewed it for NBC's Red Network and was ecstatic about Blitzstein: "Without any highbrow premise or any academic fol-de-rols he has found a way of presenting plays which is to my mind the nearest, most effective equivalent to the form of a Greek tragedy." Virgil Thomson said it was "the most appealing operatic socialism since *Louise.*"

Leonard Bernstein had no problems in finding patrons when he decided to mount *Cradle* at Harvard. One of his supporters was the poet-playwright Archibald MacLeish, Librarian of Congress, and in 1939 curator of the Nieman Collection of Journalism at Harvard. MacLeish had been at *Cradle*'s original opening night at the Venice Theater, where he had made an ecstatic speech at the beginning of the second act proclaiming the destruction of the barrier between audience and public. Other faculty sponsors were Arthur Schlesinger, Sr., and David Prall.

Bernstein and his colleagues in the Harvard Dramatic Club opted for the same style of production he had seen in New York. Staging was in the hands of Bernstein and Arthur Szathmary, a Harvard 1939 classmate. They had only ten days to rehearse—compared to the two months the original company of professionals had taken. Nevertheless they were confident enough to send a personal invitation to Blitzstein to attend the premiere. "I met his plane in East Boston," Bernstein recalled. "It was still rather daring to fly then! . . . He attended our dress rehearsal that morning and then we walked, all afternoon, by the Charles River. . . . That image leaps up in my mind: Marc lying on the banks of the Charles, talking, bequeathing to me his knowledge, insight, warmth."

Elliot Norton, drama critic of the *Boston Post,* said the performance, on May 26, featured "the most talented student cast this department has ever seen." Bernstein was on stage throughout, playing the piano part from memory, and calling out the titles of the scene changes, just as Blitzstein had done in New York; he also acted two minor roles of the Clerk and the Reporter. His sister Shirley, now fifteen, was cast as the Moll when the professional actress hired to sing the roll proved inadequate. Every evening after school Shirley had driven her mother's car to Harvard to attend rehearsals. (At the supper table before she set off her father would say gloomily that he hoped the police would catch her for driving underage without a license.) She made a big impression. Marc Blitzstein singled her out for praise in a letter he wrote when he returned to New York: he told her she was the equal of Olive Stanton, the Orson Welles discovery who had sung the part in 1937. He even requested that she make a recording for him of "Nickel Under the Foot," one of the show's best numbers. Nobody guessed at Shirley's age and the significance of her stage name, Shirley Mann, went unnoticed. "Mann" was a deliberate reference to the Mann Act, which prohibited the transportation of girls under eighteen across state lines for immoral purposes.

In the young Leonard Bernstein, Blitzstein saw an image of himself at the same age: "brash and self-assured." He told a journalist that Bernstein played the piano better than he did, and when he wrote to acknowledge receipt of the Boston reviews Blitzstein was full of compliments. "I made it fairly clear, I believe, that it all packed a thrilling wallop for me—second only to the original NY opening. I want to repeat it all; and to wave a bewildered cap in the air (I forget which Ovidian figure *that* is) at the speed, efficiency and talent with which you got it on. And it was fine to get to know you, and I keep kicking myself that I never managed to hear a note of your music. Which is a reason for us meeting soon again."

The reference to Ovid, one of Bernstein's favorite poets at Boston Latin, suggests that the two musicians had compared notes about their education and upbringings, and realized just how many parallels there were. Both came from well-to-do backgrounds. Blitzstein's father—also named Sam and also Russian-Jewish—had been a Philadelphia banker before the crash of 1929. Like Bernstein, Blitzstein was an excellent pianist. As a schoolboy he had performed the Liszt E flat Piano Concerto with the Philadelphia Orchestra. Subsequently he had briefly studied composition in Europe with both Nadia Boulanger and Arnold Schoenberg.

Blitzstein's visit bowled Bernstein over. Blitzstein played the piano at the cast party in a Harvard Square restaurant after the show, singing songs from the new musical he was writing, *No for an Answer*. He had a witty, sardonic, almost hypnotic presence, and he could put a song across like nobody else Bernstein had ever met. His single-mindedness was an object lesson for Bernstein. Here was a man who had made a firm choice when faced with multiple career opportunities: he had decided to become a professional composer. By contrast the many-talented Bernstein had frittered away the previous summer when he might have concentrated on composition. His music for *The Birds* added up to a solid effort but it was predominantly incidental music, a collection of short numbers, not a long piece for sustained listening. It cannot be coincidental that Bernstein spent part of the summer after meeting Blitzstein composing his fifteen-minute "Hebrew Lament" for voice and orchestra, though it is a sign of his innate conservatism that he chose a theme reflecting a timeless faith. The exposure to Blitzstein's up-to-the-minute professionalism triggered a spiritual response rather than another piece of music theater.

By now Bernstein was increasingly aware of his own gifts. He could take on a Broadway show such as *Cradle* and mount it in under a fortnight, galvanizing a company of thirty. He could write forty minutes of music for a play and conduct a pit orchestra. He could play concertos, write clever reviews, spout philosophy. But did he have the courage to select what was arguably the highest calling and become a composer? Did he have the gift?

The tremors within Bernstein occasioned by Marc Blitzstein's homosexuality must have gone deeper still. Blitzstein was doubtless on his best behavior at

Harvard, appearing as the distinguished composer paying a flying visit to his disciples in the cradle of the liberal establishment. But Bernstein always had very sensitive emotional antennae and the older man's ruthless honesty about himself would not have gone unremarked. Could he ever achieve a similar self-awareness and find peace within himself?

# NEW YORK, NEW YORK!

The Revuers: *Betty Comden, Adolph Green, John Frank,*
*Alvin Hammer and Judy Holliday.*
ARSENE STUDIO; COURTESY OF BETTY COMDEN

*The provincial boy swallowed by the big town.*
—Letter from Bernstein to Helen Coates,
July 8, 1939

WHEN Bernstein graduated from Harvard on June 17 he had no idea what to do next. David Prall had invited him to California as a house guest at Prall's sister's home. "But I'd much rather have a job than be a lap dog," said Bernstein in a letter to Aaron Copland. Prall had shown intense interest in Bernstein and even bought him a piano during his sophomore year. Bernstein half hoped that Copland might be able to get him a place at another creative-work retreat called Green Mansions, but nothing came of it. He needed a job, or a cabin where he could compose, and a stimulus to lift him out of the postgraduation doldrums which he reported in self-mocking vein to Copland from Sharon at the end of June:

Aaron—
    Patiently I have waited. The rains have come and gone. The sun, the moon, have seen another cycle. Millennia have elapsed. I have graduated with honors. I have been to all kinds of class days, commencements, baccalaureate services. I have grown old. And no word about cabins? Have you investigated? Are there cabins? Are they in America? Have you

forgotten me? Is there something wrong? Do you hesitate? These, and other thoughts, as Kipling would say, are my constant companions.

I am madly trying to recover my lost ergs. According to laws of nature they must be conserved somewhere, but I'm having a time finding where. I frequently stand up only to fall down. I sleep very easily (a bad sign for one who has always slept not too well). I have subtle little pains in my back. I have become positively hypochondriac. I live in waiting to hear from you. Please—before I rot in the provinces, let me know the outcome. At the above address.

He did not wait for an answer. Early in July Bernstein went to New York. Spurning his father's offer of one hundred dollars a week to work for the family firm, he accepted instead Adolph Green's invitation to share a sublet boasting a Steinway grand piano on East Ninth Street. While Bernstein was pursuing higher education at Harvard, Green had got together with four other unknown performers in New York to form a satirical group called the Revuers. Among his partners were Judy Holliday and Betty Comden. (Adolph Green had renewed his friendship with Leonard Bernstein thanks to a chance meeting with Marc Blitzstein. The Revuers had become famous within show business circles. "I went to a party between shows," Green remembers, "and met Marc Blitzstein, whom I already worshiped from *Cradle*. 'Speaking of *Cradle*,' he said, 'I just came back. I was up at Harvard and there was a young student who conducted—'" Green interrupted him. "Leonard Bernstein," he said. "How the hell did you know?" asked Blitzstein. "I just guessed," said Green: "it *had* to be Leonard Bernstein." Blitzstein was taken aback, because he didn't think anybody else had ever heard of Leonard Bernstein. Green was so excited he wrote Bernstein a letter.)

Perhaps Bernstein intended to devote himself on East Ninth Street to the life of a Bohemian composer, starving colorfully in a roach-infested garret. He had earlier told Aaron Copland that he was contemplating the composition of a sonata for violin and piano. But to Helen Coates he presented a more conventional picture, with the emphasis on practicing the piano regularly after the long layoff at Harvard. The problem was that on East Ninth Street Bernstein's piano playing was considered antisocial. He suffered, he wrote, from "violent complaints by the landlord and some of the neighbors. They won't allow it at any time—and it does seem an anomaly having this glorious Steinway grand and being able to do nothing about it. Please pray for me so that I can get a good job and find a good penthouse to live in far from the madding crowd, where I can bang away to my heart's content."

Bernstein was exaggerating. Adolph Green remembers glorious piano playing that summer at all hours of the day. And Bernstein was in New York primarily to look for a job, a depressing business since the American Federation of Musicians, Local 802, would not grant him membership until he had been living in the city for six months. The one bright light in this gloomy town,

Bernstein wrote to Miss Coates, was to have three composers giving him moral support. Roy Harris, William Schuman and Aaron Copland, he said, had it "all planned for me to become America's Great Conductor. There is even some talk of a scholarship to Julliard [*sic*] in the fall."

This first documented reference to a conducting career received an enthusiastic response from Helen Coates. "I really feel you have a great gift for conducting—tho' of course my basis for such feeling rests solely on the one performance I saw you conduct of the Greek Play."

But Bernstein had also come to New York to have fun with Green and his Revuer friends at the Village Vanguard club in Greenwich Village. Betty Comden remembered Bernstein as "very handsome and mercurial and ebullient and full of enthusiasm and fun. He came down and saw our show, which he remembered every bit of, right away, could play the whole show right back at us. . . . Around 3 A.M. [after the last performance] he got to the piano and started to play and we were there till about six or seven in the morning, with him playing away, everything, Bach, Beethoven, Brahms and finally boogie-woogie. That night I was so staggered by this marvelous man, this kid, so beautiful . . . and I knew that just knowing him would affect my life. I went home and I shook my mother—I woke her up—and I said . . . 'Mom, I've met my first genius' and she said 'Oh, that's nice,' and went back to sleep."

After that evening Bernstein became something of a fixture at the Vanguard. The witty, innocent high spirits of the Revuers were in marked contrast to the more highbrow atmosphere of Aaron Copland's loft on the Upper West Side. The long hot New York summer was a two-month jaunt for Bernstein, in which the gathering crisis in Europe seems to have gone largely unremarked. In a letter to Helen Coates, Bernstein wrote with disarming egocentricity: "Life on the world front is not bad. There is much fun shopping and cooking our own meals—budgeting very stringently, and visiting all the bon marché markets." He attended some concerts at Lewisohn Stadium in northern Manhattan, an open-air summer venue where Aaron Copland sometimes acted as host for radio audiences. Most importantly Bernstein began composing what he described as his "Hebrew song," a work for mezzo-soprano and orchestra set to a text from the Lamentations of Jeremiah. He also drafted a piano transcription of Copland's *El Salón México* and sketched some piano duets of his own entitled *Scenes from the City of Sin*. But by the time the sublet ended in late August, he had only four dollars to his name. With them he bought a clarinet in a pawnshop and returned, jobless and penniless, to Sharon. On September 1 came the news of the Nazi invasion of Poland.

Three weeks later, Dimitri Mitropoulos sent Bernstein a message asking him to come to New York to discuss a project. Bernstein seems to have taken Mitropoulos's intervention as a sign from heaven. Since he was broke he enlisted the help of his friend Bob Lubell to drive him that very night to New York.

Next morning, at the Biltmore Hotel, Mitropoulos told Bernstein he must become a conductor. He had never seen Bernstein conduct, but he knew from their talks and from their week together in Minneapolis that Bernstein had the exceptional musicality and the broad education that the conductor's task demanded. Bernstein no doubt mentioned his recent success with *The Birds* at Harvard and cited the good opinion of his composer friends Copland, Harris and Schuman. Mitropoulos dismissed any lingering doubts expressed by his young friend and pointed him firmly toward the conductor's podium.

This, at least, is the story Bernstein told over the years. It is enshrined in every magazine interview and biography of him, as well as in Burton Bernstein's book *Family Matters*. The facts, however, prove Aaron Copland to have been the moving force in Bernstein's decision to seek professional training as a conductor. In a letter from New York dated July 30, 1939, Bernstein told Aaron Copland he had been up at Juilliard to see about a conducting fellowship to study with Albert Stoessel and found he was a month too late to apply. "Can something be done? Or do I turn in desperation to the possibility of Curtis?" Copland replied on August 1, full of helpful advice: "The Juilliard story is just as I suspected. Why don't you try to get Harris [Roy Harris was on the staff] to pull one red wire and see if you can't register late? It shouldn't be impossible." The conductor in charge of conductor studies at the Curtis Institute was another friend of Copland's, Fritz Reiner, who as luck would have it was doing a series of concerts at Lewisohn Stadium. Copland proceeded to give Bernstein vital instructions. "I would approach him on or about the seventh or eighth concert (enclosed are tickets). By that time the 'friends' in the green room will be less numerous—I hope. Tell him you are dying to study conducting with him at Curtis, and that I encouraged you to ask him how to go about it. If he's in a decent mood you ought to get an answer."

Bernstein followed up the leads suggested by Copland: "Harris was very nice . . . and may be able to get me in. He also spoke very seriously about my changing my name. Something Anglo-Saxon like Roy Harris, no doubt. He thinks I might ride in on the crest of the wave of reaction against the foreign artist craze, which reaction he thinks is due for the next twenty years. Mind, he is not referring to the Jewish question(!)" One of Bernstein's legends about himself is contradicted here: it was Roy Harris rather than Koussevitzky who first urged Bernstein to change his name.

"I saw Reiner at the Stadium last night (bless you for the tickets), and he was matter of fact. When I mentioned the aspiration towards conducting he threw up his hands and yelled BAD! But write to Curtis, says he, and he'll give me an examination at the end of September. Purely routine." It was fortunate for Bernstein that Albert Stoessel's class at Juilliard was already full, since Fritz Reiner was the more distinguished teacher. Copland wrote Bernstein an enthusiastic recommendation to the Curtis Institute. Bernstein bought study scores of Beethoven's Seventh Symphony and Rimsky-Korsakov's *Scheherazade,* on which he would be tested, and went to stay for a weekend with Copland. "I can remember sitting in the train with these scores in front of me, trying to memorize them . . . and saying 'Oh, my God, this is terrible.' I arrived in Woodstock, and there was Aaron with two or three cats in his house, to which I'm allergic. It was hay fever season . . . all the pollens of Woodstock were out . . . I became so ill with running eyes and sneezing and swollen—I could barely see the notes of the score I was trying to prepare."

When Bernstein presented himself to Fritz Reiner at the Curtis Institute for his entrance examination, he was shaking with fear and still suffering from hay fever. "And there stood this stern looking, five-by-five man, who peered at me over his cruel little glasses and said, 'So, you want to be a conductor,' and at that moment I wasn't really sure if I did. . . . Dr. Reiner led me to the piano where a huge orchestra score lay open to the middle pages. 'Do you know that piece?' he asked. I stared at this forest of black notes and I admitted that I didn't. 'Mmmm,' he said. 'Do you think you could play it on the piano?' I shivered and said I'd try. I was lucky. Some heavenly fire took hold of me, opened my hayfeverish eyes and I played it like a maniac. And suddenly I realized that I was playing a tune that sounded like a folk-song that we had sung in grammar school years before.

> *What clatters on the roof*
> *With quick impatient hoof?*
> *I think it must be Santa Claus,*
> *Dear old Santa Claus.*

"And then something clicked in my mind. . . . I remembered having heard this piece on the radio many years before in grammar school, recognizing the old tune and hearing the announcer saying: 'That was the Academic Festival Overture by Brahms.' And so now, on that fateful occasion, I was able to turn to Dr. Reiner and say: 'Of course I know this piece. It's the Academic Festival Overture by Brahms.' And I was accepted into his class."

What project Mitropoulos had in mind when he called Bernstein to New York is unknown, but his clinching contribution was a financial one. Samuel Bernstein had already paid for six years of Boston Latin and four at Harvard. He refused, at first, to continue paying for Leonard's education. Conducting was not, to Sam's mind, an American profession (in 1939 he was right on this point) and in difficult economic times he had two more children to put through college. If Leonard's application to Curtis proved successful, there would be a standard scholarship to pay for tuition, but it would not be enough to live on. Mitropoulos offered the assistance Bernstein needed—seventy-five dollars a month. Bernstein never forgot this characteristic act of generosity, and thereafter ascribed to Mitropoulos a more central role in determining his career than was perhaps merited by the facts.

The sudden decision to study to become a conductor was the first of many changes of direction in Bernstein's musical life. Only a month previously he seemed set to concentrate on composition. He reported to Copland: "I've just finished my Hebrew song for mezz. sop and ork [orchestra]. I think it's my best score so far (not much choice). It was tremendous fun. . . . Eventually the song will become one of a group, or a movement from a symphony . . . unless you give it a very bad verdict." Copland responded warmly. "It is the best thing of yours I've seen so far. It's more consistent in style—and more grown-up in many ways." Two pages of criticism follow, with the postscript injunction: "write more music."

Yet here he was, switching tracks to a field in which he had no experience whatsoever, with the blessing and encouragement of his mentors, who saw in him the ideal interpreter of the American School of composers.

# THE CURTIS INSTITUTE
# 1939—1940

*Randall Thompson and (from left to right) students Leonard Bernstein ('41), Hershy Kay ('40), Albert Falkove ('41) and Annette Elkanova ('41).*
COURTESY OF THE CURTIS INSTITUTE OF MUSIC

*The old fight with Mr. Tempus. But by that fight only can one get anything done at all. . . . I've had to discipline my soul.*

—Bernstein to Helen Coates,
January 1940

STUDYING at the Curtis Institute of Music in Philadelphia was a leap in the dark for Bernstein. He had known all about Harvard well in advance. Boys from Boston Latin had progressed on to Harvard for literally three centuries. Curtis, founded in 1924 by Mary Curtis Bok, was a comparative newcomer to the musical scene and it had fewer links to the musical world with which Bernstein had become familiar through his friendships with Copland, Mitropoulos and the Harvard professors. The one exception was Marc Blitzstein, who was Philadelphia-born and had studied both at Curtis and at its older sister institution, the University of Pennsylvania. Bernstein never mentioned it, but it seems probable that Curtis was that much more attractive to him because of the Blitzstein connection.

The institute was housed in an elegant nineteenth-century building on Rittenhouse Square, with plush carpets and large high-ceilinged rooms. It was named for Cyrus Curtis, founder of the *Saturday Evening Post*. Mrs. Bok—his daughter—had personally endowed the institute with $12.5 million; she was the institute's guiding force, hiring and firing staff with a willfulness that half a century later would not have been tolerated. Bernstein's arrival coincided with the appointment of a new director, the composer Randall Thompson, who took over from the veteran piano virtuoso Josef Casimir Hofmann, after whom the Curtis's Casimir Hall was named.

The institute was a center for both composers and practicing performers. Samuel Barber and Gian Carlo Menotti were the most distinguished composition alumni; Rosario Scalero, their teacher, was still there during Bernstein's time. Among the more brilliant pianists to have emerged from Curtis in the late 1930s were Jorge Bolet and Shura Cherkassky. Stars of the future, who were young contemporaries of Bernstein, included Eugene Istomin, then fourteen years old (taught by Rudolf Serkin, head of the piano department, and by Mieczyslaw Horszowski) and Gary Graffman, then only eleven years old, who had already been studying with Isabelle Vengerova, Bernstein's teacher, for three years. Curtis was particularly important as a forcing ground for child prodigies. Despite the presence since 1931 of Fritz Reiner as head of conducting studies, it had not, by 1939, delivered an American conductor of any substance, though Lukas Foss was showing promise at the age of seventeen.

Curtis offered study in all instrumental disciplines. Marcel Tabuteau, the veteran principal oboist of the Philadelphia Orchestra, was the best known of the instrumental professors and there were enough performers to form a student orchestra of sorts. Fritz Reiner's pupils were permitted to conduct it only once or twice a term, since for the players the more valuable experience was to work under the baton of a renowned professional. Everybody at Curtis received a scholarship to cover fees and Mrs. Bok thought nothing of moving an entire family to Philadelphia so that talented youngsters could benefit from study there. Ralph and Harold Gomberg, two of America's finest twentieth-century orchestral oboists, were both students from an early age. There was no live-in accommodation, however. A number of boardinghouses within walking distance were on the Curtis student housing list. Their seediness was in stark contrast with the modern elegance of Eliot House at Harvard. And Curtis's dedication to instrumental excellence, with its emphasis on discipline and long hours of practice, was a far cry from the relaxed atmosphere of Harvard. At Curtis there were no university graduates other than Bernstein, and there was no opportunity for political debate. Not for the first time, he found himself more in sympathy with his teachers than with his fellow pupils, whom he later characterized as still in short pants, the products of a virtuoso factory. The intellectual atmosphere at Curtis was dominated, at the weekly student tea parties, by the isolationism preached by Mrs. Bok, who is alleged to have described Bernstein deprecatingly as "our little Jewish wonder."

The appointment of Randall Thompson was, however, an indication that Mrs. Bok desired to broaden the minds of her students. Besides being a composer and something of an intellectual, Thompson was a progressive liberal and an authority on education who introduced interdisciplinary musical subjects to Curtis students by way of lectures open to all. Thompson had the additional attraction, for Bernstein, of being a Harvard man; both teacher and pupil also shared a love of crossword puzzles.

Whatever his subsequent doubts about the stultifying atmosphere of Curtis, Bernstein arrived in the highest of spirits. His acceptance by Dr. Reiner and the subsequent piano auditions with Mrs. Bok and her staff all occurred within a few days. During a trip back to Boston, Sam Bernstein indicated that he would give minimum support to what he thought of as his son's misguided efforts, but even with the financial help of Mitropoulos Bernstein was closer to Sam's nightmare image of the impecunious musician than at any other time in his education. Contemporaries commented on his shabby clothing and on the way he relied on friends for food and comfort. It was his first time away from home. Newton had been only a few miles from Harvard; from Philadelphia it was a day's journey, and expensive, too.

Tackling life in Philadelphia, which he described as the "city of dust and grit and horror," Bernstein was sustained by his own inner conviction that conducting was his calling, his destiny. To suggest, as some have done, that in selecting the conductor's profession he was opting for a glamorous career is to invest his choice with too much hindsight. On the evidence of what he knew at the moment of decision, there was arguably more glory in composition. He had seen Aaron Copland's composing career blossom, first with ballet and later with feature films (the week Bernstein matriculated at Curtis, Copland left for Hollywood to write the score for *Of Mice and Men*). From Marc Blitzstein he had learned the artistic satisfaction that could result from composing socially relevant theatrical work. From his own success with *The Birds,* and Copland's praise for his even more recent "Hebrew song" for mezzo-soprano and orchestra, he had adequate evidence that he could carve out a career of sorts as a composer. But instead he chose to spend two years studying conducting—along with piano, orchestration and score reading.

Bernstein reported regularly on his progress at Curtis to Helen Coates, who had been one of the first to encourage him to take conducting seriously. "It looks like a long uphill climb," he wrote in his first letter, "but I proceed nothing daunted, despite all the venomous attacks I hear on all sides against Mr. Reiner, with whom I am studying. As a matter of fact, in the one class we've had (only 3 students) he was gentle as a lamb. Maybe only lamb's clothing. . . . I passed my [piano] audition for [Rudolf] Serkin, but am not studying with him. First, he's not yet in the country; second, I seem to be over age (!). They've tentatively allotted him a chap of 16 and a girl of 13, so that he can *mould* them. At the same time, I had impressed the worthy jury (and am consequently majoring *both* in piano and conducting). So they asked Mme. [Isabelle] Vengerova, who, I am told, is the greatest piano teacher in America, better than Serkin, a million times etc., etc.—I don't know—if she would take me. . . . The school moved a Steinway grand into my room this morning—just an old Curtis custom—since Madame insists I have just that to practice on. It's a dream of a piano—as I say, things couldn't be better. . . . I work and work and work (practice about 3 to 5 hrs. a day), and do nothing else, except sleep plenty. No social life—no friends to speak of."

With Curtis Institute providing Bernstein's training, Dimitri Mitropoulos kept faith with his offer of financial support. Bernstein reported to Helen Coates that he had "accepted Mitropoulos's offer. Not in desperation—in joy: my mind has changed drastically—I want nothing more than to have obligations to him." Mitropoulos sent a $225 check and an accompanying postcard, his normally expansive handwriting reined in to accommodate the smaller scale of the card but with his generous guiding spirit as much in evidence as ever. "I feel happy that everything seems to be welcoming you in this school, in spite of the pessimistic warnings of Mr. Reiner. . . . Don't worry, kid, and especially don't be unhappy and bitter in case these your next studies do not give you at once the opportunity to achieve your actual artistic purpose, to conduct. Don't forget, my dear boy, that our real purpose as artists is to be ready and able to *express ourselves* in all kinds of artistic fields of expression, and for that *unique* purpose, to try at any moment to increase on the extreme limit our possible or impossible technical equipment."

Bernstein's piano studies were every bit as demanding and even more daunting than his work with Fritz Reiner. In October Bernstein wrote to Helen Coates about his first encounter with Isabelle Vengerova, who like his former teacher Heinrich Gebhard had been a pupil of Leschetizky. "Speaking on Thursday," he reported, "she gave the following instructions: 'Next Wednesday play for me the Beethoven Pastorale Sonata and the Chopin C Sharp minor Etude, finished.' My God. I've seen neither before. I'm not used to this. It sounds exciting."

Isabelle Vengerova, Russian-born and -trained, and voluminous in girth, was then in her early fifties. She was an old-school authoritarian and students got into real trouble if they tried to question her approach, which of course Bernstein did, being an articulate Harvard graduate. Lukas Foss felt that the secret of Vengerova's success as a teacher was that she absolutely insisted on practice. "She would have a heart attack if we came to her class unprepared. She would get so emotional we were afraid for her health."

At Bernstein's first lesson she asked him to play the Bach fugue he had performed at his Curtis audition a few weeks earlier. "She stopped me after a few bars and said, 'Why are you banging that way? Why are you kicking the pedal? Why is the pedal down at all? You're playing Bach. Listen to your left hand. It's drowning out your right hand. . . . You're not listening to yourself. You have to listen to yourself the way you would listen to an orchestra on the podium, and you have to be critical and you have to . . .' She scared the living daylight out of me so I left the lesson absolutely trembling!"

When he went back the next week he played the Beethoven sonata he had been told to study, without daring to touch the pedal. She stopped him. " 'Doesn't it say *piano*? Doesn't it say *legato*?' I said 'yes, but I was afraid to put the pedal down.' She said, 'Alright, then make legato with your fingers.' I said, 'I can't, I only have these four fingers!' She said 'Stop! You have all the fingers you need to make legato. And I'll show you where to make pedal when the fingers can't do it by themselves.' "

Bernstein offered a detailed analysis of Vengerova's method in his letters to Helen Coates. After noting with characteristic self-assurance that he had been making "astonishing progress," he confessed: "I was mistaken about Mme. Vengerova's loading on pieces and pieces—as you say they do at Juilliard. I've been working on the same two Chopin Etudes now since I began and the Beethoven was just an experiment for tone—and so is a Chopin Nocturne I'm doing now. We're not really finishing anything—it's all terrific concentration on the 'system.' It seems that she is trying to make me relax for one thing, to end my 'percussive' touch, and to master the 'singing technique' of Leschetizky. But it's worlds apart from my experience with Heinrich [Gebhard]—she is a veritable slave driver, with a passion for *detailed* perfection—nothing less will please her. And she actually drives me during lessons so that I'm exhausted after them. Well, that's what I've been told I needed—a teacher of iron—with no sense of humor, who will make a controlled pianist of me. So says Copland, anyway."

About his conducting lessons Bernstein has left a less detailed record. Fritz Reiner was fifty when Bernstein met him. He was born in Budapest and had worked in the United States for nearly twenty years. He traveled from Pittsburgh one day a week to conduct the Curtis Orchestra and teach his students. Early on Bernstein made the mistake of calling him "Fritz," in his customary informal manner. "Yes, Mr. Bernstein," Reiner had responded, icily. Reiner could be savage with conducting students who were less than supremely gifted. He would sit in class, head bowed over his score, as a pupil plowed his way through some difficult Mozart recitative, singing the words while a fellow student represented the orchestra at the piano. Reiner would eventually look up with a pained expression and through gritted teeth growl "Give it up!"

Preparation was of cardinal importance for Reiner: the conductor, he taught, must come to the first rehearsal totally in command of his material. He should have a fully imagined sound picture of the work in his head and be familiar with every note in every orchestral part. Reiner would halt a rehearsal without warning and ask a student what the second clarinet was playing at that precise moment. Woe to the student who tried to bluff his way out. On the podium he conducted a great deal with his eyes; he was economical in his conducting gestures, doubtless heeding Richard Strauss's injunction never to look at the brass players since it only encouraged them to play too loud.

The third teacher of importance to Bernstein at Curtis was Renée Longy Miquelle, with whom he studied transposition and score-reading. His prowess in those subjects was already in evidence at Harvard; they involve being able to make instant sense at the piano of the wind, brass and string parts in an orchestra, employing up to half a dozen different clefs. Orchestral score-reading is a skill that differentiates professionals from talented amateur musicians. A conductor has to know, for example, that French horns come in many different keys; that violas generally play in the alto clef; that the English horn sounds a fifth lower than it is written; that the tenor clef is used by bassoons and tenor trombones in their high register to save the copyist having to employ too many ledger lines. Once a student has mastered the conventions of the printed musical page, he must develop the ability to decode the various keys and staffs instantly, to open a full orchestral score with individual stave-lines representing maybe twenty separate instruments and translate the score into the fingers of two hands spread over the keyboard, an act of instant comprehension that tests and stretches the brain like little else in music.

Bernstein was prodigiously gifted at score-reading and his facility, fine-tuned over two years by Mme. Miquelle, inevitably gave rise to envy among his student colleagues. They thought of him, he remembered, as "a Harvard smart aleck, an intellectual big shot, a snob and a show-off." Some students believed he was not only a Harvard snob but also a fake, secretly preparing the orchestral scores in advance and then pretending to sight read. One of the other students who had terrible trouble memorizing scores was apparently driven mad by Bernstein's prowess in Reiner's class. He bought a gun and announced to Randall Thompson that he planned to shoot Bernstein—and Reiner and Thompson as well. Thompson called the police and the student was taken away.

Bernstein's cocky manner put many people's backs up, yet he had reason to feel confident. Phyllis Moss, a fellow piano student, recalled his stand-off with Dr. Richard Stöhr, who taught species counterpoint, an academic technique which Walter Piston had already covered in his Harvard counterpoint course two years earlier. When Bernstein came to the class, he soon began to dispute Dr. Stöhr's teaching. At first annoyed with his upstart pupil, Stöhr ended up by permitting him to take over half the lesson and teach counterpoint *his* way. "They got along famously," said Moss; "it was one of my favorite classes."

Bernstein also became one of Mme. Miquelle's favorite pupils. In fact, "Renée," as Bernstein was soon calling her—a unique dispensation—developed a crush on her brilliant pupil, which he reciprocated to the extent of a physical relationship. She drove him to New York, took him to a music festival in Washington and declared that their two ages—twenty-two and forty-four—were symmetrically and mystically intertwined. Many years later he confided to a friend that Renée Longy (she was separated from her husband) had initiated him into the joys of what he called "refined" heterosexual love. (Her intense affection later became something of an embarrassment to him.) Through Mme. Miquelle, Bernstein met two artists, recently married, who shared her enthusiasm for contemporary music. Janice Levit was still at college, studying art history, and crafting handmade jewelry. Her husband, Herschel, was an artist and illustrator, a jovial fellow who later did the cover for the published score of Bernstein's *Trouble in Tahiti*. Bernstein found the Levits more sympathetic than most of his student contemporaries, with whom it was difficult to strike up friendships given the lack of social facilities at Curtis. The Levits lived close to Bernstein in a rented studio room thirty feet long with a fourteen-foot ceiling. To Bernstein, whose own quarters on South Twenty-second Street were dark, dirty and disagreeable, it was heaven. They had a lovely pink-tiled bathroom, which he made his own, and an imposing array of phonographic equipment, upon which he could play his burgeoning record collection.

It was a Jewish home away from home for Bernstein, the same sort of open house that Mildred Spiegel's mother had offered him as a teenager. He began eating with the Levits regularly. "We called him Leonardo da Vinci, except Herschel would sometimes call him Lenny Lenape, because there were Indians from the Pennsylvania area called the Lenny Lenape."

Decades later Bernstein told Janice that he had been attracted to both of them, but he kept his feelings under strict control. "We had absolutely no indication of his bisexuality," Janice remembers: the thought never crossed her mind although her husband did note some odd looks passing between Bernstein and his new friend David Diamond one day in Lenny's room.

Phyllis Moss thought Bernstein was very lonely during his early days at Curtis. "I remember taking walks around Philadelphia with him and he poured his heart out. I was quiet in general so he felt he could say things that maybe he couldn't say to other people. There were rumors that his gay life was in New York and that in Philadelphia he was not gay. That may have been one of the reasons he was unhappy. He talked very often to me about wanting to get married and particularly wanting to have children. That was his dream. He was obsessed with that."

To Helen Coates, Bernstein described a visit to New York in the fall of 1939 as "a welcome and necessary liberation." New York was home to Adolph Green, Betty Comden and Judy Holliday. His other great New York friend, Aaron Copland, was in Hollywood, but Copland's circle was still open to him and encounters with that predominantly homosexual world might well have represented a "liberation." His feeling of loneliness eventually found its way into his music in such smokily beautiful passages as the bluesy violin melody in the Coney Island dream ballet from his 1944 musical, *On the Town*. Sometimes the loneliness escalated into an overwhelming sense of panic at being alone. In September 1942, when he could afford it, he began to see an analyst, but as a student he could do no more than confide his feelings to friends such as Phyllis Moss. Still, as Lukas Foss remembers, "he never really struck me as miserable. I remember saying to him that he had such an expansive luxurious way of being miserable that it didn't seem miserable to me, ever. . . . I never worried about Lenny."

February 24, 1940, was a landmark in Bernstein's career at Curtis, and a reminder that he was still a composer as well as a conducting student. Randall Thompson decided to include four studies for two clarinets and two bassoons, which Bernstein wrote as orchestration exercises, in a broadcast program which also included works by Oscar Levant and Samuel Barber. Bernstein himself was enlisted to play the piano. "Don't be too hard on them," he wrote to Helen Coates, "—they weren't made to be heard as *compositions*." But a chorale in the third piece eventually found a place in Bernstein's first symphony.

Aaron Copland missed the broadcast, but wrote to Bernstein, "Marc Blitzstein reports it was easily the best thing on the program." Copland was back from Hollywood and in the process of selecting composition students for a great new adventure looming on the cultural skyline: the first season of the Berkshire Music Center. Copland was to be composer in residence, and the conducting classes were to be in the hands of Serge Koussevitzky. Hearing of the new venture, Bernstein was beside himself with excitement. In six months at Curtis he had rarely conducted a real orchestra, but in the Berkshires, the selected conducting students would work with the specially formed student orchestra every week for six weeks. He quickly organized letters of recommendation from Fritz Reiner, Roy Harris and William Schuman. Mitropoulos sent a supportive cable. Aaron Copland also promised to talk to Koussevitzky.

In mid-March Bernstein went to Boston to meet Koussevitzky in the conductor's greenroom at Symphony Hall. He loved to tell the story of the encounter, relishing his well-honed imitation of Koussevitzky's Russian accent. "But of coarrse I vill take you in my class," Koussevitzky announced grandly, after only a few minutes of talk. Bernstein was overjoyed.

Koussevitzky's ready acceptance was in sharp contrast to a proposal from Mitropoulos that had been preoccupying Bernstein for several months. It had begun with a letter from Minneapolis: "I must meet you because I have something very important to tell you, something that has to do probably with your next future if you are lucky. I cannot write you this. I must explain to you. On the same occasion I will bring with me the necessary [sic] for your further living and studying. Many affectionate thoughts."

Bernstein traveled to New York, where he heard at firsthand what Mitropoulos had in mind and quickly passed on the news to his family:

Dear Folks—
    I have just spent the most wonderful evening—naturally, with the maestro. And he certainly did have plans for me. I'm not supposed to tell a soul—but God, you've all got to know—but please not a *word* to *anyone!* Not even casually. Please remember.
    Dimitri wants me to finish out this year at Curtis—learn as much as I

can. Then next season—to come to Minneapolis in the following way: not as an assistant conductor, naturally, since I am in no way a conductor yet. But he is going to *build* me there. I will go and join the orchestra as pianist playing both solos (that is, concerti) and piano parts in the orch. I must attend all his rehearsals, following them with the score, and be ready at any time to take over the orchestra. And he assures me that this will happen many, many times. He has often spoken of it to the manager of the orchestra, has convinced him that I'm good; and the manager has consented, at a wonderful weekly salary. (Of course, I must first join the union.) In other words, he is going to push me in Minneapolis as piano soloist, composer, orchestra man, critic, *and conductor*—anything he can, so that the following year I can inherit the official title of assistant conductor. And then—God only knows. I am, as Dad would say, going to learn the business from the bottom up.

It's *exactly* what I want and need—and I still can't get it through my head that it's actually true. It's the most marvellous thing that could have happened—it's a job, and studying, and assisting Mitropoulos, all in one. In fact, it's wonderful.

Mitropoulos had given serious thought to his proposal, but he seems not to have made it clear to his orchestral manager that his protégé was still a student. Bernstein wrote to Mitropoulos, pointing out the problem of his lack of union membership. Mitropoulos urged Bernstein to join AFM (the musicians' union) either in Boston or Philadelphia so he would be a member when he arrived in Minneapolis. But Bernstein must have been aware from his thwarted attempt to join the union in New York the previous summer that Mitropoulos's backdoor proposal for him was impractical: he was not living in Boston and he was merely a student in Philadelphia. On April 13 the Minneapolis bubble burst when a cable, totally unpunctuated, arrived from Mitropoulos: "DONT LEAVE YOUR CLASS FOR NEXT SEASON SOME REAL DIFFICULTIES HERE BECAUSE OF MY ENGAGEMENT IN NEW YORK AND ONE MONTH OF ORCHESTRA TOUR AND SOME GUEST CONDUCTORS IT IS NOT WISE TO STOP STUDYING FOR A DOUBTFUL SEASON FOR YOU HERE AM AWFULLY SORRY"

Bernstein went into deep shock. "Today has been horrible," he wrote his newest confidant, the violinist and composer David Diamond, who was three years his senior. The extravagant vocabulary of Bernstein's letter reflects his "uncanny rapport" with the flamboyantly homosexual Diamond:

I have been missing you strangely. April is the cruelest month. I received a wire from Dimitri that knocks my world completely to hell. I have had queer forebodings about the next year affair in Minneapolis all along, and you, sympathetic to the supernatural, can certainly understand them. Today saw their manifestation. . . . I have been staggering and

pale green all day, fighting with my lifeblood that wants to stop cours-
ing. . . .

     . . . Don't think I am carrying on, please. The prospect of next year,
prefaced by a summer in the Koussevitzky class, was for me the one,
single motive of my activity, now, every move, every note studied, project
rejected, person loved, hope ignored, was a direct preparation for next
year. From the scores I chose to study to the sexual life which I have
abandoned—all.

     It is as hard to write this as it must have been for Dimitri to send the
wire.


It is revealing to learn that Bernstein had taken monklike vows of sexual
denial, but there is something uncharacteristically hysterical about his self-
pitying tone.

Three days later Mitropoulos wrote to apologize for his failure to deliver on
his earlier promise. The problem, he explained, lay with the union, which
would not allow Mitropoulos to hire somebody from outside the state. Nor
would the orchestra's manager accept the employment of a student as assistant
conductor. Mitropoulos felt terrible about the dashing of both their plans.

Bernstein was soon showing sympathy for the hapless Mitropoulos. "He's
no false promiser," Bernstein assured Diamond. "He had an integrity that is
*sans pareil*. He's simply up against a strong machine." Within a few weeks
Bernstein was able to tell Diamond that he felt much better about it. "Life has
many compensations." Chief among them was his growing self-confidence as a
conductor.

Before his first year at Curtis ended Bernstein conducted the Curtis Orchestra in Wagner's *Tannhäuser* Overture and Brahms's Third Symphony. He wrote
to Helen Coates: "It is certainly the most glorious thing one can do, and I
haven't calmed down yet—of course I was so flabbergasted by the *live* response
to my musical thoughts that I'm sure I made many mistakes, but it came
through all right, somehow or other. I've got the bug in earnest now. That was
only a taste of what it can be like to perceive the realization of a musical *desire*
by the world's most incredible instrument. Life ahead looks almost too exciting.
I hope it's practical enough to hold together."

When the term was finished, Bernstein went home to Sharon. There he
practiced Ravel's piano work *Le Tombeau de Couperin,* studied scores for his
forthcoming studies with Koussevitzky and worked intermittently at a new
violin sonata. At midsummer he went to New York, picking up the threads of
his friendship with Adolph Green and the other Revuers. A few months earlier
he had earned some money with them playing the piano in what has become a
rare record collector's item, a twenty-minute farce by the Revuers called *The
Girl with the Two Left Feet.* Betty Comden and Judy Holliday are outstandingly
funny on the recording, and Bernstein's fully integrated sound track gives the
best idea we have of his brilliance as a boogie and honky-tonk pianist. A brief

review in *Variety* described it as "a clever musical satire on Hollywood . . . written, composed and acted by five talented young people." Bernstein's next date with the Revuers was in NBC's experimental television studio to play piano for a pioneer TV "special"—seen in a few hundred homes equipped with receivers. The New York gossip columnist Leonard Lyons, a classical music buff, reported that the pages were being turned at the keyboard by none other than Aaron Copland. Ironically, he didn't mention the pianist.

At the beginning of July Bernstein went to Lenox, Massachusetts, to embark on the most stimulating six weeks of his life, the "glorious summer dream" of the music school at Tanglewood.

# 8 .
# TANGLEWOOD
# 1940

*Serge Koussevitzky in 1940 with*
*his star pupils, Bernstein (left) and*
*Lukas Foss (center).*
COURTESY OF THE ESTATE OF LEONARD BERNSTEIN

*A green fertile wooded mountain of youth and joy.*

—LEONARD BERNSTEIN

TANGLEWOOD is the name of the Tappan family estate a mile and a half southwest of the center of Lenox, a village in the Berkshire Mountains of northwestern Massachusetts. Nathaniel Hawthorne, Herman Melville and Edith Wharton had all lived and worked in the area. Tanglewood became the permanent site of summer musical activities in 1937 when the Tappan family gave the Boston Symphony Orchestra two hundred and ten acres of lawns and rolling meadows, sloping elegantly down to the north shore of Lake Mahkeenac.

Serge Koussevitzky, music director of the Boston Symphony since 1924, was in command. For its first season at Tanglewood, in 1938, the orchestra performed under a tent as it had the previous year on a nearby estate. But a spectacular thunderstorm ruined the final all-Wagner concert. Funds were speedily raised, and by its second season the Berkshire Festival at Tanglewood had a permanent concert hall based on a design by Eliel Saarinen, whom Koussevitzky had met on an Atlantic crossing. His project was judged too expensive and a local building engineer, Joseph Frantz, went ahead with a less refined version in which the roof was supported by iron girders. "You will be getting a shed instead of a concert hall," Saarinen observed, and the facility is known to this day as the Shed. "Shed" is a Bostonian understatement for a simple but elegant structure sitting in the utmost harmony with its natural surroundings. The musicians perform on a stage that forms the hub of a vast, fan-shaped hangar. There are no walls at ground level, so by day the audience can glimpse the lawns and by night the stars—and when it is low in the sky, the moon. Under the flat roof, cover is provided for five thousand people and there is room outside for at least ten thousand more, with tall firs forming a natural backdrop to the performance area.

Thirty-six thousand people from forty states of the United States came in 1938 for the six concerts in the new Shed. Tanglewood began to take on the artistic and social glamour of an international musical festival to compare with Salzburg. But Koussevitzky was not satisfied with what he had achieved. After the 1939 festival—again a series of six festival concerts—he announced that in the following year Tanglewood would begin an educational project that had no parallel in Europe or America: for six weeks in July and August, the Berkshire Music Center would provide intensive training for over three hundred students.

The creation of Tanglewood as a festival and educational center confirmed Koussevitzky's position as the most influential conductor of the twentieth century. In czarist Russia and 1920s Paris he had performed and published leading composers such as Stravinsky, Scriabin and Prokofiev. In America he pursued an enlightened policy by commissioning works for the Boston Symphony, and performing new music side by side with the classics in the winter subscription concerts. But the Berkshire Music Center was a venture on a quite different plane since it offered, as Koussevitzky explained in his prospectus, "special opportunities to all for the practice and contemplation of music in its noblest activities." Students would not receive any diploma or academic credit, but they would rub shoulders with some of the leading artists and scholars of the day. Tanglewood, he went on, "will be a place for those who wish to refresh mind and personality by experience of the best in music and the related arts."

Dr. Koussevitzky's fractured English was legendary, but on the printed page his eloquent outline for a summer school sent a thrill of excitement around the music colleges of America. In 1940 the Berkshire Music Center offered courses in advanced study of composition, conducting, orchestral playing and opera. (Less arduous courses on choral singing and general music were separately organized in a so-called Academy, which was quietly incorporated in 1941 into the body of the center.) The impressive faculty included Richard Burgin, who was both concertmaster and assistant conductor of the BSO; Aaron Copland; Olin Downes, music editor of the *New York Times;* Herbert Graf, stage director of the Metropolitan Opera; and the German composer Paul Hindemith. Among the lecturers were the composer Roy Harris and Bernstein's teacher at Curtis, Randall Thompson. Twenty-nine members of the Boston Symphony Orchestra were listed as faculty members, their task being to coach individuals and groups of instrumentalists in everything from violin to percussion. The creation of an orchestra of skilled players was one of the chief goals of the center. This student orchestra was to play one symphony concert a week, at which some works would be conducted by students and others by Koussevitzky or Richard Burgin. Thus the student players would benefit by working under professionals of the highest standing. At the end of July the rest of the Boston Symphony Orchestra would arrive to continue its annual festival series, in which Koussevitzky would conduct nine concerts over three weekends.

Second in size to the orchestra class was the one devoted to "opera dramatics," with Herbert Graf in charge. There were twenty singers in the 1940 opera class, and sixty-six players in the Institute Orchestra, which had a relatively small string section but boasted a full complement of woodwind, brass and percussion. The composing class consisted of thirteen students, among them Lukas Foss and Harold Shapero; teaching was shared between Aaron Copland, who served as Koussevitzky's deputy, and Paul Hindemith, then at the height of his powers and reputation: it was a *coup* to have secured the services of such a distinguished European. In his opening address, Koussevitzky spoke of the European landscapes as beautiful as Tanglewood's that were being destroyed by war. "If ever there was a time to speak of music, it is now in the New World." He hoped that some miracle would keep America out of war. "So long as art and culture exist there is hope for humanity."

There were 312 students in 1940, nearly two thirds from the states of Massachusetts and New York, and more than half were over twenty-four. Scholarships were given to help with board and fees (one hundred dollars general tuition, twenty dollars for special classes). Bernstein used money he had earned from NBC for accompanying the Revuers to supplement a fifty-dollar scholarship.

Living quarters were spartan. Bernstein slept at Cranwell, a Lenox prep school run by Jesuits. His room housed five students, who were all expected to study in the same space: Harold Shapero, who composed a piece called "Room 57" for his three instrumentalist roommates; a clarinetist, David Glazer; a violinist, Raphael Hillyer; and a cellist, Jesse Ehrlich. Shapero remembers Bernstein sitting at the desk in the corner screaming and yelling as he made his preparations to rehearse Rimsky-Korsakov's *Scheherazade*. Not a mention was made that summer of his compositional aspirations and not a note of his was performed in concert. He was at Tanglewood to learn the art of conducting and that is essentially what he did, morning, noon and night.

Bernstein was one of the five students chosen for active participation in Dr.

Koussevitzky's conducting class. Dozens of additional students audited the class. The other active students were Lukas Foss (studying conducting as well as composition), Richard Bales, Thor Johnson and Gaylord Browne.

What did it mean to be one of Koussevitzky's summer pupils? An appropriate analogy might be with a teaching hospital where a distinguished surgeon goes on his rounds accompanied by his interns—aristocrats in the student fraternity—who spend their waking days hanging on the master's every word. At Tanglewood there was the important distinction, however, in that the young conductors were given the chance to "operate" after only a few days of internship. Not, it is true, on the precious body of the Boston Symphony itself. That privilege was reserved for Dr. Koussevitzky and his assistant, Mr. Burgin. The students did their "carving" on the newly formed student orchestra.

Bernstein was chosen to open the Berkshire Music Center's first Institute Orchestra concert on Friday, July 12, conducting Randall Thompson's Symphony No. 2. Study began with a private coaching session at which he went through the motions of conducting the Thompson score while the orchestra parts were performed on two pianos, placed side by side—strings by the first pianist, brass and woodwind by the second. Many of the participants in 1940 speak of the excitement in the air as the sixty-five-year-old Koussevitzky, who had never before given lessons, responded to Bernstein's talent. Koussevitzky had promised the press that his Music Center would deliver five conductors of genius within five years, and twenty of value. And here he was, on his first day, teaching somebody whose talent was clearly prodigious. Bernstein remembered his early lessons vividly, and spent the rest of his life passing them on. "Between one beat and the next you *prepare*. . . . [The secret] is what is *between* the beats: it is the inner beats that are important. And Koussevitzky showed me what to do: 'When you conduct the slow movement of the Randall Thompson Symphony it must be varm like the sun come up. . . . *Varm* and a two and a three and a four and a von . . .' "

For Koussevitzky, as for a choreographer, it was essential to maintain the musical line. The comparison with dance is not fortuitous: conductors must also work with their bodies. "At the end of the first week," Bernstein recalled, "Koussevitzky decided that we all needed lessons in what he called 'die Plastik,' and so he engaged a leading dancer from the nearby Jacob's Pillow Dance Festival [Erick Hawkins, later a distinguished choreographer] to give us movement lessons; we had to stand in a certain way and then go through certain exercises and we were all supposed to do this while looking at ourselves in a mirror. I did this just one day by myself and fell about in such laughter that I couldn't repeat it. That was the only time I have ever conducted in front of a mirror."

Lukas Foss was equally skeptical about Koussevitzky's mirror advice, but the two Curtis students went different ways about the use of a conducting baton. Foss stuck to the large stick recommended by Reiner. Bernstein refused to use any kind of baton. He had seen what Mitropoulos could achieve with his eloquent bare hands—sometimes transformed into brandishing fists—and he resolved to follow his idol in this regard. "Koussevitzky pleaded with me to use this little 'baguette,' as he called it. 'Look, it's like a pencil, Lenushka, and it's very much clearer when you use this baguette!'" But Bernstein stuck to his guns.

On the eve of his first concert he wrote to his family at Sharon:

Dearest Folks,

. . . I have never seen such a beautiful setup in my life. I've been conducting the orchestra every morning, & I'm playing my first concert tomorrow night. Kouss gave me the hardest & longest number of all—the Second Symphony of Randall Thompson. 30 minutes long—a modern American work—as my first performance. And Kouss is so pleased with my work. He likes me & works very hard with me in our private sessions. He is the most marvellous man—a beautiful spirit that never lags or fails —that inspires me terrifically. And he told me he is convinced that I have a wonderful gift, & he is already making me a *great* conductor. (I actually rode in his car with him today!) He has wonderful teaching ability, which I never expected—& is very hard to please—so that when he says he is pleased I know it means something. I am so thrilled—have never been more happy & satisfied. The orchestra likes me very much, best of all the conductors, & responds so beautifully in rehearsal. Of course, the concert tomorrow night (Shabbas, yet!) will tell whether I can keep my head in performance. We've been working very hard—you're always going like mad here—no time to think of how tired you are or how little you slept last night—the inspiration of this Center is terrific enough to keep you going with no sleep at all. I'm so excited about tomorrow night—I wish you could all be here—it's so important to me & Kouss is banking on it to convince him that he's right—if it goes well there's no telling what may happen. . . .

Please come up—I think I'll be conducting every Friday night & rehearsing every morning—please come up—

All my love
Lenny

The concert, with Bales and Johnson also conducting, went well. Newspaper critics from Massachusetts and New York, among them Howard Taubman of the *Times,* were already praising the achievement of the student orchestra— on a par, it was said, with the best of the second-league American orchestras. The astonishing level of orchestral prowess, each year forged virtually overnight, has been one of the enduring achievements of Tanglewood.

Bernstein's parents duly turned up, motoring over from Sharon with Shirley, who was about to become an undergraduate at Mount Holyoke, and the eight-year-old Burtie. After nearly three weeks under his instruction, Bernstein was still reveling in Koussevitzky's attention. "He seems to like me more all the time," he wrote to Miss Coates. "He now wants me to study with him this winter in Boston. He said today that I will certainly be the *greatest* (!) conductor, if only I will work hard. 3 years—that's all. He wants to mould me, etc. He says I have everything for it—of course, I have my usual reaction of self-abasement, and get slightly depressed by that sort of confidence, but it's so wonderful here that I disregard it, and work, not even thinking of the horror of conscription that seems to be lurking in the fall. No matter—I must work while I can."

In later years Bernstein recalled the careless rapture of Tanglewood with ever-rosier spectacles. "I don't think we ever slept," he told students in 1974. "It was so exciting: we were working all the time, or playing all the time, because it became the same thing; playing music and playing with each other, making love, making music was all one thing, and it was constant, and of constant intensity. And over it all was the spirit of Koussevitzky, who held it all together and made it all so important. Everything that we did—every note, every phrase, the way we walked—was influenced by Koussevitzky because his charisma, if one can use that overused word, was so strong that his presence here at a rehearsal, for example—if I was rehearsing the student orchestra, he would be sitting there—would make it supremely important that everything you did be as good as possible."

Koussevitzky did indeed sit out front at rehearsals, occasionally using an electrical flash signal to halt proceedings so that he could make a comment to conductor or players. It may have been a daunting business for impressionable students, even psychologically damaging on occasions, but for those ready to learn—and Bernstein often said that he was like a sponge—the experience was exceptionally stimulating. In addition to the Randall Thompson Symphony No. 2, Bernstein conducted Bach's Double Violin Concerto on Saturday, July 20, the second and fourth movements of Rimsky-Korsakov's *Scheherazade* on July 25, the *Sinfonia Concertante* by Haydn on August 6, Brahms's *Variations on a Theme by Haydn* on August 13, and on August 16, Aaron Copland's *An Outdoor Overture*. Bernstein's progress was not all roses. His already flamboyant conducting style was occasionally mocked by his fellow students. During Rimsky's *Scheherazade* he acted out a cymbal clash with his hands. "We all gave him hell afterwards," Harold Shapero remembered, "for miming the obvious in such a ludicrous manner."

Bernstein also studied *L'Histoire du Soldat,* but it was not given in concert. Instead it provided the instrumental entertainment at an end-of-season housewarming picnic held at Seranak, the Koussevitzkys' newly acquired house just north of Tanglewood on the hillside known as Bald Head. Earlier in the year Natalie Koussevitzky had suffered a heart attack. She was still unwell, but she stepped out from her bedroom on to the balcony so that she and Serge Alexandrovich could look down over the front lawn where a chamber music group was performing a parody entitled *L'Histoire d'un Élève*. Bernstein was conducting and he had written a new narration, adapted specifically for Tanglewood consumption, just as *Carmen* had been updated with Sharon references five years previously. A hitchhiker was substituted for the soldier tramping "down a hot and dusty road," and as he walked past Tanglewood he heard strange music, such as the sound of ragtime, emerging from the woods. Photographs of the occasion show the Koussevitzkys presiding benignly over the scene.

Between August 1 and August 18, 1940, Koussevitzky rehearsed and conducted nine concerts with the Boston Symphony, attracting seventy thousand visitors and giving his students an opportunity to study his conducting technique. The second of the three series was organized as a Tchaikovsky-Beethoven cycle in honor of the centenary of Tchaikovsky's birth. The other weekends offered a mix of classical and modern works, so the concerts were also lessons for Bernstein in program building, a branch of the conductor's art in which he later excelled.

There were those who said Koussevitzky was not a very gifted technician, that he did not always know the scores when he began rehearsing them, and that he failed to give clear indications to the players as to his intentions regarding such basic matters as precisely when to begin playing. "Play when I touch the air above," he would say. But of his interpretive powers, and of his all-involving vision of the artist in the modern world, there was never any doubt.

In the tributes Bernstein later paid to Koussevitzky several themes can be discerned. His teaching was inspirational: "he taught the essence of the music and the spirit of the music." He was a man from whom radiance emanated, "possessed by music, by the ideas and ideals of music . . . a man whose possessedness came at you like cosmic rays." He taught devotion to music, dedication to one's work. "I remember his using the phrase 'The Central Line' . . . meaning the line to be followed by the artist at any cost, the line leading to perpetual discovery, a mystical line to truth as it is revealed in the musical art." His fundamental and indestructible lesson was summed up in a speech Bernstein made in 1963: *The composer comes first. In the beginning was the Note, and the Note was with God; and whosoever can reach high for that note, reach high, and bring it back to us on earth, to our earthly ears—he is a composer and to the extent of his reach partakes of the divine. This reach, this leap, aspiration, thrust—this is what Koussevitzky held most sacred; and he put all his vitality and concentration into serving it as well as he could. This meant not only conducting music, but teaching others to conduct it with the same blinding devotion; teaching the public to listen; and encouraging composers to reach high at every opportunity. He published new works [using his wife's fortune, he had set up a major publishing house], commissioned new works, and most important, played new works, with the same intensity, care, and beauty he lavished on the established repertoire.*"

Anybody who can inspire such high-flown praise usually has a downside, and Koussevitzky was no exception. Harold Shapero thought him unbelievably vain, preoccupied with his cape and the other trappings—vestments, one might call them—of a conductor/celebrant's working uniform. Even Bernstein felt obliged to refer to this in his centennial eulogy: "He had his share of vanity too, like all of us. I remember that when we were his students, thirty-odd years ago, at Tanglewood, we used to hear malicious rumors that he possessed upwards of ninety pairs of shoes! He liked to dress well, and look well; he did not disdain compliments in the greenroom. But—and this is a mighty conjunction—all of this was marshaled and harnessed to be at the service of music. He was simply taking all possible pains to make of himself the finest vessel for the composer's thought, the perfect instrumental link between composer and audience."

Bernstein learned something else from Koussevitzky: a sense of "gala." "When Koussevitzky stepped out on the stage, made his deft right-face to the podium, marched to it as to his destiny, raised his *baguette* (very slowly—it was *important*): no matter what the music was going to be, it was going to matter, because he was performing it. Nobody in his audience could fail to perceive that, and you listened in a heightened way . . . to each strand and caress and inflection and breath of the music." And along with the sense of gala went a sense of social responsibility, an issue over which master and fun-loving pupil would later cross swords. The conductor, argued Koussevitzky, was a leader in the community; he must behave accordingly, setting an example in conduct, speech and dress. "You must conduct your lives in such a way that when you come out on the stage to lead your orchestra you can truthfully say to yourself: 'Yes, I have the right to appear before these lovers of good music. They can watch me without shame. I have the right because my life and my work are clean.' " He advised his conducting students to begin a performance by drawing themselves up to their full height at the podium and then to spend some time— as Bernstein always did in later years—looking at the key musicians one after the other straight in the eye. "Not forgetting the trombones" he added, trombonists traditionally being the pranksters of the orchestra.

WHEN his first season at Tanglewood was over, Bernstein went home to Sharon and considered the prospect of a winter studying in Boston under Dr. Koussevitzky—as the maestro had suggested early in the summer. First he wrote a thank-you letter in the respectful, almost Victorian style he reserved from then on for communications with his mentor. "This summer to me was beauty—beauty in work, and strength of purpose, and cooperation. I am full of humility and gratitude for having shared so richly in it. These last six weeks have been the happiest and most productive of my life. I have been able, for the first time, to concentrate completely on my main purpose, with a glorious freedom from personal problems. . . . For your creative energy, your instinct for truth, your incredible incorporation of teacher and artist, I give humble thanks. Seeing in you my own concepts matured is a challenge to me which I hope to fulfil in your great spirit."

Koussevitzky kept up the high-flown tone in a note from Lenox on September 5 offering some dates for a mid-month meeting. "Nothing could have made me happier than to know that your work this summer has really given you beauty and strength and a better understanding of the gifts with which nature has endowed you."

Bernstein had already written to Mitropoulos, asking his advice about the proposal to stay in Boston. Delighted to hear of his young friend's artistic success, Mitropoulos replied on September 4: "I feel very happy that Dr. Koussevitzky is so interested in you. . . . I also think, not any more necessary to go again this winter to Curtis. The only thing left now is to work hard and be patient and wait a grand chance which I am sure will come." Bernstein drove over to Lenox to consult with his mentor and guide, who must have given him an optimistic response since ten days later Bernstein floated a new idea to keep himself tied to Boston: he would form and conduct a cadet orchestra in the Boston area under Koussevitzky's auspices. "Please don't think me presumptuous, I am just making a great effort to be practical. . . . I am sorry to intrude on your privacy even with this letter; but I am made bold by my recent reading of Nietzsche, who teaches me that I must be somewhat bolder if I, like his Zarathustra, shall ever face 'the great Noon-tide.' "

The noontide suddenly ebbed away. Fritz Reiner had earlier told Bernstein that if he went to Tanglewood to study with Koussevitzky he would not be welcome back, but Curtis was not prepared to lose its most brilliant conducting pupil. Sharp words must have passed between Lenox and Philadelphia, because on October 1 Koussevitzky sent Bernstein a telegram: "LEARN FROM DR. RANDALL THOMPSON THAT YOUR SCHOLARSHIP AT CURTIS INSTITUTE EXTENDS ANOTHER YEAR. HONESTLY BELIEVE YOU MUST COMPLETE YOUR OBLIGATION TO INSTITUTE WHICH EXCLUDES ANY OTHER PLAN FOR COMING YEAR WHICH CORRESPONDS ALSO WITH MY WISH. WITH WARM REGARDS S.K."

Bernstein capitulated. Within a few days he was installed in new Philadelphia lodgings and writing quite cheerfully to Miss Coates: "There has been a terrific tumult here concerning my return. . . . Reiner was furious (at Koussevitzky). I've heard the word *ethics* until I became immune to it. Thompson was the conciliator and he's a genius at it. He insisted that it would have been fatal, *disastrous,* to the relations between the two schools if I hadn't returned. But that's the way Curtis has of magnifying every detail. But I'm back in the arms of Reiner and Vengerova, with a school no-term loan of $40 per month and free lunches. I ought to manage. I am now a pawn in both musical and military diplomacy." (Congress had just debated a measure for a national draft.)

During the September lull in his student activities Bernstein returned to the composition of his sonata for violin and piano. He mentioned it in a postscript of an undated letter to Copland sent from Sharon some weeks after Tanglewood closed: "I've finished the Fiddle Sonata, and by God, there's something about the ending that's wonderful—almost mature. I want you to see the whole thing now—I like it better." But although the sonata was later performed in public, Bernstein never liked it enough to have it published, preferring to raid it for thematic material used in *Facsimile* (1946) and *The Age of Anxiety* (1949).

Bernstein's friendship with Copland had deepened over the six crowded Tanglewood weeks, and when they went their separate ways Bernstein felt his absence keenly. "Not seeing you is something of a shock, you understand. The summer was a revelation in that regard: neither of us (I hope) tired of the other (I had feared you might) and I came, in fact, to depend in many ways on you. I've never felt about anyone before as I do about you, completely at ease, and always comforted with you. This is not a love letter, but I'm quite mad about you." It is a touching note, especially if one recalls that Bernstein was just twenty-two and Copland was close to forty and sharing his life with the photographer Victor Kraft.

Another friendship developed at Tanglewood was with Thomas—"Tod"— Perry, already known to Bernstein from Curtis, where Perry looked after the students' radio and concert engagements. Perry used to lend Bernstein his concert tails, even though he was four inches taller—"any harbor in a storm," Bernstein observed, philosophically. Perry, who attended Tanglewood to learn about music administration, later became manager of the Boston Symphony Orchestra.

Bernstein also had friends from his Boston days in the Tanglewood Institute Orchestra. Dorothy Rosenberg had been the violinist in the trio that played summer seasons at Singer's Inn, Sharon. Jerome Lipson, a gifted viola player who was Bernstein's contemporary at Boston Latin, was one of the Sharon opera gang; he went on to Curtis and later became a prominent member of the Boston Symphony Orchestra.

Last but not least among the friends was Bernstein's roommate, the quirky composer Harold Shapero, who claimed that he chose to study with Hindemith that summer because he wanted to learn how to write music fast. Shapero and Bernstein got on famously, even to the point of sharing a girlfriend. "We took the same girl out on consecutive weekends, I remember. She was Kiki Speyer, the daughter of Louis Speyer, the English horn player with the Boston Symphony, and an absolute Parisian bombshell . . . half-Jewish . . . very slim, svelte, elegant. We figured if she couldn't sex us up nobody could, and it was very nice. She was crazy about Lenny, and they went together for quite a long time. . . . I know they had a sexual liaison. We used to discuss it in those days. . . . I think they had a fairly good time but there were problems. It didn't work."

At half a century's remove, Shapero may be forgiven for mixing up a year or a place: Bernstein's close friendship with Kiki Speyer probably dates from his 1941 season at Tanglewood and the year he subsequently spent in Boston when his friendship with Shapero was at its height. Bernstein's sexual orientation was uncertain. Emotionally he was still experimenting—or putting off the issue by immersing himself in work. As Shapero put it, "At Tanglewood sex was not a thing. You were too busy making music." Bernstein had no great love affair during these student days: no matter how trite it sounds, the love of his life was music.

# FINISHING TOUCHES

*Rittenhouse Square, Philadelphia, 1941.*
COURTESY OF SHIRLEY GABIS PERLE

*. . . in a hell of a whirl.*

—letter from Bernstein to
Helen Coates

WAR with Nazi Germany seemed increasingly possible in September 1940. The first thing Bernstein had to do when he returned to Philadelphia was to register for the newly established draft. The threat of conscription hung heavily over him all winter, giving a sense of unreality to his studies, which nonetheless continued at a frantic pace until the end of April 1941.

His new lodgings at 2122 Walnut Street consisted of a huge room—filled with massive furniture—that looked out on an alley of garbage cans. He renewed his friendship with Janice and Herschel Levit and completed a piano reduction of Copland's *El Salón México* at their apartment; their battered upright sounded, he said, like a Mexican barroom piano. Copland had accepted on Bernstein's behalf a transcription fee of twenty-five dollars (equivalent to one month's rent) and urged him to be meticulous about preparing a clean copy for his publisher Boosey & Hawkes. "Be archi-particular about dots, dashes, dynamics, etc.—as it saves endless time later when you reach the proof-correcting stage." Copland was not pleased when his protégé's efforts finally arrived in New York. "The piece came—and I've been sweating my whatchamacallits off ever since, trying to put it in shape. Your idea of a manuscript 'ready for the printer' is to weep. I'm preparing one of my best lectures for you on said subject. We need a couple of hours to talk over several points . . . I don't want to hand it over until I've seen you." This last was doubtless in response to a criticism Bernstein had made in his covering letter. "Look especially at the rather turgid and theatrical ossia [alternative version] at the end of the middle section, and if it gives pain simply cross it out. I did it only because there had to be some theatrical interest at that point (which is, I'm afraid, a bit dull—even in the orchestra). Don't take it too hard." This was not the last time that Bernstein would criticize his friend's compositions. In 1942 he shocked the choreographer Agnes de Mille by telling Copland to his face that the waltz section of *Rodeo,* his new ballet, still in manuscript, was "pretty dull." The transcription of *El Salón México* was published in 1941, the first time Bernstein's name appeared in a musical publication.

With all the excitements of his Tanglewood conducting debut still ringing in his ears, the drawbacks of the name Leonard Bernstein were again being debated. Koussevitzky wanted it changed, objecting to its Jewishness and ordinariness, and suggested Leonard S.—for Samuelovitch, son of Sam—Burns. Bernstein adamantly resisted him. (Another conductor named Bernstein who succumbed to Koussevitzky's advice and did change his name, to Harold Byrns, went on to enjoy a moderately successful career in postwar Europe.)

The fall was enlivened by Bernstein's developing friendship with Shirley Gabis, a beautiful sixteen-year-old schoolgirl who became an excellent pianist. They had first met the year before in the deli downstairs from Bernstein's apartment on South Twenty-second. "Lenny was at the counter, wearing a coat that looked ten sizes too big for him, as if he'd inherited it," Gabis remembered. "He was doing an imitation of FDR for the benefit of Mr. Lessin, the delicatessen owner. 'I hate war! Mrs. Roosevelt hates war. My little dog Fala hates war!'" Soon the two began meeting at the Delancey Pharmacy, the local hangout for the "Curtis kids," where for fifteen cents you could get a tunafish sandwich and a cup of coffee, take them to a booth, and read *The New Yorker* all day.

Their friendship moved into higher gear in the fall of 1940. Bernstein was Shirley Gabis's first romantic relationship and she was both excited and bewildered by him. She took Bernstein home to meet her divorced mother, Rae, an attractive woman who much enjoyed the company of the institute's many young musicians, notably the fifteen-year-old piano virtuoso Eugene Istomin. "Even years later," Shirley remembers, "Lenny would say to me, 'On my best days, I would like to sound like Eugene.'" Rae Gabis had a little beauty shop on the Main Line, Philadelphia's exclusive residential district. Sam Bernstein, a colleague in the beauty business, called on her. Shirley remembers him sitting in her mother's parlor saying, "I don't know why Lenny wants to be a musician. He could come into my business and I would pay him a hundred dollars a week." Bernstein described Sam to Shirley Gabis as something of an ogre: as a kid he was so frightened, he told her, that he used to hide under the table when his father came home.

For Bernstein the Gabis household was another home away from home. Shirley's grandfather had been a phonograph dealer and there were shelves of records in the basement. Shirley Gabis took over Shirley Bernstein's role in piano duets with rather more expertise. Echoes of Hindemith's piano duet sonata, which they played together, can be found in the first movement of Bernstein's clarinet sonata, begun the same year. "He used to play a lot of boogie-woogie, and, of course, the Copland *Variations.* There was so much banging away on the piano that finally the chandelier broke in the apartment below and my mother got an eviction notice."

Leonard and Shirley did a lot together that winter. "We both adored jazz and used to go to jam sessions. Lenny took me to my first burlesque show. We saw *La Bohème* together for the first time. We went to the premiere of the Schoenberg violin concerto, and heard Stokowski lecturing the audience of fidgeting ladies. And Lenny read poetry to me a lot." She never forgot the eloquence with which he recited the Keats sonnet "Bright star! would I were as steadfast as thou art."

Bernstein was tender and affectionate in his Curtis days. One night he helped Gabis with algebra homework so that she would be permitted to attend a Koussevitzky concert with the visiting Boston Symphony. She noticed that her friend behaved like a shy schoolboy in the maestro's presence backstage. She also went with Bernstein to call—uninvited—on the great Leopold Stokowski, then at the height of his *Fantasia* fame. They had just attended one of his American Youth Concerts, where the entire audience had stood to sing stirring words to the tune of Sibelius's *Finlandia.* Stokowski did not ask them in. "Thank you for coming," he called down from the top of the staircase at his Philadelphia carriage house. "And fuck you," whispered Bernstein as they turned away.

At twenty-one Bernstein was already subject to fits of deep depression— which, looking back, Shirley described as "internal conflict." There was no doubt that he was attracted to Shirley sexually. There was, she recalled, "a lot of heat between us." He must have talked to Copland about her, since in one (undated) letter he laconically wrote, "saw my 16 year old girl. I don't know." But he was also attracted to men, among them a young Philadelphia artist with whom he studied briefly. In another letter to Copland he was less guarded: "Aaron, I found someone. A young painter—twenty-one—going to give me painting lessons (among other things). I'm delighted, both at the lessons and at the teacher. Extremely mutual. This makes me very happy. But tired and skinny. To bed at 6 a.m." So he was cheerfully double-dating, even as he talked teasingly to Shirley about getting married.

In later life Bernstein used "To thine own self be true," Polonius's injunction to Laertes, as the basis for a commencement speech to students. But as a young man he had a hard time recognizing which was his own true self. A few years later he wrote the lyrics and music for a song called "Who Am I?" It was a celebration of the child in him, a side that he treasured and never entirely lost. But there was a darker self. Long before he graduated he opened his heart to

Shirley Gabis. "He expressed himself very specifically. I remember his words. He said: 'I have a canker in my soul.' "


BE that as it may, Bernstein's final year at Curtis was busy and fruitful. In November he sent Helen Coates an account of his activities. He had already conducted the Curtis Orchestra twice, in the Second Symphony of Sibelius, Beethoven's Fourth Piano Concerto and *Fêtes* by Debussy. His lessons with the tyrannical Isabelle Vengerova—"La Tirana," as he nicknamed her—were now proceeding wonderfully. But he was proudest of his activities outside the institute. For five dollars an hour he was giving piano lessons to what he called "rich brats," and coaching a boys' chorus at Meadowbrook School. And he had recently become the director of the Philadelphia People's Chorus. "I was called in to substitute for the conductor at a concert last week, and in two bloody rehearsals they had made such progress that they insisted I stay on, & I, delighted at the prospect of watching a thing grow, decided to stay. They're amateurs, of course, workers (the masses), and have a great spirit & enthusiasm. Tonight I rehearse them; & I'll have to start from scratch, teaching them to sing in tune, in time, pianissimo, and with good quality. Bach Chorales, by heck, for them!" There was also talk of conducting an all-Negro symphony orchestra that would be organized by the National Negro Congress and he gave lectures to the Youth Arts Forum, a group of young progressive artists, musicians, dancers, writers in Philadelphia, who wanted to play some of his works at an upcoming festival. "So I'm in a dither getting my fiddle sonata ready & rehearsed, and some songs that I've just completed about, of all things, the moon. I'm also to write music for the dance for it, & I've been asked to do a ballet by Merle Marscicano, an outstanding Phil. dancer. So it goes, one thing bringing along ten others."

Fritz Reiner's conducting students were sent to Chicago for a week at the end of November, all expenses paid, to attend Reiner's rehearsals for a production of *Der Rosenkavalier.* There, Bernstein plugged into Aaron Copland's nationwide music and dance network. He had dinner with Ruth Page, for whom Copland had written his first ballet score in 1934, and went to the ballet with the influential critic Cecil Smith. He dropped a card to Copland from a swanky address atop the spectacular forty-four-stories-high Chicago Towers skyscraper on North Michigan Avenue. "La vie est bien pleine de répétitions, des hommes, de la musique [rehearsals, men, music]." He listed what he had seen: *Don Giovanni, Carmen,* a ballet evening (music by Henry Brant, Kurt Weill and Tchaikovsky), a concert conducted by Frederick Stock and, above all, *Der Rosenkavalier.* When he got back to Philadelphia he wrote to Copland about the Strauss opera: *"Rosenkavalier* is puffed up, but has extraordinarily beautiful passages. Reiner is a genius! Music is a hard profession. All this have I gleaned, O richer I, from a week in Chicago!"

No sooner home than he was taking part in a radio performance of the Sibelius violin sonatina. Next day brought a letter from Helen Coates in Boston: "Mother and I listened with rapt attention and great joy to your broadcast yesterday. Half-way through, Mother said, 'Bless his heart' which shows how she feels about you." Mothers meant a great deal to him. He treasured his own, even though he sometimes neglected his correspondence with her. Letter-writing was not Jennie's forte and Helen Coates had taken over some of the mothering role. "Eat *sensibly* and *regularly,*" she had urged him earlier in the semester; "do remember all the points we talked over about your contacts with others, including the very important one of being *well-groomed* at all times (even at the earliest morning appointment)."

Bernstein had to cope with graver matters that fall. David Prall, who was only in his mid-fifties, died in October. Bernstein said it took weeks to recover from the shock of losing one of the greatest friends he ever had. And Alfred Eisner, his roommate for two years at Eliot House, died of a brain tumor three months later. Bernstein wrote to Copland: "The phenomenon of music on the brain, which has always been with me (you know that) has stopped. I have no tune to sing. My head feels like dry, brown, cracking wood."

A few days after Eisner's death, Paul Bowles arrived in Philadelphia for the tryout of *Liberty Jones,* a new political extravaganza for which he'd written incidental music. Bowles had a quandary: he had been asked to orchestrate two ballet scores for Anton Dolin, based on music by the composers Pugni and Cimarosa—but he was so busy rewriting his theater music he paid Bernstein three hundred dollars to do the ballet work in his name. Several letters from Bowles expressed gratitude to Bernstein for having carried out the task so swiftly. But in his autobiography, *Without Stopping,* Bowles claimed that "Bernstein amused himself with the instrumentation . . . which he assayed in the most perverse and unlikely fashion, giving to the brass those passages which lent themselves to strings. It was not at all what the ballet company wanted, he told me subsequently, and with glee (since only my name appeared on the scores). They had to have both ballets re-orchestrated."

In the midst of this extracurricular activity, Bernstein and a fellow pupil of Vengerova, Annette Elkanova, performed the Stravinsky concerto for two solo pianos on NBC radio. Bernstein wrote about it in advance to Mildred Spiegel, sweetly commenting that he would imagine her at the other piano. Helen Coates heard the broadcast and predictably dashed off an enthusiastic review. "I'm inclined to think you're a bit biased," he wrote back on February 7: "One of these days you'll have to redeem yourself and say something unfavorable. But it really was good. I know because I've heard the recording that was made of the broadcast. We were, in fact, quite amazing. (Pardon all this self-praise—I'm good so rarely these days.)" At the end of February Bernstein conducted the "March of the Saints" from Virgil Thomson's *Four Saints in Three Acts,* and an orchestral work of Randall Thompson's, for the Youth Arts Forum. Once or twice a week he went up to New York, which he called the "City of Sin," to

attend a concert, or visit with Copland, or simply to escape from the Philadelphia routine for a night out with Adolph Green and Betty Comden, sometimes
staying over at Comden's apartment where he had another admiring mother
figure to take care of him.

Already Bernstein was many things to many different people. He was
deeply fond of the friends he'd been seeing in Philadelphia: the Levits because
of their enthusiasm and Bohemian domesticity; Paul Bowles because of his
intense, poetic mysteriousness; David Diamond because of his mercurial, outrageous temperament; and Shirley Gabis because, as he wrote later, she kept him
on an even keel. But by the spring of 1941 Gabis had become, in her own words,
"very defensive and self-protective: I was beginning to understand what it
meant for a man to be a homosexual. And also it was already clear in Philadelphia that Lenny was there for the world. He was already busy with his extravagant ways. We'd be walking down the street and after he'd greeted five people
with kisses and arms outspread, I'd say 'Are you really so crazy about Lynn
Wainwright?' " The answer must have been yes. When he returned to Curtis in
1975 for the institute's fiftieth-anniversary celebrations, he said nothing about
how bored he had sometimes been, how stultifying he had sometimes found it.
But he did recall the "secret anti-Bernstein club, composed of students, some of
whom later became my closest friends—Julian Lutz, Leo Luskin . . . Lynn
Wainwright."

Enthusiasm was one of the secrets to his charm and it made him hard to
resist. The baritone Theodor Uppman recalls preparing a score of Schubert's
*Winterreise* in the Curtis student common room when Bernstein approached
him. "What's that you're working on?" *"The Winter's Journey."* "I've never
done that. . . . Can we work on it for a while?" And off they went to a
practice room to read through Schubert's song cycle. After he played Copland's
*Vitebsk* Piano Trio for the Russian-American Institute in the middle of March
he wrote excitedly to Copland about an idea he had to compose a piano version
of *Billy the Kid.* "It would be a kind of paraphrase in the style of Liszt (formally
only, I mean) probably a messy juxtaposition of tunes; but I think I can make it
work by fooling around with it a little. You likee? You thinkee Boosee likee?"
Publisher jokes aside, Copland was not encouraging. "Has it ever occurred to
you that nobody ever plays Liszt paraphrases any more? There must be a
reason! Still you have all my blessings so why not try?" But nothing more was
heard of the proposal.

At the end of March Bernstein was so impressed with the New York
Philharmonic broadcast of the new *Sinfonia da Requiem* by Benjamin Britten
that he wrote to the composer, telling him how moved he had been. Bernstein's
letter hasn't survived but Britten's reply suggests that Bernstein had made the
mistake of disparaging earlier Britten compositions. "Judging by your remarks," Britten wrote, "you certainly 'got' what I wrote and it was extremely
nice of you to take the trouble to write and say so. I am sure that it's the 'best so
far'—and as it's the last [i.e., the most recent] that is as it should be. I might

argue with one or two of your remarks about my earlier masterpieces—but maybe there is something in what you say. The only thing is, maybe those particular vices are less vicious than some others I can think of—such as inhibitions, sterility, self-conscious ideas of originality—but we won't go into that now!"

Paul Bowles saw Bernstein's letter on the table at Middagh Street in Brooklyn Heights where Britten was living in the same remarkable household as Oliver Smith, Wystan Auden, Gypsy Rose Lee, Paul and Jane Bowles, George Davis of *Harper's Bazaar* and Golo Mann. Bowles was prompted to write urging Bernstein to join him in Mexico that summer, but with only three hundred dollars saved, Mexico was not a realistic proposition. Bernstein could not see much further than his forthcoming Curtis diploma: that would be followed by a brief return to Harvard, where the Student Union Theater Group had persuaded him to write the music for their May production. Then he would have a second summer at Tanglewood and then—the abyss of uncertainty.

It was important to leave Curtis on a high note and this he did, making his first broadcast appearance as a conductor on April 26, 1941, conducting the Institute Orchestra in Brahms's A major Serenade. The faithful Helen Coates wrote a postcard from Boston: *"Bravo!—a thousand times!*—a lovely composition and a grand performance. I'm increasingly fond of my favorite conductor. I'm just off to a cocktail party so I'll drink one to you and a *long brilliant career."* The performance was repeated at Curtis on the twenty-eighth, when Reiner also conducted *Le Bourgeois Gentilhomme,* with Bernstein playing the orchestral piano part. Shirley Gabis remembers Fritz Reiner looking up at Mrs. Bok's loge with a quizzical look as he acknowledged the applause—she had just given him the sack, along with Randall Thompson.

Two days later Bernstein appeared in a concert given by graduating pupils of Isabelle Vengerova. He played the "Prelude" and "Rigaudon" from Ravel's *Le Tombeau de Couperin* and the Fifth Sonata by Scriabin, on which he had been laboring for months. Finally on May 3 Bernstein received his diploma in conducting at the commencement ceremony. His grades were little short of phenomenal: A-plus for piano; A's in form, orchestration and conducting, reportedly the only A Reiner ever attributed. The pianist Phyllis Moss, who graduated with Bernstein, remembers how surprised she was that he did not win the unofficial prize for the graduate most likely to succeed: that went to a singer who ended up teaching voice in Philadelphia.

Copland came to the graduation on his way home to New York from Cuba. Shirley Gabis remembers waving good-bye to her brilliant boyfriend at the station; he was off with Copland and a cellist friend for a weekend in Atlantic City. Bernstein wrote to her a few days later from Harvard, in the midst of orchestrating his ambitious score for the Student Union production of Aristophanes's *The Peace,* an antiwar satire, translated and updated with many topical allusions. He had bruised his hand playing baseball with Harold Shapero, which was worrying since he had two piano engagements as well as two performances to conduct. "Life, dear one, is hectic plus. I really need your steadying hand on mine now. It's amazing to look back and see that it really was a steadying hand. Phenomenal effect for an adolescent Galatea to have: but then you're you.

"Of course Bill [Saputelli] has told you of our Atlantic City escapade (mostly gabbing with Curtis-ites). And now you're doing algebra and going to Ivy Balls. . . . and putting your hem up and down according to your escort, and eating *Chez Saputelli*—and I've left your mind. See? I told you so."

But he had not left her mind. Once a bond had been forged with Bernstein it was impossible to forget him. They remained friends for life.

# TANGLEWOOD REVISITED
# JUNE 1941–AUGUST 1942

*The Shed at Tanglewood.*
PHOTO CHRISTINA BURTON

*Ach Gott, my life is full of Kouss and Kiki and Kiki*
*and Kouss and Kiki and Kiki and Kouss and Alex*
*and Olga and Ted and memories of you.*

—BERNSTEIN TO COPLAND,
November 3, 1941

I N June 1941, waiting for the second summer course at Tanglewood to begin, Bernstein entered a musical quiz organized by the *Boston Herald*. For the final round the competitors had to identify music recorded by the Pops and Boston Symphony orchestras, played to them over loudspeakers at Symphony Hall. Bernstein came in second but was promoted to share the first prize when it was discovered that the winner, Jerome Pastene, worked as a record buyer and therefore had an unfair advantage. The award was a free week of residence at Tanglewood. Since Bernstein was already a pupil of Dr. Koussevitzky, an extra prize was added to the hundred-and-fifty-dollar cash award: the opportunity to conduct the Boston Pops orchestra on the Esplanade, a huge outdoor facility on the parkland bordering the Charles River. Bernstein's first performance with a professional orchestra took place on Friday, July 11, before an audience estimated at twenty-two thousand people. Without a rehearsal he conducted the imposing Prelude to *Die Meistersinger von Nürnberg* by Richard Wagner, coping coolly with its tricky problems of balance and fluctuating tempos. "We all thought this was a fresh, talented young guy," the violinist Harry Ellis Dickson remembers.

At Tanglewood he again shared a dormitory with exceptionally talented musicians, among them Arthur Winograd, a gifted and witty cellist who became a founding member of the Juilliard Quartet before switching to conducting, Henry Portnoi, later principal bass of the Boston Symphony Orchestra, and Nathan Brusilow, a clarinetist from the Curtis Institute, who, according to Harold Shapero, produced the most beautiful sound, "like ambrosia in the morning."

Bernstein was the youngest of six conducting students. Among the newcomers was Richard Duncan, whose wayward sense of pulse provoked in Koussevitzky a fractured-English injunction which passed into Tanglewood history: "Donnkin, Donnkin, took it a tempo und kept it!" The orchestra was larger in 1941. The string section had fifty-three players, against thirty-six in 1940, and enlarged woodwind sections, enabling more players to perform solos. There were three-hour morning rehearsals Tuesdays through Fridays, and concert performances on Friday evenings, a pattern which changed after three weeks to accommodate the nine festival concerts given by the Boston Symphony. Then as now these were money-making activities: as many as thirteen thousand people attended the BSO's final concert. *Time* magazine said that although other venues could attract even larger audiences, Tanglewood was the premier U.S. musical event because of the polished perfection of its performances.

Aaron Copland and Paul Hindemith had eight composition pupils each. Copland's students included Gardner Read, whose *Prelude and Toccata* Bernstein conducted at the final Institute Orchestra concert on August 8. Many years later, Read wrote that no subsequent performance "ever matched the excitement and *élan* of Lenny's reading of my music." Bernstein described his first concert to Mildred Spiegel, who was away in New York studying the piano with a new professor. "These two weeks have been awful successful, but really, and I feel sort of stock-taking today, very lazy, due to a wild horseback ride yesterday and a big swim, and the greatest success of my life Friday night, and a rather romantic last night. About Friday: I did the William Schuman American Festival Overture on the same program with Kouss conducting [earlier in the concert] the Faust Symphony, and it (the overture) brought down the house. Screaming, cheering ovation. Kouss kissed me in public. Bill Schuman was there himself and said he never heard such a performance of anything before. Aaron was hopping around like a duck, and I got two more bows than Kouss had gotten." Perhaps this was because Koussevitzky did only the first two movements of Liszt's symphony, omitting the crowd-pleasing Mephistopheles. "God, I sound conceited," Bernstein continued, "but it was really marvellous that you can play a piece of modern American music full of bitonality and whatnot, and people at the end scream 'Bravo.' It's terrific. Did those kids play! Everyone really tore out his guts on the piece. I never heard anything so exciting. It even nonplussed me on the podium."

The mention of a "rather romantic last night" may allude to Bernstein's friendship with the beautiful Kiki Speyer, since Bernstein later told Shirley Gabis that Koussevitzky himself was encouraging an affair between them.

A spicier incident involved the actress Tallulah Bankhead, who was playing in summer stock at nearby Stockbridge and came to a Shed rehearsal. Bernstein, getting his first experience of work with a big chorus, was shimmying his way through Constant Lambert's *The Rio Grande*. Tallulah drawled her admiration for Lenushka's rippling back muscles and invited him back to dinner in Stockbridge. By 8 P.M., the story goes, nothing had been eaten, and even "with help from Bankhead's chauffeur, 'a roaring drunk,' Bernstein barely made it back to Tanglewood in time to navigate *The Rio Grande*'s difficult shoals at that night's concert." This much-repeated story must be treated with caution. None of the published Tallulah Bankhead biographies refers to the incident, which probably meant more to Bernstein than to Bankhead.

Bernstein's next concert appearance was to conduct the first movement of the Brahms Second Piano Concerto. The soloist was Carlos Moseley, who later became the managing director of the New York Philharmonic. Privately Bernstein was not excited to be "relegated," as he saw it, to the role of accompanist, but the concerto's epic scale gave him plenty to do as a conductor; Howard Taubman of the *New York Times* praised the interpretation, saying that among the handpicked students Bernstein was the one who had made the "biggest splash." For his part, Moseley was enchanted with Bernstein's attitude: "I started playing for him and straight away he began to show me how certain things might be better."

The summer was hot in 1941 and the elegant Koussevitzky would frequently discard his jacket at rehearsals, something he would never have tolerated of himself or others back in Boston. Winifred Schaefer, then a young cello student, recalled a warm, sunny day when Maestro Koussevitzky, accompanied by his entourage (his valet, Viktor, and the student conductors), made his usual dramatic entrance—he alone was permitted to drive his Buick into the Tanglewood grounds. Viktor removed the elegant cape and Koussevitzky mounted the podium. He worked lovingly with the students, calling them "kinder" or "mein dear yuts." But suddenly he screamed and dropped his baton, his hand flying to his face. "A vapse! A vapse his bit me!" he cried. And indeed he had been stung on the nose by a huge wasp. He was unable to go on and was quickly caped and led away by his valet.

In August Bernstein turned to chamber music, playing the piano part in Copland's *Vitebsk* Trio for the third time that year. Subtitled *Study on a Jewish Theme,* the trio is based on the folk theme used in S. Ansky's play *The Dybbuk.* For Bernstein it was an example of how a Jewish composer could keep faith with his roots and yet be contemporary in his language, a lesson he was to put into practice in his first symphony.

The 1941 summer concert season ended as the 1940 season had with a huge gala benefit to raise cash for United Service organizations and British War

Relief. A week later Bernstein was back at the family house in Sharon which his father, fearing hard times ahead, had decided to convert into an all-year-round residence, selling the big house in Newton. Bernstein was elated by the summer he'd just spent but depressed about his future. He had no immediate job prospects, and the Army wanted him. He wrote to Dr. Koussevitzky: "Again it is my privilege to be able to thank you for another great summer of glorious and inspiring study. I feel humble and grateful in the face of the added responsibility that comes with each new advance in my work. I am rather in doubt as to how to continue that advance now. As you know I have already received my questionnaire from the Army; and, as far as I know, I am perfectly eligible, except for a siege of asthma and hay fever that I am now undergoing. It is therefore difficult to formulate any winter plans; for I cannot be given a responsible position while there is the probability of my being suddenly taken away from it to join the Army."

War for the United States seemed close to inevitable. The Russians were everywhere falling back against Nazi attacks: the Japanese were threatening in the Pacific. "In the light of world events, however, I want least of all to shirk my responsibility to my country; and I therefore wonder if I might be of service in the USO [United Services Organization] where I could simultaneously serve national defense and remain in my field of endeavor. . . . Please let me know how you feel about this question, as I want to do the right thing morally and practically; and I feel that I can rely completely on your guidance."

Koussevitzky had already written letters of introduction to powerful figures in Washington and New York seeking musical work for Bernstein within the armed forces. He wrote also to Mrs. Bok in the hope that she might exert some influence with the Philadelphia draft board. But his efforts were superfluous: when Bernstein went for his medical interview he was classified 4F because of his asthma.

Bernstein's Boston year, between the Tanglewood seasons of 1941 and 1942, began with a brief holiday in Key West, undertaken, he told Copland: "to get away from people and Kiki." On the Florida train going south past Philadelphia, Bernstein scribbled a rhyming note about his plans to Shirley Gabis: "Key West for a rest, the rest can be guess'd, the best to be blest, the best for a guest, a rest in Key West. And maybe a stealthy boat trip over to Havana on the Side. All alone. No one to phone. Sounds like fone, no? I hope the Tanglewood evils have blown over, and all is in clover. 'Twas all so freaky with Kiki. And all so bleaky. And cheeky. I'll write again with a better pen. The train sways madly so I write so badly. My love to Rae and all the rest. I'm on my way, to old Key West. (For a much needed rest.) Have you ever seen a letter that naturally rhymed better?"

In Key West he lodged in an upstairs room in the southernmost house of the U.S.A., where he began work on a sonata for clarinet and piano (he completed it the following year in Boston). He listened to Cuban bands from Radio Havana and dashed off some music of his own which he hoped could be used as a ballet. He called the score a "conch concerto"; its cross-rhythmed *huapango* finale is the source of the melody "I Like to Be in America" in *West Side Story*.

Bernstein's assertion to Copland that he was running away from Kiki Speyer has to be read in the context of the special relationship between the two men and Bernstein's continuing indecision about his sexual preferences. Just as he could be absorbed with conducting one month and with composing the next, so one week he found himself flirting with "the charming boy in the Tanglewood Box Office last summer"—and the next discussing marriage with the beautiful Kiki. The end of his letter to Copland contains this significant passage: "I confessed all, like a ghoul, to Kiki, explaining the whole summer fiasco, and now it's normal again, and she wants to marry me anyway, and accept the double life, or try for my recovery."

Bernstein returned to Sharon in the fall. At the New Year, Kiki Speyer gave up the uneven struggle to capture his affection and went to Mexico "for *toute la saison*," as Bernstein reported to Copland. And for many months thereafter his letters veer bewilderingly in tone and subject from musical matters to new affairs of the heart, gleefully reporting his feelings about his latest love affair while at the same time protesting that Copland's was the affection that mattered most to him. "I don't mean this as a speech, because you are above these things; but you must know that there can never be one closer to me than you are, & I hope will never cease to be—A strange moment for a declaration of faith; but I keep thinking of that talk we once had under very personal circumstances, when you gave me a 'faute-de-mieux' speech. Remember Aaron—wish me luck and happiness; & forget all about this letter. It's silly & young, and really an insult to your great sympathy and knowledge; but I feel just a little bit terrible about The Thing. And you seemed so unhappy that night at Spivvy's [a New York nightclub]. Are you only tired? And what of Victor? Aaron, for once, tell me."

Copland wrote back calmly as he always did, gently deflating the mood but for once avoiding any of the nicknames he used for Bernstein. From Bernstein's letter and this measured reply, it seems that Copland had considered sharing his life with his friend until Bernstein had taken up with somebody else: "Dear Lenny, I'd love to be able to answer your letter solemnly like I should but the sort of things that ought to be said can't be written. Anyhow, I can't write them —I can only say them. Of course in a way it's wonderful that you should have felt the need to write yours. I'm sorry I was looking so glum at Spivvy's. I suppose I was looking the unalterable fact straight in the face for the first time. Well that's over—and I promise never to look so glum again. Naturally what I want most to happen is what you want most to happen and if you think this is really it, then I'm awfully glad. It certainly looks right from the outside. Here I am being solemn after all." Bernstein was briefly in love with a young male composer named Jean Middleton.

Some of Bernstein's emotional turmoil in the winter of 1941 derived from the fact that for once in his life he had too much time on his hands. With hindsight he realized that he should have gone to New York to seek his fortune. What kept him in Boston were vague promises of work with the Boston Symphony combined with a complete absence of financial independence. Koussevitzky had offered him the chance to appear as soloist in the piano concerto by Carlos Chávez, but the performance was canceled because of the battle being waged between the trustees of the resolutely nonunion Boston Symphony and the American Federation of Musicians, of which Chávez was a member. Bernstein had joined the union's Boston branch, too, in order to play jazz and take on nightclub gigs.

A highlight of a difficult, tense season was William Schuman's October visit for the world premiere of his Third Symphony. Disappointed in the work, Koussevitzky called in Bernstein for advice. "Lenny knew that symphony as I was writing it," Schuman later said. "I remember playing the snare drum rhythm of the last movement to him in a cafeteria on Fifty-seventh Street." The cuts Bernstein proposed were acceptable to Schuman and turned Koussevitzky into an enthusiastic advocate of the symphony.

On November 4 Bernstein was a soloist with the National Youth Administration Orchestra conducted by Arthur Fiedler, in New Bedford, sixty miles south of Boston. Twelve hundred people squeezed into the high school auditorium to hear him perform two concertos, Mozart's K. 450 in B flat and the Ravel, the latter a performance that did not go entirely without hitch for Bernstein. The *Standard Times* of New Bedford reported that the high school piano did not bring out Bernstein's gifts: "the thoughtful demeanor which he wore throughout the evening first expressed surprise and then alarm when, in the middle of the Ravel piano concerto, one of the keys which had sustained considerable pounding, suddenly refused to function and Mr. Fiedler had to stop conducting to help pry it loose."

Two weeks later Bernstein gave a morning piano recital at the Copley Plaza Hotel in Boston. His program featured *El Salón México* in his own transcription. Helen Coates had written touchingly when news of the publication had first been broached. "I remember the times—years ago it seems—when you would play me some of your arrangements of Russian and Hebrew themes and I would urge you to write them down. You would protest that you didn't know how to write them out properly and ask me how to go about it . . . I can scarcely believe how rapidly things have been happening to you since those years when you came to play to me and stayed while we talked and talked and talked."

Koussevitzky considered quitting Boston for the New York Philharmonic (which would have taken over Tanglewood) but Boston eventually settled with the union and renewed Koussy's tenure. But when the United States entered the war, the Boston Symphony withdrew from the 1942 Tanglewood festival. A defiant Koussevitzky resolved to keep it going himself, with financial help from the music foundation he formed in honor of his wife, Natalie, after her death in January 1942. The student orchestra was promoted to festival status, and Leonard Bernstein was named Koussevitzky's assistant.

But until the summer of 1942, Bernstein was supported by his father, who provided the funds for him to rent a studio apartment with a piano on Huntington Avenue. On December 5, 1941, he sent out an elegant card: "Leonard Bernstein announces the opening of his studio for the teaching of Piano and Musical Analysis." The timing was hardly propitious. Two days later Japanese warplanes struck the U.S. fleet in Pearl Harbor. Bernstein attracted only one pupil, a man called Bernie who came in once a week from the suburbs.

He played the piano in Boston's Symphony Hall for the first time in January 1942, accompanying Jean Bedetti, the principal cellist of the Boston Symphony. In February he went to New York to play piano duets at a Composers' League concert with Harold Shapero. Shapero's own sonata was given its premiere. He dedicated it "To Lenny and Myself." This unprecedented self-dedication was later adjusted: "to L.B. and H.S."

In April 1942 Bernstein appeared nightly at the Fox and Hounds in Boston, accompanying a singer named Eric Stein. It was the only formal club engagement of his career.

That spring he organized three musical events for the Boston Institute of Modern Art. At the first concert he and Shapero played duets again. At the second, "an intimate affair of evening gowns and dinner coats" featuring the clarinetist David Glazer, Bernstein's clarinet sonata had its premiere. A Boston critic noted that it was "choc-a-bloc full of jazzy, rocking rhythms."

Aaron Copland's *The Second Hurricane,* performed on May 21, 1942, was the final Institute of Modern Art concert. The two-act opera is ninety minutes long and requires seven singers, three actors, an orchestra of thirty, and two choruses, one of schoolchildren and one of adults. Orson Welles's original production in 1937 involved close to 150 people, including Joseph Cotten in the role of the aviator. Bernstein recruited his forces from all over Boston and as in Sharon days threw himself into every aspect of the production. "Things progress apace," he wrote to Copland ("Most august Diabolus"). "The usual troubles—and many unusual ones. And still I must worry about the height of the bleachers, & if there are bleachers, & they must be delivered by such a date for the dress rehearsal, which is then canceled because the hall is denied us, & can we use a rubber boat of khaki canvas, & Kouss. is in the hospital sick with I know not what, & Olga [Koussevitzky's secretary and future wife] screams at me to finish those scores, & Charlie screams at me to make copies of those songs, & the strings are inadequate (quantity *and* quality), the clarinet can't make any more rehearsals with the grownups this morning."

This homespun production of *The Second Hurricane* was a chance for Bernstein to demonstrate his devotion to Copland in the most practical way, by performing his music in his presence. The success in Boston's Jordan Hall was sufficiently great for a second performance to be swiftly arranged at the Sanders

Theatre in Cambridge, this time with piano only rather than full orchestra. The radio station WCOP played the piece all day and interviewed Bernstein at length. He talked about Copland's history—his first use of the media for musical education. "Boston is all agog and all aware! What a team! You write 'em, kid, and I'll do 'em."

The few days Bernstein and Copland spent together later that month at Copland's summer cottage allowed them to reaffirm their deep emotional ties. "It was wonderful," Bernstein wrote, "just plain wonderful. Coming home I read in Tolstoy that a truth (or a lie for that matter) never appears to two minds in the same way. But certain ones do to us, especially musical and some analytical ones, and there is great joy in that." "It was marvellous, just plain marvellous," echoed Copland of their time together. "But now it's sad and terribly quiet and no fun—only work. In two weeks you'll be *in der nahe* [nearby]—and that's some consolation."

Before he went to Tanglewood that summer Bernstein removed his belongings and rented out his Huntington Avenue studio. He had decided that whatever the future held for him, it would not take place in Boston. Wartime Tanglewood was also a disappointment to him. He had been invited to work as Koussevitzky's assistant so late in the day that the brochures did not include his name among the faculty teachers. Koussevitzky trained the first orchestra, expanded to 105 student players, in works such as Shostakovich's Fifth Symphony: its playing was by all accounts superb and the people of Lenox and the Berkshires turned out in the thousands, beating the gasoline rationing by sharing cars, hitching lifts, even commandeering a hay wagon to attend the concerts. Bernstein conducted the second orchestra, which he described as poor and overworked; his mood was little short of dejection. "The season has not measured up to its predecessors," he told Helen Coates. "I've done only very desultory conducting, and that with a poor, overworked orchestra. . . . Two scenes from *Porgy and Bess* were very successful and will be repeated for Russian Relief."

The climax of the season was another mammoth "Tanglewood on Parade" benefit on August 14, at which the outstanding event was the U.S. concert premiere of the *Leningrad* Symphony by Shostakovich, much of which had been composed in the besieged Russian city during the previous year. Bernstein was detailed to play the bass drum in the orchestral percussion section. Frederick Fennell, then a conducting student, described how they helped to build the great crescendo in the first movement: "Both of us had our mouths open at the performance to compensate for the great sound coming at the ears from all sections as Koussevitzky—forehead vein at the full—kept imploring for more."

Playing in the orchestra that summer was a young clarinetist named David Oppenheim. He and Bernstein became close and after Tanglewood they set off together for a short hitchhiking tour of New England. Bernstein wrote about his new love, as he wrote about everything else, to Aaron Copland:

We have had two glorious days. It has been like a movie, and we've been watching ourselves participate, meanwhile violently analyzing our relationship, and every little phase of it, until it's almost not there any more. You're right—talk is pernicious where instinct reigns. But we have been wonderfully happy. We've had lovely hitches, and when we didn't, we didn't care. Last night (after having seen a Bette Davis picture in Pittsfield) we got to Lanesboro, & stayed on the porch hammocks of a farmhouse. With a steaming breakfast this morning; then off on a 120 mile hitch to Vergennes, Vermont.

And all afternoon à la Whitman, nude on the shores of Lake Champlain, running around the pine woods, on the clay and slate beaches, in the luscious water,—all of this *nu*. And sun, & friendship, & friendly Vermont people—so nice & rightminded & misled—& then on to Burlington tonight where we saw *Mrs. Miniver*. A good film.

After writing this idyllic account, Bernstein huffily reported that Oppenheim had befriended a young couple and gone off to the girl's house acting as a kind of father confessor. A brief bout of introspection followed: "Why do I dare to resent situations of my own creation? There must be—and is from this moment—some strength in me and my little character." Nevertheless the friendship with Oppenheim flourished. "D.O." spent a few days in Sharon around Bernstein's twenty-fourth birthday, and the two men went down to New York together at the end of the month: Bernstein introduced him to the Revuers, who were back at the Vanguard after a spell at the Rainbow Room, and Oppenheim met the entrancing Judy Holliday, whom he would marry after the war.

In a card from New York to Helen Coates, dated September 1, Bernstein wrote, "I have come to the Big City, finally, to seek my fortune." He proved to be one of those New Yorkers who love their adopted city more than their own birthplaces.

# 11.

# THE NEW YORK BOHEMIAN

*With Shirley Bernstein, 1942.*
COURTESY OF THE ESTATE OF LEONARD BERNSTEIN

*Greenwich Village was the Mecca. I didn't find any*
*work but, instead, had a very Bohemian summer! It*
*was awful! I had no money, it was very hot and there*
*were tons of cockroaches everywhere. Did I suffer?*
*Sure! But during that summer I learned from*
*Schaunard how to transform suffering into a form of*
*art. I was the Schaunard of Greenwich Village.*

—LEONARD BERNSTEIN
(introducing his 1988
recording of *La Bohème*)

WITH his penchant for myth-making, Bernstein later called his first year in
New York his Valley Forge period. But George Washington was close to
defeat in the bleak winter of 1777, whereas Bernstein enjoyed some
success as pianist and composer in 1943, and by the summer the outlook for his
conducting career was improving. The absence of symphonic conducting and
the demeaning nature of his only regular employment colored his memories
about the period. When he reported on his occasional triumphs in other fields
Aaron Copland would pull him up short: "I keep being properly impressed by
all the offers, interests, contacts, personalities that flit through your life. But

don't forget *our* party line—you're heading for conducting in a big way—and everybody and everything that doesn't lead there is an excrescence on the body politic."

The Second World War turned in the Allies' favor in the winter of 1942–43, but it would be a desperately long haul to victory. Twelve million Americans were now in uniform. Bernstein felt "self-conscious" about being a civilian. Copland told him not to worry: "You're asthmatic and that's that." During his first nine months in New York Bernstein lived at four different addresses; for a home-loving boy who liked to be mothered this must have been hard. But the facts do not support Bernstein's image of himself as being down and out in the Big City.

"Me voici in NYC," he wrote to Aaron Copland on the day of his arrival. "This time it's real and I'm happily hunting The Job. D.O. is here making everything beautiful and harder." Next day came another card: "I'm writing a piece called 'Victory Jive' and I'm very deeply in love. Tomorrow begins the psy. Glory be. I need sleep. This morning I wrote you from a horrid room in a ghastly 42nd St. hotel, where a fat guy across the alley tried to seduce me." (He soon moved to a basement room in the Park Savoy Hotel on West Fifty-eighth Street, where the rent was eight dollars a week.)

In his reply, Copland rebuked Bernstein for writing about love and rape on wild postcards that could be read by Robert, his cook. "You sound so New-yorky," he continued, "no sleep, mauled liver, psychiatrists, etc. Not at all the sound and confident fellow that should be seeking a job." Bernstein had previously asked Copland to put him in touch with conductor André Kostelanetz, who had recently commissioned Copland's *Lincoln Portrait*. "What in God's name makes you decide that Kostelanetz is the be all and end all of jobs? It's so unrealistic of you. . . . It's too much to expect that he will create a job for you," Copland went on. He nevertheless wrote a glowing introduction to Kostelanetz on Bernstein's behalf: "His *forte* is conducting. . . . He is also a whiz at the piano—including jazz style. He can arrange, compose, coach singers, lead choral groups—in fact anything in music is up his alley." Nothing came of this, but Copland had more practical advice, suggesting that he try nightclub work for immediate cash. "Don't expect miracles and don't get depressed if nothing happens for awhile. That's NY."

Bernstein played occasionally for the Revuers that fall at Café Society and the Vanguard, and the impresario Max Jacoby reportedly wanted to build him up as a performer at the Blue Angel, but he paid his modest rent by accompanying dance classes at one of the studios at the top of Carnegie Hall. He also coached singers and individual dancers, among them Carmen Novarro, sister of the film star Ramon Novarro. But working as a rehearsal pianist was no more his métier in New York than it had been at Harvard. Agnes de Mille remembered how he would get bored with playing in the constant meter the dance class needed and slip in a bar of 5/8 or 7/8. Once he was fired because of such undisciplined behavior.

More regular employment came after a few months through the good offices of the veteran lyricist Irving Caesar, whose Broadway career stretched so far back that he had actually helped George Gershwin to get *his* first break twenty-five years earlier with "Swanee." The two had met the previous year in Boston, when Bernstein gave a party for Comden and Green, who were in the cast of Caesar's musical *My Dear Public*. The show was a flop, but the philosophical Caesar could still recognize talent in other people. Comden remembers that he got completely carried away when Bernstein sat down and played the piano. Chomping on a big cigar, he promised to arrange a job for Bernstein if he ever came to New York. He was as good as his word. Bernstein went to work for Hermann Starr, the publisher in charge of Harms-Witmark, a New York firm owned by Warner Brothers. His job was to note down for eventual publication the improvisations on records of noted jazz musicians such as saxophonist Coleman Hawkins, and to make four-hand and even eight-hand piano arrangements of music by Raymond Scott, who wrote "novelty" pieces for orchestra. Bernstein was sufficiently embarrassed to have this work published under the pseudonym Lenny Amber. However, Harold Shapero, who was often in New York in those days, points out that it was in fact a priceless job for Bernstein, "because he learned the whole *métier* of Tin Pan Alley sheet music, the actual mechanics." He was paid twenty-five dollars a week, a quarter of what his father had offered him to be a beauty supply merchant. The salary was doubled in April 1943 when Harms-Witmark, prodded by its perceptive chief editor, Frank Campbell Watson, offered him a five-year contract that provided a weekly advance on future royalties and immediate publication of his clarinet sonata. It seems a little odd that Aaron Copland, with whom he consulted, did not push Bernstein toward his own sympathetic publisher, Boosey & Hawkes. Copland may not have had much faith in Bernstein's talent as a composer. It's just as likely that he wanted his protégé to stick to conducting. But the only conducting Bernstein did during his early months in New York turned out badly: in October he was nominated by Koussevitzky as a candidate for the first Alice T. Ditson Award for American conductors but failed to win. "These are certainly times of trial for me," he reported to Koussevitzky's secretary, Olga Naumoff. "If I can come through this period of adjustment and difficulty, all will be well."

While he waited for something to turn up—Aaron Copland had promised him it would—he risked his mentor's disapproval and turned to composition. In October he started sharing an apartment on West Fifty-second Street with an artist named Edys Merrill, who was a friend of Adolph Green's first wife, Liz Reitel. She and Bernstein became good friends but were never lovers. Bernstein had the largest room, at the front, through which Merrill had to pass to use the bathroom. Copland offered to pay to have a rented Steinway grand hoisted to their top-floor apartment. On it, in the fall of 1942, Bernstein began his song cycle *I Hate Music* and completed his first symphony.

He dedicated the songs to Edys Merrill because, she remembered, "I hate music" is what she used to shout, walking around the sitting room with her hands over her ears while Bernstein coached opera singers and improvised and clowned around with the Revuers. He confessed to Copland that *I Hate Music* was "a little on the Copland side." "I want," thundered Copland in reply, "to hear about your writing a song that has no Copland, no Hindemith, no Strav., no Bloch, no Milhaud and no Bartok in it. Then I'll talk to you."

His first symphony, to which he gave the title *Jeremiah,* was written in response to a competition organized by the New England Conservatory with Koussevitzky as the chairman of the jury. It had always been his intention to make his "Hebrew song" part of a larger work. He added two movements to precede it, entitled "Prophecy" and "Profanation." He had a mad race to meet the competition's closing date, December 31. "I came to New York on vacation," recalled his sister, "and found Lenny up to his knees in manuscript, red-eyed from lack of sleep. . . . He was still deep in composing the last of the three movements, the scoring was only half done, and there remained the tedious and time-consuming job of copying the whole work neatly and clearly. Only three days remained to accomplish all this before the deadline. It would take more than one pair of hands to bring it off. A small army of friends and I were put to work helping to get the mechanical part of the job done. I was kept busy inking in clefs and time signatures, two friends took turns making ink copies of the already completed orchestration, another checked the copies for accuracy, and Lenny's current girlfriend kept us all supplied with coffee to keep us awake on this 36-hour friend-in-need task." The "girlfriend," Edys Merrill, recalled that in the middle of everything Bernstein suffered an acute attack of asthma. The helpers included David Diamond and David Oppenheim. Shirley Bernstein remembered that her brother tried to pair her off with Oppenheim while he went up to Sharon with Edys. The score had to be submitted anonymously so it was Edys who handed it to Olga Naumoff at Koussevitzky's Boston residence on New Year's Eve.

Bernstein did not win the competition, but in February 1943 the tide began to turn for him when he was asked at the last minute to play Aaron Copland's new piano sonata (commissioned by Clifford Odets) at a forum discussion in Town Hall. Copland himself had to withdraw because Sam Goldwyn would not release him from his film contract. Bernstein had only one day to practice but his performance was nevertheless a "great success," he reported to Helen Coates; he played it a second time at the end of the discussion and answered questions "with adroit wit," according to the *New York Post.* The *Herald Tribune* wrote that the sonata was "superbly interpreted" and Virgil Thomson publicly acclaimed him from the platform. "What an evening! And so sudden and accidental that few of my friends could be there. My father was passing thru' New York, though, and just made it by sheer accident. Now that's what I call a début!"

Lukas Foss, who was also in the audience that evening, recalled Bernstein's father turning to him during the applause to say, "It's all very nice to get all this applause and appreciation, but where's the money?"

A few weeks later Bernstein was at home practicing his clarinet sonata with David Oppenheim, to whom he had dedicated it, when the young composer Ned Rorem arrived at his door. Rorem was studying at Curtis and lodged in Philadelphia with Shirley Gabis and her mother. He had decided to travel to New York for the weekend and "get drunk and get into trouble, as was my wont," and Shirley had encouraged him to look up Lenny. "I was nineteen and pretty and very shy, but still not so shy that I didn't go and knock on his door. He said, 'Didn't your mother ever teach you any manners? You don't knock on people's doors in New York!' I said, 'Well, I didn't know your phone number.' And he said, 'It's in the telephone book. Anyway, come in.' He knew a good thing when he saw it."

Rorem revealed that they had a second mutual friend, Paul Bowles, whom he had met in Mexico while on a trip with his father. "Bernstein had never been in Mexico and was a little envious of my having been there. . . . I can't remember how that day progressed but David Oppenheim left and I stayed on and stayed overnight, and there was a lot of drinking going on, too. Edys came in about two in the morning. Lenny and I were on a mattress in the front room. She was very friendly and said, 'Who've you got down there? Is that Adolph?' —meaning Adolph Green. And he said, 'Oh no, it's Ned!' " Green and Bernstein were never anything but good companions. According to Edys Merrill, Bernstein had many "crushes" when she knew him but no regular partners of either sex.

When Oppenheim and Bernstein performed the clarinet sonata at the New York radio station WNYC, a crowd gathered to look through the studio window because word had gone round that Frank Sinatra was on the premises. The broadcast also included Bernstein's *Six Pieces* (later retitled *Anniversaries*) for solo piano and a brief work for clarinet and piano called *Extension of a Theme by Adolph Green*. Bernstein worked it up from a melody Green doodled at the piano one day in the apartment while the composer was taking a bath. (The theme was later incorporated into Bernstein's first ballet score, *Fancy Free*.)

On March 14 the clarinet sonata was performed in public at a League of Composers New York Public Library concert. Copland had suggested that Bernstein introduce himself with his *Six Pieces* but Bernstein took another view. "I felt the need to present my first League composition as a piece with a slightly larger form . . . and the Sonata does approach, at least, a big form. Besides it was more fun than playing alone." In a postscript he noted that the *Herald Tribune* review by Paul Bowles had not mentioned Hindemith, to which Copland tartly responded, "It's still full of Hindemith because I say so." Bowles praised the sonata's "tender, sharp, singing quality . . . alive, tough, integrated."

Bernstein finally made his New York conducting debut on March 30, 1943, with Paul Bowles's opera *The Wind Remains,* a major event on the season's avant-garde calendar. It was based on a surrealist text by Federico García Lorca, which according to Bowles "meant nothing and went nowhere," and had only two singing roles, for soprano and tenor. Spoken dialogue, dance and chorus numbers were woven together in the tradition of the Spanish *zarzuela.* Originally Bowles hoped to have it mounted on Broadway, but it ended up receiving a single performance at the Museum of Modern Art, as the third of five "Serenades of Rare Music, Ancient and Modern." The young Merce Cunningham did the choreography, and Oliver Smith designed the set. Virgil Thomson reported that Bernstein's conducting was "superb and musicanly . . . the program was unhackneyed and the audience brilliant."

Though they never worked together again, Bernstein always admired Bowles's music. Writing an appreciation in 1977 he noted that Bowles "had a genuine gift, a highly original sense of how to 'modernize' traditional materials. He has done the same thing with words, in his precise and quasi-Victorian way of presenting the primitive and the shocking. . . . I have learned a lot from him. Copland still refers to the 'Bowles' style that crops up now and then in my music." At the time of their collaboration, Bowles was thought by some to be a *poseur,* but Bernstein, always drawn to over-the-top characters, was a strong supporter: "I don't understand the theory about Paul's *badness,"* he wrote to Copland. "He's not bad, he just avoids real human relationships, and therefore seems inhuman; but that avoiding is such a human thing to do!"

News traveled fast on New York's musical grapevine. Artur Rodzinski, the newly appointed musical director of the New York Philharmonic, soon had Bernstein on his short-list to become his assistant the following season. Rodzinski wrote personally: "Please let me know what your plans are for next season and how is your military status?" He wrote again in April: "I am very glad to hear from you that you have been put in Class 4F. This is very good for the future plans which, at the present time have to be on suspension due to the crazy situation prevailing in New York. As soon as it clears up, I certainly will get in touch with you and we'll have a nice long talk about it." In the spring, Virgil Thomson lunched with Rodzinski, who spoke of Bernstein's assistantship as a fait accompli. "I haven't heard a word," Bernstein commented cautiously, in a dispatch to Copland, "but I don't expect too much." Max Goberman and Daniel Saidenberg were also being considered, he added. "What a trio we would make . . . the three prides of Goebbels."

He heard nothing more from Rodzinski, but his future as a conductor looked reasonably bright. In June he conducted the Goldman Band at the Naumburg Shell in Central Park. He was further encouraged when top players of the Boston Symphony invited him to conduct an *ad hoc* chamber orchestra for a short concert season (in Boston) at the beginning of August. Meanwhile, there was thrilling news from Harms, his publisher, who wanted the *Jeremiah* Symphony in their catalogue. Encouraged, he sent the full score to his two conducting teachers. Koussevitzky was unenthusiastic, but Fritz Reiner, the crotchety Hungarian, responded by telephone from his home in Westport, Connecticut. Bernstein could not hide his joy when he reported to Copland: "he wants to do my Symphony in Pittsburgh next fall, and he loves it, and he wants me to conduct a program anyway, and maybe to do the Symph myself. Lovely, lovely news! But he is most anxious for a fourth movement; insists it's all too sad and defeatist. Same criticism my father had: which raises Pop in my estimation no end. I really haven't the time or the energy for a fourth movement. I seem to have had my say as far as that piece is concerned and I want to get on with something else." Copland's reaction was characteristic: "I know you want me to be amazed at your successes but nothing that happens to you can ever surprise me. Isn't that too bad. Least of all your triumphs as a composer. But I am pleased that Reiner wants you to conduct in Pittsburgh. Koussie will be jealous that he didn't get you first. Maybe you can start a career as our first native guest conductor."

Within weeks Bernstein was breakfasting with Koussevitzky at the St. Regis Hotel. "He asked me up to Lenox for a few days, admitting that he hadn't really heard the Symphony very well when I played it to him in Boston, since there were so many people in the room and he was tired. I think Reiner's enthusiasm kind of pepped him up. You were right about the jealousy, though (you're always right)." When Bernstein finally got to spend a weekend with Koussevitzky early in August, his triumph was complete. "Kouss. went *overboard* about my Symphony! Gave me a great long speech about at last we have the great Jewish music! My God what am I coming to? I'm to conduct it in Boston this fall and in Pittsburgh in the winter." But Koussevitzky and Bernstein were naive if they thought Reiner would yield pride of place: Pittsburgh duly had its premiere performance in January 1944; Boston followed in February.

The only cloud on the horizon was Bernstein's medical status. In July he was reclassified 1A and subject to induction. It was an awkward moment. The assistant conductorship in New York depended on his being medically exempt. So did the conducting in Pittsburgh. Koussevitzky again acted in defense of his protégé, as he had done in 1941, writing to the U.S. Army Medical Examiner: "I wish to draw your attention to Mr. Leonard Bernstein who is to report for examination and whom I consider to be, without exaggeration, the most outstanding and exceptionally endowed musician of the younger generation. . . . I ask to protect this unique young talent for the sake of American musical art. I realize indeed that each and everyone should defend one's country, but I also believe that safeguarding such a talent for the future musical culture is equally essential for the welfare of America." But Bernstein had a genuine asthmatic condition—the revised 1A grading must have been a clerical error—and in August he was again found unfit for military service. Sam Bernstein later told journalists that his son had wept bitter tears at the rejection; Bernstein himself, in 1978, remembered that he felt he wasn't any good to his country. There is no reason to disbelieve him, but neither need one suppose that his depression was of long duration.

If there was justification for Bernstein to describe his first New York year as his Valley Forge, it was in the area of his personal life. Freudian analysis was at the height of its popularity in the forties. As soon as he got to New York he began regular consultations with a psychiatrist named Renée Mell, whom he nicknamed "The Frau." She was a refugee from Germany, and instead of a fee he gave her lessons in English—in spite of which Edys Merrill remembers Mell's accent on the telephone remaining thickly Teutonic. (Shirley Bernstein thought she was a phoney.) His loneliness was a primary topic for investigation. Away from the restraining influences of Helen Coates and his own family, he had slipped into a pattern of frequently changing relationships, sometimes intense and passionate but often merely casual encounters. Reading through his correspondence with Aaron Copland, one senses a certain desperation beneath the surface banter. The names swim in and out of focus and Copland was sometimes left gasping, although he was not above retailing the occasional titillating news item himself. At the height of the summer of 1943, when he was working on the score for *North Star,* Copland urged Bernstein to join him in Hollywood while Victor Kraft was away in Mexico. "I don't usually go in for being 2nd Fiddle but with you it looks good," was Bernstein's response, temporizing because of his forthcoming engagement to conduct in Boston. Copland wrote back: "Dear Second Fiddle Black Magic: too bad, too bad—this was the perfect moment for you to come."

The sheer volume of his sexual and social life can be gleaned from a sampling of Bernstein's and Copland's correspondence:

*Bernstein to Copland early in April 1943,* describing the cast party after *The Wind Remains:*

"All night affair, and I very drunk, and Constance [Askew] lovingly making me play all night, which I did—she's fun—and Diamond being uninvited/ unwelcome guest and really *getting* it from Constance. . . . My French has picked up enormously what with the Marquise and Alphand and my new friendy-wendy, Prince Chavchavadze. All very confusing and I still love D.O. What to do? I know—marry my new girl-friend [Rhoda Saletan]—she's lovely —my dentist's daughter. . . . My love to Farley Granger. Can you fix me up?" [Granger was the young star of *North Star.*]

*Bernstein to Copland two weeks later:* "Mad party at Arthur Berger's last night—Jean [Middleton] & Victor & Paul & Virgil & David etc. etc. oh and Colin [McPhee] and Paul Morrison. I left with Paul Morrison and it was like old times. . . . Jean was pretty dramatic, too, and left early. What a good world to stay away from! And I'm confused as ever, what with my new friend [the tenor from *The Wind Remains,* a married man] and my new girl-friend, whom I am afraid to involve unfairly, and Edys' and my decision to part company which raises all sorts of problems, like which of us to move. . . ."

*Copland to Bernstein:* "DD [David Diamond] sent a triumphant paragraph of how he had outdone you one Sat. Night. It gave me visions of a promiscuity 'sans bornes' and I tremble for you. I expect to return and find nothing but a pulpy, dismembered jellyfish."

*Bernstein to Copland:* "Don't let him [Diamond] lead you into that 'outdone me' stuff; the soldier (what a boy!) would rather have come with me but DD had done all the *work* and the soldier was afraid of a scene. As it turned out, he came to my room the next night, full of love and amusement."

*Copland to Bernstein:* "You write the most wonderful letters—just the kind I love to get: The 'I miss you, I adore you' kind, while sailors and marines flit through the background in a general atmosphere of moral decay."


IN July Bernstein had his final session of the year with his analyst. For the moment there were even more pressing priorities than his inner conflicts: "The Job" was about to become a reality.

# OVERNIGHT SENSATION

*Backstage with members of the New York
Philharmonic, following Bernstein's Carnegie Hall
debut, November 14, 1943.*
THE *NEW YORK TIMES*

*Here we go.*

—Note from Leonard Bernstein
to Helen Coates, scribbled on a press
cutting announcing his appointment as
assistant conductor of the New York
Philharmonic Orchestra

B ERNSTEIN'S account of his meeting with Artur Rodzinski was much embroidered over the years. He always implied that Rodzinski's offer came out of the blue to him on his twenty-fifth birthday, August 25, 1943. "I am going to need an assistant conductor," Rodzinski told him. "I have gone through all the conductors I know of in my mind and I finally asked God whom I should take and God said, 'Take Bernstein.' " It was a gift of a line, allowing Bernstein the comment that he'd already had recommendations from such distinguished personalities as Aaron Copland and Roy Harris, but never one from the Almighty himself. Yet the New York Philharmonic Archives reveal that as early as May 1943 Rodzinski had virtually settled on Bernstein—the only other candidate still in the running was ruled out because he was not American: the others had joined the armed forces. Rodzinski insisted, however, on an interview before the appointment could be confirmed. For his part, Bernstein was already confident that the job was his in July when he discussed his plans in a letter to Aaron Copland: "Mexico in September . . . and then home to become, God willing, assistant of the Philharmonic. Sort of a nice way to become 25 years old."

Bernstein was staying with Koussevitzky in Lenox when he was summoned late in August to Rodzinski's summer retreat, a farm in nearby Stockbridge. The meeting had more than its share of bizarre features. Much concerned with dietary reform, Rodzinski had maintained herds of goats and milking cows in his time and he loved to play the country farmer. He was dressed in shorts and wearing a beekeeper's hat when he came down the road to greet Bernstein and, gasoline being in short supply, he drove a primitive two-stroke motor scooter. God's advice was passed on to Bernstein as they reclined together on a haystack.

Bernstein spent several days at White Goat Farm. "In the evenings after dinner Artur would slump into his leather chair facing the fireplace while Lenny would sprawl on a fur carpet opposite," remembered Rodzinski's widow, Halina. "The two talked for hours, with Artur prodding information about his background, his family, his education. Artur felt bad that so gifted a young man should be earning his living copying manuscripts. . . ." Born in 1892 of Polish parents, and trained in Vienna, the new chief of the New York Philharmonic was a conductor of considerable experience. He had been brought to America in 1926 as Leopold Stokowski's assistant in Philadelphia, where he had been Reiner's predecessor as conducting professor at the Curtis Institute. He had run the Cleveland Orchestra for close to ten years; in 1937 he had fine-tuned NBC's new Symphony Orchestra to prepare it for Toscanini's opening season. Despite a reckless temperament and private eccentricities, which included carrying a loaded revolver in his back pocket whenever he conducted, Rodzinski was indisputably one of the finest conductors of the age. His interpretations of Mahler, Strauss and Shostakovich were outstanding.

Bernstein could not have wished for a better start. What Rodzinski had in mind for him was an improved version of Mitropoulos's proposal in 1940. His job would be to sit in on all the rehearsals and learn each score sufficiently well to substitute for Rodzinski or any guest conductor at a moment's notice. He was also to sift through new scores that came in and select those that were worth consideration. The reward for all the hard grind would be a Carnegie Hall concert with the New York Philharmonic toward the end of the season. Rodzinski had never heard Bernstein conduct but after their discussions the Philharmonic's official announcement described him as being "greatly impressed" by his assistant's many gifts. From Hollywood, Copland responded enthusiastically to the news: "It's one of those very rare instances when somebody worthwhile lands something. And it is so much fun to land things when one is a mere youth of 25. Oh well, I knew it all along, didn't I—and told it to you all along—and said have patience—and now I am slightly amazed at being so right."

Bernstein spent a few days celebrating with his family and friends in

Sharon, and then returned to New York to discuss his contract with Arthur Judson of Columbia Artists Management and his deputy, Bruno Zirato, who between them also managed the Philharmonic's affairs. From the letter Bernstein sent to his mentor after the meeting, one may assume that Koussevitzky had suggested he ask for a monthly salary of a thousand dollars:

Dear Serge Alexandrovich:

How I would love to be with you now to share my great joy with you! I am still so excited I can hardly write this letter. Everything seems to be going so well.

I finally had my talk with Judson and Zirato this morning. They were very nice indeed, and extremely authoritative. I realized immediately that they had the situation in hand, and that I was simply being told their terms, not asked my own. All of which was perfectly all right with me, since I feel so strongly about doing this job, and doing it as well as possible, that I would probably, in my enthusiasm, accept it if there were no salary at all.

The first thing is that there is apparently to be no contract at all. As Zirato pointed out, he doesn't believe in them. . . . I am to receive $125 a week. I realize that this is not tremendous, and that there are only 28 weeks in the season. But I am very contented with it, especially insofar as my publishers have raised my weekly royalty advance to $50 a week, which will continue all year. I simply felt that until I have proved myself to the Philharmonic and to the public, I have no real right to make any demands. On the other hand, the absence of a contract has its advantages, because then I can be free for the summer, or for any occasion that may arise. It makes finances a little bit unsure, of course, but believe me, I am very happy in spite of that. I hope you can understand the situation in which I found myself; in fact, I am *sure* that you will understand it. I simply could not ask $12,000 or any other sum for a job which thousands of conductors in this country would gladly pay to have. Once I have shown that I am of real value to the Society, then there is time enough for me to make demands. I am perfectly willing to seem naive now; as long as I know myself that I am seeming naive. The main thing is to do my job; if I can do that well enough, and if I can bear all the huge responsibilities that come with it, the rest will come by itself, I am sure. Believe me, I tried very hard to feel like Koussevitzky while I was in the Judson office, but I was only Leonard Bernstein, and I had to act as I did. Don't you think it is for the best?

And in the middle of all this, I only have to look at your picture in my room, and I am perfectly contented, knowing that there is one supreme friend that I have, who will understand whatever I do, mistakes included. I hope to see you very soon; meanwhile take good care of your health, and know that my love is with you always.

Leonard

Bruno Zirato, a big and burly Neapolitan who had originally come to America as Caruso's secretary, was affable from the beginning. The two swiftly became friends and Zirato arranged for him to rent an apartment in Carnegie Hall itself, Room 803. "It was a one-room affair," Bernstein remembered, "with a view of nothing. There was a kitchenette in the wall and I slept on the sofa, which was a fold-out bed. . . . Down the hall from me was a big dance studio. I stayed up and studied all the time. I remember going out to dinner in those little 56th Street restaurants and I'd sit alone at the table and read most of the time. I made friends little by little but at the beginning it was very lonely. . . . The closest thing to a community was a drug store, Carnegie Pharmacy, on the corner of Fifty-seventh and Seventh, which later became a Nedicks. That was a place you could meet your fellow inhabitants. That was where I had breakfast."

The designer Oliver Smith remembers the Carnegie Hall apartment as hideous and gray. At Bernstein's request Smith bought some striped wall hangings from Macy's to brighten things up. But in his current euphoria Bernstein was in no mood to complain. Hardly a day passed by without another newspaper story to cut out and send on to Miss Coates. "This publicity business is really getting fantastic," he told her. "It's rather frightening." The season was barely a week old, he added, and already he had seen his name printed in the concert programs and had met William S. Paley at a Columbia Records party. He had also had his first glimpse of the affluent Philharmonic ladies who wielded considerable power behind the scenes. Bernstein "worked the room" in those days with such assiduity that on Rodzinski's instruction Bruno Zirato had to ask him not to come to the greenroom after concerts.

Bernstein's youth was a visible aspect of the new order Rodzinski was establishing. His progressive policy included "reading rehearsals" of new American music, and for this innovation, which was expensive and did not last long, Bernstein not only selected many of the scores but also conducted the read-throughs. "Sometimes I had a chance to look at [scores] the night before and sometimes not. . . . This was tremendous practice, as you can imagine. . . . I knew what it was like to stand on that podium and conduct the Philharmonic. It was an empty hall, nobody in it but Rodzinski listening and making up his mind whether he liked the piece enough to play it." In fact a few critics were also present, but the composers themselves were banned. David Diamond was smuggled in by Bernstein for one of the sessions and immediately caused a fracas.

Bernstein's own fortunes as a composer continued to improve when his new friend Jennie Tourel decided to include *I Hate Music* in her New York debut recital at Town Hall on the evening of Saturday, November 13. The two had fallen for each other immediately when Koussevitzky introduced them the previous summer. Russian by birth, Tourel had the fiery temperament of a Carmen—one of her best roles at the Paris Opéra Comique before the war and soon to be one of the sensations of the City Center's first opera season. She could sing in half a dozen tongues, including the language of Bernstein's *Jeremiah* text, Hebrew. Twice married already and nearly ten years older than Bernstein, she had already successfully introduced his *I Hate Music* as an encore at her first American recital the previous August in Lenox, when Bernstein had been her accompanist.

Though the piece was only seven minutes long, and was placed near the end of the program along with some new songs by David Diamond, it was an important enough occasion for Bernstein to invite his parents to New York for the weekend. According to his brother, who made the trip as an eleven-year-old, Sam got his family to Boston's Back Bay Station a full two hours before the train was due to depart; almost as soon as they were installed in their hotel they were off again, arriving at Town Hall long before the concert. While they waited for the recital to begin, Leonard had time to explain that his boss, Artur Rodzinski, was taking a break after the first tense month of the new season. Bruno Walter was now conducting the orchestra for seven concerts in a fortnight, culminating in a live CBS broadcast from Carnegie Hall the next afternoon that would incorporate various works played over the previous ten days. Walter's programs had represented a lot of repertoire for Bernstein to learn but also the chance to study at close quarters the technique and style of one of the world's legendary conductors, then in his late sixties and a direct link with Gustav Mahler.

Bernstein kept to himself the news he'd just had from Bruno Zirato: Bruno Walter had fallen sick and might not be well enough to do the concert—in which case Bernstein would be expected to substitute. Zirato did not tell Bernstein that he had already telephoned Rodzinski in snowbound Stockbridge, urging him to return to New York—a four-hour drive. "Call Bernstein," was the maestro's immediate reply; "that's why we hired him." It was a grand gesture by Rodzinski, whose own first chance in New York had come in 1926 when he substituted for an ailing Stokowski.

Jennie Tourel's concert that evening was a huge success: "The best recital début since Kirsten Flagstad's in 1934," according to Virgil Thomson. Another review said Bernstein's *I Hate Music* was "witty, alive and adroitly fashioned." Tourel wore a shimmering gold lamé dress, and did encores in Russian for all the émigrés in the audience. Bernstein himself remembered that "people yelled and stamped and cheered and I had to take a bow." After the concert Tourel had a party for fifty people at her apartment on West Fifty-eighth Street. Homemade Russian food was served, and when dinner was over, the table was pushed back and entertainment began. Tourel sang Russian folk songs, Bernstein played one of his ingenious boogie-woogie improvisations, Adolph Green did some of his funny turns. Friede Rothe, then Tourel's manager, who believes Tourel and Bernstein were romantically involved for a while, recalls "Lenny and Jennie standing at the door, whispering and talking to each other and hugging each other. And then he told her he'd better get the hell out because he probably had a concert to do."

Bernstein got home some time between four o'clock and dawn, depending upon which account is consulted. "It's not true I stayed up all night studying," he told a reporter later. At 9 A.M. Bruno Zirato phoned. As Bernstein remembered the call, thirty years later, Zirato said, "Well this is it. You have to conduct at three o'clock this afternoon. No chance of a rehearsal. Bruno Walter . . . is all wrapped up in blankets at the hotel and he says he will be happy to go over the scores with you." Bruno Walter was kindness personified when they looked through the toughest work of the program, Strauss's *Don Quixote*. "He showed me a few tricky spots where he cut off here and he didn't cut off there and here you give an extra upbeat and so on. And then I just had to hang around."

The music that afternoon had been planned to fit the time slot of the broadcast's sponsors, the United States Rubber Company: the first half of the program consisted of Schumann's *Manfred* Overture, a grand work of symphonic stature; and the well-crafted *Theme, Variations and Finale* by the Hungarian-born Miklós Rózsa; the intermission was followed by *Don Quixote,* which is in effect a double concerto for solo cello, solo viola and very large orchestra. The broadcast ended there; in Carnegie Hall the audience also heard Wagner's *Meistersinger* Prelude, which was the only piece the orchestra had not performed recently. It was also the only work Bernstein had already conducted —on the Esplanade with the Boston Pops three summers previously. Because it was well known to the audience and resplendently eloquent in character, it offered him the best chance to shine on the Carnegie Hall podium.

The orchestra may have been familiar with most of the music to be played, but Bernstein's task that afternoon was still daunting. The Strauss had countless problems of ensemble; the Rózsa had its share of rhythmical intricacies, and the very first chords of the opening work, the Schumann overture, are devilishly difficult to keep together: they require a firm and clear beat. The fact that the concert was to be broadcast added to the tension; radio bound the nation together in those war-torn days in a way that no other medium could approach. Bernstein's debut broadcast would become a national event, and the telephones of the New York Philharmonic were busy all morning alerting music critics, photographers, and reporters to the story about to break. Leonard Bernstein was on the phone, too, to his family at the Barbizon Plaza. *"Oy gevalt,"* was his parents' reaction. The return train to Boston was canceled, the hotel room was booked for another night, lunch was forgotten, Shirley was telephoned at Mount Holyoke, and close friends were alerted. Sam led his family down Seventh Avenue to Carnegie Hall three hours early. They picked up the tickets for the conductor's box, and went back to the hotel.

When Bernstein dropped into the Carnegie drugstore for some coffee, the druggist wanted to know why he was looking so pale. "He gave me two little pills, a green one and a red one, and he said, 'Look, before you go on just pop these into your mouth. One will calm you down, the other will give you energy.' " One was Benzedrine and the other a phenobarbital. The long wait ended at 2:30 P.M. when Bernstein met the concertmaster and the two soloists backstage at Carnegie Hall and went over some of the danger spots in *Don Quixote*. He was already dressed in his only presentable suit, a double-breasted dark gray sharkskin. His cheap tails were hanging in his locker but he did not own a "cutaway," the standard afternoon conducting suit. It was literally decades since an assistant had been called upon to substitute at an afternoon concert.

Sitting in the conductor's box looking down at the stage, young Burtie was overwhelmed by the size and majesty of the place. The three thousand people in attendance were going to hear his brother conduct, he realized, whether they liked it or not. Sam Bernstein sighed deeply as he saw the press photographers with their big cameras beginning to assemble. Waiting in the wings, Bernstein watched the players troop onto the platform and begin their tuning. A hush fell as Bruno Zirato went out and made his announcement. Dr. Bruno Walter was ill, he said, and the public was going to witness the debut of a full-fledged conductor who was born, educated and trained in this country. Zirato asked subscribers to join him in wishing Mr. Bernstein all possible success. "He will seek to entertain you," were his final words.

When Rodzinski was conducting, one of Bernstein's more eccentric chores was to kick his boss on the backside with his knee for good luck as he went on to the platform. There was nobody in the wings to perform this ritual for Bernstein. Bruno Zirato came off, gave him a big hug, and said, "Hey, Lenny, good luck, baby." Bernstein took the druggist's pills out of his pocket, the one to calm him, the other to give extra energy. "I flung them as far away from me as I could and said, 'I'm going to do this on my own.' " The applause was merely polite when he strode out onto the platform, slim and tousle-haired, looking, as Burtie reported it, younger and less elegant than the players as he hopped onto the podium. "I remember the opening of the Schumann overture," Leonard said later; "it's very tricky because it starts with a downbeat rest, and the thing that was obsessing me was that if they don't come in together the whole concert is sunk." Once the nightmare moment was safely, indeed confidently negotiated, he was too intent on the job to feel nervous. When intermission came, the Bernstein family was ushered through the crowds of reporters and well-wishers to the greenroom. According to Burton, Sam and Jennie's faces were glazed with wonder; they had just seen their son take no less than four calls for the work by Miklós Rózsa. Burtie observed that his big brother looked hollow-eyed, like a war refugee in a news photo. "Hey, kid, how's it going?" he said, running his hands through Burtie's hair.

To judge from the recording of the broadcast, the Strauss *Don Quixote* went particularly well in the second half, and there was much kissing and embracing of the solo cellist, Joseph Schuster, when the performance ended. Then came the *Meistersinger* Prelude. When it ended, according to Burton, "the house waved like one giant animal in a zoo. . . . People were shouting at Lenny and the orchestra. Some of them moved towards the front of the stage. . . . Again and again, Lenny came out to bow, looking skinnier each time but always flashing that amazing smile." Afterward he was handed a telegram from Dr. Koussevitzky: "LISTENING NOW; WONDERFUL."

"I feel completely exhausted and completely happy," Bernstein told a reporter. Rodzinski, who had motored down from Stockbridge in time to hear the end of the second half, proclaimed to the press that Bernstein was "a prodigious talent. We wish to give him every opportunity in the future." In the greenroom crush Jennie Bernstein repeated over and over again, "I'm very proud of him." For Sam it was a pivotal moment in his relationship with his son; he was, the young conductor remembered, "all aglow . . . absolutely dazzled, bewildered, stupefied. . . . He suddenly realized that it was all possible. And there was a great moment of forgiveness and very deep emotion." At that instant Bernstein decided to dedicate his *Jeremiah* Symphony to his father.

The family celebrated ferociously that night; Bernstein told a journalist he downed four whiskies and devoured the best steak he had had in years. The next morning the story of his conquest was on the bottom of the front page of the *New York Times*. In the same size print as "JAPANESE PLANE TRANSPORT SUNK," the headline read "YOUNG AIDE LEADS PHILHARMONIC, STEPS IN WHEN BRUNO WALTER IS ILL." Inside there was a photograph of Bernstein backstage with leading players of the orchestra. In his review, the *Times* critic Olin Downes waxed lyrical: "He was remarkably free of the score, which he followed confidently but without ever burying his nose in it. . . . He conducted without a baton, justifying this by his instinctively expressive use of his hands and a bodily plastic which if not always conservative, was to the point, alive and expressive of the music." Arthur Berger, Bernstein's old friend from Harvard days, commented somewhat acidly in the *Sun* that "some of the flares of temperament . . . might fruitfully be modified and the stamping of the foot should be avoided." (Alas, it never was, to the despair of many recording producers.) On Tuesday the *Times* returned to the story with an editorial describing the debut as a new variation on one of the six great stories of the world, like the corporal taking over the platoon when all the officers are down. "Mr. Bernstein had to have something approaching genius to make full use of his opportunity. . . . It's a good American success story. The warm friendly triumph of it filled Carnegie Hall and spread over the airwaves."

The popular papers carried the story too. "BOY CONDUCTOR GETS HIS CHANCE" ran one headline. The *Daily News* used a baseball analogy, describing the debut as "an opportunity like a shoe-string catch in mid-field. Make it and you're a hero. Muff it and you're a dope." *The New Yorker* a few days later pointed out that Bernstein was the youngest man ever to direct a Philharmonic subscription concert and one of the comparatively few American-born conductors in its history. What nobody said in public but many must have thought in private, was that this was not simply a gifted and good-looking lad, but a Jewish American boy making good in one of the nation's cultural temples, until that day a citadel of European supremacy.

For Bernstein it was the end of his beginnings; from now on he had to deal with a new challenge and a new problem: fame.

# PART TWO

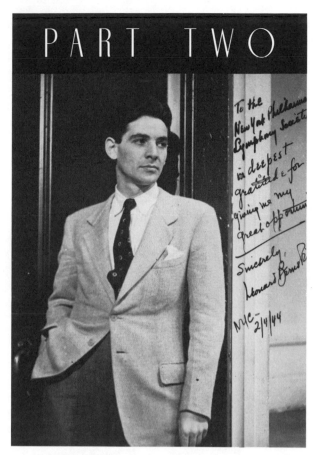

To the
New York Philharmonic
Symphony Society
in deepest
gratitude for
giving me my
great opportunity

Sincerely,
Leonard Bernstein

NYC - 2/4/44

*A 1948 portrait, dedicated to the New York Philharmonic*
*"in deepest gratitude for giving me my great opportunity."*

# 1943 – 1951

# RISE TO PROMINENCE

# THE *JEREMIAH* SYMPHONY AND *FANCY FREE*

*Fancy Free*, April 1944. Jerome Robbins, the choreographer,
is the dancer on the far left.

*". . . right up-to-date . . . strictly New York from
the sidewalk up."*

—*Fancy Free,* reviewed by
*New York World Telegram,*
April 19, 1944

I N the fall of 1943 the Japanese were slowly being forced out of the Southwest Pacific islands they had conquered and the sea war had turned in the Americans' favor. Russian armies were heading west toward a Germany already under fierce bombardment from the air: Wilhelm Furtwängler and his young rival Herbert von Karajan were conducting concerts in Berlin under frightening conditions. In New York, which was untouched by bombs and busier than ever, journalists on the lookout for heroes and good news stories found both in Leonard Bernstein's debut. American classical music had always been dominated by foreigners. Even people who knew nothing about music had heard of Toscanini, because of his dictatorial behavior with his orchestra, while Stokowski was famous for his love affair with Greta Garbo—and for his appearances in Hollywood movies. There were no comparable American-born personalities. But suddenly this short-haired, good-looking "boy-wonder" had materialized, a Harvard graduate who wore bright tweeds and a dotted bow tie for one interview and a red-and-black-checked lumber-jacket for another, who "sambas and congas and reads Dick Tracy" and "occasionally slips out for a midnight show to clear his head while it is swimming with notes." Bernstein was good for a quote on any topic from Karl Marx to the Book of Jeremiah, not omitting himself. "I look like a well-built dope fiend," he told one reporter, a self-mocking comment that stuck with him for the rest of his life. In a droll gossip column piece about Bernstein called "Famous Man," *The New Yorker* reported that he had already been interviewed by representatives of *Life, Time, Newsweek, Pic, Look, Vogue, P.M., Harper's Bazaar*, the *Times*, the *Herald Tribune*, the *Jewish Forward*, the Jewish Telegraph Agency, the *Jewish Day*, the *News* and the *Post. The New Yorker*'s writer set out to mock the razzmatazz and found a willing collaborator. " 'Do you know the biggest paper I'd been interviewed by up to last week?' And before we could make a guess he exclaimed *'The Hunter College High School News*, if you please! A couple of girls came around a week ago last Wednesday and I was pleased as a peacock.' "

Bernstein's parents were unprepared for all the publicity. Sam described Leonard as "my gift to Uncle Sam," and countered charges of having obstructed his early career with a much-quoted defense: "How could I know my son was going to grow up to be Leonard Bernstein?" A few days into the publicity barrage Jennie delivered the nearest thing to a rebuke that has survived in her correspondence with Leonard: "Lenny dear, please don't tell reporters of your personal views . . . it's very bad taste. It will not do you much good. It may have bad repercussions. From now on you should be very conservative in your statements to the public. Just a little advice from your mother and I'm sure it will not harm you." Bernstein was due to broadcast again the following Sunday, conducting the New York Philharmonic in Ernest Bloch's *Three Jewish Poems*, and she added, "We will be thrilled to hear you on the radio. *Good luck* to you honey, and success. I'm sure most of the Jews in the country will be listening to you so do your best, dear. Adoringly, Mother."

The appearance went well, and so did another concert two weeks later, in which Bernstein substituted for the ailing guest conductor Howard Barlow, a fifty-three-year-old American who was well known as the conductor of the CBS Radio Orchestra. With only one rehearsal Bernstein conducted the New York Philharmonic in a program of Delius, Brahms and Beethoven which won extraordinary praise from Virgil Thomson in his *Herald Tribune* review. "His rhythmic understanding is superior to that of any of the contemporary great, saving only [Sir Thomas] Beecham." The implied slight to Rodzinski was there for all to see.

Bernstein had always had faith in his artistic abilities, but nothing could have prepared him for the reality of celebrity. Everybody wanted to meet the wunderkind. At one party given that winter by Leonard Lyons, the *New York*

*Post* columnist, Bernstein and his sister encountered, among others, Ethel Barrymore, Bernard Baruch, Charles Boyer, Joe DiMaggio, Moss Hart, Garson Kanin, Frank Loesser, Ezio Pinza and John Steinbeck. He was even invited to appear on "Information Please," an enormously popular radio quiz show; his fund of knowledge and his Harvard accent were greatly admired.

The fan mail began to pile up in Bernstein's Carnegie studio, where he was photographed assiduously studying his scores or standing nonchalantly smoking a cigarette in a holder. He loved the outdoor life, he told one reporter, horseback riding and swimming being favorite pursuits. But these days he smoked too much, he confessed, to be able to swim far: he was on the verge of joining the YMCA and swimming in its indoor pool for a mile each day. He would stay on that verge all his life.

Sam Bernstein shared Jennie's worries about their son talking to the press. He wrote to Leonard, apologizing abjectly for his own indiscretions, and then went on, "Are you too not overdoing it a little? One statement you made—that you do not read Dick Tracy because you are not reading the News—might be controversial. You know the power of the Newspaper Organizations throughout the country. And in another publication you said you did not like them because they were Fascist. I don't blame you for feeling that way, but these newspaper syndicates can do you a lot of harm if they want to and it is best to have a thousand friends rather than one enemy so don't get in wrong with the newspapers. 'The pen,' they say 'is mightier than the sword' which is invariably a true maxim."

Bernstein was not worried by his father's strictures. He proudly told one reporter that he was composing six antifascist songs. When his *Jeremiah* Symphony was premiered in Pittsburgh he spoke to the press about his sense of identification with Jews in Europe and their terrible plight at the hands of the Nazis. The "Lamentation" movement in the symphony is a hymn of sorrow for the destruction of Jerusalem. "How can I be blind to the problems of my own people? I'd give everything I have to be able to strike a death blow at Fascism."

The week leading up to the Pittsburgh premiere was fraught with tension. No sooner had Bernstein left New York for the rehearsals than Artur Rodzinski fell ill. He was the third conductor in ten weeks to cancel, an incredible coincidence in a profession where cancellations are rare. Zirato instructed Bernstein to return to New York and take over rehearsals for Thursday's Philharmonic concert, but Fritz Reiner refused to release him. Bernstein's absence had been agreed in advance. He dispatched a cable saying he could not get a train reservation—it was wartime, after all—and Zirato and an angry Rodzinski were obliged to make other arrangements.

"I am excited beyond words at hearing my symphony," Bernstein wrote to Koussevitzky after the first rehearsal. "I must say that to me it sounds just as I thought it would: the orchestra is rough [a surprising comment in view of Fritz Reiner's renown as a trainer] but in a way like the Tanglewood orchestra—full of spirit, young and cooperative to a great degree. I am having a marvelous experience here. Even the Scherzo is almost perfect—but for a real performance we must wait for Boston." Then came a little gloat at the difficulties back home. "Have you been reading about the mess in New York since I left? They phoned me here Monday to return for the Tuesday rehearsal, but it was impossible. Then Byrns rehearsed *Rosenkavalier* and made a mess of it; so it came off the program and Hans [William] Steinberg will conduct. I derive great satisfaction from it all—it feels wonderful to have the Philharmonic really dependent on me." This rare display of *Schadenfreude* on Bernstein's part must have been prompted by a recent falling out with his boss. Rodzinski was not entirely stable in his personality and his relationships; he had bright ideas for management and made friendly gestures to his new orchestral family, but he could blow hot or cold with disconcerting speed. In the fall he had instructed the Philharmonic press office to soft-pedal on Bernstein and get his own name back in the newspaper pages. A riotous photo story ensued: two pages of bucolic reportage from the Rodzinski farm featuring bees, tractor and motor scooter. Mrs. Rodzinski was glimpsed merrily milking a cow (a birthday gift from the orchestra to her husband) while the musical director sawed a pile of logs in the background. In New York, Rodzinski crossed swords with Bernstein about a missed rehearsal and when Bernstein came to make peace Rodzinski grabbed him fiercely by the collar. The scene was witnessed by David Diamond, who was shocked by Rodzinski's violence. Many years later Mrs. Rodzinski conceded that her husband would turn on her, too, when he lost his temper.

Offers to guest-conduct were flooding in and Bernstein knew he no longer depended upon Rodzinski; their ways would part in April at the end of the season. Arthur Judson, America's musical kingmaker, had already sketched out an enticing five-year plan that would lead to Bernstein's assuming the directorship of the New York Philharmonic at the age of thirty, but Bernstein turned the scenario down, saying he wanted the freedom to compose.

The Pittsburgh performance was a complete success. "Front pages, banner headlines, a shouting audience," he told Koussevitzky. Three weeks later, in Boston, came an even greater triumph, Bernstein's first concert at Symphony Hall, with one of the world's great orchestras. The *Boston Globe* described *Jeremiah* as the best new work of the year but Virgil Thomson damned it with faint praise. "It is not a masterpiece by any means, but it has solid orchestral qualities and a certain charm that should give it a temporary popularity." Nevertheless, while Bernstein was still in Boston he received a telegram from the unpredictable Rodzinski saying, as Bernstein remembered it many years later, "Congratulations on your great success in Boston. Will you come and conduct a whole concert with the Philharmonic? Any works of your choice but including *Jeremiah*."

This was another generous act on Rodzinski's part. Though Bernstein never quite forgave him for his moment of violence he always acknowledged Rodzinski's magnanimity. In fact he would later model his relationships with his own assistant conductors on what he had learned from Rodzinski as well as from Koussevitzky.


THE success of *Jeremiah* was remarkable. In March and April 1944, Bernstein conducted it four times with the New York Philharmonic. In May the New York Music Critics Circle voted it the outstanding new classical work of the season. It was chosen at the first ballot and broadcast coast to coast on seventy radio stations by the NBC Symphony Orchestra under Frank Black. During the next three years Bernstein himself conducted *Jeremiah* in Chicago, New York, St. Louis, Detroit, Rochester, Prague and Jerusalem. Guido Cantelli conducted its Italian premiere in Venice. "It outranks every other symphonic product by any American composer of the younger generation," wrote Paul Bowles.

Bernstein went out of his way to deny any suggestion of a story line in the symphony. "As for programmatic meanings, the intention is . . . not one of literalness, but of emotional quality. Thus the first movement ('Prophecy') aims only to parallel in feeling the intensity of the prophet's pleas with his people; and the scherzo ('Profanation') to give a general sense of the destruction and chaos brought on by the pagan corruption within the priesthood and the people. The third movement ('Lamentation'), being a setting of poetic text, is naturally a more literary conception. It is the cry of Jeremiah, as he mourns his beloved Jerusalem, ruined, pillaged, and dishonored after his desperate efforts to save it."

Bernstein added, a little misleadingly, that he had not quoted much specifically Hebrew thematic material. The echoes of Hebrew liturgical music are, he wrote, "a matter of emotional quality, rather than of the notes themselves." But the Bernstein scholar, Jack Gottlieb, has identified several themes deriving from synagogue melodies. Shirley Bernstein suggests that the symphony owes a great deal to their father, Sam, who insisted that Leonard go to Hebrew school and at home frequently sang Jewish melodies in the shower. Slow tempos predominate for much of the symphony's twenty-five-minute duration. Fritz Reiner had joined Sam Bernstein in urging Bernstein to compose a fourth and brighter final movement, but he would not be budged. The concentration on a narrow range of emotions is the symphony's strength. It remains unequalled among mid-twentieth-century symphonies for the fervor with which it reaches out to audiences. Bernstein emerges from it as both a first-generation American and a modern Jew, unencumbered by the trappings of Orthodoxy, but firm in his faith, expressing in direct musical language the beauty and anguish of his Jewish inheritance. He leaves the listener in no doubt as to his anger at the way that legacy was destroyed by persecution and his belief that through tenderness and love a lost faith can eventually be restored. "How long more wilt Thou forsake us?" asked Jeremiah in his Lamentation. "Turn us unto Thee, O Lord." Bernstein set those lines, among the most hauntingly beautiful in the Hebrew tongue, in 1939, years before the Nazis put into operation their "Final Solution." But by the time of the symphony's performances in 1944 and 1945 the dreadful relevance to the Holocaust was becoming clear.

AFTER the triumphant performances of *Jeremiah* in Pittsburgh and Boston, Bernstein conducted his first concert outside the United States, standing in for yet another ailing conductor in Montreal. The gala evening included his first readings of Beethoven's Eighth Symphony and Sibelius's First. Princess Alice, wife of the Canadian Governor-General, was in the audience, as was the great trombonist Tommy Dorsey. "Solid symphony," was Dorsey's reaction to the Sibelius afterward in the greenroom: "sensational symphony. Sends me." Bernstein's plan to compose a concerto for Dorsey and the Pittsburgh Symphony was shelved, however, along with the antifascist songs. "Tempus" was still the enemy.

Shirley Bernstein, who traveled to Canada with her brother, recalls that Leonard gave her a Seconal to help her sleep on the night train. She was totally knocked out, yet Bernstein took them frequently with no after-effects. He used the drug to help slow him down, for he was full of nervous energy and had a great deal on his plate. In under five months he had led the New York Philharmonic in five different programs and appeared as guest conductor with three other important orchestras. And throughout this tumultuous fall and winter another vital thread had been spun in the fabric of his creative life: he had begun to work with the choreographer Jerome Robbins.

The two men had much in common. They were the same age and both had Russian-Jewish fathers who objected to their chosen professions. Robbins hadn't even begun to study dance until 1936, after spending a year as a chemistry student at New York University. By 1943 he was on his way to becoming a star dancer with Ballet Theatre—he was the last dancer to learn the role of Petrouchka from its creator, Fokine—but his ambition was to become a choreographer.

One evening in the fall of 1943 he knocked on Bernstein's door at Carnegie Hall. He brought with him his story outline for a one-act ballet called *Fancy Free*. He intended to create something distinctly American, observed from real life in wartime New York and derived from such social dances as the boogie-woogie, the lindy-hop and the soft-shoe shuffle. He planned to choreograph with dancers from the company, but wasn't happy with the composer who had been suggested to him; hence the call on Bernstein. Could he hear some of Bernstein's music? "Funny you should ask that," Bernstein remembered saying, "because this afternoon in the Russian Tea Room I got this tune in my head and I wrote it down on a napkin." He sang the melody. "Jerry went through the ceiling. He said, 'That's it, that's what I had in mind!' We went crazy. I began developing the theme right there in his presence. . . . Thus the ballet was born." The commissioning fee from Ballet Theatre was a modest three hundred dollars for a thirty-minute score.

Between his conducting engagements Bernstein set to work, inspired as much by his own zestful love of New York and the brash young people he saw in Harlem clubs and Times Square as by Robbins's story line, which Bernstein summarized for a program note: "The curtain rises on a street corner with a lamp post, a side street bar and New York skyscrapers pricked out with a crazy pattern of lights, making a dizzying back drop. Three sailors explode on the stage. They are on a 24-hour shore leave in the city and on the prowl for girls. The tale of how they first meet one, then a second girl, and how they fight over them, lose them, and in the end take off after still a third, is the story of the ballet."

Ballet Theatre was out of town on tour most of the winter, so with Aaron Copland as his second pianist Bernstein made piano duet disc recordings of the numbers as he wrote them and mailed them to Robbins for his choreographic sessions in nightclubs and deserted ballrooms. When the company returned to New York, Bernstein sat in on their sessions. One of the dancers, Janet Reed, remembers that he "improvised and composed right alongside us while the *pas de deux* was being choreographed." Bernstein loved such hands-on collaboration. His regular conducting job required long periods of intense private study broken up by brief frenzies of rehearsal and performance, during which he had to dominate a hundred musicians by the force of his personality and the strength of his conception. Composing was ordinarily a solitary business, but writing a ballet score for Robbins and the other dancers meant working day in and day out alongside creative partners and responding to their immediate needs, inventing a riff here to underline an action, adding extra music there to cover an exit or the follow-through of a chain of steps, giving and taking all the time and finally, as Janet Reed remembers it, collapsing together with the dancers in hysterical laughter at the end of a sweaty rehearsal session. It was a continuation at the highest level of Bernstein's teenage work as a producer and director in Sharon. But now he was working with a leading American company on a work destined for the stage of the Metropolitan Opera House, which the impresario Sol Hurok had hired for Ballet Theatre's 1944 spring season. *Fancy Free* had its premiere on April 18.

A charming sense of continuity—she had spoken a prologue to *Carmen* in 1934 and sung the opening song of *Cradle* in 1939—prompted Bernstein to invite his sister to record the blues song heard playing on a jukebox when the curtain rises. The number, "Big Stuff," with words also by Bernstein, was written for one of his idols, Billie Holiday, but she proved too expensive to hire. That Shirley's voice was heard at all was thanks to Betty Comden and Adolph Green, who had been attending all the *Fancy Free* rehearsals. Comden remembered the vital part she played on opening night: "We got down to the theater a little early and found out that . . . there was nothing on stage that you could play a record on. So we raced back to my apartment for my little table model phonograph, . . . carried it down in a taxi and got it up on stage."

Jerome Robbins was revising the choreography for his own *danzon* variation up to the last moment, and he broke a side zipper in his sailor pants while doing warm-up pliés in the wings, but the show went off without a hitch. As the curtain rose, the audience applauded Oliver Smith's nocturnal urban landscape, and they laughed loudly in all the right places throughout the performance. "It was not planned for gags," Robbins said later, tongue in cheek; "the humor is incidental. . . . I wanted to show that the boys in the Service are healthy, vital boys: there is nothing sordid or morbid about them."

*Fancy Free* was a huge success. Leonard Bernstein's music, which he conducted himself, was praised for its perfect integration with the art, the vigor, and the patterns of the dance action. "Just exactly ten degrees north of terrific . . ." was the *New York Times*'s verdict. "Besides being a smash hit, *Fancy Free* is a very remarkable comedy piece," wrote Copland's friend Edwin Denby in the *Herald Tribune. Cue* magazine compared it to *Rodeo:* "Fast and fabulous in the mode set by Agnes de Mille but louder and funnier." *Time* wrote enthusiastically about the superb dancing—"acrobatic, a specialty rhumba [*danzon,* actually], soft shoe adagio, eccentric jitterbugging, knee-drops, slapstick and a violent, half-hidden free-for-all under the bar." The *Jewish Chronicle* headlined *Fancy Free* in its inimitable style: "PRESS LAUDS BALLET BY JEWISH TEAM."

Attendance broke box office records at the Metropolitan Opera. There were seats for 3,300 people, yet standees were three-deep every night. Sol Hurok hastily arranged a fortnight's extension at the Met to be followed by a nationwide tour. Bernstein would conduct a dozen additional performances of *Fancy Free* at a fee of two hundred dollars per night. "Fun? I'll say! I'm still not over it," he wrote to Copland.

# ON THE TOWN

*Bernstein with (from left to right) Jerome Robbins,*
*Betty Comden and Adolph Green, 1944.*
MUSEUM OF THE CITY OF NEW YORK, THE THEATER COLLECTION

*New York, New York, a helluva town.*
*The Bronx is up but the Battery's down,*
*The people ride in a hole in the groun';*
*New York, New York, it's a helluva town.*

—COMDEN AND GREEN

THE *New York Times* for June 7, 1944, was dominated by reports about the
Normandy invasion and the fall of Rome. But tucked away on an inside
page was the first public reference to plans for a new Broadway musical, to
be called *On the Town,* with music by Leonard Bernstein, and choreography by
Jerome Robbins. The show was the brainchild of Oliver Smith, who had been
so impressed with *Fancy Free* that he urged Bernstein and Robbins to expand it,
and offered to be the producer with his friend Paul Feigay. Robbins had wanted
Arthur Laurents to write the book and John Latouche for the lyrics but Bernstein insisted on bringing in his friends Comden and Green. "Even in his
earliest business arrangements Lenny was always canny and shrewd," Oliver
Smith remembered. "He knew his worth and without him there would be no

show. I went with Lenny to the Blue Angel and heard their material. I was enchanted with them."

The writing took six joyous months, from June to December 1944, but first there were long and earnest discussions about the type of show it should be and the way the group should work together. Betty Comden filled a yellow legal pad with their "credo": that the action should be integrated; that music and dance and book must be all of one piece and never stop telling the story, each number being part of the action; that nothing should be permitted that was "cheap or crummy."

There was much discussion about locations, for this was to be not only the story of three sailors on their first visit to New York but also a Valentine to the monstrous city they all loved. Oliver Smith designed backdrops galore, among them the Brooklyn Navy Yard, Times Square, the Natural History Museum, Central Park, Carnegie Hall and Coney Island, a dozen in all. The show was to look as spectacular as it sounded.

While the spirit of the piece is lighthearted, the collaborators went about their work with great seriousness. Betty Comden, whose own husband was away at the war, described their aspirations in an article she and Adolph Green wrote for the *New York Times* just after the show opened. "The main thing was that having decided on three sailors we wanted them to come off as people. No matter how extravagantly treated, we wanted them to possess the qualities and attitudes of the servicemen we had seen coming into the city for the first time and at least touch on the frantic search for gaiety and love, and the terrific pressure of time that war brings. Our intention was not to bludgeon these points home, but to provide whatever fun and merriment we had to give with some basis of contemporary truth."

Comden and Green tilted the center of emotional gravity away from the men, who are always center stage in *Fancy Free,* toward the women, each of whom is a considerable character. *On the Town* reflects the way women's roles had changed in wartime America. Chip, the wide-eyed innocent sailor, is pursued by Hildy, a quarrelsome, feisty cabdriver. Ozzie, who is unashamedly looking for sexual adventure, meets his match in Claire de Loone, an unlikely sex-mad anthropologist. (Claire and Ozzie were played by Comden and Green.) Gabey, the dreamer, falls in love with that month's "Miss Turnstiles," whose photograph he sees on a poster in a subway train. Her name is Ivy Smith, and she's a singing, dancing and painting student who does hootchy-kootchy belly dancing in Coney Island to pay for her lessons.

Despite the enthusiasm, writing and composing *On the Town* was not entirely plain sailing. Bernstein had conducting commitments for much of July and August. And in June he needed surgery to clear up pain and breathing problems associated with his chronic sinus infections. The operation—for a deviated septum—was considered a minor one, and to ensure as little loss of collaboration time as possible Adolph Green decided this would be the best time to have his troublesomely enlarged tonsils removed. A gala hospital visit was planned. On June 13 Leonard Lyons's gossip column reported that "Leonard Bernstein and Adolph Green will be operated upon on the same day by the same doctor." During their stay, he added optimistically, "they will finish their new show *On the Town."*

In fact they had hardly begun to write the lyrics, and the medical operations were more grueling than anticipated. Bernstein was only partially anaesthetized during his surgery, while Green's operation left him in considerable pain. But in a couple of days they began to feel better and with Betty Comden perched on a hospital chair they started work. "The floor nurses and patients in nearby rooms were alternately amused and irritated by the singing and laughter that erupted from Room 669." In calmer moments, Shirley Bernstein noted, hordes of friends would drop in for bickering games of gin rummy. A tortured nurse, unable to tolerate Bernstein's shenanigans any longer, observed, "He may be God's gift to music, but I'd hate to tell you where he gives me a pain."

After his hospital sojourn Bernstein moved from Carnegie Hall to a high-ceilinged double studio apartment on West Sixty-seventh Street near Central Park West. Then he began his conducting season. While Comden and Green spent the month of July completing an outline of *On the Town,* Bernstein conducted outdoor concerts in Montreal, Chicago (the Ravinia Festival) and New York. After his Lewisohn Stadium concerts he was besieged by bobby-soxers screaming for autographs. It was still a limited fame, however. When he and Shirley attended a stadium concert given by another conductor, and tried to visit at intermission, a security guard barred their way. "But I'm Leonard Bernstein," said Bernstein. "And I'm Napoleon," replied the guard.

In August Ballet Theatre went to California and Bernstein rejoined the company to conduct *Fancy Free.* He took the train, composing en route. *On the Town's* first big number, "New York, New York," was written, he remembered, while passing through the plains of Nebraska. That he had no problem with composing while on the move was confirmed by Mrs. Halina Rodzinski, who had shared a train compartment with him earlier in the year on an out-of-town Philharmonic engagement: "I noticed Lenny take a pad of staved paper from his briefcase, then draw notes. I pretended not to watch, but was amazed at the speed with which he covered sheet after sheet, rarely pausing or making an erasure. He looked up for a moment, smiled handsomely as he caught my peeping eye, and said, 'You have no idea how exciting it is to hear in one's head the music that comes out in these black dots.'" The dots were the score of *Fancy Free.*

Oliver Smith sent Comden and Green to work with Bernstein and Robbins in Los Angeles, and for a few weeks the collaborators lived in the Hollywood Hills in a "dream of a Spanish villa" on Watsonia Terrace once owned by Ramon Novarro. "Hollywood is exactly what I expected, only worse," Bernstein wrote to Aaron Copland in Mexico. "Agents, agents; blood, money. But a pretty place. . . . We're getting a show done by leaps and bounds. It's amazing how hard it is—such an unwieldy thing to juggle." *On the Town* had fifteen numbers in Act I, not counting little stings of "hurry" music, and another ten in Act II. They added up to nearly ninety minutes of music, almost twice as much as *Fancy Free* and *Jeremiah* combined. Bernstein rounded out his letter to Copland with a personal note. "I miss you terribly. I need your cynical ears for my latest tales of love and limbs—from Montreal to San Francisco. Oh, what a divine one in San Francisco!"

Copland wrote back from the remote village of Tepoztlán: "Just think, not a single one in all this town has ever heard of you or me. And I moan when I think how good it would be for you to spend a month in this utter tranquility of anonymity." Copland continued with a veiled criticism. "I saw an old architect friend, name of John McAndrew. Somehow your name came up—it generally does—and I asked him if he had ever heard of you (he's lived here for the past five years). Reply: 'Oh, isn't he the boy who can never say no? I hear he's gone into musical comedy. . . .' That floored me."

On the night of his twenty-sixth birthday Bernstein conducted a concert at the Hollywood Bowl with Oscar Levant at the piano. Levant claimed in his autobiography that Bernstein telephoned, pleading that they should switch roles so that Bernstein could play the solo part in *Rhapsody in Blue*. Levant declined. Bernstein kept this exchange to himself. "My birthday was very joyful. I rehearsed the orchestra and they loved me, and the music, and really began to sound. Also they played me 'Happy Birthday'—and I received enormous wonderful flowers from them," he wrote to Helen Coates, who in early July had taken the momentous step of abandoning her teaching practice and moving to New York to become Bernstein's full-time secretary. After the Bowl concert there was an enormous birthday party to which Tallulah Bankhead was invited; according to the composer Saul Chaplin "she threw herself at Lenny like you can't believe."

September found the *On the Town* gang back in New York, giving "semi-performances" in Bernstein's apartment to what Betty Comden described later, and only half-jokingly, as "panic-stricken backers." These "readings," as she called them, "usually opened after a series of embarrassed handshakes and mirthless chuckles, with an hour and a half address by any one of us on the subject of [artistic] integration, which left our backers confused and mesmerized, but charmed. Then the four of us would proceed to plod through the story, our voices getting weaker and hoarser—and the hours wore slowly by. When it was all over the guests would flounder out of the smoke-filled room but to their eternal credit, they were still brave and smiling. What we needed more than anything else, we realized, was a director—a man not only to stage the production but to corral and tie down the roaring egos involved."

Oliver Smith went to see George Abbott, who said, "I like the smell of this." Mr. Abbott, as he was universally known, was a theatrical legend. He had been an actor, writer, play-doctor and producer, as well as the most successful stage director of musicals in his time. Smith offered Abbott a handsome deal (eventually, according to Smith, he "took half the rights to it"). He was enthusiastic about the script, but ordered rewrites. Bernstein complained to Copland, "The show is a wild monster now which doesn't let me sleep or eat or anything; in fact the world seems to be composed of the show the show the show, and little else except a *Verklärte Nacht* [by Schoenberg] or a Schumann symphony here and there. Maybe it will be a great hit, and maybe it will lay the great EGG of all time. It's an enormous gamble."

From the business angle there was no cause for alarm. Once George Abbott had agreed to direct the show, Smith and Feigay were able to supplement the basic $25,000 they had raised in the spring with investment deals involving not one but two film companies. First RKO put up $31,500 and then MGM came in for virtually double that amount, with a film deal to follow. The stage production was budgeted at just under a quarter of a million dollars and actually cost less to mount. Apart from the sense of financial security he engendered, Abbott's most important contribution was to inject *On the Town* with a sense of pace. He had the authority to override young Jerome Robbins. "He took my second act ballet—which I thought was terrific, I still believe in the conception of it—and put a scene in between the halves." Bernstein feared that Abbott had damaged the work's underlying musical unity when he cut a first-act song, "Gabey's Coming," containing the first statement of a theme which returned in various guises throughout the show.

But another number, "Carried Away," underwent drastic modification at Bernstein's own hand. He had written what he described as "a little polka-like cowboy tune. It wasn't like me, it was like 'The Surrey With the Fringe on Top.' I couldn't bear it, I hated it, but I couldn't think of anything else. After five days of trying I was in despair. Betty and Adolph said, 'Why don't you try it in the minor key?' I said, 'Come on, that's naive. So naive, it just makes it sad or agitated. It's an old fashioned thing to do. . . . I'll try it!' Suddenly we had this operatic feeling, which dictated the form of the number, the quality of those two quasi-operatic voices that brought down the house—that was the whole joke of the scene and I have them to thank for it."

Auditions and casting were completed early in November. It was a show written by young people for performance by young people; the only big names were Sono Osato, the beautiful Japanese-American dancing star of *One Touch of Venus,* whom Bernstein had convinced to play Ivy Smith, and Nancy Walker, the raucous Broadway comedienne, who played Brunnhilde Esterhazy the taxi driver. Among the chorus singers was Shirley Bernstein, who borrowed her brother's name and was listed as Shirley Anne Burton. Allyn Ann McLerie, one of the dancers in the company, still remembers the excitement of rehearsals with Robbins and Bernstein. Robbins's opening remark, she recalled, had been, "My name is Jerome Robbins but you can call me Jerry: I'm allowed to arrive late but you are not." Bernstein's appearance caused a sensation. "In bursts this apparition with his coat draped over his shoulders as a cape and his hair flying. 'Hello everybody,' he said, and sat down at the piano and played the Times Square ballet. Well, all us little kids were just struck dumb with admiration and love. . . . We would have gladly gone under trains for Jerry and Lenny because they were both geniuses."

For Bernstein there were many diversions. He was honored at a Salute to Young Americans; he spoke at a pro-Roosevelt rally; he did a series of radio concerts in Detroit. In November he conducted his tenth orchestra of the year, the Cincinnati Symphony. By now he was giving interviews as a national personality. Asked about the status of American music, he quoted the advice he had received from Aaron Copland: "Sit down and write what comes into your head; if it's good it will be American."

His fame had been reinforced by half a dozen appearances on "Information Please." At one of the shows the panel was asked to identify a line of poetry and for once in his life Bernstein was momentarily stumped. Adolph Green was in the front row of the audience that evening. He quickly leaned forward and rolled up the bottoms of his trousers. "T. S. Eliot," cried Bernstein, immediately remembering Eliot's lines from "The Love Song of J. Alfred Prufrock" about growing old and wearing the bottoms of his trousers rolled.

In the fall of 1944 Bernstein met Toscanini for the first time. Leonard Lyons reported that Bernstein called the Italian "Mr. Toscanini" while Toscanini called his guest "Maestro Bernstein." In the same week the music editor of the *Boston Herald,* Rudolph Elie, Jr., described Bernstein as "potentially the first great American conductor." Elie heard Bernstein conduct the Boston Symphony Orchestra in Shostakovich's Fifth Symphony, which became one of his "signature" works.

In New York Bernstein was sketched for the first time by Al Hirschfeld for a group cartoon of the *On the Town* creators, and attended the show's first orchestral rehearsals. Max Goberman, a fellow Fritz Reiner pupil at Curtis, had been selected to conduct and the orchestrations were in the hands of Hershy Kay, another contemporary of Bernstein's at Curtis. The souvenir program also gives orchestration credits to Don Walker, Elliot Jacoby, Ted Royal and Bernstein himself.

The ten-day tryout in Boston was full of problems. The scenery designed for New York didn't fit Boston's Colonial Theater, and at the last moment the producers had to ask the critics not to review the show on the evening of the announced premiere because it simply was not ready. For Bernstein the postponement was especially embarrassing because friends had bought most of the good tickets for a benefit for the Boston Institute of Modern Art; among the principal guests were Dr. Koussevitzky and his future wife, Olga. But Mr. Abbott exuded calm and confidence. "Backstage," Sono Osato remembered, "amidst the actors' last-minute reciting of lines and the dancers warming up, Lenny, looking very handsome in his evening clothes, paced up and down, flushed with excitement. I was wondering why he was heading to the orchestral pit when somebody told me that he, rather than Max Goberman, would conduct the first night." Next morning there was panic when it was discovered that

Jerome Robbins had left Boston. He eventually returned with a new version of Osato's important solo dance.

When the Boston critics finally got to see the show a couple of evenings later, their response was favorable but not ecstatic. One described the music as "an energetic blend of Stravinsky and Gershwin." "A little ornate but at least one popular hit in *Lonely Town,*" wrote another. *Variety* forecast that the show "could develop into a wham if properly developed up here." Fortunately George Abbott was without peer when it came to play-doctoring. Out went several more numbers. In came new dialogue, choreographic revisions and a different version of one of the best songs. Two nights before they closed in Boston, Betty Comden remembers, Mr. Abbott issued the command, " 'Freeze it! That's it!' and whatever it was, was what opened the following week at the Adelphi Theater in New York."

In the midst of all the excitement Bernstein took time out to be guest of honor at a Boston dinner organized by the Anti-Fascist League. Since Harvard days Bernstein had played at pro-left fund-raisers and demonstrated openly on behalf of his political beliefs. "The Roxbury Maestro," as twenty-six-year-old Bernstein was dubbed in the *Boston Post,* was praised for his stand for humanity and dignity; the citation spoke also of his vision, honesty and courage.

On Broadway *On the Town* had taken over one hundred thousand dollars in advance sales on December 28 and double that by January 2. The opening night was the kind of triumph that comes only once or twice in a decade when, as Jack O'Brien of the Associated Press put it, "a reviewer gets an opportunity to heave his hat into the stratosphere, send up rockets and in general start the sort of journalistic drooling over a musical comedy that puts an end to all adequate usage of superlatives." The *New York Times*'s Lewis Nichols called it "the freshest and most-engaging musical show to come this way since the golden day of *Oklahoma!*" For *P.M.*'s Lewis Kronenberger, probably the best of the theater critics in the forties, it was "not only much the best musical of the year, it is one of the freshest, gayest, liveliest musicals I have ever seen." Only the *Daily News*'s John Chapman wrote it off as "dullish." Eight months later he went back to see it again—at the prompting of the authors—and gave the play a very different verdict: "Fresh, funny and witty, a wow."

*On the Town* broke new ground on many fronts. It was the first American musical composed by an acknowledged symphonist. It was the first to have white and black dancers side by side—literally holding hands—on a New York stage, and the first to be bought, virtually sight unseen, by a film company for a subsequent movie. It went on to gross well over $2 million, on an initial production cost of $150,000, and it ran for 436 performances—a respectable tally, although not the huge hit that had been prophesied. The national tour that followed was relatively brief: the show's impact weakened with the end of the war. In the fall of 1945 sailors were still coming to New York on shore leave, but when they parted from their girlfriends they were no longer facing death on active service. Another weakness was the absence of major stars in the cast. The score was also on the clever side for theater audiences; as early as the second number the three sailors are indulging in canonic imitation, overlapping entries of the phrase, "New York, New York." None of Bernstein's melodies clicked on the hit parade. The popular Mary Martin recorded some songs from *On the Town* for Decca, but in anodyne orchestrations. Robert Shaw conducted some equally disappointing choral arrangements for RCA, but the same RCA set included a stunningly authentic performance of an orchestral suite of dances conducted by Bernstein. His second orchestral recording (he had recorded the *Jeremiah* Symphony in St. Louis earlier in the year) was made with the On the Town Orchestra—presumably the pit band. Paul Bowles, reviewing it later in the *Herald Tribune,* called *On the Town* "an epoch-making score" and especially praised an area in which he himself was less proficient: "The instrumentation is often phenomenal in its cleverness."

By the time of its first concert performance in San Francisco, in February 1946, the suite had been shortened and reorganized with the title *Three Dance Episodes from "On the Town."* It seemed only natural, Bernstein wrote on that occasion, "that dance should play a leading role in the show *On the Town* since the idea of writing it arose from the success of the ballet *Fancy Free.* I believe this is the first Broadway show ever to have as many as seven or eight dance episodes in the space of two acts; and as a result, the essence of the whole production is contained in these dances. . . . That these are, in their way, symphonic pieces rarely occurs to the audience actually attending the show, so well integrated are all the elements."

Bernstein's statement that *On the Town* arose from the success of *Fancy Free* is correct but appears to support a misunderstanding concerning the link between the two works which needs rebuttal, since it occurs in so many commentaries and program notes. *On the Town*'s story was not the same as *Fancy Free*'s. The ballet is about three sailors competing for two girls in a bar. The musical is about the interlocking fortunes of three sailors and the three girls they meet on their twenty-four-hour shore leave. "In another important sense," Bernstein himself emphasized, *"On the Town* was not an expansion of *Fancy Free:* there was not a note of *Fancy Free* music in *On the Town."*

AT the opening night of *On the Town* in Boston, Serge Koussevitzky had enjoyed the show despite the scenic hold-ups. But afterward he spoke more sternly to Bernstein than anybody had ever done. "He was furious with me. He gave me a three-hour lecture the next day on the way I was going." Koussevitzky's attitude was unequivocal: a potential great conductor must not dissipate his talents. Though Bernstein knew the worth of his Broadway music, and craved the fun of collaboration, he would devote himself almost exclusively to the conductor's art for the remainder of the decade. Composing became a holiday diversion, fitted in during conducting tours and preseason pauses. His activities as a pianist were restricted to playing the same handful of concertos with every new orchestra he conducted. He wrote a few newspaper articles, reviewed a few recordings, signed a few manifestos. But his surrender to Koussevitzky was almost as unconditional as that of the Nazis to the Allied Forces in May 1945.

# THE FIRST AMERICAN CONDUCTOR
# GETS HIS FIRST ORCHESTRA

*Bernstein's first season at the helm,*
*fall, 1945.*
COURTESY OF THE ESTATE OF LEONARD BERNSTEIN

*My manager Arthur Judson told me all conductors*
*become egomaniacs. If that happens, I'll give up*
*conducting.*

—LEONARD BERNSTEIN, March 1945

As Copland had forecast, Bernstein became the country's outstanding guest conductor. Bruno Zirato negotiated appearances for him with fourteen different orchestras in 1945. Koussevitzky remained his guiding spirit. "I think of you constantly," he wrote after more than a year of incessant travel. "Every time I lift my arms to conduct I am filled with a sense of wonder at the great insight that has flowed from you to me. It is the realization of an old and beautiful power, as if fashioned in heaven, waiting only for your magic to call it out. It is something for which I thank you every day of my life—something which has freed me and given me welcome bondage—as Prospero to Ariel. I am all in all very happy and very thankful; and when I feel this way, I always find I can express it best to you and through you to the Universal Creative Mind, to which you are closer than I." Bernstein trod the line of renunciation with every journalist he met. "It felt natural to write a musical comedy," he said in Pittsburgh in January 1945, "but from now on I intend to stick to the classics." "I'm probably through with musical comedy," he told a columnist a month later in St. Louis. "I've done that now. I like to do everything once, just to see what it feels like." And in Vancouver in March 1945 he claimed that *"On the Town* was probably the last exciting thing I will do—it took nearly ten years from my life."

Wherever he went—Pittsburgh, New York, Rochester, St. Louis, Montreal, Vancouver, Chicago—Bernstein practiced the art of public relations: all he needed to win over hitherto bored music journalists was a conference room and a piano. In St. Louis he played them a snatch of Haydn (Symphony No. 88 was on the program) and then launched into the "Weeping Willow Blues," done in authentic back-room style. He modestly acknowledged references to the similarities between his career and that of Orson Welles, a parallel first made in *Time* magazine the year before; he had a little fun at the expense of his "Information Please" rival Oscar Levant; he made mock-philosophic mention of fan clubs and of letters from girls urging him to get a crew cut. It all added up, one reporter told his readers, to a hilarious press conference. He replaced the received image of the conductor as a remote foreign autocrat with a self-portrait of the maestro as a young American, a jazz-loving, wise-cracking, boogie-playing, hat-spurning, self-deprecating fellow, still boyishly bewildered by his success. The concerts themselves attracted the biggest audiences of the season, and reviewers praised them unstintingly. In Montreal, where he was to accompany Arthur Rubinstein, Bernstein momentarily overstepped his bounds. Rubinstein took exception during rehearsal to Bernstein's tempo for the orchestral exposition to the Grieg concerto. Bernstein rashly replied that it was a second-rate work, not worth bothering about, whereupon Rubinstein stormed out, saying he would cancel the Grieg and substitute a solo piano recital. The orchestra manager ordered Bernstein to make his peace. A silk scarf was purchased and presented to Rubinstein by the crestfallen young conductor. "All right," said a mollified Rubinstein, "I'll play the Grieg but how shall we manage without rehearsal?" Bernstein assured him that would be no problem since he knew the work well—it had been his own debut piece in 1934.

Bernstein's subsequent friendship with Rubinstein endured for close to four decades: one of their last reunions was in 1977 at Maxim's in Paris; Bernstein played Chopin at two in the morning while Arthur and his wife, Nela, danced a stately mazurka on the otherwise empty dance floor. Then Bernstein demonstrated the tango, with Rubinstein at the keyboard, watched only by friends and the chef and the kitchen staff, who had crept out to see the great *maestri* entertain each other.

ONE of the central paradoxes of Bernstein's life was already in evidence by 1945: he loved home, yet he could not resist the vagabond life, even in his pioneer days when, with no wife to look after him, he did his own packing and carried his own bags. Naturally, he was asked about marriage prospects when he talked to reporters. "I meet lots of nice girls but to find one you could live with, that's a problem, a rather awe-inspiring thought."

Whenever he did spend a few days in New York he was surrounded by large contingents of friends and co-workers. In his unpretentious apartment the unlisted telephone rang incessantly. Helen Coates arrived around noon each day and dealt with the mail and the diary amid the sound of piano playing and frequent shouts of laughter. In the midst of the chaos, he completed a commission for the Park Avenue Synagogue in New York: a seven-minute setting of the choral prayer *Hashkiveinu,* part of the Jewish Sabbath service, for choir and tenor solo, accompanied by organ.

In March 1945 Bernstein chaired the jury for a composition competition created in honor of George Gershwin. When he conducted the New York Philharmonic in a program that included *Rhapsody in Blue,* directed from the keyboard, Paul Bowles saw in his friend an incarnation of Gershwin: "No other composer combines the same kind of nervous energy and the same incredible degree of facility."

In April Bernstein undertook a series of six broadcast concerts on successive Sundays with the Detroit Orchestra. Between performances his mind turned to composition. He was contemplating an opera to be adapted from Maxwell Anderson's *Winterset,* a play about the executed anarchists, Sacco and Vanzetti. Nothing came of the idea, nor of a plan for a second ballet in collaboration with Jerome Robbins, to be entitled *Bye Bye Jackie.* Writing to Helen Coates, Bernstein reported: "I have been collecting themes more than anything else these days. . . . I haven't actually written anything. I'm confused about what to do first. . . . But the ideas keep hammering at me; a piano concerto, a ballet, songs for Tourel, the Kouss. piece. . . ." Back in New York Oliver Smith tried to convince him to write a new Broadway show with Comden, Green and Robbins. Bernstein was tempted, but Koussevitzky's dire warning still rang in his ear. "What will Kouss say? Do I really want to do a new show or am I just loath to let one slip by?" When he refused, Morton Gould was named composer for the new team effort, *Billion Dollar Baby.* Bernstein kept close to his compositional agenda, however: over the next four years he wrote a piano concerto, *The Age of Anxiety* (dedicated to "Kouss"), the ballet *Facsimile* and a set of songs for Jennie Tourel.

When he returned to New York in mid-May Bernstein's social date book was crowded. He met Martha Graham at the ballet and Artur Rodzinski at a reception, he gave a copy of the *On the Town* recording to Mayor La Guardia, dined with David Diamond (who was an excellent cook), discussed summer concert plans with Mrs. Minnie Guggenheim, who ran the Lewisohn Stadium concerts, attended the premiere of his choral piece, chatted with Helena Rubinstein (a big fan) and discussed with Paramount the Tchaikovsky film for which Hal Wallis wanted him as a musical adviser. He also attended the premiere of the film biography of Gershwin. Its director, Irving Rapper, was another Hollywood suitor.

On the last Friday of May he flew to Boston to be with his family for his brother Burton's Bar Mitzvah. The siblings were not as close as they once had been. Burton Bernstein remembers that he secretly resented his elder brother's success. Shirley had briefly shared her brother's Carnegie Hall studio but with a regular job in *On the Town* she had moved into her own apartment. Leonard himself was still changing addresses every year in the quest for a place where he could play the piano to his heart's content; he had recently moved into a Broadway loft on the top of one of the big office blocks in the garment district south of the old Metropolitan Opera.

With his family obligations out of the way Bernstein embarked on the vacation his months of guest conducting had earned him. Mexico had been something of an El Dorado since the earliest days of his friendship with Aaron Copland and Paul Bowles, and on May 31 he flew to Mexico City. His plan was to meet the film director Irving Rapper at the Hotel Reforma, "one of the ritziest of hotels," hit the wild spots for a week and then head for Acapulco, where he would settle down to a few weeks of composition. He wrote to Miss Coates as soon as he was installed after a "horrible" air journey lasting more than twenty-four hours. "It looks as if this is to be a wonderful visit. . . . The people are out of this world, and Rapper has arranged a series of events that would knock your eye out; tonight a dinner party, then the Chávez concert, tomorrow afternoon the races, at night a party. Sunday the bull-fight, at night another party; then the opera opens, etc., etc." To Aaron Copland, a week later, he was less discreet about how he had been enjoying himself. "Mexico ist schain! But it's worn me out. I have never seen or experienced such a round of parties, cliques, drinking, sex, lassitude, futility and expatrié snobisme." He had lunched, he added, with Carlos Chávez. "He told me that he's giving up the orchestra next year in favor of composing. He thinks of you especially in this matter, because you once told him that he was first of all a composer." The subtext to Bernstein's letter was that Copland had never urged Bernstein himself to stop conducting and concentrate on composition; indeed when Copland, who'd won the Pulitzer Prize in 1945 for his ballet score *Appalachian Spring,* was asked to compile a list of the top ten American composers apart from himself, Bernstein's name was not among them—the ten were Barber, Diamond, Gershwin, Harris, Ives, Piston, Schuman, Sessions, Virgil Thomson and Randall Thompson. Bernstein never knew about the list, but he may have suspected that Copland still thought little of him as a composer, despite the substantial success of *Fancy Free* and the *Jeremiah* Symphony.

One of Bernstein's Mexico City acquaintances was Tennessee Williams, fresh from a huge Broadway success with *The Glass Menagerie,* which paradoxically had left him feeling empty and depressed. Bernstein and Williams, two of the most flamboyant creative artists of the twentieth century, were invited to lunch by what Williams described in his memoirs as "a pair of very effete

American queens. Bernstein was very hard on them and I was embarrassed by the way he insulted them. 'When the revolution comes,' he declared, 'you will be stood up against a wall and shot.' Bernstein has since been accused of something called 'radical chic,' " Williams continued, "but looking back on that luncheon, I wonder if he is not as true a revolutionary as I am. . . ." Bernstein's only recorded comment on the playwright was a laconic postscript to his letter to Copland: "Tennessee Williams is here—*que fastidio* [what a pain]."

Instead of going to Acapulco, Bernstein rented a villa for a fortnight, sight unseen, in Cuernavaca, sixty miles south of the capital. He described it to his parents: "a lovely pool, a grand piano, a charming house with many terraces and gardens. . . . Can you picture me running a staff [of seven] in Spanish? . . . I'm doing absolutely nothing but lying in my garden in the tropical sun with a G string on. I interrupt it only to eat, or shop, or write a measure of music. And I'm beginning to feel like a human being again. How you'd love this place."

En route to San Francisco and his next conducting date, Bernstein had an appointment in Hollywood with his director friend Irving Rapper—"Rappersody in Blue," as the trade papers called him because of his Gershwin movie— for talks about a film version of the ballet *Fancy Free*. He played the piano at a party where the guests included Somerset Maugham, Ethel Barrymore, Joan Fontaine, George Cukor and his idol Bette Davis. When he got to San Francisco he told a reporter that he was "a confused young man. . . . They want to give me a screen test. They want me to play Rimsky-Korsakov in a movie."

It comes as no surprise to find Bernstein flirting with Hollywood. Copland had already won fame and fortune with his movie scores. Virgil Thomson had composed distinguished documentary film music. Even Stravinsky and Schoenberg had been approached. None of those illustrious names had ever been considered for an acting role, however, and Bernstein was quite tickled when Hal Wallis of Paramount actually sent a director to New York to shoot a screen test in a studio. The project under discussion was a "biopic" in which Bernstein would play Tchaikovsky and Greta Garbo would be Madame von Meck, the composer's protector. According to one early press release, Vladimir Horowitz was to record "the famous Tchaikovsky sonata," although Bernstein himself played the piano in the test. Shirley Bernstein remembers helping her brother to learn the dialogue: "Most of the study time was spent roaring helplessly with laughter over the silliness of the writing and the spectacle of Lenny's taking the whole thing seriously enough to say the lines with a straight face. It was a terribly written script, and Lenny's acting was equally terrible. . . . He didn't have the talent and he was far too quick to see the ridiculous side of himself."

Back and forth across the continent the roving young conductor traveled. From San Francisco he took the *Streamliner* train to Chicago, and then a plane to New York, just in time to make a 10 A.M. rehearsal at Lewisohn Stadium. For one of his four stadium concerts he put together the equivalent of a symphony by Richard Wagner. *The Flying Dutchman* Overture constituted the first movement. The slow movement was the Prelude and "Love Death" from *Tristan und Isolde*. That was followed by "Siegfried's Rhine Journey" from *The Twilight of the Gods* and "The Ride of the Valkyries" made a rousing finale. This was Bernstein's first substantial exposure to Wagner's orchestral magic: he was indifferent to the man's avowed anti-Semitism.

Later in July he made a recording of his blues number "Big Stuff" with Billie Holiday; it was released as the introduction to his high-spirited Decca recording of *Fancy Free*. Then it was back to Chicago for a four-concert engagement at Ravinia Park, where the *Chicago Tribune* critic Claudia Cassidy observed that he conducted the way Joe DiMaggio played baseball. (Another critic said he had "a terrific windup, like a big league spitballer.") Opinions were already dividing as to his merits on the podium. Better heard and not seen was the tenor of those who objected to his physical exertions.

Plans were afoot to modify Bernstein's hectic vagabond life. Dr. Koussevitzky recommended him to Mayor La Guardia as a replacement for Leopold Stokowski as the director of the New York City Symphony Orchestra, which had been formed in 1943 to play concert seasons at Manhattan's new temple of the arts, the City Center for Music and Dance on West Fifty-fifth Street. The City Center was run by the municipality on a shoestring and the appointment had its disadvantages. For one thing, there was no salary: the music director had a seasonal expenses allowance of three thousand dollars. There was nothing in the city's budget to support the concerts—even the renting of the hall had to come out of revenue. The musicians were paid basic union scale for a short season that nevertheless made it difficult for them to take alternative theater work. But for Bernstein the post was irresistible: he would have a chance to plan an entire season and show what he could do with his own orchestra. Salary wasn't a big problem: *On the Town* and *Fancy Free* (161 performances in its first year) were earning substantial royalties, and he had an escape clause inserted in his contract so that if an offer for a major conducting date elsewhere turned up he would be free to accept it.

The formal offer to take over the orchestra was made to Bernstein in Lenox on his twenty-seventh birthday, August 25. The season was due to begin on October 8, but he had no qualms about the brief planning period. The subscription brochure, complete with a moodily handsome portrait of the new music director, promised "vital music old and new, superbly performed under a stimulating young conductor at prices within the reach of all." The concerts were on Monday nights, and there were repeat performances with no intermission on Tuesdays at 6 P.M. for those who preferred music before they went home to dinner. "We're getting together a tremendously vital group of young people," Bernstein told *P.M.* Because the orchestra was an ad hoc group, he was not required to employ the previous year's players. With the Pacific war at an end (the Japanese surrendered on August 14), there would be a good supply of demobilized musicians looking for work. In his mind's eye he saw the possibility of re-creating the prewar Tanglewood student orchestra in Manhattan. "Last year's personnel was much older. I have sought an orchestra consisting of people young enough, eager enough, so that they're still in a self-critical stage." He auditioned three hundred musicians. Some came to play for him at his new penthouse apartment: "I tried to call them off because of the elevator strike but several people I couldn't reach came anyway. They climbed seventeen floors carrying heavy instrument cases and came in feeling perfectly fine. They rested a bit, played their heads off and walked down again." The new democratic order was made visible in the way the orchestra was listed in its concert programs, instrument by instrument in strictly alphabetical order, the concertmaster Werner Lywen halfway down.

A rivalry quickly developed with the Philharmonic a few blocks uptown at Carnegie Hall; Artur Rodzinski was no slouch when it came to program building—the Philharmonic scheduled three Mahler symphonies in the 1945 season and two in 1946, as well as music by Creston, Diamond, Harris, Jerome Kern, Piston, Poulenc and Vaughan Williams. Yet Bernstein's programs were the more imaginative and concert lovers could buy the best orchestra seat on subscription for under two dollars or pay seventy-five cents for a seat upstairs. The Philharmonic had higher technical standards, but the City Symphony played as if its very existence depended on it. "New life was injected into the orchestral world," reported the *Brooklyn Eagle*. "Enthusiasm ran over on both sides of the stage. If he did nothing else Mr. Bernstein created a kind of white heat while putting on an excellent show."

Bernstein's first City Center season ran from October 1945 to April 1946, and he conducted nine pairs out of the twelve fortnightly events. During the second and third seasons, which ran from September through November in 1946 and 1947, there were ten weekly concerts and Bernstein conducted them all. Every concert contained a premiere or a second New York performance or a work of especial interest. The first year's novelties indicate the scope of the series: Shostakovich's First Symphony, Hindemith's *Concert Music for Strings and Brass,* Randall Thompson's Second Symphony, *La Création du Monde* by Milhaud, Beethoven's C sharp minor Quartet, op. 131 (in Mitropoulos's edition), Stravinsky's *Symphony of Psalms,* Diamond's Second Symphony, Chávez's *Sinfonia India,* Bartók's First Violin Concerto and finally Blitzstein's *The Airborne* Symphony, with Orson Welles narrating.

It was a fine achievement for a conductor still in his twenties. It involved sacrifices; Bernstein's gadfly presence at the City Center meant that he was no longer invited to conduct the New York Philharmonic. But he established himself firmly in the city's musical life, he enlarged his repertoire, improved his conducting technique, and served notice to every orchestra in the country that he was a potential music director. Early on, Olin Downes wrote a rave notice to match his account of Bernstein's debut concert in Carnegie Hall two years earlier: "For vividness, conviction, imagination, we do not expect soon to see this concert surpassed. . . . Here is a conductor."

Bernstein's busy life in the first postwar New York season included interviews for magazines as far apart in the political spectrum as *Commentary* and *Vogue,* broadcasts about the City Center programs with Arthur Berger on WQXR, and appearances on a panel game called "So You Think You Know Music?" He was photographed by Gjon Mili for *Vogue* and by Arnold Newman for *Life*. The kaleidoscope whirled ever faster. But at its center, Leonard Bernstein remained in some ways alone, emotionally uncommitted. One night in February 1946, at the City Center, he accompanied the great Chilean pianist Claudio Arrau in a performance of the Brahms D minor Concerto. After the concert a party was held at Arrau's house in Queens. There Bernstein met a beautiful young Chilean actress who had been taking piano lessons in New York with Arrau. Her name was Felicia Montealegre Cohn, and she would change his life.

# FINDING HIS WAY

*The international conductor.
Bernstein's passport photo at
the time of his first visits to Prague
and London, 1946.*
COURTESY OF THE ESTATE OF LEONARD BERNSTEIN

*Leonard Bernstein would be a delightful conductor if
he could ever forget . . . that he is being considered
by Warner Brothers to be a potential film star.*

—Virgil Thomson,
*Herald Tribune,* 1946

FELICIA Montealegre Cohn was born in Costa Rica in 1922. According to
family legend, her Chilean mother, a staunch Catholic, had aristocratic fore-
bears stretching back to the kings of Navarre. Her father, Roy Elwood Cohn,
was a mining engineer who became president of the American Smelting and
Refining Company in Santiago, Chile. His grandfather had been a rabbi, but
Felicia and her two sisters were educated by Catholic nuns. Felicia was bilin-
gual and opted for American nationality at the age of twenty-one. She loved

music, literature and the theater and she was clever with words. She had a sharp sense of humor as well as good taste. In her teens she decided that she wanted to be an actress, but her parents disapproved. She switched disciplines to music, and was allowed to go to New York to study piano with her compatriot Claudio Arrau. In New York she began calling herself Felicia Montealegre, studying at Herbert Berghof's Drama Studio at the New School. Berghof was reputed to have been crazy about her. She made her stage debut in the summer of 1945 in a García Lorca play, *If Five Years Pass,* at the Provincetown Playhouse in Greenwich Village.

The night Bernstein met Felicia Montealegre, February 5, was the eve of her twenty-fourth birthday. Friede Rothe, who was Claudio Arrau's agent, remembered the meeting as love at first sight: "Felicia was built like a boy. She was very slim and delicate and *raffinée.* Well educated. A lady. She had all the qualities that Lenny adored." In later life the Bernsteins observed Felicia's birthday, the sixth, as the day of their first meeting, which confirms Friede Rothe's impression that they went home together that evening and celebrated the dawning of her birthday itself. David Diamond, who was also at the party, recalls Leonard and Felicia sitting together on a sofa, talking to each other a mile a minute.

Felicia had already seen Bernstein conducting at City Center and reputedly expressed her intention of marrying him, even before she met him. Over the next few months she would learn the hard way, through his absence, about his peripatetic lifestyle, with its pattern of incessant travel and hotel meals, new orchestras to conquer and other relationships to pursue.

Bernstein left New York the day after Felicia's birthday for concerts in San Francisco and Vancouver. The letters he sent back to Helen Coates were full of references to someone else entirely—a friend named Seymour, who was with him in San Francisco, and a week later in Vancouver. There he wrote to Helen Coates: "This is a heavenly evening. S. and I have made no appointments, but have remained in the room with dinner and talk and reading and writing and infinite love. These days have been beautiful beyond belief. S. is accepted everywhere, by everyone, not only as my friend, but for himself; and we have had so much joy to share. San Francisco is now a marvelous memory: Vancouver is a real honeymoon."

This is hardly the language of somebody who has just fallen in love with a Chilean actress. Yet Bernstein was inspired to new musical heights by the emotional euphoria Seymour induced. "The rehearsal today [Beethoven's First Piano Concerto, directed from the keyboard] was amazing. The orchestra outdid itself, never having played 'conductorlessly' before. And I have never played so well. This is sincere. The slow movement . . . was so beautiful I was almost weeping." After the Sunday afternoon concert he took part in a play reading of *Hamlet* at the Vancouver Players Club. Bernstein, predictably enough, read the title role.

There is no further mention of either Seymour or Felicia in his date book until the end of April. Indeed his life was so crowded with musical excitements throughout the spring and summer that there would have been little time for romance. In March he conducted the last two City Center programs of his first season. The Hungarian violinist Josef Szigeti combined Bartók's early *Violin Rhapsody* and *Portrait No. 1* in the first of these concerts, to form the premiere of what became known as Bartók's Violin Concerto No. 1. The second saw the world premiere of Marc Blitzstein's *The Airborne* Symphony, with Orson Welles as the narrator.

Very much a product of its time, reminiscent of both radio documentary and poetic drama, *The Airborne* is scored for orchestra, tenor and baritone soloists and male chorus. It was dedicated to the U.S. Eighth Air Force, and its evocation of the mystery of flight and the harsh reality of wartime flying conditions gave the public what the *Journal-American* called "a thrill and excitement." A work that dealt with grand issues and combined narrative and music in an accessible style, *The Airborne* would exert an influence on Bernstein's *Kaddish* Symphony of 1963.

On May 3 Bernstein set out on his first visit to Europe to represent America at the inaugural Prague Spring Festival in Czechoslovakia. The composer Samuel Barber and the pianist Eugene List were also in the delegation organized by Carlos Moseley, then working for the U.S. State Department. Bernstein flew into Prague from Paris in a U.S. Army plane. In his luggage he carried a consignment of violin and cello strings, the gift of the New York Philharmonic to their Czech orchestral colleagues. He was soon swept up in a wave of celebrations marking the first anniversary of the city's liberation from the Nazis. "And are they celebrating, as no American would ever dare to do!" he wrote to Helen Coates. "Outside in the streets the whole town is dancing—to miked-up records of boogie-woogie and Strauss waltzes! People have come from all the provinces—Moravia, Slovakia—in their heavenly national peasant costumes, and the gaiety is beyond description. . . . Last night there were fireworks on the Moldau and up in the great Hradcany Castle. It is the only place on earth to be this week."

Bernstein took an attractive program of American music to play with the Czech Philharmonic. William Schuman's sparkling *American Festival Overture* was followed by Barber's *Second Essay*—with the composer present—and the *Rhapsody in Blue*. Eugene List almost missed this: his car broke down en route from Berlin and he failed to make the morning run-through. Bernstein rehearsed the *Rhapsody* from the keyboard and was probably disappointed when List turned up just in time to perform in the evening. In the second half Bernstein conducted Roy Harris's Third Symphony and the exhilarating *El Salón México*. At the second concert Bernstein substituted his *Jeremiah* Symphony for the *Rhapsody in Blue;* it got the best reviews of the week.

On his way back to the United States Bernstein stopped in Paris and met

Nadia Boulanger, who had been alerted to his coming by Aaron Copland. They hit it off together famously and she introduced him to François Valéry, the diplomat son of the poet Paul Valéry, who came as close as anybody at that period to penetrating Bernstein's inner life. "Frankly speaking, I found him rather pretentious," wrote Valéry many years later, "a little too familiar, not even very good looking. I was of course dazzled when he went to the old piano on which Ravel, Milhaud, Chausson, Debussy (and André Gide, four hands with my mother) had played, and even more so when, on Marie-Blanche de Polignac's Bechstein (we went to visit her with Nadia after dinner) he gave a pot-pourri recital, Verdi, Chabrier, Beethoven—the whole cadenza from the so-called First Concerto—and Marc Blitzstein. Because his [New York] plane was canceled, he remained one more day in Paris, and we spent it together. . . . For the first time in my life, I had met the one thing which I envied: *gift,* real genuine unquestionable gift 'à l'état pur.' It was a shock, and also a fantastic reward, but it put our relations on the wrong track. I did not accept easily a certain facility in the way Lenny behaved with people, who—at least I thought —were unworthy of him, and this tended to create between us, whenever we met . . . a certain tension."

EARLY in June Bernstein flew from America to England with Helen Coates to conduct six concerts with the London Philharmonic, only two of them in London. He was out of sorts from the day he arrived, mostly because nobody had heard of him. Nor was he happy with the "miserable, 'Ford-Hour' type programs" he'd been asked to conduct. "The only redemption is *Appalachian Spring* (*Jeremiah,* of course, is out) and my one comfort these days is studying it," he wrote to Aaron Copland. "I manage somehow to borrow some of that fantastic stability of yours, that deep serenity. It is really amazing how the clouds lift with that last page. And I feel better. Thank heaven for you. The state of music here is ghastly. As is the state of everything (food, morals, housing, politics, India, clothing)."

Copland's London publisher, Ralph Hawkes, did his best to entertain Bernstein, but there were no press conferences such as had been organized for him in the smallest of American cities, no diplomatic receptions, no parties in his honor, nothing more glamorous than an early evening talk to the members of the London Philharmonic's Supporters Club. "I have rarely felt so lonely," he wrote to his sister. "I react to everything with big soggy depressions." When he was not walking the West End streets in search of company ("I've worn out Piccadilly in invitation and rejection," he told Copland; "my loneliness has become a monster"), Bernstein was in his hotel room, shivering. Leaving New York in a heat wave, he had brought the wrong clothes. London was unseasonably cold and since clothes were still rationed foreigners could not even buy a hat or gloves without the vital coupons.

On the musical front rehearsals were difficult because the orchestra was in a transition stage with many of Britain's best players not yet demobilized after the war. It was hard, he reported, to get the London Philharmonic to play in tune. The city had been without a proper concert hall since 1942, when the Queen's Hall was destroyed in an air raid; rehearsals took place on makeshift stages awkwardly dotted around the city, and Bernstein made his London debut in a West End theater. But his despondent account must be treated with some skepticism. He told Copland he had problems teaching the London Philharmonic the irregular rhythms of *Appalachian Spring,* yet his first concert, on June 16, was well received by the critics, notably *The Times:* "He gave vivid performances of Walton's *Portsmouth Point* Overture, *Till Eulenspiegel,* and a work new to us, the ballet *Appalachian Spring* by his fellow countryman and contemporary [*sic*] Aaron Copland." The second half of the program consisted of "Siegfried's Funeral March" and the "Immolation Scene," two glorious bleeding chunks from Wagner's *Götterdämmerung. The Times* thought Bernstein "threw away the last degree of tautness and brilliance" by not using a baton but said he was "plainly a Wagnerian conductor by temperament, and it was indeed an exciting experience to hear again after seven years the closing scene from *Götterdämmerung* built up to climax and consummation under his impulsive direction."

The London Philharmonic lived a grueling life in those austere days: Bernstein was caught up in a punishing series of out-of-town concerts, and came down with a sore throat and a fever. The doctor who was called when he returned from Leicester to London prescribed a dose of penicillin. This was a thrill, arguably the high point of the tour for Bernstein. "I was one of the first people in England to have penicillin, which had just been invented. The army got me penicillin. Gloves they couldn't get me but penicillin saved my life." That was how Bernstein used to tell the story whenever he visited London and drove past the Hyde Park Hotel where he had stayed on his first visit. In fact he was only in bed for one day; the penicillin treatment was remarkably effective and next morning he went down the road to the Royal Albert Hall in Kensington promptly at 10 A.M. for his regular LPO rehearsal. This concert was sold out —despite the fact that in Bernstein's recollection the newspapers consisted of only two pages and carried virtually no advertising. The main work on the program was Tchaikovsky's Fifth Symphony. "A great experience," he wrote to Koussevitzky. "Some people in the audience came back and told me it was better than Nikisch!"

After a visit to Glyndebourne to see Benjamin Britten rehearsing his new opera, *The Rape of Lucretia,* Bernstein returned to London to make his debut recording as a concerto pianist, playing the Ravel concerto with the recently formed Philharmonia Orchestra. He was due in Tanglewood to begin rehearsals of Britten's opera *Peter Grimes,* but Ralph Hawkes convinced him to extend his stay a week and conduct *Fancy Free* at Ballet Theatre's Independence Day gala opening at the Royal Opera House. On that occasion he was praised both for his score and his conducting; the *Evening News* gossip column said London office girls had his photograph pinned up next to their typewriters. He dined with Jerome Robbins on the evening before he flew back to New York: Ballet Theatre wanted to commission a new ballet from them but Robbins was hesitant as to theme and treatment.

Transatlantic flight was still a dreary business. Bernstein's plane stopped to refuel in Iceland, Greenland and Labrador on the way to Idlewild. Traveling up to Lenox with Helen Coates in his newly acquired station wagon was not much fun either; they had two blowouts on the 120-mile journey and had to make an overnight stay. He took lunch next day with Koussevitzky and dinner with Aaron Copland, and then launched into rehearsals for *Peter Grimes*. They continued every day—six, nine, sometimes even twelve hours a day—until the first performance on August 6.

*Peter Grimes* was far and away the toughest conducting project of Bernstein's career so far. The story of a misfit fisherman who accidentally causes the death of his boy apprentices, the opera consists of more than two hours of music and requires a large cast, chorus and orchestra. It had first been mounted at London's Sadler's Wells Theatre in June 1945 after Koussevitzky, who commissioned the work, had generously waived his rights to the world premiere. Successful with critics and public in England, it had nevertheless caused serious tension within the opera company, some of whose members resented the opera's modernity. Koussevitzky and his Tanglewood colleagues ignored these storm warnings concerning the work's complexity and went ahead with what to all intents and purposes was a student production. The scenery and costumes were made on site in a theater which had been out of commission since 1942 and had never been used for anything more elaborate than a few scenes from *Porgy and Bess* and *La Bohème*. Almost all the roles were sung by students. The opera was produced with alternate casts and with a double orchestra, one group playing for Act I and Act III, the other for Act II. In theory, this division of labor was an admirable procedure for an educational venture, but it placed an additional strain on Bernstein and the production team. They were given only five weeks to mount a brand-new opera in an unfamiliar style that required half a dozen sets. Even in an experienced professional opera house, this would be a dangerously short rehearsal period. But Bernstein flourished under such conditions; he had a picture in his mind of how "Grimey Pete" should go, and the flair to communicate his conception, which could be epitomized by the memorable command he once gave the orchestra: "Give it all you've got and then crescendo!"

As the performances grew closer, the number of friends and family visiting Bernstein's cramped quarters at Bull Cottage on the edge of Lake Makheenac grew accordingly, with Helen Coates valiantly attempting to maintain some kind of order. His sister Shirley came up whenever she could—she was in rehearsal for a new Broadway show. Marc Blitzstein visited several times, as did Oliver Smith, who came to talk to the Opera Workshop program and had to sleep on the floor. Other guests included David Diamond, Adolph Green, his new fiancée, Allyn Ann McLerie, and Bernstein's young brother Burton, who got a summer job in the *Peter Grimes* lighting department. Burton's *Family Matters* memoir suggests that Felicia Montealegre was among the house guests, but there is no mention of her in Bernstein's date book, and she was acting in a Broadway play throughout the summer.

The most important visitor was Benjamin Britten, who dined with Bernstein twice in the week leading up to the premiere. The slim, boyish-looking Englishman, almost five years older than Bernstein, was by now a hardened professional, mild in appearance but tough as nails underneath. Burton Bernstein noticed that Britten was somewhat excited by the large contingent of young men working that summer at Tanglewood. The dashing Burtie, then fourteen, was invited to perch on Britten's knee when he came to dinner; his elder brother was self-righteously indignant when told about it. Britten's comment to *Time* magazine after the premiere of the opera was devastating: "There's no use pretending it was professional—this was a very lively student performance." W. H. Auden, Britten's former mentor and collaborator, told a friend that the performance was "dreadful." Irving Kolodin sourly described the opera as "a drain on the attention and a trial to the patience." He referred to Bernstein's "unrelenting baton," an odd phrase when used to describe a conductor who did not use one.

But "Peter und Grimes," as Koussevitzky called it in a proud curtain speech, was far from being a flop. For Edmund Wilson it was an "extraordinary music drama." Phyllis Curtin, who sang one of the nieces, was "thrilled to death; it was so real and alive." The conductor Sarah Caldwell, then a twenty-two-year-old student, was put in charge of the complicated lighting plot. "I hope you know the music," Bernstein said to her in the wings before the opera began, looking at the cues in her score. "I hope *you* do," was the redoubtable Caldwell's swift rejoinder.

Bernstein always adored *Peter Grimes* and shortly before his death was making plans for a full-scale recording in 1993 for Deutsche Grammophon. He had an affinity with the work at several levels: he would have identified with the loneliness of Peter Grimes and with the ambivalence of Grimes's sexuality. More immediately, he reveled in the music simply as music: the nocturnal trio of gorgeously blending women's voices, reminiscent of *Der Rosenkavalier;* the spirited pub chorus "Old Joe Has Gone Fishing," in 7/4 time, one of Bernstein's favorite meters; the grim energy of the "Storm"; and the yearning tenderness of the "Night Interlude." The *Four Sea Interludes* were included in the last concert Bernstein ever conducted.

Within hours of the conclusion of the premiere, Bernstein was playing boogie-woogie at the cast party. As Eric Crozier, the English director, remembered, Bernstein was more interested in talking to Auden, whom he revered, than to Britten, who was no great shakes as a party-goer. Reciprocally, perhaps, Britten did not warm to his flamboyant interpreter and never invited him to perform at the Aldeburgh Festival, which he founded two years later.

BERNSTEIN seemed to have an inexhaustible fund of nervous and creative energy in 1946. No sooner had he finished the run of *Peter Grimes* than Jerome Robbins arrived in Stockbridge to work on a new ballet project, *Facsimile*. In five days they had hammered out the story line; Bernstein spent the rest of August composing and orchestrating, taking a brief break in Sharon for his twenty-eighth birthday. He made a piano recording of the ballet for Robbins and the dancers to work on soon after he got back to New York. The premiere took place on October 24.

*Facsimile*—twenty minutes in length—represents the somewhat bitter fruits of the psychoanalysis sessions both Robbins and Bernstein had been undertaking for as long as either of them could scrape together a few dollars. (For a time Bernstein went to a woman analyst recommended to him by Robbins, who had heard about her from Martha Graham.) The new ballet was less obviously beguiling than *Fancy Free;* nobody suggested turning it into a musical. Later in the year Bernstein wrote a program note for the concert hall adaptation. "The inspiration of [Robbins's] scenario, with its profoundly moving psychological implications, had entered into this music in a degree which, I believe, produced what one might almost call a 'neurotic music,' mirroring the neuroses of the characters involved. The action of the ballet is concerned with three lonely people—a woman and two men—who are desperately and vainly searching for real interpersonal relationships. They meet for the first time, develop quick and passionate connections, and, inevitably, find themselves left in a state of ennui and resentment: inevitably, because they are unintegrated personalities with little if any capacity for real relations." A triangular relationship develops and the climax is reached when all three perceive the emptiness of their feelings. "This point is accomplished in the ballet by the desperate cry of 'Stop!' from the woman, followed by a minute of silence in which only her sobbing is heard. The men stand by, abashed and motionless."

The psychological basis of the plot line prompted some unfriendly reactions: "To a frantic score by Leonard Bernstein," wrote *Time,* "the three insecure people . . . rolled on the floor, kissed indiscriminately, tussled, then the two men tossed Nora Kaye back and forth like a shuttlecock until she fell sobbing on the floor. On opening night she went down so hard that many seat holders thought she had sprained her ankle. At this point Ballerina Kaye cried out 'Stop.' One unkind critic felt she had said everything that needed saying." But Oliver Smith's design was universally admired—the "open space" was an empty beach, with irregular iron breakwaters running out to sea—and Robbins was given credit for being his own man: as Walter Terry put it in the *Herald Tribune,* "the fact that Jerome Robbins with four smash comedy hits behind him (two in ballet and two on Broadway) endangered his not yet rooted success as a designer of gay dances by creating the bitter and not-pap-for-the-audience *Facsimile* proved that . . . contrived shadows of past successes could not hope to rival the fresh substance of a new creation." The score of *Facsimile* was dedicated to Robbins. The ballet has not been revived since December 1951 and the hard-driving concert version has been equally neglected.

*Facsimile* was the cause of a rift between Bernstein and Koussevitzky. Bernstein was booked for two weeks as guest conductor with the Boston Symphony in January and February 1947, and he included the new ballet score in his plans for a concert that would be broadcast. Dr. Koussevitzky called him to object, and after their conversation dictated the following letter:

> Dear Leonard:
> My last talk over the telephone with you left a very disturbing impression. And these are the reasons:
> Speaking of your programs you stubbornly insisted on the performance of your own composition, even for the broadcast. Do you realize that you are invited as a guest conductor, to show your capacities as interpreter of great musical works? May I ask you: do you think that your composition is worthy of the Boston Symphony Orchestra and the Boston Organization? Can it be placed on the same level as Beethoven, Schubert, Brahms, Stravinsky, Prokofieff, Bartok or Copland? . . . You may answer my question saying that I often perform also works of lesser value and scope. But you must not forget that I am the permanent conductor, that I stand at the head of this organization to further and develop the musical culture of this country, and, therefore, have the obligation to help young composers. Thus, my responsibilities are very different from yours or other guest conductors.
> I am writing in this direct manner because I consider it superfluous to talk to you as if you still were a "spoiled child." You are fully grown up and have to realize that you are responsible for every word you say and all of your actions, especially responsible on account of your gifts and the position you are beginning to occupy.
> Think it over, and I hope you will understand the motive which dictates this letter.

In his reply, Bernstein pulled out all the stops to effect a reconciliation with his master.

> Dear Serge Alexandrovich:
> I have been deeply grieved all day on account of your last letter. I immediately sent you a telegram, trying to explain the misunderstanding, but I canceled it, realizing that it was not a thorough clarification. I must write you instead, because of my love for you, and my need for you to understand.

Why do these misunderstandings happen? Is there an evil element in my nature that makes me do and say immoral things? Is it that I say one thing and mean another? Or is it that communication between two people who are so close to each other is so difficult? If so, then life is too difficult; something is missing in the human constitution. . . .

And you know I am happy to play only what you suggest and approve in my Boston concerts. Whenever I conduct in Boston I am conducting for *you,* deep inside, and whatever I may do well is a tribute to you. My main concern is to make you proud of me, and justified in all your efforts for me. So when you asked me suddenly on the phone to take off my own piece, I was surprised, and merely questioned why? Certainly I believe in my music, or else I would not have written it—not on a level with Beethoven and Bartok, naturally, but in its own smaller terms. But if you feel it is wrong to play it, I will certainly follow what you say, and gladly.

I have had a very difficult year trying to adjust myself to the conventions of my profession. The réclame means absolutely nothing to me—in fact, it only complicates further my already complicated life. Managers, agents, public charm, the terrifying sense of competition in other conductors—the whole desperate race with time would be worth nothing if it were not for the magical joy of music itself. And this joy is bound up tightly with you, who are my only "spiritus genitor." That is why I become so depressed when misunderstandings come between us.

Forgive me, and

Believe me,
Leonard

Once again Bernstein capitulated to Koussevitzky. *Facsimile* was removed from the Boston program and premiered as a concert work by the Rochester Philharmonic in March 1947. He began to worry that his work as a composer might forever be sacrificed on the conductor's altar. To what must have been his secret chagrin, Dimitri Mitropoulos never programmed his music (although he championed David Diamond's) and Koussevitzky had just made his opinion of Bernstein's compositions brutally clear.

Even before his run-in with Koussevitzky, Bernstein would have felt concern about how he was going to maintain his earnings. In December 1944 he had received forty thousand dollars as his share in the sale of the film rights of *On the Town* to MGM. But his royalty payments had dwindled now that *On the Town* had concluded its national tour. He had a small guaranteed income from his music publisher but his serious compositions were making no headway. So when the producer Lester Cowan came to him in September 1946 with a project for a feature film, Bernstein immediately expressed interest. Cowan was well known in Hollywood. He had produced W. C. Fields's *You Can't Cheat an Honest Man,* and war movies such as *The Story of G.I. Joe.* He wanted to make a musical film—partly because his wife, Ann Ronell, was a songwriter. His idea was to take a novel called *The Beckoning Fair One,* by an English writer, Oliver

Onions, and have it rewritten so the male lead would be a conductor and pianist. "A real debut vehicle for me," Bernstein told Helen Coates. He summarized his role for Aaron Copland: "It involves score, authorship (of the screen play), acting and conducting. *My* picture." Copland was deeply skeptical. "I'm intrigued by your story of the quadruple threat to the movies. I'm utterly mystified how you can fit it in. Have you considered 1) the general effect on your conducting career? 2) having somebody outside yourself read the script? 3) having someone advise how much dough you ought to get? Keep the angles in mind!"

While Bernstein was flirting with Hollywood during the fall of 1946, momentous changes were occurring in his personal life. He had taken a new apartment on the top floor of 32 West Tenth Street when he moved back from Tanglewood to New York in September. (Paul Bowles lived literally on the other side of the wall. On warm evenings they opened the windows and played two-piano music, one piano in each apartment.)

Felicia Montealegre had a small basement studio nearby at 69 Washington Place. On September 28 Bernstein attended the closing performance of *Swan Song,* the Broadway play in which she had been performing all summer. Subsequently, they saw each other regularly, and when he set off in December for California to confer with Lester Cowan, Leonard took Felicia with him to look for acting work in Hollywood. "Felicia is wonderful and very happy," Leonard wrote to Helen Coates from Cowan's ranch in the San Fernando Valley, "she fits so well into any situation—on a horse or bicycle, in a party, or alone together. We are a big hit with the servants, and enjoy unlimited service. The Cowans are away most of the time, and we are practically masters of the ranch."

In his next letter he told Helen Coates that he and Felicia were growing closer all the time. "She's an angel and a wonderful companion. I shouldn't be surprised if it worked out beautifully in the end." By December 22 he was edging toward a decision. "I'm toying with the idea of becoming engaged to Felicia," he wrote to Miss Coates. "No marriage yet—she must stay here and do a movie contract [wishful thinking on Bernstein's part], and I must travel. We think of it for June, and it's an exciting and somewhat confusing prospect. . . . Listen to Winchell Sunday night. If I decide, he will announce it." In the same letter Bernstein confided that Koussevitzky was pressing him to marry immediately.

Bernstein's parents, who had met Felicia in the fall when they went to Manhattan to see *Facsimile,* were divided in their response to the news of his impending marriage. Sam was vacationing in Miami when his son told him he was contemplating an engagement. "It was the most wonderful news I heard of for a long time. You have my full blessing, Lenny. I have the utmost confidence in you, that you know what you are doing. One thing I want you to promise me, that you'll have her turn completely to Judaism. It is very important for the future of both of you that you know where you are going. Drifting is a sad situation. Knowing where you are going is an insurance for a successful trip."

Back home in Brookline with only Burtie to keep her company, Jennie responded like the archetypal Jewish mother. "I tell you dear that I'm not too happy about this affair of yours. Aside from the religious angle I still don't think she is the girl for you. You deserve someone better. Don't let that accent fool you. However I'm sure you will not heed me nor Dad if you make up your mind to do it. Dad and I love you very much and we want nothing but the best all around for you, someone who will help keep that shining light glittering. I know I sound as though I broke into poetry but nevertheless it's true."

Jennie's appeal for caution fell on deaf ears. At the end of the year press releases announced that Bernstein had made two agreements, one to make a movie, the other to take a bride. The film deal, from which Bernstein hoped to net twenty thousand dollars as a down payment, was reported in all the trade papers, while the engagement was celebrated at a ranch party thrown in Bernstein's honor by the Cowans. It was a publicist's dream and Leonard Lyons had a field day: "This is how Leonard Bernstein's engagement to Felicia Montealegre was announced. Lester Cowan, producer of 'The Beckoned [*sic*] Fair One' in which Bernstein will co-star, conduct and compose the musical score, gave a hoe-down for them on his ranch. Sinatra sang, Gene Kelly danced and John Garfield donned boxing gloves. . . . Then came a song written by Ann Ronell, author of 'Willow, Weep for Me,' 'Big Bad Wolf,' etc. The tune was a blending of Haydn's *Surprise* Symphony, Mendelssohn's *Wedding March*, and Bernstein's *Fancy Free, On The Town* and *Jeremiah*. The lyrics ended with this announcement:

> " '*This party has been staged*
> *Because they got engaged.*
> *Len and Felicia*
> *Are now officia-*
> *Lly two.*' "

The sophisticated banality of the rhyme turned out to be a bad omen for the young couple. Almost five years elapsed before they married.

# THE CONDUCTOR AS MESSIAH

*Talking to settlers at Tel Joseph, after his*
*Ein Harod concert, Palestine, 1947.*
COURTESY OF THE ESTATE OF LEONARD BERNSTEIN

*If you ever wanted to be involved in an historical*
*moment, this is it.*

—Bernstein, in Palestine, to Dr.
Koussevitzky, April 1947

MMEDIATELY after the engagement party Bernstein had to leave California to begin his winter conducting season. Felicia stayed in Hollywood, looking for film work. On January 21, 1947, a rumor appeared in the gossip column of *Variety* that when Serge Koussevitzky retired from the Boston Symphony Orchestra Leonard Bernstein would replace him. Bernstein's decision to get married surely had a relevance, however subconscious, to the drama of Koussevitzky's succession which was soon to be played out in Boston. Bernstein's feelings for Felicia were not fabricated or dissembled; he was not that kind of a man. But their engagement announcement was made less than a month after the couple had begun spending time in each other's exclusive company. It would do no harm to present himself as a respectable married man if he were about to be considered for the musical direction of the country's leading orchestra. Not that there was any hint of such reasoning in the letter in which he had broken the news to Koussevitzky. "I have become engaged to a wonderful girl from South America named Felicia Montealegre. We plan to be married in June, when I return from Europe. I am very happy, and I hope you will be. This news seems to have leaked out into the papers already, and I did want to be the first to tell you, before you might read it." But Bernstein seems to have become ambivalent about his commitment to marriage when he left Felicia in Hollywood. The engagement announcement said that they planned to marry in June, when Bernstein got back from conducting engagements in Europe, yet his subsequent instructions to Helen Coates indicate otherwise. After informing her that he had decided to cancel his unrealistic film plans, he asked her to seek additional concert engagements, specifically "Paris, into June." He later admitted to Shirley that he had treated Felicia cruelly that winter.

Still hoping for a film contract, Felicia waited in California, sustained by her friendships with Adolph Green, Gene Kelly and Saul Chaplin, but somewhat apprehensive for the future, to judge from a series of touching letters to her fiancé and this one to Helen Coates: "It was wonderful to get your blessing! Please don't think that my silence meant I'd forgotten you—on the contrary your friendship means so much to me, and I always look back on that conversation we had before I left, as something very special and heart-warming. I hope we will always be able to sit down and talk our heads and hearts off that way— you are a very understanding person and I really feel I can count on you; so just consider me a very poor correspondent and write me a line once in a while.

"Oh Helen, I know everything is being left unsaid but it is very difficult for me to write. Believe me though, I'm very very happy and full of faith and strength—there will probably be very hard times ahead, I know that, but good times too. Please help us have them—if you can."

A few months later Miss Coates gave an interview about her boss to the *New York World-Telegram* that would have left Felicia in no doubt as to her position. With Leonard Bernstein, she declared, "music comes first and it always will. If he ever does marry, his wife will have to recognize that from the beginning."

Music-making dominated his daily life. February found him conducting a three-week season with the Boston Symphony. He loved being back in his hometown. "Somehow I really relax here," he wrote Helen Coates from his parents' Brookline house. "Sleep comes naturally. I've bought two suits, had a massage and gotten a haircut. And this phenomenal orchestra makes me terribly happy. What a response they give me." A week later he wrote that his Friday afternoon concert, featuring Schubert's "Great" C major Symphony, had been "one of my top jobs of all time. I've been sailing ever since. And apparently my sermon last night in Temple Israel (in rabbinical robes!!) was a slight bombshell. It was real fun." The subject was "What Is a Jewish Composer?" and his choral work *Hashkiveinu* was performed.

Bernstein had some strong meat in his programs, including the Boston premiere of Bartók's *Music for Strings, Percussion and Celesta,* and Stravinsky's *Le Sacre du Printemps,* which the orchestra had not done since 1939. They played *Le Sacre* from an edition Nicolas Slonimsky had made for Koussevitzky. Legend had it that the version was simplified and something of a cheat, but Slonimsky merely rationalized the way the bar lines were organized: the sound of the music was unaltered. Bernstein had loved Stravinsky's score since hearing it as a boy on a radio broadcast. "The whole modern movement, as I look at things, begins with the *Sacre du Printemps.* It stands as the primary example of continuous, consistent dissonance." The *Sacre* is still a tough work to bring off and in the 1940s it was thought to be of ferocious difficulty. When Bernstein conducted it at Carnegie Hall, at one of his two appearances in New York with the Boston Symphony, Virgil Thomson, often his sternest critic, wrote, "One felt that he loved the music, understood it, and submitted his will in all modesty to its relentless discipline. . . . He is a real interpreter." "He felt its whole structure and germination," echoed Olin Downes in the *Times;* "felt it in his bones and so released it that it seemed almost to rend the orchestra itself with its elemental power. He is a born conductor, a musician of his period and one of its voices in his art."

With recommendations like these, Koussevitzky had high hopes that Bernstein would be his successor. No other guest conductor had led the Boston Symphony in New York during his twenty-two years as director. Bernstein was of two minds about whether he wanted the job, but the music world clearly thought it likely and when the Rochester Symphony chose Toscanini's protégé Erich Leinsdorf as its music director, in February 1947, Bernstein expressed himself keenly disappointed. "It's a shame," he wrote to Helen Coates from Rochester, where he had been given the news confidentially at the start of a three-week concert tour with the orchestra. "They wanted me very badly but were told I was too involved with Boston! Why don't they ask me? It's a shame."

In March, *Newsweek* pointed out that Koussevitzky was in his seventies and was doing only thirteen weeks of the orchestra's twenty-four-week season. There were three names on the magazine's list of possible successors: two of Bernstein's inspirations, Fritz Reiner and Dimitri Mitropoulos, and Bernstein himself, described as ". . . Boy Wonder of Carnegie Hall, Broadway and *Information Please."*

By that time Charles Munch had also entered the running. Munch, who came from Alsace in eastern France, was in his mid-fifties, elegant and, thanks to his wife, a Nestlé heiress, rich. Boston prided itself on its French connection —Pierre Monteux had preceded Koussevitzky—and on its understated but undeniably patrician approach to culture. Bernstein, on the other hand, took a positive delight in democratizing the role of the conductor. The week before his New York debut with the Boston Symphony, he wrote to Miss Coates that there were "no dress shirts in Boston, but I've taken to T-shirts for concerts. Just a fad, probably." His love of jazz, his sexy ballets, his youth and his success on Broadway all made him in the eyes of the Boston establishment a "flaky" prospect for the music directorship. It has also been suggested that his un-doubted Jewishness and his rumored homosexuality also told against him with the orchestra's trustees. But Koussevitzky had been born Jewish (and was soon to reaffirm his faith) while Bernstein had just announced his engagement.

As if to confirm that his hat was in the Boston ring, Bernstein issued a pathetically late but vigorous denial to the two-month-old story that he had been signed up for the movies. *Variety* reported that he was furious at the advance publicity, which he claimed had never been cleared by him: "He denies that he has any intention of becoming a 'motion picture' star." Helen Coates seems to have thought that the engagement announcement was a similar kind of publicity stunt. In all her voluminous scrapbooks of press cuttings for 1947 there is nothing about Felicia, who reluctantly shelved her quest for a screen career after a few months and returned to New York. The entries reflect only "LB's" life: LB being awarded the Audubon Society's Order of Merit, along with the Secretary of State James F. Byrnes and the author John Hershey; LB's ballet *Facsimile* censored in Boston (a moment of erotic kissing was removed); LB named to conduct in Belgium as part of an American arts and cinema season; LB accompanying Isaac Stern in Prokofiev's First Violin Concerto ("we had to repeat the scherzo as an encore, right away, before we went on," Stern recalls; "it has never happened to me since"); LB inviting four hundred students from seven different high schools to attend a Gershwin orchestral rehearsal at the Brooklyn Academy (a trail-blazing gesture for which he dressed "casually in maroon pullover and slacks"); and most intriguing of all, LB invited to conduct the Vienna Philharmonic in May 1947.

F O R Bernstein all other honors and opportunities that year faded into insignificance by comparison with his forthcoming conducting engagement in Palestine. The Palestine Symphony Orchestra had first approached him in November 1945 but at that time couldn't pay his travel expenses. Although he was willing to waive his fee, he couldn't afford to travel to Palestine until 1947, when he also had conducting engagements already confirmed in Europe. With his father and sister as companions he set sail from New York on April 9, 1947, on the SS *America.* They landed in Cherbourg and took the train to Paris where, Shirley Bernstein remembers, they ate dinner out of cans in their hotel bedroom. Travel to Palestine was possible only via Egypt, but Bernstein's outspoken support of Zionist causes had made him unpopular in Cairo, and the Egyptian embassy in Paris refused to issue the Bernsteins' visas until an American official who was a fan of *On the Town* helped smooth things over.

In Cairo the nine-seater connecting plane to Palestine was allegedly too small to cope with all the Bernstein luggage—even in those days the family did not travel light. "The atmosphere was tense and hostile," Shirley recalled. "We were about to count ourselves lucky to lose our luggage and get *ourselves* out of Egypt when the Customs inspector's position shifted. He finally ruled that the matter could be arranged for a $300 payment for 'overweight baggage,' in addition to the 'gift' of Lenny's fountain pen, which the inspector had been eyeing throughout our negotiations."

They arrived to find Palestine, then a British protectorate, in turmoil. The

Jews, about a third of the population, were pressing for the establishment of the independent Jewish state they had been promised in 1917 by the Balfour Declaration. The pro-British Chaim Weizmann and the Jewish Labor party led by David Ben-Gurion wanted a negotiated settlement, but terrorist activity was on the increase, notably from Menachem Begin's right-wing Irgun group and its equally violent splinter party, the Stern Gang. In such troubled times the newly retitled Palestine Philharmonic Orchestra was a symbol of Jewish identity, and attending its concerts offered a positive way for Jews to express their Jewishness and their links with Europe's cultural mainstream. Toscanini had conducted the opening concerts late in 1936; when Bernstein finally arrived in Palestine it was to conclude the orchestra's tenth-anniversary season.

Writing to Koussevitzky two days after his arrival Bernstein emphasized his feeling of being present at a crucial period for the Jewish people's future. "There is a strength and devotion in these people that is formidable. They will never let the land be taken from them, they will all die first. And the country is beautiful beyond description."

In his excited letter to Helen Coates, which he instructed her to show to Felicia, he wrote, "Palestine opened on us like a fresh sky after the storm. We were met, taken care of, calmed. Daddy is in Paradise—he loves every minute. . . . The situation is tense and unpredictable, the orchestra fine and screaming with enthusiasm (first rehearsal this morning). I gave one downbeat today to the accompaniment of a shattering explosion outside the hall. We calmly resumed our work. That's the method here. An Englishman was kidnapped at our hotel last night, the police station was blown up today, a truck demolished in the square—and life goes on; we dance, play boogie-woogie, walk by the Mediterranean (which is out of a fairy book) and we hope for the best."

In a letter about himself to Leonard Lyons, he added a graphic final paragraph: "The café sitters don't put down their newspapers, the children continue to jump rope. The Arab goatherd in the square adjusts another milking bag, and I give the next downbeat. The orchestra's fine. Shalom."

The program he planned was a classic Bernstein triple bill: his *Jeremiah* Symphony, the Ravel piano concerto and Schumann's Second Symphony, music he knew backward and was expert at inspiring players to perform. On May 1, when he introduced the *Jeremiah* Symphony to the Jerusalem public at the crowded Edison Cinema, which did double duty as a concert hall, the impact was apparently overwhelming. Here he was in a country where the Hebrew of Jeremiah's lament was the living language and where Jerusalem was a real city as well as the symbol of Zionist yearning. ("Next year in Jerusalem" is the last line of the annual Passover service.) Not since Toscanini's opening concerts in 1936, reported the *New York Times,* "has a conductor been recalled so many times and given a similar ovation."

Bernstein felt a tremendous empathy with his audience. "They rise with the crescendi and sink down with the decrescendi," was how he described it to the *Palestine Post;* "They are like a barometer—there is nothing more subtle." *Time* magazine noted that the nightly ovation was caused in part by Jewish pride in the presence of a young Jewish maestro. "I was in tears," Bernstein said. "I have never seen anything like it—that hysterical, screaming audience." Apart from his youthful good looks there was an even more obvious reason for his success: he was simply the best conductor since Toscanini to have worked with the orchestra. In 1947 he was at a youthful peak in his career. There was also a bobby-soxer faction; "Palestine has its share," reported Dorothy Kilgallen; "the impressionable young girls of this land have been waiting for him at the stage door." Shirley Bernstein remembers that after one of the concerts the audience flatly refused to go home. The maestro came out in his dressing gown to take a final bow, then got dressed—not a speedy business, even then—and still they were clapping when he was finally driven away.

Tel Aviv, Haifa and Jerusalem were visited in turn, sometimes at considerable risk from Arab or Irgun terrorists. From the holy city of Jerusalem, Sam, Shirley and Leonard made the steep descent to the weirdly buoyant waters of the Dead Sea. They all came back, Shirley remembers, feeling desperately queasy. When they visited the Sea of Galilee with the German-born composer and journalist Peter Gradenwitz and his wife, Rosie, Bernstein taught them the conga on the beach at Tiberias. Bernstein referred to this concert tour several times in his letters as his "tropical vacation," and his list of expenses included the purchase of quantities of swimming trunks, sun lotion and camera equipment, as well as two handsome white suits.

The last concert of Bernstein's idyllic two weeks was given at Ein Harod, a large kibbutz in the Yesrael Valley. The orchestra played under a ceiling of stars and against the backdrop of historic Mount Gilboa. The biggest audience of his tour, approximately 3,500, jammed the spacious amphitheater. "They had come by truck or wagon and on foot, they lay atop cars, stood in the aisles and spilled over onto the platform. Because of government road restrictions, many of them would have to spend the rest of the night until dawn lying in trucks or in the open fields," reported Arthur Holzman in the *Boston Morning Globe*. "It was as if Heaven had sent them this genius to help them forget their troubles."

While he was still waiting to hear whether he would succeed Koussevitzky in Boston, a new mission presented itself to Bernstein in Palestine: to be the savior, if not of the Jewish people, then at least of what he later would call "the Jewish orchestra." The orchestra did not have a permanent conductor; it depended on a handful of locally based conductors and the goodwill visits of international figures. Isaac Stern described it as "a mixed bag," made up of average quality musicians from various East European countries. "The very worst didn't make the orchestra and the very highest quality did not go to Palestine, they went to Western Europe or the United States—particularly the United States." But the players took to Bernstein enthusiastically. His first advantage was that he spoke Hebrew, which in those days facilitated rehearsal. Secondly, he was already a brilliant orchestral trainer. Since his debut in Carnegie Hall less than four years previously he had conducted twenty different orchestras in America and Europe. Working with a new orchestra was for Bernstein a kind of seduction process. He loved the act of making music together and he loved making audiences a third partner in this act of love. In Palestine, however, he met his match: audiences and orchestra seduced him. He had been in Palestine for only a week when the orchestra invited him to come back the following year for the months of February and March. On the eve of his departure from Palestine in May 1947 to give concerts in Europe he wrote a memorandum to the chairman of the orchestra:

"The orchestra of Eretz-Israel has . . . the possibility of attaining to the first ranks of the orchestras of the world. Its potential is enormous, largely because of the innate musicality and intelligence of its personnel. . . . But the realization of the goal is highly dependent on certain material prerequisites. No orchestra can fully succeed which must play in one week twice as many concerts as rehearsals. The proportion must be quite reversed."

He called for a new concert hall, a permanent conductor, a larger string section, a well-stocked music library and a pension fund. At the time he clearly hoped to be the one entrusted with the task of building the orchestra. Aaron Copland was not on hand to ask whether he had thought this proposal through. Could Bernstein have regular jobs on two continents? How would a long-term Palestine link fit in with his plan to become the first great American conductor, the eloquent spokesman for America's new school of composers? Jewish audiences in Palestine were, by contrast with Americans, enthusiastic but conservative and unsophisticated. Was it really his destiny to perform the standard classics over and over again in jam-packed, sweaty cinemas for virtually no fee?

The Palestine Orchestra certainly hoped so. After their next board meeting, on June 6, they sent him an important message: "Would you accept permanent or long-term musical directorship our orchestra minimum stay Palestine three months yearly? Functions include general artistic line, building programmes, nominating orchestra leaders, soloists, guest conductors." The invitation got lost as Bernstein traveled around Europe: duplicates had to be sent, and it was not until July 8 that he replied. Citing previous commitments he sorrowfully refused the musical directorship, at least for the time being, but he had another proposal: "My deep attachment to Eretz-Israel and to the orchestra inspire me to keep as close a connection as is possible under the circumstances; and I would, therefore, accept with pleasure the title and the role of 'musical advisor.' This would enable me to make suggestions by mail, and other means of 'remote control.' I would be glad to contribute my criticism to your seasonal planning, with a view to the possibility of a more integrated and longer association in succeeding years."

A combination of factors pulled Bernstein away from Palestine. In Boston, Koussevitzky was now proposing that the next Boston Symphony season be conducted by a triumvirate consisting of himself, Bernstein and another Tanglewood protégé, the Brazilian-born Eleazar de Carvalho. Bernstein's American management was not in favor of a permanent link with Palestine. Bruno

Zirato put it succinctly in a letter to Helen Coates: "I don't think it would be possible for him to assume the Musical Directorship if he cannot be there all the time." And Bernstein's unabashed delight to be working again in Europe was a further cause for caution. "I'm awfully happy," he wrote Helen Coates from Prague, "my big regret being that I cannot stay longer." He had engagements still to come in Belgium and Holland but had already pulled out of his planned visit to Austria to conduct the Vienna Philharmonic. "They wanted Bach, Mozart and Schumann, which is silly," he told Helen Coates. "And then my reports were that the orchestra was still 60% Nazi and the whole town follows suit—which you can imagine sounded uninviting in Palestine where I was so much 'chez moi.' "

A T the end of May, in Prague, Bernstein led the Czech Philharmonic in the first European performance of Aaron Copland's Third Symphony, just seven months after Koussevitzky had conducted its premiere in Boston and declared it to be the greatest American symphony. The confident, almost arrogant tone of Bernstein's letter to Copland reporting on the Prague premiere is a measure of how much their relationship had changed in the decade they had known each other: "First, I must say it's a wonderful work. Coming to know it so much better [he had attended only a rehearsal in Boston the previous October] I found in it new lights and shades—and new faults. Sweetie, the end is a sin. You've got to change. Stop the presses! We must talk—about the whole last movement, in fact. The reactions were mixed. Too long, said some. 'Too eclectic,' said Shostakovich (he should talk!) 'Not up my street,' said Wee Willie Walton. It lacks a real Adagio, said Kubelik. And everyone found Chaikovsky's Fifth in it, which only proves their inanity. I haven't seen the press yet, but I think it will be good. It just wasn't a wow, that's all; it was solid, it was serious."

Copland had taken two years to write this symphony: Bernstein was giving his first reactions to his closest musical friend and adviser. On the page his cockiness suggests that the adulation in Palestine and Prague had gone to his head. But his devotion to the symphony knew no bounds, and Copland testified in his autobiography to his friend's intuitive understanding of his music. Bernstein conducted the Third Symphony again in Israel in 1948. "After the fourth performance it has begun to sound, and quite magnificent at that," he wrote Copland. "I must confess I have made a sizable cut near the end and believe me it makes a whale of a difference." Copland thought it "pretty nervy" of Bernstein to make unauthorized cuts but conceded that taking out eight bars did improve the finale.

F R O M The Hague, Bernstein brought Helen Coates up to date on his European progress: "PARIS BRUSSELS WONDERFUL SUCCESSES HOLLAND COLD AND LOVELY REPLACING MILSTEIN TONIGHT WITH

RAVEL FEELING TOPS LOVE LENNY." Bernstein had conducted his *Jeremiah* Symphony with the French Radio Orchestra at the beginning of June, with Jennie Tourel as soloist: he loved Paris but it was close to humiliation—for which he never quite forgave his European manager—to be making his Paris debut in a radio studio. Paris was followed by concerts of American music with the Belgian Radio Orchestra in Brussels, and two popular concerts at The Hague—three different European orchestras in less than a fortnight. Then Bernstein and his sister flew home. Miss Coates was in the welcoming party at La Guardia Airport. "Felicia arrived a little later," she noted in the date book. At least Felicia was still considered part of the family.

After four concerts in five days with the New York Philharmonic at Lewisohn Stadium, Bernstein went to Tanglewood for its opening on Sunday, June 29. His tempo there was less hectic than the previous year. He lectured and coached students, and to celebrate Koussevitzky's seventy-third birthday he composed "Fanfare for Bima," for eleven brass instruments and one violin, its theme based on the whistle Koussevitzky used to summon his dog. He recorded two Stravinsky chamber pieces for RCA, the *Octet* and *L'Histoire du Soldat,* using players from the BSO. And he conducted the full Boston Symphony in two festival concerts. Never before had Koussevitzky allowed another conductor to take over from him in the Shed: it was a gesture as significant as the two Carnegie Hall opportunities he had provided Bernstein earlier in the year.

Felicia came up to Tanglewood for two long spells that summer. A home movie shot by Burton shows Bernstein and his family arriving for a Tanglewood concert, Leonard dapper in a bow tie and blazer. Felicia is slightly to one side. She looks beautiful in a white dress, but also rather frail and vulnerable; hovering outside the artists' entrance, she seems a little anxious about where to go next. It makes a poignant image. Life was not easy for her despite her official status as Leonard's fiancée. There was rivalry with Shirley, ostensibly about such mundane matters as who should sit next to Leonard at meals. Helen Coates was also fighting to maintain her old position. Felicia said later that her self-confidence was undermined as Leonard constantly found fault with her. In mid-August he and Felicia left for New York to see Gian Carlo Menotti's new opera, *The Medium.* A few days later he visited his family in Sharon alone, spending Sabbath eve with them and celebrating his twenty-ninth birthday. Then he returned to his cottage in the Berkshires.

In a letter he wrote to David Diamond on August 23, Bernstein revealed a sudden crisis of self-confidence at both personal and professional levels: "I've made a few decisions. I'm canceling my whole European trip, with the possible exception of Palestine, to which I feel such an obligation. This means composing, analysis, solitude, maybe getting to know myself again (or for the first time) . . . I know you'll approve. I feel better for it already. I had a home-going . . . this week which turned to be a splendid and relaxing visit! What a wonderful family I have! Once I can break those old chains I can feel very warm about them." Perhaps the pace of his life as an itinerant conductor was getting him down. To judge from the frequent medical appointments he made that summer, he was not feeling well. He had been on a three-month emotional roller coaster, wallowing in the adulation of his audiences. But he had not been writing any music and his conducting career was without a center. He had turned down the music directorship of the Palestine Orchestra, yet there was no certainty that he would inherit the Boston Symphony. Meanwhile, despite heroic efforts led by Helen Coates to sell subscription tickets, the New York City Symphony Orchestra was beset with financial problems.

The indecision seems to have spilled over into his relationship with Felicia, although this was not mentioned in his letter to Diamond. Burton Bernstein believes that neither Felicia nor Leonard was ready at that point for the sacrifices involved in marriage. Felicia wanted an acting career. Being Bernstein's wife would be something else. She had seen her fiancé "Lennuhtt" in close-up, surrounded by his clan in the campy world of Tanglewood and she had probably been disturbed by the flattery as well as stimulated by the fun. For his part, Bernstein seemed unwilling to commit himself: despite his affection for Felicia he was still looking over her shoulder—perhaps for a more intellectual partner, perhaps for the alternative homosexual life practiced discreetly by Aaron Copland or flamboyantly by David Diamond. Arguably the strength of his feeling for the pianist John Mehegan, with whom he spent happy Tanglewood days that summer playing jazz, warned him against marriage. The pressure on Felicia was intense. She found it increasingly difficult to bear. "I can take it alright," she wrote, "but for *what?*"

Early in the evening of September 10 the couple met at the bar of the St. Moritz Hotel in New York. They were going on to a farewell dinner later that night in honor of Judy Holliday. Next morning Dorothy Kilgallen's gossip column in the *Journal-American* carried a bleak, one-sentence story: "Composer conductor Leonard Bernstein's matrimonial plans have been canceled."

# THE MAN FROM ANOTHER WORLD

*Budapest, 1948.*
COURTESY OF THE ESTATE OF LEONARD BERNSTEIN

*He has reviewed the 20th Century for us and brought
up a nugget practically every time.*

—VIRGIL THOMSON on Bernstein's
tenure at the New York City
Symphony Orchestra

A T the opening concert of his third City Center season, on September 22, 1947, Bernstein conducted the first of two performances of Gustav Mahler's Second Symphony, the *Resurrection*. It was his first Mahler interpretation; he dedicated the performances to what he called the resurrection of Palestine. Both were sold out. Nonetheless, journalists sniped at the music's alleged lack of popular appeal. The depth of the prejudice against Mahler which Bernstein fought—joining a crusade on behalf of Mahler that he was later to lead in triumph—can be measured by the critic Irving Kolodin's sneering reaction to Mahler's rarely performed score: "The most bumptious, empty noise ever contrived." Bernstein had learned the symphony when Rodzinski performed it in December 1943. The symphony's emotional intensity made it an ideal work for Bernstein's expressive instincts; he turned it into a concerto for conductor and orchestra, squeezing out of it every moment of electricity and drama, from the primeval stirrings of the first movement to the vision of Judgment Day with which the work rises to its epic climax.

In October, Bernstein presented an evening dedicated to Mozart, another composer who aroused strong sympathies in him. Conducting from the keyboard, Bernstein offered a deft performance of Mozart's sprightly Piano Concerto in B flat, K. 450, "music to make a man sweat," to use Mozart's own unforgettable phrase. He also conducted the early G minor Symphony, K. 183, and accompanied Jennie Tourel in three rare operatic arias. Later in the season he conducted an all-Stravinsky evening and a triumphant staged performance of *The Cradle Will Rock*—the world premiere of the orchestrated version—sponsored by the League of Composers in honor of its twenty-fifth birthday. Bernstein took two small acting parts and was even praised for his histrionic performance, a moment which fortunately was without sequel.

With *Cradle,* Bernstein's third short season came to an end. *The New Yorker* called it "an altogether stimulating fall series," and the *Times,* summing up the year, gave equally good marks. The season was, said Olin Downes, "more varied and progressive than the New York Philharmonic," offering "performances of exceptional vitality." They included excerpts from *Wozzeck* and Ralph Vaughan Williams's Fourth Symphony. Virgil Thomson later noted Bernstein's success in attracting to his concerts a young and twentieth-century-minded public, which he identified as the "Bernstein Audience."

But there had been worrying signs during the fall that orchestra standards were slipping. The critic Robert Bagar commented on "lack of precision, poor intonation and uneven balance," and Olin Downes said bluntly that technically the orchestra was not as good as the previous year. The toughest criticism, because it was so personal, came from Virgil Thomson, who wrote that Bernstein lacked sympathy for West European culture and had "embraced a career of sheer vainglory . . . he worries us all a little bit." Thomson never concealed his dislike of the physical way in which Bernstein conducted; he castigated the "chorybantic choreography" and "the miming of facial expressions of uncontrollable states."

Two days before Thomson's potentially damaging review came out, Bernstein had lunched with Newbold Morris, chairman of the City Center. He asked for more cash for his orchestra—better salaries for the musicians, more rehearsals, a longer concert season, some kind of remuneration for himself. But Morris was unable to promise anything. Mayor O'Dwyer, the more conservative successor to Mayor La Guardia, was not prepared to increase municipal spending.

All through the fall the question of who would take over Koussevitzky's post in Boston also remained unresolved: it was a job Bernstein said he did not want but would surely have accepted had it been offered. The absence from his life of a permanent orchestra with which to build a long-term relationship was matched by an inability to settle on a personal companion. He still saw Felicia occasionally in the fall of 1947, and never confirmed the gossip columnist's story that their engagement was off, but he had also started taking out a new girl-friend, Ellen Adler, the vivacious and beautiful teenage daughter of the actress Stella Adler. Ellen's stepfather, Harold Clurman, the dean of American theater, had quipped of Bernstein that he was a young man "doomed to success." Ellen was a princess in New York's Bohemia and on the face of it would have made a good match with Bernstein. His parents probably thought as much when they all went to see *Me and Molly* at the Belasco Theater. He talked to her incessantly about marriage, but although she had always found him immensely attractive she also thought he was exhausting, even for a single evening. In the spring of 1948 she moved to Paris, where she later lived with René Leibowitz, France's leading proponent of the music of Schoenberg and the twelve-tone school of composers.

Since his trip to Palestine Bernstein had become more active in his support for political causes. In November 1947 he joined the Progressive Citizens for America and went on nationwide radio to speak up for the First Amendment and against the House Un-American Activities Committee, along with George Kaufman and Moss Hart in New York, and Lauren Bacall, Humphrey Bogart and Danny Kaye in Hollywood. In the same month he published a trailblazing article in the *New York Times* blaming the educational system for the disturbing lack of trained black musicians in New York orchestras and pit bands. Shortly afterward he joined Albert Einstein and Linus Pauling in an appeal to cancel the deportation order placed on the German composer Hanns Eisler, and was one of the sponsors of a New York Town Hall concert of Eisler's music. (Eisler, who was a Communist, was deported nonetheless.)

DESPITE his critical success with the New York City Symphony Bernstein felt himself to be at a career crossroads. One of his dreams, he told the writer Henry Simon, was to settle in Palestine, where the UN was on the point of passing a resolution calling for the establishment of a separate Jewish state, and there become the country's leading musician, the "premier musician d'état," as he put it. Another was to abandon conducting in favor of composition: it was impossible, he asserted, to combine the two careers in the United States.

But in the winter of 1947–48, there was too much "fun" involved in the conducting projects for which he was already committed for him to take such a decisive step. (There was, as well, his commitment to Koussevitzky.) *The Cradle Will Rock* had been so successful at the City Center that the show, starring Alfred Drake, was swiftly transferred to Broadway for a five-week run. Bernstein agreed to conduct the first three performances for a handsome fee of five hundred dollars per night. On December 26 a snowstorm almost forced the cancellation of the premiere when twenty-six inches fell on the city. But just as the government had failed to close the premiere of *Cradle* ten years earlier, Mother Nature failed to defeat the company's efforts this time. The cast picked its way through the snowdrifts, the first-nighters took to the subways, the show went on, and at the end Bernstein led the cast in a round of applause for the plucky audience. In his dressing room, he had received a telegram from Blitzstein: "IN SPITE OF GLITZSTEINS [*sic*] BLIZZARD MY UNDYING THANKS HIT IT BOY LOVE MARC."

Though many critics praised the show, it did not draw a big enough audience for it to make money on Broadway, even when a second producer took over and tried charging less than five dollars for orchestra tickets. Harold Clurman called the production "labor's only victory in many months," but he also dismissed its dated political message, noting it had been "just as boyishly sentimental and comically theatrical in 1937." In public Bernstein remained loyal to his friend: in early January he told a reporter that Broadway was pioneering, for once in its history, and that *The Cradle Will Rock* was "a forerunner of American opera." But watching the fate of his friend's agit-prop music drama, he must have felt in his bones that he could do better. A week later he set his position down on paper: "Most of my scores have been in one way or another for theatrical performance, and the others—most of them— have an obvious dramatic basis. I rather glow at this discovery. . . . Where it will lead I cannot tell; but if I can write one, real moving American opera that any American can understand (and one that is, notwithstanding, a serious musical work), I shall be a happy man." The challenge he set himself remained dear to his heart for the rest of his life.

In December Felicia finally conceded defeat and wrote a disconsolate letter to Leonard calling off their marriage plans. "Being engaged this long should have brought us closer together but somehow it has defeated its purpose. Per- haps if we were both certain we would get married eventually there would be less tension and resentment. But you're still not sure I'm the right one for you. It's not so much that you're afraid to hurt me as that you may be 'stuck with the salad.' So here's one less decision for you to make—let's call it off. If some miracle happens and some day you want me very much, ask me again." It was, she confessed, a horribly difficult letter for her to write: she was still very much in love with him. "Your life has become mine and I feel so involved in it and you, that cutting myself off seems preposterous, but I know that I can't go on this way. . . . What affection you had for me you have somehow stifled. You really don't give yourself a chance. By being unbearably critical you've made me self-conscious. . . . In any case, and whatever you decide to do, don't, for our sake, talk it over with anybody. I'm so tired of having everybody 'au courant.' "

Nothing has survived to indicate Bernstein's reaction at the time but he did not forget Felicia's letter. Meanwhile he commenced a new conducting odyssey in the United States. After concerts in Minneapolis and Houston he went to Boston, where he created a sensation conducting Mahler's *Resurrection* almost every night of his third week. None of the critics mentioned the possibility of Bernstein succeeding Koussevitzky, however, although the issue was now close to settlement.

Bernstein had originally intended to travel to Palestine after his Boston concerts. But on December 29, 1947, he wrote a long letter to the orchestra's secretary, Menahem Mahler-Kalkstein, which began with a bombshell: "I am being pressed on all sides not to go to Palestine in February. It seems clear to many people that I, as an American, and as a Jew, representing America in the

East, would be target number one for Arab hostility. Of course I don't object to violence *per se,* having seen a little of it on my last trip . . . but those were at least Jewish bombs. There is another school of thought which thinks it may all blow over by February. In any case, I have not yet been persuaded or dissuaded."

He had reviewed the situation in January and cabled the orchestra, pleading health reasons for his withdrawals: "PLEASE UNDERSTAND FINAL DECISION TO CANCEL PALESTINE VISIT THIS SEASON. DOCTORS ORDERS TO REMAIN IN AMERICA FOR PERIOD OF REST PLUS UNCERTAINTY OF YOUR SITUATION. AM HEARTBROKEN WITH REGRET BUT FEEL IT ONLY FAIR TO LET YOU KNOW AT ONCE SO THAT YOU CAN MAKE OTHER ARRANGEMENTS. PLEASE FORGIVE AND UNDERSTAND. LETTER FOLLOWS. HEARTFELT GREETINGS."

The reply from Tel Aviv was fierce: "YOUR ATTITUDE INCOMPREHENSIBLE AND UNACCEPTABLE ALL GUEST CONDUCTORS AND SOLOISTS FULFILLED CONTRACT STOP VIOLINIST IDA HAENDEL ARRIVED YESTERDAY MOST CONCERTS TAKING PLACE ACCORDING SCHEDULE STOP AMERICAN VISITORS ARRIVING DAILY STOP PALESTINIAN AND WORLD JEWISH OPINION WOULD UTTERLY DISAPPROVE YOUR DECISION STOP IF YOU FAIL US NON-JEWISH GUEST CONDUCTORS WILL FOLLOW SUIT WHICH IN TURN WILL MEAN FINANCIAL CATASTROPHE FOR OUR INSTITUTION STOP PLEASE RECONSIDER AND CABLE REGARDS. PALPHILORC."

Bernstein was not to be shaken, even by these dire threats of financial catastrophe. "YOU MUST BELIEVE ME," he cabled next day. "DOCTORS ORDERS RESPONSIBLE FOR MY DECISION. OTHERWISE I SHOULD GLADLY COME. IMPOSSIBLE TO REVOKE DECISION. PLEASE HAVE FAITH IN ME. TRYING HARD TO GET STEINBERG AS REPLACEMENT. SECOND PERSONAL EXPLANATORY LETTER FOLLOWS. BLESSINGS. BERNSTEIN."

"STEINBERG UNAVAILABLE," came the reply. "PLEASE FOR SAKE ALL OF US REVISE YOUR DECISION. . . . ASSURE YOU IF NOT SAFE WILL PLAY TEL AVIV ONLY." Bernstein was lobbied by his father to reconsider. A conductor, Sam Bernstein wrote, was like a clergyman giving comfort to the soldiers on the battlefield. Sam's intervention was to no avail. His son had already canceled. The private note he sent to Tel Aviv, revealing his need for urgent medical treatment, silenced objections.

The nature of Bernstein's health problem remains a mystery—it was possibly the first attack of emphysema. A newspaper cutting from November 1947 reads "LEONARD BERNSTEIN TO UNDERGO SURGERY." In her scrap-book Helen Coates wrote "Not true!!" in the margin. By canceling the Palestine engagement Bernstein had at least created a breathing space for himself; for the next two months he took things easy. One newspaper said he was thinking out his American opera; another had it that he was composing a new symphony.

In the middle of his rest period, his standing as a composer was attacked from an unexpected quarter. Writing in the *New York Times* in March 1948, Aaron Copland included Bernstein among the new school of American composers. "At its best Bernstein's is music of vibrant rhythmic invention and irresistible *élan,* often carrying with it a terrific dramatic punch," wrote Copland. He added that the music had "an immediate emotional appeal, a spontaneity and warmth which speak directly to the audience." But his opening statement must have stabbed Bernstein to the heart. "At its worst, Bernstein's music is conductor's music—eclectic in style and facile in inspiration." However unjust the criticism (Copland did not indicate to which of Bernstein's compositions he was referring) here was another reason to concentrate on composition.

Despite his claim to David Diamond the previous August that he was canceling everything, plans were still in place for him to return to London and conduct in Copenhagen and Amsterdam in the spring. But as part of a more radical attempt to create some composing time Bernstein pulled out of those engagements. He also made a longer-term decision: he gave up the New York City Symphony. He had learned that neither the musicians' union nor the City Council could give the orchestra any financial support. Had he stayed on, he would have been forced to retrench. He sent his resignation letter to the music editors of all the New York papers. "I am proud and happy that there has been a steadily mounting attendance during the last three seasons. . . . The enthusiasm of public, press and the musical world has been gratifying. But financially the going has been rough." The reaction of Newbold Morris, the chairman of the City Center, was immediate: "I, along with millions of other New Yorkers, regret Mr. Bernstein's resignation and I still hope he will reconsider it." In a private letter he added, "these things cannot be done without some form of subsidy. . . . Your stature has grown tremendously these past three years."

Two days after he resigned, Bernstein met Henry Haftel, one of the Palestine Philharmonic's concertmasters, whose mission in America was to persuade sympathetic artists to give benefit concerts for the orchestra. It is a measure of how much Bernstein meant to the players that Haftel also handed him a renewed invitation to become the orchestra's first artistic director, for the following season. The offer was gratifying but Bernstein did not respond immediately. He was waiting for the Boston succession to be resolved. The next meeting of the Boston Symphony's Trustees was on March 15. Koussevitzky had written on the tenth urging them to consider the appointment of a young American.

IN April Bernstein left Harms and signed a new contract with the music publisher G. Schirmer. Schirmer's announcement listed four Bernstein works. The most substantial was his Second Symphony, called *The Age of Anxiety,* for piano and orchestra, inspired, it was said, by W. H. Auden's poem, and commissioned by Koussevitzky. Another work, *Four Anniversaries,* was a set of short piano pieces dedicated to people who had been close to Bernstein in 1947: Helen Coates, David Diamond, the jazz pianist John Mehegan and Felicia Montealegre. The third was a witty group of songs called *La Bonne Cuisine,* consisting of settings of four nineteenth-century French recipes, dedicated to and inspired by Jennie Tourel. The last, a set of pieces for brass instruments commissioned by William Schuman for the Juilliard School, were all dedicated to dogs: "Fanfare for Bima," Koussevitzky's cocker spaniel (rescored for trumpet, horn, trombone, and tuba); three "Mippy" pieces, named for three dogs owned in succession by Burton Bernstein (to whom the suite is dedicated); and "Rondo for Lifey," named for Judy Holliday's Skye terrier. On paper Schirmer's list looked impressive: it must have gone some way to assuage the guilt Bernstein felt about neglecting his muse.

A T the end of Serge Koussevitzky's final concert of the Boston Symphony season, on April 13, 1948, it was announced that he would retire the following year, which would be his twenty-fifth season, and that his successor would be Charles Munch from Paris. "This announcement took the Hub by surprise," *Variety* reported, adding that Munch was a man of private means. "Two names most prominently mentioned . . . have been Leonard Bernstein and Dimitri Mitropoulos."

To be passed over for an important position, even if one is unsure whether one wants the job, is a chastening experience. Bernstein had waited too long in the wings for Boston's decision not to hurt. But at least he could give the Palestine Orchestra a positive answer now, even as he tried to console his disappointed mentor. A few days before he was to leave for Europe he wrote a long letter to Koussevitzky. "I want to tell you how deeply grateful I am for all the fighting you have done on my behalf these last years. . . . I realized how upset you were at the appointment of your successor, and I have the greatest sympathy with your feelings. But I know that somewhere there is the inscrutable law that makes everything balance in the end."

Then he went on to announce his own news—his decision to accept the artistic directorship of the Palestine Orchestra. "I could no longer resist their plea. They need me so badly, and I can really help. The first thing I want to accomplish is to have the joy of seeing you there, inspiring and leading this orchestra. They love you so; and I have a profound conviction that you would have a deep joy and sense of rightness in this experience. Won't you please try to come this winter? I shall be there only two months—October and November; but I will direct the policy and program of the entire year. I keenly feel the justice of this decision, and I pray that you do also." Koussevitzky duly made his debut in Tel Aviv the following season.

Before he left New York Bernstein held a press conference on board the

*Queen Mary*—he was already doing such things in style. "It will be an honor and a privilege to have this opportunity to serve the Jews of Palestine," he told the journalists, noting with pride that the Palestine Orchestra was obliged to travel in armored buses over dangerous roads to fulfill its engagements.

Early in the morning of April 22, the RMS *Queen Mary* weighed anchor and was towed out of her moorings at Pier 90. Bernstein's duties in Palestine were five months away. Meanwhile he was heading for his third European spring, conducting in cities new to him on both sides of the Iron Curtain—Budapest, Milan, Vienna and, most important, Munich, the cradle of Nazism.

I N the wake of the Holocaust many outstanding Jewish artists such as Arthur Rubinstein and Isaac Stern refused to give concerts in Germany. Yehudi Menuhin, a natural bridge-builder among peoples, adopted a different stance. In 1945 he and Benjamin Britten gave recitals for Jewish audiences in the concentration camps of Belsen and Buchenwald, and in 1946 Menuhin played concertos in Germany conducted by Wilhelm Furtwängler, who had been head of the Berlin Philharmonic during the Nazi era. Menuhin felt that as a musician he was offering Germany "something to live for," while as a Jew he was "keeping alive German guilt and repentance." In 1947 Bernstein had had last-minute qualms about making music with the Vienna Philharmonic when he heard that its membership was still 60 percent Nazi—a highly improbable statistic—but by 1948 he had changed his position and accepted invitations to conduct in both Austria and Germany. He relished the process of winning over the players of the Bavarian State Orchestra. "I had expected great hostility from the orchestra," he wrote to Koussevitzky, "since I was so young, American (which here means no culture) and Jewish. But they seem to love me and play with great *lust* [joy]."

The invitation to conduct the orchestra, which also played for the Munich Opera, had come from Georg Solti, its dynamic music director. Bernstein's friend Carlos Moseley, now the U.S. Music Officer in Bavaria, organized Bernstein's accommodation and alerted the local Displaced Persons camp (which was supervised by the American military) that the newly appointed artistic director of the Palestine Philharmonic was coming to town. Bernstein listed his horrified reactions to Helen Coates:

> First, it's all ruins. Second, the people starve, struggle, rob, beg for bread. Wages are often paid in cigarettes. Tipping is all in cigarettes. It's all misery. Third, the Jews are rotting in the [refugee] camps. Fourth, Nazism is in every corner.
>
> As I stepped off the train in that shell-shocked Bahnhof, I was greeted by Moseley . . . who told me that the orchestra was on strike because some of them fainted of hunger at rehearsal. It's fixed now, through Military Government prestidigitation, and there will be a concert on the

9th. (Not the 10th, though.) No rehearsal yet. I've made many friends, heard Bruckner's 8th tonight, had two very full days. But what a mess!

In the midst of this misery, I live in luxury [in] the Geislgasteig which is the Hollywood of Bavaria. I live in a villa . . . surrounded by stars, pines, a pool, wonderful food, a private Army car. I am rated a V.I.P. This is all illegal, since I'm not Army-sponsored, but the Military Government here thinks it important enough for America's reputation, so they wrangled me in. . . . I shall give a special concert for Jewish D.P.'s in one of the large camps, or in the opera house in Munich. There has been much trouble and fuss over this, but I insisted. I may have to hire the orchestra myself, but it's worth it.

To avert the threatened orchestra strike, Carlos Moseley amassed a hoard of cigarette packs from his American friends and had them distributed to the players at Bernstein's first rehearsal. His program consisted of Roy Harris's Third Symphony, Ravel's piano concerto and Schumann's Second Symphony. "One violinist told me at this morning's rehearsal [he was writing to Helen Coates] that there were *maybe* two conductors in all Germany who could do Schumann as well as I, and they were both over eighty! My greatest compliment yet, and from a German!"

The *New York Times* reported the May 9 concert, which was given to a mixed German and American audience, as a triumph. "At the close of the performance of the Ravel piano concerto, the audience stood on its feet and applauded him for more than ten minutes in repeated curtain calls, amid a storm of 'bravos.' " Carlos Moseley remembers "a great crowd waiting for Lenny to come out and they carried him on their shoulders through the street." He was the first American to conduct in Munich after the war and German critics hailed his "astounding, demonic gifts." He was, wrote one, a Paganini of the symphony orchestra.

Bernstein sent his own account to Helen Coates: "The Munich concert was the greatest success to date. . . . There's nothing more satisfying than an opera-house full of Germans screaming with excitement. . . . It means so much for the American Military, since music is the German's last stand in their 'master-race' claim, and for the first time it's been exploded in Munich. [Bernstein was probably exaggerating the anti-Semitic prejudice against him in Munich. The career of Georg Solti, another Jew, was flourishing in Bavaria.] Almost more exciting were the two concerts in D.P. camps. I was received by parades of kids with flowers, and the greatest honors. I conducted a 20-piece concentration-camp orchestra (*Freischütz,* of all things!) and cried my heart out."

The Jewish Representative Orchestra was made up of musicians who were the survivors of a concentration-camp orchestra that had performed at Dachau, a few miles north of Munich. The camp had been liberated in May 1945, but three years later two nearby refugee camps at Feldafing and Landsberg still housed a tragically large number of homeless Jews. Many hoped to go to Palestine, where strict entry quotas were being enforced by the British. Bernstein was told that five thousand refugees attended each of his performances; the front three rows at both concerts were occupied by what Bernstein called "the Nazi Orchestra," the Staatstheater Orchester. Bernstein accompanied Jewish soloists and played *Rhapsody in Blue*.

Afterward, as a token of gratitude, Bernstein was given a striped camp uniform belonging to the wartime founder of the Dachau orchestra, a flute player killed by the Nazis. He sent it home to New York but no amount of dry cleaning could get rid of the stench of Dachau, and much to his chagrin the garment eventually had to be thrown away.

The concerts coincided with momentous political events in Palestine: on May 14 the state of Israel was formally proclaimed. Many musicians in the Dachau orchestra begged Bernstein to take them with him to the promised land. He eventually obtained jobs for two of the players. But after Munich he did not conduct a German orchestra again for close to thirty years.

BERNSTEIN made his Italian debut in Milan with the Teatro Nuovo chamber orchestra. His program included *Appalachian Spring* and Bach's Fifth Brandenburg Concerto, in which he played the solo keyboard part with Claudio Abbado's father as the violinist. He wrote to Helen Coates following his visit to Leonardo da Vinci's *Last Supper*. "They call me 'the other Leonardo' which almost made me cry. . . . I'm invited to La Scala for next spring [the orchestra, not the opera] plus at least *two* weeks with the Teatro Nuovo, and they say I can do both. . . . I'm in love with all the kids in the orchestra—and they're so devoted to me. They want me as permanent conductor. . . . Also, I'm invited to the great Venice Festival in September."

In Budapest his program with the Metropolitan Orchestra included Schumann's Second Symphony and Bartók's *Music for Strings, Percussion and Celesta*. The concert was broadcast and many people who had listened to the first part on the radio rushed to the hall to hear part two in the flesh. It inspired reviews of a different order from those written in other cities, as if the very swiftness of his coming and going created its own legend. "We have witnessed one of the miracles of our own century." "This young genius brings to the surface the tremendous power and elementary energy of the jungle. . . . His virtuosity is not an end in itself. He inspires the orchestra to a performance without precedent." Again he was carried shoulder-high through the streets. "They say there hasn't been such a scene in a Budapest concert hall since Toscanini was here," he wrote to Helen Coates.

At the Sudbahnhof in Vienna Bernstein marched down the platform to greet the U.S. embassy officials singing chunks of his beloved *Der Rosenkavalier* at the top of his lungs. He found himself in the middle of a typical Viennese intrigue. Although politically the city was divided into four occupied zones, the musical world recognized only two: the Vienna Philharmonic, based at the Musikverein and the State Opera; and the rival faction, which had hired Bernstein, the more progressive Vienna Symphony, based at the Konzerthaus, where the manager was the young impresario Egon Seefehlner. He wanted a program change to make room for the Bartók work with which Bernstein had just had such a success in Budapest. It transpired that Herbert von Karajan had just performed it with the Vienna Philharmonic and it had caused something of a scandal, with fights erupting in the audience and many people walking out. (Bartók's music had been banned during the Nazi period.)

Seefehlner made no bones about wanting to score a point against his rival Rudolf Gamsjäger, the impresario of the Karajan camp. To his credit, Bernstein would have nothing to do with this conductor's war, or *Dirigentenkrieg,* as he dubbed it. He had hardly heard of Von Karajan at this point—"Karryan" was his eccentric spelling when he subsequently made notes for a Tanglewood lecture—and his only concern was to score a success with the Viennese public. "It was the toughest city of all to conquer, a characteristic provincial, materialistic town, convinced that only Viennese can do anything at all, and that all Americans are fools. . . . It's the first time it ever took me three rehearsals to overcome the natural hostility of an orchestra. . . . The final trouble was that I had to cancel *Jeremiah*—it would have been impossible . . . with such a hostile, exhausted orchestra. It's just as well: the house came down, and as the management said, 'Ganz Wien in ein [einem] Schlag! [All Vienna at a single blow!]' "

Several Viennese music critics disliked Bernstein's conducting style intensely. One compared his concert to a sporting event, and said he conducted like a boxer. The bad notices he shrugged off, but Bernstein never forgot the players' hostility; he did not work again with the Vienna Symphony and it was nearly twenty years before he overcame his prejudice and accepted another Viennese conducting engagement.

He was much happier with the musicians in Paris. "The orchestra here [of French Radio] is angelic," he informed Helen Coates. "They learned Jeremiah in one rehearsal and are so fast and good and in love with me that I actually cancelled today's rehearsal. First time I ever felt I could dispense with a rehearsal in Europe. Jennie [Tourel] is greater than ever. . . . It just angers me that this second year I still don't have a debut in Paris—after all the ego-building of these triumphs, to do just a broadcast here is an anti-climax." That the broadcast was only on a local station turned out to be a blessing in disguise. "I had a bad moment. . . . I came to the Beethoven Concerto and the old thing happened with my fingers—they went dead. I played horribly. I was terribly depressed of course, especially as everyone insisted it was so good. I guess it was sheer fatigue . . . but what a nightmare to have to go through that 35-minute piece on the air with paralyzed hands!"

Bernstein saw Ellen Adler again in Paris. He bought a book of Baudelaire poems and translated them off the page into English as they walked together in the Tuileries. But Adler was disappointed by his lack of intellectual curiosity. While she wanted to talk about existentialism, Leonard preferred to hear Nadia Boulanger and Soulima Stravinsky play through Stravinsky's *Orpheus* or have drinks with Oliver Smith at Maxim's. Adler urged him to explore the new literature of Sartre and Camus but Bernstein was more interested in searching for presents for his friends or consulting his little black book of Paris's gay nightclubs. He always wanted to visit twenty places the same evening and his restlessness spilled over into his thoughts about his future. There was nobody around to counsel him regarding his career. Only a few weeks after his resolution to clear the decks for composition, he was entertaining very different plans for the following year, writing to Helen Coates about engagements in Paris, London, Milan and Holland. "I may live April 1 to Sept. 1 in Europe . . . although I had another idea, to chuck conducting for a year and be a pianist. Both ideas excite me. We'll see."

Leonard Bernstein was the first American-born conductor to enjoy international fame. But the adulation he received in Europe weakened his sense of direction. Virgil Thomson's warning words the previous fall seemed increasingly relevant: "It would be a pity if our brightest young leader should turn out to be just a star conductor."

# HISTORY-MAKING DAYS

*Bernstein with Koussevitzky at Tanglewood,
1949, after performing* The Age of Anxiety.
PHOTO HOWARD S. BABBITT, JR., COURTESY OF THE ESTATE OF
LEONARD BERNSTEIN

*You should hear Beethoven's* Leonora *trumpet solo
with an accompaniment of artillery shots.*

—Bernstein reporting from Jerusalem,
October 1948

WHEN Bernstein returned to New York in July 1948 he had a deadline to meet. His new symphony, *The Age of Anxiety,* had been announced for the Boston Symphony's spring season, and it was far from finished. He had also accepted a thousand-dollar commission to write a jazz work for Woody Herman. And his summer and fall schedule was crowded with conducting engagements. But first he had to cope with a political storm brought about by his own naïveté. In the summer of 1948 Israel was besieged by the surrounding Arab states and torn apart by internal dissension. David Ben-Gurion, Israel's first Prime Minister, was challenged by the right-wing extremists of the Irgun group, led by Menachem Begin. Bernstein had links with both sides, and when he agreed to organize a benefit concert for the Palestine Resistance Defense Fund at the Waldorf-Astoria in New York in July 1948 he apparently didn't understand that Israel was on the brink of civil war. In April Irgun extremists had massacred 254 Arabs. Late in June an Irgun-sponsored ship flouted Israeli government orders and attempted to land weapons destined for Begin's private army. It was shelled by government guns.

Bernstein soon learned that his friend Jennie Tourel, the "Met" baritone Robert Merrill and the film star Henry Fonda had all withdrawn from his concert because the Resistance Defense Fund was linked to the Irgun terrorists —the proceeds of the benefit were to be used to buy fighter planes, despite the truce that had been negotiated. Two thousand guests were booked to attend the concert and Bernstein moved to defuse the criticisms by announcing that the cash raised from the sale of tickets was to be used instead "to repatriate displaced Hebrews to Palestine." He added the funeral march from the *Eroica* Symphony to the program "in memory of 20 Irgun soldiers who had died on the beaches of Tel Aviv." Picketers demonstrated outside the hotel, and during the proceedings a telegram was read from Menachem Begin, thanking Bernstein for his courageous participation. The music was performed by "Leonard Bernstein and his Symphony Orchestra"—a unique billing in Bernstein's career.

It was a relief to get to Tanglewood. As usual, Bernstein spent six weeks teaching score-reading and basic principles to fifty-seven conducting auditors, who in 1948 included the future conducting star Thomas Schippers and the composer Robert Starer. Bernstein also conducted two concerts with the Boston Symphony; an all-Russian program was followed by his new pièce de résistance, Mahler's *Resurrection* Symphony.

To celebrate Koussevitzky's seventy-fourth birthday, the three conducting fellows, Irwin Hoffman, Seymour Lipkin and Howard Shanet, joined Bernstein on the porch of the main house to perform his "Koussevitzky Blues."

> *I've got those Koussevitzky blues, and, baby,*
> *    That ain't good:*
> *'Cause he's the best dressed man in all of*
> *    Tanglewood.*
> *We wear dungarees, we dress like apes,*
> *But come the Revolution, we'll all wear capes.*

Bernstein was already a Tanglewood legend himself, famous not only for his conducting but for his skills as a raconteur, his late-night jazz playing and the peacock pleasure he took in wearing a cape like Koussevitzky's.

At the end of the festival Bernstein set off for New Mexico with a new friend, the poet Stephen Spender. D. H. Lawrence's widow, Frieda Lawrence, had given Spender the use of her ranch in Taos; Bernstein, needing somewhere quiet to compose *The Age of Anxiety,* offered to drive him there. Burton Bernstein, now sixteen, shared the driving with his brother, while Spender sat rather regally in the backseat of Leonard's convertible, nicknamed "Greena." The adventures en route of the three men in a Buick involved frequent blow-outs, or "burst tires" as Spender called them in what for the Bernstein brothers was a laughably English accent. While the Bernsteins sweated on the repairs, the poet would find a quiet stream and patiently read a book. Both brothers wrote entertainingly about the trip, Leonard in one of the "imaginary conversations" published in his *The Joy of Music,* Burton in *Family Matters.*

In the Lawrences' Taos retreat, eight thousand feet up in the Rockies, Bernstein spent the days banging away on a jangling upright piano completing the first part of his symphony, while Spender worked on his autobiography, *World Within World,* and Burtie made friends with the local Indians. Each evening at six they would bathe in an icy stream and as the sun set behind a mountain ridge Spender would sing a verse from a Victorian hymn which W. H. Auden had appended to the Prologue of his poem *The Age of Anxiety:*

> *Now the day is over,*
> *Night is drawing nigh;*
> *Shadows of the evening,*
> *Steal across the sky.*

But, as Burton Bernstein wrote, "a week was all Lenny could take of the extreme isolation and the deficient piano." In a letter to Miss Coates, Bernstein himself preferred to blame the altitude, the goldenrod and his defective
sinuses.

While he was in Taos he celebrated his thirtieth birthday. His life seemed less hectic and precarious than it had a few months earlier: he was making good progress with his symphony; his clever new song cycle, *La Bonne Cuisine,* was soon to be premiered in New York by the soprano Marion Bell, and he was about to start his first season as artistic director in Israel.

On their roundabout way home from Taos the Bernstein brothers visited Gus Rudolph, a Tanglewood student, at his ranch in Sheridan, Wyoming; it was the first of many trips the brothers took together while Burtie was a student at Dartmouth. Their friendship blossomed as they drove north swapping jokes in Rybernian, playing word games and talking philosophy. "We plunged into the strenuous Wyoming life, working in effect as hired ranch hands from dawn to dusk and then drinking beer in town at night with the local cowboys." Bernstein used a snapshot of himself on horseback as his 1949 holiday greetings card.

THE mood in Israel was exceptionally tense in September, following the assassination of the United Nations mediator Count Bernadotte. Frontiers and airports were closed. When Bernstein and Helen Coates (who was traveling with him abroad for the first time since 1946) eventually touched down in Haifa six days late, they had a hair-raising night drive to Tel Aviv in a car without headlights. But they soon settled into wartime routine. Bernstein's fence-mending after the New York benefit concert and February's cancellation began immediately. "I feel closer to this orchestra and this country than a mere guest would feel," Bernstein told the *Palestine Post*.

He had been obliged to accept a redesignation of his title, dropping from "artistic director" to "musical adviser." The Palestine orchestra had changed its own name to the Israel Philharmonic, but its daily grind was no less harsh in 1948 than it had been the year before. Bernstein's first subscription program was given nine times. Four other concert programs were also repeated many times over. The devoted players traveled the country in battered old buses; their instruments were wrapped in shock-absorbing blankets and transported in specially constructed cases. At his first Jerusalem concert, on October 14, artillery explosions punctuated the trumpet solo in Beethoven's *Leonore* Overture No. 3.

After a month Bernstein wrote from Tel Aviv to Serge Koussevitzky:

> How to begin? Which of all the glorious facts, faces, actions, ideals, beauties of scenery, nobilities of purpose shall I report? I am simply overcome with this land and its people. I have never so gloried in an army, in simple farmers, in a concert public. I am in perfect health, and very happy—only a little tired from the fantastic schedule we have here: 40 concerts in 60 days, here, in Haifa, in Jerusalem, Rehovoth, and so on. The concerts are a marvelous success, the audiences tremendous and cheering, the greatest being special concerts for soldiers. Never could you imagine so intelligent and cultured and music-loving an army!
>
> And Jerusalem—what shall I say of my beloved Jerusalem, tragic, under constant Arab fire, without water (only a pail a day)—with machine-guns outside accompanying our performances of Beethoven Symphonies! I have visited the fronts, entered Notre Dame, where we hold out a few paces only from Arab-British guns, inspected the strategic heights around the city, and the Palmach bases. I have played piano in hospitals for the new wounded of the Negev, and in camps for soldiers and "kibbutzim" people. I have been decorated with the Jerusalem Defense medal and the Palmach insignia. I have almost grown to be part of all those wonderful people and history-making days. Believe me, it will end well: there is too much faith, spirit, and will to be otherwise.
>
> I am holding auditions for young conductors next week (I have reason to believe there are real talents here). Our good friend Mrs. Frank Cohen advises me that she wishes to donate a scholarship for an Israeli conducting student at Tanglewood next summer. Would you be willing to accept one, as an active pupil if possible, if we find a very talented one? Do please let me know as soon as you can, so that I can make arrangements while I am still here.

I hope the season [Koussevitzky's last in Boston] goes as wonderfully as always.

He added a postscript: "I feel that I shall spend more and more time here each year. It makes running around the cities of America seem so unimportant —as if I am not really needed there, while I am really needed here!" (Koussevitzky, in response, authorized Bernstein to go ahead in selecting a student conductor for Tanglewood.)

In his third subscription series Bernstein introduced Copland's Third Symphony to Israeli audiences. The cautious reviews reflected the local conservatism, but Bernstein himself was now calling it "a fantastic piece!" In his letter about the symphony's reception, Bernstein also informed Copland that he had fallen in love with the young Israeli army officer who had been assigned to him as a personal guide, Azariah Rapoport. "It's the works; and I can't quite believe that I should have found *all* the things I've wanted rolled into one. It's a hell of an experience—nervewracking and guts-tearing and wonderful. It's changed everything."

During a concert at Rehovoth attended by the future President and Mrs. Chaim Weizmann, Bernstein was called to the wings at the end of the first movement of the Beethoven First Piano Concerto and told there were air raid warnings. The *Palestine Post* reported that he "returned to the piano as if nothing had happened." "I never played such an Adagio," he said afterward; "I thought it was my swan song."

IN October 1948 the Israeli Army pushed south into the Negev desert and captured Beersheba, an important crossroads town of biblical significance. On November 19 the UN ordered Israeli forces to withdraw. In Jerusalem Bernstein called for volunteers from the orchestra to perform for the Israeli troops who remained stationed there in defiance of the UN instruction. Thirty-five players set off next morning to drive through the desert in an armored bus and at 3:30 P.M. Bernstein led an extraordinary concert for troops and settlers.

The site was an archaeological dig, where high walls on three sides created an outdoor amphitheater. A newspaper report by the noted South African writer Colin Legum caught the atmosphere. "A solitary minaret looks down in haughty aloofness. . . . The early winter sun beats down mercilessly over scenes of unaccustomed bustle. . . . The well of the amphitheater is alive with chattering soldiers—men and women of the front line army. Jews from Palestine and the British Commonwealth and U.S., Morocco, Iraq, Afghanistan, China, the Balkans, the Baltic, even one from Lapland. . . . An ambulance 'presented in honor of Eddie Cantor' drives up to the entrance, bringing wounded soldiers from the nearby hospital to participate." For the first time in his career Bernstein played three concertos in a row: Mozart in B flat, K. 450, Beethoven's First Piano Concerto and the *Rhapsody in Blue,* which he did as an encore, playing in his shirtsleeves. "MOZART IN THE DESERT" was *Time* magazine's headline. During the concert Bernstein's chair started slipping on the shingle of the makeshift concert platform. "I had to keep on playing in a sort of half crouch," he recalled, "while a violinist got behind and stacked up the stool again." Afterward he enjoyed describing the impact his concert had on Egyptian military plans. His audience in Beersheba was variously estimated at one to five thousand. When scout planes reported large numbers of troops massing on the town, the Egyptians pulled back their units threatening Jerusalem in order to prepare for new Israeli attacks in the Negev. Dr. Chaim Weizmann confirmed this story when he met Leonard Lyons in New York. The Egyptians were sure that this was a military maneuver, he said, "because who'd take time out in war to listen to a Mozart concerto?"

DURING his two months in war-stricken Israel, Bernstein saw a great deal of suffering. Six thousand Jews died during the struggle for independence and twenty thousand were wounded. The fourth section of W. H. Auden's poem *The Age of Anxiety,* from which he was drawing inspiration for his piano-symphony, was entitled "Dirge," and evoked a sobbing world remote from happiness. Bernstein completed the movement in Israel and immediately orchestrated it, so that it could be included in a fund-raising concert in Tel Aviv held to mark the first anniversary of the UN partition resolution which had legitimized Israel's claim to independence.

Bernstein's final visit to Jerusalem was to conduct a gala performance of Mahler's *Resurrection* Symphony, which he insisted on including in his programs—bringing his own set of orchestral parts with him—despite the Israel Philharmonic's objections to its technical and logistical demands. The German text was translated into Hebrew. Following the concert his appreciative admirers presented him with a handsome silver Kiddush cup and a miniature Holy Scroll. His popularity was at its zenith and when he left for home he had in his pocket the outline agreement of a long-term contract to become the musical director and permanent conductor of the Israel Philharmonic Orchestra at a fee of twenty thousand dollars for six months' presence in Israel. "In the event of rejection," the letter concluded lamely, "you agree to accept an alternative plan for coming as guest conductor during the season 1949/50."

Bernstein loved what he thought of then as his second country, and wanted to do well by it. But the repetitive conditions of performance remained exhausting and artistically limiting, and left little time for serious composition. Eventually he would turn down the invitation. "That broke my heart," he remarked to an American journalist at the time. "I wanted to do it. But I can't do everything." It was a rare flash of insight. To the Philharmonic's Mahler-Kalkstein he explained that he could not accept a permanent responsibility until he had worked out his own problems: "I can serve music and Israel much better by being careful now and doing the job when I'm ready for it." Sam Bernstein was heard to observe of the episode that it was fortunate his son had not been born a woman because he was incapable of saying "no."

Despite his rejection of their offer, Bernstein continued to feel that he had a special relationship with the Israel Philharmonic, and he was decidedly put out when in June 1949 they appointed the French conductor Paul Paray as their music director without consulting Bernstein in advance. Earlier, in a private letter to Mahler-Kalkstein, Bernstein had suggested the young American Izler Solomon as music director instead of himself. The letter was circulated to the Philharmonic's board without permission. Bernstein felt betrayed: "The list of instances of my humiliations I shall leave to another and more formal letter. Likewise my detailed opinion of the course the orchestra management has recently embarked upon. . . . [Paray had insisted on importing a new wood-wind section en bloc from France.] How could you, having respect for my function, have behaved so secretively on a matter of greatest importance to me, so that I had to learn of your actions through friendly hints in my miscellaneous mail from Israel? . . . It will also be difficult for me to come next spring with such an atmosphere prevailing. I hope there is something you can do to dispel it."

But Bernstein could not expect to have his cake and eat it so far as being music director was concerned. The fact of the matter was that rightly or wrongly the players preferred Paul Paray to Izler Solomon. Assuaged by Mahler-Kalkstein's grief-stricken explanations, Bernstein's anger subsided and he returned to Israel in 1950 for further triumphs. Paray lasted only a year.

I N 1948, on his way home from Israel, Bernstein made his debut in Rome, the city which he came to love more than any other in Italy (even though *Fancy Free* was booed). He conducted the Orchestra dell'Accademia Nazionale di Santa Cecilia at the Teatro Argentina. In December he traveled back and forth between concerts in Boston, Philadelphia and New York. While in Philadelphia he went to a pre-Broadway tryout of the new musical *Kiss Me, Kate*. Next morning he attended a brunch party in Felicia Montealegre's Washington Place apartment in New York, where he hammered out Cole Porter's tunes and lyrics virtually word and note perfect after that one hearing. Felicia's friend Mike Mindlin remembers being astonished by Bernstein's feat of memory.

Although their engagement had been over for more than a year, his friendship with Felicia was still a reality. On New Year's Day 1949 Bernstein took her with him to a dinner in honor of Jean Cocteau. A fortnight later they attended a Boston Symphony concert together at Carnegie Hall conducted by Koussevitzky. Azariah Rapoport was also in New York in January, but his allure faded when Bernstein was back in his New York milieu and concentrating on his creative work.

The month of January was punctuated by conducting engagements in Buffalo and Pittsburgh, but what dominated Bernstein's thoughts was the need to complete *The Age of Anxiety*. The Boston premiere was only three months off and the finale was still not written. It was at this most unpropitious of moments that Jerome Robbins came to him with the irresistible proposal for a serious musical that could perhaps become the "real moving American opera" Bernstein had dreamed of a year earlier. Robbins's idea had been born when he was asked by his friend Montgomery Clift for guidance in playing Romeo in a contemporary way. The story line Robbins sketched out eventually became part of Broadway history. Its working title was *East Side Story*.

Nearly a decade later, in September 1957, the month of *West Side Story*'s premiere, Bernstein published what he described as a log of the musical's gestation period. It begins: *"January 6, 1949.* Jerry R. [Robbins] called today with a noble idea: a modern version of *Romeo and Juliet* set in slums at the coincidence of Easter-Passover celebrations. Feelings run high between Jews and Catholics. Former: Capulets; latter: Montagues. Juliet is Jewish. Friar Lawrence is a neighborhood druggist. Street brawls, double death—it all fits. But it's all much less important than the bigger idea of making a musical that tells a tragic story in musical-comedy terms, using only musical-comedy techniques, never falling into the 'operatic' trap. Can it succeed? It hasn't yet in our country. I'm excited. If it can work—it's the first. Jerry suggests Arthur Laurents for the book. I don't know him, but I do know *Home of the Brave*, at which I cried like a baby. He sounds just right."

The *Herald Tribune* published the news on January 27. "The production is scheduled for next year. . . . This is an idea that Mr. Robbins has had for some time."

A month later, while touring the South with the Pittsburgh Symphony, Bernstein provided more information. "Prejudice will be the theme of the new work. It will not be a feud of aristocrats that keeps the lovers apart, but rather the prejudice of their Jewish and Italian families. The music will be serious music," he added. "Serious yet simple enough for all people to understand."

But by spring the collaborators were at a creative impasse for which, in his *West Side Story* "log," Bernstein puts the blame on his own work and travel schedule. But a comparison of the 1957 *Playbill* log with the actual dates and places in Bernstein's life during the period it purports to cover reveals it to be a creative reconstruction, factually inaccurate, of the discussions held eight years earlier. The truth is that Bernstein's absence wasn't the problem, he was free in mid-April. But Arthur Laurents was having mixed feelings about the project for both personal and professional reasons: he did not want to be the forgotten opera librettist of the collaboration and he was emotionally drawn toward California rather than New York by the demands of a pressing love affair.

*East Side Story* was quietly shelved. No announcement was made—Robbins, Laurents, Smith and Bernstein simply went their separate ways. For Bernstein it was a set-back, the first of many occasions in his composing career when a proposal for a major collaboration ran out of steam and left him without a strong project. In fact, between *The Age of Anxiety,* first performed in April 1949, and *Trouble in Tahiti,* begun in May 1951, he wrote nothing of substance.

Yet he had cleared the decks for creative activity with high intentions. After declining the music directorship of the Israel Philharmonic in January 1949, and while *East Side Story* was still under discussion, he had written to Menahem Mahler-Kalkstein: "I have decided to make 1949 a composing year, and have given up *all* conducting beginning in April until 1950. . . . I have great plans for a theater work here, and a few other pieces. All this, too, will enable me to grow inside as a person, which this life of running around utterly prevents. I don't have a chance to get acquainted with myself!"

The pattern was similar to the summer of 1947: an agonizing (but brief) reappraisal of his circumstances, and a firm resolution to pause, take stock, explore his inner motivations, followed by a long period of hectic activity carried out in much the same spirit as before. And thus it was that in January and February 1949, while working on both the new musical and the nearly completed symphony, Leonard Bernstein embarked on a seven-week season with the Pittsburgh Orchestra. After three weeks in Pittsburgh itself, the orchestra toured the Southern states of the United States. Bernstein conducted twenty-five concerts in twenty-eight days, and orchestrated all but the closing movement of *The Age of Anxiety* while having what he described to Helen Coates as "a beautiful summer holiday, basking in Georgia sunshine, happy to have found fine people, beautiful vistas and a reasonable division from the seamy side which I usually seek out first."

THE world premiere of *The Age of Anxiety,* in which Bernstein played the piano solo, was the crowning moment of his relationship with Serge Koussevitzky. The work was dedicated to Koussevitzky "in tribute" and was performed on April 8, 1949, in the final month of the Russian conductor's twenty-five-year tenure with the Boston Symphony.

*The Age of Anxiety,* Symphony No. 2 (after W. H. Auden), to give the work its cumbersome full title, was Bernstein's most substantial work yet for the concert hall. Auden's eighty-page poem, a "baroque eclogue" in six parts, won a Pulitzer Prize in 1948 but it is long-winded and self-consciously clever. The critic Richard Hoggart summed it up as "brilliant, perverse, disjointed . . . a structural experiment that does not succeed." Bernstein used Auden's section titles for the six musical movements and claimed that the music reflected Auden's "general form"—a series of conversations (with linking narrative) between three men and a woman, set mostly in a bar in wartime New York. At the time Bernstein said it was "absolutely necessary" for the listener to have read the poem, calling it "fascinating and hair-raising . . . one of the most shattering examples of pure virtuosity in the history of the English language." But it would be a waste of time to try to follow the score as program music:

Bernstein wanted his listeners to enter Auden's imaginative world but did not seek to reflect the poetry page by page. Indeed, he was seduced by his admiration for Auden into overstating his debt to the poem. The musical language is considerably less adventurous than Auden's pretentious if occasionally riveting poetry.

"The Prologue" is a duet for two clarinets, one overlapping and echoing the other, *pianissimo*. The critic Howard Taubman detected phrases from the children's song "Rockabye Baby," which led him to suggest that the age of anxiety began in the cradle. "The loneliest music I know," was Bernstein's own description. Paradoxically the music is in only two parts, two voices, although four people are supposed to be gathered in the Third Avenue bar. "The Prologue" ends with a long descending scale on the flute, acting, according to Bernstein, "as a bridge into the realm of the subconscious, where most of the poem takes place."

Part One continues with "The Seven Ages," beginning with a sweetly dissonant chorale-like theme for solo piano. Labeled "Variation One" to conform to the Auden-derived framework, it is the first of a set of seven short pieces, played without a break and linked one to the other by fragments of melodies or rhythms which are planted at the end of one "variation" and then developed in the next. In his program note Bernstein describes this movement as a "four-fold discussion" which is "reasonable and almost didactic in tone." In fact, it sounds very much like a concerto, with echoes, surely conscious, of Brahms and Rachmaninov. Bernstein's music is symphonic in its technique of musical development but it would have been more accurate to describe the work as a concerto than a symphony.

In "The Seven Stages," after Auden's description of a dreamlike state, deep in the unconscious, Bernstein continues with seven more variations of the same modest dimensions as "The Seven Ages," beginning with a brief passacaglia that recalls his affection for Benjamin Britten. Later the fugal writing for the brass is reminiscent of Hindemith and there is a dash of Shostakovich for good measure. In truth, Part One of *Age of Anxiety*—"The Prologue" and first two movements—is even more eclectic than the *Jeremiah* Symphony, brilliant and sometimes breathtaking in its kaleidoscopic variety of mood and musical texture.

In "The Dirge," the slow movement that begins Part Two, we are being asked to mourn for the twentieth century's loss of faith. Bernstein responds with what he describes as "almost Brahmsian romanticism." "The Masque" follows without a break; Bernstein's musical transitions are managed with considerable cunning. Here there is more divergence between Auden's work and Bernstein's. Far from mirroring Auden's "mirthless discourse," Bernstein's scherzo is a five-minute jazz frolic. The Boston critic Cyrus Durgin described "The Masque" as "the finest single movement in the American idiom and feeling that I have ever heard . . . A triumph of rhythmic interplay, subtle and unexpected accents, a marvelous distillation of the movement of jazz."

The large orchestra of the other movements is reduced to an unusual jazz-inflected combination consisting of harp, double bass, timpani and a variety of percussion instruments. After an exuberant display of syncopated piano playing by the soloist, the trumpets burst in with four bars of an ear-splitting riff. And then the tremendous energy fades into nothingness; the soloist sits with his hands in his lap while we hear the distant tinkling of a second piano, mocking the jazzy bravura of a few moments before. This is the most theatrical moment in the symphony. Bernstein described it as "a kind of separation of the self from the guilt of escapist living."

The glittering parade vanishes like a soap bubble and Bernstein launches into "The Epilogue," which is a triumphantly resolving finale. The movement represents the reassertion of faith (although it is impossible to read such a straightforward theme into Auden's own more pessimistic text). Yet here at last Auden and Bernstein converge. In Auden's "Epilogue," Rosetta, the Jewish female character, contemplates her history. She refers to the Jews' exile in Babylon, ending her monologue with an assertion, in Hebrew, of monotheism: *"Sh'ma Yisrael, Adonai eloheinu, Adonai echad* [Hear O Israel, the Lord our God, the Lord is One]." Bernstein found a musical equivalent to this Jewish credo with a simple but stirring melody derived from synagogue music.

Composing "The Epilogue" gave Bernstein the most trouble. Living dangerously, he did not get the last page done until March 20, less than three weeks before the premiere. In the original version, the solo piano remains silent—a detached observer of the composer's struggle to find his faith in musical terms—until, at the very end, the pianist plays a single chord, symbolizing the oneness of man and God when faith has been restored. But Bernstein was never happy with this concept. Years later, in 1965, he recast the movement so that after a long orchestral prelude the piano joins in the argument and reflects on the earlier movements in an extended cadenza.

Even in the revised version there are passages reminiscent of a Hollywood film score. Was the renewed faith he wished to express genuine, or was it, as he suggested in his 1949 program notes, an artificial, celluloid version of what faith should be like? In his rush to reach a musical conclusion Bernstein may perhaps have been confused as to his motives. But when the finale is played with purity and serenity, as the composer instructed in the score, it communicates a sense of overwhelming love. The brashness falls away to reveal pure beauty.

Auden's influence on Bernstein's work should not be exaggerated. Bernstein told journalists that he read the poem in the summer of 1947 "and almost immediately the music started to sing to him." But the singing had started much earlier. The opening duet for two clarinets is derived, almost note for note, from a duet for muted violin and cello in his 1939 score for *The Birds* at Harvard. The flowing melody of the third variation first appears in Bernstein's unpublished violin sonata, written around 1940, and the catchy tune in "The Masque" was originally a song called "Ain't Got No Tears Left," dropped from *On the Town*. The falling fourths of the principal theme of "The Epilogue" appear in a piano piece Bernstein wrote for Aaron Copland while staying with him in the summer of 1942. Throughout his life Bernstein was determined never to let a good tune languish in a bottom drawer.

Bernstein never revealed another of the inspirational sources of *The Age of Anxiety*. In July 1944, just before he set off to Hollywood to write *On the Town,* he wrote a seventieth-birthday letter to Koussevitzky. "I am sending you, with my love and deepest congratulations, a few notes on your birthday, which form a small sketch for the piece I hope soon to have for you. Life is so busy and complicated now that I cannot set any really definite date when I expect the composition to be finished, but I am trying to make it as quickly as possible without sacrificing any quality!—I want this to be as fine as I can make it, since it is for you, who represent quality itself to me. Please accept the sketch now, and let us hope it grows into a composition worthy of your greatness."

The accompanying "small sketch" was the sixteen bars from *The Birds,* which became the echo duet for two clarinets in *The Age of Anxiety.* Almost five years were to elapse before the work came to fruition but one can feel the spirit of Koussevitzky hovering over one of Bernstein's most deeply felt and romantic compositions.

# THE END OF THE FIRST CONDUCTING CAREER

*Cuernavaca, May 1951.*
COURTESY OF THE ESTATE OF LEONARD BERNSTEIN

*I've been on a merry-go-round so long I've lost my sense of values.*

—LEONARD BERNSTEIN, February 1951

I N the spring of 1949 Bernstein moved to a new apartment on Park Avenue in the shadow of the Empire State Building. Not long afterward he traveled to Hollywood, where MGM was about to shoot *On the Town,* starring Gene Kelly and Frank Sinatra. Kelly had been at the opening night of *On the Town* in December 1944. "I loved it so much I phoned Hollywood that evening," he remembered. "I called Arthur Freed and said, 'You must buy this musical for MGM.' " A documentary filmmaker himself while serving in the U.S. Navy, he planned to eliminate the chorus and shoot much of the film on location in New York.

When the producer Arthur Freed got the green light for production four years later, he assigned Stanley Donen to share the direction with Gene Kelly. The toughest problem facing the filmmakers was what George Abbott had called the Prokofiev element, the cleverness in Bernstein's music. The studio complained that there were no hit tunes. But according to his sister Shirley, Bernstein still had a legal hold on his score. MGM bought his approval to change the score with a five-thousand-dollar consultation fee, and Roger Edens, who was Judy Garland's vocal coach and one of MGM's most successful arrangers, got the job of writing six new songs. Betty Comden and Adolph Green— experienced Hollywood practitioners by now—were hired to revise the book and write new lyrics. Privately, Bernstein felt let down by their collaboration with the undistinguished Roger Edens. The lovely ballad "Lonely Town" was dropped in favor of the movie's banal song "Main Street." But there is no denying the ebullience of the film adaptation, nor its good humor. When the movie version opened at Radio City Music Hall in New York, just in time for the 1949 Christmas holidays, it received a sheaf of good reviews. "A happy film," *Variety* said, "gay with comedy and lilting song numbers." Bernstein himself was privately appalled by all the changes but he put on the best face he could. He told a reporter that *On the Town* was "the best musical Hollywood has ever turned out," although he was a little disappointed, he added with unusual self-restraint, "because several of his favorite ballads were left out."

Bernstein spent a week working on the second-act ballet. Saul Chaplin had already cut and pasted various sections of the original dance number to fit Gene Kelly's choreographic wishes. "We had to shorten the ballet," Kelly reported. "I worked with Lenny over at MGM. We worked very quickly together and very pleasantly, because we had a real affinity. We were [at my home] every night, singing and playing the piano and having fun."

After this midsummer break Bernstein plunged back into conducting, the renunciation forecast by his letter to Mahler-Kalkstein quite forgotten. First he did three concerts at the Robin Hood Dell, the Philadelphia Orchestra's outdoor venue, including a concert version of *Tristan und Isolde* "conceived" by the soloists and "synthesized" by Ernest Knoch. This was Bernstein's first encounter with a work that came to obsess him. Tristan was played by the great Lauritz Melchior, who had sung the role before the war in Bayreuth. Helen Traubel as Isolde looked resplendent in a black gown but spoiled the effect by adding obviously false eyelashes. "It was like Venus de Milo wearing a bra," reported an irreverent journalist.

In July and August at Tanglewood, Bernstein served again as Koussevitzky's chief assistant. Together they gave a repeat performance of *The Age of Anxiety*. All the students were whistling "The Masque," which Koussevitzky had decided was "a noble jezz" and "very eclectical." Oliver Smith came up specially to hear it: he was planning the designs for a new ballet by Jerome Robbins which was to be danced to the score of *The Age of Anxiety*.

On August 25 Bernstein celebrated his thirty-first birthday with his family in Sharon; two days later he was feted in New York for a second time at a party in his honor at which Judy Garland sang with Bernstein at the piano, and Ray Bolger later joined her for a dance. Much of the fall, Bernstein's quietest since coming to New York, was devoted to composition—the jazz piece for Woody Herman and songs for a new version of *Peter Pan*—and to the grind of preparing for his next conducting season. But his social life continued at madcap speed. "I've been going to parties, lots of parties, a strange new occupation for me," he wrote to his brother at Dartmouth College. He countered the alcohol intake by playing squash three times a week.

Before Marc Blitzstein's new opera, *Regina,* based on Lillian Hellman's *The Little Foxes,* opened on Broadway on October 31, Bernstein published an appreciative essay in the *New York Times,* describing it as a significant milestone on the road toward a genuinely American opera. But *Regina* received mixed reviews. After a month attendance fell off, and a testimonial advertisement in the *New York Times* by eleven of *Regina*'s most celebrated supporters—including Cole Porter, Tennessee Williams and Moss Hart, as well as Bernstein—could not save it. The Broadway public did not seem to be interested in experiments in music theater.

Bernstein's season of guest-conducting began in Boston in November 1949 with the world premiere of a Koussevitzky Foundation commission, the *Turangalîla* Symphony by Olivier Messiaen. *Turangalîla* is the Sanskrit word for love, and Messiaen's ten-movement symphony was voluptuous and orgiastic by turns. Included in its exotic orchestration was an Ondes Martenot, an electronic keyboard instrument whose sound resembled the wailings of an old-fashioned musical saw. Messiaen had been picked out for a Boston Symphony commission back in 1945 by Koussevitzky, whose nose for the best in the avant-garde rarely failed him; deeper links were forged when Messiaen spent the summer of 1949 in the Berkshires as composer-in-residence at Tanglewood. Koussevitzky hoped (in vain) that *Turangalîla* would have the same sort of impact on the postwar musical world that Stravinsky's *Rite of Spring* had had in 1913. Messiaen wrote to Bernstein in advance from Paris: "I am forty-one years old and I have put into my symphony all of my strengths of love, of hope and of musical research. But I know you are a man of genius and that you will conduct it the way I feel it." In Boston the reviewers were impressed by the mountains of percussion requested by the composer, and by the brilliance of Yvonne Loriod's piano playing, but as the *Christian Science Monitor* noted, "If Bostonians suffer, they suffer in silence."

*Turangalîla* is intended to be performed in one seventy-five-minute uninterrupted span, and Bernstein may have miscalculated by introducing an interval after the fifth movement; momentum was lost and with it the sense of cumulative rapture that has since assured the work a special place in the concert hall repertory. But in fact Bernstein was obliged to interrupt the work—union requirements specified that musicians play for no longer than one hour without a break. Despite this musical *coitus interruptus,* Irving Kolodin innocently hailed "a really arousing experience" when Bernstein conducted *Turangalîla* at Carnegie Hall later in the week. Other critics proved deeply hostile. Cecil Smith felt that "the trashiest Hollywood composers had met their match"; Arthur

Berger, the most trenchant of New York's reviewers, summed it up as "an amazing performance of the most pretentious nonsense."

Later the same day, still at Carnegie Hall, the Boston Symphony took part in its very first telecast. Leonard Bernstein replaced an unwell Serge Koussevitzky at an event marking the first anniversary of the signing of the Universal Declaration of Human Rights. The ambitious program included Yehudi Menuhin playing Bach, and speeches by Eleanor Roosevelt and Trygve Lie, the first UN Secretary General. Aaron Copland had used the stirring words of the introduction to the UN Charter as the text of his *Preamble* for narrator and orchestra, commissioned by NBC for the event. It was to be spoken by Laurence Olivier, fresh from his film success as Hamlet. Olivier flew in from London for the performance and, delayed by bad weather, arrived in mid-rehearsal. No one had told him in advance when and how he was to make his entrance for the Copland work, which has a slow and stately musical introduction. Olivier's petulant plea for instructions was heard around the hall. "Well, what am I to do, Lenny? Stand here like a green cunt?" In the performance Olivier narrated the piece with the appropriate solemnity, but his colorful phrase passed into Bernstein's personal anthology.

In December Bernstein took a holiday in Florida to compose the incidental music for a new production of J. M. Barrie's play *Peter Pan,* in which Jean Arthur and Boris Karloff were to play Peter and Captain Hook. "Losing his head," as he put it, over J. M. Barrie's fantasy, Bernstein delivered more than had been asked for. Along with the various dances and segments of mood music he'd been commissioned to write, he supplied both music and lyrics for five songs as well as for two choruses for the pirates. The production eventually opened on April 24, 1950, a month after Bernstein had sailed for Europe. Before leaving he asked Marc Blitzstein to cope with last-minute problems. Blitzstein wrote to him in Italy a week before opening night: "Your casual throwaway phrase: 'If you run into any trouble on lyrics (in *Peter Pan*), consult Marc—he's my deputy'—has borne all kinds of fruit; raw, ripe, rotten." The best song, "Dream with Me," had to be cut. For the lyrics he rewrote, Blitzstein was paid from Bernstein's royalties. "Don't be upset about the small amount: $200. I really didn't do much," he told Bernstein; "just about enough to disturb you."

*Peter Pan* was a solid success, earning Bernstein over twelve thousand dollars in its year on Broadway and collecting unanimously good notices. "Leonard Bernstein has taken time off from serious work to write a melodic, colorful and dramatic score that is not afraid to be simple in spirit," Brooks Atkinson wrote in the *Times.* Bernstein's songs display the innocent directness of the child's mind and because of the limited singing skills of the *Peter Pan* cast they are simpler and more diatonic than anything in the *I Hate Music* cycle. But far from "taking time off from serious work," this is Bernstein in search of a "serious yet simple" language; the songs are modest steps along the road leading to his opera *Trouble in Tahiti.* After four decades of neglect they are finally establishing themselves in the concert recital repertoire.

❦

BERNSTEIN may still have been feeling his way as a composer, but as a conductor he was already aware that he was part of a great line that stretched back through Koussevitzky to Nikisch. Bernstein prided himself on the friendships he built up with the great conductors of his day, among them Bruno Walter, Pierre Monteux and George Szell. The most legendary figure was Toscanini, whom he met again when he was preparing a program that included excerpts from Berlioz's *Romeo and Juliet* for the Philadelphia Orchestra. He had listened to Toscanini's recording, and also to a live broadcast where the "Love Scene" had been taken at a considerably slower tempo. He wrote to Toscanini asking for a meeting to go over the score, and an audience was granted at the maestro's Villa Pauline in Riverdale, a few miles north of Manhattan. "He was in rare form," Bernstein recalled, "running up the stairs two at a time and bouncing all over the place." Toscanini insisted that there could be only one correct Toscanini tempo. However, the old man promised to listen again to both radio and recorded versions and a few days later he wrote to Bernstein in his customary red ink, confirming the fact that his tempo on the recording was much faster. "And I confirmed another fact," the letter continued, "namely that every man, no matter the importance of his intelligence, can be from time to time a little stupid. . . . So is the case of the old Toscanini. Your kind visit and dear letter made me very, very happy. . . . I felt myself 40 years younger."

When Bernstein conducted the Philadelphia Orchestra at Carnegie Hall, Harriett Johnson of the *Post* said his "controlled and meaningful" conducting was getting better all the time. "He is almost overcome by the elixir of the music he is performing," she observed. Marc Blitzstein dashed off an equally appreciative note:

Lenny dear:

I'm inept at writing fan letters—but the Berlioz last night threw me completely. I don't know when I have been so shattered by the concatenation of piece, orchestra and conductor. It had a beautiful sober romanticism, an innate tragic sense I had dimly sensed when I studied the score years ago, but had forgotten. How original a work it is! And the technical address, the tonal sheen and rhythmic ease of your performance was not only a delight—it was that subterranean delight that should underpin a big spiritual experience, but so rarely does.

Does this tell you? I took it to my heart, and I took you to my heart. Thank you, baby.

Marc

Bernstein's 1950 winter season took him to Pittsburgh, Detroit, Los Angeles and San Francisco. Between trips, on January 15, he signed his first contract with Columbia Records. His friend Goddard Lieberson was director of the

Masterworks Series and later became president; he was soon to be joined by David Oppenheim as producer of classical music. The agreement was the beginning of a fruitful relationship that lasted more than a quarter of a century, with literally hundreds of recordings to show for it. At last Bernstein could make recordings with his beloved Jennie Tourel, who was also under contract to Columbia. The first projects were Ravel's song cycle *Shéhérazade,* accompanied by the Columbia Symphony Orchestra, and Mussorgsky's *Songs and Dances of Death,* with Bernstein at the piano. In February, after the New York Philharmonic's public performances, Columbia also recorded *The Age of Anxiety,* with Lukas Foss as soloist.

A New York journalist dubbed the last days of February "anxiety week." On the twenty-sixth Bernstein conducted the orchestral version of *The Age of Anxiety* in the afternoon concert at Carnegie Hall, while Jerome Robbins's new ballet, set to the same music, was performed that evening at the City Center. The ballet, featuring twenty-eight dancers, divided dance critics much as *Facsimile* had done in 1946: John Martin, a Robbins enthusiast, thought it "tremendously distinguished," while Douglas Watt in the *News* wrote it off as "a tiresomely sentimental piece of claptrap." *Newsweek* reported that the audience gave it an ovation "probably not equalled since *Fancy Free,*" but made fun of the "Colossal Dad" character from Auden's poem, who was "gotten up like a hooded beekeeper on stilts."

Bernstein's appearances in New York as both composer and conductor prompted an analytical interview with Louis Biancolli in the *World-Telegram.* Bernstein described himself as a dual personality. The composer in him represented, he said, "an introspective person with a strong inner life; his primary mode of activity is to stay home and compose, whenever he feels the impulse. He can have a strong private life, too. The conductor is an extrovert. He is dealing constantly with audiences, orchestras, critics—people, great numbers of people. In other words, he is a performer. That's the basic conflict. As a conductor you are not supposed to have too much of a personal life."

Two days after the "analysis," another aspect of his extrovert personality appeared in Leonard Lyons's column: "Leonard Bernstein, who jammed Carnegie Hall three times last week, introduced a new fashion note for conductors and recitalists—black cowboy boots or moccasins, with white tie and tails. . . ." Bernstein's private life, however, was still at sixes and sevens. Back in January, Walter Winchell's syndicated column reported—two years after the event—that "Maestro Leonard Bernstein and Felicia Montealegre canceled their altar plans at the last moment." That something had set the story in motion again can be deduced from a gossip column in the *Pittsburgh Press* during Bernstein's brief visit there in January 1950: "Take heart again girls: handsome Leonard Bernstein, the musical man of all trades, is still very eligible. This corner the other morning had him married to Felicia Montealegre, television's No. 1 dramatic actress. 'Taint so. They were once engaged but the romance stopped short of the altar." Bernstein's date book yields few clues as to whom he was seeing at the time. Felicia's name is not recorded, and in fact she was in the middle of a love affair with another man.

Felicia had made great strides in her career since 1947. In the burgeoning world of television drama, when every show was broadcast live, she had become a force to be reckoned with. At the end of 1949 the *Motion Picture Daily* balloted the country's television editors and Felicia was elected as the female Most Promising Star of Tomorrow. By the spring of 1950 she commanded a fee of $750 to $1,000 for television performances, and she was understudying Eva Gabor on Broadway in a play called *Happy Time.* Playing opposite Gabor was a dashingly handsome young actor named Richard Hart, with whom Felicia fell in love. There were drawbacks to her romance. Hart drank heavily, and when he drank he became violent. In addition, he was married, with three children. But friends reported that he was the love of Felicia's life. They set up house together in Manhattan's West Side. When Burton Bernstein visited them for supper, Hart was "sloshed." Shirley Bernstein was also close to Felicia, and Leonard himself may well have met Felicia with Hart. She was certainly much on his mind when he set off for Europe on the SS *Atlantic.*

The hectic mood of Bernstein's chaotic three-week conducting season in Italy was epitomized by a letter to Burtie from Turin. "They lost my tails at the Naples hotel half an hour before the concert (which was at six, and the rehearsals lasted til four, with many chills and fevers and a raw cold hall) and the piano broke down mitten der [in the middle of the] Ravel in Milano, and every city I come to there's always a mess. But such fun and fury!"

F R O M Italy, he traveled to Israel for a punishing schedule of concerts, including no fewer than ten performances of *The Age of Anxiety,* which he conducted from the keyboard. His parents arrived in Haifa for a visit on May 1; after they departed he made a high-spirited excursion with Alexis Weissenberg, Jennie Tourel and Helen Coates to Eilat on the Red Sea to play for the Israeli troops stationed there. The visiting musicians, wearing Druse headgear and brightly striped pullovers, flew down in a tiny open-doored military plane, and performed at sunset from the balcony of the clubhouse with the soldiers drawn up below them. "Sigi" Weissenberg, a brilliant and good-humored young man who was adored by Bernstein at the time, played popular piano solos, audience requests, and imitations of the great pianists, while Jennie Tourel sang numbers from *Carmen* and Yiddish songs, with Bernstein accompanying. Finally Bernstein was persuaded—after a great show of reluctance—to play the piano alone. The local correspondent of the *Ha'aretz* newspaper caught his unique concert persona: "Bernstein approaches the piano—opens his shirt like a man who has to cope with a hard labor [the piano was out of tune and reacted "like a stubborn and wayward bull"] and starts performing the 'Sad Rhapsodie' by Gershwin. He puts his whole soul and energy into his playing, he struggles with the piano, an open fight in order to achieve the maximum. When finishing, his face was tired and outworn and he remarks to his fellows, 'this was the strang-est and most sublime concert.' "

At midnight the musicians went for a swim in the Red Sea. Discreetly the members of the group slipped away, two by two, to watch each other's seem-ingly phosphorescent bodies sliding through the water and to enjoy the beauties of the night. It wasn't until four, *Ha'aretz* reported, that they went to bed.

FROM New York, Shirley continued to send Lenny news of Felicia. The letters Bernstein wrote to his sister in reply during his two-month concert season in Israel indicate that beneath the surface he was experiencing a dramatic shift in his feelings. He wrote from Herzlia on April 26:

> How strange that you should have written just now of Felicia! Ever since I left America she has occupied my thoughts uninterruptedly and I have come to a fabulously clear realization of what she means—and has always meant—to me. I have loved her, despite all the blocks that have consistently impaired my loving-mechanism, truly and deeply from the first. Lonely on the sea, my thoughts were only of her. Other girls (and/or boys) meant nothing. Even the automatic straining toward general sexual-ity of the moment—which had always carried a big stick with me, was of no importance. I have been consistently aware of the great companionship of this girl—seen clearly and independent of the damnable tensions that discolored it, the fears melting into thin air. I feel, for the first time in my life, jealousy—a growing resentment of her current affair, and a certain knowledge that D.H. [Dick Hart] was horribly wrong for her. Over all this, a real knowledge that she and I were made for each other, then as now: that we have everything to give each other. Just as right is my feeling that it would have been wrong to marry when we planned in '47, in struggle with the complex tensions of both our young lives then. It is right now: I would marry her tomorrow, sight unseen, ignorant of all she has lived through these two years or so, willing to learn, insatiably eager to learn.
>
> On the boat I was seized by these feelings—and more: a grave intu-ition that she was in trouble, and needed someone. I prayed it might be me she needed. So strong was this conviction (though I admitted to myself that intuitive deductions are all too easy in mid-Atlantic) that I wrote her a letter explaining my urge. I felt humble writing it, vastly apologetic for the indifferent treatment I had afforded her during her troubled time in California, and in fact all through our "engagement." After mailing it, I was afraid that I had been guilty of bad manners, of possibly trying to disrupt what may have been a good relationship with Hart, of possibly yielding to the impulse of a moment of loneliness. Now I know, weeks later, how sincere and deep the impulse was. . . .
>
> I would write all this directly to her, but the unknown fate of my first

letter to her gives me pause. I don't mean to use you as a go-between—I know you understand that as deeply as you do my desire to have her know my feelings. So many things become clear when abroad—so many cow-webs [their father's phrase] are cleared away: the tongues of dear friends persuading me that she was wrong for me, etc., the psychiatric womb wherein one is safe from the need to cope with sexual adjustment, etc. My feeling is one totally apart from analysis: I want only to cope, and through my own powers, without aid—especially of the indulgent, personal sort that was forthcoming from Miss Nell [Renée Mell].

How is Felicia? Did [Eva] Gabor leave, as I heard she might, and did Felicia replace her? Is she still in the show? How does she feel about her career? Is her health OK? These things, of course, I would love to hear directly from her; but if that is not possible, let me hear them from you. I am thrilled that you are close again: that should always be: you have so much for each other.

Only one thing more: last night I dreamed at length that I had found her and solved our problems together. It was a hard dream, but full of richness. And, on awakening, I was desolate at the thousands of miles that still lay between us, and the grayness of doubt and not-knowing. My day-dreams are of her flying to Israel, and our being married in Jerusalem, . . . my world changes from one of abstractions and public-hungry performance to one of reality, a world of creativity, of Montealegre-Cohn, of Spanish and French and travel and rest and love and warmth and intimacy. I've never felt so strongly as these weeks in Italy how through I am with the conductor-performance life (except where it really matters) and how ready I am for inner living, which means composing and Felicia. I'll probably never stop conducting completely; but it will never again be in intensity and emphasis what these last seven years have been.

In a second letter to Shirley, written three weeks later, Bernstein was testing his ability to resist his homosexual instincts:

. . . I have been engaged in an imaginary life with Felicia, having her by my side on the beach as a shockingly beautiful Yemenite boy passes —inquiring into that automatic little demon who always springs into action at such moments—then testing: if Felicia were there, sharing with me that fantastic instant when the Khamsin is suddenly gone, and a new wind, west from the sea comes in to cancel the heat with its almost holy approach—and the test works. It's surprising how true some of the old parts out of the analysis book can be: "to establish a good relation to yourself is the prerequisite to any other relation." This self-relation is what I have begun to find: I have discovered the core in myself of human relationship (words, words til now)—the core of a sunburst of quiet energy, and always à propos of Felicia. This, after years of compulsive living, of driving headlong down alleys of blind patterns, dictated by God knows what vibrations—this is a revelation. Not that the demon absents himself: he still pokes me when his occasions arise—the french horn player, the artist in Jerusalem, but the old willingness to follow him, blind to any future, blind to the inner knowledge of the certain ensuing meaninglessness—that is gone. So the demon diminishes. . . .

I feel such a certainty about us—I know there's a real future involving a great comradeship, a house, children, travel sharing—and such a tenderness as I have rarely felt. I want to comfort her for all her heavy wandering, and to make it right. Only one thing: why does she insist on prolonging the suffering? Is she as sure as you that her present life is not her future? I hope she is—I know from some almighty source that Dick was created for other things. And Felicia is for me. . . .

A month later, near the end of his Israel season, Bernstein remained obsessed with establishing a future for himself with Felicia. The Israel Philharmonic was again urging him to take over the orchestra, he told Shirley, and while he was inclined to accept, he claimed he couldn't do it without Felicia by his side. He hoped she would consider giving up her career to become his wife. But Felicia had committed herself to Dick Hart; her own dreams were fashioned on her hopes of taking over Eva Gabor's role so that she could appear on stage with her lover, whom she hoped to marry when he was free. In the summer of 1950 she had submerged her feelings for Leonard Bernstein. She was twenty-eight and she was getting on with her life.

Unaware of her rejection, Bernstein threw himself into his music. At his farewell concert in Jerusalem he performed Mahler's *Das Lied von der Erde.* "When it's over," he told Shirley, "one wants only to crawl away and die somewhere. It's a summation of conducting. Now I can quit." Less than a week later he was conducting Mahler again, at the Holland Festival, in what the *New York Times* described as "an overpowering revelation." Bernstein's identification with Mahler had grown incredibly strong: "I love Mahler's music very deeply. . . . Sometimes I feel clearly that his difficulties were the same as my own. Mahler was also 'possessed' by music and his compositions, too, originated during his occupations as a conductor. . . . With works by Mahler I seem to be playing some of my own."

Bernstein returned to the United States to find Tanglewood in an uncomfortable mood, with the aging Koussevitzky no longer master in his own house. He was nominally still director of the Berkshire Music Festival, but the BSO board had invited Victor de Sabata, musical director of La Scala, Milan, to conduct concerts without consulting him. Bernstein delivered a lecture about nationalism in the music of Israeli composers—he had read dozens of scores while preparing programs for the Israel Philharmonic's forthcoming American tour—and conducted his customary two concerts with the Boston Symphony. In his three weeks of teaching, he picked out a young auditor named Charles Roth and gave him the chance to conduct the Prelude to *Tristan und Isolde* with the student orchestra. A brief friendship developed between the two men—one that would return to haunt Bernstein in the mid-fifties.

That summer Bernstein unexpectedly fired Helen Coates after six years of faithful, if sometimes overpowering, support. A letter he wrote to Coates from Holland in July had given no hint of dissatisfaction. But when he returned to New York he met with Felicia, and learned that she was not ready to give up her lover or career for him. One of the problems she would have certainly voiced was Bernstein's reliance upon Helen Coates, who ran every aspect of his life and had all too obviously disapproved of their engagement. "She doesn't scare me any more," Felicia had written in June 1947, "she just makes me mad." Perhaps Bernstein wanted to prove his newfound independence of spirit, or perhaps, as he had written to Shirley, Miss Coates was getting on his nerves. On August 7, while she was still, as she put it, "on a mission in a foreign country," he sent her a crushing letter of dismissal.

Her angry reply, written when she returned to New York—Bernstein was already back in Europe—called him unethical for having sacked her when she was abroad. "You have the right to run your life in any way you choose," she went on; "I was completely unaware of any of the difficulties you described in what you called 'our relationship.' . . . Your own sense of dependency was the result . . . of your turning over more and more for me to look after. . . . You told me it would be such a relief to you not to have to think of anything connected with finances or money. . . . As for the 'over involvement' in your personal life, as you put it, I think you must share some of whatever blame there is by drawing me into it as much as you did. . . . I can only say that I did my job to the very best of my ability and out of complete devotion to you. I have always had great faith in you as a human being and in your musical genius, and I had no other desire, during the last six years, than to serve both as selflessly as possible."

Helen Coates described how she had been asked to manage Bernstein's daily life. She had handled constant telephone calls, made appointments, acted as a screen between him and the countless people calling on him, arranging auditions, even taking some auditions herself "at your request," writing letters, looking after his clothes, packing and unpacking for his trips, and so on. In New York, she reminded him, she had "saved him *hundreds* of dollars on the six moves I have made for you (in and out of apartments, and in and out of storage) when I packed all of your personal belongings, all of the office supplies, records, etc., and unpacked all of these."

Bernstein must have recognized how much he needed Helen Coates, for within a few days she was back in his employ, at first on a part-time basis but soon with all her administrative powers restored. She had been his guardian angel, and in his heart Bernstein knew that despite her fusspot, schoolmarm manner, she was indispensable to his career, whatever Felicia's feelings to the contrary. Besides, it was easier to hire her again than to face the guilt of having fired her.

While Helen Coates was still seething with justified rage, Bernstein took his brother and sister on his next conducting trip. "From the moment we fastened our seatbelts on the airliner to Paris," wrote Burton in *Family Matters,* "the three of us regressed to our old puerile Rybernian form. The private jokes and allusions, the uncontrollable giggles and mad laughter, the infantile sense of sheer pleasure in one another's existence poured out nonstop, no matter how many eyebrows were raised in amusement. . . . Were we being vulgar Americans, loud Jews? We didn't care." In Paris Bernstein was already described as a *chef d'orchestre distingué,* but for the "dribbling siblings," as Burton described himself and Shirley, no reaction could be too outrageous. "Lennuhtt" would mumble asides in the family's private language even as he was being lionized by "some terribly grand *comtesse.* . . . We could hardly wait to leave elegant receptions and special excursions to cultural landmarks so we could rush back to the hotel for some unmuffled jokes and, of all things, a long game of canasta. Canasta—loud, riotous, hysterical canasta—was the obsession of the tour."

Bernstein's first music engagement was with the French Radio Orchestra, appearing at the Edinburgh International Festival, Scotland's postwar answer to Salzburg. In the *Daily Express,* the critic Arthur Jacobs wrote that he found Bernstein almost too fascinating to watch at the piano. "Look at the split-second timing as a hand ceases to wave at the strings and drops dead in place on the keyboard. Mark the film-star figure, the easy kissing of hands to the audience. But make no mistake, here is a fine, if not quite mature musician."

After two weeks of concerts in Holland, where Bernstein made his debut with the Concertgebouw Orchestra, the trio flew to Ireland to stay with their eccentric Philadelphia friend Henry McIlhenny (the manufacturer of Tabasco sauce) at his castle in County Donegal. The height of their canasta madness was reached in a game between Lenny and Burtie which they played, according to Shirley, "in a taxi taking us from Shannon Airport to our hotel. . . . I got out of the car and looked back, staring in disbelief at my brothers. Oblivious to the fact that we had arrived, the two of them sat in the back seat, surrounded by luggage, melded cards stuck into any convenient part of the upholstery, intent only on finishing their wild game."

Glenveagh Castle was an imposing estate on the west coast of Ireland, and Bernstein fell in love with it, warmly singing its praises in a letter to David Diamond. "How you would love this place! Wild, unbelievably human woods, glens, lochs, gaps, weather. Everything moves constantly." In a postscript he added, "Hey, I'm resting at last!" But it was an energetic kind of repose: "I've hunted deer, fished and danced 'The Siege of Carrick' all night." McIlhenny had taken his guests below stairs to join the domestics in an evening of Irish reels.

The deer hunt was a farcical affair. The Bernstein brothers rose before dawn, eager for the fray. They waded through peat bogs and clambered up treeless mountainsides in the soft Irish rain in search of game. But whenever they came upon a proud stag making a perfect target, the head stalker begged them not to shoot—the animal was pregnant, he would say, or nursing foals, or to shoot would risk killing nearby does. Leonard became so frustrated at not being allowed to fire his deer rifle that he abandoned the hunt altogether. He was back at the castle having afternoon tea when his exhausted and equally frustrated brother stumbled in. Not a shot had been fired all day.

When the Irish idyll was over Burton flew back to begin his sophomore year at Dartmouth. Leonard and Shirley spent a few days at a rented house in Èze in the south of France and moved on to Majorca by way of Barcelona, where they were joined by Bernstein's journalist friend Rosamond ("Peggy") Bernier, whose father was a big wheel in the Philadelphia Orchestra. At the Ritz in Barcelona, Bernier remembers, it was hard to know which the management disapproved of more, the unruly dachshund puppy they brought with them from France or the fact that brother and sister shared a bedroom.


LEONARD and Shirley stayed in Europe through November. That month he conducted the Orchestra of La Scala for the first time, performing Mahler's *Resurrection* in one concert and *Le Sacre du Printemps* in the other. "The concerts in Milan have been wonderful," he wrote to Burton, "and my future at La Scala seems to be a great one. They want me back not only for concerts but opera as well—imagine, in the world's greatest opera house! All this is very confusing to a guy who wants to compose, and choices are hard to make. I don't seem to know what I prefer at this point. But living is fun."

The canasta craze continued. While staying at the Israel Philharmonic's guest house in Tel Aviv, Leonard got so furious during a game, Shirley remembers, that he ripped the window curtain off its rail. He had been more successful on the ski slopes. On a postcard of the Matterhorn dispatched to Burton, he wrote triumphantly: "You'll never believe it but I made the entire descent yesterday. 2½ hours but that's almost a record for a beginner. I feel great and miss you. Shirley's resigned to walking forever."


IN January of 1951, the Israel Philharmonic was scheduled to make its first visit to America. The tour would preoccupy Bernstein for the next four months. Then he intended to give up conducting altogether and devote himself exclusively to composition. Bernstein was to share the conducting with Koussevitzky, who had made a triumphant debut with the orchestra after Bernstein had convinced his Israeli friends that the maestro's teenage conversion from Judaism to Russian Orthodoxy had been an aberration. Koussevitzky fell ill, however, and Bernstein and his conductor colleagues Eleazar de Carvalho and Izler Solomon had to take over many of his concerts. The aim of the tour was to raise money for the institutions of the infant state of Israel and to increase the American awareness of Israel's cultural achievements. In day-to-day terms such pious goals involved a great deal of socializing with Jewish community leaders in every port of call. Events ranged from a grand fund-raising concert at the Waldorf-Astoria in New York to a modest mayoral reception in Tucson, the smallest city on the itinerary. Out of town, the press was enthusiastic about the orchestra's performances, but Virgil Thomson led the New York reviewers in deploring the absence of Israeli composers in the programs—the solitary Israeli work of substance was a viola concerto by Oedoen Partos; other Israeli pieces were performed only as encores. Olin Downes wrote in the *Times* that he was moved by the presence in the orchestra of "men and women who had been branded in prison camps and had fought on Israel's battle front," but Kurt List in the *New Leader* thought the indifferent woodwind and brass playing pulled down the standard to that of "a pre-war German provincial orchestra." A critic in Toledo, Ohio, wrote Bernstein off as a charlatan: "He cajoles, he grimaces, he hams outrageously. . . . a most profligate waste."

It was a relief for Bernstein to slip away from an arduous tour to fulfill a previously made conducting commitment with one of the nation's leading orchestras, the Chicago Symphony. "I find that conducting can still be a joy with an orchestra like this. . . . Chicago itself is fun—full of depravity and jazz and old friends." The critic Claudia Cassidy—"the great Bitch Cassidy" as Bernstein dubbed her—noted greater serenity than when he had performed six years previously. Another critic wrote that Bernstein's way with *Le Sacre du Printemps* was "like going over Niagra Falls on a bar-stool: a procedure immensely exciting but somewhat incautious."

In February 1951 he made history conducting the New York Philharmonic in the world premiere of the Second Symphony of Charles Ives. It had been completed a full fifty years earlier yet had not been performed anywhere. Its composer, too frail to attend the performance, heard the Sunday afternoon CBS radio broadcast on the kitchen radio at his home in Danbury, Connecticut, and was so thrilled that he shaved off his beard.

In March, near the end of the Israeli tour, Bernstein wrote to Aaron Copland. "I am giving up conducting next month for at least two years, and since my last date is in Mexico City, I shall probably remain there for some months, and write big, loud pretty music for the American Theatre." In an almost identical sentence to the one he had used in his letter to David Diamond in August 1947, he went on: "I've never felt so happy and strong about a decision: it will be so good to get in contact with myself again, live a little more innerly . . ." He defended his decision to give up conducting to a Salt Lake City reporter: "I don't think I'm deserting art for low communication. I think I'm going into a form [opera] that is intrinsically more difficult, challenging and vital to the long-range history of American music."

The Israel Philharmonic tour wound up in New York, where Bernstein conducted the last three concerts. The marathon was almost over. But Koussevitzky summoned Bernstein to a crisis meeting at his winter ranch near Phoenix; supposedly he wanted to commission Bernstein to write a big work for the festival he was planning for Jerusalem in 1953. "But the dark hints began to emerge," Bernstein reported to Helen Coates, "as to the real subject of my visit: that in case he should find himself not well enough at the beginning of the Tanglewood season, the whole thing would devolve upon my shoulders; concerts, festivals, teaching and all. I demurred, of course, matching my poor health against his, and we agreed not to discuss it further. . . . I must say he didn't look well, even resting in the desert."

The last stop on a twelve-month odyssey which had seen him conduct a hundred concerts with a dozen different orchestras was a week with Carlos Chávez's Mexico City orchestra, before going on to Cuernavaca to look for a house where he could write. He selected Cuernavaca not merely because he had liked it so much in 1945, but because the author Martha Gellhorn now lived there. Gellhorn, ten years Bernstein's senior, had met him in Israel in 1948. Married in the forties to Ernest Hemingway, she was an intriguing personality, a distinguished writer who was both brave and beautiful. Having abandoned journalism to return to fiction, she was living in Cuernavaca with her three-year-old adopted son, Sandy (to whom Bernstein later dedicated one of his *Anniversaries*). Bernstein announced to Gellhorn out of the blue that he was coming to live with her.

"I regarded this with undisguised horror," Gellhorn recalled. "The very first thing he wanted was a grand piano and the other thing he wanted to do was play Scrabble. . . . He exhausted me within twenty-four hours." Gellhorn lived on the Avenida del Parque, where Bernstein had rented a house for a few weeks in 1945. The house he had rented before was available again by a strange quirk of fortune, improved and more beautiful. It came with five servants and was grotesquely expensive to rent, but his other expenses were small. He ate, slept, played tennis, swam, talked and read. "I will shortly be speaking Spanish and writing like a boiler factory—book, libretto, music," he told Helen Coates. "It is only a matter of getting back my lost health, letting ideas flit about my battered brain, stewing and growing, and then the explosion will come."

Less than two weeks after settling in, he wrote to Helen Coates that his muse was functioning at full speed. "This is a really nice surprise from the gods, as I didn't expect anything to happen for at least a month or two. I'm knee deep in my opera idea *Trouble in Tahiti* and loving it. Full of problems of every description and each one is a joy to solve. (I assume that they will be solved, cockily enough. That's what comes from sun and air and swimming and eating like a horse.) I have cut off my hair . . . sit in my beloved Laurel de India tree, and find there is a lot of life I know nothing about, especially the life inside me. It's more than fascinating learning about it." He instructed Helen Coates to inform his concerts manager that he was not able to commit himself for anything. "I have ceased (O blessed state!) to be a conductor." And he passed the word to his producer friend Peter Lawrence in Hollywood that he was not interested in refurbishing his *Peter Pan* score for a proposed movie version. Four days later, in another letter to Helen Coates, he was discussing the possibility of investing the thirty thousand dollars he had in a checking account and living off the interest so he could devote himself to composition.

Another Mexican week went by and the first careless rapture of creativity gave way to something approaching a routine as he settled into a groove, alternating between periods of hard work and periods of relative (for Bernstein) inactivity. He had already sketched four scenes and had reached a point where he had begun to doubt the merit of his work. "But there is always a reassuring voice the next day to tell me there is something really valuable in it."

In the month of May he wrote the libretto and sketched out the music for the entire work, "wrestling delightedly," as he put it, "with the problems of getting Americanese to sound sensible when sung." Although only a short opera of some forty-five minutes duration, *Trouble in Tahiti* contains some richly varied arias and three substantial duets. Marc Blitzstein had struggled for years to complete *Regina;* by comparison Bernstein's compositional speed was little short of phenomenal, and he had started from scratch with his own libretto. It was all very promising.

But it was not to last. Only days later his creative mood was shattered. On June 4, 1951, Serge Koussevitzky died in Boston, signaling for Bernstein the end of an era. He had long outgrown Koussevitzky's mentorship, but the debt he owed the great maestro would never be forgotten.

# 21.

# RITES OF PASSAGE

*The honeymoon couple, September 8, 1951.*
PHOTO BY BACHRACH, COURTESY OF THE ESTATE OF LEONARD BERNSTEIN

*Good or bad, the thing has been simmering for so long*
*a time I am relieved.*

> —MARC BLITZSTEIN, following the
> announcement of Leonard Bernstein's
> second engagement to Felicia
> Montealegre

BACK in January, Bernstein and his sister had returned from Europe by ocean liner. When their ship docked in New York, Felicia was waiting at the pierside and they all went off for a drink, without pausing to unpack their bags. After a while Felicia called her service to collect her messages and learned that her lover, Dick Hart, had collapsed in a coma. He died in her arms in a hospital waiting room the same day. The obituary in *Variety,* published eight days later, reported that Hart's death came "after suffering a heart attack." But around New York's theater and television world there was talk of suicide. He suffered from acute cirrhosis of the liver and he had ignored doctor's orders to stop drinking. As Burton Bernstein remembers it, Hart was found collapsed and unconscious in a Third Avenue bar. Earlier, while living with Hart, Felicia had written to Bernstein: "Lenny dear, wait till you fall in love, deeply wonderfully in love, before you get married. Anything else is second best and you'll be cheating yourself and someone else." But the humiliating reality of her relationship with Hart was that as the "other woman" in his life, she could not even attend his funeral. Her Chilean sisters were never told of her relationship with him. With Hart dead, her affections swung back to Bernstein.

Prompted by his sister, Leonard helped Felicia through her first days of mourning and saw her in New York whenever he was home from his Israel Philharmonic tour. When he moved to Mexico for his "sabbatical" year of composing Felicia went bravely off to Europe on her own. "When are you going to decide to take care of me?" she wrote from Paris in April. "This futsing around is ludicrous and unbecoming to people your age. Do grow up my darling. Life is so unbearably short and I am so tired. It is a shame that our last few days in N.Y. were so strained and full of tension. You must understand that mine [tension] was not solely due to you—I too am going through my private 'whatsis'—it distressed me to find I could not lean on you for support. Knowing that you love me (in your own peculiar way, I grant you) I cannot understand why it is you don't accept and even enjoy the responsibilities that loving entails. But that is more of that same bloody talk—it does get monotonous, doesn't it? I wish we could stop discussing things and start *doing* them!"

In Paris Felicia got to know Bernstein's friend Rosamond Bernier. Felicia told her that she had made up her mind to marry Bernstein. A few weeks later, over dinner in Florence, she told Oliver Smith as well. But she mentioned nothing about her intentions to Bernstein when next she wrote. In fact, she was at pains to prove her independence. "I know now that I no longer 'need' a someone to relate to—the mere fact of living is exciting enough and I want to work not because there is nothing else to do but because I love it and I feel it is important. . . . I think that you'd be pleased at the way I look. I must have gained ten pounds and can hardly fit in my clothes. Very sexy!" She was even more cool and self-possessed in subsequent letters: "I think of you a lot but somehow in a different way now. The string must have snapped somewhere along the way, perhaps in Florence. I don't belong to any place or to anyone and yet I'm not afraid or lost—maybe I'll be a good actress, maybe not, it doesn't matter. I feel a great urge to live, the 'how' is not important. Boss darling, write me again soon. . . . I would like to meet Martha [Gellhorn]—give her my love. Don't get bored too soon."

No matter how endearingly Felicia expressed herself, Leonard remained in Mexico, consumed by the composition of *Trouble in Tahiti* and apparently impervious to her appeals, despite the warmth of his own feeling a year previously. "Who knows when we shall meet again?" Felicia wrote forlornly. When fate intervened, it was in the form of a phone call from Olga Koussevitzky, with the news he had been dreading. Koussevitzky had become too ill to manage Tanglewood alone; worse, he seemed on the brink of death. Twenty-four hours later Bernstein was in Boston, at Koussevitzky's bedside. The two musicians, master and disciple, spiritual father and devoted son, talked long into the evening about music, life and love. The following morning Koussevitzky died.

A double service, Russian Orthodox and American Episcopal, was held in Boston and next day a second service took place a hundred miles west in

Lenox's Church of the Hill. Koussevitzky had prudently reserved for himself the last plot in the Lenox cemetery, in the shade of a large red maple tree on a velvety green southward slope, the nearest consecrated ground to Tanglewood. With Bernstein standing in respectful attendance behind her, Olga Koussevitzky threw down onto the coffin a handful of the Berkshire earth her husband had come to love so much.

There was little time for sadness and reflection. Tanglewood's summer season was due to start in less than a month. Charles Munch, the Boston Symphony Orchestra's music director, was away conducting in Europe. The center's deputy director, Aaron Copland, was living in Rome, at the American Academy. Despite his unfinished opera, Bernstein felt he had no choice but to assume Koussevitzky's duties as head of the conducting school. At the opening exercises on July 1 Bernstein evoked for a new generation of students the spirit of Serge Alexandrovich. "We ate and drank and dreamed music," he told them, "always under the aegis of a standard that knew no compromise, that tolerated no mediocrity."

Felicia returned from Europe in July, determined to force a decision from Leonard regarding their relationship. Finding nobody to greet her when her ship docked in New York, she left her trunk at Shirley Bernstein's, and took the train to Lenox to join Bernstein at Tanglewood. Shirley, who'd missed Felicia at the pier and again at her apartment, sensed that a moment of high drama in her brother's life was about to be played out. She borrowed a car and drove north in hot pursuit. She had no cash, and had to leave her wristwatch at a gas station to buy fuel for the final miles to Bernstein's rented cottage on the grounds of the Blantyre Hotel in Lenox. "Where were you?" both Felicia and Leonard asked her when she stepped in the door. Soon, as Shirley put it in her biography, "the whole thing had become funny and calm was restored. By the end of the weekend, Lenny and Felicia had decided to get married."

But Bernstein was still not completely resolved about their relationship, despite the second engagement. He continued to question whether Felicia was the right person for him. His brother Burton remembered a protracted decision-making process. "Lenny and I were roommates [that summer], so we'd have long talks at night and I just kept working on him. I'd say, 'Well you know, you're not going to find anyone better. You know each other so well and you love each other. That's it!' So finally he said, 'Okay.' "

Felicia herself later told a journalist that she and Leonard proposed several times to each other; the clincher, as she called it, had been made by Bernstein over dinner at the Blacksmiths Arms in Millbrook, New York, on another trip up to Tanglewood.

The news of their engagement was broken by Olga Koussevitzky at the annual Seranak party after the final afternoon Tanglewood concert on August 12. Less than four weeks later the couple solemnized their union. "Engagements are horrible things," Bernstein later told a reporter, no doubt with some

*Jennie and Samuel Bernstein with their four-year-old son. Their breakfast-time quarrels inspired the opening scene of* Trouble in Tahiti.
COURTESY OF THE ESTATE OF LEONARD BERNSTEIN

*Father and son on a hike in New Hampshire.*
COURTESY OF THE ESTATE OF LEONARD BERNSTEIN

*Graduation photo from Boston Latin School, 1935.* COURTESY OF THE ESTATE OF LEONARD BERNSTEIN

*Bernstein's childhood friend and first pupil in music theory, Sid "Syd" Ramin became a lifelong collaborator.*
COURTESY OF THE ESTATE OF LEONARD BERNSTEIN

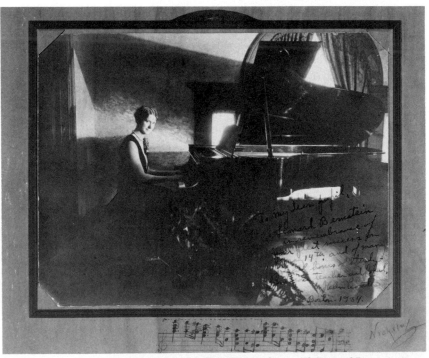

*Helen Coates in her studio. The inscription begins: "To my dear pupil, Leonard Bernstein, in remembrance of your great success on May 14th." Underneath, Bernstein added the opening bars of the Grieg piano concerto which he played at his debut concert. Boston, 1934.*
COURTESY OF THE ESTATE OF LEONARD BERNSTEIN

*Beatrice Gordon. In 1934, she played Don José to Leonard's Carmen.*
COURTESY OF THE ESTATE OF LEONARD BERNSTEIN

*Dimitri Mitropoulos, 1937. "You have everything to make you great."*
COURTESY OF THE ESTATE OF LEONARD BERNSTEIN

*Camp Onota Rhythm Band, 1937. The first photograph of Leonard Bernstein the conductor. As camp music counselor, "Uncle Len" directed* The Pirates of Penzance.
COURTESY OF THE ESTATE OF LEONARD BERNSTEIN

For HELEN
La commencement
de "L'Histoire
d'un élève"
with much love
Lenny
aug. 19

*Tanglewood tea party. "Lenushka" conducts an informal performance of* L'Histoire d'un élève *at the end of the first year's summer course. Koussevitzky and his wife Natalie look down from the balcony.*
COURTESY OF THE ESTATE OF LEONARD BERNSTEIN

*Shirley Anne Bernstein in 1940. A year previously, Shirley had sung the Moll in Marc Blitzstein's* The Cradle Will Rock.

*Rittenhouse Square, near the Curtis Institute, 1941. Renée Longy Miquelle (left) taught Bernstein score-reading, among other things; his friend Shirley Gabis (right) played duets with Lenny and listened to him reading Oscar Wilde.*

*An early photo printed for fans requesting an autograph.*

December 5, 1941

## ◦LEONARD BERNSTEIN

*Announces the opening of his studio for the teaching of* . . . .

### PIANO and MUSICAL ANALYSIS

**295 HUNTINGTON AVE., BOSTON**

Room 403                    Gainsboro Building

KENmore 4364

*Open for business—two days before Pearl Harbor.*

*Jennie Tourel, who sang* I Hate Music, *Bernstein's first song cycle, as an encore at her recital in Lenox on Bernstein's twenty-fifth birthday, 1943.*
COURTESY OF THE ESTATE OF LEONARD BERNSTEIN

*With Artur Rodzinski, musical director of the New York Philharmonic, August 1943. Rodzinski conducted with a loaded revolver in his back pocket. He claimed that God told him to hire Bernstein.*
COURTESY OF THE ESTATE OF LEONARD BERNSTEIN

*Fritz Reiner, the Hungarian-born conductor of the Pittsburgh Symphony, who taught Bernstein for two years and gave him his breakthrough as a composer, inviting him to conduct the premiere of his first symphony in January 1944.*
COURTESY OF THE ESTATE OF LEONARD BERNSTEIN

*The great conductor Serge Alexandrovich Koussevitzky. He was sixty-five when he started to teach at Tanglewood; Bernstein was his first pupil.*
COURTESY OF THE ESTATE OF LEONARD BERNSTEIN

*With Aaron Copland, 1945. Their friendship, stretching over fifty years, is one of the most remarkable in the annals of music. Copland saw in Bernstein the genuinely "Amurikan" conductor that he and his fellow composers needed to champion their music.*
COURTESY OF THE ESTATE OF LEONARD BERNSTEIN

*"Here is a conductor," wrote Olin Downes of the* New York Times. *Bernstein rehearses in the famous Studio 8H with Toscanini's renowned NBC Symphony Orchestra.*
PHOTO JEAN DALRYMPLE,
COURTESY OF THE ESTATE OF LEONARD BERNSTEIN

*With Shirley Bernstein and Marc Blitzstein on the lawn at Tanglewood. Blitzstein exerted a powerful influence on Bernstein in his twenties: his music "…seduced my soul."* PHOTO © RUTH ORKIN

On the Town, *1944. Betty Comden as Claire de Loone and Adolph Green as Ozzie at the Museum of Natural History.* MUSEUM OF THE CITY OF NEW YORK, THE THEATER COLLECTION

*...ollywood, 1944. Bernstein's portable typewriter was ... constant companion.*

*America's favorite guest conductor with Helen Coates in 1946.*

*...Vith Igor Stravinsky at a New York City Symphony concert, 1946. ...oncertmaster Werner Lywen is on the left. To the right of Bernstein ...e his manager Bruno Zirato; Robert Shaw, the chorus master; and ...eo Smit, the pianist and composer.*

*The composer at home on West Tenth Street in 1947. He used pen and ink for personal letter writing and fine-copies of his scores.*

*Felicia Montealegre Cohn as a child; Bernstein's future wife, great granddaughter of a rabbi, was brought up a Catholic in Santiago, Chile. Elegant and rebellious, the essential Felicia was already visible.*
COURTESY OF THE ESTATE OF LEONARD BERNSTEIN

*Felicia: the young screen actress hoping for movie stardom. "Just love and kisses from me," she wrote.*
COURTESY OF THE ESTATE OF LEONARD BERNSTEIN

*Engagement photograph. New Year's Eve, 1946.*
COURTESY OF THE ESTATE OF LEONARD BERNSTEIN

*At Tanglewood, 1947. "You're still not sure I'm the right one for you," Felicia wrote later to Leonard. Soon after this picture was taken, the gossip columnist Dorothy Kilgallen reported the cancellation of their marriage plans.* PHOTO © RUTH ORKIN

*The impromptu concert at Beersheba, November 1948, during the Israeli War of Independence.*
COURTESY OF THE ESTATE OF LEONARD BERNSTEIN

*Home on the range—Bernstein's 1949 New Year greeting card. Leonard and his brother Burton worked at a cattle ranch in Wyoming in September 1948.*
PHOTO BURTON BERNSTEIN, COURTESY OF THE ESTATE OF LEONARD BERNSTEIN

*Alone again. Bernstein made late night raids on the refrigerator all his life.*

PHOTO BEN GREENHAUS, COURTESY OF THE ESTATE OF LEONARD BERNSTEIN

*The "Koussevitzky Blues." With Seymour Lipkin at the piano, Bernstein celebrated his mentor's seventy-fourth birthday in 1948.*
PHOTO © RUTH ORKIN

*The writer Martha Gellhorn. Bernstein sometimes joked (even in front of Felicia) that he ought to have married Martha, who was ten years his senior.*
COURTESY OF THE FRANKLIN
DELANO ROOSEVELT LIBRARY

*Shirley and Leonard coming home from Europe and Israel, January 1951.*
COURTESY OF SHIRLEY BERNSTEIN

*Felicia's mother, Clemencia, and Bernstein's parents.
The bridegroom is wearing a suit presented to him by
Koussevitzky's widow, Olga.*

*The jacket had also belonged to
Koussevitzky.*

*The bride with the "dribbling siblings," Leonard,
Shirley and Burton.*

*Farewell to the best man, David Oppenheim.
Helen Coates keeps a stiff upper lip.*

*In Jerusalem, 1953, with Felicia. "Lenny is their God, his name is magic everywhere."*
COURTESY OF THE ESTATE OF LEONARD BERNSTEIN

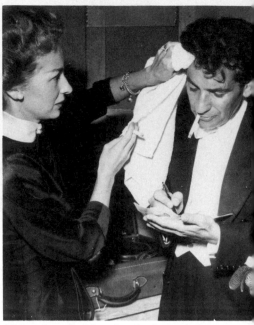

*The conductor's wife tends to her husband after a concert.* COURTESY OF THE ESTATE OF LEONARD BERNSTEIN

Wonderful Town, *1953, starring Rosalind Russell. Comden and Green, Bernstein's collaborators, shared with him an unabashed affection for the thirties.* MUSEUM OF THE CITY OF NEW YORK, THE THEATER COLLECTION

*Bernstein made his opera house debut at La Scala, Milan, in December 1953. Maria Callas is on the left, while Felicia and Leonard are accompanied by Contessa Emanuela Castelbarco, Toscanini's granddaughter (right).*

*Bernstein's television debut on "Omnibus," November 14, 1954. Members of the Symphony of the Air indicate Beethoven's orchestration changes as Bernstein lectures on the Fifth Symphony and what is to be learned from the composer's sketchbooks.*

*Jamie's third birthday party, 1955.*

*Lillian Hellman with Jamie at
Martha's Vineyard, 1954.*

*Felicia cut her husband's hair
for many years.*

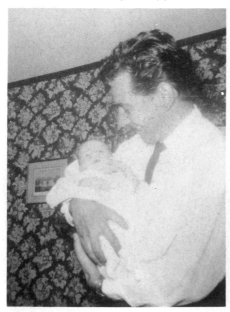

*Alexander Serge Leonard was born in
July, 1955.*

*The Bernstein family always celebrated Christmas.*

feeling, remembering his and Felicia's previous engagement in 1947, "so we just got married."

The decision to marry cannot have been as easy as that. Felicia had learned a lot about herself in the five years since she and Leonard had first met, and she knew that marriage would inevitably involve a major readjustment in her life. Over those years she had risen from bit parts to television stardom. Although she intended to resume her television work after their honeymoon, and still had hopes of becoming a movie star, she must have seen that marriage to a man who led such a public life, who created for himself—and required—so much attention, would necessarily jeopardize her career. Perhaps she believed that becoming Leonard Bernstein's wife and having a family with him would offer as high a fulfillment as her acting career.

However, the idea that she wanted to marry Bernstein because he represented the entrée to the glamorous milieu of the celebrity conductor can be discounted. She knew him to be a towering talent (she had often sat in on his New York City Symphony rehearsals) but she was also aware that he had renounced conducting for the life of a composer working not on Broadway but in the risky field of American opera. Fame was certainly not the spur; indeed she could claim to be better known than he was. Her performance as Nora in Ibsen's *A Doll's House* had been seen by millions of American television viewers.

Did Felicia marry Bernstein knowing that he was bisexual? The answer must be that she knew about his past but she thought she could change him, since he had never been exclusively homosexual. It was true that many of his love affairs had been with men, but he had loved women, too, and he felt strongly attracted to Felicia. She evidently felt that she could cope with what Bernstein had described to Shirley Gabis as his "dark side," mostly by ignoring it, although Bernstein frequently referred in his correspondence to his special difficulties in the first months of the marriage. For all his sophistication, Bernstein was also an old-fashioned family man who desired to please his own parents and obey the Hebrew scriptures by going forth and multiplying. He trembled uncontrollably at the marriage ceremony, but he went through with it: it was one of the most difficult and important decisions in his life.

Felicia was so determined to marry Leonard that she embraced the Jewish faith before the wedding, upsetting her mother but placating Sam and Jennie Bernstein. Felicia was half-Jewish, after all, and according to Burton Bernstein, half her humor was Jewish, too. "She had more Yiddishisms than almost anybody else. Her beloved little dog, which she had acquired in 1947, was named Nebbish. She was the only non-born, non-genetic Bernstein who could really speak Rybernian."

Before the wedding, the Bernstein brothers spent a week in Cuba together as Leonard's last bachelor fling. One of the people they met, Burton remembered, was a Jewish refugee from Europe who had become a Cuban citizen. "[He] did quite well making pastry for the rich. When we came back everybody wanted to know what happened to us and we said, 'Well, we met this man named Andy. He was a pastry-maker and he was a Jewish refugee.' It had no punch-line. It was like a Leonard Lyons story. You had to be there to see the interest in it. So Shirley and Felicia said, 'Do you have any more pastry-maker stories?' Any dull, interminable travel story became known as a 'pastry-maker.' So now everybody says, 'Have I got pastry-makers from my last trip!' "

Driving back north to prepare for the wedding, the two brothers stopped for the night at Virginia Beach. They had decided on a very grand, very WASP hotel which they feared might bar Jews. "We were very nervous about it," Burton recalls, "even though it was Leonard Bernstein, so to speak, so we decided to compromise: we would call from the phone booth outside of the town and just give our names—why be humiliated in the lobby, right? So both of us crammed into a phone booth and Lenny got his best Harvard accent going, rather grand, and he says, 'Hello, I'm coming down your way,'—we were about half a mile away—'and we thought we'd like to spend a day or two playing tennis. Is there any accommodation available?' The clerk said, 'Yes sir, we have a room.' 'My brother and I will be there.' 'And your name?' And I heard Lenny saying this, and I never let him forget it: 'This is Leonard Bernstein. Of Boston.' . . . as if that somehow made it all right. Not Leonard Bernstein the famous conductor, but Leonard Bernstein of Boston."

The wedding eve was passed in a state of near hysteria. "Everybody was on edge," Burton remembers. "Lenny was so nervous. Felicia was coming to dinner. My parents were sort of half-thrilled that she was half-Jewish. Shirley and I realized that it was going to be a nightmare dinner. So we went into Boston and went shopping at a place called 'Daddy & Jacks,' the premier joke shop of the U.S.A. We bought out the store and set up the dinner table with gadgets: the plate lifters, the dribble glass, the rubber cockroach, the ants, the vomit thing, the itching powder, the matches that exploded into a million sparks. All the cigarettes were booby-trapped. . . . Just when they thought it was over there'd be this spider crawling on the table cloth. . . . It got to be an hysterical joke. We were all exhausted from laughing but we got through the evening. We often thought the wedding took place merely because of that evening."

Felicia and Leonard were married at the Parthenon-like Temple Mishkan Tefila on September 9. Bernstein wore a splendid white suit bequeathed to him by Serge Koussevitzky. It was exquisitely tailored but made him look a touch ridiculous, since the trousers were several inches too long and Koussevitzky's shoes, part of the package, were crampingly tight. When the official wedding photograph had been taken in his parents' garden—Leonard looking dashingly handsome in the sunshine, his bride radiant in a short white dress and carrying yellow roses—he quickly changed into casual trousers and a striped sports jacket that had also been Koussevitzky's. He had lent his father three thousand dollars to pay for the reception. A fountain in the front hall of the Bernstein residence in Brookline flowed with pink champagne, but no amount of alcohol could entirely defrost the social and religious barriers between Felicia's family of aristocratic Catholics, led by her mother, Clemencia, and the Bernstein clan of Ukrainian Jews, joined for the day by Leonard's forbidding paternal grandmother, Dinah, who after a decade in America still spoke no English. Burton Bernstein and David Oppenheim were best men.

Love conquers all, as Bernstein used to say after two or three rehearsals with a hostile orchestra, and late in the afternoon the newlyweds set off in his convertible for their honeymoon. Their eventual destination was Cuernavaca, where Bernstein planned to resume his sabbatical year, but they got lost driving out of Boston and spent their first wedded night at the seaside resort of Gloucester, where Felicia had once acted in summer stock. On the second day they stopped at Schenectady, New York. "I miss you something awful," Leonard wrote to his brother; "we both do—and every once in a while wish you were along. But better this way. It gets better all the time—I think we'll make it. We are heading for Detroit and the Marcuses. My functions have stopped—eating, sex, thought—but they are slowly returning and normalcy is in sight. F. is a great human being."

A week later, from the Remount Ranch in Cheyenne, Wyoming, Bernstein wrote to Helen Coates. "We are truly happy on this fabulous ranch where we are the only guests and are living like royalty. . . . I don't know how to thank you for all your help with this wedding; especially your sweetness to Felicia and your spirit of joy and willingness to cooperate and facilitate. You are a real joy to me." The letter was dated September 16; underneath Bernstein typed "first anniversary!" It was the date on which, a year before, Miss Coates had been reinstated as Bernstein's secretary.

On the way to Mexico Leonard gave Felicia lessons in English grammar. The trip took five weeks, including a stop-off with Felicia's family in California, and Felicia found it excruciating. Every day they would climb back into the car and Leonard would begin, "So you remember in yesterday's lesson . . ." From California they retraced the tour route of the Israel Philharmonic—Phoenix, Tucson, El Paso—and saw the friends Leonard had recently made. The odyssey must have given them confidence about sharing their lives together. If two fastidious people could survive five weeks of living out of suitcases and five thousand miles of driving, they could probably survive anything. There had apparently been a "crisis" early in the trip, at the Detroit home of Philip and Barbara Marcuse, who had been friends since Bernstein's earliest engagements with the Detroit Symphony. "The tensions (do you recall this word?) accumulate still, are fought, lived through," Bernstein told the Marcuses soon after his arrival in Cuernavaca. "Every once in a while a state of comparative ease is reached which promises well for the future. . . . I am not quite sure what F. is going to do all winter while I am at the piano and in my own world, so to speak. But most of that, of course, depends on what security she will manage to feel in a marriage contracted in insecurity. We hope and pray and we wait."

Martha Gellhorn helped them to find a new place in Cuernavaca about fifteen minutes' walk from her own. The decor was "tourist Mex," wooden furniture painted with flowers, but the garden was pretty. Their plan was to spend the fall and winter in Mexico and return to New York late in the spring. Bernstein turned down all conducting offers in the meantime. "I am not committing myself to anything . . . until I see what sort of composer I turn out to be."

To Copland he wrote of his composing plans. "I have written an extra aria for Captain Hook [for a touring production of *Peter Pan*] . . . and am now starting on the long hard road of writing some real things. I have decided, *coute que coute,* to finish my little opry [*Trouble in Tahiti*] and then write a few more little opries. [He had in mind a trilogy like the Puccini *Trittico,* to make a full theatrical evening.] There may be some stray notes—like even a piano sonata and a new idea for an orchestra piece, but the main stem is still that old devil theatre, and I just have to see what my connection with it is." Referring to Copland's friend Victor Kraft, who had also just got married, he asked, "Does he find marriage as fascinating as I do? . . . It is the most interesting thing I have ever done, though there are times when one's interest must be that of a person in an audience, or one would go mad. It is full of compensations—and rewards and reveals more to me about myself than anything else ever has, including a spotty array of analysts."

Martha Gellhorn remembered that Bernstein was nervous and confused at times about being married, as was Felicia about being married to him. "She was very in awe of him, I think, at that point. Anxious but unable to know how to please him. He was feeling . . . trapped." Gellhorn and Bernstein would occasionally play tennis together, giggling as they coped with a much-cratered tennis court. Other days Martha went for a walk with Felicia. She saw herself as a kind of nanny to the "troubled pair"; their marital unease was almost comic. Bernstein related to Gellhorn the trauma of Dick Hart's death, and the terrible ordeal it had been for Felicia; Gellhorn had the impression that he felt he was in a way rescuing Felicia, but that Felicia loved him for very straightforward feminine reasons—not because he was rescuing her any more than most women are "rescued" by marriage. He was the one having the major problem and "Feli" had to cope.

To the outside world Felicia presented a contented face. "She is a busy housewife," reported Bernstein to Helen Coates, "busier than one could imagine, running the house and buying things and instructing the servants." " 'Things' are going rather well," Felicia later wrote to Helen, "and in spite of the more than expected off moments, we stand a good chance of having a wonderful marriage. It takes patience and love, and I seem to have plenty of both. It is difficult for Lenny of course to have given up the mad, hectic and glamorous life and gotten married to boot. Marriage is bound to take the blame for much that he must be missing . . . however it's all possible to cope with."

For the first month of their stay Bernstein was optimistic about his compos-ing work. "The days whizz by. . . . *Trouble in Tahiti* is practically finished," he wrote to Helen Coates in October. And by mid-November, he had started on a piano sonata, "probably in defense against actually FINISHING the little opera." But a month later the opera was still not finished. He wrote to Burton, "Maybe you can tell me how to finish my fucking little opera." By late January his mood was even blacker. "About my opera: I have abandoned it, decisively. It just will not come. . . . Something seems to have happened to the creative flow."

What had dried up his creative juices since the optimism of the fall? Felicia had done her best to provide good working conditions, but finishing a work was rarely easy for Bernstein, and in Mexico he seems to have suffered from the *mañana* syndrome. "Nothing ever went slowly before," he wrote to Phil Mar-cuse; "now everything goes slowly. We have long chess games with each other, we take hours to eat, we sleep late, I compose very slowly and then throw it away, we make our adjustments slowly . . . slow, slow, nice days. Nothing may ever come of it except perhaps a better digestion, but it is well worth it. F. is an angel and I love her."

The two spent their evenings mostly with Martha Gellhorn and Flavia, an Italian countess who was staying with her: "We invite each other to dinner," Felicia told Helen, "and dress up in our swankiest clothes and feel very gay and festive." They also explored Mexico by car for a week in November, attending the Night of the Dead on the island of Janitzio in Lake Pátzcuaro and spending two days of shopping and sight-seeing in Mexico City.

A few days later Bernstein went back on his own to the capital, where he ran into the young pianist "Sigi" Weissenberg at a party. "L. looked marvelous, though sad," Weissenberg wrote to his friend Helen Coates, "and was for the first time I can remember completely natural with me and sincerely affection-ate. . . . We made an appointment for the same night at 11 P.M. I also saw him yesterday all afternoon and evening . . . and by the time I left . . . I was ready to cry. Helen, Helen, I don't know how long it will last, alas! Oh yes, he spoke wonders about F., but said he had to come to town alone, he had to have the 'make the town' satisfied, on the other hand he could not lie to her, he loved her so, yet, he didn't quite know why they married, he guessed it had pulled along so far over the years that they both got tired of the game and decided to get married. Yet, was a marriage by calculation right? Then again he spoke about Martha Gellhorn, if she were only ten years younger [she was forty] they could have been such a perfect team, she had the brains, the vitality, they were just the right team, why did he have to speak to her so often alone etc. etc. And all that time, praising F. to the Heavens. Of course I hadn't asked any questions and that made me feel even worse, because he spoke not out of necessity to answer but out of necessity to confess. . . . I insisted that we don't but he just had to go to the bars and oh Helen—what bars! and with each place he felt worse. . . . I was a wreck by the time I left. But I am sure it was just a curiosity moment with him, nothing else. Because all the rest said about F. couldn't have been more wonderful."

In December the newlyweds faced a new hazard: a family invasion. First they were visited by Burton during his winter break from Dartmouth. Later both Felicia's parents and Leonard's parents came to stay. "The apes [folks] are here in force, all four of them," Leonard reported in a letter for Burton's twentieth birthday at the end of January 1952. "The Cohns have just left, though, and we are now painfully restricted to our apes who are as incredible as always. You would have enjoyed last night's discussion of the J.[ewish] Problem between Daddy and Flavia. That was one for the books. And every few minutes punctuated by one of Mama's staggering generalizations apropos of nothing at all."

After three months in Cuernavaca the honeymoon was brought to a premature end. Felicia was invited to appear in a television play in mid-February and Leonard received an SOS cable from the Boston Symphony Orchestra asking him to stand in for the ailing Charles Munch for three weeks in February and March. It was worth five thousand dollars, with another thousand in expenses to get them home from Mexico, and there would be a chance for Bernstein to perform a new Mozart concerto (K. 271) that he had been studying. The deciding factor, however, made it seem as if fate were again directing the proceedings. "WE ARE PREGNANT," Bernstein informed Helen Coates triumphantly. "We have just had the confirmation and we are positively dancing with excitement. I'm sure my parents will dance likewise. Felicia is aglow with happiness."

# PART THREE

*With Felicia and Jamie, 1953: "Family picture, second to none, / In the little white house . . ."* —Trouble in Tahiti, *Scene 4*

# 1952—1957

# SOMETHING'S COMING—THE COMPOSING YEARS

# RETURN TO SHOW BUSINESS

*Bernstein at Lewisohn Stadium,*
*New York City, 1953.*
PHOTO I. W. SCHMIDT, COURTESY OF THE ESTATE OF
LEONARD BERNSTEIN

*BROADWAY BARRAGE OF B.O. BONANZAS REVERSES*
*TREND OF PAST SEASON.*

*—Variety,* March 1953

FELICIA Montealegre had written to Leonard five years earlier from California: "Please let's get married some day and I can bear you a masterpiece of a child." The impending prospect of parenthood finally seemed to sweep away Leonard's secret doubts about the wisdom of the marriage. Felicia flew back to New York in early February to perform in *Crown of Shadows* and *The Wings of the Dove* on television. Meanwhile Bernstein, longing for some time to himself after the family invasions, took a slow boat home from Tampico.

The previous summer he had accepted an invitation to become the visiting music professor at the new nonsectarian Brandeis University at Waltham, outside Boston. His annual salary was nine thousand dollars. His first task was to direct an ambitious Festival of Creative Arts in June 1952, and he was persuaded by the composer Irving Fine, his colleague at Brandeis, to finish *Trouble in Tahiti* in time for it. After his three weeks' stint with the Boston Symphony

Orchestra, Bernstein made his way to Yaddo, the artists' colony outside Saratoga, New York, to compose. He took over the cabin where Marc Blitzstein had been working on his new opera, *Reuben Reuben,* and did not reemerge until his own opera was ready for production, fully orchestrated. "It's hard on Felicia, but necessary," he wrote to Fine, "and maybe it's less hard than having me around all the time. By the way, we are doing awfully well, for us, and have every reason to hope for a lovely future." The five-week separation cannot have been easy for Felicia, her work in New York finished and halfway through her first pregnancy, but she knew how important it was for Bernstein to deliver his musical child on time.

The Brandeis festival ran for four days, from June 12 to June 15, 1952. Its aim, Bernstein wrote, was to seek a key to the future by examining the creative arts. *Trouble in Tahiti* was part of the inquiry. It was performed on the first night, following an overlong symposium on the state of the arts in America, moderated by Bernstein. The three thousand strong audience was reportedly in "a grave state of impatient fidgets" by 11 P.M. when the curtain went up. Faced with copy deadlines, few of the journalists could stay for the performance. One who did complained that "the technical direction and lighting were hampered by the newness of the stage." (Workmen were still banging away at the dress rehearsal.) The amplification system of the open-air theater was poor and there were unwelcome noises from the wind in the trees and nearby railway tracks. *Time* magazine added "librettist, lecturer and festivalist" to the list of Bernstein's attainments, but complained of a disjointed effect in *Tahiti* and said the drama was "a little too real to be funny." Bernstein expressed his frustration in a letter to Irving Fine: "I don't know whether to thank or curse you for making me finish *Tahiti* in time for the Festival; it turned out half-baked and it's a shame, since it's so hard to go back and re-do something which already boasts a double bar."

Bernstein had no time for postmortems during the festival. The next afternoon he presided over a remarkable jazz session organized by his friend John Mehegan. The program included a heated discussion on the relative merits of the new "bop" and traditional Dixieland, followed by two groups with radically different styles improvising on the same standard melodies. Performers included Miles Davis, Percy Heath, Lee Konick, John Lewis and Max Roach. Bernstein said that Charlie Mingus's string bass solo was "the most thrilling musical experience in years." There were also poetry readings, literary conferences, art exhibitions and documentary film screenings, all part of Bernstein's exploration of the contemporary scene, which was being undertaken at the height of Senator Joseph McCarthy's baleful influence. Lillian Hellman's brave defiance of the House Un-American Activities Committee (or HUAC) had occurred three weeks earlier.

The HUAC witch-hunt invested the second evening of theatrical entertainment with unusual topicality. Marc Blitzstein narrated the first performance of his American translation of Kurt Weill's *The Threepenny Opera.* The text was by the playwright Bertolt Brecht, who had insolently denied being a Communist party member when he was arraigned by the HUAC in 1948 but had left the next day for East Germany. Blitzstein's lyrics, including "Mack the Knife," caught Brecht's rasping tone to perfection. With Lotte Lenya in the cast at Brandeis, and Bernstein conducting, the show was a triumph. In the first half of the same program, Merce Cunningham danced to the fashionable *musique concrète* sound track of *Symphonie pour un Homme Seul* by Pierre Schaeffer and Pierre Henry, and provided choreography for Stravinsky's *Les Noces,* a Boston-area premiere.

"Is this a possible time for the arts?" the critic Elliot Norton had asked earlier in the week. In the shadow of the hydrogen bomb—the first testing at the Eniwetok atoll took place four months later—Bernstein's festival came up with positive answers even if some of the key works dated from the 1920s. At the final event, he conducted a vigorous program of contemporary music for string orchestra, dedicated to the memory of Serge Koussevitzky. Aaron Copland introduced each work to the audience of five thousand at the outdoor auditorium. The program included William Schuman's *Symphony for Strings,* the *Nocturne* by Irving Fine, a new piece by Ben Weber and Britten's *Serenade for Tenor and Horn.* The concert concluded with David Oppenheim performing Copland's 1950 clarinet concerto. The festival's launch was pronounced a clear success in the press. Bernstein had given Brandeis University a national profile.

FOLLOWING the festival, Bernstein was determined to take another year off for composing. He planned to spend one day a week teaching at Brandeis but otherwise there was to be "no conducting, no concerts, nothing." But first he had to fulfill his obligation to Tanglewood, where he was again in charge of the conducting school, with Lorin Maazel the outstanding student that year, as he had been in 1951. His main concern, however, was "to erase the awful memory" of the *Trouble in Tahiti* premiere. He rewrote the final scene, and *Trouble in Tahiti* was performed twice that summer at Tanglewood's Music Theater. Seymour Lipkin conducted and Sarah Caldwell was the stage director. Caldwell was disconcerted by Bernstein's lack of conviction about his own work. He and his wife would attend a run-through of a scene at the end of the morning's rehearsal and give notes. In the afternoon they would return with friends who contradicted their first opinion. "It didn't make much difference who they were," Caldwell recalls, "it seemed to me that everybody had a vote and it made it difficult to work."

Caldwell put a stop to this production by committee, and the Tanglewood performances were well received by the public, if not the critics: Olin Downes in the *Times* complained of unconvincing characters and a lack of dramatic motivation. Bernstein wrote to his Detroit friends, the Marcuses, who had attended the premiere at Brandeis: "Tahiti was 200% better at Tanglewood. It's a real work now, all revised and pretty: but we still can't get the critics to take it seriously. Tant pis, yawn, and I really wish they would, if only for poor old Schirmer's sake." But the publisher had already negotiated a telecast for the fall.

On August 25 the Bernsteins moved into a rambling fourth-floor apartment in the Osborne, the second-oldest luxury family apartment building in Manhattan, with one of the grandest entrance halls in the entire city, standing diagonally across the street from Carnegie Hall. Two weeks after the move, on September 8, Felicia gave birth at Doctors Hospital to a daughter weighing seven pounds and three ounces. Marc Blitzstein, who was to be a godfather, wanted the girl to be called Nina, after the heroine of the opera he was writing. The Bernsteins agreed at first, but by the next morning Leonard had changed his mind. Since Blitzstein's opera was not yet finished he felt it would be unlucky to take the name Nina. So the baby was christened Jamie Anne Maria. "Jamie is a raving beauty—fearless and healthy," Bernstein wrote to Irving Fine.

Six weeks after Jamie's birth, Felicia went back to work, performing in a televised play in October, and two more in December. And Bernstein himself had his first experience in a television studio since the experimental prewar telecasts of the Revuers. At 3 P.M. on a Sunday afternoon, November 16, he conducted a live television broadcast of his opera.

Bernstein misleadingly described *Trouble in Tahiti* as a "light-weight piece . . . popular song inspired," with roots, he said, in American musical comedy, "or even better the American Musical Theater." Only the last part of this statement is wholly accurate. In its violent juxtaposition of moods *Tahiti* is more like a Mahler symphony than a musical comedy. Its sustained and poignant lyricism, in both solo arias and duets, its savage Strindbergian portrait of a marriage on the rocks, and its satirical lyrics intoned by a vocal trio functioning as Greek chorus, all place *Tahiti* in a different world from the popular song forms Bernstein claimed to be at the heart of his score.

The opera lasts just under forty-five minutes. It depicts a day in the deteriorating married life of a young American couple, Sam and Dinah, who live in a typical American suburb. He is a successful businessman who commutes downtown each morning. She is a housewife with time on her hands. They have a son, Junior, whom they neglect shamefully; he does not appear in the opera. There are no other dramatic roles, although a business colleague and a secretary are both addressed by Sam, and Dinah talks to an unseen analyst and a shop assistant. The theme of the opera is timeless: the death of love. "Years have passed and what has happened to dull our mystery?" asks Sam of his wife; "can't we find the way back?"

The first scene plunges us into domestic drama: Sam and Dinah bickering at breakfast with lyrical asides as each one pleads for understanding. The second and third scenes alternate between Sam at the office, pompous, self-satisfied, and occasionally brutal, and Dinah on her psychiatrist's couch describing her troubled dream of a quiet place where "love will teach us harmony and grace." In scene four, Sam and Dinah meet by accident in the city at lunchtime;

in the end they go to their separate appointments, and yet the music tells us how deep is their yearning for each other. "We like the same movies, the same parties, we have our little child; what makes this emptiness?" The central duet in *Tahiti* comes very close to achieving what Bernstein had been talking about for four years: something simple yet serious and wholly American, something everybody would understand.

Part two begins promisingly with a second helping of the trio's sardonic evocation of American suburbia. The two set-piece arias that follow delineate character without advancing the drama. Scene five finds Sam at a gym celebrating his victory in a handball game with an Iago-like "Credo" of male chauvinism. Next Dinah recounts the story of a film she's just seen. Her showstopping number, "What a terrible, awful movie!," is a five-minute comedy burlesque which pokes brilliant fun at American colonialism and Hollywood escapism. The trio joins in the hip-swaying melody of "Island Magic," the hit tune of the imaginary movie.

The finale recapitulates the themes and tensions of the opening scene. Dinner is over, Junior is tucked up in bed, presumably nursing his latent hatred for his parents, who were both too self-absorbed to attend his school play. Sam and Dinah try to have a "serious talk." The trio becomes a true Greek chorus, commenting musically on the domestic tragedy of the couple who cannot recover their lost love. Pedal points pound in the orchestra. Eventually husband and wife sink back exhausted and the music collapses into the banality of everyday speech. When Sam suggests a visit to the movies Dinah does not demur at his choice of *Trouble in Tahiti*. They leave to the mocking accompaniment of the trio singing "Island Magic."

"It is lively musically but dreary in subject," was Marc Blitzstein's harsh assessment. Irving Kolodin was even more severe: "Two emptier, duller people never lived." Arthur Berger felt that *Tahiti* suffered "from a weak libretto and seems like a mere sketch for an effective spry Broadway show." Only the critic John Crosby grasped the true measure of *Tahiti* when it was telecast. "The trio sings deadpan with only the faintest hint of a dry smile suggesting life in suburbia is not quite as enchanting as the lyrics proclaim. . . . The lines, innocent-appearing in print, are extraordinarily pointed and malicious when sung." Crosby saw in the opera the contrast between material plenty and spiritual emptiness, the "psychic havoc caused by bowing low before materialism."

There is an autobiographical element in the opera. In his first libretto draft, Bernstein called the husband "Sam" and the wife "Jennie." "Dinah," the more singable substitution, was his paternal grandmother's name. Bernstein was administering a public rebuke to his father for the misery, as he saw it, of his childhood, although the real Sam was nothing like his operatic counterpart. It was an extraordinarily vengeful act on Bernstein's part, and revealed a streak of cruelty in him, a trait that was to surface occasionally in his private life, causing pain to his family and friends.

*Trouble in Tahiti* was dedicated to Marc Blitzstein, the man who showed

Bernstein the way toward music theater. But there is arguably more heart, more genuine pathos and more lyric impulse in a single duet from *Tahiti* than can be found in the entire *Regina*. Bernstein was pushing forward into emotional territory that nobody in American music theater had previously dared to explore. *Tahiti* was a key work in his development and one that returned to haunt him thirty years later when he composed its sequel, *A Quiet Place*.


H A R D on the heels of the telecast of *Trouble in Tahiti,* between early November and mid-December 1952, Bernstein composed the entire score for a new musical, *Wonderful Town.* Set in Greenwich Village, it was based on *My Sister Eileen,* a book of autobiographical stories by Ruth McKenney that had been made into a successful play by Joseph Fields and Jerome Chodorov in 1940, and then into a movie and a long-running radio show. The play had been adapted as a musical by Fields and Chodorov, and the producers Robert Fryer and George Abbott had already signed Rosalind Russell as the star when they approached Comden and Green to write lyrics and Bernstein to do the music. Another composer and lyricist team had already failed to turn in a satisfactory score. Could the new team pull off the impossible and do a complete musical in a month, before their option on Rosalind Russell expired?

Chodorov and Fields thought the book was dated and wanted to reset the story in the 1950s, but Comden and Green were excited by its original thirties flavor. The period was an inspirational trigger for Bernstein. "Lenny ran to the piano," Betty Comden recalled, "and played the famous Eddie Duchin vamp [Duchin was a society bandleader]. The thirties gave us the musical style and that Duchin vamp opened the show." The tight timetable acted as a stimulus: the three friends spent the next five weeks closeted in what Bernstein labeled his "thinking room" at the Osborne. Daylight was shut out and the walls were painted a dull gray. The air was so blue with cigarette smoke that they could barely see each other across the room from piano to typewriter.

What emerged was a sparkling entertainment. There is no sign of the breathtaking pace at which lyrics and music were turned out—in fact the autobiographical elements make it seem as if Comden, Green and Bernstein had been preparing this piece all their adult lives. *My Sister Eileen* is about Ruth Sherwood, a wisecracking fledgling writer and her more obviously attractive actress sister Eileen, who move from Ohio to New York in search of jobs and end up part of a Bohemian crowd in Greenwich Village. The Village had been headquarters for Comden, Green and Bernstein a decade earlier when the Revuers had performed at the Village Vanguard. Before her marriage Felicia Montealegre rented a Washington Place basement apartment not unlike the one occupied by the Sherwood sisters. Ruth shared with Leonard Bernstein a passion for grammatical accuracy. She also resembled him in her tendency to deliver pedantic lectures on any subject under the sun. A song satirizing this trait, "One Hundred Easy Ways to Lose a Man," was added to the show during the tryout month.

Ruth gets a job as a reporter and goes off to interview a group of Brazilian sailors in the Brooklyn Navy Yard. The questions she fires at them illustrate the collaborators' encyclopedic knowledge of the thirties: "What's your opinion of Harold Teen? Mitzi Green? Dizzy Dean? Who do you love on the silver screen?" "We were writing to meet the period," said Adolph Green. "And to make rhymes." The libretto is as packed with often-incomprehensible contemporary references as a Shakespeare comedy. The Brazilian sailors do not understand Ruth's questions: all they want to do is conga. And so the first act finale boils over with a riotous conga, a dance Bernstein had himself loved to organize at parties from Beverly Hills to Galilee.

In the opening number of the second act, "My Darlin' Eileen," a chorus of absurdly warmhearted Irish cops serenades the younger Miss Sherwood (played in the original production by Edie Adams). The scene owes something to the Irish reels Bernstein had danced all night in County Donegal three years earlier. The composer's musical autobiography continues in "Swing," an affectionate tribute to one of Bernstein's earliest musical enthusiasms. In *Wonderful Town*, swing music is performed at the Village Vortex; in real life it was heard at the Village Vanguard. The surrealist, word-associating humor of the lyrics for "Swing" is like a game of "consequences" masterminded by James Joyce.

The production was swiftly assembled at the end of 1952. The show came in 10 percent under its budget of $250,000, and a month before the New York opening advance sales already totaled over $600,000. In both Boston and Philadelphia, *Wonderful Town* broke box office records. Not that it was all plain sailing. An early casualty for Bernstein was the excision of a balletic scene based on *Prelude, Fugue and Riffs,* the music he had composed for Woody Herman four years earlier but shelved when Herman had been unable to come up with the check (or even an acknowledgment of receipt). Apart from a riff that can still be heard in "Conversation Piece" in Act I, the music went back to the bottom drawer. Jerome Robbins was brought in—uncredited at his request—to "show-doctor" the dance routines, reportedly after Miss Russell was accidentally dropped by a male dancer at a performance in Boston. It was an "acrobatic production," according to the *Times* in a preview: when Rosalind Russell was hoisted aloft on a crowd of sailors' hands, she seemed to be "wallowing on nothing more tangible than the Good Neighbor Policy." As a renowned Hollywood star, Miss Russell was an enormous draw, and there was great dismay when she lost her voice in New Haven and missed most of a week of previews. She was a real trouper, however: she described her voice as "so bass it's viol," and she hinted at her difficulty with music when she told a reporter that Leonard Bernstein was a nut for changing keys: "a new one on each word!"

In New Haven, Bernstein had a joyful reunion with his childhood friend Sid Ramin, now a skilled orchestrator, who was recruited to cope with the volume of orchestration work caused by the tight deadline. Ramin remembers both "Swing" and "Conga" being rewritten and refined during the rehearsals; Bernstein was stimulated by direct contact with the singers and dancers, just as he had been in 1944 when preparing *Fancy Free*.

George Abbott had done such an efficient job of fine-tuning the production that the first-night critics at the Winter Garden Theater turned in uniformly enthusiastic reviews. Brooks Atkinson said it was the best musical since *Guys and Dolls*. John Chapman, the reviewer who had criticized *On the Town* eight years earlier and spectacularly eaten his words after he saw it again, had no doubts this time: "Wonderful Town—wonderful score—wonderful book, etc. etc. . . . There hasn't been anybody around like [Bernstein] since George Gershwin for jauntiness, tricky and intriguing modulations and graceful swoops with simple and pleasant melody." For Harold Clurman, in *The Nation*, *Wonderful Town* summed up a kind of fervent Bohemianism that was typical of New York in the mid-thirties. "It was light without being empty, a triumph of good nature."

*Wonderful Town* won a Tony Award for Best Musical for the 1952–53 season. Bernstein won a Tony for the music, as did Joseph Fields and Jerome Chodorov for writing the book. Rosalind Russell, Lehman Engel, the music director, Donald Saddler, the choreographer, Betty Comden and Adolph Green, and Raoul Pene du Bois, the scenic designer, also won awards. In addition the musical won nine Donaldson awards—a poll of theater workers on Broadway—as well as the Best Musical award from New York's Drama Critics Circle and the Outer Circle, which polled the national and international newspaper writers. Bernstein had spent a total of fifteen weeks in a whirl of composing, rehearsing and rewriting; his share of the royalty income came to over sixty-six thousand dollars in the first year alone. "I need the money," Bernstein observed drily to a journalist in Israel.

*Wonderful Town* is as perfectly poised between lyrics, plot and music as an operetta by Gilbert and Sullivan. The sustained musical invention lifts it into the highest league of Broadway musicals. Olin Downes said of it, "This is an opera made of dance, prattle and song. . . . In days to come it may well be looked upon in some museum exhibit as the archetype of a kind of piece which existed peculiarly in the America of neon lights and the whir and zip of the twentieth century. We are coming to believe that when the American opera created by a composer of the stature of the Wagners and Verdis of yore does materialize, it will owe much more to the robust spirit and the raciness of accent of our popular theater than to the efforts of our emulators, in the upper aesthetic brackets, of the tonal art of Bartok, Hindemith and Stravinsky."

*Wonderful Town* may have seemed like a diversion from Bernstein's declared ambition to write an American opera but it can be considered part of his training. True, it was composed in a hectic rush, but so were many of Rossini's operas. Agreed, there is a lot of "prattle," as Olin Downes put it, but spoken dialogue is a feature of Mozart's German operas and Offenbach's French operettas. Bernstein remained excited about composing music for the theater. "That is what I feel I write best, what I ought to do and what I most enjoy," he said in February 1953. Yet it was almost four years before he returned to Broadway. And all subsequent attempts at a collaboration between Bernstein, Comden and Green were to come to naught. *Wonderful Town* stands as the final fruit of a brief but glorious Broadway partnership.

# DIVERSIONARY TACTICS

*Isaac Stern was the soloist in the world premiere of*
*Bernstein's* Serenade, Venice, 1954.
PHOTO: DAVID DIAMOND, COURTESY OF THE ESTATE OF LEONARD BERNSTEIN

*I'm condemned to choose the activities that interest me*
*most, instead of those that pay, and I'm stuck with it.*
*I think they call it artists' folly.*

> —Letter from Leonard Bernstein
> to Philip and Barbara Marcuse,
> May 1954

IVING in New York together for the first time, Felicia and Leonard found that their interlocking circles of friendships expanded rapidly: Leonard received nearly a hundred telegrams of good wishes on the opening night of *Wonderful Town*. But Felicia's acting career went into decline and she busied herself with creating a home at the Osborne. "Most of our time is spent shopping and going to auctions," Bernstein wrote to Irving Fine. "The place ought to be fine when finished, if ever. And I find that the domestic life is by far the most exhausting of any I have yet tried. More than atoned for, of course, by the fun; but when between all the drapes and rugs and tables and irons does one write music?"

As he had promised himself, Bernstein did very little conducting in the 1952–53 season: there were a few fund-raisers for Israeli causes, a modest concert at Town Hall, honoring the tenth anniversary of the Koussevitzky Foundation, and in the summer a set of eight symphony concerts at one of his favorite venues, the Lewisohn Stadium. These were one-rehearsal affairs, with members of the New York Philharmonic masquerading as the "Stadium Symphony." When each concert was over, Bernstein and the orchestra would spend half the night, starting at midnight, making recordings for American Decca. The master sound tracks of five symphonies were eventually sold in 1955 to the Book-of-the-Month Club and marketed with Bernstein's introductory talks and analyses. This brought him in a good sum in advance royalties, but the stadium was an unsatisfactory recording location and the experiment was not repeated.

The most important artistic event of his summer was the 1953 Festival of Creative Arts at Brandeis, where after teaching a hundred students once a week for a semester he'd been named the first holder of the Sylvia and Frederic Mann Chair of Music. When Irving Fine suggested "Classicism and the Comic Spirit" as the festival's theme, Bernstein responded: "We discovered at the last festival that we are not living in experimental times: that our times are cautious in the extreme: that we are not producing real tragedy. On the other hand we are not producing real satire either; the caution prevents it, all the fears prevent it; and we are left, at the moment, with an art that is rather whiling away the time until the world gets better or blows up. Good and Evil are still valid and oft-used subjects in the abstract (*Billy Budd* and *The Rake*), and will always be the best subjects; but since our time doesn't major in this field, let's be amusing, or pretty, or diverting."

The letter provides an inkling of the fun-loving Bernstein's deflated mood in the early Eisenhower era. It was a bad time for liberals. During the out-of-town run of *Wonderful Town,* Jerome Robbins had shocked his friends and colleagues by slipping away to Washington to give evidence in a private session concerning his political record. A month before the Brandeis festival, on May 5, Robbins was called to appear at an open meeting of the House Un-American Activities Committee. Unlike Lillian Hellman, he chose to testify—which meant naming friends who had been members of the Communist party. He cited nobody who had not already been named by other witnesses, but his more radical friends did not forgive him: Marc Blitzstein, who had worked with Robbins on a ballet in 1948, described his conduct as "miserably revolting." Bernstein was more conciliatory. His political instinct was tempered by a desire to work with the best people in the field: Robbins was among his most important collaborators.

"The Comic Spirit," as the second Brandeis festival was called, spread its net wide to be amusing, with Al Capp, S. J. Perelman and Saul Steinberg among the participants. The budget for music had been cut back since 1952. Bernstein offered only one program, performed twice: in the first part he conducted a four-movement concerto for tap dancer and orchestra, composed by Morton Gould at the invitation of the renowned Danny Daniels; after the interval he conducted the American premiere of Francis Poulenc's witty opera *Les Mamelles de Tirésias,* with Phyllis Curtin in the lead role and costumes and scenery by *Wonderful Town*'s award-winning designer Raoul Pene du Bois.

Bernstein moved on to spend his customary six weeks in Tanglewood. Four days after arriving, he wrote to his university's president, Abram Sachar, announcing his withdrawal from both teaching and the festival: "It has finally dawned on me that I have been dancing at far too many weddings. I have always faced a rather severe problem in trying to balance the creative and performing side of my life—either of which should properly be a full-time matter. As I reach thirty-five I find I have not yet found the way. But I have learned that putting one foot, however tentatively, into the academic world constitutes a real plunge. I love to teach: and therefore I agreed to try a one-semester plan last year, experimentally. I cannot carry that experiment forward next year, since the other active ogres have caught up with me. [He planned a conducting season in Israel and Italy, after which he wanted to work on new composition projects.] I am afraid this will rule out teaching in the second semester. Something has to give somewhere, before my mind does. . . ."

He continued to teach at Tanglewood as a labor of love; his salary there was minuscule compared with the fifteen hundred dollars a week he earned in 1953 from *Wonderful Town*. He received a thousand dollars for his position as head of the conducting school and another two thousand for conducting the Boston Symphony in two concerts. But Tanglewood kept him in touch with the latest trends. A forum on the problems of communication in contemporary music allowed him to discuss an issue which had been worrying him for months. Since leaving the New York City Symphony he had had no orchestra of his own with which he could fulfill Copland's dream and become the first "American" conductor, the interpreter of the American school of symphonists. But over and above his own contribution, which was now primarily that of a composer, he saw that since the death of Koussevitzky no conductor was consistently championing American music. "Serious music composed today in this country doesn't interest anybody," he said, "not even musicians. Our future lies in what some future genius will take out of American music theater and work up into some new, large and abstract form. But that won't happen quite yet."

His mood may have been pessimistic but he delighted Tanglewood's young people, to whom he was as much of an institution as Koussevitzky had been in the 1940s. His rehearsal methods, if unorthodox, were effective. As a way of persuading the choir to sing a truly soft *pianissimo* at the beginning of the finale of the *Resurrection* Symphony, he lay down on the podium and refused to get up until they achieved the hushed effect he wanted. An Israeli musician was struck by Bernstein's unforgettable flair for matching words to every possible theme and melody, "singing them loud, enjoying himself, and conveying his temperament and charm."

The Bernsteins spent the summer in the little town of Hillsdale in upstate New York, across the state line from Massachusetts and a forty-minute drive from Tanglewood. The remoteness mirrored Bernstein's feeling, perhaps encouraged by Felicia, that it was time for a gradual withdrawal from his commitment to Tanglewood, where the atmosphere was undoubtedly flatter without Koussevitzky's inspirational presence. Even the levelheaded Aaron Copland seemed noticeably depressed that summer, following an uncomfortable brush with Senator Joe McCarthy at a Senate subcommittee hearing.

Bernstein had his own problems with the witch-hunt in the summer of 1953 when the State Department refused to renew his passport. He wrote to his brother, "I finally went down to Washington and had to have a hearing with an ape at the State Department. *I got it!!* The great experience of it all was my lawyer, whom I was insanely lucky to get—Jim McInerney, formerly head of Criminal Investigation in the Dept. of Justice—an old Commie-chaser—just the right person to have on my side. And what a great person he is. It was worth the whole ghastly and humiliating experience just to know him, as well as the $3500 fee. Yes, that's what it costs these days to be a free American citizen. All too depressing: but at least it's settled. I am told that the other things will be cleared as a result: the Committee files, and even Red Channels. McI. knows all these people on first-name terms: he's a great and valuable ally. But it's shameful that one needs such an ally to retain 1st class citizenship."

According to Robert Joseph, a producer colleague of Shirley Bernstein's whose father had pulled strings on Bernstein's behalf, McInerney had a folder which listed all the "communist front" petitions and organizations to which Bernstein acknowledged he had given his name. "Don't you ever say no?" McInerney had asked. "It doesn't look that way," a chastened Bernstein had replied. "I don't think you're a Communist," McInerney had concluded. "Go across the street and get your passport, and don't get into any more trouble." Bernstein may have been disappointed never to have been subpoenaed but he was undoubtedly relieved that the threat hanging over his international career had been lifted.

With passport in hand he left New York on September 5, 1953, on his first trip to South America—he was to miss his daughter's first birthday and his second wedding anniversary. Eleazar de Carvalho had invited Bernstein to conduct the Orquestra Sinfônica Brasileira and he had squeezed in the three-week engagement before a long-planned return to Israel. He was distinctly underwhelmed by his reception, however. "There was absolutely *no* advance publicity," he told Miss Coates, "no press conference, nothing: and nobody in Rio knew I was there. . . . The orchestra is only so-so, but I've worked like a horse with them, and the progress they have made is astonishing."

Felicia was still without acting work. "I have been steeped in domesticity since you left," she wrote, as if to underline the contrast between his high life on the beach at Copacabana, and her placid routine at the Osborne. She was kept busy getting the apartment back into shape after the summer expedition to the Berkshires, but she missed her husband dearly, and couldn't help but feel, to some extent, abandoned. "No word from you since Sao Paulo," she complained; "I'm very depressed and hurt—I don't care how busy you are, there is always a tiny moment for at least a post card. I don't suppose you've ever waited desperately for a letter from someone for two weeks. Take it from me it's hell!" This was their first overseas separation since their marriage. Yet Bernstein took nearly two weeks to write to her again. When his letter arrived, Felicia was overjoyed. "I can't tell you how I needed that particular 'missive'—someday I'll tell you all about it, but in the mean time I want you to know (as if you didn't) that I love you deeply and marvelously and I wouldn't change *anything* about my life or you—I know this as I know my nose—or your nose." She soon resolved to stop hanging around New York in the hope of getting work, and instead spend two months in Israel and Italy with her husband, leaving Jamie in the care of her faithful nanny, Paula Marks.

Bernstein's journey from Rio to Israel took more than four days. On his travels he had new professional arrangements to consider. His lawyer Abe Friedman had been handling his business deals up to now; for subsequent theatrical work he was taking on an agent, David Hocker of MCA. His relationship with Schirmer, his publisher, was being renegotiated by Friedman. Eventually he would establish his own company, which would enable him to retain the copyrights on his compositions.

Bernstein's financial situation was a little precarious. Helen Coates wrote to him that his current bank balance was a mere six thousand dollars. He had a separate "thrift account" of ten thousand dollars, but despite the high earnings from *Wonderful Town* his living expenses had risen so dramatically since his marriage that he was doing little more than make ends meet. The concerts in South America brought in several thousand dollars, and his five weeks in Israel netted him another five thousand. His situation was far from dire but he was not the rich man some people imagined him to be. Royalties from his serious music—the clarinet sonata, the song cycles, the two symphonies and the piano music—didn't amount to more than a few hundred dollars a year.

F E L I C I A joined Leonard in Tel Aviv. She was not enamored of the rough-and-ready Israeli lifestyle in the pioneer days of 1953, but she put on a good front when she wrote to Helen Coates. "The concerts have been brilliant. Lenny is their God, his name is magic everywhere. I never saw such a thing. It's really very touching." Bernstein gave twenty-one concerts with the Israel Philharmonic in the space of four weeks. He was pleased with the orchestra's development and included Mozart's Wind Serenade, K. 388, to show off the improvement in the section's playing. His most challenging choice of repertoire was the "Adagio" movement from Mahler's uncompleted Tenth Symphony. "The music is saturated with Wagner's musical world, especially the 'Tristan,'" commented the *Jerusalem Post*. "The present ban on the works of Wagner appears as an intolerable misinterpretation of the functions of cultural education." But not even Leonard Bernstein could succeed in breaking that embargo.

Bernstein and Felicia next traveled to Italy, where he was scheduled to conduct twice in Milan with the orchestra of La Scala and twice in Florence, before moving on to Rome to conduct three different programs with the Santa Cecilia Orchestra. He had been hoping for a December engagement in London to follow, but something decidedly more interesting intervened—an opportunity to conduct Cherubini's *Medea* at La Scala, with Maria Callas as his prima donna. In his book *My Wife, Maria Callas,* the diva's husband and manager claimed that Callas heard Bernstein conduct on a broadcast and suggested him as a substitute for the ailing Victor de Sabata, but La Scala had cabled him weeks earlier in Israel, hoping to engage him if de Sabata's health should fail. They had unsuccessfully approached him several times in years past to conduct *Wozzeck, Billy Budd* and *Gloriana.*

"Never heard of [Cherubini's *Medea*] before, but it is fascinating, and the soprano Calas [*sic*] who does the title role is terrific," he wrote to Helen Coates. "All this depended on Scala's being able to cancel, or rather postpone, my Rome dates, which they couldn't. So they then came up with a plan whereby I run back and forth between Rome and Milan next week, rehearsing both orchestras. It's a bit mad, and Felicia is furious at me for accepting so much, but I couldn't resist it." It meant he would spend an extra month in Italy.

La Scala was at the pinnacle of its postwar eminence, and working there was an incomparable experience for Bernstein. In Callas he found a soprano who outclassed even Jennie Tourel in vocal expression, a singer who despite her girth acted with the intensity of a Sarah Bernhardt. Once he had been persuaded to do *Medea* he went at it with such a ferocious appetite that the Italians must have wondered what hit them. He demanded and got extra rehearsals. "We learned the music together," he said of the orchestra. He even persuaded Callas to make an unusual cut in her tremendous third-act aria. John Ardoin, the Maria Callas expert, explains that by omitting the passage expressing her remorse at having murdered her own children, she gave additional strength to her resolve of vengeance, "so that her fury would strike with full force in the final pages of the act." The recording made of the first-night performance confirms the Italian critics' enthusiasm for the two Americans, both born of immigrant parents, who shared the spotlight. According to Franco Zeffirelli, who was present, "the world of opera was transformed that night. There was BC and AC, before and after Callas." The respected *Corriere della Sera* spoke of an authentic revelation, of Bernstein's miraculous intuition, of a *"grandioso succèsso."* From the opening bars of the overture the dramatic urgency in Bernstein's conducting placed the opera firmly on a tragic plane worthy of the late Mozart style which it sometimes resembles. (Cherubini was born three years after Mozart.) Callas's performance, in which there were countless inflections of dynamics and tempo suggested by Bernstein, was among the best in her career. In her interpretation, Ardoin notes, "benign classicism became vibrant emotionalism." Across the decades the stridency of her voice can still strike terror in the listener, mixed with awe at the moments of tenderness and with sheer physical excitement when she soars up to a high B for one tremulously arching phrase after another. No conductor pushed Callas further to the limits of expressivity and sometimes beyond; in the name of drama he tolerated, perhaps even encouraged, some downright ugly sounds. The result was thrilling. Leonard Bernstein and Felicia became the toast of the opera world's capital city. Toscanini's daughter was among the first to praise him, having gloomily forecast that he would be "scalped, slaughtered, roasted alive."

His intoxicating new relationship with La Scala left Bernstein in something of a frenzy, torn between composing and conducting opera. The idea of living in Europe was increasingly attractive to him. But Felicia's work was tied specifically to America. The Bernsteins flew home to New York on December 15 for the end-of-year holidays, and in the first six weeks of 1954 Felicia performed in three television plays in quick succession, beginning with *Moment of Panic* (for NBC), an apt title for her mood. The homecoming had been miserable for her—she had felt swamped in her own apartment by the Bernstein clan and cut off from her baby by the nanny. Ten days later, Leonard returned to Milan to continue the performances of *Medea*. Confused and disheartened, Felicia sat down and wrote one of the strongest letters of her life:

> What I have to say is hard—before I start I want you to accept the possibility that most of what I say is true. I know that I tend to dwell on things till they get way out of proportion, but not now.
>
> I was happier in Italy than I have ever been with you—we had fun, we shared everything, we were truly relaxed for once. (I am sorry now I ever suggested we come home—I needed to see Jamie but I should have waited.) Here in New York all the old problems and tensions seemed to be lying in wait—plus the whole Bernstein clan. I love Burt and I love Shirley but they are *your* brother and *your* sister, there is no wall keeping me out, but there is blood and a shared past between you—they are, with Sam and Jennie, your family. I have no family really apart from you and Jamie—and this is all I need. This place is our home—yours and mine—it is beautiful because we have made it so and both our personalities are blended in it . . . but all of a sudden it became so "Bernstein" that I have a hard time keeping in touch with myself, but mostly keeping in touch with you. I cannot change this, it is the way things are; put yourself in my place and admit that it can be a little wearing. You will probably say that all this is a sign of possessiveness—it isn't. My objecting to Jamie being called "Jamela" comes from the same source—it isn't our way of calling her, it is the Bernstein way—something quite foreign to me, something I cannot share in.

From St. Moritz in Switzerland, where he had gone for two days to ski after the final performance of *Medea,* Bernstein typed a long and conciliatory reply:

> Darling Goody: Did you think that I was unaware of all that "bad trouble" you were going through? That arrival home must have been one of the worst, with all things conspiring to exaggerate your feeling of left-

outness: first Miss Marx vying with you for the role of mater-familias; then your feeling that Jamie was being presented to me rather than to you; and then all the "clan" business. All at once. Each one of these is soluble and understandable enough by itself, I suppose: but all three at once must have been too much. I don't think it will ever again be like that. This was our first time away and first time returning; it was a crisis. . . . You mustn't take it so hard. And I hope you and Shirley and Burtie can exist again on a relaxed level. There is so little I can do to prevent that particular tension: I had missed them both a lot on my long trip (and had not seen Burt for six months), and I was conscious every second we were together that I must not display too much affection or invoke the past overmuch. That was as hard for me as it was for you, and it seems silly to deprive us all of a warm, easy relationship. You wouldn't want that, I know, especially since all tensions between S. and B. and myself only provoke more tensions between you and me, as well as between you and them. I don't really think it will ever again be so hard as it was this last time, with everything hitting you in the face at once. At least let's hope so, lovely Goody; and please be happy. We have so much to be happy and grateful for; let's both try not to injure it.

Despite its affectionate and concerned tone, Leonard's response was as Felicia had predicted. He found it hard to understand her feeling that she, as his wife, should take precedence over the clan. The subtle threat about injuring their relationship must have hurt even more. But the truth was that the Bernstein world seemed to revolve around her husband and that he had become, even for his own parents, a father figure.

In his letter to Felicia, Bernstein laid out a plan for 1954 that would give them nearly a year in Europe. He had decided to take a sabbatical from Tanglewood so the summer was free for composition, and he had been offered a place to work at the American Academy in Rome for the fall; in between there were inquiries from many European festivals, a conducting invitation from the Berlin Philharmonic, a firm date at the Holland Festival, a request from Karajan to appear in Vienna. He had become, he told Felicia, "real good friends with von Karajan, whom you would (and will) adore. My first Nazi." It was as if he had already forgotten his wife's loving description of the home they had built for themselves at the Osborne. He wrote as if he had no inkling of what bringing up a child entailed.

Bernstein was daydreaming again—adrift in a fantasy where every week there would be a new orchestra to conduct, a new opera house to conquer, London, Copenhagen, Lucerne to take by storm. Nor was he through outlining plans for the coming year. "I have decided to go along with Lillian [Hellman] on *Candide*—imagine, after having written her a letter saying no and tearing it up. I think it will be more feasible than the David piece this spring [the television magazine "Omnibus" wanted to commission an opera based on a J. M. Barrie play called *The Boy David*], and will allow me to do other things as well, like the violin piece." (Isaac Stern had asked Bernstein to write a work for violin and orchestra.) Hellman and Bernstein had abandoned an earlier idea to collaborate on an opera about Eva Perón, but in the fall Hellman had suggested adapting Voltaire's *Candide*. Bernstein conceived it, he told Felicia, as "a big, three-act opera with chorus and ballet."

When he returned to New York at the end of January Bernstein publicly confirmed that he and Lillian Hellman were "having a fling" at *Candide*. It was to be the "real satire" he had written of in 1953, his and Hellman's creative response to the excesses of McCarthyism and to a generally shameful chapter in American public life. But *Candide* plans were interrupted when he was approached out of the blue to write a film score for *On the Waterfront*. At first he declined the producer Sam Spiegel's invitation because of his many prior commitments. He was also reluctant to work with the director, Elia Kazan, who had been one of the most notorious and reviled informants to the House Un-American Activities Committee. The very subject of the film was the glorification of an informer. Spiegel begged Bernstein at least to look at Kazan's rough cut. When he did, he was so impressed by Marlon Brando's spellbinding performance, and by Budd Schulberg's dramatic account of union corruption in the New York dockyards, that he changed his mind. He started work as soon as he had been through what he called, in a letter to Philip Marcuse, "the ugly experience of being cleared to work for the motion picture industry."

*On the Waterfront* occupied Bernstein from February to May 1954. He claimed to have hitherto resisted all invitations to compose film music on the grounds that it is "a musically unsatisfactory experience for a composer to write a score whose chief merit ought to be its unobtrusiveness." This hardly accords with his earlier efforts to get into the movies, or his often-expressed admiration for Aaron Copland's film music, notably *Of Mice and Men*. But he had never been asked to work on anything as good as *Waterfront*. At the rough-cut screening, Bernstein already felt a surge of excitement: "I heard music as I watched: that was enough. And the atmosphere of talent that this film gave off was exactly the atmosphere in which I love to work and collaborate. . . . Day after day I sat at a movieola, running the print back and forth, measuring in feet the sequences I had chosen for the music, converting feet into seconds by mathematical formula, making homemade cue sheets."

Without detailed instructions from Kazan to hem him in, Bernstein wrote his music in much the same way he had done in the past for the theater; the scenes varied in length from thirty seconds to two and a half minutes and had titles like "Roof Morning" and "Kangaroo Court." The bustle of the Hoboken dockyard is expressed by a fierce *fugato* for three sets of timpani; a later scene, played out on a desolate stretch of wasteland dominated by a dump of old tires, has a stabbing violin motif which is reminiscent of the North Sea music Benjamin Britten composed for *Peter Grimes*. Over and over again Bernstein establishes a decisive mood in a few brilliant bars: the *furioso* fight passages are as terrifying as anything to come in *West Side Story,* and among the sequences of innocent tenderness there is a rooftop night scene between the inarticulate lovers Edie and Terry (Eva Marie Saint and Marlon Brando), where despite Bernstein's complaint that his contribution was sacrificed to the dialogue at the dubbing session, the music rises to a *Tristan*-like climax. Bernstein's finest achievement is the thematic integration of the whole score. Its symphonic nature is easier to grasp in the orchestral suite he was to produce the following year, but even when watching the film one is at least subliminally aware that the opening music is brought back at the end, having earlier been combined with the yearning love theme in a fine piece of contrapuntal writing.

It was something of a coup for Sam Spiegel to have lured Bernstein to the movies—and to have signed him up for only fifteen thousand dollars. The last major composer to have worked in Hollywood had been Aaron Copland, in 1949; he had won an Oscar for *The Heiress.* Surprisingly, Bernstein did not conduct his own music for the sound track, but this was for contractual rather than artistic reasons. André Previn attended the recording sessions and remembers how on edge Bernstein became over delicate points of balance. But Bernstein did contribute the moment of elegant jazz piano playing which can be heard in the background of the saloon bar scene.

Despite the hassle of last-minute rewrites in "Upper Dubbing"—the name on the music studio door at Columbia—Hollywood remained a fun place for Bernstein. "I've made millions of good new friends," he told Helen Coates, "and I find I actually like it here—for the very reasons Hollywood is usually attacked: namely, that there is nothing to do but see people." He kept himself going with steaks. He had a steak for breakfast, he told a reporter, and looked forward to two more steaks during the day—"That's how I get energy."

At the Academy Awards for 1954 *On the Waterfront* won eight Oscars, including Best Picture, but the award for Best Musical Score went to Dimitri Tiomkin for *The High and the Mighty.* Tiomkin was a well-known Hollywood composer who organized his Oscar campaign very intensively. Bernstein's support may have also suffered from his earlier left-wing sympathies, especially given the political climate in Hollywood at that time.

When *On the Waterfront* was shown at the 1954 Venice Film Festival, where it won the Silver Lion, the screening was interrupted five times by applause. *Newsweek*'s review observed that music gave the film "dramatic universality." While not on the same scale as Prokofiev's collaborations with Eisenstein— there is less than thirty-five minutes of music to be heard in *Waterfront,* as a result of Kazan's sparing use of music in general—Bernstein established himself as a major international film composer. The Austrian-born critic Hans Keller, writing in the English magazine *Score,* hailed Bernstein's work as "about the best film score that has come out of America. In sheer professional skill, it surpasses everything I have heard or seen of the music of his teacher [*sic*] Aaron Copland (himself one of the very few contributors of musical music to the American film), while in textural style and harmonic idiom it is more daring even than many more individual film scores by our own leading composers." He was approached many times—and not only by Sam Spiegel—but Bernstein was never to score another film.

I N the summer of 1954 Leonard and Felicia rented a house on Martha's Vineyard. "My life is all Lillian Hellman and *Candide*," Leonard wrote to the Marcuses, "and the violin concerto for Isaac Stern to première at the Venice Festival in September. . . . I've canceled all my conducting for the year . . . all of which means financial idiocy on my part."

But creatively the summer was immensely productive. First he completed the *Serenade*. After hearing a run-through, a holiday visitor, Marc Blitzstein, called it "the finest work you ever wrote; [it] haunts me all the time." Then serious work began on *Candide*. Leonard and Felicia wrote the lyrics of one song together ("I Am Easily Assimilated") but he and Hellman had decided to collaborate with John Latouche, a lyricist with a track record for brilliant satirical wit. His "syphilis" songs in *Candide* are triumphs of elegant bad taste, technically on a par with the intricate versifying of W. S. Gilbert.

The show progressed slowly, however; the first act was sketched out but by the end of the summer there was much work left to do on the second half. Production plans were still vague: Bernstein and a few friends auditioned some numbers for Sol Hurok's deputy, Walter Prude, upon which Hurok promptly canceled his plan to present *Candide* on Broadway.

Life was very pleasant at Martha's Vineyard. Bernstein went snorkeling and sailing in his rented sloop, and, with his experience of Hollywood fresh in mind, inaugurated a holiday tradition of making elaborate silent movies involving house guests and family.

At the end of August Felicia went off to Woodstock, New York, for a fortnight's acting in a summer stock production of *The Last Tycoon*. Happy to be back on stage, she nonetheless wrote to Leonard, "I miss my family and for the first two days had an alarming case of homesickness. I hadn't felt like that since I was a child."

Bernstein stayed long enough to see Felicia in the play, before flying to Venice to conduct the premiere on September 12 of his *Serenade* with Isaac Stern at La Fenice opera house. Once again he missed his daughter's birthday, as well as his third wedding anniversary. He made amends with a cable: "MISS YOU TERRIBLY TONIGHT OF ALL NIGHTS GIBBOUS MOON OVER GRAND CANAL LOVE YOU LOVE JAMIE—LENNY."

In the letter to Felicia which followed, he reported that an orchestra rehearsal had run on until 2 A.M. "Isaac plays the Serenade like an angel. If it all goes well tomorrow it should be a knock-out." Stern remembers Bernstein being at his most socially attractive during the week in Venice. After a rehearsal, the two had supper and drinks, "and then started to talk about life and music, about ideas, about family. . . . The greatest times I had with him were always alone. You could never talk with Lenny this way if one other person entered the room; [he] immediately went on stage."

I T is doubtful whether Bernstein did the *Serenade* any service by giving it a cumbersome subtitle, *Serenade* (after Plato's "Symposium") for Solo Violin, Strings, Harp and Percussion. The *Symposium* is Plato's imaginative reconstruction of the speeches made at a drinking party attended by the philosopher Socrates and his Athenian friends. The subject of their discourse was love. But Bernstein's reference to Plato smacks of elitism: readers of the Greek philosopher were probably no more numerous than those of W. H. Auden's *The Age of Anxiety*. The composer made things more complicated by publishing a substantial preface to his score. "There is no literal program for this Serenade," he announces at the beginning, but he then gives many examples of "literary allusions" which concert annotators have ever since seized upon with gratitude and unquestioningly reproduced. Innocent listeners have thus been caused considerable anguish since many people are unable to pronounce the names of the speakers, let alone to distinguish the various arguments put forward at the symposium. Erixymachus, for example, is not a name to trip lightly off the tongue, and perhaps only one in a thousand will recall what Bernstein was pleased to describe as "the famous interruption by Alcibiades" in the finale.

Bernstein wrote that the *Serenade* "resulted from a re-reading of Plato's charming dialogue." On June 30, 1951, just after Koussevitzky's death, he had been commissioned to write an orchestral work by the Koussevitzky Music Foundation; the *Serenade* was eventually dedicated to both Serge and Natalie Koussevitzky. Bernstein had Plato by his bedside in Cuernavaca in 1951 but did not begin composing until the fall of 1953, at which time he described the work as a concerto; he finished it the following summer. Exactly when the idea to base it on Plato occurred is unknown, but it was possibly not long before the completion of the work, since a glance at Plato reveals obvious discrepancies between Bernstein's adaptation and the original. Bernstein names the individual movements of the concerto after the various speakers at the banquet but has changed the order of the speeches and modified their character. Thus in Bernstein's version, Aristophanes, the comic playwright, becomes a "bedtime story-teller, invoking the fairy-tale mythology of love." Moreover, Bernstein shifts the emotional center of gravity from Socrates to Agathon. The fourth movement of the concerto, dedicated to Agathon, contains some of the most beautiful music of any twentieth-century score. But in Plato it is Socrates who has the longest and most important speech.

Why did he opt for the title *Serenade* rather than the more conservative "Violin Concerto"? Tchaikovsky and Elgar used "Serenade" as the title for works for string orchestra which were sophisticated entertainment music, similar to divertimenti, and intellectually less ambitious than a symphony. But Bernstein was harking back to the earlier usage when serenades, literally "evening music," from the Italian *sera,* were love songs delivered beneath the balconies of fair ladies. Bernstein's *Serenade* is at one level a profoundly felt and technically deft violin concerto in which, as the composer put it, the musical material of each movement "evolves out of elements in the preceding one"—his favorite compositional method. But Bernstein described *Serenade* as "a series of related statements in praise of love," and the very nature of love was a preoccupation when he was working on it. Returning from Italy to New York by ocean liner in January 1954, he wrote a radio talk for an Ed Murrow series called *This I Believe.* "I believe in people," he began. "I feel, love, need and respect people above all else. . . . One human figure on the slope of an Alp can make the Alp disappear for me. . . . I believe in Man's unconscious, the deep spring from which comes his power to communicate and to love. For me, all art's a combination of these powers; art is nothing to me if it does not make contact between the creator and the perceiver on an unconscious level."

What Bernstein surely meant us to understand was that his *Serenade* embodied all his loving feelings toward all his fellow human beings. Complete movements from Bernstein's *Anniversaries,* short piano pieces dedicated to loving friends, are woven into the musical fabric of three of the *Serenade*'s five movements. But the work can also be perceived as a portrait of Bernstein himself: grand and noble in the first movement, childlike in the second, boisterous and playful in the third, serenely calm and tender in the fourth, a doom-laden prophet and then a jazzy iconoclast in the finale.

Critical response to the *Serenade* was mixed in Venice. Virgil Thomson, reporting for the *Herald Tribune,* was waspishly unappreciative: "A negligible contribution to music . . . Meditative passages of a conventional nature alternate with dance-like movements. . . . It might with drastic cuts be made into a repertory work." Cynthia Jolly, writing in the *New York Times,* praised Bernstein's luminous communicative powers and his buoyant musicianship. The *Serenade* has emerged as his most satisfying work for the concert hall.

B A C K in New York in the fall of 1954, Bernstein resumed composing *Candide,* meeting Hellman and Latouche three or four times a week. He also returned to Brandeis, where for two days each month he taught a seminar on musical theater based on *Candide.* Students were assigned to write the same scene Bernstein was working on at the time, and then they compared results. According to Jack Gottlieb, a young graduate who later became Bernstein's assistant, the course was immensely stimulating while it lasted. But one semester was all he could spare.

In addition to his teaching and composing, Bernstein had a new preoccupation in the fall of 1954: he was asked to deliver a television essay for Robert Saudek's "Omnibus," the CBS culture magazine show funded by the Ford Foundation. Saudek's associate Paul Feigay, who had been co-producer of *On the Town* in 1944, took Bernstein to lunch with Mary Ahern, the "Omnibus" feature editor. Ahern proposed a program about Beethoven's notebooks and showed him the sketches Beethoven had discarded from his Fifth Symphony. Bernstein immediately saw the possibility of doing some intriguing musical detective work. He would orchestrate the rejected material and explain the creative process that lay behind the composition of a masterpiece. "Thus," Robert Saudek recalled, "was born a new Bernstein—television's star teacher."

Bernstein wrote his own script, which he polished in lengthy editorial sessions with Saudek and his team. During the week preceding the telecast he memorized his lines, together with the musical extracts he was to conduct and play at the piano. The live transmission took place at 5 P.M. on Sunday, November 14, eleven years to the day after his New York Philharmonic debut. He was introduced by the program's host, Alistair Cooke. Looking dapper in a bow tie and dark suit, Bernstein spoke with a velvety voice and a Harvard accent. "We are going to perform for you today a curious and rather difficult experiment. We're going to take the first movement of Beethoven's Fifth Symphony and rewrite it. Now don't get scared: we're going to use only notes that Beethoven himself wrote." He showed viewers the sketchbooks, which are remarkable, he said, "as a bloody record of an inner battle." Even more striking visually was the way the studio floor had been painted with the first page of Beethoven's printed score. Musicians carrying the various instruments of the orchestra stood on each stave: Bernstein was able to demonstrate visually as well as aurally how Beethoven decided to omit most of the woodwinds and brass in order to achieve a particularly dark sound for his opening unison. Walking on the actual score he pointed with an elegant black shoe to Beethoven's V for Victory opening motif—"three Gs and an E flat"—as the camera craned down for a close-up. "Almost every bar of this first movement is a direct development of these opening notes," he explained.

It made gripping television. "Beethoven, more than any other composer before or after him, had the ability to find exactly the right notes that had to follow his themes. But even he, with this great ability, had a gigantic struggle to achieve this rightness: not only the right notes but the right rhythms, the right climaxes, the right harmonies, the right instrumentation. And it's that struggle that we would like to investigate," Bernstein told the audience.

He spoke for more than twenty minutes, playing earlier versions of familiar melodies, splicing in bars of development Beethoven had abandoned and offering reasons for Beethoven's composing decisions. A complete performance of the first movement followed. The *Times* described it as "an absorbing and adult half hour." *Life* gave the program a full-page spread in its following issue. In San Francisco Bernstein was compared to a young Abe Lincoln and hailed as "one of the more electrifying personalities of our time." *Variety* pointed out that he had "opened up a new field in television," and the *New York Post* suggested, prophetically, that he should be given a regular program.

The thirty-five hundred dollars Bernstein was paid for his Beethoven essay was much needed. He and Lillian Hellman had completed only one act after their first summer's work on *Candide,* and there was a further holdup in November when they broke with Latouche and resolved to write the lyrics themselves. On short notice, Bernstein canceled conducting Milhaud's *King David* and set out to finish *Candide* by the first of February, when he had to leave for Italy. His experience over the previous summer should have warned him that Hellman did not work that quickly. Months had been spent already on breaking down Voltaire's novel into theatrical scenes. (The task was never concluded to everybody's satisfaction.) Nor could Bernstein cope with writing the lyrics for half an operetta. Within weeks of the brilliant but uneven Latouche's withdrawal, Hellman was suggesting new writers for his approval, first E. Y. "Yip" Harburg, then Dorothy Parker and finally James Agee. *Candide* was effectively stalled: Bernstein and Hellman saw their producer, Ethel Linder Reiner, half a dozen times in January; the meetings led to a contract and a down payment of twenty-five hundred dollars—and the decision to postpone production until lyricist and director had been selected. Then he headed for La Scala and a second collaboration with Maria Callas.

# FROM LA SCALA TO BROADWAY

*Maria Callas "La Divina"*—
La Sonnambula, *La Scala, March 1955.*
PHOTO: ERIO PICCAGLIANNI, TEATRO ALLA SCALA, MILAN,
COURTESY OF THE ESTATE OF LEONARD BERNSTEIN

*Some day, preferably soon, I simply must decide what
I'm going to be when I grow up.*

—Bernstein, aged thirty-eight, to Philip and
Barbara Marcuse

B ERNSTEIN spent four months in Italy. At La Scala, Milan, he conducted a controversial new production of Bellini's *La Sonnambula,* with a drastically slimmed-down Maria Callas in the title role, directed by the aristocrat Count Luchino Visconti. An underrehearsed revival of *La Bohème* followed, replacing a planned new production of *Cavalleria Rusticana* which was dropped.

"I've gotten all steamed up about *Sonnambula,* as with *Medea*—getting wild ideas for cutting and staging and tempi," Leonard wrote to Felicia soon after his arrival in Milan. "Luchino has planned a small production, perfect in every stylistic detail, just as I have planned a small orchestra, with emphasis on buoyancy and youth. . . . Callas is greater than ever. She has shrunk to a pinpoint, and is positively beautiful, even offstage. . . . We had our first reading of *Sonnambula* today, and she made me cry."

Because she was expecting her second child, Felicia had to withdraw from the Broadway-bound play *Tonight in Samarkand,* in which she played a tiger-tamer. She made her final appearance in Boston, receiving flowers and an ovation at the curtain call. The whole company applauded, she wrote to her husband: "They pushed me out for a solo call, the audience cheered, the tears streamed down their faces, etc., etc. I must say I'll never forget it Lennuhtt! . . . *Promise me:* do not commit yourself to anything until I arrive and we can talk it over." A few days later she chided Leonard for ignoring her birthday. ". . . don't feel too badly however, 'cause no one but Helen and the servants remembered. That angel of a Jamie pranced into my room singing Happy Birthday. I could have eaten her up." Leonard, deeply involved in his rehearsals, working with a director whose devotion to detail matched his own, replied with a long letter reveling in the domesticated life:

> My darling:
>
> I miss you terribly, and love your letters. They carry a whiff of something warm and familiar and joyful. Imagine—after three years: joyful! Isn't it wonderful: home has always been the spot in which I happened to be: and now it is *a place,* with all that one place connotes: the dining room one apologizes for, and my studio where you get blind with cigarette-smoke, and the two "modern" chairs you hate in the library, and the marvelous sala, and the hall wallpaper you can't stand, and our country bedroom, and the loud canary, and Jamie spreading her presence like a marigold, and the difficulties below-stairs, and Bill [the doorman] with his weather, and all the problems and tensions and joy and noise and quiet. Home. A new experience.
>
> . . . I visited the sartoria of The Scala the other day—an incredible experience. On the outskirts of Milan—a huge warehouse with 40,000 costumes, and thousands of new ones constantly being made—all by hand, and such materials and designs and care and work! (I'm going to have tails made for me there!)
>
> . . . I've never worked so close to a show: really into everything—painting the sets, and spending one hour arguing about the color of the cuff of a sleeve of one costume for one chorus-lady, and kind of co-directing with Luchino, and planning out every second. I'm learning, learning. It's a glorious theatre.
>
> . . . I hope you can get here in time to see Sonnambula at least once: it will be a sweet production, slightly campy, with the stage apron advanced way out so that Callas sings in the middle of Scala, and sings her last fabulous aria with all the houselights up, and flowers flying from the boxes and—you must see it.

The premiere of *La Sonnambula,* deferred because Maria Callas had been suffering from a painful boil on the back of her neck, took place on March 5. Franco Zeffirelli called it the best thing Visconti and Callas ever did together.

"Piero Tosi designed the production in pastel colors, silks and frills. It was a romantic vision. . . . Maria was exquisitely dressed in Swiss peasant style—though with all her jewels, since no diva sang without them, no matter what the role. . . . I remember the third act aria, 'Ah, non credea mirarti. . . .' She sang with her lips barely apart, almost like a ventriloquist, the ultimate pianissimo, and everyone was straining to hear her. The tension was incredible. Today [1986], when Lenny wants more pianissimo from an orchestra, he asks them for a 'Callas pianissimo.' "

In spite of Bernstein's exhilaration during *Sonnambula* rehearsals, and the artistic excitement of the production, all was not well in Milan. Charles Roth, the young conducting student Bernstein had taught in 1950 and 1951 at Tanglewood, turned up to threaten him with blackmail. Roth, whom Bernstein called "the black fairy," demanded that Bernstein make him "the world's top conductor," or he would make public the letters Bernstein had written to him. Bernstein sent him back to Vienna, assuring Felicia, ". . . there is nothing in any of those letters, nor has there ever been any relationship between us of any kind." The mentally unbalanced Roth continued to badger Bernstein with letters and parcels, which were returned unopened. Later Roth threatened to expose Bernstein and his circle of friends as Communists. Bernstein asked Helen Coates to trace the mental hospital where he had been treated. "I cannot understand," he wrote, "why he was released so quickly. He needs *constant* surveillance." To Felicia he added, "Crazy people always scare me, especially this one."

After the premiere of *La Sonnambula* Bernstein plunged into rehearsals for what turned out to be a routine revival of *La Bohème*. It opened only two weeks after *Sonnambula*. The company had done the production before, and not in Bernstein's style. "I have had terrible notices from the critics, who are stupid and pick all the wrong reasons; but they are basically right," he wrote to Helen Coates. "Oh well, the stars are wrong this month."

Meanwhile Bernstein was doing his best to persuade Antonio Ghiringelli, La Scala's artistic director, to produce Marc Blitzstein's *Regina,* with Callas singing the title role. A vocal score had been sent and some sample lyrics were translated, but the Italians temporized, and Blitzstein, hearing nothing, got mad at Bernstein: "What do you want me to do, crawl?" It transpired that Victor de Sabata, La Scala's music director, liked the music but hated the libretto, finding it sadistic, cruel and nonoperatic. The La Scala audience would object, he said, to the spectacle of a woman letting her husband die. Blitzstein wrote to Bernstein in early April. "I've had de Sabata's personal letter—and I have answered it, expressing my disappointment and my surprise that 'compulsory matrimony' (his term), and money-as-the-root-of evil should be unacceptable as an operatic theme. Where has he learned about opera-texts?"

Bernstein himself, "furious and disgusted," was turning against La Scala—but he still looked forward to a second stab at *La Bohème* with a more gifted cast, led by Giuseppe di Stefano. After a short vacation on Capri with Felicia, who spent a month with him in Italy, he went happily back to rehearsals. The holiday had been "sheer heaven," he told Helen Coates. But despite his optimism he suffered the rare indignity of being hissed after the new cast's first performance.

The even tenor of his personal life perhaps consoled him. From New York, Felicia wrote, "Lennuhtt, my stay in Italy now was the happiest time I've had in my life—the feeling is still with me, an aura of *warmth* and quiet fun—and I don't think it all has to do with my being preg.—it is really much deeper and impossible to talk about anyway so you might as well ignore this whole paragraph."

T w o Bernstein compositions were successfully launched in America while he was away. On April 15 Isaac Stern gave the first American performance of the *Serenade* with the Boston Symphony Orchestra, conducted by Charles Munch. And four days later *Trouble in Tahiti* opened on Broadway. "I feel I ought to be composing like mad, now that two of my works have had success in one week, and the composer feeling is with me again. But nothing comes out," he told Felicia.

*Trouble in Tahiti* was part of a triple bill that included Tennessee Williams's *Twenty-Seven Wagons Full of Cotton,* a short play Bernstein had once thought of using as a libretto. Brooks Atkinson of the *Times* called it "an evening of superb theater art." Blitzstein wrote Bernstein that *Tahiti* was a hit. But Helen Coates thought it was a terrible mistake to substitute two pianos for the orchestra—an economy move—and Felicia, who said she'd fallen in love with the piece all over again, was sharply critical: "I sat through the performance doing 'a Lennuhtt'—quivering at the tempi and shooting notes to Shirley who was equipped with pad and pencil! I don't want you to fret and get the impression that it's a fiasco—it is really rather good, but it could be so much better! The main musical faults were in the tempi of the first scene and the rain duet—they cannot understand that the first scene is a serious ugly quarrel. They sing it so slow and measured without really interrupting each other so it becomes endless and dull."

"Why won't people realize that it is the touching parts that the opera is about?" Leonard replied. "The rest is only either comment or diversion. I'd love to see you direct it one day."

With time on his hands while he awaited his next conducting engagements, Bernstein went to Rome to stay with Luchino Visconti, whom he had recommended to Lillian Hellman and Ethel Linder Reiner as a possible stage director for *Candide.* Felicia wrote, wishing him, in Rybernian, a delicious ("delashadü") time, adding that she hoped the atmosphere would not be too "perverty." Leonard replied:

Darling Bubbles:

Rome is beautiful as I have never seen it: blue blue sky, cool air, and the warm sea, and everything blooming away luxuriantly. I am glad I came; but I miss you here. . . . Perverty it is, of course, as is to be expected, but it is not all so. . . . I have seen a lot of Gina Lollobrigida . . . with *Serenade* in mind. . . . The indicated combination would be Lollo and Luchino, a marvellous combo. . . . I would be happy for a postponement of a year on Candide: I'd like to have that time to let it cool and see what should really be done with it. It's wrong the way it is. [*Serenade* was to be a musical based on the James Cain novel. Lollobrigida would play a Mexican tart with a heart of gold.]

Bernstein still worried about money. He had less than three thousand dollars in his checking account plus the ten thousand dollars in a savings account that he was loath to touch. Prospects were improving, however. *Wonderful Town* had just opened in London, and for the first time his quarterly check from ASCAP (American Society of Composers, Authors and Publishers) was over three thousand dollars. Still, the Bernsteins were obliged to turn down the idea of renting a large house near Tanglewood for the summer season. "We really are so broke," Felicia told Helen Coates.

After conducting orchestras in Trieste and Florence, he joined the Israel Philharmonic in Genoa for a brief Italian tour featuring Berlioz's *Romeo and Juliet* and his *Serenade,* again performed by Isaac Stern. He wrote to Felicia: "it was a job and a half teaching them the Serenade and the Berlioz, neither of which they knew, and at a time when they were so tired they could barely read the notes . . . and then there was the concert, and the report is that never before has Genoa seen such a success. Imagine, with my funny modern music and unpopular Berlioz! I had feared for the size of the audience as well as for their applause, and was surprised delightfully on both counts. The papers are raves, and Isaac played better than ever, and the orchestra really did miracles, everything considered. . . ."

During his Italian season Bernstein conducted ten performances of *La Sonnambula* and seven of *La Bohème* and gave eleven concerts, seven of them on the Israel Philharmonic tour. For all this activity, he would take home, when travel costs and agents' commission had been deducted, thirteen thousand dollars. But his commitment to finish *Candide* made him reluctant to accept too many future conducting dates. The production had definitely been postponed once again—hardly surprising since the producer and the author were still wrangling about stars and director, and Bernstein knew he did not yet have the right score, or even a workable set of lyrics. *Candide*'s gestation period seemed interminable.

Seven months' pregnant and showing "what is discreetly called a profile," Felicia was increasingly anxious for her husband's return to New York. She wrote that Jamie was in the tantrum stage. "I'm very worried as to your reaction—our little angel is asserting herself and can be an absolute devil. Please don't be too shocked and impatient and leave us forever."

"You can't scare me with Jamie's tantrums," Bernstein replied. "I've been expecting them all along. . . . Darling girl, it won't be long now. Please stop yourself up with adhesive tape or corks till I get home. LOVE."

Two days after the tour ended in Milan, Bernstein was in Paris meeting the film director René Clair, one of Lillian Hellman's wilder suggestions to direct the uncompleted *Candide*. (Another was Gene Kelly.) Soon he was in New York, plunging into the meetings with writers, directors and producers that were to determine the course of his life for the next two years. La Scala was no longer on his agenda. "It was a mistake to give three months to it," he wrote to Philip Marcuse; "I lost my glamour." It was almost a decade before he was to work in an opera house again.

H is first concern was not *Candide* but the brand-new project he had dreamed up in Rome. On June 13 the *New York Times* reported that he had signed to write the score for a music-play Arthur Laurents had adapted from James Cain's novel. Only six days later, however, *Serenade* was shelved, before it had even been started. It was being replaced, according to the *Times,* by *East Side Story,* a collaboration between Bernstein and Laurents with Jerome Robbins as choreographer and director.

It was Robbins who convinced his friends to turn back to the Romeo and Juliet idea. He and Laurents came to see Bernstein the morning the news item about *Serenade* was published. "I don't know why you're wasting your time on that trash," he said, "when here I'm presenting you with [an] idea which is a much more noble thing to do." Bernstein met Laurents again half a dozen times before he went up to Tanglewood. It was essential to him, both artistically and financially, to develop a realistic work plan for the following winter and beyond. He and Hellman had not solved the lyricist trouble in *Candide*. Dorothy Parker wrote only one song and James Agee died before he could complete anything. Bernstein decided to wait on *Candide* until a new lyricist was found, and in the meantime start composing *East Side Story* straight away, with himself and Laurents handling the lyrics.

Disillusioned by La Scala's routine and by the hard slog of touring with the Israel Philharmonic, Bernstein temporarily abandoned his European conducting career. He did not leave America again for two years. And despite the success of his *Serenade,* he was drawn irresistibly to the theater. It was now as a composer of musicals that he saw himself leading the field. "Don't think it's easy to be a theater composer!" he wrote in November 1954 in one of his Imaginary Conversations. "In some ways it's harder. There is a discipline of the stage. You're not your own boss. It's the whole work that counts! . . . A great theater composer is a rare thing: he must have the sense of timing of a Duse, a sense of when to go easy and when to lay it on. . . . He must have wit and sentiment, pathos and brilliance. . . . What is alive and young and throbbing with historic current in America is musical theater."

ON July 7 Felicia gave birth to a seven-pound-four-ounce baby boy, named after Koussevitzky: Alexander Serge (Leonard) Bernstein. "The parenthetical name is for Goyim only," Bernstein explained to his friends the Marcuses. "He is perfect, with a sloping intellectual brow, and pronounced intellectual (Bernstein tradition) nose and very, very manly. Broad shoulders and loud lungs and a glorious head and just what we wanted."

Three days before Alexander was born, Bernstein completed his *Symphonic Suite from "On the Waterfront,"* which he later dedicated to his son. It was premiered at Tanglewood on August 11. In an introductory article for the *Berkshire Evening Eagle,* Bernstein wrote about the *Waterfront*'s thematic integration, which was intended, he said, to compensate for the inevitable fragmentariness of music used to underscore drama and dialogue in a film. "The main materials of the suite undergo numerous metamorphoses, following as much as possible the chronological flow of the film score itself." But it is not necessary to be familiar with the film to enjoy the music as a piece of symphonic writing. Despite the title, it is not a suite, but rather a tone poem, and incidentally the longest single movement in Bernstein's orchestral output—the slightly longer *Symphonic Dances from "West Side Story"* he was to compose in 1961 are clearly defined as separate dance movements with obvious transition sections. The metamorphosis composition technique derives from Liszt's tone poems; *On the Waterfront* can be seen as a twentieth-century equivalent of Tchaikovsky's fantasy overture *Romeo and Juliet,* with the film's principal characters, Terry and Edie, as the star-crossed lovers.

From Tanglewood Bernstein flew to Los Angeles to serve as artistic director of an ambitious new "Festival of the Americas" conceived by the Hollywood Bowl's administrator, Wynn Rocamora. Despite the grandiose title, there were only five concerts in this hype-laden event. Bernstein had originally been asked to come for two weeks but had talked it down to one, at the same handsome fee, seventy-five hundred dollars. His opening concert, attended by Vice President Nixon, featured contemporary American music. Latin-American composers were featured in another concert and Martha Graham's company made an appearance. The only sold-out evening was dedicated to jazz: Bernstein chaired a symposium similar to the one at Brandeis in 1952; this time Billie Holiday and André Previn were among the performers.

It was not the most arduous of weeks for Bernstein. His expense account suggests that he did a fair amount of drinking and sunbathing. The most significant part of the trip was a poolside meeting with Arthur Laurents at the Beverly Hills Hotel to discuss the development of their new musical, *East Side Story.* While they were talking, Bernstein noticed a newspaper headline: "GANG

RIOTS ON OLIVIERA ST.," a story reporting violence between Mexicans and Anglos. At last they had found a viable modern equivalent to the rivalry between the Montagues and Capulets. As Bernstein and Laurents developed their idea, the setting was transferred from Los Angeles to New York, and the Mexicans were recast as Puerto Rican immigrants. Bernstein's imagination caught fire, he said, as the Latin-American rhythms began to pulse in his mind.

"This is to be a composing year," Bernstein wrote to Martha Gellhorn when he returned to Great Barrington at the end of August; "all winter on 57th Street with my ever-widening family circle; a new show (tragic this time) and rewriting the old show (the interminable *Candide*) and a big orchestral work for the Boston Symphony's 75th Anniversary. . . ."

In mid-September Bernstein and his wife appeared on Ed Murrow's popular "Person to Person" program, playing duets and sitting side by side on a sofa in their Osborne living room, devastatingly charming, almost relaxed and both smoking away like chimneys (as was Murrow). Felicia told Ed they were at the beginning of a very crowded season. She rattled off Lenny's activities in such detail that her husband joked feebly that she knew more about him than he knew himself (which in some ways was true). He had recently announced that he was going to compose the incidental music for *The Lark*, Lillian Hellman's translation of *L'Alouette,* a 1953 play by Jean Anouilh about Joan of Arc (who, like Miss Hellman, had defied repressive authorities). The play opened later in the fall, and ran for 229 performances on Broadway. (Bernstein's Renaissance-style music for seven voices took on independent life in 1988 as his *Missa Brevis*.)

The sheer profusion of projects in Bernstein's professional life at this point can be seen from a glance at his datebook for the last week of September 1955. On the twenty-sixth he met Joseph Anthony, the director of *The Lark*, and Noah Greenberg of Pro Musica Antiqua, who was to conduct his score. On the same evening he saw Arthur Laurents for dinner to discuss *East Side Story.* He met Laurents again on the twenty-seventh, the twenty-eighth, and the thirtieth. On the twenty-seventh he had a meeting about a forthcoming "Omnibus" program on jazz. The next day he dined with Tyrone Guthrie, who in July had agreed to direct *Candide.* Two days later he and Arthur Laurents had a meeting with Comden and Green, hoping to persuade them to do the lyrics for *East Side Story.* (They were too busy on *Bells Are Ringing.*) The same day Bernstein lunched with Guthrie and dined with Hellman. "I suppose it's a little crazy to do all these things I do," he told a journalist, "but that's my curse." He described himself as suffering from double schizophrenia, his loyalties split first between composing and performing, and split again, in both activities, between concert hall, opera house, Broadway theater and television studio. "I have never wanted an orchestra of my own," he declared, "because immediately I'd become bogged down. I might be able to compose symphonies but I'd never be able to do theater work."

The first of his autumn labors to reach completion was an "Omnibus" program called *The World of Jazz.* Looking, *The New Yorker* noted, like a young Burgess Meredith, Bernstein delivered a "splendidly lucid primer" on some of the essential elements in jazz, such as improvisation, syncopation, blue notes, and the different colorations created by vibrato and by mutes on trumpets and trombones. The live music—in a variety of jazz styles—was performed in the studio by an unnamed group of "sessions" men, clever, all-purpose white musicians who were adequate for Bernstein's educational purpose. Nobody who saw the program or has heard the Columbia recording derived from the original script could forget Bernstein's discussion of the structure of the twelve-bar blues and the pleasure he expressed in his discovery that the typical blues couplet is stressed in iambic pentameter:

*My man / don't love / me, treats / me aw / ful mean*

Bernstein proceeded to growl out a blues to the iambic pentameters of William Shakespeare, *Macbeth,* Act V, Scene 3:

*I will not be afraid of death and bane*
*Till Birnam forest come to Dunsinane.*

Then he tackled improvisation, attempting to draw a parallel between Mozart's variations in the piano work *Ah Vous Dirai-je, Maman* and the way jazz players embellish a popular song like "Sweet Sue." He spoke warmly about improvisation in jam sessions, about swing in the 1930s and about the new "bop" style, which he suggested, astonishingly, was "the real beginning of serious American music." In the same paragraph he unceremoniously dismissed all American symphonic works up to 1955 (including, by inference, his own) as being no more than personalized imitations of the European symphonic tradition from Mozart to Mahler. He was leading his audience around to a performance of a jazz work of his own, the *Prelude, Fugue and Riffs* with which the "Omnibus" program concluded.

The work, which plays just under ten minutes, is scored for solo clarinet and a conventional 1930s swing group. The "Prelude" is played by the trumpets and trombones, the "Fugue" by five saxophones and the "Riffs," the longest section, by a solo clarinet and a hard-driving rhythmic piano, backed by the entire band, which is "jumping" by the end—after Bernstein combines the riff music with both his fugal themes. Only here, when the composer calls for free-flowing *ad lib* repetitions, can the piece be truly described as jazz. Behind the scenes, Benny Goodman, a Tanglewood neighbor and friend since the 1940s, had encouraged Bernstein to perform the work. He made the first recording with him for Columbia.

Bernstein's knowledge of jazz was cheerful and enthusiastic, but essentially superficial. Jazz musicians never thought much of his gifts as an improviser. But his next "Omnibus" essay, on the art of conducting, was a field in which he knew more than any other American. On December 4 he gave an estimated sixteen million Sunday afternoon viewers a detailed and illuminating description of the conductor's job.

At the beginning of the program an orchestra is seen in dramatic silhouette, playing the somber opening bars of Brahms's First Symphony. The conductor is in a pool of light, his back to us. After a few seconds Leonard Bernstein—for it is he—ceases to gesticulate and turns away from the orchestra, which continues to play behind him as he walks toward the camera and addresses the audience at home. "You see, they don't need me. They do perfectly well by themselves," which indeed they do, quietly continuing under Bernstein's dialogue until they reach letter A in the score, a tactful moment to stop. It is a stunning *coup de télévision*. Bernstein proceeds to make us all into conductors. He shows us how to beat time in different signatures from one in a bar upward and how to express feelings and character in the music by the body language employed to do the stick-wagging—by turns poetic, energetic, and decisive. He explains how to find an appropriate tempo and how to manage a tasteful rubato. He reminds us that a conductor needs to be an artistic historian, with an informed opinion on the cultural and stylistic standing of anything he conducts. He analyzes the first page of the Brahms First Symphony, identifying the upward-straining melody and the downward-dragging counter-melody and the throbbing pedal note on timpani and double basses which, according to the conductor's conception, may either be pushing the movement forward or emphasizing its doom-laden solemnity. He shows how the conductor must decide how loud is loud (*forte*), or, in the specific case of the brass at the beginning of the Brahms First Symphony, how soft the *forte* should be in order not to drown the rest of the orchestra. He demonstrates the different tonal qualities obtained when the violins play with *vibrato* and without it, when they use a little bow or a lot, when they pluck the string *pizzicato* with the hard fingertip or with the soft flesh of the finger.

This is all entertaining, behind-the-scenes stuff, beautifully delivered by Bernstein in a relaxed manner. Then he moves the discourse on to a higher plane—into Koussevitzky country. He talks for nearly ten minutes straight to the camera with no examples to distract us. "We now begin to deal with the intangibles, the deep magic of conducting." A true conductor is one with "great sensitivity to the flow of time . . . a kind of sculptor whose element is time instead of marble. . . . He must judge the largest rhythms, the whole phraseology of a work. He must conquer the form of a piece not only in the sense of form as a mold, but form in its deepest sense, knowing and controlling where the music relaxes, where it begins to accumulate tension, where the greatest tension is reached, where it must ease up to gather strength for the next lap, where it unloads that strength." None of the foregoing is of real value, Bernstein adds, without the power to communicate to the orchestra. Long romantic speeches about "the beauty-meanings of a piece . . . [are] of no earthly use." In Bernstein's view, the conductor is a benevolent dictator. "Everything must be shown to the orchestra before it happens . . . so the conductor always has to be a beat or two ahead of the orchestra. . . . The basic trick is in the preparatory upbeat. . . . It is exactly like breathing: the preparation is like an inhalation, and the music sounds as an exhalation."

His peroration is magnificent—and deeply personal. "Finally, the great conductor must not only make his orchestra play, he must make them want to play. He must exalt them, lift them, start their adrenaline pouring, either through cajoling or demanding or raging. But however he does it, he must make the orchestra love the music as he loves it. It is not so much imposing his will on them like a dictator; it is more like projecting his feelings around him so that they reach the last man in the second violin section. And when this happens —when one hundred men share his feelings, exactly, simultaneously, responding as one to each rise and fall of the music, to each point of arrival and departure, to each little inner pulse—then there is a human identity of feeling that has no equal elsewhere. It is the closest thing I know to love itself. On this current of love the conductor can communicate at the deepest levels with his players, and ultimately with his audience."

Bernstein rounded off the program by rehearsing sections of the finale of the Brahms First Symphony. Work never stops, he said: "the conductor is an eternal student." *Variety* called the program "the perfect teleshow." It was among the best things Bernstein ever did in a studio.


In November 1955 Bernstein reappeared on New York's musical scene, after accepting an invitation to conduct a season of six Carnegie Hall concerts with the Symphony of the Air, formerly Toscanini's personal orchestra at NBC, now fighting for its life. He needed the money and he wanted to help save a fine orchestra. He initiated the series with Mahler's *Resurrection* Symphony and ended it in April 1956 with the New York premiere of his *Serenade*.

The position seemed on the face of it a satisfactory halfway house between a full-scale music director's job and the hired-hand status of guest-conducting for an established orchestra. But there were difficulties. The players were a self-governing and talkative bunch, with whom it was difficult to negotiate and who meddled publicly with Bernstein's program plans. The orchestra management had problems paying their bills. Finally, in March 1956, a congressional subcommittee in Washington, chaired by Representative John Rooney from Brooklyn, alleged that some of the orchestra's members had Communist sympathies. Bernstein was not named in the congressional hearings but was widely assumed to be the mysterious "No. 5" on the list of politically dubious personalities connected with the orchestra. When the transcripts of the hearings came out he summoned the Symphony of the Air's manager, Jerome Toobin, for a conference with his lawyer, Abe Friedman, and his secretary, Helen Coates. Toobin described the scene in his memoirs, *Agitato:*

> He literally clutched at his throat when he talked, and shook his head from side to side, and groaned: "My God, what a time for this. What a time. The show [*West Side Story*] is almost ready and now this. Oh. What are we going to do, it's so—so—stupid, for Christ sake." And he wrung his hands, and chain smoked, and thrashed around. And he stroked his throat. Most of the time he lay on a sofa. He'd sit up, but only briefly, and lie down again.
>
> And Friedman said, "Now take it easy, let's look at the stuff and see what it's all about. You know how ridiculous this stuff usually is."
>
> And Helen said, "Now Lenny, stop taking on so. Gracious. It's all foolishness. Stop taking on so. Goodness."
>
> And I sat there and agreed with everybody.
>
> We began going through the material on number five, who it was agreed by all was Bernstein. Bernstein didn't remember half the organizations he was supposed to have joined and had never heard of the other half. He admitted in a calmer moment, with a giggle, that in his extreme youth he would join anything if they would put his name in print— Committees for Greek, Polynesian, Eskimo, or Transylvanian Freedom. He remembered letterheads, he told us, that read: "Agranapos, Avanopoulos, Bajoulopoulos, Bernstein, Cachamapoulos. . . ." No idea what the outfit really did, but he was a joiner if his name got in print. . . . This was the grist for Rooney's mill. So Bernstein alternated between angry contempt and hysteria. Friedman soothing, Helen "my graciousing," Toobin sitting there. . . . The contrast between the self-contained Bernstein I knew in Carnegie Hall and the writhing, throat-clutching man on the sofa before me was startling.

A few days later, Bernstein went up to Boston to take part in an "Omnibus" program about life at Harvard. One of his co-hosts in an elaborate seventeen-camera show about the venerable university was John F. Kennedy (Class of 1941). The two struck up a friendship, and two days later, on March 27, Bernstein lunched with Kennedy in Washington and attended a debate at the Senate. Perhaps Senator Kennedy was able to offer advice about Bernstein's security-clearance problems. At all events, Bernstein was not bothered again by the Rooney hearings.

In the end his relationship with the Symphony of the Air was superseded by something altogether more promising. On November 18, 1955, he had received a telegram from Bruno Zirato confirming a four-week guest engagement with the New York Philharmonic in December 1956 and January 1957. Two months later he lunched with his old friend Dimitri Mitropoulos, who since 1951 had been the Philharmonic's musical director. Mitropoulos had recently received an early intimation of mortality in the form of a heart attack. He wanted to spend more of what time was left to him conducting opera at the "Met" and he wanted Bernstein to follow him at the Philharmonic. Mitropoulos was no more empowered to name his successor than Koussevitzky had been in Boston— but he did have considerable influence with the Philharmonic board. For his part, Bernstein could not contemplate a full-time conducting job—he had not yet completed either of his Broadway shows—but the prospect of regular, well-paid prestige employment with the Philharmonic was beginning to appeal again. So when the orchestra under Mitropoulos received a critical bashing from the *New York Times* and *Herald Tribune* in the spring of 1956, negotiations got under way for a more formal relationship with Bernstein.

During his 1955–56 season with the Symphony of the Air, Bernstein's friendship with Aaron Copland became strained. As a prelude to Mahler's *Resurrection* Symphony, Bernstein scheduled the New York premiere of Copland's new work for chorus and orchestra, entitled *Canticle of Freedom*. Copland attended a rehearsal and was deeply disappointed. "The piece seemed to have no conviction; the playing and singing were very tentative because the performers had no chance to familiarize themselves with the music. It was obvious that Lenny had cut the rehearsal time for my work in favor of Mahler's *Resurrection Symphony*. I told him so and threatened not to go to the performance—and didn't."

Bridges were quickly rebuilt between Bernstein and Copland—the concert had gone well—but their old intimacy was a thing of the past. Bernstein had new friends now, none more creatively important than Stephen Sondheim, who in October 1955 was chosen as the lyricist for *West Side Story*. (The title *East Side Story* was dropped when it was discovered that the notorious tenements on Manhattan's East Side had all been pulled down. Gang war had moved west.) Sondheim was a family friend of Oscar Hammerstein, Jr., and had been in love with music theater since childhood. A music major at Williams College (class of 1950), he was comfortably well-off. Jewish . . . "but very Park Avenue" was how his composition teacher Milton Babbitt once described him. He was accustomed to spending time with celebrities and expected to become one himself. At their first meeting he told Bernstein that he had been trained as a composer and had already written words and music for his own show, *Saturday Night*. Bernstein was loath to give up his own lyric-writing entirely, and offered Sondheim only a shared credit as lyricist. "I can't do this show," Sondheim told Oscar Hammerstein; "I've never been that poor and I've never even *known* a Puerto Rican." But Hammerstein convinced him that the chance to work with some of Broadway's most outstanding talents simply could not be turned down.

Bernstein and Sondheim worked quietly together all through the winter of 1955–56. "I could explain musical problems to him and he'd understand immediately, which made the collaboration a joy," Bernstein later said of Sondheim. "It was like writing with an alter ego. We also found we shared a love for words and word games and puzzles, to say nothing of anagrams. In fact, I think we spent more time doing puzzles than we did writing lyrics for *West Side Story*." Work moved forward so confidently that in January 1956 the *Post* reported that production was set for the fall. The paper called it an "off-beat musical . . . done and ready for serving but the cooks are busy with other projects."

# CANDIDE

*The original Broadway production of* Candide, *with (from left to right) Max Adrian as Pangloss, Louis Edmonds as Maximilian, Barbara Cook as Cunegonde and Robert Rounseville as Candide, December 1956.*
BILLY ROSE THEATRE COLLECTION, THE NEW YORK PUBLIC LIBRARY FOR THE PERFORMING ARTS, ASTOR, LENOX AND TILDEN FOUNDATIONS

*A triumph of stage arts molded into a symmetrical whole.*

—BROOKS ATKINSON,
*New York Times,*
December 3, 1956

BERNSTEIN'S "other project" was *Candide.* In December 1955 he and Hellman finally found the right lyricist for *Candide:* Richard Wilbur, a thirty-five-year-old poet whose witty translation of *Le Misanthrope* had just been performed at the Poet's Theatre in Cambridge, Massachusetts. He taught English at Wellesley College and had recently been in Italy on a Prix de Rome fellowship. He was already recognized to be one of the leading figures of his generation. The bulk of Wilbur's work on *Candide* was to be done in the summer and fall of 1956. He provided lyrics for the second act, and he revised his predecessors' work on the first act, often with startling improvements.

Bernstein spent the winter and spring of 1956 juggling his many activities as he waited for Wilbur to join him. As Felicia put it: "Lenny never does anything in moderation. If we go to the opera, we go to a midnight movie on the way home. He always carries a pocketful of anti-acid pills; if he decides he must eat a raw onion sandwich, he first eats the sandwich and then the pills." He kept himself in the public eye, and had some fun at the same time, by accepting an invitation to be on a television panel show for ABC called "Down You Go," hosted by Bergen Evans, an erudite and charming college professor. Shirley Bernstein was the show's producer. Appearing weekly from February to May Bernstein earned more than $1,750, and the *Detroit News* nominated him, only half-jokingly, as the season's "best Male TV panelist." "It doesn't do me any good but it pays the maids," was Bernstein's pronouncement.

In May he moved to Martha's Vineyard. "Here we are," he reported to Phil ("Pfil") Marcuse, "painfully as before, like a déjà vu, once again ensconced in the same house on Martha's Vineyard, with Lillian H. hard by, writing *Candide*. It doesn't seem possible. I even got a crewcut at the same barber shop in Falmouth en route, and have said the same hellos to the same rabbits." Richard Wilbur and Tyrone Guthrie, hired as director, were also in Martha's Vineyard, but even now Bernstein had to interrupt himself for various conducting engagements, among them a Lewisohn Stadium concert at which he accompanied Louis Armstrong in the "St. Louis Blues" for a film called *The Saga of Satchmo*. In Chicago he conducted a miniature Bernstein festival with performances of *Jeremiah, Anxiety* and the *Serenade* on successive evenings. The *Serenade,* played by Tossy Spivakovsky, received more appreciative notices than it had at its New York premiere back in April. Then, Howard Taubman in the *Times* had not been seduced: it was, he wrote, "attractive in places and ought to be better in sum." But the *Chicago Daily Tribune* thought Bernstein was "as near an authentic genius as there is." The jazzy music of the last movement, disliked by Taubman, was praised by the *Chicago Daily News* as "wonderfully salubrious. . . . The kind of thing Haydn might have written if he had lived in New York City in the 1940s."

Bernstein also traveled to Cambridge, Massachusetts, to see Felicia play the Queen of France in Shakespeare's *Henry V*. "Lenny was there for opening night," she told a journalist. "He makes me nervous." At the New York premiere of his *Serenade* she had been the one with the nerves. She paced up and down outside her box, unable to sit still. "It's like childbirth," she had told Leonard Lyons of the *Post*. "Leonard paces when I'm in labor and I pace when he is." In Cambridge she was frank about the disjointed nature of her career. Nowadays, she said, she took television work only when her husband was also in New York so that their children would see at least one parent every day. She took pride in what she'd achieved for his sake: "His career is more important than mine. He's been composing more devotedly since we've been married."

*CANDIDE* was virtually completed in August 1956. It was Bernstein's most substantial achievement as a composer. The score consists of close to two hours of music and over thirty numbers: solos, duets, trios, quartets, ensembles, cho-ruses and purely orchestral music, frequently interspersed or combined with spoken dialogue. Thanks to Richard Wilbur, *Candide* is throughout impeccably versified. The problem lies in the adaptation of the story. Voltaire's *Candide,* first published in 1759, is a picaresque novella, only eighty-seven pages long, in which, as the satirist John Wells put it, "every page takes us to a different country and every paragraph contains some new adventure." Hellman and Bernstein saw in its satirical attacks on the Catholic Church and the bland optimism of the philosopher Leibnitz a way of hitting back at Eisenhower's complacent America. But Voltaire's mockery of the philosophy that "all's for the best in the best of all possible worlds" and the novel's cynical acceptance of war, greed, treachery, venery, snobbishness and mendacity as staples of civiliza-tion are achieved by short sharp sentences contained in thirty chapters of comic-strip brevity. Lillian Hellman's expertise, on the other hand, was in the field of the "well-made" three-act play; she had never written a comedy, although she was by many accounts a witty woman. Yet Bernstein would not have agreed to collaborate with her had he not believed that her sense of theater and play structure, combined with her anger at what was happening to America, could be productively harnessed.

Bernstein and Hellman worked together in New York and Martha's Vine-yard, so no written correspondence exists to show how they devised their adaptation. But it is not surprising to learn that Hellman went through fourteen different versions: she faced a well-nigh impossible job creating a workable theatrical structure, and it has to be conceded that in the intervening years nobody else has been entirely successful either. At the time of his death in 1990 Bernstein had collaborated directly on at least seven versions (London 1959, Los Angeles 1966, Chicago 1967, San Francisco 1971, New York City Opera 1982, Scottish Opera 1988 and LSO Concert 1989) and had also allowed Harold Prince and Hugh Wheeler to create a high-spirited pocket-version, first seen in an off-Broadway theater, in 1973.

*Candide* is "based on" Voltaire in much the same way that *The Age of Anxiety* is "after" W. H. Auden and the *Serenade* is "after" Plato. Many of the best moments in the Hellman adaptation are not even hinted at in Voltaire's original: Voltaire mentions no interrogation during the auto-da-fé, no waltz in Paris, no gambling casino in Venice; in the novel Candide expresses no lament after the butchering of Cunegonde and no bitter sadness at her fall from grace. Voltaire's Candide receives advice from two philosophers: the genial Dr. Pan-gloss's sugary conclusions are mirrored by the bitter reflections of old Martin. Hellman has the same actor play both parts, which is a neat solution. But her overall scheme for *Candide* runs into problems caused by the bewildering num-ber of locations. Voltaire's skepticism is finally subverted on the home stretch when Bernstein's incurable optimism turns "Make Our Garden Grow" into a stirring and positive hymn full of hope for a better world. Voltaire's moral, *"Il faut cultiver son jardin,"* translated in the operetta as "Make our garden grow," contains an element of hope, to be sure, but it is more passive, quietist, in spirit than Bernstein's ecstatic music would have the audience believe.

The important question is not whether Bernstein has been true to the spirit of Voltaire, but whether he has created a rounded work of art. Although a perfect stage production of *Candide* may never be achieved, the work has proved to be a deeply satisfying piece, exemplifying the credo Bernstein expressed at the 1953 Brandeis festival: "Man's capacity for laughter is nobler than his divine gift of suffering." The rival elements of fun and thoughtfulness that jostle for supremacy throughout *Candide* are a reflection of Bernstein's own complicated, almost schizophrenic personality. On the other hand, *Candide* is far from being the "real, moving" American opera Bernstein had promised himself. The music of "Candide's Lament" and the chorales is "simple yet strong," but much else is ultrasophisticated. The language is English but its relevance to contemporary American life went over many people's heads, largely because the incisive satire on the House Un-American Activities Committee was edited out of the Inquisition scene by a nervous Tyrone Guthrie before the show opened in Boston; it was successfully restored in Gordon Davidson's Los Angeles revival of 1966, but disappeared from all subsequent versions.

The score of *Candide* was described by Bernstein as a Valentine card to European music. European dance forms such as the gavotte, mazurka, polka, schottische and waltz pop up all over the place. The conventions of European opera are gently mocked: when the lovers are reunited for the surrealistic duet "You Were Dead, You Know," they warble in thirds and sixths in the best *bel canto* style, remembered from *La Sonnambula*. When the chorus repeats the closing couplets of Dr. Pangloss's syphilis song, "Dear Boy," it is as if the ghosts of Gilbert and Sullivan have entered the theater. Bernstein's past has come to haunt him with the echoes of *H.M.S. Pinafore* at Sharon.

It was suggested at the time that Bernstein was deriding opera and operetta. Nothing could be further from the truth. Cunegonde's comic aria "Glitter and Be Gay" is much more than a parody of the "Jewel Song" from Gounod's *Faust;* the basic humor is derived from the way the bathos of Cunegonde's slow waltz recitative—"Here I am in Paris, France"—is contrasted with her insouciant coloratura warblings as she bedecks herself with pearls and sapphires—"If I'm not pure, at least my jewels are!" And when Bernstein resorts to a complex feat of counterpoint in the "Venice Gavotte," combining "I've got troubles of my own" with "Lady Frilly, Lady Silly," he does not trumpet his cleverness but rather lets us enjoy his compositional dexterity as a side product of the action. There never was a Broadway show fashioned with more musical skill. As it turned out, the cleverness worked against it at the box office.

A Broadway production is always a team effort. *Candide*'s was led, nominally at least, by its producer, Ethel Linder Reiner, a wealthy New Yorker who had once been a sculptor. She had had considerable success in the 1953–54 season with *The Rainmaker* and had recently produced a European tour for *Four Saints in Three Acts* by Virgil Thomson. She was a woman of artistic ambition prepared to take risks on a project that was not an obvious candidate for Broadway. She estimated costs for the show at three hundred thousand dollars, a hefty sum in those days, and she traveled to Dallas and five other cities seeking to raise half the investments out of town at fifteen hundred dollars maximum per investor. Richard Wilbur thought her well intentioned but something of a dilettante.

The director, "Tony" Guthrie, looked like a British Army colonel and talked like an Irish don. Tall and ebullient, he had been the chief of the Old Vic in London, had directed Laurence Olivier in *Hamlet* at Elsinore, had staged opera at the Metropolitan and had most recently directed *The Matchmaker* by Thornton Wilder. Unfortunately, he had no experience at all with the Broadway musical. Oliver Smith and Irene Sharaff, on the other hand, were show business veterans. Sharaff designed three hundred costumes, ranging in period over two centuries, for a cast of kings and cardinals, courtesans and beggars. It was the most elaborate production since the previous season's *My Fair Lady*.

*Candide* was cast without a major star. This has never been cited as a reason for its disappointingly short Broadway run but it must have been a contributing factor. Alfred Drake, star of *Kismet,* had been talked about for Dr. Pangloss but the part eventually went to Max Adrian, a witty British actor unknown on Broadway. Robert Rounseville, the Candide, had sung Captain Macheath in Peter Brook's film of *The Beggar's Opera* and Tom Rakewell in the world premiere of Stravinsky's *The Rake's Progress.* Barbara Cook, the irresistible Cunegonde, had only a small role in *Carousel* the previous year to her credit.

The show opened in Boston for three weeks of tryouts. The dress rehearsal overran catastrophically and the reviewers were asked to come back later in the week. "We have a little trouble," Tony Guthrie told the charity benefit audience in his disarming way, "but we're going to get this thing on tonight." *Variety*'s account, when it came, began promisingly: "It's a spectacular, opulent and racy musical, verging on operetta. It's replete with eye-filling costumes, lavish settings, a big cast and fine musical score." Then came the warning: "A major hurdle to popular acceptance of the show is the somewhat esoteric nature of its satire (and the public's unfamiliarity with the Voltaire original). The musical also needs severe cutting, especially in the second act."

Many other Boston reviewers were enthusiastic about *Candide,* but the book was criticized for being slow and heavy and hard to follow. Behind the scenes the mood was close to panic. When Lester Osterman, Mrs. Reiner's associate producer and fellow investor, came up from New York to see a performance, he arrived late, in time to catch only the last fifteen minutes: " 'I was almost knocked down by people trying to get out of the theater,' he told a crisis meeting next morning." Bernstein and Hellman pruned to clarify the show and wrote extra material to provide more time for costume changes. An especially hectic rewrite period began when it was decided that a new number was needed to brighten up the start of the scene in the Venice casino. Script conferences, Richard Wilbur remembers, took place in the men's room at the theater. "Let's do a vulgar rousing number," Bernstein said. He wanted the kind of song that might be sung on the way to a college football game—but with echoes of "Carnival in Venice." The result was "What's the Use?" Bernstein improvised a refrain there and then, after which he and Wilbur went back to their separate hotels; every hour or so Wilbur would phone through another verse or a refinement to an existing idea. Hershy Kay came up from New York the same day to do the orchestration, and that evening the number was part of the show.

When *Candide* opened in New York at the Martin Beck Theatre, on Saturday, December 1, 1956, the critics saw a production from which probably too much had been cut. Guthrie lacked the experience to do his own show-doctoring and nobody was in command of the creative talent in the way that George Abbott had been for Bernstein's two previous musicals. Backstage there was a sense of disappointment. Yet the work was received with acclamation in many quarters. Brooks Atkinson wrote an unqualified rave in the *New York Times.* "Since Voltaire was a brilliant writer it is only right that his *Candide* should turn out to be a brilliant musical satire." John Chapman, in the *Daily News* called it a "work of genius"; in a follow-up piece he hailed it as "wonderfully enjoyable and a very important event in the theatre . . . so good that it stands in a class by itself." Howard Taubman offered a music critic's opinion: "the popular instincts of the Broadway theatre have been seasoned with delicious sophistication and immense gusto."

One or two New York critics were openly hostile. Walter Kerr in the *Herald Tribune* was the most damning. "A really spectacular disaster," he called it, lambasting Lillian Hellman's attempts to match Voltaire's satire as "academic, blunt and barefaced." Tyrone Guthrie's hand was, he said, for once unsure: "ensemble songs are sung with a vote of no confidence, cluttered crowds trample one another." The lyrics, he claimed, "had no purposeful edge"; for "a great part of the evening Mr. Bernstein is composing little pastiches."

But a few bad reviews could not on their own kill a show as good as *Candide.* The truth seems to be that there were not enough theater-goers of sophisticated taste in New York to support the show past a couple of months. *Candide* suffered the same fate as Blitzstein's *The Cradle Will Rock* in 1948 and *Regina* in 1949, and Menotti's *The Saint of Bleecker Street* in 1955. Four of the seven New York daily critics gave *Candide* rave reviews, yet receipts were dipping badly within a month. The reason, John Chapman suggested, was that "it was O.P.E.R.A." While he loved the show personally, Chapman admitted that there was also the Broadway view that *"Candide* is a great big bore because it does not have a romantic plot according to Broadway standards, and it does not have any songs in it which can be understood by disk jockeys or hung on the appallingly dispiriting record racks of juke boxes in saloons and dining-car hash-houses."

When attendance fell off, Bernstein and his partners took a 50 percent cut in royalty payments. Letters for and against *Candide* appeared every Sunday in the correspondence columns of the *Times*. After a provisional closing was announced in mid-January, box office bookings rose dramatically, and the show grossed over forty-four thousand dollars in each of its last two weeks, double the previous fortnight's take. By the time Ethel Reiner closed *Candide,* on February 2, it was beginning to sell well. Oliver Smith believes it was an unnecessary failure, that Mrs. Reiner "arbitrarily closed it" because she was mad at Lillian Hellman. The two women had a tremendous row at his house, Smith recalled; "Hellman could be very cruel, screaming and yelling at her, and Mrs. Reiner had just had it and said 'the heck with it.' "

All that remains of the original show is a lively cast recording, produced by Goddard Lieberson for Columbia. Conducted by the show's devoted musical director, Samuel Krachmalnick, it became a collectors' item on both sides of the Atlantic. The show had run for only seventy-three performances at a cost of $340,000. Bernstein earned less than $10,000 for a task that had been in progress for three years. (Voltaire had written his novella in only three weeks.)

In their postmortems the participants blamed themselves as well as others. Tyrone Guthrie, in his autobiography, said his direction had "the effortless grace of a freight train heavy-laden on a steep gradient." Guthrie was generous to Bernstein—"the stuff of genius is here"—but suggested that Bernstein's artistic collaborators were in some way dimmed as an "unconscious reaction to the diamond quality of Bernstein's brilliance." Bernstein is reported to have complained that Richard Wilbur "shuts himself off in a phone booth and talks to God!" Wilbur remembers that Bernstein "thought rather highly of himself as a writer." On one occasion Wilbur was so exasperated by the way Bernstein came up with his own version for a lyric that he would have quit had he not been strapped for cash. Instead, he made a joke of it; when he left Martha's Vineyard briefly in the summer of 1956 he asked Hellman to protect his interests: "if you catch [Lenny] re-writing my lyrics, clip his piano wires."

As Richard Wilbur saw it, "There was no single villain. Lillian Hellman doesn't really like musicals. Lenny's music got more and more pretentious and smashy—the audience forgot what was happening to the characters. Lillian's book got to be mere connective tissue." Hellman called *Candide* "her most unpleasant experience in the theater." Oliver Smith remembers she fought tooth and nail with Guthrie over his cuts, denouncing him at one rehearsal. "You've sold out," she screamed; "You're just a whore." Smith, for one, disagrees with the often-repeated claim that *Candide* suffered because there were too many talents at work. Bernstein was working with equally distinguished collaborators on *West Side Story*.

I N the fall of 1956 Bernstein wrote and hosted an elaborate Sunday night spectacular for "Omnibus" (now on ABC Television) entitled *The American*

*Musical Comedy.* With *Candide* going into production and *West Side Story* virtually finished, he was well placed to discuss the subject. He identified the great unifying factor in the Broadway musical: it is "an art that arises out of American roots, out of our speech, our tempo, our moral attitudes, our timing, our kind of humor." Then he talked about what might happen next in American musical theater. In the eighteenth century, he said, Mozart had taken *Singspiel* —literally a "singing play"—and made it into art. "After all, *The Magic Flute* is a *Singspiel;* only it's by Mozart. . . . All we need is for our Mozart to come along. If and when he does we surely won't get any *Magic Flute;* what we'll get will be a new form, and perhaps 'opera' will be the wrong word for it. There must be a more exciting word for it. And this event can happen any second. It's almost as though it is our moment in history, as if there is a historical necessity that gives us such a wealth of creative talent at this precise time."

It was a muddled yet prophetic message. The Broadway shows of the forties and fifties that Bernstein loved so much were in no way the equivalents of the forgotten *Singspiel* composers who preceded Mozart. On the contrary, Irving Berlin, Jerome Kern, Frank Loesser, Frederick Loewe, Cole Porter and Richard Rodgers were composers of a golden age. And yet Bernstein and some of his collaborators were genuinely approaching their "moment in history." Not the *Candide* team: *Candide* will eventually take its place in opera houses as a satirical operetta. But Bernstein was right about a new form: the other musical on which he was working was indeed something original. It could not be called "opera," because it relied on an element he hardly mentioned in his television show—the dance, used creatively to tell the story. The work was the modern tragedy *West Side Story,* and 1957, the year of its production, was also the year when Bernstein drew near to the pinnacle of his American career.

# WEST SIDE STORY

*The Rumble,* West Side Story.

PHOTO: FRED FEHL, MUSEUM OF THE CITY OF NEW YORK, THE THEATER COLLECTION

I N early December of 1956, immediately after the opening of *Candide,* Bernstein fled to Nassau to get away from it all. He talked to no one for three days, except to order his meals, as he rested and licked his wounds far from the madding crowds of Broadway. Even had the show been an unqualified triumph, too much of his music had been jettisoned along the bumpy road from Boston to New York for him to feel comfortable about the hit-and-miss business of composing a Broadway show. As it was, he must have experienced a brief sense of despair at all the hard work and agonized hours that had failed to jell.

*West Side Story* was still waiting in the wings, but Cheryl Crawford, who had become the show's producer the previous April, had not yet succeeded in assembling a production package. Meanwhile, Bernstein had committed himself in the months ahead to a heavy new load of conducting and television programs. In November 1956, shortly before *Candide* opened, he had been appointed joint principal conductor of the New York Philharmonic, effective the 1957–58 season, sharing the title with Mitropoulos, who was stepping down as musical director. The appointment was widely seen as an interim move which would test Bernstein's willingness and ability to devote a substantial portion of his time to the Philharmonic. His first contact with the orchestra, after a six-year hiatus, would be the month-long engagement arranged before negotiations for a more permanent position had begun. This was brought forward an additional two weeks to December 13, as a result of the death in a Paris airplane crash of the Italian conductor Guido Cantelli. Bernstein kept to Cantelli's planned programs, which meant restudying among other music the grand *Mathis der Maler* Symphony by Hindemith.

His own programs began after Christmas with three performances of a virtually complete *Messiah,* presented in two parts rather than three—in Part One, the Christmas music, culminating in the "Hallelujah Chorus," and in Part Two, after the intermission, the music for Easter. There was controversy immediately. His interpretation was "grotesquely unauthentic," according to Paul Henry Lang, who had succeeded Virgil Thomson at the *Herald Tribune,* and "one of the finest things yet to his credit" if one was to trust Irving Kolodin. Altogether he conducted twenty-two concerts in six weeks. His repertoire included Prokofiev's Second Violin Concerto with Isaac Stern and Beethoven's Second Piano Concerto, his first collaboration with the eccentric but brilliant Canadian pianist Glenn Gould. The two concertos and *Messiah* were immediately recorded by Columbia. The recording company was beginning to influence repertoire and soloist choices, but it also gave the orchestra a strong profile. Emphasizing his commitment to American music, Bernstein conducted Roy Harris's Third Symphony and the American premiere of Copland's challenging *Short Symphony* of 1933, as well as the first performance of the full orchestra version of his own *Candide* Overture. "A smart sophisticated little piece," judged Harold Schonberg, then a second-string critic of the *Times;* it rapidly became Bernstein's most popular concert hall composition.

In between concerts Bernstein wrote and hosted another major "Omnibus" essay, *An Introduction to Modern Music.* Essentially he wanted to persuade his enormous audience that twentieth-century music was as beautiful in its own way as that of earlier centuries. He demonstrated convincingly that "beauty" and "dissonance" were relative terms, and explained the tonal system of harmony in terms of a baseball diamond on which the home plate represented the tonic key. Though he granted that a composer like Alban Berg could use Schoenberg's system of composing with all twelve tones to compose beautiful and moving music, his skepticism concerning the universality of the twelve-tone system and his preference for Copland and Stravinsky were clear for all to see. Dimitri Mitropoulos had led the Philharmonic in major works by Schoenberg every year from 1950 to 1954. Bernstein was choosing instead to highlight contemporary American music, and his "Omnibus" lecture gave early notice that he would be an articulate spokesman for musical conservatism, while all around him the tide was flowing toward serialism.

A few days before *Candide* closed, Leonard and Felicia left town for a two-week holiday in pre-Castro Cuba with Marc Blitzstein, who was recuperating from a hernia operation and was depressed by the impasse in his composing career since the production of his musical *Reuben Reuben* had been canceled before its Broadway opening in the fall of 1955. Ironically, he now earned higher praise as the translator of Brecht than as a composer. Bernstein was equally disconsolate following *Candide*'s failure, but the two friends and their families consoled themselves with ever more elaborate word games, incorporating French, German, Italian and even Latin words to add spice.

Their professional prospects could hardly have been more different. Although *Candide* had been a box office flop, Bernstein's music for it had been widely praised—only Irving Kolodin wrote it off as "padded out by formula"— and he was ready to bounce back with *West Side Story*. Several important developments would soon improve his finances. An exclusive recording contract with Columbia, signed in April 1956 and announced to the public in the fall with the issue of five Bernstein LPs in a single month, provided an annual fifteen-thousand-dollar advance against royalties, and he was promised a busy schedule of new recordings. His television fee was almost doubled when "Omnibus" switched to ABC and Sunday night screenings. Even his concert work was set to expand in a new direction: it was announced that he would take over artistic control of the Philharmonic's "Young People's Concerts."

While Bernstein was still on holiday in Cuba, *Time* published a profile of him in which it listed five different Bernstein careers and had laudatory comments about them all. His portrait appeared on the magazine's cover, the first time an American conductor had ever been singled out for such acclaim. Significantly, the caption read "Conductor Leonard Bernstein"—this in the very week when his most ambitious composition, *Candide,* was set to close. It seems fair to assume that during their Cuban vacation Felicia encouraged him to concentrate for the next few years on conducting. (The *Time* article said Mitropoulos was "very likely to quit soon.") There was no certainty that *West Side Story* would fare any better on Broadway than *Candide* had done. The immense effort involved in preparing a musical no longer seemed commensurate with the uncertain reward. In any case Bernstein was not a natural commercial Broadway composer. He had just sailed through six weeks of Philharmonic concerts with great panache. Now he had the chance to follow Gustav Mahler's footsteps and become New York's music director. Like Mahler, he could be a conductor in the winter months and a composer in the summer. On the financial side there would be handsome additional income from the television shows and the Columbia recordings. Whatever the grumbles to his friends, he loved being in studios and he loved teaching. Above all, he reveled in being a celebrity, as he had ever since the heady days following his Carnegie Hall debut in 1943.

Felicia, too, enjoyed the society role. There was tremendous status in being the wife of New York's leading musician. In the fall of 1956 she had been photographed for the *Herald Tribune* in the dress she would wear for the opening concert of the Philharmonic season. "It was of floor length white faille," the report read; "the pearl and gilt embroidery began just under the empire bodice." She looked breathtakingly beautiful. To maintain that kind of elegant lifestyle, money was essential, lots of it. A gossip columnist estimated that from all sources Bernstein earned one hundred thousand dollars in 1956;

examination of his financial records indicates that before taxes he actually did slightly better. But a nine-room Manhattan apartment at a prestige address was not easy to keep up, and there were the Chilean cook and nanny to pay for. (Julia Vega joined her compatriot Rosalia Guerrero in 1954.)

Decisions taken in the weeks following his Cuban holiday reshaped Leonard Bernstein's career still further. The first move, the assumption of the "Young People's Concerts," was soon followed by successful negotiations with William Paley of CBS (a member of the board of the Philharmonic) to have four programs a year televised on Saturday mornings at noon. And in April, before he had given a single concert in his official role as joint principal conductor, negotiations began for him to become the Philharmonic's music director when Mitropoulos stepped down.

Two weeks after receiving his first Emmy Award, for Best Musical Contribution to television, he demonstrated his versatility as a conductor with an hour-long "Omnibus" feature broadcast on Easter Sunday. The subject was the grandeur of J. S. Bach, and the program featured excerpts from the *Magnificat* and the *St. Matthew Passion*. Considering how rarely he had performed the choral music of Bach, his enthusiasm and knowledge were impressive—he conducted, played piano and harpsichord, even sang a little. His talk touched on many aspects of Bach's genius—the strength and beauty of his counterpoint, his numerological complexities (which Bernstein compared to the Talmud), his musical pictorialism, the mystic fusion of words and music in the chorales, the high drama of the Passion story. He spoke finally of Bach's religious spirit; simple faith, he argued, was the spine of Bach's enormous output.

By late spring of 1957 the eleventh hour for *West Side Story* had arrived, and with it the crisis without which no Broadway story is complete. Having nursed the production for more than a year and seen it postponed in March, allegedly because of casting difficulties, Cheryl Crawford called its creators into her office on the morning of April 22 and told them she was quitting. Bernstein felt suicidal. "I don't know how many people begged me not to waste my time on something that could not possibly succeed . . . a show full of hatefulness and ugliness." Sondheim remembers his sense of shock and surprise at being rejected. But when Crawford's partner Roger Stevens was telephoned in London he confirmed his interest and urged them not to give up. That night Sondheim enlisted the support of his producer friend Harold Prince, to whom, unbeknownst to Bernstein, he had already played much of the score. Prince and his partner Robert Griffith flew down from Boston the following weekend. Prince recalled the subsequent audition in his memoirs: "Sondheim and Bernstein sat at the piano playing through the music and soon I was singing along with them, and Bernstein would look up and say, 'My God, he's so musical!' "

There was a rapidly approaching deadline: Bernstein had to leave in September for concerts in South America and Israel, to be followed by his first New York appearances as joint principal conductor of the Philharmonic. Production had to be now or never. Robbins threw in his own bombshell. He wanted Herbert Ross to do the choreography so that he could concentrate on directing. Prince threatened to pull out unless Robbins agreed to be in charge of the dancing (his was the hottest name among the collaborators). Robbins relented, on condition that he could have eight weeks rehearsal instead of the customary four: there was to be more dancing in *West Side Story* than in any previous Broadway show and extra rehearsal was essential to block all the numbers. Even so, Robbins entrusted some of the dance numbers to the choreographer Peter Gennaro.

In their brief careers as producers, Griffith and Prince had had three hit shows in a row. With Roger Stevens behind them, they quickly raised the cash and established a production schedule. They chose a big New York theater, the Winter Garden, and booked a five-week pre-Broadway tryout, three weeks in Washington and two in Philadelphia.

Fine-tuning on the score of *West Side Story* went on throughout the early summer. They dropped what Bernstein described as the "militantly aggressive" opening chorus, "Mix," sung by the Jets and the Sharks. The replacement number, "Prologue," was another big chorus for the rival gangs with, as Bernstein put it, "millions of lyrics to insanely fast music." Eventually, the lyrics were dropped in favor of pure dance; the only sounds the chorus produces in the opening five minutes are a whistle and the rhythmical click of fingers snapping.

Bernstein had originally intended his song "Somewhere" to serve (with a different lyric) as the love music for the balcony scene between Tony and Maria played on a tenement fire escape. Laurents and Robbins were not convinced, so Bernstein and Sondheim created a new love duet, using the "Tonight" music from the quintet heard later in the act. "Somewhere" found its ideal position in the second act as the introduction to the dream ballet.

Composing *West Side Story* and *Candide* in tandem led to some surprising switches of material between the two works. Tony and Maria's duet, "One Hand, One Heart," was originally intended for Candide and Cunegonde. The music of the satirical number "Gee, Officer Krupke" was annexed from the Venice scene in *Candide,* where its punch line (to Latouche's lyrics) had been, "Where does it get you in the end?" The traffic flowed both ways. The marriage duet in *Candide,* "O Happy We," started life as a song for Tony and Maria in a tea party scene that was dropped.

Once the green light had been given, Bernstein had two main tasks: coaching the company in his music and supervising the orchestrations, which began in late June, with Sid Ramin and Irwin Kostal carrying out Bernstein's wishes.

Ramin was especially knowledgeable about jazz and vaudeville. He suggested some of the slapstick effects in "Officer Krupke." Kostal had been a student of Stefan Wolpe: he did the music for the weekly "Show of Shows" starring Sid Caesar. He described Bernstein as a great orchestrator. "If he'd had the time he wouldn't even need us. . . . When it came to *West Side Story* every note is his: still, he would say once in a while, 'Who said that orchestration can't be creative?' He was entirely appreciative of anything that we did. Jerome Robbins, if you changed anything, would really get angry. Lenny would say, 'Jesus, why didn't I think of that?' " Bernstein once told Kostal he was like a sponge; "I learned everything I know from everyone I meet. I pick their brains." Kostal's wry comment was: "Yeah, sure. He learned everything I know, but I didn't learn everything he knows."

As a first step in their preparation, Bernstein and his orchestrators went to the Winter Garden to hear the resident band. Under the prevailing union rules, certain players came with the theater; they were officially known as house men but Bernstein called them "Shuberts," after the name of the owners of the theater. "How would you guys feel if we got rid of the viola Shuberts?" he asked his orchestrators. "If they don't come to the theater we'll have to pay them anyway," warned Kostal. "Okay," Bernstein said, "Let's just do without them, because I couldn't stand listening to my show every night and hearing what those guys would do to the viola parts." The two "guaranteed" cellists were also disappointing, and Kostal suggested dividing the cello parts so that the freelance musicians on the first desk would play the difficult music while the Shuberts "played the potatoes." A similar procedure was adapted for the violin sections. Doing away with the violas created a little more room in the crowded pit for the elaborate percussion section Bernstein needed for a score that was heavy with jazz and with Latin-American rhythms.

With Bernstein totally preoccupied with preparations for his musical, Felicia and the children flew to Chile on July 9 for two months with Felicia's mother in Santiago. Bernstein's letters provide a more accurate and detailed "log" of the weeks leading up to *West Side Story*'s first night in Washington than the one he subsequently published in *Playbill*.

*Leonard in New York to Felicia in Santiago, July 19, 1957*: "Darling: The work grinds on, relentlessly, and sleep is a rare blessing. Jerry continues to be— well, Jerry: moody, demanding, hurting. But vastly talented. We start on the book Monday, trepidation in hand; and the score is still not completed. At the moment the Problem is the usual one of the 2nd act ballet, which is finished, and will probably not work at all and be yanked and we'll have to manufacture a new one. It's going to be murder from here on in. My nights are all spent in work, so no fun at all."

In Chile Jamie, nearly five, and Alexander, just two, met their cousins—the children of Felicia's sister Nancy. "Jamie is the queen, the glamorous beautiful imperious pixie and they're at her feet ready for her slightest whim," Felicia wrote in her first letter. "I miss you so that it hurts—I think it's the incredible depressing distance between us."

*Leonard to Felicia, July 23*: "The show—ah yes. I am depressed with it. All the aspects of the score I like best—the big, poetic parts—get criticized as 'operatic'—and there's a concerted move to chuck them. What's the use? The 24-hour schedule goes on—I am tired and nervous and apey. *This is the last show I do.* The Philharmonic board approved the contract yesterday and all is set. I'm going to be a conductor, after all."

A few days later Bernstein had to interrupt work on *West Side Story* in order to attend a Columbia Records sales convention in Miami. "Home tomorrow, in time . . . for a RUN-THRU of Act One! Imagine—already! Where does the time all go to? In a minute it will be August, and off to Washington—and people will be looking at West Side Story in public, and hearing my poor little marked-up score. All the things I love most in it are slowly being dropped—too operatic, too this and that. They're all so scared and commercial success means so much to them. To me too, I suppose—but I still insist it can be achieved with pride. I shall keep fighting.

"I miss you all terribly—especially you, who have come to mean something miraculous to me. You reside at the very core of my life, my darling."

Felicia responded with the kind of emotional support Bernstein needed: "Don't give up the ship, Lennuhtt. Fight for what you think is right—you are so far ahead of all that mediocrity and in the long run they're only interested in the 'hit' aspect of the theatre. What you wrote was important and beautiful. I can't bear it if they chuck it out—that is what gave the show its stature, its personality, its poetry for heaven's sake! From way down here I <u>protest</u>!! Promise me you'll make an effort to get enough sleep—and don't take too many pills. Are you eating correctly or just pastrami sandwiches and coffee in cartons? Lennuhtt?"

On August 3, Leonard wrote:

Darling:

. . . I signed the Philharmonic contract. . . . Big moment. Bruno arrived at 10:30 A.M.; contract in one hand and a huge chilled bottle of Brut in the other. . . . I made a coup. The lawyers had fallen out so far that the contract was up to 20-odd pages, and growing: and the disputes were growing correspondingly. So I scotched it by tearing up the whole thing, and writing a one-page letter that said I was engaged for such a period for so much money, sincerely yours. They loved it. Simple, and trusting. We'll settle the details as they come along.

Other events—nothing but the show. We ran through today for the first time, and the problems are many, varied, overwhelming; but we've got a show there, and just possibly a great one. Jerry is behaving (in his own way) and Arthur is doing well. But the work is endless: I never sleep: everything gets rewritten every day: and that's my life for the moment. And imagine, we open two weeks from Monday.

A week later, he reported on a last-minute change:

8 Aug already!

. . . I missed you all terribly yesterday. We wrote a new song for
Tony ["Something's Coming"] that's a killer, and it just wasn't the same
not playing it first for you. It's really going to save his character—a
driving 2/4 in the great tradition (but of course fucked up by me with 3/4s
and whatnot)—but it gives Tony balls—so that he doesn't emerge as just a
euphoric dreamer.

These days have flown so—I don't sleep much; I work every—literally every—second (since I'm doing four jobs in this show—composing,
lyric-writing, orchestrating and rehearsing the cast). It's murder, but I'm
excited. It may be something extraordinary.

The show had its first run-through—for an audience of Broadway dancers
and singers—on August 10. It is traditionally done without sets or lighting or
costumes, but on this occasion, Arthur Laurents remembered, "the cast came
out on stage in colors they had chosen for Jets and Sharks and their girls. They
did it on their own, by themselves, and it was very, very touching." During
rehearsals Robbins had kept the rival groups separate offstage as well as on. "I
thought it was pretentious," Stephen Sondheim said, "but of course it was
perfect, because without any animosity or hostility, there was a sense of each
gang having its own individuality, so that you had two giant personalities on
stage."

On Tuesday, August 13, the company moved to Washington. Two days
later Leonard wrote to Felicia again:

Dear Beauty,

Well, look-a me. Back to the nation's capital and right on the verge.
This is Thurs. We open Mon. Everyone's coming, my dear, even Nixon
and 35 admirals. Senators abounding, and big Washington-hostessy type
party afterwards in Lennuhtt's honor. See what you miss by going away.
Then next Sunday, which is my birthday, there is the Jewish version—a
big party for me, but admission is one Israel bond. All helps the show. We
have a 75 thou. advance, and the town is buzzing. Not bad. I have high
hopes.

. . . If I sound punchy, it's because I am. Up all night trying to put
together an overture of sorts, to carry us through until I do a real prelude.
[He abandoned this idea, preferring to have no music before the Prologue
began. Later he claimed not to have written the overture, but this letter
surely confirms that he wrote *something*.] Orchestra reading all day yesterday—a thrill. We have surprisingly good men, who can really play this
terribly difficult stuff (except one or two of them)—and the orchestrations
have turned out brilliant. I tell you this show may yet be worth all

the agony. As you can see, I'm excited as hell—oh so different from *Candide.*

The show opened on August 19. Relying on adrenaline to get his performers through the evening, Jerome Robbins called a final dress rehearsal at 3 P.M. It was a risky move, but it paid off. The evening performance had none of the embarrassing stumbling that had marred the first performance of *Candide* in Boston. President Eisenhower's chief of staff, Sherman Adams (later famous for the scandal surrounding his vicuña coat), was in the audience. So were senators Fulbright and Javits, together with Mrs. Robert Kennedy, three ambassadors, and Justice Felix Frankfurter, whom Bernstein found in tears at the intermission. In Felicia's absence, Helen Coates went to the postperformance party on Bernstein's arm. When the reviews arrived—all of them "raves"—Bernstein read them out to the guests before going on to the cast party where he played jazz piano with the dancers until five in the morning. When she received a cable from her husband next evening, Felicia was beside herself with happiness. She wrote back: "Oh joy oh bliss, oh rapture! Your cable with the frabjous news has just arrived—*thank you!* I'd been desperate for some word all day long. Congratulations to one and all—how happy, how marvelously happy you must be. As for me I'm bursting with pride and frustration—of all the moments to miss sharing! . . . Oh God how exciting it must have been! Were you very nervous—did you sit through it or pace?"

Later in the week Bernstein went to the White House for lunch. "Such credenzas, such breakfronts!" he exclaimed to Felicia. "I really felt in. . . . All were talking of nothing but *West Side Story.* I think the whole government is based on it." But despite the pressure to return to America (she had also just received two offers to do television plays) Felicia preferred to make her mother happy by remaining in Chile for another week. When the Washington reviews reached Santiago, she was once again trembling with excitement—"such reviews, my God, I carry them around with me to read over and over again." The *Washington Post* called *West Side Story* "a uniquely cohesive comment on life. . . . The violence is senseless but Leonard Bernstein's score makes us feel what we do not understand." The *Daily News* said it opened "a new field in the American stage." A critic for the *Seattle Times* perceptively noted that "perhaps the love story is a little too reminiscent of *Romeo and Juliet.*"

Flushed with success, Bernstein told a journalist that he felt like he did after his first dance. A celebrated photograph caught him leaping for joy outside the National Theater. He had just been told that the box office had "gone clean" for the entire run. "It's only Washington, not New York," he wrote to Felicia; "don't count chickens. But it sure looks like a smash . . . the book works, the tragedy works, the ballets shine, the music pulses and soars, and there is at least one history-making set." (Bernstein is referring to Oliver Smith's magic moment when the tenement walls fly up to reveal a sky filled with stars.)

❧

I N Washington the program credits read "Lyrics by Leonard Bernstein and Stephen Sondheim." "I can see you're upset," Sondheim remembers Bernstein saying to him as they drove back to their hotel from the day's rehearsal. "The lyrics are yours and you should have sole credit and I will arrange that." Sondheim thanked him. "And we'll make the financial adjustments too," Bernstein went on. "Oh, don't bother about that," said the grateful Sondheim. "After all, it's only the credit that matters." When Sondheim told the story later, he would ruefully add: "I'm sorry I opened my mouth."

As Bernstein's most intimate collaborator, Sondheim recognized early on that his task was "to bring the language down to the level of real simplicity. The whole piece trembles on the brink of self-conscious pretentiousness anyway . . . and Lenny's idea of poetry was much more purple than mine. Backed up by Arthur Laurents, I got stronger about it as I felt more sure of myself." Out went Bernstein's draft lyric of "Maria"—a song he had already sketched for *East Side Story* in 1949 when Maria was going to be Jewish and Tony was an Italian Catholic from Greenwich Village. "I had a dummy lyric," Bernstein said later: "Lips like mine . . . divine—very bad! Like a translation of a Neapolitan street song." Sondheim perceived that since Tony had only just met Maria the song should not be about the girl herself but about the loveliness of her name—"the most beautiful sound I ever heard / All the beautiful sounds of the world in a single word." Bernstein later claimed that it "took longer to write that song than any other. It's difficult to make a strong love song and avoid corn."

The melody of "Maria" begins with the tritone interval Bernstein pinpointed as the kernel of *West Side Story* ". . . in that the three notes pervade the whole piece, inverted, done backwards. I didn't do all this on purpose. It seemed to come out in 'Cool' and as the gang whistle [in "Prologue"]. The same three notes."

When it was decided to add Tony's first-act song "Something's Coming," Bernstein and Sondheim raided the scene-setting page in Laurents's outline. "Something's coming," Laurents had written: "it may be around the corner, whistling down the river, twitching at the dance—who knows?" The lines were incorporated in the lyrics. "We raped Arthur's play-writing," Bernstein said. "I've never seen anyone so encouraging, let alone generous, urging us, 'Yes, take it, take it, make it a song.'"

Like Sondheim, Laurents was working on his first Broadway musical, but he was an experienced dramatist and screenwriter. His invention of a teenage language and his skillful updating of Shakespeare's plot intricacies are at the heart of *West Side Story*'s success. The show's climactic moment when, with a gun in her hand, Maria makes a speech over Tony's lifeless body, is one of Laurents's most striking contributions. According to Sondheim, Bernstein wanted at this point to create a mad scene for Maria, but he could not find the appropriate style. "It cries out for music," Bernstein said himself. "I tried to set it very bitterly, understated, swift. I tried giving all the material to the orchestra and having her sing an *obbligato* throughout. I tried a version that sounded just like a Puccini aria, which we really did not need. I never got past six bars with it. I never had an experience like that. Everything sounded wrong." So Maria's words, which Laurents had written merely as a guide to lyricist and composer, became the dramatic text. "I made," Bernstein confessed, "a difficult, painful but surgically clean decision not to set it at all." *West Side Story* is a true marriage of all the arts. It is emphatically not an opera.

The *West Side Story* creator whose name receives especial prominence in every form of billing is Jerome Robbins—his "original conception" is contractually protected by a "name in a box" clause. Robbins in rehearsal is a formidable personality. Sid Ramin remembers an early cast meeting at which Robbins said, "I know I'm difficult. I know I'm going to hurt your feelings. But that's the way I am." Bernstein remained in awe of him. When there was the threat of confrontation about music to be cut or an orchestration to be changed, Bernstein would back down. "I hate scenes," he confided to Ramin. At the dress rehearsal in Washington, Sondheim, who was sitting with Bernstein, was startled to see Robbins go down to Max Goberman at the conductor's podium and give orders for a rhythmic pulse to be added to the second verse of "Somewhere." Instead of remonstrating, Bernstein slipped out of the theater. Sondheim found him with several scotches lined up at a nearby bar.

What counted was the chemistry between Robbins and Bernstein, which was as strong as it had been for *Fancy Free*. "I remember all my collaborations with Jerry in terms of one tactile bodily feeling: composing with his hands on my shoulders. . . . I can feel him standing behind me saying, 'Four more beats there,' or 'No, that's too many,' or 'Yeah—that's it!'" Robbins described their work together as one of the most exciting collaborations he ever had. After Bernstein's death he spoke of "the amount of fuel that we fed each other, the ideas and chemistry between us, each one taking hold of something and saying, 'Hey, I think I can do that,' or saying, 'No, don't write it as music, we can do it better in book'—or 'Don't do it in song, I can do it better in dance.' The continual flow between us was an enormous excitement."

Robbins had no problem defining the genre of *West Side Story*. "It's an American musical. The aim in the mid-50s was to see if all of us—Lenny who wrote 'long-hair' music, Arthur who wrote serious plays, myself who did serious ballets, Oliver Smith who was a serious painter—could bring our acts together and do a work on the popular stage. . . . The idea was to make the poetry of the piece come out of our best attempts as serious artists; that was the major thrust." For Robbins it was a "musical"; for Bernstein "a tragic musical comedy." In his heart Bernstein refused to yield primary authorship to his colleagues. Writing to David Diamond from Philadelphia he insisted that "this show is my baby. . . . If it goes as well in New York as it has on the road we will have proved something very big indeed and maybe changed the face of American Musical Theater."

*West Side Story* ran for nearly two years (772 performances) then toured nationally for close to a year before returning to New York in 1960 for another 253 performances. In 1961 it was released as a feature film.

BERNSTEIN was criticized by the critic Brooks Atkinson for having "capitulated to respectability" when he withdrew from Broadway to become music director of the New York Philharmonic. The truth is more complicated: Bernstein knew that the creative collaborations he had enjoyed (and endured) with Lillian Hellman and Richard Wilbur on *Candide* and with Sondheim, Robbins and Laurents on *West Side Story* were experiences too intense and exhausting to be renewed on an annual basis. The creators were not permanent teams like Rodgers and Hammerstein or Gilbert and Sullivan. Besides, the rival attraction of being sole lord and master of the New York Philharmonic, encouraged week in and week out to journey among the masterpieces of two centuries of music, was for Bernstein too strong. Coupled with *Candide*, *West Side Story* made a splendid climax to Bernstein's composing years. But it was neither the end of an era nor the new beginning for Broadway Bernstein claimed it to be. *West Side Story* was a singular marvel of style and substance created by what Stephen Sondheim dubbed a "unique concatenation of people."

The New York premiere on September 26, 1957, was not a total triumph. "The show is, in general, not well sung," wrote Walter Kerr, the man Bernstein most feared, in the *Herald Tribune.* "It is rushingly acted. . . . And it is, apart from the spine-tingling velocity of the dances, almost never emotionally affecting." But Kerr led off his review with two much-quoted phrases: "The radioactive fallout from *West Side Story* must still be descending on Broadway this morning." He applauded "the most savage, restless, electrifying dance patterns we've been exposed to in a dozen seasons." All seven morning newspapers were strongly positive; Brooks Atkinson of the *Times,* the most important of the bunch, called it "a profoundly moving show . . . as ugly as the city jungles and also pathetic, tender and forgiving. . . . Everything contributes to the total impression of wildness, ecstasy and anguish. This is one of those occasions when theater people, engrossed in an original project, are all in top form. . . . The subject is not beautiful, but what *West Side Story* draws out of it is beautiful. For it has a searching point of view."

The only consistently hostile review was Harold Clurman's in *The Nation:* he called it a "phoney" and accused the writers of intellectual slumming for the purpose of making money. The offended Sondheim informed Bernstein, tongue in cheek, that he was canceling his *Nation* subscription immediately. Sondheim's handwritten note to Bernstein delivered on the afternoon of the New York premiere provides a touching epitaph to an important chapter in the history of American musical theater: *"West Side Story* means much more to me than a first show, more even than the privilege of collaborating with you and Arthur and Jerry. It marks the beginning of what I hope will be a long and enduring friendship. Friendship is a thing I give or receive rarely, but for what it's worth, I want you to know you have it from me always.

"I don't think I've ever said to you how fine I think the score is, since I prefer kidding you about the few moments I don't like to praising you for the many I do. *West Side Story* is as big a step, Leonard, for you as it is for Jerry or Arthur or even me, and in an odd way, I feel proud of you. . . . May [it] mean as much to the theater and to people who see it as it has to us."

# PART FOUR

*Backstage with his parents at his first concert as music
director of the New York Philharmonic, October 2, 1958.*
UPI/BETTMANN ARCHIVE

# 1957 – 1969

# THE NEW YORK PHILHARMONIC
# ERA

# 27.

# THE HEIR APPARENT TAKES COMMAND

*1957, Carnegie Hall.*
PHOTO: WALTER DARAN, COURTESY OF THE ESTATE OF
LEONARD BERNSTEIN

*There are no words to describe the success here
in Chile—Lenny is a national hero.*

—FELICIA BERNSTEIN to Helen Coates,
May 23, 1958

O N the day after the New York opening of *West Side Story,* Felicia and
Leonard Bernstein set off for Tel Aviv where, after years of lobbying
and fund-raising, the Frederic R. Mann Hall, named after its principal
benefactor, was to be inaugurated with a series of gala concerts given by the
Israel Philharmonic Orchestra. Isaac Stern and Arthur Rubinstein were to be
the soloists; Bernstein, making his first visit to Israel since 1953, had been the
obvious choice as conductor. After being presented with a baton made of local
olive wood, he departed from his customary baton-less style at the inaugural
concert on October 2 and used this gift to conduct the chorus, orchestra and
audience in the American national anthem. Conservatives deplored the playing
of "The Star-Spangled Banner" before the Israeli national anthem, but it had

been done, it transpired, at the Prime Minister's suggestion, as a compliment to Leonard Bernstein and the concert hall's American benefactors.

The filmmaker Richard Leacock shot a *cinéma vérité* documentary of Bernstein's trip for "Omnibus." The travelogue element resembled a tourist board commercial—Felicia and Leonard watching folk dancing at a Druze village, Leonard teaching orphan children the words of a Yiddish song—but there is a striking moment of truth filmed at a rehearsal with the Israel Philharmonic. Bernstein had conducted sanitized rehearsals in front of television cameras for his "Omnibus" programs on Bach and the art of conducting, and some of his Boston Symphony rehearsals had been broadcast in the 1940s. But nothing would have prepared the viewing public for the ferocity with which he was to be seen attacking the music of Ernest Bloch. *Schelomo* (Solomon)—for cello and orchestra—is subtitled a *Hebrew Rhapsody:* working on it, Bernstein displayed the exhortatory side of his personality, while Paul Tortelier, substituting at the last moment for an indisposed Gregor Piatigorsky, tore into the solo part with the same abandon Bernstein had encouraged in Maria Callas for her interpretation of Medea.

Bernstein hurt his back during his Israel season and for several rehearsals was obliged to conduct sitting down. He had resisted using a baton for eighteen years, but he found that even a pencil was useful when his body movements were restricted. He decided to adopt his new Israeli baton for regular concerts while he was temporarily disabled, and after a few months took to employing a stick regularly. "He found a suitable baton at the Half Price Music Shop in Carl Fischer's," reported the ubiquitous Leonard Lyons. "He believes a baton will add ten years to his career." Bernstein settled for a relatively small baton, just over a foot long. At the base was a pear-shaped ball of cork that he held between the thumb and the first two fingers. (In later years his batons were made for him by Dick Horowitz, the veteran timpanist of the Metropolitan Opera Orchestra.)

Bernstein used a baton when on January 2, 1958, he inaugurated his only season as joint principal conductor of the New York Philharmonic. But before he conducted a note of music, his status with the orchestra had been dramatically transformed. At a press conference held at the Century Club on November 20, 1957, the Philharmonic made public its decision, taken in July, to appoint Leonard Bernstein as its first American-born music director, to take effect beginning in September 1958. He was the first conductor to bear this specific title; Rodzinski and Mitropoulos had been called musical directors. It was not a full-time, year-round position but it required first-call loyalty nevertheless. As well as conducting concerts for a guaranteed minimum number of weeks during the season and on tours by agreement, wrote the Philharmonic, "he plans the format for each season; determines the general content of the programs; selects and co-ordinates guest conductors and soloists; handles orchestral personnel problems; studies scores; and plans concert tours including selecting artists and programs for tours."

It was Dimitri Mitropoulos who actually broke the not unexpected news of Bernstein's succession. Mitropoulos's presence that morning emphasized the friendliness of the proceedings. He said he was not leaving but "abdicating with joy" in favor of his protégé and choice for the job. In his twenty-year relationship with the orchestra, Mitropoulos conducted more than five hundred performances, a record at the time. His conducting style was memorably described by *The New Yorker* as resembling a Byzantine monk frantically shaking martinis. His concert performances of operas, most famously *Elektra* and *Wozzeck,* were high points of New York's musical life in the 1950s: he said himself, "every time I have an opportunity to conduct an opera I feel immensely happy," and he gave as his reason for his withdrawal from the management side of the New York Philharmonic his wish to spend more time at the Metropolitan and La Scala. "Opera," he told the journalists at the press conference, "is a very tempting mistress."

Bernstein's three-year contract as music director, which was intended to see the orchestra established at Lincoln Center, was straightforward: in the first year he was to receive $52,000 for sixteen weeks, with $3,500 for each additional week of conducting; in the second year $57,000; and in the third $62,000. (As a comparison, Toscanini received $110,000, all taxes paid, in 1931.) He was also to receive one third of the royalties paid to the orchestra by Columbia Records, reduced to 20 percent when a soloist was involved. There was an additional fee of $1,000 for conducting each of the "Young People's Concerts": CBS-TV paid separately, and much more handsomely, for the scripts of those talks and for the television rights. These financial arrangements were not revealed at the press conference, nor did the Philharmonic draw attention to the part-time nature of the music directorship since it was nothing new: Mitropoulos conducted only sixteen weeks in 1956, Rodzinski nineteen in 1943.

Subscribers, the backbone of the audience, demanded variety and conductors expected to travel. Yet a great deal of subsequent sniping about Bernstein's absentee landlordism might have been avoided had Bernstein's commitments been publicly defined from the outset. Instead, Bernstein spoke sentimentally at the press conference of the cyclical seven-year coincidences involved in his appointment. It would soon be twenty-one years, he said, since his first meeting with Dimitri Mitropoulos and only a few days had passed since the fourteenth anniversary of his 1943 debut with the New York Philharmonic. The withdrawal of Mitropoulos, he told the press, visibly moved, "is . . . heartbreaking and yet it fills me with such a great sense of responsibility. Mr. Mitropoulos is a great genius and I hope I'll be worthy to follow him." He got a laugh by pointing at Mitropoulos, his friend and champion, and adding: "I am like the actress who had to follow Tallulah Bankhead."


FOR his debut as principal conductor and music director–elect on January 2, 1958, Bernstein chose two of the works with which he had made his debut in

November 1943, Schumann's *Manfred* Overture and the *Don Quixote* tone poem by Richard Strauss. To these he added Ravel's *La Valse* and, with himself as soloist, the North American premiere of Shostakovich's Second Piano Concerto. It was the first new piano work he had learned in three years. "With concerts like this, a lot of the Philharmonic's problems will be solved," wrote Howard Taubman in the *Times*. Bernstein's parents were in the audience to share the triumph.

Two weeks later came the first televised "Young People's Concert" and a fortnight after that the preliminary announcement, linked to a drive for new subscriptions, of the plans he was hatching for his first season. He set himself a staggering pace and confessed as much after his first month (during which he conducted sixteen concerts) in a letter to David Diamond in Italy. He was engulfed, he said, "by an endless new series of meetings, interviews, conferences, et al. about next year's soloists, programs, details for the South American tour we are making with the Orchestra in May and June . . . and all the rest of the administrative detail that goes with being *the* conductor. But so far it's been a joy, far surpassing any expectations. The orchestra has played marvellously, newly, joyously; the men are happy and proud; there is better morale; more money for them (TV, etc.); full houses week after week, in spite of a tremendous amount of contemporary music, Webern and Strav. on one program, for example Haieff and Macero together on another; you, of course, Shosty, Shapero, Foss, Bartok—all in a month. . . . We're doing the *Young People's Concerts* on TV now, they're a smash but oh so difficult and tiring! And *Omnibus* coming up, two more *Young People's* shows, new [concert] programs to prepare for April. . . ."

THE twelve months of transition from his success with *West Side Story* in September 1957 to his assumption of full power at the New York Philharmonic in September 1958 were among the most exhilarating in Bernstein's entire career. Yet for his alternative life, as a composer, the decision to accept the New York Philharmonic position could only be damaging. Publicly Bernstein insisted that composing remained essential for him, even if "a return to Broadway would have to wait for quite a few seasons." The reason he advanced for accepting the Philharmonic appointment, only two years after asserting he would never do so because it would limit his freedom, was a desire to simplify his life. "We're getting old, you know," he had conceded at his press conference. "We just don't have the energy we had at twenty. One begins to center on certain things." "I want to think deep thoughts about music," he told the man from *Newsweek*. "Up till now I have been hedging," he observed to another reporter, striking a familiar chord: "I should know more about myself than I do."

Felicia Bernstein told an interviewer that she had persuaded her husband "to settle down to a single job, so that he can learn a few things about being a father and a husband." But there was not much settling down, and Bernstein underestimated the drain on his creative energy from his whirlwind activities as a conductor, administrator and television pundit. Two decades later he told Mike Wallace of the CBS "60 Minutes" program that the greatest regret of his life was that he had composed so little. Yet whatever the pressure from Felicia, the decision to accept the New York position had in the end been his. It was not that the choice he made was in any sense ignoble. To take on a fine orchestra and make it great again was a grand ambition. To become spokesman for the nation on musical matters, to give a generation of Americans a genuine interest in music, to serve as America's cultural ambassador to the world—these were causes of which he could be proud. But it was his tragedy that being endowed with so many talents, he was forced to neglect one part of his divided self in favor of another. Between 1957 and 1971, the year of his *Mass,* he completed only two works: the *Kaddish* Symphony (No. 3) of 1963 and the *Chichester Psalms* of 1965. Their combined durations amount to slightly less than sixty minutes of music composed in more than a decade: it was a meager harvest for a composer who in the years between 1951 and 1957 had written three Broadway musicals, a one-act opera, a film score and a violin concerto, averaging more than an hour of music each year.

Bernstein's decision to concentrate on his conducting career may however have been a matter of playing his strongest suit. It can be interpreted as a form of self-defense, a shelving of the internal debate as to what musical language he should employ as a composer. The *Kaddish* Symphony has long, often strident passages using the twelve-tone technique of composition, but *Chichester Psalms,* two years later, is almost defiantly tonal throughout. After the *Psalms* came silence for half a decade, while Bernstein the conductor busied himself with opera productions and increased activity in Vienna and London. To the walling up of a fruitful stream, to the dominance of the extrovert side of his personality over introspection, can perhaps be attributed the increasing number of black depressions experienced by Bernstein from his forties onward, and the occasional impression that he was not completely in touch with reality. His worldly success was great indeed, but sadly it was also accompanied by occasional signs of hubris.

ALL this was very much in the future as Felicia described her husband to a journalist profiling Bernstein during his 1957–58 season with the New York Philharmonic. "He is like a child in many ways. He enjoys being a celebrity but his biggest pleasure is collecting other celebrities. He was overwhelmed when he met Garbo at a party. . . . He's getting fat. He will eat seconds on everything. When I see that he needs a rest I just cart him off to hospital." Bernstein entered a hospital briefly in November 1957 (when he returned from Israel) for treatment of a slipped disc. Felicia added the incongruous detail that her husband had found a new and weird way of relaxing; he persuaded his doctors to allow him to observe their operations on other patients.

In another interview, Felicia described her husband's routine on days when he was conducting. Again she emphasized his appetite. "He dresses before dinner. Then he eats an enormous meal. He's a big eater anyway. He will have a coffee but nothing else to drink. And dinner will end just before he goes across the street to Carnegie Hall. He's generally relaxed." She might have added that she was still responsible for putting Koussevitzky's cuff links in his shirt and rubbing him down with Jean-Marie Farina cologne before each performance. Bernstein's exceptional appetite was nothing new. Bruno Zirato remembered nostalgically, in the same newspaper profile, that when Bernstein lived in Room 803 at Carnegie Hall he would often cross the street to the Zirato apartment saying "God I'm hungry" and raid the icebox.

During the months before he took over at the New York Philharmonic *West Side Story* was earning Bernstein two thousand dollars a week in royalties. Nor were earlier musicals forgotten. In December 1957 *Candide* had its first campus production at Indiana University, decked out in the original Broadway costumes. Three months later, *Wonderful Town* was revived by Herbert Ross at the City Center, with Nancy Walker in Rosalind Russell's role: John Chapman said it was even better than the original, and the show went on to represent the U.S.A. at the Brussels World Fair in the summer of 1958. In April *Trouble in Tahiti* was included in a New York festival season of ten American operas. Julius Rudel, the new head of City Opera, persuaded Bernstein to conduct the premiere himself—it was the only occasion when he conducted a staged opera at the City Center. The surprise setback that season was that *West Side Story* won only two Tony Awards—for choreography and scenic design. It was eclipsed in every other department, including music, by the old-fashioned charms of *The Music Man* by Meredith Willson.

His final concert program of the 1957–58 season at Carnegie Hall was a collaboration with his wife in Arthur Honegger's *Jeanne d'Arc au Bûcher (Joan of Arc at the Stake),* a melodramatic oratorio made famous earlier in the fifties when Roberto Rossellini staged it for Ingrid Bergman. As St. Joan, Felicia scored a big success. "She looked exquisite in a slate-gray robe with a red cape across her back," the *New York Times* reported. "Designed by Valentino, it fell in soft folds about her slight, girlish form, giving her the simplicity of the peasant with the nobility of a saint. . . . Her voice, completely bereft of stereotype, was that of a frightened girl, and not the valiant actress of the Bergman school." It was exciting for Leonard and Felicia to be able to work together. Joel Friedman, who coached Felicia for the role, remembers attending a choral rehearsal with the two of them at Princeton. "The whole thing went marvelously well and on the way home he made violent love to Felicia in the back of the car. . . . It didn't seem to bother them that I was there. . . . They had a marvelous time."

Joan of Arc was scarcely off the bonfire before the New York Philharmonic departed on April 27 for a seven-week tour of Latin America, performing in twenty-one cities in twelve countries and covering fifteen thousand miles. Bernstein and Dimitri Mitropoulos were co-conductors of what was the most ambitious tour ever undertaken by the Philharmonic to date. But Mitropoulos was conducting opera at the Met until the end of May, and Bernstein conducted every one of the first twenty-six concerts. Each program contained a work by an American composer. Funded by President Eisenhower's Special International Program for Cultural Presentation, the tour was part of a good neighbor campaign that also sent Vice President Richard Nixon touring the Latin-American state capitals. U.S. oil companies' exploitation of South American oil fields angered populations in several countries and Nixon was often greeted by hostile demonstrations. By contrast, the New York Philharmonic was received with rapture wherever it went.

In Panama City the theater was stifling and so small backstage that half the orchestra had to dress in the street. "It rained madly," Bernstein reported, "and many fiddlers had soaked tails by concert time." A zealous stage attendant used furniture polish to brighten the piano keys, making the piano unplayable (it was cleaned off with scotch whiskey) but Bernstein described the concert (he played the Ravel concerto) as "one of the best." In Caracas, he wrote to Felicia, the New York Philharmonic was "the all-time smash." The orchestra gave three sold-out concerts, and Bernstein was given a loki-liki, ". . . a great beige linen national garment, very handsome, with a high collar held by gold links."

The orchestra's arrival in Bogotá coincided with a relatively peaceful revolution. Addressing Felicia in serviceable Spanish, Bernstein described his joy at the beauty of the Colombian landscape and his anticipation at soon seeing Chile. "It seems all wrong for you not to be on this trip; everyone asks for you and misses you and your whole 'This Is Your Life' turns up every minute— Yolande this and Carmen that and Miguel the other. And think of all the receptions and . . . pastry-makers you're missing! *Y te compré una esmeralda barjata* [I bought you a cheap emerald]—the national industry here—only it's a beautiful little Cabrochon *[sic]* set in diamonds."

After Bogotá the orchestra played in Quito, Ecuador, where Bernstein's path finally intersected with Nixon's and the two shared a press conference on the lawn of the U.S. embassy. "We exchanged notes," Bernstein recalled. "I reported to the Vice President tumultuous receptions, record crowds, cheering stamping audiences; kisses; roses; embraces; while he reported to me the unpleasant distasteful incidents of his visit [rocks were thrown at his motorcade in Caracas]. . . . Where did the difference lie? In music: in the exchange of the deepest feelings and revelations of which man is capable—those of art."

Felicia flew to Lima on the thirteenth and traveled with Leonard and the orchestra on the daunting journeys across the Andes to Bolivia and Paraguay. Another revolution was waiting for them at La Paz—gunfire could be heard as they emerged from their DC-6s. But the high altitude proved to be a greater threat to the orchestra. For the woodwind and brass players, who depended on their lungs to create a good sound, oxygen tanks became standard equipment backstage in cities like La Paz, which is situated at over twelve thousand feet above sea level. Bernstein himself was photographed gulping from a mask between movements of the Ravel concerto, but despite the altitude, his energy was undiminished. Serving on the tour as the Philharmonic's press director, Carlos Moseley remembers that in some countries people slept in the streets waiting for box offices to open. "Lenny was hailed as a hero in city after city. . . . It was a grueling schedule . . . but . . . Lenny would be fresh as a daisy after a concert and want to go and hear the local musicians perform. He would want to know all the places where the young people gathered. He would be up half the night after the concerts. It nearly killed the rest of us, but Lenny survived it very easily in those days. [Once] we were flying over the Andes, the snowcapped mountains below us . . . when . . . we saw Lenny go into the cockpit. And five minutes later, sure enough, the plane suddenly took an enormous drop, and some of the men got airsick from it because they were terrified, knowing that Lenny had probably talked his way into the pilot's seat."

In Santiago, Felicia experienced an overwhelming thrill at the opening concert in the Teatro Astor. "I had never imagined I'd hear my husband conduct the national anthem there, where I grew up. It was a beautiful extraordinary moment and the tears were streaming from my face. It meant coming home in glory." Chileans have never forgotten the performance: Bernstein chose a much brisker tempo than normal. The anthem has been played faster ever since. During his stay Bernstein learned to love the folk music of Chile through the magical singing of Violetta Parra. His *Mass* of 1971 contains a direct quote from one of her songs.

The Philharmonic crossed the Andes once again to perform in Argentina, Uruguay, Brazil, and finally Mexico, with Mitropoulos now doing the majority of the concerts. Felicia had to stay behind with her family in Chile; she had fallen ill after eating oysters and was rushed to the hospital. She caught up with her husband a few days later for his concert in Buenos Aires, and they returned to Chile for a week's holiday. Bernstein had arranged with Mitropoulos that he would feign illness in order to skip a Philharmonic concert and have a longer break, but as bad luck would have it he really did fall ill in Santiago—from overeating, according to Felicia's account to Helen Coates. *"Mon mari ne cesse pas de vomiter,"* Felicia explained to the French-speaking doctor who attended Bernstein. *"Vomir,"* groaned the pedantic maestro from his sickbed. Bernstein rejoined the tour in Rio de Janeiro, as planned, to conduct the final concert there. "18,000 people listened in intent silence," wrote the orchestra's president, David Keiser, in the official tour history, ". . . and exploded into a thunder of applause and cheering after each number. Many of the audience openly wept as the crowds joined in the singing of the National Hymn of Brazil."

The South American odyssey was a success both artistically and politically. Mitropoulos and Bernstein had both gone out of their way to press Latin-

American flesh. Mitropoulos was photographed wearing a sombrero at a piñata party in Mexico City and greeting hospital patients at an open-air concert attended by thirty thousand in São Paulo; Bernstein listened patiently to Peruvian folk musicians from Lake Titicaca, and was personally congratulated by six South American presidents, most of them, be it said, dictators. He gave innumerable breakfast press conferences, once—in Panama City—clad in nothing more than red swimming trunks, and he autographed countless concert programs. Most important, he slipped easily into his coming role of music director. He had known some of the players since 1943 and had already conducted nearly a hundred concerts with the orchestra. The tour gave him a chance to get to know individual players during airplane journeys and postconcert receptions and water-skiing afternoons.

The City of New York officially celebrated the Philharmonic's return with a reception in front of City Hall. On hand to play "The Star-Spangled Banner" was the Sanitation Department Band. Like J. P. Sousa before him, Bernstein borrowed the bandmaster's baton to give the downbeat. It was probably the only time he conducted an ensemble of garbage collectors.

For their summer holidays Leonard Bernstein took his family to Martha's Vineyard. Even here there was work to do—a revision of *Candide* for a new production to be mounted in London the following spring—but at last the pace slackened. The most important creative business of the summer was the shooting of a new silent-film home-movie drama, with camera work and direction by Leonard Bernstein. Felicia Montealegre played a dowdy woman who makes a fateful visit to a plastic surgeon (played by Burton Bernstein). Felicia's big moment came in a scene worthy of a Joan Crawford movie. After her operation the bandages on her face are removed and by a piece of cinematic trickery (the film was run in reverse) she emerges as a ravishing beauty, champagne glass in one hand, cigarette holder in the other. Burton's character falls in love with her. But his jealous nurse (played by Burton's current girlfriend, Ofra Bikel) reverses the operation and the unfortunate patient loses her newly acquired good looks. It was a far cry from the Hollywood films they were dreaming of at the time of their first engagement, but for Leonard and Felicia, for the entire Bernstein clan, it was fun. By September, however, the last summer days were, as Bernstein wrote to Helen Coates, "rushing away with the speed of lightning: and it's absolutely terrifying to confront what's coming. I pray every night."

# MUSIC DIRECTOR AT THE NEW YORK PHILHARMONIC

*Modeling the Philharmonic's new
preview concert uniforms, October 1958.*
COURTESY OF THE NEW YORK PHILHARMONIC ARCHIVES

*He is starting a renaissance and this takes a
courageous man.*

—DIMITRI MITROPOULOS, 1957

"MY job is an educational mission," Bernstein told the *New York Times* a few weeks after his appointment as music director was announced: "Programs should have a theme running through them. Programs should be built not singly but in series, cycles, blocks . . . a festival of a particular composer, or a particular time or a particular movement. There should always be a sense of festival about going to the Philharmonic." It was the gospel according to Serge Koussevitzky.

One of his first acts as music director was to change the way concerts were scheduled. The traditional Thursday concert was scrapped and replaced by a separate full-price subscription series entitled Preview Concerts. They were in effect public dress rehearsals at which the conductor would include a little talk about the music on the program and would be free to stop the orchestra to make a point to players or public. Some people, Bernstein argued, preferred the informality of rehearsals to performances given in an atmosphere of high-culture solemnity. To emphasize the novelty and the relaxed mood of the proceedings he decided the orchestra would wear "Nehru jackets," loose-fitting rehearsal coats of the type worn by Bruno Walter and Arturo Toscanini. The public was intrigued and the critics took with fortitude the news that they were to be kept out of Thursday evenings and invited to review instead the regular Friday afternoon concerts, hitherto the preserve of society ladies of a certain age whose tinkling jewelry and teatime gossip formed a noisy counterpoint to the sounds of the orchestra.

The new arrangements turned Saturday into a regular subscription night, boosting the number of Saturday evening concerts from 16 to 30. Sunday afternoons remained popular in tone, and provided an opportunity to experiment with less well-known soloists. Taken together with an increase in touring, the total number of concerts per year was to rise from 131 in the Mitropoulos era (1951–57) to 165 in the first five years of Bernstein's directorship and to 192 in the last five years.

Bernstein outlined his program plans for his first season in more detail in a memorandum which he typed himself and sent to the board on February 4, 1958. He would conduct, in his eighteen weeks, "a general survey of American music from the earliest generation of American composers to the present," interspersing this grand exploration with standard works of the orchestral repertoire, including a Handel Festival for the 1959 bicentenary. He invited his guest conductors—Schippers, Karajan, Barbirolli and Mitropoulos—to conduct music of other nationalities, both classical and contemporary.

For the board the document must have seemed like manna from heaven. Some of Mitropoulos's enthusiasms had been for obscure composers such as Artur Schnabel, the pianist, and the iconoclastic Ernst Krenek. Bernstein by contrast offered controlled experiment, sensible exploration, surrounded by popular classics, and all wrapped up in the patriotic reexamination of America's own musical heritage at a time when the City Center and the Metropolitan Opera were also promoting American composers.

Bernstein's opening season, 1958–59, will always be seen as a turning point in the Philharmonic's affairs. For professional musicians, the most significant development was his root and branch exploration of American music, offering Philharmonic subscribers an opportunity to hear the music of the New England pioneers like Henry F. Gilbert, Arthur William Foote and George Chadwick, alongside works by more familiar composers such as Edward MacDowell and Charles Ives. From the period of the 1920s Bernstein conducted Copland's *Music for the Theatre* and Gershwin's *Rhapsody in Blue*. Several of the composers in the survey were teachers or supporters from Bernstein's student days, among them Roy Harris, Walter Piston and Randall Thompson. But Bernstein was careful to be even-handed; there were also works by Samuel Barber, Paul Creston and Virgil Thomson. Among the postwar American composers he included friends like Irving Fine and Lukas Foss, but also progressive figures from the next generation such as William Russo and Gunther Schuller. The most substantial world premiere was Ned Rorem's Symphony No. 3. Rorem recalls that he had written it in France and Morocco—without a commission—and shown it to Bernstein on his return to New York in March 1958. "It was a big affair for big orchestra, about twenty-six minutes long in five movements. He liked it immediately. 'It's exactly what I'm looking for . . . on condition that you reorchestrate the whole slow movement for strings only!' I thought about it and I said 'Okay' and didn't do it. And he forgot that he said it."

Many a symphony orchestra has announced a new era with imaginative programming schemes. But making an orchestra play well, week in and week out, is quite another matter. Here Bernstein inherited a major problem. "The odor of failure had hung heavily over the New York Philharmonic in recent seasons," according to Howard Taubman, Olin Downes's successor as chief music critic of the *Times*. Morale among the players was low, Bernstein told his board at their first meeting. But the orchestra's self-respect and sense of well-being soon advanced by leaps and bounds. Television appearances gave the musicians a sense of being valued members of the community as well as providing additional income. Also appreciated were the extra weeks of engagement on major international tours during the early years of Bernstein's music directorship. Yet even this factor was peripheral to Bernstein's central achievement, which was to revitalize the orchestra as a musical instrument. He yielded to none, he said, in his admiration for Dimitri Mitropoulos, calling him "the greatest genius I have ever known in music." But he also admitted that Mitropoulos had, "like all of us, his faults. I remember during that first year [1957–58] listening to his performances and observing . . . a raggedness, a lack of ensemble, of precision, of intonation. He'd never asked for these things, you see. As long as he had his dynamics he was happy. . . . The orchestra, especially in Mozart or Beethoven, had begun to sound quite coarse with him. . . . As he confided to me in a personal conversation, he had grown to a point where this [repertoire] was kind of dull because it didn't challenge him enough. . . . I hate to say all these things because it sounds as though I am denigrating Mitropoulos, whom I worshiped. I'm just trying to say what I think is the truth."

Early on in his reign Bernstein flexed his directorial muscles by spending most of a morning's rehearsals taking Mendelssohn's *Italian* Symphony to pieces and working on it bar by bar, erasing instructions for bowing and breathing that went back to the days of Toscanini. For the players it was chastening at the outset to be treated like students, but the improvement was there for all to hear. Moreover, they were encouraged to listen to each other, to make music like chamber musicians. To facilitate internal listening—and the projection of the sound into the hall—Bernstein reorganized the layout of the orchestra and introduced platform risers for the sections situated near the back and sides of the concert platform.

At the personal level Bernstein, like Mitropoulos before him, gave a sympathetic ear to individual musicians, sometimes helping quietly with private loans in cases of hardship. At the musical level he treated the players with courtesy and good humor. He was one of them and yet demonstrably he was their master. His taste in music was perhaps too progressive for the conservative members of the orchestra, but his conducting technique, his ear and his memory were immensely impressive, while nobody could match his skill in handling the complicated rhythms of twentieth-century music from Stravinsky to Copland. All in all, he was a *mensch* of the first order, and the musicians played their hearts out for him.

"What a difference one year has wrought in the New York Philharmonic!" wrote Howard Taubman, reviewing Bernstein's first season in command. "The orchestra played with fresh pride and rediscovered coherence. The programs were venturesome. The public grew. The box office rejoiced." More impressive than Leonard Bernstein's versatility, Taubman added, was his "spirit of drive and curiosity, humor and sincerity that had struck one as distinctively of our time and country. . . . He took chances, made mistakes and publicly confessed his guilt in one case. . . . [At the Previews] Mr. Bernstein tended occasionally to exaggerate, oversimplify and oversell. But there is no doubt he entertained most of his listeners. . . . His conducting, like his musicianship, has grown in maturity."

When the enthusiastic Howard Taubman switched from music criticism to drama in 1960, he was succeeded as the *New York Times*'s chief critic by Harold Schonberg, who early on gave notice that he would take a more critical line. Schonberg disliked what he considered Bernstein's overly romanticized interpretations of the nineteenth-century classics and argued that organizing seasons in "themes" was no substitute for the careful planning and execution of individual concerts. Bad notices, whether for his conducting or his compositions, always wounded Bernstein. He said himself that he read his reviews because he retained a childish delight in seeing his name in the paper and wanted to know what people were saying about him. After a decade of attacks from Schonberg he concluded: "I have been hurt and I have been overjoyed by it, and I have been bored by it and I have been incensed, but mostly not embittered. None of this has lasted. It is all ephemeral." As Sibelius once tartly observed, nobody has ever erected a statue to honor a critic.

The Philharmonic was certainly not rattled. When it became clear that the new hall at Lincoln Center would not be ready before 1961 the board approached Bernstein about extending his contract. He proposed and the board accepted a seven-year extension which, with a sabbatical year thrown in, would take Bernstein's directorship to May 1969. He remained tremendously popular with the New York audience throughout the decade.


W I T H the continuity of artistic leadership assured, and a strong management team behind him, the New York Philharmonic under Bernstein's leadership made swift progress to regain its position as one of America's leading orches-tras. Much of its expansion in the 1960s can be ascribed to Bernstein's own enthusiasms, and to the mood of confidence and preparedness to take risks that he engendered. There were three times as many guest conductors in the sixties as there had been in the fifties. Starting in 1959, Bernstein gave three young conductors a year the opportunity to work with him as assistants. From 1963 onward the assistants were chosen from prizewinners in the Mitropoulos Com-petition, which the New York Philharmonic and Leonard Bernstein's own foundation administered jointly. Claudio Abbado, Alain Lombard and Edo de Waart were among the incumbents. There was also a much greater diversifica-tion in the choice of soloists. With subscription tickets fully sold, the orchestra could gamble occasionally with relatively unknown young pianists such as Philippe Entremont, Malcolm Frager and Vladimir Ashkenazy, while the An-dré Kostelanetz Promenade Concerts, begun in 1963 in the air-conditioned Philharmonic Hall, brought in a wider range of conductors; André Previn made his New York Philharmonic debut in this way. Bernstein's willingness to experiment may be demonstrated by the fact that almost a third of the works he himself conducted were by American composers; the annual percentage of American works in the repertoire rose under his aegis from 5 to 15 percent.

Bernstein was a born educator. In addition to the "Young People's Con-certs," one of his ideas was to invite New York high school students to attend a Philharmonic rehearsal; immediately afterward he would hold an informal question and answer session with them. Even his regular subscription concerts took on an instructional slant—one series in 1959–60 had the ring of a univer-sity lecture prospectus: "The Twentieth Century Problem as Reflected in Mu-sic," was how he announced it to the board.

Bernstein's "lurking didactic streak," self-proclaimed, was not to every-body's taste. Guest conductors declined to treat the Thursday Previews as opportunities for informal chats. When Sir John Barbirolli and Herbert von Karajan conducted, the orchestra abandoned their Preview uniforms for con-ventional white tie and tails and the conductors said not a word. The young American Thomas Schippers was the only conductor in the first season who actually stopped a Thursday performance to make a comment; Bernstein lim-ited his prefatory remarks to one or two of the works on the program and always played the pieces straight through. But by bringing on composers to talk about new or unfamiliar compositions and by sitting down at the keyboard himself to provide a brief analysis, Bernstein established a precedent for what has become known in many concert halls around the world as the "preconcert talk."

The informal "uniforms" lasted only a few months: they were abandoned in January 1959 and labeled "Bernstein's Folly." But Previews continued until 1962, and the policy of building the season's programs around themes was retained throughout the Bernstein decade. In 1959–60, the main theme was a centennial retrospective of the music of Gustav Mahler, conducted by Dimitri

Mitropoulos and Bruno Walter as well as Bernstein. In the course of the decade, Bernstein himself conducted all nine symphonies and recorded them for Columbia Records. Another overtly educational project was a two-season survey exploring twentieth-century symphonies. In the summers of 1965 and 1966 the Philharmonic also mounted festivals under the artistic directorship of Lukas Foss: in 1965 a concert series of French and American music and in 1966 "Stravinsky—His Heritage and His Legacy." Bernstein took part in both.

Festivals cause a stir at the time but the memory of even the finest performance eventually fades. What most music-loving Americans remember of Leonard Bernstein at the New York Philharmonic in the sixties are his television appearances and his phonograph recordings. Columbia Records built up an entire classical music library around him. Literally hundreds of different titles were recorded. Up to half a dozen overtures and tone poems would be taped in a single session, many of them not part of the season's concert hall programs. In his date book Bernstein would write the single word "Junk" to describe such sight-reading sessions, but the performances are often vital and full of fun; many were issued on Columbia's two-disc compilation, *The Joy of Music*.

In terms of national recognition, however, even Bernstein's recording output pales in significance by comparison with his position as a television personality. Bernstein hosted and conducted "Young People's Concerts" on television for fifteen consecutive seasons, from 1958 to 1972, first at Carnegie Hall, and from 1962 in Philharmonic Hall. The urge to teach was, he said, a constant factor in the fluctuating tides of his New York career: "the Young People's Concerts are among the favorite, most highly prized activities of my life." When he finally withdrew it was because the preparations for his six Norton Lectures at Harvard were demanding his undivided attention. For the first five seasons of his Philharmonic decade, 1958–62, Bernstein also wrote and delivered scripts for more than a dozen adult programs, first for "Omnibus" and later for a new series featuring the New York Philharmonic, which was sponsored by the Ford Motor Company. They were filmed in television studios in New York and Berlin, at La Fenice in Venice, on tour in Japan, in the Moscow Conservatory and on the bare stage of the Metropolitan Opera. They ranged from explorations of romanticism and humor in music to essays on the creative performer, the grandeur of grand opera and the transformation of Greek drama into opera achieved by Stravinsky in *Oedipus Rex*. They have never been rivaled in popular television education.

Ford stopped sponsoring Bernstein and the New York Philharmonic in 1962; Bernstein's inventive use of the television medium was thereafter restricted to the modest format of the "Young People's Concerts." These programs (over fifty in all) meant a lot to Bernstein but they were produced on a shoestring budget and were never intended to rival the intellectually ambitious adult programs made for "Omnibus" and Ford.

After Newton Minow, chairman of the Federal Communications Commission, had lambasted the TV networks in 1961 for turning prime time television into "a vast wasteland," the "Young People's Concerts" were shown by CBS at 7:30 P.M. for six years. They became a national institution, parodied in television comedy and immortalized in the comic strip "Peanuts." Films of the concerts were loaned to schools through the Bell System and the McGraw-Hill company. Two books of Bernstein scripts were published by Simon and Schuster. The programs were dubbed into twelve different languages and syndicated in forty countries, providing handsome revenue for Bernstein and the Philharmonic. From Hungary it was reported that the "Young People's Concerts" were as popular as "The Flintstones" and were actually beating "Bonanza" in the ratings.

Before the televised "Young People's Concerts" were inaugurated in 1958, a *Variety* article entitled "A Concert is a Show" misled Bernstein into thinking that his friend since 1946, the director Roger Englander, planned to introduce theatrical presentation gimmicks to Carnegie Hall—a narrator in costume, Broadway stars, dancers to illustrate the music. Soon after the article appeared, Englander received a telephone call. " 'Roger! This is Lenny! . . . A concert is *not* a show.' " According to Englander the "Young People's Concerts" were probably the most straightforward shows on television. "The script conferences were happily anticipated rituals held at Bernstein's apartment. . . . The search for the exact word, the most illuminating phrase, continued right up until we went on the air. Bernstein wrote every word of each script himself. He invited our suggestions and comments, but . . . could not comfortably deliver someone else's words."

The first "Young People's Concert" was called *What Does Music Mean?* Bernstein began by conducting the "cowboy" music from Rossini's *William Tell* Overture. "What do you think this tune is about?" he asked his audience. "You will understand, I am sure, what my little daughter Jamie said—she's up there somewhere—when I played it for her. 'That's the Lone Ranger's song, Hi-ho Silver! Cowboys and bandits and horses and the Wild West. . . .' Well, I hate to disappoint her, and you, too, but it isn't about the Lone Ranger at all. It's about notes: Cs and As and Fs and even F sharps and E flats. No matter what stories people tell you about what music means, forget them. Stories are not what music means. Music just *is*. It's a lot of beautiful notes and sounds put together so well that we get pleasure out of hearing them. So when we ask 'what does it *mean;* what does this piece of music mean?' we're asking a hard question. Let's do our best to answer it."

The programs were a happy way for Bernstein to keep in touch with his own children as they progressed from nursery to high school. He delighted them when he included references to the Beatles in his talks, in 1964 to illustrate the structure of a melody and in 1966 when describing the "church" modes— his daughter Jamie had been finding it difficult to pick out the modal harmonies of a Beatles' tune on her guitar. Jamie and Alexander loved their father's television days, and would get up before dawn to go to the hall with him. Lighting checks and teleprompter rehearsals began as early as 6:15 A.M. At eight, the orchestra would arrive for rehearsal and a sound test and there would be a full dress rehearsal (attended in later years by an overflow second audience) from 10 A.M. to 11 A.M. The concerts were at noon. Subscription tickets for the season were always sold out months in advance. Eager parents put their children's names down at birth.

In 1960, when the orchestra was on tour in Denver, Bernstein went for a walk in a public park with Carlos Moseley, by then promoted to be assistant general manager of the New York Philharmonic. All of a sudden, Moseley remembers, a little boy of four or five marched up to Bernstein and hit him. "Lenny was absolutely astonished, as I was too. And the little boy said, 'You didn't say good night to me!' He repeated it until Lenny exclaimed 'Oh my goodness, the last children's program was the program when we were running overtime and I didn't have time to say my usual farewells.' And this child said, 'You were talking about Mahler!' That this little thing had resented the fact that Lenny hadn't signed off, but had remembered the name Mahler, pleased Lenny and me no end."

Glenn Gould provided this irreverent but professional assessment of Bernstein's educational work. "Bernstein is content to use television as a means to an entirely worthy end—the musical enlightenment of the American public. And consequently the typical Bernstein television effort is a straightforward 'This is your life Ludwig Spohr' sort of show—taped before a live audience . . . with all the sound liabilities thereunto pertaining and with coy cutaways to some cute little kids in the balcony specially imported for the occasion from the Westchester Home for Insufferable Prodigies. The camera work isn't very elaborate, and if the director allows us a tight shot on the tuba, likely as not the tuba player will be holding up a banner reading '10 seconds to countdown for second theme.' Bernstein's purpose is entirely didactic, and he simply isn't willing, or isn't asked, to compromise his podium-and-lectern stance to accommodate the demands of the camera. Yet, for all that, such is the force of his personality, the intensity of his performing style, and the constant insight of his analytic comment that Bernstein's innumerable television appearances have unquestionably, in the best and strictest sense of the phrase, 'done a great deal of good.' "

# TO RUSSIA WITH LOVE

*A bear hug for Boris Pasternak, with Jack Gottlieb
and Felicia Bernstein looking on.*
PHOTO: DON HUNSTEIN, COURTESY OF SONY CLASSICAL

*Leonard Bernstein is lifting the Iron Curtain
in Music.*

—ALEKSANDR MEDVEDEV, in *Sovetskaya
Kultura,* August 28, 1959

B ERNSTEIN'S first season with the New York Philharmonic, and the tour of
Western Europe, Poland and the Soviet Union that followed it, was arguably the most dramatic and eventful in the history of that orchestra. The
society columnist Elsa Maxwell called the opening night, October 2, 1958, "the
most socially important affair of this or any season." Photographs of Felicia
Bernstein, looking exceptionally glamorous, had appeared in the *Times* a few
days previously. She was described as "a leader in the movement to make the
opening concert a fashion event for the first time ever." "I'm all for snobbism,"
she said; "fads can become serious. Some people may attend to show off their
mink, find they enjoy the music and become devoted to the Philharmonic."

To a Carnegie Hall made festive by flags and flowers, Bernstein's new
policies had attracted more young people than in previous seasons, many of
them wearing casual clothes that contradicted the formality of the conservative
members of the audience. Pillars of New York society were joined by the UN
ambassadors of the twelve South American countries recently visited by the
orchestra, and by Henry Cabot Lodge, America's ambassador to the UN. An oil

painting of George Washington was hung in the cocktail lounge to emphasize the Americana theme of the season.

Opening night was also the first of the Preview Concerts, in which a new informal atmosphere was supposed to reign. To mollify some worried subscribers, it had earlier been announced that works would definitely be played straight through, as at a normal concert. But Bernstein revealed his hand by making a speech as soon as "The Star-Spangled Banner" had been performed. As the *Daily News* put it, he was taking the starch out of the stuffed-shirt brigade. He welcomed the audience, described the season's plans, introduced new players in the orchestra, and immediately added an extra item to the program, "as a gift from us to you." The choice of "pre-encore" was the *Roman Carnival* Overture by Berlioz, already thoroughly prepared during a brief preseason out-of-town concert tour. "The sound was radiant, the precision remarkable, and the spirit warm and communicative," reported the *Herald Tribune*. Bernstein then conducted one of his earliest Tanglewood successes—the *American Festival Overture* of William Schuman—before slipping into his professorial mode for a talk at the piano about Charles Ives's Second Symphony. In what one report described as "an hilarious as well as illuminating *tour de force*," he sang some of the American folk tunes and hymns Ives embedded in his Brahmsian symphonic structure. Although he praised the "whistle-clean articulation" of the performance, Irving Kolodin described the Preview event as "cultural vaudeville" and "Box Office slanted." But Kolodin's was a solitary voice of hostility. At the intermission Leonard Lyons asked Samuel Bernstein about his son's latest success. "I have no quarrel with the Lord," responded Sam, who with experience was becoming adept at delivering one-liners.

Bernstein offered no talk before the second half, in which he conducted Beethoven's Seventh Symphony. The press office informed journalists that the new music director had again been busy at rehearsal removing the sometimes contradictory pencil markings in the orchestral parts which went all the way back to Toscanini, perhaps to Gustav Mahler. Howard Taubman wrote lyrically of the orchestra's "shining morning face." After the performance and the cheers, Bernstein changed into a silk dressing gown, looking for all the world like a champion heavyweight boxer. Adolph Green greeted him, "Attaboy, Sugar, you fought a good fight!" Later in a long evening, Bernstein and his wife attended a postconcert party. They waltzed together when the band played "I Feel Pretty" from *West Side Story*. Two nights later they went to another postperformance party—at Sardi's—to celebrate the first anniversary of *West Side Story*'s New York opening. Times were good.

Bernstein kept up the festive atmosphere for four weeks of concerts, during which the Texan pianist Van Cliburn made his Philharmonic return after his enormous success winning the Tchaikovsky Competition in Moscow the previous spring. At another emotional concert, Bernstein brought out of relative obscurity the works of three veteran American composers, John Becker, Wallingford Riegger and Carl Ruggles, all in their seventies, and gave them each fifteen minutes of Philharmonic fame. A touch tactlessly, Bernstein told the Preview audience that they would be listening to "a large dose" of modern music.

A T the end of October Bernstein flew to Paris with Felicia to make his long deferred public debut. This time, instead of conducting in a radio studio, he was to be the guest of the respected Lamoureux Orchestra, whose principal conductor, Igor Markevitch, had been a friend since the 1940s. The trip began badly. When the Bernsteins arrived at the Ritz Hotel in Paris they were told it would not be possible, as previously arranged, to have a practice piano in the suite. A gossip columnist reported that they turned on their heels with their ten suitcases, rejoined their taxi and installed themselves at the Hotel George V.

Bernstein had allowed his French affairs to become so hopelessly muddled over the years that three different artists' managements claimed to be negotiating on his behalf. His characteristically optimistic solution was to invite all three impresarios to lunch after his first rehearsal. (Nothing was settled, and it was eight years before he conducted again in Paris.)

For his opening concert he scheduled *Le Sacre de Printemps,* by now his most impressive warhorse. He was so anxious to do it in Paris (where it had been premiered in 1913) that he agreed to pay for the seventeen extra players needed to perform the huge and exotic score. "It's cost me three hundred thousand francs," he told Art Buchwald of the Paris *Herald Tribune,* "and I didn't even write it." A French journalist attended one of the rehearsals. *"Vous jouez trop français,"* she heard Bernstein telling the players; "it is too French. Stravinsky, *c'est bar-bar-re,"*—spoken with much rolling of the Rs. *"Soyez barbares!"* The orchestra applauded at the end of the rehearsal and the performance, according to François Mauriac, was *superbe.* Friends old and new were there, among them François Valéry, Nadia Boulanger, Peggy Bernier and Sam Spiegel, who gave a party after the concert which the recently widowed Lauren Bacall also attended. During their Parisian stay the Bernsteins went to a fashion show at Christian Dior, heard a concert conducted by Karajan and a Poulenc opera privately performed, drove out to Versailles, shopped in the flea market, called on Alice B. Toklas, had a drink with the Olivier Messiaens, lunched with Janet Flanner and attended a party at Nadia Boulanger's in honor of Bernstein's visit and Aaron Copland's fifty-eighth birthday. There was a dinner for six at Maxim's, a large cocktail party at Peggy Bernier's and a formal lunch with Nicolas Nabokov and Igor Stravinsky at UNESCO. It was a way of life after Cunegonde's heart: "We'll round the world enjoying high life: all bubbly pink champagne and gold."

Bernstein's second Lamoureux concert consisted entirely of keyboard concertos, in all of which he appeared as both pianist and conductor. *France Soir* provided a ringside summary of the audience response: *"Après Bach* [Branden-burg Concerto No. 5] *un franc succès. Après Mozart* [K. 453] *un triomphe. . . . Après Ravel une explosion et après Gershwin un délire sans fin"*—an endless delir-ium. But the critics were less enthusiastic. An excellent circus act, wrote one. Had Bernstein chosen Ravel's concerto for the left hand alone, observed another acidly, he could have conducted *all* the time as well as playing. Bernstein shared with Franz Liszt an exhibitionist element in his makeup: he reveled in the opportunity to display himself. But he was not just a "numéro" for the leading Paris critic, Bernard Gavoty, who wrote in *Le Figaro* that "a success of this quality goes far beyond being a merely *sportive* occasion. I regard Leonard Bernstein as being a prodigiously gifted musician."

Bernstein's performance of Mahler's *Resurrection* Symphony the following week, with the Orchestre Nationale, did little for his Parisian reputation, how-ever. The orchestra had performed the work a few months previously with Carl Schuricht, and the German conductor's austerity on the podium was preferred by several critics to what were described by Claude Rostand as Bernstein's *"vaines convulsions."*

The Bernsteins flew to Milan next morning, where Leonard conducted two programs with the La Scala Orchestra following a memorial concert in honor of Arturo Toscanini in the maestro's birthplace, Parma. That made three Euro-pean orchestras in three weeks. When he returned home he had made a deci-sion. He announced it at the annual luncheon of the Friends of the New York Philharmonic. "While away I found myself missing my own orchestra and wondering how it was behaving with other conductors," he said. "Then I fully realized how remarkable the New York Philharmonic is. It's the greatest or-chestra and the most flexible." After discussions with his wife, he told his audience, he had decided to conduct no other orchestra during the period of his contract. Though his one-page Philharmonic contract letter made no mention of exclusivity, he subsequently turned down dozens of prestigious projects, among them conducting *Lohengrin* at Bayreuth, *Carmen* at La Scala and con-certs with the Berlin Philharmonic.

BERNSTEIN's hair was already graying at the temples when he took over the Philharmonic. He stood five feet eight inches tall and weighed a modest 145 pounds. He was still very handsome and many society women were attracted to him. Elsa Maxwell commented on his magnetism in her *Journal-American* col-umn on October 18, 1958. "After the concert we repaired to El Morocco for supper. Leonard Bernstein, as usual, was the star. So many women call me up and say, 'We know you know Mr. B. How is it possible to meet him? We are mad about him'. . . . The old, old cry. But in this case, gals, there is a Mrs. Bernstein, and a beauty, and the Bernsteins love each other. And that's that." The Bernsteins' public togetherness was suitably acknowledged on Valentine's

Day 1959. When Schrafft's, the New York restaurant chain, invited the public to nominate loving couples in various walks of life, the Bernsteins were chosen Valentine of the Year in the Arts category.

Apart from the glamour of the job, Felicia liked having her husband at home. She confessed ruefully to an interviewer that she had never in her acting career been in a "hit." So Bernstein, she said, was "used to having me around in the evenings." She revealed a little of the domestic side of her husband. "He's extremely organized—puts his laundry in the hamper every night, goes around emptying ash-trays. He's very neat and very interested in decoration and fashion—he always notices what I wear and even picks out my clothes. . . . He's always saying he will write a show for me but can never find anything original enough."

Felicia understood that it was essential for her husband to concentrate his efforts on the Philharmonic. "It's a superhuman job," Bernstein told Leonard Lyons. There were TV scripts to write, new orchestral scores to read, research to be done on every other aspect of his conducting work. In the summer of 1958 Bernstein hired the composer Jack Gottlieb as his regular musical assistant. With the Philharmonic contributing to his weekly salary for the next decade, Gottlieb became Bernstein's amanuensis and colleague and occasionally his musical spokesman, and remained so, with only one break, until Bernstein's death.

That Bernstein hankered after his alter ego, the composer, can be deduced from an interview with Richard Schickel published in *Look* in November 1958. "The feeling is never far away from me that I should be working on a wonderful symphonic piece." In composing, Bernstein continued, "you get close to the depths of yourself, you have a really deep experience when you face the despair of not being able to find the right notes. The only thing to match it is ecstasy. . . . [Composing] is like a religious experience." Bernstein had spoken about the quasi-religious nature of the composing experience a year earlier at a lecture he gave to students at the University of Chicago. "Mostly I compose in bed, lying down, or on a sofa lying down. . . . Now this is a trance state, I suppose, which doesn't exactly sound like a very ideal condition for working but rather a condition for contemplating, but there is a very strong relation between creative work and contemplation. . . . What is conceived in this trance? Well, at the best, the utmost that can be conceived is a totality, a *Gestalt,* a work. . . . The next-to-greatest thing that can happen is to conceive an atmosphere . . . which is not the same as a totality of a work, because that doesn't involve the formal structure. . . . But if you're not that lucky, you can still conceive a *theme* . . . It can be a basic, pregnant idea or motive which promises great results, great possibilities of development. You know without even trying to fool with it that it's going to work, upside down and backward, and that it's going to make marvelous canons and fugues. . . . This is very different from conceiving only a tune. Tunes can't be developed; themes can."

At the Philharmonic, Bernstein talked himself into believing that he was somehow composing even while functioning as a full-time conductor. In November 1958 he told a journalist that "the composing part of me is left out now, but in a sense it's still active." When he conducted, Bernstein claimed, he temporarily *became* the composer. "If I don't feel I'm Beethoven, I'm not doing it well." It was the rationale to which he returned over and over again and it was confirmed by a composer colleague. "When he performs my music," Ned Rorem wrote, "his metabolism is so in tune with my own that he might have written the music himself. Other composers will attest to this—his bloodstream is theirs during the length of their piece."

I N May 1959, when Bernstein had rounded off his first Philharmonic season, he and Felicia went to England to see the London productions of his shows. *West Side Story* had been running at Her Majesty's Theatre in the Haymarket since the previous December. Jerome Robbins had directed an all-American cast: in those days no British dancers could cope with the syncopated intricacies of the Robbins choreography and the Bernstein music. Those who had seen both productions said the London one was superior, but London's critical response varied from the rapturous to the stony-faced. In the *Observer,* Peter Heyworth said that Bernstein's music was "quite without a distinctive lyrical idiom." The influential *Sunday Times* critic Harold Hobson complained that *West Side Story* lacked what he called an inspirational flash.

Hobson had worse things to say when *Candide* opened at the beginning of May 1959. His target was Lillian Hellman. Hobson blamed her book for what he saw as the failure of *Candide.* "Miss Hellman has no irony because irony needs style and Miss Hellman has no style." *Candide*'s London fate was probably sealed by his concluding line: "the entertainment is ignoble and at the end it was deservedly booed." In fact, the booing came from a small contingent in the balcony led by Sandy Wilson, composer of *The Boyfriend.* Wilson was angry because his own new show, *Valmouth,* had had to close to make way for *Candide.*

Bernstein enjoyed himself hugely when he attended the show on May 6. It was his first opportunity to hear "We Are Women," the new duet he had composed for Cunegonde and the Old Lady. "I laughed, carried on, just loved every bar everywhere." But when he appeared on "Monitor," BBC Television's influential Sunday arts magazine, he lashed out at Harold Hobson for daring to suggest that Lillian Hellman, to his mind one of the great playwrights of the age, lacked style. Britain had very perceptive critics, he said, citing young David Drew, who had written a coolly favorable piece about *Candide* in the *New Statesman.* But its gutter press was even worse than New York's, and the *Sunday Times,* he suggested, was the yellowest of the yellow.

The assault made breathtaking television, and Bernstein's hostile remarks were reported back to America by *Variety.* They were reminiscent of his blunt attack on Paul Henry Lang of the *Herald Tribune* the previous year after Lang complained that Callas had sung flat. In fact she had sung sharp, but only in order to stay in tune with a nervous tenor.

The interviews Bernstein gave in England provided an informal progress report at the end of his first year with the New York Philharmonic. He reacted sharply when the BBC interviewer, Huw Wheldon, suggested that success had come to him too easily. Nothing was easy for him, he said. "I'm extremely humble about whatever gifts I may have, but I am not modest about the work I do. I work extremely hard and all the time." In another interview he surmised that his serious music was not often performed because "conductors don't like conducting other conductors' music." There was probably some truth in that, although the *Candide* Overture was swiftly making friends—in its first two years nearly a hundred orchestras performed it. According to a letter from his publisher at Schirmer's, Hans Heinsheimer, his two "concertos" were also admired. *Serenade* was played in Russia and featured at the Spoleto Festival that summer as the score for a new ballet by Herbert Ross. *The Age of Anxiety* had already been used for a ballet in Mannheim, Germany.

Piano playing remained part of his essential life, he added: each year he learned a new concerto. Currently he was studying the Beethoven triple concerto, which he was to play in July with the concertmaster and principal cellist of the New York Philharmonic. But had he got any closer to deciding on his long-term future? He confided to the *Daily Express* (circulation four million) that the idea of concentrating on the New York Philharmonic "was to discover my focal point. But after a year I still can't say what that is." In the 1940s, he went on, he had felt much more confident than he did now. "The amazing rush of creation and events left no time for introspection. The time was full of glory. As I become older I get more self critical. . . . There is no composing time for me. And I doubt whether I can get any done for two years, which is a great grief."

WHEN he returned to New York in mid-May Bernstein conducted the New York Philharmonic (housed in a tent) at the ground-breaking ceremony for the new Philharmonic Hall, the first building to be built at Lincoln Center. *West Side Story* was to be filmed three blocks to the north in 1961, just before the final site demolitions occurred. Then the Bernsteins drove up to Martha's Vineyard for a two-month holiday. The car journey remains a vivid memory for Bernstein's daughter Jamie. "It was an all-day trip in those days. . . . You had to drive through Providence expiring from the heat. . . . My father was at the wheel of one of the cars, with everything piled up to the rafters, and my mother had the station wagon with the maids and the fish and the birds and the dog. It was preposterous. . . ." Bernstein had recently been loaned a big Lincoln convertible as part of his television contract. Jamie still remembers the ignominy she felt when the push-button mechanism of the folding roof got stuck halfway up and they had to crawl along the highway for miles with a protruding canopy.

Once installed at the spacious rented house, the Bernsteins led a lazy and comfortable summer life. "There was always lots of laughter and goofing around," Jamie recalls. Bernstein taught his daughter the Cyrillic alphabet. He was studying Russian himself in preparation for a grand New York Philharmonic tour that was part of the cultural exchange program between the United States and the Soviet Union. The orchestra went to Greece, Turkey, Lebanon (without Bernstein, too prominent a target), the Salzburg Festival, Warsaw and the Soviet Union, where it stayed for three weeks, performing eight concerts in Moscow, six in Leningrad and four in Kiev. Then came a further month in Western Europe. In every concert an American work was played and all three conductors were American, Bernstein sharing the honors with Thomas Schippers and Seymour Lipkin, who was also the pianist in seven performances of *The Age of Anxiety*. Bernstein had the lion's share of the conducting—thirty-six concerts in fifteen states. Felicia traveled with him.

In Salzburg a problem threatened the good-will mission: tickets for the Philharmonic's concert were said to be unavailable through hotel porters. There were rumors the concert was sold out when in fact very few tickets had been sold. It was the orchestra's first visit to the festival, which was dominated by Salzburg's most famous native musician since Mozart, Herbert von Karajan. Carlos Moseley of the Philharmonic was sent ahead to rectify the situation. "We started a big campaign to make sure that the public knew there were tickets. We ourselves bought a lot to get the ball rolling and went on the radio in both German and English. The rumors were that tension between Bernstein and Karajan had accounted for it." The warmth of their Milan friendship had cooled the previous fall, when Karajan had privately had harsh words for Bernstein's decision to do a television feature about Beethoven's Ninth with the New York Philharmonic the day after four public performances conducted by Karajan with the same musical forces.

Moseley did a good job: the hall was packed when Bernstein conducted his *Age of Anxiety,* coupled with Barber's *Second Essay* and Shostakovich's Fifth Symphony. The Vienna Philharmonic, the resident orchestra in Salzburg, gave a party for the Americans which Karajan and Mitropoulos attended: whatever the ugly gossip, all was sweetness and light on that occasion.

In Warsaw Bernstein discovered a jazz club to which he invited the director of the Chopin Institute, the conductor of the Warsaw Philharmonic and various Polish musical dignitaries after a concert. At the club an eighteen-year-old student astonished him by reciting in English the opening section of his Columbia LP recording *What Is Jazz?* "There was a great deal of merriment," Carlos Moseley remembers. "Lenny and the local conductor were becoming very chummy until Lenny pulled him up on his back and rode him piggy-back through the streets of Warsaw with everybody singing at the tops of their voices." *Time* magazine added that "The party broke up at 3 A.M. and Lenny was accompanied to his hotel in a long, gay, noisy procession that only dispersed after scores of students of both sexes kissed him farewell."

The final Warsaw concert, in the vast Congress Hall, drew an ovation—partly a political, antiregime demonstration—lasting forty minutes. In the end Bernstein sent the orchestra off the stage and returned to play solo piano pieces, including a nocturne and a mazurka by Chopin. He had not played them in public for decades. He probably made mistakes. But the gesture was unforgettable and the audience would not stop cheering.

From Poland the orchestra went to Moscow, where Prime Minister Khrushchev and Vice President Nixon had recently had a celebrated clash of words during Khrushchev's visit to the dream kitchen installed at the American National Exhibition at Sokolniki Park. It was the era of the Sputnik and intense Soviet-American rivalry.

Bernstein conducted all five concerts of the first Russian week, each with a different program, in the modestly proportioned but elegant hall of the Tchaikovsky Conservatory. The *New York Times* carried a prominent report of the opening concert. The audience had been excited from the beginning by Bernstein's brisk tempo for the Soviet national anthem, and by the unfamiliar sight of the conductor directing a Mozart piano concerto (K. 453 in G major) from the keyboard. "But the enthusiasm rose to an almost overwhelming peak at the final great crescendo of the last number of the program, Shostakovich's Fifth Symphony. . . .

"The excitement of the music and the power of the orchestra combined to bring the audience to its feet . . . with cheers of 'Bravo! Bis, bis! Encore, encore!' . . . Mr. Bernstein, who said he had been studying Russian for two weeks, shouted back: 'Bolshoi spasibo!'—'Many thanks!' "

After the concert many prominent Soviet musicians went backstage to congratulate Bernstein. Shostakovich was away on vacation and missed hearing his Fifth Symphony, but the composer Dmitri Kabalevsky was reported by Tass as saying it was "the finest interpretation ever heard here," and in *Izvestia* another leading Russian composer, Aram Khachaturian, wrote of the Philharmonic: "Their ensemble is wonderful. . . . Listeners are captivated by the purity of intonation and the beauty of tone of the solo instruments."

At the second concert Seymour Lipkin was the soloist in *The Age of Anxiety*. Bernstein became angry when he learned that the Russians, perhaps for ideological reasons, perhaps by custom, had not printed his long program note. Without it, he felt, the work was impossible to follow. He suspected the sinister hand of censorship in what may well have been nothing more than bureaucratic incompetence. Outwardly, however, the Moscow visit continued well. "Bernstein's force and magnetism," wrote Carlos Moseley, "has been everywhere pervasive. He has hurled himself with high spirits and a burning zeal into the task of reaching people—in the concert hall through electrifying performances and outside the theaters in a combination of ways uniquely Bernstein. In Russia as in other countries, the young have flocked to him. He has learned enough Russian to bring laughter and applause from the stage and to keep crowds entranced in stores, on the sidewalks and before the Macy-furnished house at Sokolniki Park." Grinning broadly, he had his hair cut at the exhibition, in full view of a huge crowd of Russian visitors. On his forty-first birthday David Keiser, the Philharmonic's president, gave a luncheon in his honor with vodka, caviar and birthday cake. That morning the orchestra had rehearsed *The Unanswered Question* by Charles Ives. "We rigged it," Keiser reported to *Life* magazine, "so that after Leonard called for muted strings out came *Happy Birthday* with drums and cymbals."

The New York Philharmonic's concert of twentieth-century music, given that evening, created a sensation when Bernstein broke with Russian tradition and talked directly to the audience. The program began with *The Unanswered Question;* through an interpreter Bernstein explained Charles Ives's philosophy "and his theory of accidental music, in which several themes in different tempos are woven together accidentally at unpredictable times." This was a revolutionary notion for a Russian audience restricted to a musical version of social realism. The *New York Times* man, Osgood Caruthers, reported that the most unexpected event after the performance of Ives's brief work was "a rousing demand by the cheering stomping clapping throng for a repeat." There was no doubt, he wrote, that Bernstein's remarks had intensified the interest of the audience.

But two mornings later Aleksandr Medvedev, music critic of the Cultural Ministry's own newspaper, *Sovetskaya Kultura,* came out with a stinging attack. "Before the Ives, Bernstein violated all traditions and spoke to the public. . . . It is difficult to see why the conductor did it—whether he was not sure the music of Ives would speak for itself or whether he was uncertain of the qualifications of the audience in the number-one concert hall of this great musical capital. . . . Before this four-minute piece L. Bernstein spoke for six minutes. . . . Only the good manners of the hospitable public resulted in a ripple of cool applause. Nevertheless the conductor, setting modesty aside, himself suggested that the piece be repeated." Medvedev was on thin ice in this assertion. Even the Russian news agency, Tass, reported that the Ives was "encored at the insistence of the enraptured audience." The attack made Bernstein furious. He called Medvedev's critique "an unforgivable lie . . . in the worst possible taste" and insisted he had been so surprised by the warmth of the audience's ovation that "in my very best Russian I asked if they wanted the piece again, and when they responded with cheers I played it."

Medvedev hit the nail on the head, however, when he criticized Bernstein for, as he put it, putting on a show called "Leonard Bernstein Is Lifting the Iron Curtain in Music." That was undoubtedly Bernstein's intention. In the same contemporary music program he scheduled two works by Igor Stravinsky: the

Concerto for Piano and Woodwinds of 1922, an example of Stravinsky's neo-classical style which had never been performed in the Soviet Union, and *Le Sacre du Printemps,* which had not been performed there, Bernstein told the Russians, for thirty years. ("Not true" muttered a Soviet official; in fact there had been a performance recently, in far-off Tallinn, Estonia.) "I want it to be possible for you to hear Stravinsky," Bernstein told the Moscow audience, which burst into applause. With *Sacre,* he went on, giving the Russians a lecture on their own artistic heritage, "Stravinsky created a revolution five years before your own revolution. Music has never been the same since that performance." Nine players from the Moscow Symphony Orchestra joined the 106 musicians of the New York Philharmonic to play a work officially classified as "bourgeois" and "decadent" in the Soviet Union. Caruthers of the *New York Times* described the occasion: "When the savage rhythms and weird melodies had reached their climax, there was a moment of breathless silence and then a great explosion of wild cheering."

The official news agency, Tass, described Bernstein's introductory remarks as "highly interesting critical essays," contradicting the party line laid down by Medvedev. But en route to Leningrad Bernstein was persuaded (probably by David Keiser) to respect the wishes of their Russian hosts. There were no more lectures from the podium about the contemporary music.

Bernstein's personal success in the Soviet Union was as all-embracing, literally so, as in the palmy days of his first visit to Palestine. "They want to touch me, shake my hand, embrace me, even kiss me," he said of the music-lovers who mobbed him and cheered him in a double line all the way back to his hotel. "I feel we are this much closer. Nothing else will be worth a hill of beans if we don't have peace." The Cold War continued, but Bernstein had helped a more musical cause: his concerts prepared the way for Igor Stravinsky's return to Russia in 1962 after nearly half a century of voluntary exile.

He had another card to play in his personal campaign to shake the Russian ideologists. Nine months previously the poet and novelist Boris Pasternak had been awarded the Nobel Prize for literature. First he had accepted, joyfully. Then the Soviet authorities had made him write a letter declining the honor. Greatly admired around the world, Pasternak's *Dr. Zhivago* had never been published in the Soviet Union because it was openly critical of Marxism. In August 1959 Pasternak was living in disgraced seclusion in a *dacha* somewhere outside Moscow. The Bernsteins had sent invitations to him to attend the first Moscow concert but they went unanswered. In Leningrad Bernstein obtained Pasternak's address, and sent a cable inviting Pasternak to his final concert back in Moscow on September 11. Pasternak responded in a strange, formal English, his beautiful broad handwriting flowing over three pages in all:

> September 1st. Dear Mr. Bernstein, I am exceedingly touched and
> most thankfully surprised by your kind friendly wire. If other interjacent

notes from me will not anticipate this my uttermost decision I hope to have the happiness to attend your concert on the eleventh. To this end, not daring or intending to trouble you with anything, I shall by my own care look after four passes (for me and my family) to the performance. Only please indicate my name to the attendant before the door of your artistic room on the evening, that I may be admitted to you after the concert.

Besides that I shall try to get the luck, the honor and the right to invite you to dinner at Peredelkino Wednesday the ninth at three o'clock. I shall confirm it afterward once more.

Obediently yours,
B. Pasternak

On the same page is a lengthy postscript dated September 2:

No it will not go—I think it better to renounce to that great pleasure and not to meet apart from the concert evening (the 11) when I shall experience myself the delight and ecstasies all the town speaks of, whereupon I am congratulating you fervently in advance.

Excuse my unexplainable discourtesy. My unvoluntary ungraciousness is my misfortune, not my fault. But I shall hear and see you.

With the same devotion
Idem

Heaven knows what battles were going on in Pasternak's mind and perhaps with the authorities too, for on a third page, dated September 3, came what Pasternak described as a "last note."

Last Note. Please be welcome on the day and hour you dispose the best, except the intervals between 1–2½ and after 8 in the evening, when I can be absent on walks. The best hour remains that of the dinner (3 o'clock). *Come as it were unawaitedly.* Ask the guidance of the concert organization to provide for the return car. Agree with them upon my being admitted to you on the evening of the concert in the entr'acte.

I wish you the renewal of your habitual triumphs I know of from hearsay.

Respectfully yours, B. Pasternak.

The Bernsteins returned to Moscow from Leningrad and Kiev on September 8. They had not yet received the Pasternak triple letter of September 1, 2 and 3 (perhaps because it was addressed to Bernstein c/o the Moscow Conservatory) but they had been sent another message from him through an intermediary and were not to be thwarted. Bernstein had to remain in Moscow preparing a television script so Felicia, accompanied by Steve Rosenfeld, a Russian-speaking member of the Philharmonic's staff, hired a cab to drive to Peredelkino, an old Russian village well outside the Moscow boundary, complete with log-wood cottages, grazing chickens, and peasant women nursing babies. Through the rear window of the cab, Felicia Bernstein caught a glimpse of the great writer walking in the forest. "Felicia rushed to Pasternak," Rosenfeld recalled, "and began talking, first in French, then in Italian, and in Spanish. She was so excited and talked so fast he probably couldn't have understood her in Russian. Then it occurred to us that Pasternak spoke perfectly good English, and we established contact. . . . When she dropped her glove one of the *babushka* ladies standing by picked it up and said, 'Your glove, *Dama* [Milady].' . . . She must have looked to them like a princess out of a fairy tale."

The Bernsteins dined with Pasternak that very afternoon, the eighth anniversary of their wedding. Bernstein found Pasternak (then sixty-nine) "both a saint and a *galant*. He has enormous warmth and great humor. . . . We hit it off, straight away. We talked for hours about art and the artist's view of history. He knows a great deal about music, his son is a pianist and a professor of music and music is very important in his household." Bernstein was later asked whether Pasternak had discussed his abandonment of the Jewish religion. "My conversations with Pasternak never touched on this point," he replied. "They were in fact virtually monologues by him on aesthetic matters. But he conveyed the impression of a Tolstoyan Christian, a worshipper of nature and the divine spark in man." Bernstein played excerpts from *West Side Story*.

On September 11, true to his word, Boris Pasternak and his family attended the Philharmonic's final concert. The program repeated works already heard the previous month in Moscow, including the Shostakovich Fifth. This time the composer was in the audience and an American film crew was there to record the embrace he bestowed upon Bernstein at the end of the performance. (The shots were spliced in at the end of Bernstein's lecture concert—for American television viewers—about the similarities between Russian and American musical cultures. It had been filmed earlier in the day, using Copland's *Billy the Kid* and Shostakovich's *Leningrad* Symphony as examples. The Moscow audience had loved the music but listened to Bernstein's untranslated talk with blank incomprehension.)

For Moscow's Western journalists the lead story that evening was the presence of Pasternak, making his first public appearance since the Nobel Prize scandal and his expulsion from the Writers' Union. Pasternak's reaction to the concert was the climax of Bernstein's tour. "You have taken us up to heaven," Pasternak exclaimed in the conductor's loge. "Now we must return to earth. . . . I've never felt so close to the aesthetic truth. When I hear you I know why you were born." Seated with Felicia beside him in his dressing room, Bernstein blushed for once in his life. Choking with emotion (according to the Associated Press reports), he said in reply: "I only want to listen, not to speak." In Richard Leacock's documentary footage, shown on U.S. television a few weeks later, Bernstein and his wife appear overwhelmed by the sheer physical energy of the great Russian writer.

✑

BERNSTEIN had a personal matter to attend to in the Soviet Union. His uncle Shlomo, Sam's younger brother, and Shlomo's son Mikhoel were allowed to come to Moscow to see him. Bernstein later described the scene at the Hotel Ukraina. "What I remember most about Shlomo was his mouthful of stainless-steel teeth. What a shock! He was big and muscular, a completely different type from Sam." Like Sam, Shlomo had wanted to escape from the ghetto, but he had preferred to align himself with Communist Russia, rather than emigrating to the U.S.A. Bernstein felt closer to his cousin Mikhoel who expressed sadness at being unable to live a Jewish life.

Bernstein phoned his father in Boston. "Look," he said. "I have your brother standing in this room. Talk to him." The conversation—restricted to a few halting words in Russian and Yiddish—persuaded Sam, who had first planned to make the trip and then backed out, to fly over after all. But the reunion was an anticlimax. According to Bernstein "the two brothers collided with bear hugs, their eyes glistening, and then . . . had absolutely nothing to say to each other." The only excitement came when Shlomo showed them his internal passport, marked "Jew." Bernstein was shocked. "What would have happened to me if I'd grown up here?" he said.


AFTER the mind-numbing austerity of the Soviet Union, the Philharmonic spent its last month on tour positively wallowing in the comforts and choices on offer in Western Europe. When he arrived in his favorite Dutch resort of Scheveningen, Bernstein wrote to Helen Coates, "I find myself talking in patri-otic clichés, crowing with pleasure over Dutch coffee, smiling faces, good old bourgeois luxury and *freedom!*" In London, the tour's last stop, the reviewers praised the orchestra but criticized the conductor. Even in a "stunt perfor-mance," thundered *The Times,* "it is not good conducting technique to leap into the air." "He looked as if he was playing a part choreographed for him by Jerome Robbins," echoed the *Daily Express.* "He swayed, stabbed, crouched and leaped in the air, both feet clear of the ground several times, like a pocket-sized Tarzan." But in a sympathetic *Spectator* review David Cairns showed that at their best, London critics had an articulated perception of Bernstein's gifts as well as his shortcomings. "At times he conducts [Brahms Symphony No. 1] as if utterly at the mercy of restless, adolescent emotional urges. In the violently fluctuating tempos of the Brahms *Finale* he always appeared to be succumbing to his first excited reactions to the music, never to be thinking beyond them. The missionary and publicist in him seems unable to let the music alone to make its own points but has to put his arm around its shoulders and introduce it to us as a very very warm and lovely human being. There is a shrewd truth in the American wisecrack 'unfortunately the composer was unable to carry out Bernstein's intentions.' . . . The hopeful sign in Bernstein is his impatient unpredictable humanity—if he can only master it. He is already, at forty, a fabulous conductor. I trust we do not have to wait until he is eighty before he becomes a great one."


I N an astute piece of self-promotion the New York Philharmonic flew home to Washington, D.C. The orchestra arrived at 8 A.M.; twelve hours later they performed for an audience that included the ambassadors of all the countries they had visited. As Paul Hume put it in the *Washington Post,* they showed "a responsiveness to Bernstein's soaring demands that is the mark of a great orchestra."

For a second time in twenty-seven months, Bernstein was given a key to the city of Washington. The first had been presented by the mayor to mark the opening of *West Side Story;* this time the commissioner of the District of Columbia did the honors as Felicia looked on, holding a massive bouquet and smiling radiantly despite the two months of traveling. Privately she had resolved to quit the touring business.

Before returning to New York and the start of the 1959–60 Philharmonic season, Bernstein addressed the National Press Club. He called for an expansion of cultural export programs. "If military strength is a nation's right arm, culture is its left arm, closer to its heart." Where did all his energy come from, he was asked: "Do you use Milltown, happiness pills or penicillin?" "I have no more energy than anybody else," he replied, "but I will say this. Whatever I do is with my whole heart, for the love of it."

# LAST YEARS AT CARNEGIE HALL

*On tour in Hawaii, 1960.*
CAMERA HAWAII, INC., COURTESY OF THE NEW YORK
PHILHARMONIC ARCHIVES

*There is a secret relationship between your soul and
Mozart's soul: perhaps you know it.*

—KARLHEINZ STOCKHAUSEN
in a letter to Leonard Bernstein

BERNSTEIN's years as music director of the New York Philharmonic fall into three distinct periods. Until 1962 he was forging his relationship with the orchestra and the New York public, undertaking major overseas tours and preparing for the move to Lincoln Center. For the next two seasons he supervised the establishment of what was in effect a new Philharmonic. After a year's sabbatical he resumed the leadership of New York musical life but also began looking to Vienna for new stimulus and fun.

Bernstein's second season at the Philharmonic, 1959–60, was expected to be the last at Carnegie Hall before it was replaced by an office development. He organized a stunning farewell. His guest conductors included his first teacher, Fritz Reiner, and his first inspiration, Dimitri Mitropoulos. Leopold Stokowski came back after a decade's absence and lectured his audience about the folly of pulling down Carnegie Hall. Bruno Walter returned in his eighty-fourth year to say farewell to the New York Philharmonic with four performances of *Das Lied von der Erde,* the climax of the Mahler centenary celebrations. Mahler's widow, Alma, came often to Bernstein's own Mahler rehearsals. She was in her late seventies, but according to Bernstein she did her coquettish best to add him to her formidable list of genius conquests. One concert she did not attend, however: "My dear great friend," she wrote to Bernstein, "I will not be at the rehearsal of the 'Kindertotenlieder' [*Songs of the Death of Children*] . . . as I relive again now, more than ever, my great sorrow at the loss of my own child and of my grand husband who was never strong and never regained his health after that loss—nor myself!"

Bernstein's other Philharmonic programs included a survey of the concerto form from Bach to Bartók, and a five-week festival of music for the theater, including part of Virgil Thomson's opera *Four Saints in Three Acts* and a new mini-opera, *Introduction and Good-byes,* by Lukas Foss. A series called "In Search of Style" explored Stravinsky's neoclassical music; another series, entitled (to the derision of certain journalists) "In Search of God," presented music for Christmas, Easter and Passover. "The Search for Nothingness" surveyed the fashionable minimalist music, including scores by Pierre Boulez and Henry Brant.

Though he was hemmed in by concerts and television programs with the Philharmonic, and immersed in music politics in a way that would have seemed unthinkable to him only a few years earlier, Bernstein's family life flourished. His children, Jamie and Alexander, were both musical and Bernstein enjoyed giving them informal instruction. "He's a marvelous teacher," Felicia told a journalist. "He goes straight to essentials and makes everything clear. He gives them tonality and the relationship of chords and all kinds of things children aren't usually taught. . . . He likes to make up songs for them, too. When he was about to leave on a trip a few months ago, he wrote a three voice lullaby for us to sing. 'Evenings, when it's booze time, that's the time we think of Daddy.' "

In the late fall of 1959 the Bernsteins paid forty-eight thousand dollars for their first country house, in Redding, Connecticut. It was a pleasant four-bedroom property set on a hill in rural countryside yet close enough to Manhattan for the family to drive out on Friday afternoons after the Philharmonic concert. Bernstein had to return to the city for Saturday evening concerts but the weekend retreat became a fixture in the family calendar.

In November 1959, Simon and Schuster published Bernstein's first book, *The Joy of Music.* The first part contained three humorous "imaginary conversations," forty pages in all. The first, called "Bull Session in the Rockies," was with Stephen Spender and Burton Bernstein, en route to Taos. The second, "Whatever Happened to the Great American Symphony?," was actually not a conversation but an exchange of letters between Bernstein's ego and his id, thinly disguised as a Broadway Producer. The third, "Why Don't You Run Upstairs and Write a Nice Gershwin Tune?," had Bernstein arguing self-defensively about the elusive ingredients of a musical hit with a friendly Tin Pan Alley publisher.

The book's most substantial section, 230 pages, was devoted to seven of the best "Omnibus" scripts, copiously illustrated with music examples. Other articles were reprinted from the *Atlantic Monthly* and the *New York Times*. The book stayed on the best-seller list for six months and sold over a hundred thousand copies in hardcover, helped no doubt by the appearance on television of nine music shows by Bernstein during the winter months. Bernstein dedicated the book to Helen Coates "with deep appreciation for fifteen selfless years."

In February 1959 Bernstein created a music publishing company called Amberson Enterprises, Inc., which was later expanded to administer all his business affairs. Amberson's directors were Bernstein's accountant, H. Gordon Freeman, his lawyer, Abe Friedman, and Helen Coates. The existence of such a company prompted a few private sneers but was a necessary development, given the increasing complexity of Bernstein's activities in popular and classical composition, publishing, recording, television and theatrical licensing. He was ultra-conservative in financial matters, never borrowed money, and preferred the safe advice of his accountant to the speculation urged on him by others. *West Side Story* performance royalties were bringing in at least $125,000 a year in 1959 and 1960 yet his most ambitious tax shelter was the purchase of a ranch and a few thousand dollars' worth of cattle. He later added a Florida orange grove to his interests.

Bernstein's recording contract was due for renewal. When Schuyler Chapin joined Columbia Records in 1959 his first task was to conclude the new deal. Abe Friedman drove a hard bargain in return for exclusivity. Bernstein's contract was to run for an astonishingly long period, twenty years, and guaranteed him the right to nominate his repertoire, an unheard of freedom in the recording business. It reflected Bernstein's strength and Columbia's determination to prevent him from defecting to RCA, which offered him a blank check and his own orchestra. He was guaranteed a basic forty-five thousand dollars annually in conducting royalties. This was in addition to copyright recording income from existing Columbia recordings, among them the original cast album of *West Side Story,* which brought in tens of thousands of dollars each year well into the 1960s. Giving Bernstein a free hand to choose the repertoire was a dangerous precedent, but Goddard Lieberson's philosophy was that Columbia was making so much money from music in other fields that the company had a duty to take an occasional loss in the classics. The policy of going along with Bernstein's wishes made sense economically in the long run: the New York Philharmonic nearly doubled its recording income between 1959 and 1969.

BERNSTEIN's work was exhilarating, but he began to experience more serious trouble with his health. His back continued to plague him—especially when he took holidays. Insomnia was a familiar foe. The guilt he felt about not composing, combined with the frenetic pace he maintained in New York, disturbed his equilibrium. In May 1960 he missed a rehearsal. "I had a collapse-o," he told the *Post*. "Never happened to me before. I couldn't get out of bed. Ran out of fuel." In the same *Post* article he spoke of his depression at the way world events were turning. On May 1, the Russian National Day, the Americans carelessly allowed a U-2 photographic surveillance flight across the Soviet Union to be intercepted. Bernstein called the U.S. Government "blunderers" and yearned publicly for a strong man at the top.

His reaction was probably colored by his most recent meeting with President Eisenhower. On April 5 the New York Philharmonic had performed at the White House. Bernstein played two movements of a Mozart piano concerto and Gershwin's *Rhapsody in Blue*. The President, whose favorite conductor was the relentlessly middle-brow Lawrence Welk, told Bernstein he had enjoyed the Gershwin. "It's got a theme. I like music with a theme, not all them 'arias and barcarolles.' " The phrase lodged in Bernstein's memory.

·*W EST Side Story* reopened in New York on April 27, 1960, after nine months on the road. The producers wanted to maximize the show's theatrical potential before the film version was released late in 1961, and Bernstein agreed to add to the glamour by conducting the second premiere. In the thirty months since the show's first opening he had become, through his television appearances, one of the best-known men in America. He arrived outside the theater in his Lincoln Continental and instead of entering through the pit, like a regular show conductor, he waited until the houselights were dimmed and then walked down the aisle in a single spotlight, sporting his Koussevitzky black silk cape, pausing to greet his friends on left and right and being applauded all the way to the orchestra, like a toreador in white tie and tails. He had the full score under his arm, tattered and illegible. When he greeted Sid Ramin halfway down the aisle, he whispered, "How the hell does this goddam thing begin, with an upbeat or a downbeat?" He did not stop for an answer. He conducted only the overture, a conventional assembly of the show's top tunes. He had slaved away on it with Sid Ramin and Irwin Kostal one sleepless night in Washington back in 1957; he subsequently claimed to dislike it, and did not include it in his 1985 recording for Deutsche Grammophon, but its success that night was overwhelming. Bernstein spent the best part of five minutes acknowledging the applause. Then he handed over the baton to Joseph Lewis, the pianist of the original band, and the show, in which Larry Kert was still singing Tony, finally got under way.

A month later he conducted an LP of *On the Town* with four of its original stars—the only occasion on which he recorded one of his own musicals with a Broadway cast. Two months of vacation followed, "lovely but utterly unproductive." Gustav Mahler's example was proving unworkable. "I was so fatigued," he told David Diamond, "that I never managed the switch to composing at all."

When he returned to New York at the beginning of August it was to prepare for a seven-week American tour with the Philharmonic. An early biographer, John Briggs, found him on August 5, "back in steaming Manhattan, looking more jaded than words can say. His appetite was poor, and insomnia, that dreaded enemy of all who live on nervous energy, was taking its toll. He had slept badly for a month." Yet a few days later Carlos Moseley phoned Briggs: "You need not have concerned yourself. Lenny's appetite has come back, he's sleeping like a baby and his back doesn't hurt anymore. Once the tour got under way he was fine."

Wherever he went that summer, Bernstein attracted huge crowds. Some of the biggest were in Hawaii, where the Philharmonic was the first mainland orchestra ever to perform in the fiftieth state. Traveling without Felicia, who had stayed behind with the children, Bernstein's flamboyance was unrestrained. At his Honolulu press conference he was photographed stripping to the waist to don an *aloha* shirt he had just acquired. "Hawaii was Paradise," Bernstein told David Diamond. "I would never have believed I'd like it—I've always detested leis and alohas and the shit-music, but there I was, moved and exalted by all the affection and warmth, alohas included. The intermingling of races there, with no self-consciousness, is a joy: the people are so beautiful you can't keep your eyes or hands off them; and the life is an object lesson to the other 49 states."

From Martha's Vineyard Felicia wrote to tell her husband that he "sounded contented and independent on the phone—a very special sound to me which is hard to describe. Perhaps akin to your bachelor days, very pleased to hear from me, and yet full of the 'other' life, the 'other house,' the 'other' others—I must be jealous."

Partying with his parents in Hollywood during the record-breaking tour, Bernstein reported to his sister that "the top moment was Mama meeting Anita Louise. . . . 'I've always adored you. Never missed a picture you were in! I even named my daughter Shirley after you!' (General bewilderment and dismay.)"

At the end of the tour Bernstein and the Philharmonic set off from New York on a visit to the 1960 Berlin Festival to give concerts and tape a television program. Bernstein's sponsor, Ford, paid for the trip. One mood a night was never enough in a foreign city. On his first evening Bernstein went *shul*-hopping—it was Rosh Hashanah—then ate a heavy German dinner and drank with members of the orchestra until 3 A.M. The concert at the Sender Freies Berlin radio studio went well. "It will never cease to amaze me," wrote Bernstein's brother, who was taking time off from his *New Yorker* staff post to accompany him, "what a genuine ovation will do for Lenny. He can be grey-green and sunken eyed with fatigue, but with a round of sincere applause he can bounce back with the resiliency of Herb Elliott [world record holder in 1960] on the last lap of a mile race. Backstage, Lenny looked suddenly healthy, energetic and vital." After a long wait for autograph signing and a meeting with Seiji Ozawa, due to work as his assistant in 1961, the two brothers set off for a tourist nightclub called the Rififi, where the musical entertainment was provided by a feeble but raucous imitator of Elvis Presley. Bernstein brought along some German students who had been at the concert. " 'Isn't it amazing,' he said to them. 'You were born when I was finishing college and the war was just breaking out here. All I could think of that year was how much I hated Germans. . . . Here it is in 1960 and here we are, sitting together in Berlin listening to ghastly American popular music. Where else could this happen in the world? I hope you kids are coming to the taping tomorrow, because that's what it's all about.' "

The subject of the program was in fact Beethoven's music, which comes closer than any other, Bernstein argued, to the idea of the universal language "because of the German genius for development [which] is the fountainhead of everything we call 'symphonic.' " By development, reported Sydney Gruson, then the *New York Times*'s man in Berlin, Bernstein meant "the dissecting, testing and proving of each thematic idea." The year before Bernstein had had the chutzpah to explain Stravinsky and Shostakovich to the Russians. Now he was describing Beethoven to an audience of Berlin students and making political observations on Berlin's increasing isolation from the West. He ended his talk with a benediction, spoken in Hebrew and then in English. "May the Lord lift up His face to you and give you peace." There was a momentary silence, wrote Gruson, "then a great wave of applause."

Next day Bernstein played Beethoven's First Piano Concerto three times in twelve hours: at the morning television dress rehearsal, at the afternoon's taping and at the evening concert. For many musicians it would seem inartistic to perform so often. But Berlin had an energizing effect on Bernstein. His desire to demonstrate for universal peace and the brotherhood of man led him to make gestures, like this visit to Berlin, that were matched by very few other musicians in the twentieth century.

CARNEGIE Hall was reprieved in the summer of 1960, and its savior, Isaac Stern, played the Beethoven violin concerto at the Philharmonic's opening concert in the fall, just four days after the orchestra returned from Berlin. The harsh touring schedule finally caught up with Bernstein that week: he conducted the first half of the Saturday evening concert but had to go home at intermission, suffering from bronchitis. His assistant, Gregory Miller, took over Schumann's Fourth Symphony. (An earlier biographer's assertion that the collapse was brought on by reading a bad notice from Harold Schonberg is untrue. He survived many worse ordeals.)

It was the beginning of a wretched season of cancellations at the Philharmonic. Worst of all, Dimitri Mitropoulos died, at La Scala, Milan, while rehearsing Mahler's Third Symphony. He crashed unconscious into the orchestra and was carried to the prompt corner at the side of the stage; a plaque marks the spot where he expired. A friend of David Diamond's who was at the concert retrieved the silver Greek cross with a dove carved on it that Mitropoulos always wore around his neck. Diamond passed it on to Bernstein, who adopted it as his talisman.

For a conductor only recently recovered from a heart attack to die at the podium had about it a feeling of inevitability, almost of ritual, that moved Bernstein greatly. He later compared his dear friend's death to that of Socrates, who calmly prepared his own suicide. Bernstein had already conducted memorial concerts in New York for Toscanini and Rodzinski. He marked the passing of the Philharmonic's third great musical director with a performance of the "Urlicht" movement from Mahler's Second Symphony (Jennie Tourel was the soloist), promising also to take over the complete performance of Mahler's Third Symphony, which Mitropoulos had been scheduled to conduct later in the season.

John F. Kennedy was elected President in November 1960. Bernstein was the only classical musician invited to participate in Frank Sinatra's gala fund-raising concert on January 19, the eve of the inauguration, at the Washington Armory. Sinatra asked Bernstein to compose a fanfare and to conduct two festive works, J. P. Sousa's "Stars and Stripes Forever" and the "Hallelujah Chorus" from Handel's *Messiah*. Other stars included Harry Belafonte, Milton Berle, Nat King Cole, Bette Davis, Jimmy Durante and Gene Kelly. The Bernsteins received a summoning telegram from Sinatra. First he outlined the rehearsal arrangements. Then he discussed what he called "the social side of this hoe-down": "EXHIBIT A WILL BE A SUPPER PARTY THAT AMBASSADOR KENNEDY IS GIVING IN HONOR OF THE ENTIRE CAST IMMEDIATELY AFTER OUR GALA PERFORMANCE. . . . EXHIBIT B IS THE INAUGURAL CEREMONY ITSELF AT NOON OF THE TWENTIETH AND THE PARADE WHICH FOLLOWS. . . . EXHIBIT C IS THE LITTLE WING DING DINNER WHICH I AM TOSSING FOR ALL OF US AT SEVEN THIRTY ON THE EVENING OF THE TWENTIETH. WE WILL ALL GO EN MASSE FROM THIS DINNER TO THE INAUGURAL BALL AT THE MAYFLOWER, WHICH IS PRETTY DRESSY FOR BOYS AND GIRLS. BLACK TIE OR WHITE TIE DIAMONDS AND EMERALDS AND ALL THAT JAZZ. EVERYTHING IS SHAPING UP FOR SOMETHING THAT WE ALL WILL BE REMEMBERING FOR A LONG LONG TIME AND BELIEVE YOU ME I DON'T THINK I HAVE EVER BEEN SO EXCITED. LOVE AND KISSES AND I'LL BE WAITING FOR YOU."

On the morning of the nineteenth, snow began to fall in Washington. It snowed solidly all through the day. The gala was due to begin that evening at 8:45 with Bernstein's new fanfare. At 10:15 P.M. the President-elect and his wife finally arrived, having navigated Washington's dangerously snow-encumbered side streets with a posse of Secret Service outriders. The orchestra was in place but the show could not go on. Everyone had to wait for Leonard Bernstein.

Bernstein had become trapped in traffic on his way back to his hotel after the rehearsal to change into white tie. He was sharing a limousine with Bette Davis. Jack Gottlieb left the car to get help and quite by chance he knocked on the door of Congresswoman Marguerite Church. Church called the police and Bernstein and Davis were returned to the armory in a patrol car. When Bernstein eventually raised his baton to conduct at 10:35 P.M. he was wearing a flamboyant Mexican-style shirt two sizes too big for him lent by Harry Belafonte's dresser. The cuffs were held together with a pair of Jack Gottlieb's cuff links.

Bernstein was proud of his friendship with the Kennedys. In November 1961 he and his wife were among the distinguished group of American composers and conductors who gathered at the White House to salute the Spanish cellist Pablo Casals. Bernstein had a meeting at noon next day at the White House and went back for dinner that evening. Mrs. Kennedy had begun wooing him to become artistic director of her pet project, the cultural center being planned for Washington.

Two months later the Bernsteins were back at the White House for a dinner party to honor Igor Stravinsky on his eightieth birthday. When Stravinsky had departed, the Bernsteins were among the small group invited to the family quarters. Bernstein was so excited he sat himself down in President Kennedy's favorite rocking chair, oblivious to Felicia's asides in Spanish urging him to make way for the President. "Who's taking care of the candy store?" he later asked, enjoying the chance to talk politics with the top man. Bernstein always kept a signed photograph of President Kennedy on his grand piano. Their friendship whetted Bernstein's appetite for other meetings with presidents and crowned heads around the world.

IN February 1961 Bernstein was elected to the Institute of Arts and Letters, then the outer circle of the American Academy. Among the other nominations that year were Ludwig Mies van der Rohe, Langston Hughes and Arthur Schlesinger, Jr. Bernstein was pleased because the academy honored creativity rather than interpretative skills. Membership entitled him to sport a purple and yellow rosette: his suits from then on were modified to include the appropriate size of button hole.

Meanwhile, on February 13, at a "Valentine for Leonard Bernstein" gala concert—a fund-raiser for the orchestra's pension fund—the New York Philharmonic laid on the equivalent of a lifetime tribute for its forty-two-year-old maestro as a thank-you present for staying another seven years with the orchestra. Apart from the show biz razzmatazz (the sort of thing to which Harold Schonberg took offense) the event was important for the premiere of the *Symphonic Dances from "West Side Story,"* conducted—from an unwieldy manuscript score—by Lukas Foss. Sid Ramin and Irwin Kostal had recently completed the scoring for the film musical so they knew the work inside out. Early in 1961 they submitted a list of potential numbers to Bernstein, who decided upon a running order. Every note in the suite is taken from the score. The collaborators found it difficult to decide upon a finale; Jack Gottlieb suggested the lonely flute solo of "I Had a Love." The suite ends, like the musical, on a tense, unresolved, and haunting tritone chord. Why are they described as *symphonic* dances? Because even in its show form *West Side Story* is symphonically conceived. Jack Gottlieb noted at the time that the dances consist of "relatively few thematic ideas, combined with each other and metamorphosed into completely new shapes." It's one of Bernstein's most popular works.

Harold Schonberg had already complained in the *Times* when Bernstein took a four-month mid-season break from subscription concerts (but not from the "Young People's Concerts"). In April Schonberg produced his first end-of-season report on the Philharmonic. Not only did the orchestra sound less good, he wrote, but the atmosphere at Carnegie Hall had deteriorated since Bernstein had taken over. "At all times the aura of show business rather than music-making is present. Thoughtful people are beginning to complain more and more of Bernstein's antics on the podium . . . and asking if Lenny is ever going to grow up." *The New Yorker*'s music critic, Winthrop Sargeant, a former violinist in the Philharmonic, also objected to Bernstein's podium movements, which included, he said, "fencing, hula-dancing and calling upon the heavens to witness his agonies. I care about Mahler's agonies," he went on, "but I do not care a bit about Mr. Bernstein's. . . ." The sniping had begun.

When the New York season was over Bernstein and the Philharmonic embarked on their first tour of Japan. Government support for such tours dropped away under the Democrats; CBS Television underwrote the visit, with additional funds coming from the East West Music Encounter, a festival being held in Tokyo under the auspices of the Congress for Cultural Freedom, a C.I.A.-funded organization. The Philharmonic arrived in Japan to find itself in the middle of a row between the well-established Osaka Festival, supported by the newspaper *Asahi Shimbun,* and the brand-new Tokyo Festival, of which the East West Encounter was a part. Both festivals were in full swing. The New York Philharmonic had to make its Tokyo debut in a brand-new hall, acoustically unproven, on the same night that the venerable Leipzig Gewandhaus Orchestra under Franz Konwitschny was making its Japanese debut at the Hibiya Hall down the road. For good measure the Royal Ballet was also in Tokyo that night, performing *Giselle.*

The new Tokyo Festival had been boycotted by Japanese left-wingers because of its anti-Communist sponsorship and it was under attack from other quarters because its program policy was dictated by a Westerner, Nicolas Nabokov. It was Nabokov's intention to challenge Japan's conservative taste in Western music, formed by German musicians early in the twentieth century. In the festival, the New York Philharmonic presented three programs of contemporary music, including Bartók, Berg, Hindemith, Ravel, Stravinsky, Ives and Copland. Elsewhere, in a six-city tour, they also performed Beethoven, Brahms, Schumann, Tchaikovsky and Bernstein's own *Jeremiah* Symphony.

Bernstein's reviews were mixed. One report described him as the Karajan of America, which cannot have greatly pleased him, although Karajan was already treated as a god by Japanese music-lovers. Some critics did not take kindly to what *Time,* echoing Harold Schonberg, described as "Bernstein's gaudy podium antics." One writer called his conducting "too American." Another said he made the slow movement of the Ravel piano concerto sound Jewish rather than French. But the orchestra impressed almost everybody with its dynamism and its body of tone. "Hearing such a wonderful performance as this," a famous Japanese singer observed in the intermission of Bernstein's first concert, "I feel as if many beefsteaks are eaten in America." Coached by the young Japanese conductor Seiji Ozawa, who served as his assistant on the tour, Bernstein came out and talked to the public in Japanese—a gesture of friendship that was warmly received.

Bernstein wanted to conquer wherever he went, but he felt a special sympathy for Japan, its landscape, its Zen philosophy, its Old World lifestyle. He wrote to Felicia:

> Darling: How can I describe the last two days? Paradise. At last, really Japan—once we got out of mad gay Tokyo. About 16 of us were put up at that famous Japanese inn called Minaguchi-ya, where I think I had the most beautiful day and night anyone has ever had. The gardens—the beauty—the sea—the quiet—the deep charm of Japanese rooms, the smell of new tatami [the straw mats used for carpeting]—the elegance of simple flower arrangements—the marvelous food—and oh, the girls. We were welcomed in a way that made me feel I'd never been really welcomed before. The girls crowd around, laughing, attending, bubbling, dressing and undressing you, preparing your kimono, your bath (oh, that wonderful bath of old scoured wood)—and with none of the artificial gaiety of the Geisha (who embarrass the wits out of me) but with a natural spontaneous *joie de vivre* and delight in making you happy. I had the Emperor's suite, mind you, and slept in his bed, and had his breakfast (about 17 courses) and it was coincidentally the Emperor's birthday, so Lennuhtt was the Emperor (which is *Tenno* in Japanese, so now you can call me Tennuhtt). The morning after we visited the famous nearby temple Shenken-ji [actually, Seiken-ji], a terribly moving Zen sanctuary with the most overwhelming gardens I have ever seen. The entire side of a mountain, covered with every green imaginable, spotted with huge red azalea and pierced by a long, narrow graceful waterfall from top to bottom. I shall never forget the sound of that silence, or the doors, the colors, the peace. . . . I bought me two black kimonos today—one silk, one wool: saw nothing for you, don't dare, really. Bought Axel [Alexander] a great boy-doll in honor of Boy's Day, which is the big festival tomorrow. It's a Samurai-boy on a horse, in a glass case, and featuring a huge phallus, which I don't know how I'll explain to him. Then visited Nagoya Castle, a breathtaking piece of architecture, and a museum reminiscent of the

Hermitage in terms of costumes, prints, and paintings. Now sleep. Then a koto-player is coming for to play the koto. Then sleep. Day off. Thank God. My big nose is still sick, and needs a big rest. All else is great, concerts et al. are smashes. Minimum of Saudeks, etc. [Robert Saudek was producing a film record of the tour for a Ford show on CBS.] All under control. Only I miss you terribly.

My love, my little maid of Orleans, my swan, I miss you. My dearest love to the littles.

L

30 April '61

[P.S.] O, that inn! I had always thought the idea that Japan made men happy was a commercial notion from Brando movies: but it's true!


Bernstein was writing from Nagoya, where, encouraged by Helen Coates, he finally met the English-speaking Kazuko Amano, a former piano student in Paris who had been writing fan letters to him since 1947. Kazuko went to Tokyo for Bernstein's second and third East West Encounter concerts. She remembers how anxious he was about the overresonant acoustics of the new Festival Hall. "Lenny needed many rehearsals with the help of Seiji Ozawa, who was running in all directions, shouting, 'No Lenny, it's too *forte,* or too sharp . . . I cannot hear the strings. . . .' Sometimes he asked Seiji or Ely-akum [Shapira, the Israeli conductor, another Bernstein assistant] to conduct certain passages and this time it was Lenny's turn to listen, adjust and make a good balance. A difficult job but worth doing: the concerts were brilliant, everything was sensational and, though I am reluctant to admit this fact, *shocking* for a conservative country like Japan." As Kazuko Amano saw it, Bernstein's friendly attitude toward the audience opened a new path for the music world in Japan, which was still under the influence of "the old German music-teaching approach. Middle-aged and older audiences indulged themselves by being for Karajan and against Bernstein. . . . For Lenny it was a great shock. How often he said: 'No one here made a standing ovation for me. I heard that Karajan has that always.' I denied it," writes Kazuko, "but Lenny was still unhappy, so my family and friends decided to make a standing ovation, which needs a lot of courage. But we did it, shouting 'Bravo Lenny!' The members of the orchestra looked happy and smiled. I hope Lenny saw us! The Japanese audience around us was angry, finding our action just disgusting."

At the second East West Encounter concert on May 5, Bernstein told the audience that a work by a Japanese composer, Toshirō Mayuzumi, deserved a talented Japanese conductor. He introduced Seiji Ozawa and handed him his baton. Here was the Koussevitzky legacy at work. In Ozawa, then twenty-five and winner of the Koussevitzky award at Tanglewood, Bernstein had found the first of a dozen conductors of international reputation to whom he gave active encouragement. When the Tokyo concerts were all over, Ozawa took Bernstein to his parents' small house in Kawasaki. "My mother went crazy," he remembers. "Every possible Japanese family dish was on the table. Lenny had a great time, eating, drinking and praying at our family shrine." Afterward, in the car, Bernstein realized with a shock that in the Ozawa house he had not smoked a single cigarette.

Flying home across the International Dateline, the orchestra played in Anchorage on the evening of May 9, the same day they left Tokyo. The announced performance of the Ravel piano concerto had to be canceled when Bernstein arrived in Alaska minus a slice of his left thumb. Eating dessert in his hotel while engrossed in the sumo wrestling on television, his latest passion, he had gashed himself with a fruit knife.

Homecoming in those days was a happy ritual. Jamie Bernstein remembers her father's walking in "with his own bags, all tanned, with a big smile and those really white teeth—they got yellower as the years went on. And everybody would make a big noise and carry on and we would jump up and down on his knees and shoulders and climb all over him, and it was always very exciting. He would always be jazzed up and exhilarated and full of funny stories about things that had gone wrong."

But there was a darker side to the Bernsteins' long separations. According to Judith Braun, an actress friend of the family who lived in the Osborne, when Bernstein was away Felicia became "a Persephone-like creature, depressed about the turn her life had taken. She'd chosen this life, and she wanted this life, and she loved Lenny, but it was driving her really crazy. I remember her sitting in the kitchen . . . really so unhappy and I said, 'Why don't you have an affair?' She said she could never do that. She loved Lenny too much. They needed each other really desperately. She served such incredible functions in his life: his morality, his spine. She was a martinet [with] such strict standards about what was acceptable and what was unacceptable."

Felicia insisted that he drop a few of his friends from the 1940s but got on well with most of the important players in Bernstein's life as well as creating her own little court of close friends, among them the director Mike Nichols, the photographer Richard Avedon and the composer and lyricist Stephen Sondheim, who was a fanatic competitor in the anagram parties organized regularly at the Osborne. In the summer of 1961 Sondheim directed his friends in a wicked home-movie parody of *Tosca,* lip-synched to the Maria Callas–Tito Gobbi sound track. Bernstein played Scarpia in a joke false nose and mustache, while Felicia wore an Empire-style nightgown. As the music dies away the crucifix on the murdered baron's chest is surreptitiously replaced by the family menorah.

Felicia was never totally at ease with her parents-in-law, however. According to Burton Bernstein, it wasn't simply a matter of religion since his own first wife, Ellen Hora-Siccama, was not Jewish. "Ellen and my parents grew close over the years, closer than Felicia and my parents ever did. Jennie and Sam often spoke of Ellen as their 'other daughter'—a phrase they couldn't bring themselves to use about Felicia." Felicia almost always acted correctly toward them, but there was no real warmth in her welcome.


IN the spring of 1961 the Bernsteins conceived their third child. The prospect of a new baby, coupled with the certainty that Philharmonic Hall would replace Carnegie Hall as the orchestra's headquarters, prompted the decision to find a larger apartment. They moved in November to a fifteen-room duplex at the top of a substantial if somewhat characterless 1920s apartment building at 895 Park Avenue. The new place divided neatly in two. The lower floor was for the Bernsteins' bedroom, the children's quarters and the live-in help. The penthouse floor consisted of a library and the rooms where the Bernsteins entertained: a splendid reception room, equipped with two grand pianos and a harpsichord, and an equally handsome dining room. Unlike the Osborne, the new apartment was not a place where friends would drop in unannounced for a drink or gossip. The Bernsteins continued to entertain the same small circle, but there was no mistaking their change of status. Bernstein himself spoke about it to his old friends, relishing the fact that he, a Jew whose father had lived in a ghetto in the Ukraine, was driving downtown from his Park Avenue duplex in a Lincoln convertible.

Moving house was part of the process whereby Bernstein became public property. In truth the much photographed penthouse floor did resemble an official residence. Felicia once told a journalist that she did not dare admit how many servants she employed, and Schuyler Chapin recalls a whole line of Chilean maids in black dresses serving the guests at a dinner party. In making the change the Bernsteins symbolically distanced themselves from the Philharmonic's day-to-day affairs. From Park Avenue at Seventy-ninth Street it was too far to walk to work at Lincoln Center. A chauffeur-driven car took Bernstein to and from rehearsals, concerts and recordings. It was no doubt part of Felicia's calculations that Helen Coates's proximity was also greatly reduced. "La Belle," as they called her, after the Offenbach operetta *La Belle Hélène,* remained in the Osborne apartment that had been bought for her in 1958. Bernstein also kept his study there to house the burgeoning shelves of Bernstein memorabilia Miss Coates had been accumulating since 1932. The family eventually referred to it jokingly as "The Shrine."


ON October 18, 1961, Robert Wise's long-awaited film version of *West Side Story* had its world premiere in New York. Pauline Kael jeered at what she described as two gangs of ballerinas, and *Time* accused the film of becoming "wildly, immorally sentimental when it attempts the apotheosis of alley rats," but Bosley Crowther's *Times* verdict, "Nothing short of a film masterpiece," was endorsed by the award for Best Picture when the Oscars were announced the following spring. Bernstein had little to do with the making of the film, and he was personally ineligible for an Oscar because his score was not an original work for the screen. But Academy Awards went to the conductor Johnny Green, the associate producer Saul Chaplin and the orchestrators Sid Ramin and Irwin Kostal. The co-director, Jerome Robbins, had been pulled off the project ten weeks into the shooting because his perfectionism had led him to fall behind schedule, but he shared the Oscar for direction with Robert Wise and received a special award for film choreography.

The film's structure was significantly different since there is no intermission. "Krupke" was switched with "Cool" as part of the screenwriter Ernest Lehman's intention to create "a rising line of conflict," and "America" became a number for the boys as well as the girls—which had been Sondheim's original plan. All in all, *West Side Story* is one of the best of Hollywood's musical adaptations from stage to screen. Still seen regularly on television all over the world and screened at home on untold numbers of videocassettes, *West Side Story* is the work which has given Leonard Bernstein's name universal recognition.

With the passing of the decades the status of *West Side Story* has been transformed from an innovative and daring piece of music theater into a classic, frequently performed by school children who are even younger than the gang kids they are portraying. What were once awkward melodic intervals, such as the tritone C–F sharp–G at the beginning of the song "Maria," have become easily negotiable parts of everyday musical language. Impossibly tricky syncopations have become literally child's play. Most of the singing, acting and orchestral playing required is within the bounds of practicability for good amateurs. And yet the work's emotional charge has not been diminished. A 1992 production at a Brooklyn school, directed by Alexander Bernstein, the composer's son, featured a sixteen-year-old Puerto Rican girl as Maria. She was in tears at the end, along with many in the audience.

On Sunday January 7, 1962, Samuel Bernstein celebrated his seventieth birthday at an event organized by his favorite charity, the Boston Lubavitz Yeshiva, in Boston's Sheraton Plaza Ballroom. Eight hundred prominent citizens were in attendance, including the mayor of Boston, the lieutenant governor and the attorney general of Massachusetts. When his turn came, Leonard spoke with great seriousness about the relationship between father and son. The speech offered a glimpse of his creative preoccupation. He had recently begun grappling with a new composition, his *Kaddish* Symphony, in which a narrator, the Speaker, holds a defiant, sometimes violent, debate with God. The symphony was not to be completed until August 1963, but Bernstein was thinking aloud about its theme almost two years earlier: "What is a father in the eyes of a child? The child feels: My father is first of all my Authority, with power to dispense approval or punishment. He is secondly my Protector; thirdly my

Provider; beyond that he is Healer, Comforter, Law-giver, because he caused me to exist. . . . And as the child grows up he retains all his life, in some deep, deep part of him, the stamp of that father-image whenever he thinks of God, of good and evil, of retribution.

"For example, take the idea of defiance. Every son, at one point or other, defies his father, fights him, departs from him, only to return to him—if he is lucky—closer and more secure than before. Again we see clearly the parallel with God: Moses protesting to God, arguing, fighting to change God's mind. So the child defies the father and something of that defiance also remains throughout his life."

It was powerful stuff for a birthday party, and Bernstein had sufficient sense of occasion to lighten the mood for his conclusion. He acknowledged that since becoming a father himself, nine years previously, he had a better understanding of "the complex phenomenon that is Samuel J. Bernstein, for he is a great and multifaceted man." Finally he took his audience back thirty years to what he remembered as his first public performance as a pianist, in the vestry of Temple Mishkan Tefila. "I was playing a composition of my own. It was a series of variations on a tune my father was singing in the shower and from hearing it sung so often I had gotten to be rather fond of it myself." In honor of his father's seventieth birthday he had composed a new variation in his own style. He called it "Meditation on a Prayerful Theme My Father Sang in the Shower Thirty Years Ago," and he later incorporated it into his *Kaddish* Symphony.

O N February 28, 1962, Nina Maria Felicia came into the world, weighing seven pounds three ounces. There was no problem now, as there had been when Jamie was born, with using the name "Nina." Bernstein dashed off to the hospital to inspect the newborn child, taking with him his beloved Nadia Boulanger, who was in New York at his invitation, the first woman ever to conduct the Philharmonic. He stood pressed up against the window of the delivery ward, furious at being kept outside. Boulanger never forgot the scene and when Nina's birthday came around would often write from France to relive the memory of Bernstein's frustration at not being allowed to take his daughter in his arms.

Two weeks later he was in a fit of depression. He left Felicia and the new baby to spend a week in the Virgin Islands with Lillian Hellman in another attempt to make a workable version of *Candide*. He island-hopped to Puerto Rico, where he fell in with Leon Danilian, a Ballet Russe dancer from New York who had been a good friend of Felicia's. Danilian's young companion, Charles Wellrich, recalls that Bernstein was deeply depressed about the fate of *Candide*. Danilian was equally depressed about his own retirement. They went to a gay bar called Michael's, got very drunk and ended the evening dancing on the steps of the cathedral in Old San Juan.

A shadow was passing over, but it was quickly thrust into the background

—as, over the years, were countless other depressions and brief encounters—by Bernstein's hectic schedule. His ambitious 1962 spring program included Bruckner's Ninth Symphony, Mahler's Seventh (which had not been heard in New York since 1948), the *St. Matthew Passion,* and in April the tragicomical episode of the Brahms D minor Piano Concerto with Glenn Gould, one of the few pianists he positively enjoyed accompanying because of the originality of his interpretations. Gould often gave unexpected prominence to accompaniment figures and sometimes disregarded composers' tempo indications, but his musical ideas were unpredictable and fascinating. Bernstein and Gould made recordings of keyboard concertos by Bach and Beethoven and they became personal friends, too, insofar as anybody could break through Gould's idiosyncrasies—he wrapped up in overcoat, cap and muffler on the warmest of summer days, crouched on a piano stool so low that his nose was hardly higher than the keyboard and hummed loudly and uncontrollably with the music, to the despair of the same Columbia recording engineers who had to deal with Leonard Bernstein's stamping feet.

Gould telephoned Bernstein from Toronto to warn him that his interpretation of the Brahms D minor would be unorthodox. He intended to play the work less forcefully than was customary, so that it would sound like celestial chamber music, and he felt that the concerto's first and second movements were so closely integrated they should share the same tempo, a very deliberate six beats in the bar. For Bernstein and the orchestra this basic pulse was embarrassingly slow. But Bernstein had too much respect for Gould's musicianship to withdraw and leave the accompaniment to an assistant—an action that would inevitably have caused a furor. He resolved instead to use their disagreement as the subject for his Thursday Preview. He scrapped the talk he had prepared on Carl Nielsen's Fifth Symphony and after obtaining Gould's agreement backstage, he announced to the audience that there had been a difference of opinion. Gould's unusual interpretation should be listened to, he said, in a spirit of adventure—"what Dimitri Mitropoulos used to call the *sportive* element" in music. Then Gould made his entrance. He never shook hands for fear of damaging his fingers, but the two friends touched fingertips in greeting before Gould sat down for the performance. "He played it," Bernstein remembered, "exactly the way he had rehearsed it, and wonderfully, too." With Gould's agreement Bernstein made the same speech at Friday afternoon's concert, when normally he said nothing. This time music critics were present. Harold Schonberg's astonishingly offensive review in the *Times* was couched in the form of a chatty letter from a Russian crony to the long-dead pianist and conductor Ossip Gabrilowitsch. It suggested that by making his disclaimer, Bernstein had publicly washed his hands of his soloist. "So then the Gould boy comes out, and you know what, Ossip? . . . He played the Brahms D minor concerto slower than the way we used to practice it. (And between you, me, and the corner lamppost, Ossip, maybe the reason he plays it so slow is maybe his technique is not so good.)"

It may have been a miscalculation for Bernstein, who leaped at any excuse to talk to his public, to make a big issue over a borderline case of musical taste. Gould himself was said to have deplored Bernstein's action privately, but in public he gave it his endorsement. A recording of the performance confirms that the tempos were serene and magisterial but sometimes perilously slow. Gould gave up performing in public soon after; the Brahms concerto made a disappointing end to a brilliant creative partnership with Bernstein. (It can be seen at its best in the "Ford Hour" of January 1960 entitled *The Creative Performer,* where Gould plays the Bach D minor keyboard concerto.)

Bernstein taped his last Ford program, *The Drama of "Carmen,"* in February 1962. "It's been grueling beyond words," he told David Diamond, "and I've learned my lesson about the television business: it eats up my life and has absolutely stopped me cold as a composer. . . . Yet the TV shows have been immensely satisfying and creatively rewarding." But around the time that his Ford television features were dropped Bernstein agreed to take the New York Philharmonic on tour to England in 1963 and to conduct a season of ten *Falstaff* performances at the "Met" in 1964. However loudly he asserted his heartache at not having enough time to compose, the suspicion grows that consciously or unconsciously he accepted alternative assignments in order to put off composing or to confine the activity to impossibly short periods, such as the three weeks he spent at the MacDowell Colony in June 1962, working on his third symphony.

He was also in search of "fun." In July and August he and Felicia took a five-week holiday in Europe. After a brief cruise on the Mediterranean they spent a fortnight in Monaco where Leonard conducted Prince Rainier's house orchestra in a pair of concerts. He didn't need the money but he enjoyed the change of air. He described the scene to his brother:

Dearest Beebles and Ellen

Of course I wouldn't want to live here, but it's been an incredible experience. *Le Monde Entier, très haut,* has furnished me with an unforgettable week. The concerts were smashes—but that's the least. Monte Carlo is like a great glorified prison, where everyone is stuck with everyone else, climbing away on someone's back to get —where? Princes and princesses drip from the trees, the villas are cloud cookoo-land. I'm the thing of the moment, lionized to the bitter end, and adoring it. Water skiing as you never saw it, sailing on a junk, lunch aboard yachts, squash three times with Rainier (I finally beat him the 3rd time, after my diarrhea had stopped). I've practically lived at the palace; I've taught Grace the chachacha, not knowing it myself, of course. Today was lunch (for five hours) at the incredible villa of Prince Trubetskoy—tomorrow Prince Chervatidze—tonight Prince Pierre de Monaco (Rainier's father, whom I adore); last night Elsa Maxwell's revolting party; the night before the Maharani of ******, with 100 pounds of emeralds, practically fucked me on the dance floor while I tried to nibble some of the emeralds, in vain.

All this, needless to say, Felicia loathes, and she is this moment in Paris seeing dresses. . . .

Following their two weeks in Monaco, Leonard finally delivered on a promise he had made to Felicia before they married: they spent ten days together in Spain. Mike Nichols traveled down from Paris with Felicia, and Stephen Sondheim joined them all a few days later in Madrid. On their last evening together they had dinner with Ava Gardner, who was living in Spain after the collapse of her marriage to Frank Sinatra. Then Felicia and Leonard drove all the way to Paris, making overnight stops in Biarritz and Chartres. It was the last touring vacation they spent together without the children.

A month later Bernstein conducted the Philharmonic at the opening night of Philharmonic Hall at Lincoln Center, September 23, 1962. It was hailed as "the most glamorous premiere in the city's history." Bernstein planned a program of works that were appropriate to a grand occasion and would test and show off the new hall's acoustical properties. He began with the "Gloria" movement from Beethoven's *Missa Solemnis,* which he said expressed "the joy and excitement and religious fervor of the undertaking of a great new enterprise." That was followed by *Connotations,* a twelve-tone commissioned work by Aaron Copland. The concert's second half featured Ralph Vaughan Williams's *Serenade to Music,* with twelve soloists from the Metropolitan Opera, and the first movement of Mahler's Eighth Symphony, "Veni Creator Spiritus," written for eight soloists, a double chorus, a boys' chorus, an organ and extra trumpeters calling across the deep at the climax.

The program was arguably too rarefied for a festive occasion attended by an audience of middlebrow dignitaries, but Harold Schonberg's advance reaction was woefully wide of the mark. He dismissed it as a mere extravaganza, "a big patchwork that has neither the virtue of consistency nor taste, a gaudy affair that rings as hollow as a broken drum." John Chapman of the *Daily News* was much more favorably impressed on the night. "It was a beautiful, exciting, memorable evening . . . When Leonard Bernstein gave the downbeat . . . a profound emotion must have seized the most distinguished audience this city has seen in decades."

The CBS telecast was the top-rated show from nine to eleven that evening. Don Hewitt, who was in charge of the intermission feature, remembers that the great attraction was the chance to see the First Lady "live." When the intermission began, the urbane host, Alistair Cooke, told viewers that Mrs. Kennedy was waiting in the greenroom with the maestro's wife to meet the conductor. According to the *New York Post,* "the exuberant conductor, clutching a cloak around his wet soup and fish, kissed his wife's cheek before he kissed Mrs. Kennedy." Another reporter noted that he first said, "May I?" to the First Lady but did not wait for an answer before launching into his embrace. The full-blooded nature of the kiss shocked the more straitlaced of the public, although it would have come as no surprise to anybody who has been the recipient of a

Bernstein embrace after a performance. "I'm all sweated up," one report had him saying. Another quoted Mrs. Kennedy as telling Maestro Bernstein: "You look ten pounds younger—er, lighter." To which Bernstein replied *"Connotations* takes a lot out of you. . . . Mr. Copland's work is strenuous as well as magnificent." (The *New York Post*'s Harriett Johnson described it as "twenty minutes of dissonance.") Bernstein then introduced Aaron Copland to the First Lady, who was at a loss for words to describe her reaction to *Connotations,* but taking her cue from Bernstein she pronounced the new hall magnificent. "Tell me about the acoustics," asked Bernstein gamely. "I never saw anything like it," replied Mrs. Kennedy enigmatically. Their comments were noted by reporters who were permitted to eavesdrop in the room, but the television audience was less fortunate. Bernstein's remarks came over loud and clear but Mrs. Kennedy spoke so quietly that the microphone failed to pick up her voice. Directing the telecast, Don Hewitt promised in vain a case of champagne to the audio man who could make Mrs. Kennedy audible. He found himself praised next morning by the press for his good taste in allowing the First Lady her privacy.

Mrs. Kennedy left New York after the intermission to return by helicopter to Hyannis Port, where fog was closing in. She missed an uplifting second half, tumultuous applause and the sight of the audience members drinking celebratory champagne before they went home. Critics might carp but New Yorkers were proudly aware that they had acquired a wonderful air-conditioned temple of the arts, at whose dedication ceremony Leonard Bernstein had been the celebrant. His apotheosis as America's leading musician was complete. Five years, almost to the day, after the opening of *West Side Story,* Bernstein had scored an equal triumph in the alternative career he had chosen.

# 31.

# A KADDISH FOR A PRESIDENT

*1963.*

*All our lives are spent in the attempt to resolve
conflicts . . . it is only after death that it can finally
be perceived whether we ever succeeded.*

—LEONARD BERNSTEIN in the
*New York Times,* October 24, 1965

THOUGH Bernstein began conducting abroad again in 1962, New York remained the center of the Bernsteins' world. They went frequently to the theater, much more than to musical events. Their friend Michael "Mendy" Wager was an opera buff—the model for the opera-lover in Terrence McNally's play *The Lisbon Traviata*—and occasionally Bernstein went to the Metropolitan with him, usually when other personal friends, like Maria Callas, were singing. He took his daughter Jamie to see *Swan Lake,* but he was not interested in classical ballet unless Margot Fonteyn and Rudolf Nureyev (both friends) were dancing. He felt closer to contemporary dance. He admired Martha Graham and loved American Ballet Theatre, mostly because of his close personal ties with the choreographer Jerome Robbins and the designer Oliver Smith. He rarely visited art galleries, but through Lukas and Cornelia Foss he got to know the iconoclastic "pop" artist Larry Rivers, enjoying his quick wit and high spirits. (Unfortunately, Rivers's various portraits of Bernstein are not very successful.) Bernstein did not appreciate abstract art. For a time he mocked it openly, hanging a painting done by a chimpanzee over his living room fireplace and inviting comments from his friends on his expensive acquisition.

Although Leonard and Felicia were prominent in New York's high culture world, the inner circle of friends with whom they dined regularly remained small. Many were professional theater collaborators such as Adolph Green and his third wife, Phyllis Newman, Betty Comden and her husband, Steve Kyle, Stephen Sondheim, Lillian Hellman, Marc Blitzstein and Franco Zeffirelli—until Felicia stopped inviting him because he always arrived an hour and a half late. Other close friends had been drawn into the Bernstein orbit by similarities of style and outlook, among them Lauren Bacall, who had first dazzled Bernstein in Hollywood in the 1950s. "If that guy [Bernstein] is coming into town, I'm going on my boat," her late husband, Humphrey Bogart, used to tell her. Mike Mindlin, the feature film publicist, had admired Felicia since 1947 and attended the Bernstein wedding. He was a good storyteller with a huge circle of friends. "Din-dins with Mindlins," reads one entry in the date book. Shirley Bernstein lived in London for several years in the early 1960s, but when in New York she was often a guest, as were Louis d'Almeida, Bernstein's regular squash partner, Richard and Evelyn Avedon and Patrick and Cynthia O'Neal. Burton and Ellen Bernstein were also part of the circle. And once or twice a year Sam and Jennie came down from Boston to attend an important concert or to share Thanksgiving turkey.

Musicians made up a different, occasionally overlapping, New York circle. Bernstein's oldest friendship, dating back to Curtis Institute days, was with Lukas Foss, who had been married to the painter Cornelia Brendel since 1951. David Oppenheim was another old friend. He had left the record business in 1959 to work (often with Bernstein) as a television producer. His second marriage was with Ellen Adler. Other regular guests (and reciprocating hosts) were Isaac Stern and his second wife, Vera, Schuyler and Betty Chapin (Chapin was with Columbia Records until 1964 and then moved to Lincoln Center), Willie Weisel from the New York Philharmonic, and his wife, Carmine, the piano duo Arthur Gold and Robert Fizdale, and the critic and cultural reporter John Gruen, whose wife, Jane Wilson, later taught Felicia painting. Friends from an older generation included the William Schumans, Goddard Lieberson and his wife, Brigitta (Vera Zorina on stage), and Jennie Tourel, whose seder the family attended almost every year at Passover.

Dinners at the Bernsteins were occasionally grand and formal affairs—Schuyler Chapin remembers one at which the elegant mood was shattered when not once but twice a temporary dining table collapsed, spilling first the Chilean stew—*pasto de choclo,* one of Felicia's specialities—and then the roast beef into the lap of a former lover of Lillian Hellman, the director Herman Shumlin. Chapin sent Felicia flowers next morning inscribed to "Herman Shumlin Hostess of the Year." Mostly the evenings were informal and characterized by tasty Chilean food followed by long and desperately competitive games, which Bernstein imposed on his friends whether he was host or guest. Prince Rainier wrote to him in October 1962. "It was such fun this summer—even if you do want to play those terrible little lap-slapping vocabulary games."

Squash was Bernstein's chief form of city recreation in the sixties. He was delighted when he was made an honorary Doctor of Music by Yale University —it meant he could finally use the Yale Club squash courts in New York, which he greatly preferred to those of his own Harvard Club. Bernstein's figure remained trim in the mid-sixties, but he was plagued by insomnia and on days when he was not rehearsing he would often stay in bed all morning: frequently his first appointment was with his psychiatrist. He consulted nearly every day with Dr. Willard Gaylin, the author of several "touch and feel" counseling books. Dr. Gaylin believes that for a time Bernstein probably talked to him more than anybody else in the world except Felicia. Had Bernstein devoted as much time to composition as he did to analysis, he might well have produced a fourth symphony.

Bernstein worked equally hard to maintain his physical well-being. He had frequent appointments with his tailor, Otto Perl—friends called the fittings "dress rehearsals" because the peacock element in Bernstein's nature enjoyed showing off his new, often garish clothes—and with a small army of doctors, dentists, chiropractors, masseurs and hair preservers. For many years he employed a woman named Rita Harbinger to look after his scalp. Nicknamed the Popper, her task was to yank Bernstein's hair until the scalp separated from the skull sufficiently for blood to irrigate the hair roots. You could hear the scalp pop, Jamie remembers. It was a painful but apparently efficacious treatment; unlike his father and his brother, Bernstein never lost his hair. But at one time or another he was a victim—or thought himself to be—of most of the other ailments to which flesh is heir. He was still an incessant smoker and his capacious lungs had long been troubled by emphysema, but apart from a bout of hepatitis—his own diagnosis—in the late autumn of 1961, he was never ill for longer than a few days. Often he would ask an assistant to take a rehearsal, or even—in London in 1972—the final run-through of a major concert, but he always came through on the night to deliver a resounding performance.

THE move to Lincoln Center was not easy for the New York Philharmonic. In 1962, Carnegie Hall was seventy years old and without air-conditioning, but the auditorium was beautifully proportioned and graceful to the eye. Despite elaborate consultations and comparative studies the new Philharmonic Hall's acoustics were unsatisfactory and fiercely criticized. Bernstein had the difficult task of privately calling for urgent remedial action but publicly expressing long-term confidence in the Philharmonic's new home. In his first "Young People's Concert" there he recited the "Tango" from William Walton's *Façade,* accompanied Shirley Verrett in a Schubert song and conducted the *1812 Overture,* before pronouncing the new hall marvelous.

But by the end of 1962, having conducted his five hundredth concert with the New York Philharmonic, he was expressing regrets at having renewed his contract and neglected his composition. "O Lenny, what is all this regret business?" asked Lukas Foss. "You did not do wrong in staying with the Philharmonic. How could you abandon it? It's yours now—like a child you may like or not like it, [but] you cannot cast it off because of irrational grumblings. Your programs are not getting worse. I'd like to go to most all of them. I think the [Philharmonic] Hall business took too much out of you. It cast a shadow. Criticism in N.Y. distorts things out of all proportions: I came twice. The orchestra sounded fine, made music. You looked so sad. Maybe you need what I need—to finish that new piece."

The *Kaddish* Symphony stayed unfinished. In January 1963 Bernstein introduced a sixteen-year-old pianist named André Watts to the television public in a "Young People's Concert" featuring young soloists. He gave Watts a complete concerto to perform and in a departure from the program's regular format he conducted the Philharmonic himself, instead of entrusting the task to one of his three assistants. He was so impressed with the way Watts acquitted himself that two weeks later he turned to him to substitute at the Philharmonic for the ailing Glenn Gould. Watts's acclaimed performance of Liszt's First Piano Concerto was immediately recorded by Columbia. The episode must have reminded Bernstein of how a dramatic substitution had launched his own career twenty years earlier. Later Watts was to sum up Bernstein's response as being characteristically extravagant: "Here, kid, you wanna career? I'll give it to you—on a plate."

In April 1963 Bernstein made a rare appearance as a chamber music performer, joining the Juilliard Quartet for two performances of Schumann's piano quintet at the Library of Congress and taking part in a tribute to Francis Poulenc, who had died suddenly in January. He accompanied Benny Goodman in the world premiere of Poulenc's clarinet sonata. At Easter the Philharmonic gave the posthumous premiere of Poulenc's *Sept Répons des Ténèbres,* commissioned for the first season of Lincoln Center. The work, for chorus and orchestra, offended the substantial Jewish section of the audience because of the passage in the text asserting that Christ was murdered by the Jews. Observing Passover, Bernstein had not been the conductor, but as the Philharmonic's music director he admitted that had he been consulted he would not have printed the English translation in the program notes. Freedom of expression, for which he had argued with such passion in the Soviet Union, did not seem so sacrosanct when the feelings of the Philharmonic's Jewish subscribers were involved. Bernstein admitted that the previous year he had cut the short sections of Bach's *St. Matthew Passion* based on the same Gospel text. The whole affair must have lodged in the back of his mind as he prepared his *Kaddish* Symphony, in which the spoken narration contains outbursts of fury against the Almighty that perhaps are better heard than read. The text of *Kaddish* was not printed in the program books when the work came to be performed in America.

Late in April Felicia's mother fell mortally ill. Bernstein had the closing five weeks of the Philharmonic season to contend with, so Felicia flew alone to Santiago, arriving in time for a bedside meeting while her mother was still conscious. "She had put on some makeup for me," Felicia reported to her husband, "but still I was shocked and heart-broken to see her so thin and frail —we talked for fifteen minutes, about the children, you, her garden—that was it. She never spoke again." In New York Bernstein attended the funeral of the Philharmonic's veteran second trumpeter, Nat Prager. Bernstein's funeral tribute was appreciated by Prager's widow. "Whenever Nat mentioned your name," she wrote, "it was always 'Lenny,' not out of disrespect, but because he was so proud you were able to come up from the ranks. Thank you . . . for helping me in my agony."

In June the family moved into "Springate," their new Connecticut home, a colonial revival two-story country house in Fairfield. There were a pool and a tennis court, lovely lawns and grand old trees; the grooms' quarters, next to the old stables, served as Bernstein's study until they were replaced by a prefabricated wooden house. Bernstein was gripped that summer by a passion to finish *Kaddish*. It had been commissioned by the Koussevitzky Foundation way back in 1955, during Charles Munch's music directorship of the Boston Symphony Orchestra, and Munch wanted to include it in his first return visit as a guest conductor at the end of January 1964. But as Bernstein clarified its shape and content—it was to be a threefold setting of the Jewish prayer for the dead, interwoven with narration—he decided it should receive its premiere in Israel. Boston generously waived its rights, and the Israel Philharmonic set aside concert dates in December. Now the challenge was to have the symphony ready for the copyists before the New York Philharmonic began a preseason American tour in California at the end of August.

Work on the *Kaddish* Symphony was the priority, but even in the summer there were distractions galore—recording sessions, conferences about acoustics, public appearances in support of other conductors. A different personality might have denied himself all this: Bernstein, repeating a pattern of procrastination followed by feverish activity that had characterized the composition of both the *Jeremiah* Symphony and *The Age of Anxiety,* squeezed everything in. "On August 1st," he wrote Shirley, "I made the great decision to go forward with *Kaddish,* to try to finish it, score it, rehearse, prepare, revise, translate into Hebrew. . . . It's a monstrous task: I've been copying it out legibly for the copyists, night and day and now it's ready, except for a rather copious finale that remains to be written. . . . I'm terribly excited about the new piece, even about the Speaker's text, which I finally decided has to be done by me. Collaboration with a poet is impossible on so personal a work, so I've found after a distressful year of trying with [Robert] Lowell and [Frederick] Seidel; so I'm elected, poet or no poet. But the reactions of various people to whom I've read it have been so moving (and moved) that I was encouraged to keep at it. I think you'll be surprised by its power."

It could be argued that working feverishly against the clock was not the best way to compose a symphony. However, as with *The Age of Anxiety,* Bernstein could claim that the new work had been part of his composing life—when he allowed it to peep above the surface of his consciousness—for nearly three years. With the deadline to spur him on, he completed *Kaddish* on August 19, just a week before the start of the Philharmonic tour. His daughter Jamie remembers that he came walking across the garden from his studio at Fairfield, waving the manuscript and shouting, "I've finished it, I've finished it." Felicia was so happy she jumped into the swimming pool with all her clothes on.

September and October were taken up with New York Philharmonic. After a flying visit with his son Alexander to San Juan, Bernstein settled down at the end of October to the substantial task of orchestrating close to forty minutes of music. Much of it, Jack Gottlieb remembers, was done on the kitchen table at Fairfield. On Friday, November 22, Bernstein went to New York to prepare for the second "Young People's Concert" of the season. The lunchtime conference at Philharmonic Hall was cut short when Joe Zizza, the orchestra's assistant librarian, brought the news that President Kennedy had been assassinated. Driving back to the Park Avenue apartment, Jack Gottlieb remembers that Bernstein had no doubt now to whom his new symphony should be dedicated. The father of the nation was dead; to him, Bernstein would dedicate *Kaddish*.

That Sunday at 8 P.M. Bernstein and the orchestra gave a memorial performance for President Kennedy of Mahler's Second Symphony on CBS television. Never has the *Resurrection* Symphony, a work composed by a Jew who converted to Catholicism, had a larger audience or one more greatly in need of spiritual sustenance. Bernstein's face as he conducted was for once grimly controlled. His choice of a Mahler symphony was unexpected. Bernstein justified it when he spoke in tribute to Kennedy the following night to an audience of eleven thousand at Madison Square Garden, where a United Jewish Appeal Gala benefit had been transformed into a wake:

> Why the "Resurrection" Symphony, with its visionary concept of hope and triumph over worldly pain, instead of a Requiem, or the customary Funeral March from the "Eroica"? Why indeed? We played the Mahler symphony not only in terms of resurrection for the soul of one we love, but also for the resurrection of hope in all of us who mourn him. In spite of our shock, our shame, and our despair at the diminution of man that follows from this death, we must somehow gather strength for the increase of man, strength to go on striving for those goals he cherished. In mourning him, we must be worthy of him.
>
> I know of no musician in this country who did not love John F. Kennedy. American artists have for three years looked to the White House with unaccustomed confidence and warmth. We loved him for the honor in which he held art, in which he held every creative impulse of the human mind, whether it was expressed in words, or notes, or paints, or mathematical symbols. This reverence for the life of the mind was apparent even in his last speech, which he was to have made a few hours after his death. He was to have said: "America's leadership must be guided by

learning and reason." Learning and reason: precisely the two elements that were necessarily missing from the mind of anyone who could have fired that impossible bullet. Learning and reason: the two basic precepts of all Judaistic tradition, the twin sources from which every Jewish mind from Abraham and Moses to Freud and Einstein has drawn its living power. Learning and Reason: the motto we here tonight must continue to uphold with redoubled tenacity, and must continue, at any price, to make the basis of all our actions.

It is obvious that the grievous nature of our loss is immensely aggravated by the element of violence involved in it. And where does this violence spring from? From ignorance and hatred—the exact antonyms of Learning and Reason. Learning and Reason: those two words of John Kennedy's were not uttered in time to save his own life; but every man can pick them up where they fell, and make them part of himself, the seed of that rational intelligence without which our world can no longer survive. This must become the mission of every artist, of every Jew, and of every man of goodwill: to insist, unflaggingly, at the risk of becoming a repetitive bore, but to insist on the achievement of a world in which the mind will have triumphed over violence. . . .

The assassination gave a hideous new relevance to Bernstein's *Kaddish* Symphony. In the text, Bernstein's Speaker challenges the Almighty in a moment of high anger: "You let this happen, Lord of Hosts! You with your manna, your pillar of fire! You ask for faith. Where is your own?" Even before the assassination, Bernstein had worried about Israeli reaction to the boldness of words like these. On September 23 he wrote to Abe Cohen, manager of the Israel Philharmonic, offering to withdraw the premiere for fear "that this text may excite some controversy or problem with the Israeli public." Cohen sent the script to an authority on Hebrew literature and philosophy. "It was his unqualified opinion," Cohen reported, "that this recitation can be made without hesitation whatsoever, as there were many precedents of this type of poem in Jewish and Hebrew literature."

The Speaker's text was translated into Hebrew, to be delivered at the premiere by Hannah Rovina, Israel's most famous classical actress. At the first rehearsal Bernstein fell to his knees when Rovina began the narration. It was, he exclaimed, exactly the sound he had imagined. Felicia arrived in time for the final rehearsals; she was to be the narrator at the American premiere two months later. It had been the beauty of her performance in Honegger's Joan of Arc back in 1958 ("grave and inspiring and unforgettable," he had called it) that had prompted Bernstein to compose a work in the same narrative genre.

Hannah Rovina had trouble reading the speaker's text in rhythm but eventually Bernstein coached and coaxed her through it. Jennie Tourel sang the symphony's solo setting of the *Kaddish* prayer. The part is identified in the score as being written for soprano, but Tourel, a mezzo-soprano, pleaded to be allowed to do the premiere. After running through the movement with her at Fairfield, Bernstein felt committed to her dark-hued mezzo timbre. "Whenever she stood to sing," he remembered later, "that stage was the Holy of Holies."

The choral writing is advanced for its time. The singers are required to stamp loudly with their feet in unison at one point and at another to clap in a jazzy 3:2:3 rhythm. A couple of bars must be shouted at the top of their voices like a football crowd and there is a choral cadenza during which the unaccompanied chorus divides into eight groups. Getting the professionals and amateurs to understand their music was an exhausting business and the premiere had to be postponed twenty-four hours. "FANTASTIC SUCCESS WITH PUBLIC AND PRESS DESPITE SHAKY FIRST PERFORMANCE," Bernstein cabled Helen Coates. "SPREAD THE WORD." Whatever his secret hopes to the contrary, there were no demonstrations. The only sect that might have taken offense apparently regarded all concert halls as being little better than brothels and always gave them a wide berth.

Of all Bernstein's major works, the *Kaddish* Symphony has been the least performed and the most misunderstood. Charles Munch led four performances in Boston at the end of January 1964: Bernstein conducted five performances in New York in April and his highly charged Columbia recording was released soon after. Several other conductors performed the work in the United States in 1964, with either Felicia Montealegre or Patricia Neway as narrator, but it was rarely performed thereafter.

It is a common mistake, encouraged by the title, to think that *Kaddish* is in some way exclusive in its appeal because of its Aramaic and Hebrew texts. But they are no more difficult to grasp than the Latin verses uncomprehendingly sung by choruses around the world in countless Te Deums, Stabat Maters and Requiems. Indeed, the fact that most of *Kaddish*'s text is in Aramaic, the language actually spoken by Jesus Christ to his followers, should be seen as adding poignancy to the work for Christian performers and audiences. The *Kaddish* is a mourning prayer, spoken by Jews at the graveside. It is also spoken in temples as part of a service and in homes during a period of mourning. Paradoxically its text is a hymn of praise that never mentions death. In the course of the symphony Bernstein sets the hymn three times. The first version is troubled; the second (for solo soprano and women's voices only) is peaceful, a cradle song; the third is exultant. The three movements of the symphony are performed without a break, combining to make a single forty-minute statement that is authentically symphonic in its systematic development of the musical material. The symphony also makes a spiritual journey in words and music from darkness to light, from wild dissonance without a key center to a calm and peaceful F major.

Bernstein's starting point, as already mentioned, was the desire to compose a dramatic work in which his wife could play a leading role as the narrator—in October 1963 she had appeared in Debussy's *Le Martyre de Saint Sébastien* in

New York. That the *Kaddish* Symphony would also jolt concert-going audiences out of their seats by the brutality of its assault on received ideas of religion and man's relationship with God was characteristic of Bernstein's flair for the grand gesture. The exciting theatricality of *Kaddish* undoubtedly owes something to the Honegger St. Joan, and to Marc Blitzstein's *The Airborne* Symphony. But primarily it is a reflection of Bernstein's own sense of the dramatic. In 1961, when he began work on *Kaddish,* a nuclear confrontation seemed ever more likely; his intention was to express in a spectacular way the loss of faith experienced by people of all religions, not just the Jews, in a century dominated by senseless killing and destruction. And what could be more dramatic than a frontal attack on God?

The Hebrew tradition of disputing with God goes back to Old Testament heroes like Moses, Job and Jacob. It was renewed in eighteenth-century Russia by rabbis of the Hasidic sect to which Bernstein's own family originally belonged. "I intended no sacrilege," Bernstein told a reporter in Israel. "The argument with God has its origin in love; this is the great conflict in man's soul." On the psychological level *Kaddish* is also concerned with the struggle between father and son, discussed openly by Bernstein at his father's seventieth birthday. Musically the symphony embodies yet another struggle, between atonality and tonality. Its second movement contains a lullaby as sweetly languorous as Ravel's *Shéhérazade.*

The symphony was extravagantly praised in Tel Aviv in December (Max Brod's was the only dissenting voice), and so great was public interest that two extra performances were added to the nine subscription dates in Israel. But at the American premiere in Boston the *Globe*'s newly appointed critic, Michael Steinberg, assaulted its "unashamed vulgarity" and charged that the music was "strongly derivative." He described the text as "a lava-flow of clichés wherein a few cozy intimacies (Speaker to God: 'We'll make it a sort of holiday') are contrasted against the tinny rhetoric of Norman Corwin's radio plays from the 1940s." Bernstein removed some of his own excesses when he revised the piece in 1977, but he left in other lines of embarrassing condescension.

> *Look up: What do You see?*
> *A rainbow which I have created for You!*
> *My promise, my Covenant!*
> *Look at it Father: Believe! Believe!*
> *Look at my rainbow and say after me:*
> *MAGNIFIED . . . AND SANCTIFIED . . .*
> *BE THE GREAT NAME OF MAN!*

One of the finest musical moments in the symphony follows this passage: the boys' choir enters with the opening line of the *Kaddish* prayer sung to a simple melody in the radiant key of G flat major. Bernstein's passionate belief in the perfectibility of man shines through his sometimes awkward text.

Harold Rogers, the music critic of the *Christian Science Monitor,* praised *Kaddish*'s emotional thrust and dramatic power. "Never has the word 'Amen' been so acridly set to notes," he wrote. "At such times the music is apt to become completely atonal, with percussive punctuation, asymmetrical rhythm, poly-rhythmic augmentations and diminutions—name it and he's done it. At other times—when the prayer becomes more repentant—the music becomes tonal, severe, aspiring, lyrical." *The Nation*'s critic commented favorably on Bernstein's eclecticism, comparing him to Norman Mailer in his embrace of every sound and style. And under the headline "THE PRODIGAL SON CAME HOME YESTERDAY," the *Boston Herald* concluded that "Leonard Bernstein had for so long occupied the role of flawed genius that his triumph must be regarded as the release of a talent freed from the lashings of its own facility."

I N Boston Leonard and Felicia Bernstein prepared for the *Kaddish* premiere while nursing a new and shocking cause for private mourning: the death in humiliating circumstances of their dear friend Marc Blitzstein. Blitzstein, then fifty-eight, had been wintering in Martinique. Late one evening, during a session of heavy drinking, he had picked up three Portuguese sailors in a bar, one of whom slipped into a nearby alleyway with Blitzstein in response to his sexual advances. The other two followed and all three robbed him of the four hundred dollars he had carelessly displayed in his wallet. They beat him up and stripped him of all his clothes except his shirt and socks. The police found him moaning and crying, and took him to a hospital in the middle of the night. He appeared to be only superficially hurt, but he was bleeding to death from internal contusions and he died the next evening, January 22, 1964. "Marc is dead and I've lost an arm," Bernstein wrote to his sister in London. "It's open season for Kaddish. Do you realize we have loved Marc for 25 years?"

Bernstein was in his Philharmonic Hall dressing room preparing for a concert when he learned of Blitzstein's death. He immediately dedicated the performance of Beethoven's *Eroica* he was about to conduct to Blitzstein's memory. "The work was performed as if the conductor were re-writing Beethoven as he went along in order to express his grief," wrote Eric Salzman in the *Herald Tribune.* "It was an incredible, agonized, unbearable reading, which with its bursts of nervous energy and wild relentless drive, left clarity, accuracy and indeed everything but anguished, frenetic intensity far, far behind."

Bernstein was named musical executor in Blitzstein's will. In the eulogy he delivered at the memorial concert organized by David Oppenheim, he impetuously promised to complete Blitzstein's unfinished opera based on Bernard Malamud's story "Idiots First." But he had trouble enough completing his own works satisfactorily and he never tackled the Blitzstein. Moreover he offended some of Blitzstein's admirers by referring in a tribute to his friend's "long chain of beautiful work failures." The truth is sometimes better left unspoken.

After the enormous elation he had experienced in Israel, the first six weeks of 1964 were tough going for Bernstein. In the rough and tumble of New York's musical life he was the object of more fierce attacks from Harold Schonberg in the *Times* and from Alan Rich, the newly appointed *Herald Tribune* critic, for what they took to be a poorly planned Philharmonic series examining the latest in avant-garde experiments. Bernstein had announced an exploration, in six concerts, of new developments in orchestral writing, but because of the conservative tastes of the Philharmonic subscribers he sandwiched the unfamiliar works between standard classics. Schonberg deplored the way that Xenakis and Ligeti were "snugly fitted" between Beethoven and Saint-Saëns. Bernstein reportedly gave the new music a twenty-minute hard-sell introduction which combined "good humor and deep philosophy; metaphysics and folksy man-to-man talk." Schonberg and Rich had no patience with Bernstein's bedside manner. "This is bad," thundered Schonberg; "bad psychology, bad music-making, bad show business, bad everything. If Mr. Bernstein wants to conduct modern music, and he should, why can't we have it without the fancy trimmings and hoopla?" "He tried everything short of a Flit gun in his attempt to kill off the *avant-garde,*" cried Rich, who deplored not only the condescending introduction—"Mr. Bernstein practically passed out the ripe tomatoes"—but the performance as well, "tentative, scratchy and superficial."

Each week brought a new press scandal. Pierre Boulez was sick in Paris and had to cancel a premiere. Stefan Wolpe's symphony proved so difficult that there was time to rehearse and perform only two of its three movements. Bernstein was accused of approaching the season carelessly and scheduling the music from ignorance. To make things worse, he left his assistants in charge for a week and went up to Boston to supervise the premiere of *Kaddish*. In the final avant-garde program, entitled "Music of Chance," America's leading experimenter, John Cage, was roundly booed by hundreds of patrons in some of the noisiest scenes ever witnessed at a Philharmonic concert. Perhaps because of the furor, Bernstein emerged with a modicum of credit. Alan Rich conceded that for all its ups and downs, the avant-garde season "has enlivened the musical scene no end."

BERNSTEIN'S happy collaboration with Franco Zeffirelli on Verdi's *Falstaff* at the Metropolitan Opera that spring was a welcome relief. He came to the opera knowing every note of the score and every word by heart. Working with singers on such a joyful masterpiece was exactly the tonic he needed. Regina Resnik, singing Mistress Quickly, emerged from her first ensemble session wreathed in smiles. It had been like the old days of rehearsing with Fritz Reiner and Bruno Walter, she exclaimed. Bernstein reveled in the long rehearsal hours. With singers there was time to polish musical nuances in a way rarely possible at regular orchestral rehearsals.

He went to all Zeffirelli's stage rehearsals and offered his own ideas for the staging, just as he had done in Milan in 1955 with Zeffirelli's master, Luchino Visconti. Far from resenting Bernstein's intrusions, Zeffirelli welcomed them. "Lenny and I speak the same language," he wrote in his autobiography. "In some ways we are both isolated in a world of gloom, boredom and arrogance, too often surrounded by people who don't really know what theater or even life is about. Doing *Falstaff* with him was one of the most riveting, revealing, charming experiences of my life. We had fun like children, real genuine fun, exactly the way old Verdi wanted it, the way Shakespeare imagined it."

Bernstein's own feelings were similar: the excitement he generated in the theater was almost palpable. Jean Uppman of the Metropolitan Opera Guild remembers slipping into the orchestral rehearsals at every lunch hour, enchanted with the quality of music-making that Bernstein inspired. He was never satisfied, she recalled, with the moment near the beginning of Act III, Scene I, when Falstaff, soaked to his skin, climbs out of the River Thames. He made the orchestra repeat over and over again the series of trills that grow louder and louder as the hot wine supplied by the host of the Garter Inn seeps into every damp cranny of Falstaff's immense body. He knew the sound he wanted and he went into overtime to get it.

"*Falstaff* is just Leonard Bernstein's cup of champagne," wrote John Chapman in the *Daily News,* reviewing the premiere of March 12. Harold Schonberg hailed "a magnificent production," and said Bernstein's timing and pacing were "surprisingly adept." Opera historians agree that it was one of the finest productions ever mounted at the old Metropolitan Opera House.

BERNSTEIN chose what would have been his seventh season with the Philharmonic, 1964–65, to be his sabbatical year. The orchestra's management swallowed hard and appointed four solid, dependable conductors to share the leadership of the orchestra during his absence: Josef Krips, Lorin Maazel, Thomas Schippers and William Steinberg. The up-and-coming Seiji Ozawa was named assistant conductor. Even without Bernstein, the season was a total sellout. Bernstein maintained a degree of contact with the Philharmonic by continuing to conduct the "Young People's Concerts" (for which CBS-TV paid him eleven thousand dollars for each of four shows).

THE *raison d'être* of the sabbatical year was to create time to compose. He was planning a new Broadway musical based on Thornton Wilder's *The Skin of Our Teeth,* with book and lyrics by Comden and Green; direction and choreography were to be by Jerome Robbins. But the year did not turn out the way he had hoped. When it was all over, Bernstein described his time "off" in the following poem:

*In glad compliance with your request,*
*O* New York Times, *that I testify*
*On my late sabbatical (dubious rest!)*
*And the fruits thereof, I now comply.*
*But why in verse? I do not know.*
*This is the way it wants to go,*
*Spontaneously. It may be rhymed,*
*Or not; and tetrametric, though*
*Here and there I may add a foot or so,*
*Indulge in quatrains, couplets, or*
*In absolutely blank pentameter—*
*Anything, only not in prose.*
*End of apology. Here goes.*

*Since June of Nineteen Sixty-four*
*I've been officially free of chore*
*And duty to the N.Y. Phil.—*
*Fifteen beautiful months to kill!*

*But not to waste: there was a plan,*
*For as long as my sabbatical ran,*
*To write a new theater piece.*
*(A theater composer needs release,*
*And* West Side Story *is eight years old!)*
*And so a few of us got hold*
*Of the rights of Wilder's play* The Skin of Our Teeth.
*This is a play I've often thought was made*
*For singing; and for dance. It celebrates*
*The wonder of life, of human survival, told*
*In pity and terror and mad hilarity.*
*Six months we labored, June to bleak December.*
*And bleak was our reward, when Christmas came,*
*To find ourselves uneasy with our work.*
*We gave it up, and went our several ways,*
*Still loving friends; but there was the pain*
*Of seeing six months of work go down the drain.*

*The picture brightens, come New Year;*
*The next nine months restore some cheer*
*That vanished when our project died.*
*I firmly brushed regrets aside,*
*And started a whole new sabbatical,*
*Forgetting all projects dramatical,*
*And living, for once, as a simple man,*
*Partaking of life, as you never can*

*With a full Philharmonic season to run.*
*Now, here was a project that* could *be done:*
*Stay home, go out; see friends, see none;*
*Take walks with the children, study for fun;*
*Practice the piano, attend the Bonnard*
*Exhibit; visit your neighborhood bar;*
*See more of the people in other arts,*
*Meet your nonmusical counterparts;*
*Read the new poets; play anagrams, chess;*
*Complete the crosswords in the British press;*
*Restudy Opus 132;*
*Do, in short, what you want to do.*


*All these I did, but inevitably*
*One finds that sabbaticals aren't* that *free;*
*There are certain commitments that cannot be*
*Unmet or interrupted—e.g.,*
*The Young People's Concerts, recording sessions,*
*And similar nonsabbatic digressions.*
*These took time, and a certain amount*
*of adjusting,*
     *But kept my baton from rusting.*
*Meanwhile, there lurked at the back of my mind*
*The irrational urge (too late!) to find*
*Another theatrical project, which meant*
*That hours and days were now to be spent*
*In reading plays and considering oceans*
*Of wild ideas and desperate notions.*
*None took fire, which is just as well,*
*For I then had the luxury, truth to tell,*
*Of time to think as a pure musician*
*And ponder the art of composition.*


*For hours on end I brooded and mused*
*On* materiae musicae, *used and abused;*
*On aspects of unconventionality,*
*Over the death in our time of tonality,*
*Over the fads of Dada and Chance,*
*The serial strictures, the dearth of romance,*
*"Perspectives in Music," the new terminology,*
*Physiomathematomusicology;*
*Pieces called "Cycles" and "Sines" and "Parameters"—*
*Titles too beat for these homely tetrameters;*
*Pieces for nattering, clucking sopranos*
*With squadrons of vibraphones, fleets of pianos*

*Played with the forearms, the fists and the palms*
*—And then I came up with the* Chichester Psalms.
*These psalms are a simple and modest affair,*
*Tonal and tuneful and somewhat square,*
*Certain to sicken a stout John Cager*
*With its tonics and triads in E-flat major.*
*But there it stands—the result of my pondering,*
*Two long months of avant-garde wandering—*
*My youngest child, old-fashioned and sweet.*
*And he stands on his own two tonal feet.*

*Well, that was my major sabbatical act—*
*At least, the most tangible; but in fact*
*There were other boons from my newfound leisure*
*Which brought me (and, I hope, others) pleasure.*
*In doing research for this résumé*
*I've looked through my datebook since New Year's Day*
*To see what I actually did, for fun—*
*Things I could otherwise not have done.*
*I cannot go into the bulk of it:*
*Let suffice one item per month. To wit:*
*Jan. Conducted Stravinsky's* Histoire du Soldat
*For a benefit. Staging and all. A ball.*
*Feb. Flew out to Aspen. Institute Seminar*
*With skiing on the side. Came back revivified.*
*Mar. Conducted new Robbins ballet* Les Noces.
*Stravinsky again. Now, there's a blessed pen.*
*Apr. Practiced and played and recorded Mozart*
G-minor, *with Juilliard Quartet. Not to forget.*
*May. To Denmark. The Sonning Prize. As thanks,*
*Played Nielsen's* Third. *A marvel, take my word.*
*Jun. To Puerto Rico. Conducted before*
*Casals, musician supreme. A lifelong dream.*
*Jul. To Chichester,* en famille, *to hear*
*My Psalms in the place for which they were written. Smitten.*
*Aug. To Tanglewood, scene of my happiest youth,*
*To conduct, on its quarter-centennial, Carmen, Act IV.*
*Tanglewood! Twenty-five years! So much to remember!*
*For instance . . .*
                    *. . . and suddenly here it is September.*
*Refreshed and rejuvenated, I*
*Regard the new season with eager eye.*
*Tanglewood's brought back a breath of my youth:*
*Stravinsky and Mozart, Beauty and Truth.*
*Denmark provided a glorious spring.*

*In Chichester I heard angels sing.*
*Skiing at Aspen has brought me health.*
*This whole sabbatical's been like a tonic.*
*Can't wait to get back to the Philharmonic!*

The collapse of the musical based on *The Skin of Our Teeth*—glossed over in Bernstein's poem—was a blow to all the collaborators. There had been frequent meetings all through the fall of 1964, business talks with the producer, a writing trip together to Martha's Vineyard for ten days—all the outward signs had been propitious. But something in the renewed collaboration did not click as it should have. Writing to David Diamond in January 1965, Bernstein called the cancellation "a dreadful experience. The wounds are still smarting. I am suddenly a composer without a project, with half that golden sabbatical down the drain. Never mind, I'll survive."

After a two-week escape to Chile *en famille* over Christmas and the New Year, Bernstein had a flurry of meetings with Stephen Sondheim, Arthur Laurents and Jerome Robbins—the *West Side Story* team. But nothing solid came of the five months of consultations that ensued.

In May, Bernstein flew to Denmark to accept the Sonning Prize, a Danish award worth over seven thousand dollars, whose previous recipients had included Winston Churchill, Albert Einstein, Bertrand Russell and Igor Stravinsky. While in Copenhagen, Bernstein added the Royal Danish Orchestra to his list of conquests, conducting a glowing performance of Nielsen's Symphony No. 3, the *Espansiva*. "The orchestra is splendid," he wrote to Helen Coates the day after his arrival. "First rehearsal a triumph. Lunch unforgettable." A film documentary (for Scandinavian television) about the performance, and the hard work and smorgasbords leading up to it, was one of the first substantial examples made in Europe of the new film genre featuring the conductor as "pop" hero—Leonard Bernstein was seen sweating and singing his way to an exalted musical finale, described by the Danish newspaper *Politiken* as "wild in its force, glowing in its love, irresistible in its gentleness." The King of Denmark, himself a conductor, was there to greet Bernstein and Felicia. It was all very different from the staid uniformity of subscription concerts at Philharmonic Hall, accompanied by the sniping of the *Times* and the *Herald Tribune*.

Bernstein's last sabbatical excursion was to Chichester in England, to hear his latest composition, the *Chichester Psalms,* sung by the combined cathedral choruses of Winchester, Salisbury and Chichester. Dr. Walter Hussey, the dean of Chichester Cathedral, had been encouraged by Bernstein's physician friend Cyril "Chuck" Solomon to offer him the commission.

Once Bernstein had accepted, Dr. Hussey wrote to give details of the restricted musical forces that would be at Bernstein's disposal: "The string orchestra will probably be the Philomusica of London, a first rate group. In addition there could be a piano, chamber organ, harpsichord and, if desired, a brass consort (three trumpets, three trombones). It is not really possible to have a full symphony orchestra for reasons of space and expense and the fact that the combined strength of the three Cathedral Choirs is about 70 to 75 (all boys and men). . . . I hope you will feel quite free to write as you wish and will in no way feel inhibited by circumstances. I think many of us would be very delighted if there was a hint of "West Side Story" about the music. I hope you will not mind my writing like this, but I talked of it the other day with Chuck Solomon when he was here recently, and he said I was certainly to say it to you."

Dean Hussey got more than "a hint" of *West Side Story*. The male chorus's dramatic intervention halfway through the second movement of *Chichester Psalms* is a reworking of the chorus cut from the "Prologue" to *West Side Story*. Stephen Sondheim's lyric "Mix—make a mess of 'em! Make the sons of bitches pay" was transformed into *"Lamah rag'shu goyim Ul'umim yeh'gu rik?"*—"Why do the heathen so furiously rage together?" Furthermore, the principal melodic material in all three movements of *Chichester Psalms* was adapted from music Bernstein had just composed for *The Skin of Our Teeth*. He had decided to set the psalm texts in the original Hebrew; by a combination of significant coincidence, minor miracle, and sheer good luck, he found appropriate texts to match the rhythms of Comden and Green's Broadway-oriented lyrics. Thus the second half of the boy alto's song—Psalm 23—in the second movement was originally set to:

> *Spring will come again,*
> *Summer then will follow:*
> *Birds will come again,*
> *Nesting in the hollow,*
> *Once again we'll know all we know:*
> *After the Winter comes Spring.*

Bernstein composed *Chichester Psalms* in the spring of 1965 at his Manhattan apartment, between visits to the ballet with Mrs. Jacqueline Kennedy, a "game night chez Jerry R," and reunion drinks with Martha Gellhorn and Bob Presnell (his Cuernavaca lodger in May 1951). There was a more substantial interruption when on March 24 he flew to Alabama at Harry Belafonte's invitation to join a group of entertainers who put on a show in support of the civil rights march from Selma to Montgomery.

In early May he wrote to Dean Hussey to describe the finished piece. "It is quite popular in feeling . . . and it has an old-fashioned sweetness along with its more violent moments. The title has now been changed to 'Chichester Psalms.' ('[Psalms of] Youth' was a wrong steer; the piece is far too difficult.) The work is in three movements, lasting about eighteen and a half minutes, and each movement contains one complete psalm plus one or more verses from another complementary psalm by way of contrast or amplification." He concluded with a request: "I am conducting a program of my own music with the

New York Philharmonic in *early* July, and I have been asked if I could include the *Chichester Psalms.* I realize this would deprive you of the world premiere by a couple of weeks; do you have any serious objections?" Surprisingly, the dean did not attempt to stop the American "tryout." New York audiences heard a mixed, adult choir: Chichester would host the premiere of Bernstein's preferred, all-male version, with boys' voices singing the soprano and alto lines.

Philharmonic Hall was sold out for the New York premiere of *Chichester Psalms,* and the work received sustained applause. The *Herald Tribune* tactfully sent its second-string critic, Raymond Ericson. After the frequently hostile judgments of Alan Rich, Ericson's verdict seemed almost too friendly to be true: "extremely direct and simple and very beautiful." Irving Kolodin was equally positive: "it parades not neither does it posture." The performance was immaculate, Kolodin thought; Bernstein was clearly entering a new, more confident period as a composer.

At the end of July the Bernstein family (without Nina, who was only three) flew to England at the dean's invitation to attend the concert in Chichester Cathedral. Leonard and Felicia stayed at the deanery, where Felicia said the beds were "like sleeping on grapefruit." The family went sight-seeing to Stonehenge and saw King Arthur's famous round table in Winchester. It seems not to have occurred to anybody to ask Bernstein to conduct his own music, but this may have been a fortunate oversight since the logistics of the three-choir event turned out to be terrifying and the orchestra did not begin to rehearse until the day of the concert. "All we can do now is pray," Bernstein was heard to mutter at the end of the final run-through. When it was all over he wrote to Helen Coates: "The Psalms went off well, in spite of a shockingly small amount of rehearsal. The choirs were a delight! They had everything down pat, but the orchestra was swimming in the open sea. They simply didn't know it. But somehow the glorious acoustics of Chichester Cathedral cushion everything so that even mistakes sound pretty."

After the performance the Bishop of Chichester said he had seen David dancing before the Ark. The dean told Bernstein that he was "especially excited that [the *Psalms*] came into being at all as a statement of praise that is ecumenical. I shall be tremendously proud for them to go around in the world bearing the name of Chichester." Shocked perhaps by the sound of bongos in a cathedral nave, one English critic wrote the *Psalms* off as a "shallow experience," offering "slick professionalism without much else," but Desmond Shawe-Taylor in the *Sunday Times* observed that Bernstein was a religious composer "of the kind Luther must have had in mind when he grudged the devil all the good tunes." Partly because of their Broadway elements, the *Chichester Psalms* quickly established themselves as Bernstein's most popular choral work.


A T the end of his sabbatical, Bernstein claimed to have spent much of the year pondering "the present crisis in composition and its possible consequence in the

near future. Are symphonies a thing of the past? . . . Is tonality dead forever?" To mark his return to the concert platform he inaugurated a survey of
symphonic forms in the twentieth century. With the exception of Haydn's
*Creation,* every one of Bernstein's programs—thirty in all over the next two
years—was to contain a substantial twentieth-century symphony or concerto.
The emphasis was on Mahler and Sibelius, whom Bernstein described as the
"key turning points" in the development of the twentieth-century symphony.
Columbia Records—which in 1966 changed its name to CBS Records—
planned to record all seven Sibelius symphonies. To these Bernstein added a
cross-section of symphonies by European composers, among them Schoenberg,
Webern, Nielsen, Prokofiev, Shostakovich, Vaughan Williams, Roussel and
Hindemith, together with a substantial selection of American symphonies. He
went back as far as Charles Ives's Third (which Mahler had wanted to conduct
when he was the director of the Philharmonic) and included symphonies by
Harris, Copland, Randall Thompson and Blitzstein—*The Airborne*—as well as
recent symphonies by Irving Fine and Leo Smit, and the world premiere of
David Diamond's Fifth. It was one of the grandest pieces of program planning
in American orchestral history.

When Bernstein took up regular conducting again in New York, a Kousse-
vitzky-derived sense of "gala" increasingly marked out his performances. His
interpretations in the fall of 1965 of the last three Mahler symphonies (he held
off the Tenth for another decade) represented the pinnacle of his conducting
power as director of the New York Philharmonic, in retrospect a golden age
even in the eyes of those who had formerly been severe critics. Harold
Schonberg called the Ninth performance "a high-powered, apocalyptic evening." Noting that Mahler's Eighth had only once before been performed by
the Philharmonic, under Stokowski in 1950, Alan Rich was overwhelmed:
"Leonard Bernstein laid himself bare in the service of the score, and the cohesion, the motoric energy, the pure driving brilliance of his conception, can stand
as a landmark among many in his musical career." The unnamed London
*Times* correspondent in New York sent back an equally glowing report. The
Mahler Eighth was, he wrote, "one of the towering moments in my life in the
concert hall . . . the ultimate statement of Bernstein's deep-rooted conviction
of Mahler's genius. . . . The bond between them is both undeniable and a
glory."

In the midst of the musical excitements Bernstein was photographed for the
social pages of the *New York Times.* "Leonard Bernstein at home is relaxed,
sipping scotch-on-the-rocks, joking with his children and twitting his wife
about her embarrassment at showing her first oil painting." Alexander was
reported to be playing in a group at school called the Beatles—"but I think we
are going to change the name to the Four Fifths." The real Beatles had become
important in the family circle. Bernstein arranged to take his children backstage
to meet the Fab Four during a dress rehearsal for "The Ed Sullivan Show" in
the summer of 1965. He talked of setting some of John Lennon's Lewis Car-

roll–style poetry to music, and he told journalists how much he admired John Lennon and Paul McCartney's compositions. It was fun for Bernstein to play the iconoclast. Pop music, he said many times in the mid-sixties, is more adventurous "than anything being written in serious music today."

Yet among professional musicians Bernstein's standing had never been higher. In January 1966 he took part in a fund-raising concert for the America Israel Cultural Foundation, playing a Mozart violin sonata (K. 305, in A major) with such style that Arthur Rubinstein rose to his feet afterward to offer comprehensive tribute. Bernstein, he said, was "the greatest pianist among conductors, the greatest conductor among composers, the greatest composer among pianists. [He played the Mozart] as I wish I could play it. He is a universal genius."

That was nice to hear, even if it offered little consolation for Alan Rich's continued attacks on his compositional gifts. In February 1966 Zino Frances-catti performed Bernstein's violin *Serenade*. While the *Times* reported that it charmed the New York audience, the *Tribune* dismissed the work rudely as "drab, tawdry and derivative—leaving a listener with the feeling of having spent the time nibbling on a dietetic cotton candy." Rich returned to the attack three weeks later, deriding Bernstein's defense of tonality as the basis for com-position. "His own serious style is so embarrassingly derivative that he seems often to be using the past more as a crutch than as a source for new technique."

But by the time these wounding words appeared, Bernstein was a continent away in Vienna, on the eve of a new conducting triumph that inaugurated a radical realignment of his professional life and ultimately of his private life too.

# THE CONQUEST OF VIENNA

*The Golden Hall of the Musikverein, Vienna.*
PHOTO: FRANZ GITTENBERGER, COURTESY OF THE ESTATE OF
LEONARD BERNSTEIN

*Leonard Bernstein is the only conductor who has the ability, the authority and the musical sex appeal to surpass you-know-who.*

—JOSEPH WECHSBERG in *Opera,*
May 1966

AT a party at 895 Park Avenue one evening in 1964, Leonard Bernstein surprised his friend Robbie Lantz, a well-known film and theater agent, by inviting him out of the blue to look after his business affairs. "Of course I would love to represent you," Lantz remembers saying, "but I don't know the first thing about it." Bernstein immediately asked Lantz to go to Vienna to work out a deal with Egon Hilbert, impresario of the Vienna State Opera. Hilbert had invited Bernstein to make his Viennese opera debut in 1966, during a mid-season break from the New York Philharmonic. The choice of opera was *Falstaff,* with his friend Luchino Visconti as director and Dietrich Fischer-Dieskau in the title role. Bernstein found the combination irresistible. He didn't even brief Lantz about singers or money. The vital subject was adequate preparation time. He needed twelve orchestral rehearsals, he said, two for each of the six scenes, as well as a goodly number of separate piano rehearsals with the singers.

Lantz never forgot his first visit to Vienna. Armed with Bernstein's instructions and his own knowledge of film world negotiations, he was shown into Dr. Hilbert's palatial office at the opera house. "He got up very nicely and shook my hand, then in the same movement opened with his left hand a drawer in his desk from which he took out a file, put it in front of me, and said, 'This file conclusively shows that I was never a Nazi.' . . . We then discussed the rehearsal periods and that was absolutely no problem. Anything Maestro Bernstein wanted. And then we talked money and expenses. I cannot recall what the figures were, I only know that after this was all agreed I went back to the Sacher Hotel and called Lenny. When I told him the figures he said, 'That's not possible. That much money nobody pays a conductor. How did you ask for such a figure?' 'I come from the movies,' I said; 'I figured that you are the equivalent of Robert Redford. Now what would Redford have?'"

So Bernstein was on a different footing from other conductors from the moment he arrived in Vienna on February 26, 1966, for a momentous five-week stay. His first impressions of the city were colored by the disagreeable memory of his brief visit in 1948. "There's still something about a shouting German crowd that makes my blood run cold," he wrote to Helen Coates. "I don't know if I shall ever really *love* Vienna." But it soon proved impossible to resist the attractions Vienna had to offer: luxury, style, adulation, dedication to music and history: in the pit at the opera house Bernstein was standing on the very spot—reconstructed after the American bombing—where Gustav Mahler once had reigned supreme.

He took with him to his first rehearsal with the opera-house orchestra a long list of notes, gleaned from his experience of *Falstaff* at the "Met." He tended to talk too long to orchestras when he was nervous. After ten minutes or more of instructions in his still rather halting German, the players became impatient. The Vorstand, the orchestra's elected chairman, pointed discreetly to his watch. Bernstein took the hint and began the music for the first scene. It was a love affair from the first downbeat, he remembered later. "We were off and flying. By the third bar there was no catching us and we knew this was a lifetime relationship."

Bernstein virtually blushed in public at the satisfaction he got from working with the Viennese players. "I am really married to the New York Philharmonic," he told a journalist. "I have done very little guesting in the past decade. This is an illicit affair I'm having." But he did nothing to conceal his pleasure in the liaison. "This is a wonderful orchestra," he said in the Austrian newspaper *Express*. "They play with their hearts. They are very willing to work, very concentrated and very humorous, too." There was a marked contrast with New York, where the union was strict about timekeeping. When recording sessions in Vienna ran fifteen minutes over, "the players didn't seem to notice. There were neither scowls nor mutters." After the very first rehearsal the players applauded him. "They want me to take over everything," he reported to Coates, "operas, tours, concerts, Lord knows what. . . . The cast is generally fine, Fischer-Dieskau extraordinary." Again the admiration was mutual. With Bernstein, Fischer-Dieskau noted, "you have a feeling that he's not out there at the podium. You feel he's on the stage with you. He conducts right to the backcloth. He catches everybody with his eyes and the point of his stick. He makes you feel good."

Opening night was on March 14, a mere eighteen days after Bernstein's arrival. The ensemble had been forged at breakneck speed, and Bernstein took chances with his mercurial tempi—but at the end there were forty-eight curtain calls as the audience applauded for half an hour. The critics agreed with the public: this was primarily Bernstein's *Falstaff.* Visconti's was an effective production, but it was in the music that a sense of revelation was to be felt. Karl Löbl, one of the most reliable of Vienna's music critics, described Bernstein as "world class on the podium. A genius in the service of Verdi." The unsigned London *Times* review applauded his "fiery musicianship and winning personality. His *Falstaff* (or rather, his and the Philharmonic's—the partnership was emphasized at every bow) has pretty much everything Verdi put into it— sparkle and headlong dash, suavity and sentiment, plus Bernstein's own ingredients: scrupulous attention to dynamics and a fanatical approach to precision which left everyone the winner."

Legends grew up around Bernstein immediately. One concerned the single rose mysteriously left on the conductor's desk each night before he entered for the performance. The donor, it was rumored, was Karajan's divorced second wife. Certainly Bernstein thought so. The television director Brian Large, who was in Vienna to tape a BBC interview with Bernstein, remembers sharing a box for a *Falstaff* performance with Anita von Karajan. Bernstein entered and saw the customary rose awaiting him. In one continuous gesture he picked it up, gestured toward the box in salute, turned to the orchestra and gave an imperious downbeat for the opening scene at the Garter Inn. "Das *ist ein Dirigent!*" Anita von Karajan whispered admiringly to her neighbor. *"That* is a conductor!"

Bernstein ordered a traditional Austrian loden coat, silver gray, made to measure; it had green facings and horn buttons. "I wear it as a therapy against German Nationalism," he told an English journalist, "which I still remember and still dislike." But he had no compunction about making music in Vienna, whatever his doubts about his musical partners. Although Egon Hilbert could point to his resistance to the Nazis, the business manager of the Vienna Philharmonic—the trumpeter Helmut Wobisch—had been active in the Nazi party from 1933 onward. Bernstein brushed aside his past: he would refer to him openly as his "SS Man."

Another Viennese friend, Marcel Prawy, had lived in the United States during the war. He had become a prominent broadcaster and television host who planned the productions at Vienna's second opera house, the German-language Volksoper. Back in 1956, Prawy translated and produced *Wonderful Town,* and had since produced a German language *Candide* for the radio. He was to remain Bernstein's most ardent Viennese fan. Yet another ally proved to be Peter Weiser, then the director of Vienna's Konzerthaus, where Bernstein had conducted the Vienna Symphony Orchestra back in 1948. Weiser was planning a Mahler Festival, and in his memoirs, *Wien Stark Bewölkt,* he describes going to see Bernstein at the Bristol Hotel and inviting him to conduct a Mahler symphony the following year. Bernstein asked if it was true that Weiser had first offered the whole Mahler cycle to Karajan. Weiser said yes, it was true. Bernstein asked why he'd admitted the truth, when the Viennese never admitted anything. Weiser said, "I'm not from Vienna. I'm from Mödling." "Where is that?" "Thirteen kilometers to the south." Bernstein smiled, and agreed to return to Vienna in 1967 to conduct the Second Symphony. He and Weiser became friends for life. He had more friends in Vienna than in any other European city. They included bankers, politicians, priests and princesses—notably Lili Schönburg, a vivacious pianist who turned up at parties looking like the young aristocrat Octavian in *Der Rosenkaualier.*

Bernstein was determined to record *Falstaff* while the Vienna production was still white-hot. His "Met" *Falstaff* had not been recorded because Columbia Records, with whom he had an exclusive contract, had stopped making opera recordings in the mid-fifties. This time Goddard Lieberson struck a deal with Decca's Maurice Rosengarten. Decca would record and produce *Falstaff* on behalf of CBS. The "price" was two hours of Bernstein conducting in Vienna for the Decca label. One LP would contain Mahler's *Das Lied von der Erde,* the other was to feature two Mozart works, the *Linz* Symphony and the Piano Concerto in B flat, K.450.

Recording sessions of *Falstaff* were slotted in at the Sofiensaale, a seedy complex of ballrooms a ten-minute drive from the State Opera. The Decca team was led by Erik Smith. They used the auxiliary studio in the Blue Ballroom to create an unearthly quality for the offstage voices at the end of Scene I of Act III, and for Nannetta's Queen of the Fairies aria in the final scene. Bernstein coaxed playing of infinite subtlety from the musicians. Under the leadership of the legendary Willi Boskovsky, the Philharmonic's violinists performed staccato thirds and sixths (in the fairy scene) "as sweet as anything the Sacher Hotel pastry cooks turn out" and earlier in the same scene—at the moment in Windsor Forest when Falstaff counts the chimes of midnight—Bernstein rebowed the violin parts "so that on every 'chime' chord each player, never using more than half the bow, made the swiftest, lightest possible downstroke, *flautando,* before continuing up slowly on the same note to the middle of the bow for the next chord." Bernstein claimed that this sound was his own invention: "a swishing sound, the sound of night and zoom, zoo-oom, zoo-oo-oom." Between "takes," singers and musicians crowded into the control room to share the maestro's reactions to the playback. His informed, unstuffy approach was invigorating.

As soon as *Falstaff* was over and recorded, Bernstein had a week of concerts to conduct with the Vienna Philharmonic, which was made up of the leading players from the opera house orchestra. Dietrich Fischer-Dieskau and the American tenor James King sang the alternative version of Mahler's song symphony *Das Lied von der Erde,* in which the mezzo solos are taken by a baritone. Bernstein conducted the Mozart B flat Piano Concerto from the keyboard. "This is your Mozart," he said respectfully to the players before the first rehearsal; "I hope I can learn something from you." His first subscription concert, wrote the *Express,* assumed "the atmosphere of a great artistic event." At the Saturday afternoon concert a crowd stormed the standee area demanding places; on Sunday morning the traditional eleven o'clock concert saw equally frenetic audience reactions. The *Salzburger Nachrichten* wrote that Bernstein was *"der Wiener Musikfreunde liebstes Kind"*—"the favorite child of Vienna's music-loving public." At the end of the *Das Lied* performance, after the music had taken what seemed an eternity to die away into silence, Bernstein remained at the rostrum motionless, as if in a trance. According to the *Arbeiter Zeitung,* "it was clear that in spite of the ovations he was unable to come back to reality. The secret of this complete musician seems to be that he can identify himself with such intensity with the character of the music that it shapes his outward appearance—in Mozart's simple genius as well as in Mahler's bleeding *Weltschmerz."* The critic Joseph Wechsberg said it was the best performance of *Das Lied von der Erde* since Bruno Walter's, more than a decade previously.

If Bernstein had brought new vitality to Viennese musical life the same might be said of Vienna's effect on Bernstein. "I've got the opera bug now," he told William Weaver after recording *Falstaff.* He summed up his feelings about Vienna in another letter to Helen Coates. "What a joy being involved constantly in such music—Verdi, Mozart, Mahler! It makes up for the fatigue: the rewards are enormous. And the public—I can't describe it to you: the greatest love affair I've ever had with the public. Odd, isn't it?"

Felicia flew to Vienna for the last performance of *Falstaff.* She had mixed feelings about her husband's triumph. She didn't share his enthusiasm for Viennese food and she was made uneasy by the fawning subservience with which the Austrians treated him. At the end of a brief visit to Monte Carlo (the Vienna Philharmonic flew in and out in a day to play Mozart for Prince Rainier on the centenary of the principality) she wrote her own letter to Helen Coates, bemoaning the price Bernstein seemed to be paying for his success in Vienna. "He has aged visibly and it is unbearable to accept the fact that it all starts again in London—it is insane!"

Bernstein had been persuaded by Ernest Fleischmann, the innovative manager of the London Symphony Orchestra, to spend a fortnight in London conducting Mahler's Seventh and Eighth symphonies, so that CBS could record the Eighth for Bernstein's Mahler cycle without paying what they thought were exorbitantly high New York fees for choral singers. Working with Bernstein for the first time, the orchestra rose to both occasions magnificently but the much-respected Leeds Festival Chorus proved to be inadequate to their task in the Eighth. By Bernstein's own account, "we had a chorus of . . . ladies in hats who couldn't sing at all except in tea-time voices." Fortunately, the BBC had decided to televise the performance: extra funds were found to enable the LSO to hire a substantial stiffening of London's most experienced professional singers. Sidney Edwards in the *Evening Standard* painted a vivid picture of Bernstein at the Royal Albert Hall, "arms outstretched, urging with demonical charm elderly grandmas in white from Leeds in front of him, schoolboys from Highgate and Finchley to the right and left, with brass from the LSO right behind."

During this stay in London his British friends got a glimpse of the brash arrogance that sometimes characterized Bernstein's actions. After his first concert he invited a group of admirers gathered in the greenroom to accompany him to a private party being given in his honor by Princess Lee Radziwill, Jacqueline Kennedy's sister. All protestations that they had not been invited were brushed aside and a fleet of taxis proceeded to the house in Buckingham Gate where the innocent princess awaited her prize guest. She blanched when she saw a small army standing at her doorstep. "I've brought some friends," said Bernstein guilelessly. "But, Lenny," she said, "I don't even have enough chairs."

Bernstein had had eight free weeks between his New York Philharmonic dates in February and April and had filled every one with guest appearances. "I don't think he will ever do again what he did this season," Helen Coates confided to her new English friend, Alan Fluck, whose musical work at Farnham Grammar School had attracted Bernstein's attention the previous year. "I know he used up every ounce of his energy, but the elation of the tremendous success and acclaim of his performances everywhere kept him going. But this is really taking too much of a risk with one's health, and I hope it will never happen again. And what makes it all worse is that he is very poor at sleeping and never gets enough rest."

After the excitements of the previous two months it might have seemed a let-down to resume the New York Philharmonic's academic-sounding "Survey of Twentieth Century Symphonic Forms," but Bernstein had promised to conduct the premiere of David Diamond's Fifth Symphony as a present for Diamond's fiftieth birthday the previous July, and he plunged straight into rehearsals. The new symphony, he told the composer, "is your absolute *best* to date. . . . The fugue is a killer. I hereby accept the dedication with due formal ceremony and much affection."

Bernstein's reviews for the last four weeks of the season were restrained by comparison with the accolades he had received in Austria, but Harold Schonberg was definitely shifting his position. "Maturity seems to be creeping in. . . . Ideas were logical rather than calculated or super-imposed, and above all there was a feeling of musical confidence." The critic suggested that Bernstein had somehow undergone a mystical conversion during his sabbatical. "The old Leonard Bernstein was a didact. . . . He seemed to think that unless he made a big thing of a specific composition, audiences would miss the point. Look (he in effect would say) now comes the second subject of the exposition. You have to realize it is a second subject. And so in his eagerness to emphasize the point he would slow up to make sure everybody understood. . . . Often the result was uncomfortably obvious and vulgar. Now he is developing into the extraordinary musician that his extraordinary talents had indicated. A few more years and musicians will call him 'Maestro' instead of 'Lenny.' "

Bernstein did not need to put up with such condescension. He had seen another music capital where music making and music criticism were much more in harmony with one another. He was beginning to sense that he was at a turning point. "I am very close to having lived two-thirds of my allotted time," he told a journalist, referring to the biblical three score years and ten which already obsessed his ailing father. "The last third, if I live it, is when all the trouble will start. You begin to need glasses. Your teeth fall out."

At the end of a prodigious conducting season, Bernstein the composer reemerged. It was announced in June 1966 that he had accepted an invitation from Jacqueline Kennedy to write a major dramatic work for the 1969 opening of the National Arts Center in Washington, renamed the Kennedy Center. Mrs. Kennedy had earlier pulled off a tremendous coup by persuading Bernstein to accept the post of artistic director. "Jack would have wanted it," was her clinching argument. Bernstein then made his wife furious, their daughter Jamie remembers, by having Felicia break the news that he could not after all accept the post. It was the story of the music directorship of the Israel Philharmonic all over again. But he did not refuse the new commission, indeed he called it "the highest honor I have ever been accorded." There was no price tag. "He hasn't asked for any money," the Center's chairman and artistic director, Roger Stevens, told the *Times,* "and I haven't offered any."

In mid-July the composer Bernstein was given a further boost when the young stage director Gordon Davidson mounted a brilliant new professional production of *Candide* at Royce Hall in Los Angeles. Since the box office failure of *Candide* in London in 1959, Bernstein and Hellman had been too depressed about the work to authorize further productions. Permission was granted on this occasion only because the conductor, Maurice Peress, had been an assistant of Bernstein's back in 1961 and Peress and Davidson wanted to rescue some of the material cut in 1956. The production, Davidson remembers, "had an unpretentious, *Beggar's Opera* quality to it." Carroll O'Connor, who later rose to fame as Archie Bunker in the television comedy "All in the Family," played Dr. Pangloss.

Bernstein flew in for the dress rehearsal. "We had restored a couple of songs," Davidson recalls. " 'Ring-Around-A-Rosy'—the syphilis song—and the ballad 'Nothing More Than This,' which is sung by Candide when he faces up to the reality of what his life has meant chasing this golden dream which turns out to be tarnished. . . . It was a very important song and when David Watson stepped forward to sing it, Lenny dissolved. It was my first encounter with Lenny's tears and they were genuine. He was moved; he turned around and hugged me." He spent a long evening with the cast giving notes. "He did exactly what he was always capable of: he communicated criticism and love.

The company was nervous and apprehensive and he galvanized them. . . . He went up and kissed everybody on the stage."

The veteran Los Angeles theater critic Cecil Smith called *Candide* "an immensely gratifying experience, pulsating with life, visually exciting, charged with ribald wit, a swirling rag-tag world pinned to the stage." Martin Bernheimer noted that the show was better than the original, "partly because of the revisions and additions, but also thanks to Gordon Davidson's stress on bitter satire—as opposed to shiny showbiz cheer—the music now takes on a degree of theatrical irony it lacked before," referring to the hilarious send-up of the HUAC interrogations which Davidson, alone among all *Candide*'s directors, insisted on including. Lillian Hellman never quite forgave Davidson for adapting her text without prior permission, and despite its success Bernstein allowed Davidson's revival to become merely the first in a long line of alternative *Candide* versions.

A second collection of Bernstein's writings, *The Infinite Variety of Music,* was published in August 1966. It included the scripts of five television essays, five analyses of famous symphonies, and individual pieces on the gap between composer and audience and on the nature of the creative process. It's a pleasant collection of discussions on music but a little haphazard; without Bernstein in person to hold one's attention, the reader may occasionally remember Oscar Levant's wicked bon mot: "Leonard Bernstein has been disclosing musical secrets that have been well known for over four hundred years."

A hint of weariness with his routine can be detected in the letter he sent Helen Coates from Fairfield at the end of summer of 1966. "August here has been my usual dubious vacation: lots of tennis, lots of insomnia, some score-studying, and no composing at all. As you can imagine, this leaves me suffused with guilt; but then all my vacations are guilt-ridden. . . . The children are fine and Jamie and Alexander performed a magnificent original musical play about me at my birthday-do, which was a charming party. Felicia is splendid, painting and sculpting away. . . . And so, the summer ends, much too soon, and we will all be reunited on the 12th, back in those exhausting salt mines."

As Bernstein contemplated yet another Philharmonic season, Jerome Robbins was calling him daily with projects for a musical; he had a new acting company with which to experiment, new writers, ideas for a new type of show. It was too tempting. Early in the fall Bernstein decided to quit the Philharmonic. He told Carlos Moseley and Frank Milburn, the Philharmonic's press man, on the way to an out-of-town pre-season concert. They were on a train, Milburn remembers, discussing plans for the following year, when Bernstein suddenly said, "I can't go on this way any longer. I can't be pinned down for so many weeks at a time. I'm really a composer and I don't have any time to do my other work."

He informed the Philharmonic Board at the end of October 1966 that he would not seek a renewal of his contract after May 1969. He said he would be happy to maintain his connection with the orchestra by continuing to do the televised "Young People's Concerts" and to make records with them for CBS, and by doing a month of guest-conducting each year for as long as they wanted him. But he needed freedom from administrative responsibility. Meanwhile, he planned to round off his ten years as music director with two splendid seasons. The 1967–68 marked the 125th anniversary of the Philharmonic. Twenty-five composers were commissioned to write new works, and in addition all through the year Bernstein planned to conduct compositions that had been given, over the decades, world or American premieres by the Philharmonic, going back as far as Wagner's *Die Walküre,* first performed in 1876. In his final season, 1968–69, he decided that the programs were to be chosen by subscribers' votes from the previous decade's complete repertoire. He reserved Mahler's Third Symphony for his farewell performances.

The board created a new title to bestow upon Bernstein following his retirement: lifetime Laureate Conductor. The public announcement of his resignation in 1969, made on November 2, 1966, was described by the press as the most decisive moment for change in New York's musical life since Toscanini's retirement from NBC in 1954. Bernstein's statement reverberated with a sense of historical importance:

> It is a wonderful thing to know that relinquishing this post does not necessitate my severing the deep-lying, almost familial bonds that bind me to this great orchestra. The years I have so far spent as Music Director have brought me immense satisfaction, joy, and spiritual rewards; and our personal relationships within the orchestra are of an intimacy and brotherhood so strong as to merit the word Love. And this is as true of the Management of the Board as it is of the players themselves. It will, of course, be a wrench for me to leave my post, but it must be done. A time is arriving in my life when I must concentrate maximally on composing; and this cannot be done while retaining the great responsibilities inherent in the Philharmonic post, which is a full-time commitment, and indeed more than that.
>
> I am therefore especially pleased at the arrangement that has been evolved, whereby our music-making can continue indefinitely. I shall always regard the Philharmonic as "my" orchestra; and it is for that reason that I am so proud of, honored by, and grateful for the distinguished title to be bestowed on me.

It was not the first time that Bernstein had told the world that he proposed to "concentrate maximally" on composing.

Late in November 1966 Bernstein returned to London to conduct a series of television programs with the London Symphony Orchestra. Three works from the twentieth century—Stravinsky's *Sacre du Printemps* and the Fifth symphonies of Sibelius and Shostakovich—were telecast separately and linked under the title *Symphonic Twilight*. The first rehearsals for the Shostakovich, Bernstein's first encounter with the orchestra since April, was held in one of the big BBC television studios at White City. The intention was to record both sessions and edit from them an hour-long documentary of rehearsal highlights.

Herbert Chappell, a composer and television director who had looked after Bernstein when he spoke at the Oxford Opera Club in 1959, was assigned to the production. Bernstein was late to the recording, and Chappell had to ask everybody in the studio to be patient. "When LB arrived, he was in a foul mood. His car had driven him to the wrong BBC building. Whatever the reason he was spitting fire. He was ill. He was exhausted. He was in his dressing room and he wouldn't come out. I had never faced this problem before, an orchestra waiting to go and a conductor unwilling to start. Finally the ill-tempered maestro swallowed another handful of pills from his medicine chest (which bore a brass-plate inscription from some adoring fan club) and dragged himself across the floor of the studio towards the conductor's podium. He carried no musical score. He neither looked at the orchestra, nor apologized to the musicians for keeping them all waiting. Instead, without so much as a hint of a preparatory upbeat, he plunged into the first fortissimo 'double-dotted' strings entry in the first movement.

"The LSO responded immaculately with complete precision and gave him back as good as he gave them. Their unison attack was impeccable, violent and faultless. 'Again,' barked Lenny, stopping them after only one measure and once more the LSO, in fury, played the opening notes. 'Again!' . . . Any conductor who behaves like an autocrat does so for one reason only—to break the orchestra's spirit and to show off. Lenny's behavior became increasingly outrageous. Under the hot lights each and every musician in the LSO turned into his implacable enemy; each and every one of them would happily have throttled him.

"After an hour's rehearsal," Chappell continues, "we were no further. Time and time again Lenny played the same few opening bars, again and again, now upper strings only, now cellos and basses only. The microscopic attention to phrasing and rhythm drove the players insane. At one point he drilled the strings not section by section or desk by desk, but player by player, treating London's finest orchestral musicians as if they were recalcitrant children who had failed to practice. The TV studio became a bull-ring, a torture chamber, an *abattoir*."

It was electrifying program material; television is never happier than when it witnesses violence, bloodshed and grief. That afternoon there was an abundance of all three. The footage was so powerful that David Attenborough, who was then controller of BBC-2, decided to cancel the late night talk show that normally followed the news so that the Bernstein rehearsal documentary could run for an unprecedented two hours. And the relationship between conductor and orchestra, forged in blood, went from strength to strength over the next decade.

Before returning home the Bernsteins spent a few days in the English Lake District at Levens, the ancestral pile which was the family home of Erik Smith's fiancée, Priscilla Bagot. They were lodged in the royal bedroom—Queen Elizabeth I was said to have slept in the same four-poster—and despite the freezing temperature, indoors as well as out, Bernstein was captivated by the Bagot family. The sonnet which he wrote in their guest book concluded with this quatrain:

> *The harpsichord declaims within the hall—*
> *The woodcocks boil like brothers in the pot.*
> *No hand can devastate, no voice recall*
> *What God has wrought and Bagot hath Begot.*

# 3 3 .

# END OF AN ERA

*With Nina, Jamie, Felicia and Alexander on the balcony of
their Park Avenue apartment, 1969.*
PHOTO: DON HUNSTEIN, COURTESY OF THE ESTATE OF LEONARD BERNSTEIN

*I feel very young.*
—Bernstein on the eve of his fiftieth
birthday

EARLY in 1967 Bernstein was approached by several publishers with requests for an official biography, to be published in time for his fiftieth birthday in August 1968. He disliked both the existing biographies (by David Ewen and John Briggs—his sister's more intimate account had been written specifically for young people) and he decided to accept a proposal for an informal portrait of himself and his family with photographs by Ken Heyman and accompanying text by his cultural journalist friend, John Gruen. Gruen and his family would spend part of the summer in Italy down the road from the villa that the Bernsteins planned to rent in the village of Ansedonia, near Porto Ercole on the Tyrrhenian Sea. Felicia's objections to having outsiders observe their family holiday were mollified by the prospect of studying painting with Gruen's wife, her friend Jane Wilson.

Earlier in the year Bernstein conducted his first Verdi *Requiem,* at a New York Philharmonic concert marking the centenary of Toscanini's birth. A poll on WQXR, the *New York Times'* radio station, found that Toscanini was still the second most popular conductor with its listeners, despite the fact that he had been dead for a decade. Bernstein was the hands-down favorite. In March he worked for the first time with Jacqueline du Pré, the charismatic young English cellist—"Golly, she can upstage Lenny," was Harold Schonberg's reaction—

and in May he concluded his Philharmonic recordings of the Mahler cycle with the Sixth Symphony, after three public performances which were warmly greeted by the critics. In the same program he gave the world premiere of a new work by Lukas Foss entitled *Phorion,* a Greek word meaning "stolen goods." The first movement deconstructs the thematic material of a Bach violin partita. Foss remembers that Bernstein called him up at 11 P.M. the night before the first rehearsal. "I don't understand your music any more. It's gotten so violent. Would you please come over and explain it to me." Foss loyally walked the fifteen blocks from his Fifth Avenue apartment and the two friends went through the score together. "By 2 A.M.," Foss recalls, "he was explaining the music to me." At the rehearsal next morning Foss was surprised to see Bernstein bring out twenty pages of notes. He had evidently worked through the night. "He made the players not just understand but *want* to play my music. It was a great performance." Alas, the audience greeted it with a round of boos.

Bernstein himself was criticized for his television special for CBS (produced by David Oppenheim) called *Inside Pop—The Rock Revolution.* In it he addressed his own generation, the parents of rock-loving teenagers, and expanded on the controversial opinion he had expressed in the preface to his book *The Infinite Variety of Music.* At a time when jazz was dormant and tonal music lay in abeyance, "Pop music seems to be the only area where there is to be found unabashed vitality, the fun of invention, the feeling of fresh air. Everything else suddenly seems old-fashioned: electronic music, serialism, chance music—they have already acquired the musty odor of academicism." Critics decried Bernstein for condescension and inconsistency—"praising rock in one breath and slapping it down in the next," and Bernstein became less vocal in his support for rock and pop thereafter, until his enthusiasm reemerged in 1971 in his theater work *Mass,* which was to draw much of its energy from blues, rock and electronic instrumentation.

In advance of the summer holiday in Ansedonia, Bernstein had asked his European agent to organize some Italian concerts for him. It was a mistake, he soon realized. In Florence he had an "intense struggle" to get the Maggio Musicale Orchestra to play well. When he appeared in Rome, a headline described his concert as a *"SUCCESSO ECCEZIONALE,"* but he was upstaged by Karajan, who was at the Vatican to conduct a concert for the Pope.

The same day, June 5, 1967, war broke out in the Middle East. In six days of fierce fighting, Israel scored a momentous victory over the Arab countries surrounding her. Jordanian troops were driven from areas of Jerusalem they had controlled since 1948. When Bernstein flew to Vienna to conduct the *Resurrection* Symphony at the State Opera House—"the undisputed major event of the Festival"—he donated his fee to the Israeli Red Cross. His two soloists, Hilde Güden and Christa Ludwig, followed suit, as did the Vienna Philharmonic. The elating news of the "liberation" of Jerusalem, as Jews saw it, inspired Bernstein to propose a celebratory concert in the Holy City. After returning briefly to the United States to receive an honorary doctorate from

Harvard and conduct yet more *Resurrection* Symphony performances at the first Lincoln Center Festival, he flew to Israel on July 1 to conduct three special concerts marking the "peaceful reunification" of the city of Jerusalem. His friend Mike Mindlin had swiftly organized a film documentary which was to be released in art house cinemas under the title *Journey to Jerusalem*. Ernest Fleischmann, the former manager of the London Symphony Orchestra and now head of CBS Records in Europe, set up a parallel LP recording.

Bernstein thrived on being once again the center of political excitement and upheaval. Richard Leacock, a member of Mindlin's film team, remembers Bernstein's visible emotion when he prayed for the first time at the Wailing Wall. Another scene in the film showed Bernstein visiting wounded soldiers at an Army hospital. One man—a bearded Hasidic Jew—was seen throwing away his crutches after Bernstein had entertained them with foot-tapping Yiddish songs at an upright piano.

The climax of Bernstein's trip was the outdoor concert in the amphitheater on the slopes of Mount Scopus (part of the newly liberated original campus of Hebrew University and a regular concert venue before the War of Independence). Given under Mayor Teddy Kollek's patronage, the concert was described in the official program as "the cultural opening of the united city of Jerusalem." The audience included the Israeli President and Prime Minister. Isaac Stern played the Mendelssohn violin concerto and Bernstein conducted the last three movements of Mahler's *Resurrection* Symphony. The soloists were Jennie Tourel, who had flown with Bernstein from the United States, and the Israeli soprano Netanya Dovrat, who had a dress rehearsal of *Madama Butterfly* in Tel Aviv at 6 P.M. She arrived and departed by helicopter, a *diva ex machina* for the day.

Before the music, Bernstein recalled from the podium the performances he had conducted in Israel in 1948 during the War of Independence. "The idea of resurrection at that time was momentous; after all this land had just been reborn. But still the ancient cycle of threat, destruction and re-birth goes on; and it is all mirrored in Mahler's music—above all the expression of simple faith—of belief that good must triumph. *En b'rerah!*—there is no alternative."

The Israel Philharmonic performed in shirtsleeves, open-necked against the heat. When the concert began with the national anthem, "Hatikvah," "scores of men and women in the audience wept openly at its moving strains." Adolph Green, who had accompanied Bernstein to Israel, noted that despite the hazards of a sandstorm, land mines being exploded and a fierce wind which knocked over music stands and rendered the offstage brass inaudible, "Lenny conducts with a look of almost angelic peace on his face."

Bernstein's choice of conducting clothes in Israel matched the milieu—a high-necked natural linen tunic with matching trousers. The suit looked vaguely militaristic; he had been given it, ten years previously, in Venezuela. "I'm amazed the concert came off so well," Bernstein said afterward. "Everything was against it—the wind, the sun. But somehow nothing seemed to matter." The *Jerusalem Post* noted "the extraordinary warm and intense reception accorded the artists who had come [to] Israel . . . out of solidarity."

All week in Israel Bernstein had been going from doctor to doctor between rehearsals hoping to find relief from an aching back. After a four-hour cortisone drip treatment in a military hospital, he was still in pain. As he left, an old Jewish doctor asked what was wrong and offered his own solution. A small man, he locked arms with Bernstein, facing away from him, and suddenly hoisted the maestro onto his back so that he was like an upturned beetle, his legs in the air. He stayed there for two minutes and was then returned to his feet. The pain had disappeared. "See that man," cried Bernstein to the doctor, pointing at Mike Mindlin, who had accompanied him. "Teach *him* to do whatever you just did!" Mindlin remained Bernstein's physiotherapist for the rest of the stay.

I N mid-July, Bernstein finally joined his family in Ansedonia, having paused in Rome to take delivery of a convertible Maserati sports car. Unfortunately the vacation was not the Italian idyll he had hoped for. "My back has been in agony for a month," he wrote to Lukas Foss in August. Felicia had to spend most of her time indoors because sunshine gave her itchy, angry-looking rashes. Both had trouble sleeping. Leonard's heavy snoring when he eventually did go to bed often drove Felicia to seek unlikely places to sleep in the house, where she would be discovered early in the morning by the Italian maid.

When John Gruen arrived for the interview sessions that were to form the basis of the biographical portrait he had been commissioned to write, he noted that Bernstein looked pale and drawn, even though he was exalted after his experiences in Israel. "Something weighed him down," Gruen went on. "He was depressed and he was restless." A month later, in a long letter to Aaron Copland prompted by news of the imminent delivery of Copland's new symphonic work, *Inscape* (his first in five years), Bernstein described his sorry state:

Dear A:
    Can't sleep (haven't for weeks) and thinking very much of you, of music, of impasses. Haven't found a work to write (after almost a month of *dolce-far-niente* in this beautiful house): not a note on paper, not a score studied, a very few books read: no thoughts to speak of, no nothin. Much pleasure in children, Hebrew lessons (!) to Alexander (we adore them and laugh a good deal [Alexander was preparing for Bar Mitzvah]); in the sun-air-sky-water-boat department, diving from my new rubber boat (singing all the while "All we've got is a rubber boat we can't blow up and a single flashlight" [a chorus from Copland's opera *The Second Hurricane*] and nearly weeping with nostalgia) and enjoying all my diving gear— black spaceman type wet-suit, flippers, helmet, knife, watch, depthometer, oxygen tanks on back; enjoying driving my new silver-gray Maserati—my

first (and last) sheer playboy acquisition. Sailing, snorkeling, seeing a very
few people, not even going to see Etruscan ruins nearby, logey, paralyzed
with sea and sun. And no sleep. Somewhere in all this I must be restoring
my soul, recharging my transistors, "resting." I never have rested well;
I'm happy only when I work. But I can't work. And there you are.

To another composer, Lukas Foss, he wrote: "I am tortured by the passing
of time. . . . Each day is a horror because it leads me one day closer to the end
of summer; and the guilt of not working is intolerable. . . . John Gruen sits
with me for hours, a tape-recorder between us, and I talk, talk, talk. I have been
photographed to a crisp."

The assertion that he was "seeing a very few people" must be taken with a
grain of salt.

The Gruens were not the only visitors. A visit by Adolph Green was
followed by others from Betty Comden Kyle and her husband, Steve, Martha
Gellhorn, Erik and Priscilla Smith, Princess Lili Schönburg, and Thomas and
Nonni Schippers. The highlight of the season was an evening when Charlie and
Oona Chaplin came to dinner with two of their eight children. In his book
Gruen gives a vivid description of Chaplin, seventy-eight years old, performing
silent movie comic routines, with Bernstein at the keyboard. "He becomes the
young Chaplin caught in a thousand dilemmas. He takes his little steps. He
pivots. He reels. Lenny plays faster and faster. The company howls." The
entertainment developed into a parody of Italian opera. Chaplin became the
compliant tenor, sobbing out an aria in mock Italian. Betty Comden joined him
in what Gruen describes as "a mad, frenzied duet, which seems to end on the
highest notes ever sung by living man, woman or beast. Everyone, including
Lenny at the piano, is completely overcome with laughter. Lenny rushes from
the piano to embrace Chaplin."

There were quieter days when the only guests were the ubiquitous Gruen
and his artist wife, Jane Wilson, who gave professional instruction to Felicia
and volunteered to paint portraits of the Bernstein children as well. Bernstein's
sister-in-law Ellen, an occasional visitor that summer, thought Jane Wilson was
"trying to be nice about things, trying to cover up for John Gruen being such a
pain in the ass." But Gruen was there on invitation, and he stuck doggedly to
his task. In search of biographical detail, he recorded hour after hour of late-
night scotch-lubricated confessionals with Bernstein, accompanied only by the
hum of cicadas in the pines and the rumbling of Bernstein's digestive system.

At Bernstein's forty-ninth birthday party Gruen acted as master of ceremonies for a make-believe radio program—faithfully transcribed for his book—in
which Jamie and Alexander made fun of their famous father as they sought to
define in what ways they resembled him. "It has always been a sort of duty,"
Bernstein explained, "sworn on oath, by all the members of all my family, to act
as bringers-downers, so that Daddy doesn't go off on Cloud 9 with a swollen
head." He added that Felicia was fond of an intimate, teasing kind of criticism.

Bernstein knew how important Felicia's critical eye was in keeping him in touch with reality. "I don't know what I would do without it, in fact," he said to Gruen, adding that Felicia was "the most critical single person I've ever met in my whole life. It's a wonderful thing to be."

But an inner trouble was gnawing away at Felicia. Perhaps she was depressed by the inevitable comparison she made between her own paintings and those of Jane Wilson. Perhaps she was anxious about the way exposure to the sun made her body ill. Perhaps she was simply bored, as she suggested in a note to Helen Coates. While the cause of her frustration is a matter of conjecture, its effect was startlingly real. One afternoon, in front of Jamie and Alexander, Felicia threw all her paintings into the sea. It was an act of fury, Jamie remembers. "We were so horrified that she actually threw them over the wall onto the rocks of the beach of the house next door." The twelve-year-old Alexander heroically fished the canvases out of the Mediterranean.

Living nearby with friends in Porto Ercole, Burton Bernstein and his wife, Ellen, found their famous relatives' proximity intrusive. "There was a problem a day and then they would phone us," Ellen recalls. ". . . Lenny was the only one who was trying to have fun. Then the Queen of Holland [vacationing in the area] heard that Lenny was in Ansedonia and she sent a message saying would he like to come over to her house and play piano for her after dinner. It was a total put-down. To top it off, his dentist and his wife arrived by seaplane and she promptly had a heart attack and Don Stewart [Ellen's host] had to drive her to Rome because the Maserati didn't work."

For Alexander and Nina Bernstein (now aged five) the Italian holiday had its merits. Nina was enjoying it: "it meant that I was actually more with my parents than I would have been, because I was getting my picture taken with them." Alexander spent a lot of time with his father, too. "I had a blast. I didn't even realize that nobody else was having a good time." Jamie was the most unhappy. "We were made to be very self-conscious about who we were and who we appeared to be to the public. We sensed that we were being observed and photographed as this perfect, happy and larger-than-life family. . . . I was this lumpish fourteen-year-old. I didn't know what I was doing there. . . . Of course the other thing was that I developed this mad crush on John Gruen. *Faute de mieux,* I guess; nobody else around."

Bernstein himself became increasingly despondent. The hours of meditation looking out over the moonlit Mediterranean seem to have confirmed in him a mood of pessimism that the previous months of concert-giving—which included eight performances in three countries of Mahler's *Resurrection* Symphony—could not dispel. "It all ties up," he told John Gruen in the last of their Italian conversations, "with my almost Spenglerian feeling about the decline of Western man, or of Faustian man, as we have known him. . . . Twenty-five hundred years, let's say, of glorious culture—which seems to be grinding to a halt except, of course, scientifically."

In the end the prospect of conducting restored Bernstein's spirits. He received the score of Copland's new work and immediately sent off a telegram: "ADORE INSCAPE BRAVO LOVE SEE YOU NEXT WEEK." His love of music kept him "glued to life," as he put it, even when he was at his most depressed. But his preoccupation with Mahler's music reinforced the mood of gloom and doom when he returned to America. He wrote an article for *High Fidelity* called "Mahler: His Time Has Come," to introduce his CBS recordings of the nine symphonies—presented in a leather-bound boxed set costing one hundred dollars for fourteen discs. "My time will come," Mahler had said; according to Bernstein, the musical world had been obliged to endure half a century of holocausts before it could "finally listen to Mahler's music and understand that it foretold all. And that in the foretelling it showered a rain of beauty on this world that has not been equaled since." The catalogue of disasters provided by Bernstein makes woeful reading: "The smoking ovens of Auschwitz, the frantically bombed jungles of Vietnam, through Hungary, Suez, the Bay of Pigs, the farce-trial of Sinyavsky and Daniel, the refueling of the Nazi machine, the murder in Dallas, the arrogance of South Africa, the Hiss-Chambers travesty, the Trotskyite purges, Black Power, Red Guards, the Arab encirclement of Israel, the plague of McCarthyism, the Tweedledum armaments race." Bernstein could not help taking it all personally, right back to Stalin's show trials of the 1930s. To onlookers the list seemed almost comical in its determination to omit nothing from the blacklist, but for Bernstein himself the unbroken melancholy had a deadening effect on his creativity. An increasing sense of shame at what was happening to America in the sixties kept his previously optimistic spirits dampened as he approached his fiftieth birthday.

THE opening event of the New York Philharmonic's 125th season was a gala at Lincoln Center starring the Vienna Philharmonic, which was also celebrating its 125th season. Karl Böhm shared the conducting with Leonard Bernstein. Bernstein opened with Beethoven's *Leonore* Overture No. 3 and according to the *Times* he made the Viennese play like the New Yorkers—"much more powerful, sharper in dynamics, more strident in sound." Böhm reciprocated a week later by conducting the New York Philharmonic in Mozart's *Haffner* Symphony. While the Vienna Philharmonic was in town its members gave Bernstein a ring as a personal birthday present from the orchestra. It was yellow gold, noted the *Daily News* reporter, "with diamonds twinkling sinfully about the perimeter." Bernstein's illicit orchestral affair had become a public relationship.

Later in October Bernstein taped a "Young People's Concert" entitled *A Toast to Vienna in ³/₄ Time,* which aired on Christmas Day and was seen by twenty-seven million people. (In New York it was billed as the first stereo simulcast.) He "looked as if he might dance off the podium at any moment" as he conducted the waltzes from *Der Rosenkavalier,* a work he was preparing to conduct in Vienna itself. Songs by Gustav Mahler were also part of the program and his musical life continued to be imbued with Mahler both in live performances and on disc. His recording of Mahler's Eighth Symphony with the London Symphony Orchestra was at the top of the classical best-seller list for several months, and eventually won a Grammy; Mahler even displaced Beethoven in *Billboard*'s list of Best-Selling Classic LPs. Eric Salzman, in reviewing the complete symphony set of Mahler recordings, noted that in Bernstein's hands even the vulgar elements in Mahler's work did not sound vulgar: "they emerge as part of life."

Preparing the premiere of *Inscape* in the fall of 1967 brought Bernstein closer again to his old friend Aaron Copland. Copland attended rehearsals at Ann Arbor in September. "When Aaron heard that big crashing first chord," remembers Copland's friend Phillip Ramey, "his eyes gleamed with pleasure and excitement. . . ." Backstage after the concert Bernstein exclaimed, "Aaron, it's amazing how, even when you compose in a completely 'foreign' idiom [he meant the twelve-tone system] the music *still* comes out sounding like you." Copland thought the performance was excellent. But when he heard *Inscape* again in New York, coupled with Mahler's Fifth Symphony, he grumbled to Ramey that " 'Lenny's been conducting too much Mahler. *Inscape* has gotten too slow . . .' " Bernstein himself felt overwhelmingly sentimental as the thirtieth anniversary of his first meeting with Copland approached:

> Dear A:
>
> It's two days before your birthday, but I'm already thinking hard and tenderly about you; and this note is your birthday present carrying with it such abiding love as I rarely if ever get to express to you in our occasional meetings. I don't know if you're aware of what you mean, have meant for 30 years, to me and my music and so many of my attitudes to life and to people. I suppose if there's one person on earth who is at the center of my life it's you; and day after day I recognize in my living your presence, your laugh, your peculiar mixture of intensity and calm. . . . I hope you live forever.
>
> A long strong hug—
> Lenny

The Philharmonic celebrated its 125th birthday at Lincoln Center on December 7, with a repeat of the orchestra's very first program, given at the Apollo (on Broadway between Canal and Walker streets) in 1842. Bernstein played in a piano quintet by Hummel and conducted the orchestra in Beethoven's Fifth Symphony. Eileen Farrell, Nicolai Gedda and Reri Grist sang arias by Weber, Mozart and Beethoven respectively. Finally Bernstein came out to introduce an overture by Johann Wenzel Kalliwoda, a Bohemian composer much admired

*"I'm So Lucky to Be Me"—Carnegie Hall, 1956. Bernstein was a guest conductor of the New York Philharmonic in the 1956–57 season.* PHOTO V. MAZÉLIS, COURTESY OF THE ESTATE OF LEONARD BERNSTEIN

*"O happy pair, O happy we…" Leonard and Felicia at the control room playback of* Candide, *December 1956.* PHOTO DAN WEINER, COURTESY OF SONY CLASSICAL

*Bernstein leads Felicia and members of the staff of Columbia Records in an impromptu chorus at the* Candide *playback.* PHOTO DAN WEINER, COURTESY OF SONY CLASSICAL

*"I'm going to be a conductor after all." With Helen Coates and Felicia.* PHOTO DAN WEINER, COURTESY OF SONY CLASSICAL

West Side Story, *1957. With Stephen Sondheim at the piano, Bernstein rehearses a bevy of Shark ladies in* "America." *From left to right: Chita Rivera (who sang Anita), Marilyn d'Honau, Carmen Guiterrez, Nanette Rosen, Elizabeth Taylor, Lee Becker, Lynn Ross, Wilma Curley and Carol Lawrence (who sang Maria).*

*"What is Sonata Form?" Young People's Concert, 1964. Bernstein gave fifty-three televised hour-long concert lectures with the New York Philharmonic between 1958 and 1972.*

*Backstage after his last Moscow concert in 1959, Bernstein is congratulated by his father. The onlookers include the Russian composers Dimitri Shostakovich on Bernstein's left, and opposite, the tall Dimitri Kabalevsky.*

*In Japan with Jennie Tourel and Seiji Ozawa, Bernstein's assistant for the 1961 New York Philharmonic tour.*

*Herbert von Karajan (left) and Dimitri Mitropoulos (center) with Leonard Bernstein in Salzburg, 1959.*

*Local musicians entertain the "little drummer boy" in La Paz on the New York Philharmonic's 1958 South American tour.*

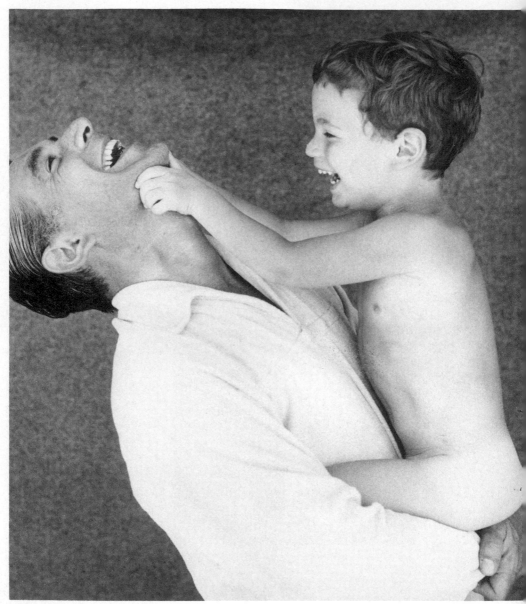

*Leonard Bernstein with his son Alexander, as photographed by Richard Avedon, Jamaica 1960.*

*Felicia Bernstein with her daughter, Jamie, as photographed by Richard Avedon.*
*"Jamie looks like a princess...unnaturally blond and delicate and fey."*

*Winter sports at Sun Valley, Idaho, 1958. "He should wear a bell on the slopes," said his friend Mike Mindlin.*
COURTESY OF THE ESTATE OF LEONARD BERNSTEIN

*Bernstein and his dog Henry.*
PHOTO DON HUNSTEIN, COURTESY OF SONY CLASSICAL

*Bernstein with Glenn Gould in 1961. Bernstein's partnership with the electrifying Canadian pianist concluded bizarrely with a controversial interpretation of the Brahms D minor Piano Concerto.*
PHOTO DON HUNSTEIN, COURTESY OF SONY CLASSICAL

*The 125th anniversary of the New York Philharmonic was celebrated in December 1967. Bernstein conducted the orchestra in nearly thirteen hundred concerts between 1943 and 1989.*
PHOTO DON HUNSTEIN, SONY CLASSICAL, COURTESY NEW YORK PHILHARMONIC ARCHIVES

*"My first and last sheer playboy acquisition." Ansedonia, Italy, 1967.*
PHOTO © KEN HEYMAN, COURTESY OF THE ESTATE OF LEONARD BERNSTEIN

*Felicia's drawing of Springate, their home in Fairfield, Connecticut, was used as the family greeting card in 1963.*
COURTESY OF THE ESTATE OF LEONARD BERNSTEIN

*Bernstein and Mike Nichols commandeer Alexander's walkie-talkies. Bernstein's Fairfield work studio can be seen in the background.*
COURTESY OF THE ESTATE OF LEONARD BERNSTEIN

*Felicia as Floria Tosca in a Bernstein home movie directed by Stephen Sondheim.*
COURTESY OF THE ESTATE OF LEONARD BERNSTEIN

*Leonard as Baron Scarpia.*
COURTESY OF THE ESTATE OF LEONARD BERNSTEIN

*The famous "Lenny Leap"—caught at the dress rehearsal for the Verdi* Requiem *in St. Paul's Cathedral, London, 1970. Bernstein is a foot clear of the podium. From left: Martina Arroyo, Josephine Veasey, Placido Domingo and Ruggiero Raimondi, with the London Symphony Orchestra.*
LONDON WEEKEND TELEVISION, COURTESY OF THE ESTATE OF LEONARD BERNSTEIN

Lenny – "I loved it, yes, I did"
and I love you too ——
Thank you for making <u>Mass</u> so beautiful. Jackie

*After attending Bernstein's* Mass, *Mrs. Jacqueline Onassis signed a commemorative photograph.*
*Looking on is Roger Stevens, chairman of the Kennedy Center and supporter of Bernstein since 1950.*
COURTESY OF THE ESTATE OF LEONARD BERNSTEIN

*The Bernstein family with their Chilean housekeeper, Julia Vega (left), as they prepare to meet Pope Paul VI in 1973.* PHOTO GIROLAMO DI MAJO, COURTESY OF THE ESTATE OF LEONARD BERNSTEIN

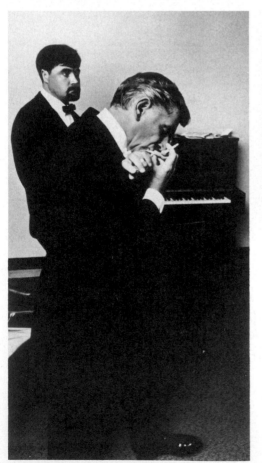

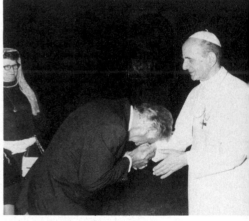

*Papal Audience. "Remember, the ring, not the lips!" Mike Mindlin had cabled. Behind Bernstein is Helen Coates.*
PHOTO THE VATICAN, COURTESY OF THE ESTATE OF LEONARD BERNSTEIN

*Before he went out to conduct, Bernstein would always kiss the cuff links bequeathed to him by Koussevitzky.* PHOTO © KEN HEYMAN

# COLLABORATORS

*With Schuyler Chapin (center)and John McClure (right), key figures in the 1960s when Bernstein recorded a cycle of Mahler symphonies for Columbia (later CBS) Records.*

PHOTO © KEN HEYMAN

*With Michael Tilson Thomas at the 1974 Charles Iveys centenary concert.*

PHOTO © DAVID GAHR, COURTESY OF MICHAEL TILSON THOMAS

*With Alan Jay Lerner in 1976, preparing* 1600 Pennsylvania Avenue.

PHOTO © HENRY GROSSMAN, COURTESY OF
THE ESTATE OF LEONARD BERNSTEIN

*Humphrey Burton filming Bernstein in Vienna, 1978.*

PHOTO UNITEL/LAUTERWASSER

*Bernstein with Franco Zeffirelli, the stage and film director, 1981.*

COURTESY OF THE ESTATE OF LEONARD BERNSTEIN

*With Stephen Wadsworth, co-librettist of* A Quiet Place, *1983.*

PHOTO © ARTHUR ELGORT

*With John Mauceri in Scotland, 1988, for the Scottish Opera's production of* Candide.

PHOTO CHRISTINA BURTON

*Füschl, Austria, 1975. The Bernstein family was joined by Michael "Mendy" Wager (front row, left) when Bernstein conducted at the Salzburg Festival for the first time since 1959.*

PHOTO JOHN WALKER, COURTESY OF JAMIE BERNSTEIN THOMAS

*With Tom Cothran at a party in Frankfurt during the New York Philharmonic's bicentennial tour of Europe in June 1976. Bernstein left his wife for Cothran a month later.*

CBS/SONY MUSIC GERMANY, COURTESY OF THE
ESTATE OF LEONARD BERNSTEIN

*The bearded maestro, conducting Mahler's Sixth Symphony in Vienna, 1976. "I decided that I had to lead the rest of my life as I want."* PHOTO UNITEL / LAUTERWASSER

*With President Carter and Nina in 1979. "Please come and see me any time," President Carter wrote on Bernstein's place card.*
COURTESY OF NINA BERNSTEIN

*With (from left) Quincy Jones, Michael Jackson, Jamie Bernstein Thomas and David Pack.*
PHOTO © LESTER COHEN

*Bernstein visits the Hiroshima Peace Museum in 1985 with one of his conducting protégés, Eiji Oue.*
COURTESY OF THE ESTATE OF LEONARD BERNSTEIN

*Conducting class in the Rehearsal Barn, Salzau, Germany. Bernstein's friend Aaron Stern is standing in shirt-sleeves at the rear, left. Seated on Bernstein's right is the pianist and festival director Justus Frantz; Bernstein's manager, Harry Kraut, is on his left.* PHOTO UNITEL

*Four generations of Bernsteins. David and Jamie Thomas introduce their newly born daughter Francisca to Jamie's grandmother, Jennie Bernstein, who had just turned eighty-nine.*
COURTESY OF JAMIE BERNSTEIN THOMAS

*A birthday party at Fairfield in 1986. Burton Bernstein pays homage to his brother "Lennuhtt."*
COURTESY OF THE ESTATE OF LEONARD BERNSTEIN

*Encouraged by Craig Urquhart, his assistant, Bernstein takes a chisel to the Berlin Wall on Christmas Eve 1989.*
PHOTO ANDREAS MEYER-SCHWICKERATH

*Lighting the menorah in front of a ruined synagogue in East Berlin between performances of Beethoven's renamed Ode to Freedom.*
PHOTO SAMUEL J. PAUL

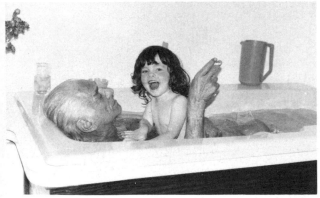

*In the bath with his granddaughter Francisca, whisky and cigarette close at hand as always.*
PHOTO JAMIE BERNSTEIN THOMAS

*At Villa Wahnfried, Bayreuth, April 1990. A visibily aging Bernstein, in duffel coat and cowboy boots, plays* Tristan *on Wagner's piano to the approval of Wagner's granddaughter Friedelind.*
PHOTO THOMAS GAYDA

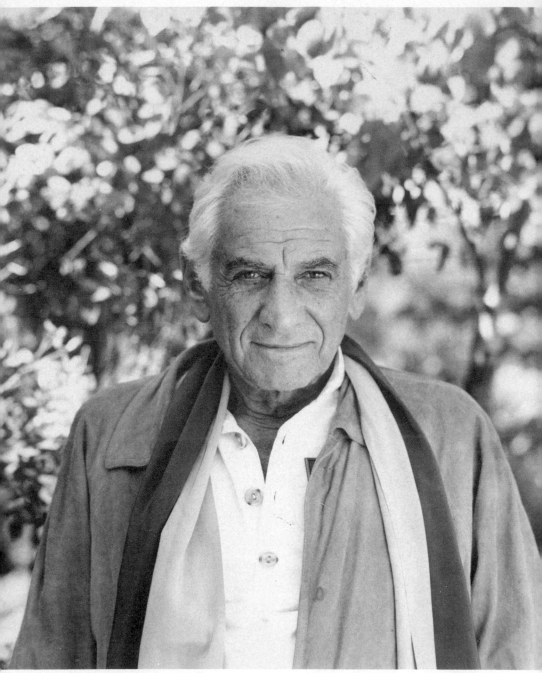

*The last portrait, July 1, 1990, Sapporo.*
PHOTO © EIICHIRO SAKATA

by Robert Schumann. "To conclude this evening honoring the mighty Philharmonic," said Bernstein, "we will have the star on its own." He gave the downbeat and left the stage. Among the musicians in the audience that night was Pierre Boulez, who was mentioned next day by Harold Schonberg as a possible contender for Bernstein's position as music director. The gossip columns were already hard at work on the subject. Karajan had signaled that he was tied to Berlin for life. Leinsdorf had just resigned from Boston, citing ill health. But Lukas Foss's name was in the ring, along with Colin Davis, Lorin Maazel, Seiji Ozawa and Zubin Mehta. The Philharmonic seemed in no hurry to fill Bernstein's post permanently. Much to the resentment of William Steinberg (sixty-eight) the current principal guest conductor, it announced that George Szell (seventy) had been selected to serve as the orchestra's musical adviser when Bernstein became Laureate Conductor in 1969. A few days later, as Bernstein was driving up Third Avenue with his friend Irma Lazarus in his Maserati convertible (license plate LB7), five teenagers in a rattling jalopy drew alongside them at every traffic stop. At the fifth light, Irma Lazarus remembered, one of them yelled over to Bernstein: " 'Hey Lenny, wanna change cars?' Lenny looked at me very severely and said, 'They wouldn't talk to Szell like that!' "

Reviewing the Philharmonic's 125th anniversary, *Time* quoted Bernstein's often-reported litany that "the natural growth and decline of the symphonic literature has left us with a great repertory of masterpieces from the eighteenth and nineteenth centuries but only a few from the twentieth. The orchestra is booming today as never before, but as a museum. The conductor today is a kind of curator." *Time* disagreed. "A museum it may be, but at its 125th birthday the New York Philharmonic is a far healthier celebrator, with a longer life expectancy, than it has ever been in the past." The credit, it said, was Bernstein's. He has "made symphony-going once more a galvanizing experience."

Felicia saw her husband's progress differently: "In five years I have seen the orchestra take so much out of him. He has become quite gray-white." She was confiding home secrets to a Philadelphia journalist while on a short tour playing Birdie in Lillian Hellman's *The Little Foxes*. Interviewers on tour always wanted to know about her famous husband, and she obliged with tantalizing tidbits: "I fell in love with Lenny at first sight and he with me. . ˙ . . At night when he's hungry he spoons baby food out of jars in his music study rather than raid the ice box for snacks."

Much of Felicia's energy was now devoted to political work. In 1968 she was active in fund-raising for Eugene McCarthy, who some saw as the best hope for ending the five-year Vietnam War. For his part Bernstein composed a touching antiwar song called "So Pretty," with lyrics by Comden and Green for Barbra Streisand to sing at a fund-raising event called "Broadway for Peace." In the summer of 1968 Bernstein introduced Senator McCarthy to the crowd at huge rallies in Boston and New York. Sometimes he said, only half jokingly, that he was thinking of running for political office.

⟲

IN May 1968 Bernstein returned to Vienna to conduct *Der Rosenkavalier*. By choosing to tackle this most Viennese of operas in Vienna, he was walking into a lion's den. Every taxi driver in Vienna, he observed, knew the piece backward. But Bernstein had loved the opera since his student days, when he had watched his teacher Fritz Reiner conduct it in Chicago, and he intended to offer the Viennese public a new interpretation. In practice this meant paying great attention to orchestral detail. Instead of giving the singers their head and keeping the orchestra damped down, Bernstein encouraged the musicians to relish one of the most elaborate and sophisticated opera scores ever composed. "I took the score apart, cleaned up the rhythms, re-bowed the string parts. [He also reseated the orchestra, all strings to the left of him, woodwinds and brass to the right.] I trembled because I knew I had removed all the nice lazy sloppiness, all the whipped cream that the Viennese treasure."

Karl Löbl found the result "in part fascinating, always extraordinary and often breath-taking." The Welsh soprano Gwyneth Jones sang Octavian, Reri Grist was Sophie, Walter Berry sang Baron Ochs, and his wife Christa Ludwig was the Marschallin. "She was so marvelous [at the end of Act I] that I cried watching her," Bernstein said. His own nonchalant tour de force at the beginning of Act III, standing impassively, arms folded, very obviously not conducting when the orchestra has a whirlwind prologue, took the audience's breath away. The first-night ovation was similar to *Falstaff*'s, with forty-eight curtain calls. *Time*'s review summed up the Viennese enthusiasm for Bernstein: "He captured the elegiac bitterness which is at the heart of the autumnal work, he freed it of the sentimental encrustations that Strauss never intended; as a result it was sharper, livelier, nobler." Joseph Wechsberg, on the other hand, was occasionally quite hostile: "It was the longest *Rosenkavalier* on record and at certain times the most boring. . . . Where was the lightness, the exhilaration?" Peter Heyworth, writing in the London *Observer,* felt the interpretation lost something of the "music's insinuating grace, its irony and shy self-mockery," but he admired Bernstein's "radical re-thinking of a fatally familiar score."

Altogether Bernstein spent a month in Vienna. At a Philharmonic subscription program he played Mozart's G major Piano Concerto (K. 453) and introduced his *Chichester Psalms.* At the Konzerthaus he accompanied Christa Ludwig and Walter Berry in an evening of Mahler songs which prompted comparisons with Bruno Walter and Gustav Mahler himself. At the Volksoper he received an ovation when he attended a performance of *West Side Story,* with Julia Migenes as Maria, in a translation by the ever-faithful Marcel Prawy. Meanwhile word spread through Vienna about Bernstein's common touch. At the Atrium night club, *Newsweek* noted, "he peeled off his jacket, loosened his tie and frugged far into the night."

Felicia came to the opera premiere but stayed for only five days. While she still found the Viennese atmosphere of hand-wringing adulation somewhat oppressive, her husband thrived on it. He was made an honorary member of the Gesellschaft der Musikfreunde, and received a prize from the Vienna Loyalty Club. His name was even put forward as a candidate to become artistic director of the Vienna State Opera—the job Mahler had held for ten years. "I am through with attaching myself to institutions," he responded. "I need time to compose." But he admitted to *Newsweek* that his Viennese month had been *"himmel"*—heaven.

Another episode in the simmering rivalry between Bernstein and Karajan took place in the spring of 1968. After his return from Vienna, Bernstein conducted a concert performance of Act I of *Die Walküre* as part of the New York Philharmonic's retrospective 125th season. Six months earlier the Metropolitan Opera had imported Karajan's Salzburg production of the entire *Die Walküre*. Harold Schonberg compared the two conductors in his review of the Bernstein concert, in which Eileen Farrell, Jess Thomas and Michael Langdon were the soloists:

> The Karajan approach had as much Karajan as Wagner. It was a scaled-down, almost chamber-music *Walküre* . . . notable for its refinement and detail of texture. But was it the rich, surging Wagner we remember from the past? Many thought not. It remained for Leonard Bernstein last night to restore the dramatic, romantic Wagner. In recent years Mr. Bernstein has been turning more and more toward opera, though this was the first time he has conducted so lengthy a Wagnerian sequence. And it was brilliant. The playing was textually note-perfect, in that every marking in the score was scrupulously observed, every note value adhered to, every dynamic faithfully followed. But in addition to all this, there was an unusual degree of tension and excitement. Mr. Bernstein's dynamic palette was very wide. This is the way Wagner should sound and Mr. Bernstein's avoidance of artificial effects was testimony to his continued growth as a musician.

Only days after the Wagner concert an event occurred to confirm Bernstein's pessimistic mood about the future of civilization. Early in the morning of June 6 Robert Kennedy was assassinated in Los Angeles. Jacqueline Kennedy called Bernstein later that day to ask him to supervise the music for the funeral at St. Patrick's Cathedral in New York. With some trepidation, Bernstein accepted the request. He persuaded the appropriate monsignor at the cathedral to agree to the inclusion of the "Adagietto" movement for strings and harp from Mahler's Fifth Symphony, but the soprano solo with unaccompanied chorus from the last movement of Verdi's *Requiem* was vetoed because women were not allowed to sing at St. Patrick's. While Bernstein was talking to the priest, Jacqueline Kennedy telephoned again, this time from the presidential Boeing 707. She informed him that she was on her way back to New York, and that she was sitting next to Robert Kennedy's widow, her sister-in-law Ethel, who had certain wishes about the funeral. One was that the nuns from her old school, Manhattanville, sing songs from her youth. "Well how am I going to get them [the monsignors] to allow nuns to sing if they won't allow female voices?" Bernstein asked. "You can tell them that's Ethel's wish," Mrs. Kennedy replied. Another wish of Ethel's was that her friend Andy Williams sing "The Battle Hymn of the Republic." Bernstein felt that he was being used as a messenger boy. He said he had to draw the line at Andy Williams.

At seven-thirty the next morning Ethel Kennedy visited the archbishop of New York at St. Patrick's, after which as Bernstein put it, "all the Monsignors flew about their duties: the Requiem was in, and the sopranos were in, and the Manhattanville nuns were in." Bernstein's two contributions were Mahler and Verdi—and, as he understood it, his wishes had been obeyed in the matter of Andy Williams.

The day of the funeral started disconcertingly for Bernstein. "A telephone call came just as I was about to leave the house. I was told not to go to the cathedral until police detectives arrived—there had been a threat on my life. . . ." It was Bernstein's first death threat. " 'It's probably a crank call,' they said, 'but we can't take any chances.' I arrived at St. Patrick's surrounded by detectives and plainclothesmen. [Incongruously, the Secret Service men were searching the violin cases of the Philharmonic musicians, but not their pockets.] I was greeted by an assistant manager of the Philharmonic with the news that Andy Williams was in the choir loft and had been there since 7:00 that morning."

It was, Bernstein recalled, a beautiful service. "The Mahler part of it was made more beautiful by the Kennedy children's procession up to the altar carrying the Communion articles. . . . The Verdi also sounded very beautiful sung from the choir loft. Then came the big surprise of the day: suddenly this lone voice issued from the choir singing 'The Battle Hymn of the Republic.' Partly because it was so unexpected, partly because it was so simple, it turned out to be *the* smash of the funeral. I say this in my own disfavor because I would have done anything I could to avoid it."

THAT summer Bernstein stayed at home in Fairfield most days writing music for *The Exception and the Rule,* a one-act Brecht morality play about racial exploitation that Jerome Robbins had persuaded Bernstein to consider as the basis for a new serious Broadway musical. His children became so bored by his interminable recounting of the plot when visitors called, and by his grumblings about insomnia, that they took a sweet revenge at the cabaret they put together for his fiftieth birthday party. In one sketch the author, Jamie, played herself and Alexander played his father.

(Enter Daddy)

J:  Good morning, Daddy. How'd you sleep?

D:  TERRIBLE. I went to bed at two, tried to sleep, got up, raided the ice box, watched the Late Late Show, watched the dawn come up, and finally around 6:30, I fell asleep.

J:  Didn't you take anything?

D:  I took EVERYTHING.

J:  You mean like:

(To the tune of "Another Opening, Another Show")

Effedrin, Milltown and Placidyl
Then Noludar and Suponéryl
Then Seconal Nembutal and then
The NTZ Nose Spray's at work again!

You wake up groggy and drugged to here
You wonder how you'll get through the year
And then at breakfast what could that be?
It's Theragran and Vitamin C!

But there's one drug that keeps you alive
It gives you pep, stamina and drive
Unroll the carpet and roll the drums
For indigestion's foe, a pack of Tums!

The Bernsteins appeared to be as happy a family unit as one could imagine. "As this horrifying birthday approaches," he had told a *Time* reporter, "I feel better than I have in a long time. . . . I play better tennis. I have more endurance. I'm happier in spite of the thoroughly ghastly state of the world. I feel that I have enough energy to do what it is I am going to do." But Thomas Cole, in a fiftieth-birthday profile for the *New York Times,* sent out a contradictory signal: "The television glamor cliché evaporates and you see a pair of soft, almost painfully sensitive brown eyes [actually hazel]. . . . [They appeared] wounded, like those of a man who always says yes to life no matter what. . . . The strong large nose and craggy jaw strike a note of strength and the wavy, greying hair lends coolness, dignity." Cole detected in Bernstein many ambivalences and opposites: "Longing and resignation blend with sturdy health, exhaustion with vitality, the burned out with the still burning. At fifty he's looking towards seventy and racing his engine."

⟩⟨⟨

ON August 22, shortly after the Soviet Union invaded Czechoslovakia, the New York Philharmonic set off on a five-week goodwill tour of Western Europe. Jamie and Alexander traveled with their father; Felicia stayed behind with Nina at Fairfield to work for Senator McCarthy. America was much less popular in Europe than it had been at the time of the orchestra's previous grand tour in 1959: after five years of the war in Vietnam and the agonies of the civil rights battle at home, Bernstein could no longer play the role of pugnacious fighter for democratic freedom. Instead, the tour stressed the quality of the Philharmonic's music-making. Two basic programs were given, one featuring Mahler's Fifth Symphony, the other the *Symphonie Fantastique* by Berlioz. The twenty-four European concerts were all conducted by Bernstein himself, except for two performances of William Schuman's Third Symphony, which he handed over to Alain Lombard, the tour's associate conductor. After Lombard conducted in Venice in Bernstein's place, false rumors flew round the musical world that Bernstein had had a heart attack, even though he returned after the intermission to do the Berlioz.

Belgium was the orchestra's first destination and Bernstein celebrated his fiftieth birthday at the Hilton Hotel in Brussels. Norman Rosten composed a consolatory poem for him:

> *Relax, friend it's only fifty*
> *Ten big ones short of sixty.*
> *You can still bend and touch your knees,*
> *When you run you do not wheeze*
> *And what is even more rare:*
> *You've got your own teeth and hair.*
> *So on your day in dear old Brussels*
> *Take a bow and flex your muscles.*

Appreciations were published in many American and German newspapers. Perhaps the most generous, in view of his past antagonism, came from the critic Alan Rich: "For all his flaws as a conductor, for all the aura of slickness which surrounds his work as a salesman for the art of music, there is in Bernstein a blend of artistic integrity and tangibility that has given to music in his time of activity a transfusion badly needed. . . . His own youth touched other youth and brought them once again into contact with musical excitement."

Such high-flown phrases were no consolation to an apparently despairing Bernstein on the morning of his birthday. Ernest Fleischmann of CBS Records was keeping at bay what he described as a "fifty-strong mob" of media people in the hotel lobby when he received a call. "Lenny wanted me to come up to his suite and have breakfast with him. He was looking terrible. . . . [He had been up to the small hours the night before at a party in Bruges.] 'Here I am at fifty and I have nothing to show for it,' he cried, beating his breast. For well over two hours I was there consoling him."

The New York Philharmonic's European tour also included its first-ever visit to Israel. At Caesarea they played in the spectacularly sited Roman amphitheater, where the moon dipped into the Mediterranean to the accompaniment of the "Adagietto" from Mahler's Fifth Symphony. On the flight from Israel to Italy, Bernstein, Jamie and Alexander read in a newspaper about Eugene McCarthy's defeat at the Democratic Convention in Chicago, and the shocking police violence that had accompanied it. "All three," Evelyn Ames, the wife of the president of the New York Philharmonic, recalled, "were in tears of rage and grief and stunned horror." Bernstein's pacifist position was not endorsed at the Democratic Convention. Delegates voted three to two against a policy of immediate peace.

When the orchestra played in Germany, some of the players were uneasy. William Lincer, the principal viola player, said to the *New York Times* in Bonn, "They gave flowers to Mr. Bernstein today. Twenty-five years ago they probably killed fifty of his relatives. I can't wait to leave." But the Germans loved Bernstein. Three thousand people turned up for his record-signing session at Ka De We, the biggest store in West Berlin. Ernest Fleischmann had persuaded his CBS colleagues to market the new recording of the Berlioz *Symphonie Fantastique* at a bargain price; more than two hundred thousand copies were sold in Germany in a month.

Only in London was there still a pocket of resistance to Bernstein's conducting charisma. The audience gave him an ovation of "frenzied proportions" but the critic Eric Mason thought the Berlioz *Symphonie Fantastique* was "too high—in the drug addict's sense—by half: horribly vulgar, often distorted." Henry Pleasants suggested that Bernstein conducted Berlioz as one imagined Booth or Irving to have played Hamlet. The *Telegraph* critic Anthony Payne grumbled, as only an Englishman could, that there was "too much brilliance and excitement, too often achieved at the expense of formal clarity." Five days later, at the opening of Bernstein's last New York season, Harold Schonberg disagreed. "The orchestra was in splendid shape. Mr. Bernstein has learned to curb his natural ebullience."

In November 1968 John Gruen's book, *The Private World of Leonard Bernstein,* was published. "Look, it's Lenny doing push ups!" was Donal Henahan's quip in the *Times.* An Atlanta, Georgia, review said Gruen's text had "all the judgment of a teenage autograph hound" and added that Ken Heyman's photographs—Bernstein shaving, Charlie Chaplin dancing, the family running through autumnal woods at Fairfield—were embarrassingly banal. In fact, Heyman's photographs are remarkable for their tenderness and intimacy. The embarrassment came from seeing famous people apparently so keen for publicity that they would allow a photographer to watch them do everything but perform their bodily functions. There were hard feelings, too, about the book's revelation that Artur Rodzinski had once tried to throttle Bernstein. Rodzinski's son Richard wrote to the *Times* asking how somebody of Bernstein's stature could stoop so low as to speak ungenerously about the man who had done so much to help his career. Without consulting Gruen, Bernstein responded to the *Times* that the inclusion of such material was due to an editorial function over which he had very little control before he left for Europe. But Gruen recalls offering to let Bernstein see the text. Since everything Bernstein told Gruen about Rodzinski was true (and has since been corroborated by an eyewitness, David Diamond, and by Rodzinski's widow) he might have done better to stand by his friend instead of seeking to repudiate him. On the morning Bernstein's letter was published Gruen telephoned him to remonstrate. "Lenny, you *said* those things." Gruen remembers Bernstein's cavalier reply: " 'Well, you know, I choose to do what I choose to do. Please don't dictate to me how I must answer my letters.' A great coolness descended between us for a long time."

Helen Coates spelled out the party line. "There is much in the book that we do not like. Lots of things that Lenny talked about . . . were only meant for background. As Lenny said, the book was not supposed to be about his past, but about his present and future. There are no pictures from the past in the book, so why should there be any discussion of it? Lenny saw the galleys of the book twice and asked for many things to be cut out, but the last time he saw it was the night before he left on the tour and then he never knew how much they really did take out."

It is a lame defense. Bernstein cannot have been so disingenuous as to believe that the interviews Gruen was taping day after day were for background only. Bernstein's account of his childhood and early career is fundamental to an understanding of the man he became. Had Bernstein been worried before he left for Europe, he could have insisted that his approval be delegated to his lawyer or his wife. As published, the book is a useful document in the American tradition of full-length reportage, but it falls between the two stools of biography and coffee-table gossip.

THE fall of 1968 marked the climax of Bernstein's professional partnership with one of his favorite singers. In October Dietrich Fischer-Dieskau sang the *Kindertotenlieder* with the New York Philharmonic, and on November 8 the two men gave a memorable recital of Mahler songs to raise funds for UNICEF. "To have Bernstein behind you in the concert hall at the grand piano," Fischer-Dieskau recalled in his autobiography, meant "not 'accompaniment' in the usual sense but something more like the 'Tiger Rag.' Between his hands and the keyboard . . . an electrified zone is created; it seems as if he were advancing into a dangerous area that gives him no choice but to fight or flee. When we were recording the Mahler *Lieder* in New York he had five concert grands set up in a circle and he moved—more or less outraged—to the next instrument as soon as he found something to dislike in the mechanics of the previous one. During a concert, as if reluctant to start playing out of the blue, he will always let his hands glide silently across the keys while the audience is still applauding. But then there is one electric shock after another—continually paraphrased *rubati,* always surprising coloration, something exceedingly intimate and yet extending far beyond the edge of the stage—and the singers must prove themselves the match for these if they are to succeed."

Bernstein had planned to devote November and December to the completion of *The Exception and the Rule.* He had already worked on it for a year, first with Jerry Lieber (the lyricist famous for writing "Hound Dog" and other Elvis Presley hits), and then with Stephen Sondheim and the young playwright John Guare. Zero Mostel was engaged to be the star of a cast consisting for the most part of black singers. But it was another promising musical project that withered on the vine. Helen Coates noted in December that her boss was in a deep depression, just as he had been in 1964 when *The Skin of Our Teeth* was dropped.

At the end of December he flew to Rome to discuss with Franco Zeffirelli the idea of writing a musical film about St. Francis of Assisi. Their concept was for a film in which music would play a leading rather than a secondary role—Bernstein's old dream from the days of *The Beckoning Fair One* in 1946. But he wouldn't commit himself to it until he could approve a script.

Back at the Philharmonic he had his last brush with the American avant-garde during his musical directorship when in January 1969 he conducted the world premiere of Milton Babbitt's *Relata II.* The piece had been commissioned by the Philharmonic, but there were so many copyist's errors in the original parts that its premiere had been postponed from the previous October. "I have tried to exploit the most subtle resources of a most sophisticated orchestra," Babbitt told the *New York Times,* "but rather than flattering the musicians by giving them a challenging score, I managed only to anger them considerably." Babbitt underlined the point Bernstein had been making for a decade about contemporary music: "The regular Philharmonic audience does not want to hear this piece. And why should they have to? How can it be coherent for them? It's as though a philosophy colleague of mine were to read his paper on the Johnny Carson show. The milieu is inappropriate for the event."

Bernstein persevered. He made extra time for rehearsals, and to keep the musicians cheerful he devised a limerick composition, with one hundred dollars as the first prize. He gave as the opening couplet:

> *There was a composer named Babbitt*
> *Who had a peculiar habit.*

Martin Eshelman, one of the Philharmonic's second violins, contributed the winning lines:

> *Each day around noon,*
> *He'd go into a swoon*
> *Scoring piece after piece like a rabbit.*

The last few months of Bernstein's reign was a rich period in the Philharmonic's history. He conducted Bruckner's Ninth Symphony, Beethoven's *Missa Solemnis* and the Verdi *Requiem*. And as part of his continuing survey of Wagner's music dramas, he mounted a whole evening of scenes from *Tristan und Isolde* with Jess Thomas and Eileen Farrell as soloists.

Early in April Sam Bernstein, whose health had been failing for seven years, suffered a series of heart attacks. Jennie nursed him night and day. "Only she knew how many slices of banana he preferred on his Cream of Wheat," wrote her son Burton in *Family Matters;* "only she understood what he meant when he said, 'My legs are drawing.' " Sam died, with Jennie holding his hand, on April 30, 1969, at the age of seventy-seven.

His funeral eulogy at Temple Mishkan Tefila was spoken by Rabbi Israel Kazis, who had officiated at Leonard's wedding and Alexander's Bar Mitzvah. When the rabbi defined Sam's Judaism by describing its Hasidic roots he might have been describing Leonard Bernstein at the podium: "This form of worship evokes the complete involvement of the individual—his mind in contemplation, his heart in love, his voice in song and his limbs in dance—the resultant experience is one of exquisite joy reflected in radiant face and a quickened spirit."

Bernstein shared his sadness with the Philharmonic subscribers. In Sam's honor he rescheduled his program to include his own *Jeremiah* Symphony, which had been dedicated to Sam. In the second half he conducted the Second Symphony of Robert Schumann, a particular favorite of his father's. Bernstein conducted, said Harriett Johnson, "with quiet, eloquent intensity."

In the space of a few weeks he lost his father and said farewell to the most important job of his life. He was prepared for the death because of Sam's long illness, and he publicly longed to relinquish the Philharmonic's administration, but when the final concerts were upon him there was a powerful underswirl of emotion with which to come to terms. It was over twenty-five years since his Philharmonic debut. He had conducted more than eight hundred concerts as music director, including thirty-six world premieres. If his era had to be remembered for just one achievement it would be for his interpretations of the orchestral works of Gustav Mahler, and it was with Mahler's Third Symphony that he chose to say good-bye.

"In the performance," wrote Leighton Kerner in *The Village Voice,* "the finale spun on as if conductor and orchestra, and indeed the audience, were refusing to let it go. Finally it did vanish and in the first long burst of applause Mr. Bernstein did not turn to the audience but stood facing his orchestra for what seemed like more than a minute. It was as if their years together were being remembered in private silence—no words spoken, just glances back and forth and more than one hundred musicians with no more cues to be given and the cheers from the audience perhaps unheard."

Amyas Ames, David Keiser's successor as the orchestra's president, presented the laureate conductor with a four-foot-high laurel wreath. (The board's gift was a nineteen-foot Chris-Craft motorboat named *Laureate*.) The poet Archibald MacLeish sang Bernstein's praises in a prose poem, describing him as "one of the very few who have truly *lived* an art in these days." MacLeish ended by quoting Rilke: *"Du musst dein Leben ändern"* (You must change your life). Such was Bernstein's vowed intention.

At the postconcert party, Bernstein expressed his chagrin that he had not thanked the orchestra while he was still on the platform. "I just couldn't find a word. I was too moved. But I should have said something about . . . the most sophisticated orchestra in the world." He had already said good-bye to them at a private party the previous afternoon; the players had presented him with a silver and gold *mezuzah,* inscribed with lines from Deuteronomy. The *mezuzah* is the symbol of faith fixed by Jews to the doorposts of their homes. The orchestra was telling him that the Philharmonic remained his home.

The music directorship had been an anchor for Leonard Bernstein. For the rest of his life, for better or worse, he was on his own.

Mike Mindlin was among the group of somewhat nostalgic friends who lingered in Bernstein's dressing room after the final concert. It was already known in backstage circles that Pierre Boulez, the serialist composer and conductor, would become music director, although not until 1971. At the moment Bernstein was finally ready to depart, Mindlin appeared from the lavatory, carrying four toilet rolls and some hand towels. "We leave Boulez *nothing,"* he said triumphantly, as he marched to the door. The Bernstein era was at an end.

# PART FIVE

*London, 1977.*
PHOTO: ANNETTE LEDERER, COURTESY OF DEUTSCHE GRAMMOPHON, HAMBURG

# 1969–1978

# COMING APART

# RADICAL CHIC

*With Black Panther "field marshal" Donald*
*Cox at the Bernsteins' apartment, 1970.*
PHOTO STEVEN SALMIERI

*Everybody has talent at twenty-five. The difficulty is*
*to have it at fifty.*

—EDGAR DEGAS

I N a bird's eye view of Bernstein's life, his twenties and forties can be seen as conducting decades, while his thirties were largely devoted to composition. In his fifties he established an equilibrium: he kept his links with the New York Philharmonic and built up even stronger ones with the Vienna Philharmonic, but he also composed more. His output was neither as substantial nor as immediately successful as in his thirties, but it included two big theater works, a song symphony and a ballet. He enjoyed tremendous success as a conductor, broke fresh ground in the field of television and returned to an old role as university professor. Yet his fifties were to end in tragedy and despair.

O N May 18, 1969, the night after his farewell concert as music director, Bernstein plunged into the world of rock for a few hours when he attended a Jimi Hendrix concert. Next day he flew to Vienna to conduct Beethoven's *Missa Solemnis* for the Vienna State Opera House's centenary. Hendrix and Beethoven made a potent juxtaposition. Bernstein's creative juices often flowed on long air journeys. He had had his first insight of what *Candide* might become on a 1953 flight to Milan. Perhaps he began to plan his *Mass* while heading for Vienna: he eventually decided to write a work for the opening of the Kennedy Center in which rock music would be interwoven with a setting of the Catholic Mass.

Although he had accepted no official post in Vienna, Bernstein had become, in three years, a leading personality in Austrian musical life. The Austrian President and Chancellor were at the Staatsoper for the *Missa Solemnis,* along with such great singers of the past as Lotte Lehmann and Ljuba Welitsch, each sitting in her rose-bedecked box. "EKSTASE, EXZESS, EXALTATION" was one of the newspaper headlines summing up Bernstein's interpretation. He entertained princesses and cardinals in his loge after each of his three performances, while Franco Zeffirelli bombarded him from Rome with pleas to come and work on the St. Francis film project. Bernstein was interested only if he could do every-thing together from the beginning. "I wouldn't call it an opera. I suppose it may just develop into a new art form," he said. "I'm not just writing the score. I've had that." Unfortunately ideas did not come easily. Each year he seemed to take a little longer to switch to a composing state of mind at the end of a conducting period. "There is a certain amount of decompression that has to take place between one and the other," he explained, but he was rarely to leave himself enough time to make the transition.

He spent the first half of June with Zeffirelli in Italy and in July Zeffirelli came to stay at Fairfield. According to Bernstein a lot of music got written, but they continued to disagree about the script, and three months later Bernstein withdrew: when Zeffirelli eventually made the story of St. Francis, as *Brother Sun, Sister Moon,* Bernstein was replaced as the composer of the score by the singer and songwriter Donovan. The medieval hippies who would have been featured in the Bernstein version of the film found a place as the unruly "street people" in his next theater work, *Mass.*

St. Francis had another link with *Mass.* In the summer of 1969 Bernstein invited Paul Simon, the immensely popular composer and lyricist, to collaborate on writing songs for his film project. Simon, who had never written works for somebody else's music before, recalls going to Bernstein's Fairfield studio in some trepidation. "He played a melody and asked me what I thought. I said, 'It's fine.' He said, 'If we're going to collaborate, you really have to be honest and say what you think.' So I said, 'I think it's lousy. It's just generic rock and roll. Why would you be writing that? Everybody wrote that ten years ago.' I think he was surprised. 'I don't know why you said that. This is not generic rock and roll. This is Leonard Bernstein music.' I said, 'Okay, well it's great, I can write to that.' "

The partnership with Simon did not prosper, but a year later Bernstein telephoned to ask if he could use part of a lyric he had found among Simon's sketches. Simon gave him the rights as a Christmas present in return for an acknowledgment (duly made on page 112 of the score) and a pair of opening night tickets—which Bernstein forgot to deliver. Simon's lines were among the most frequently quoted in *Mass:*

> *Half of the people are stoned*
> *And the other half are waiting for the next election.*
> *Half the people are drowned*
> *And the other half are swimming in the wrong direction.*

On the rebound from St. Francis, Bernstein had still not settled down to write *Mass* when in November 1969 the Israeli actor Chaim Topol came to him with a proposal to turn Brecht's *The Caucasian Chalk Circle* into a musical. "I was immediately at the piano," Bernstein remembered, "and found myself writing music and re-adapting the original Brecht lyrics." He wrote half a dozen of the thirty songs envisaged. They never saw the light of day. Topol persisted for six months but couldn't pull a production together. Bernstein's infatuation with Brecht waned once he had determined on a structure for *Mass.* "Is the world waiting for another Bernstein masterpiece?" he asked mockingly in January 1970. Roger Stevens at the Kennedy Center certainly was, and the further postponement of its opening, to September 1971, gave him the breathing space he needed.

False starts on the creative front were mirrored by several blows to Bernstein's public reputation. The first came in October, when the City Commission on Human Rights ruled that the New York Philharmonic had discriminated against black musicians in its employment policy. As Bernstein saw it, the episode would have been "farcical had it not been heartbreakingly bad." Two black freelance musicians who had been turned down for permanent posts by the Philharmonic charged that the orchestra's audition policy during Bernstein's directorship discriminated against black musicians. Bernstein testified that only 7 blacks had been among the 250 string players who had applied to fill vacancies in the orchestra. The two in question had been invited to play at the final audition even though they had failed or could not attend the preliminary round. They had asked to be heard in a "blindfold" test, playing behind screens, but Bernstein had insisted on upholding the Philharmonic policy that candidates should be seen as well as heard. It was essential, he said, to be able to observe the candidate's physical technique. Neither of the black musicians had been chosen. In his evidence Bernstein explained that any potential player for the New York Philharmonic would have to undergo a long apprenticeship. He would need "money, guidance, orientation, psychological preparedness, psychological optimism." Not enough young black students, he felt, were being encouraged to undertake such a rigorous preparation. "You're saying that society is guilty, not the New York Philharmonic?" "We're all guilty as members of the society we inhabit, yes." But Bernstein had spoken up for black orchestral musicians as early as the 1940s. He had approved a black conductor for *On the Town* in 1945, appointed a black assistant conductor, James de Preist, at the

Philharmonic in 1965, regularly hired black soloists and frequently argued publicly for reforms in the education system. He had appointed a black violinist, Sanford Allen, to the Philharmonic in 1962. Sad though it was, he felt the other black applicants he had auditioned were simply not good enough to be part of the country's premier orchestra. The musicians lost their case. The commission found a pattern of bias in the way substitutes were hired, but not in the Philharmonic's audition procedures.

In the fall the Juilliard School moved into its new Lincoln Center quarters two blocks north of Philharmonic Hall. As a loyal supporter of Juilliard, Bernstein gamely decided that his first Philharmonic program in January 1970, a concert performance of Beethoven's *Fidelio* marking Beethoven's bicentennial, should be sung by students from Juilliard's new American Opera faculty. It would be a useful dry-run for Bernstein, who had agreed to conduct *Fidelio* at the 1970 Vienna Festival. And there was an underlying political relevance in the opera to which Bernstein referred in a "Young People's Concert" about the opera. *Fidelio* was, he said, "a celebration of human rights, of freedom to speak out, to dissent, a political manifesto against tyranny and oppression." Dissent had been part of Bernstein's recent activity. In November 1969 he had gone to Washington to take part in the great moratorium against Vietnam. In New York next day he joined Lauren Bacall, Ed Koch and many others in reading the names of U.S. soldiers killed in Vietnam from the pulpit of Riverside Church.

In the midst of preparations for the Philharmonic *Fidelio,* Bernstein was interrupted by another appeal from Franco Zeffirelli. A long strike had disrupted the fall season at the Metropolitan Opera. Now that it was resolved Zeffirelli was determined to rescue his new production of the *"Cav* and *Pag"* double bill. His original casts had long dispersed and Thomas Schippers, the conductor, now had another commitment. Would Bernstein please come and rescue them? Bernstein, who could never resist a challenge, agreed to take on *Cavalleria Rusticana.* For the rest of December he rehearsed the *Fidelio* singers in the mornings, and the *Cavalleria* singers, among them Franco Corelli and Grace Bumbry, in the afternoons. He announced that he had completely restudied the opera. "I've worked and written and changed and erased and thrown out junk that's accumulated, the encrustation of generations of what are called traditions." He considered his musical archaeology sufficient reason to suggest that the customary order of the operas be reversed. The stature of the work was what mattered, not the incidental fact that he would then take the final bow of the evening. But to mount an evening of *Pag* and *Cav* was not a practical possibility; the stage staff would need at least three quarters of an hour to build Zeffirelli's architecturally realistic Sicilian piazza. The request was quietly dropped. Whether played last or first, Bernstein's very measured interpretation would never have been a crowd-puller. *Pagliacci* (under the veteran conductor Fausto Cleva) was better liked but the beautiful production itself was the real star of this *Cav* and *Pag.*

Zeffirelli later criticized Bernstein's broad tempos for tending "dangerously towards self-indulgence," while Schonberg in the *Times* wrote that Bernstein had "somewhat devitalized the score" with his painfully slow speeds. Bernstein used an interview with John Gruen to strike back at such criticisms. "They wrote a lot of nonsense about why *Cavalleria* didn't work. . . . *Cavalleria* is more like a music drama and I tried to make . . . a big arch from beginning to end, discouraging applause. . . . I set tempi that attempt to give the work a stature and nobility it customarily lacks in performance." The timings were not as slow as Mascagni's own, he added; he had checked with an old recording. The defense was spirited but Bernstein did not conceal his disappointment. "Have you ever read such a collection of put-downs? When I read those reviews I suddenly realized why I do opera so rarely. Every time I do I swear never again! Because I forget that the best you can hope for is an approximation." This petulant outburst was totally unjustified by the facts: his two *Falstaffs* and his Vienna *Rosenkavalier* had been received with almost unanimous enthusiasm.

Bernstein's reviews for *Fidelio* a week later were as bad as those for *Cavalleria*. Although he loyally announced that he was proud of his Juilliard singers, the *Post*'s critic, Harriett Johnson, felt they were hopelessly out of their depth and Schonberg in the *Times* suggested that it was unprofessional to put such inexperienced artists into so difficult an opera.

On January 14, the day before *Fidelio*'s first performance at the Philharmonic, Bernstein had two rehearsals for the opera, followed by an informal meeting with Tanglewood's manager at that time, Harry Kraut. He casually invited Kraut to a meeting his wife was holding at their apartment. The two men drove across Central Park to 895 Park Avenue, arriving late but not too late for Bernstein to put his foot in things in a way he was never allowed to forget.

In the 1960s Felicia Bernstein had become active in civil rights causes. She had helped to found a women's division of the New York branch of the American Civil Liberties Union. (She had also demonstrated against the Vietnam War and supported many other causes, including indigent Chileans, Israeli student scholarships, Church World Service and a Greek boys' school.) Recently she had become concerned with the issues of civil liberty underlying the nine-month detention of twenty-one Black Panthers awaiting trial on charges of plotting to kill policemen and bomb midtown police stations, department stores and railroad facilities. The Panthers were a revolutionary group organized in military style, anti-Zionist, and violently opposed to discrimination against African-Americans. The legal outrage, as Felicia Bernstein and her group saw it, was that the bail of one hundred thousand dollars set on ten of the Panthers was so high as to be tantamount to preventive detention. Because the defendants were Black Panthers they were being denied a fair trial; they were being kept in solitary confinement and were without resources to organize their defense. Moreover, their wives and children needed support.

Felicia organized a meeting at which drinks and canapés were to be served before guests moved into the living room to hear speeches and an appeal for funds for the legal defense of the imprisoned "twenty-one." Ninety people turned up at 895 Park Avenue; among them were several Panthers and their wives, show business friends and black civic leaders, one of whom arrived with four bodyguards. Because the Bernsteins never gave big parties, there was considerable social cachet attached to the invitation and many more guests appeared than had been anticipated. The room was uncomfortably crowded.

Leon Quat, one of the lawyers representing the Panthers, got off to a bad start, pronouncing Felicia's name "Mrs. Bernsteen," and was loudly corrected— BernSTINE!—from the back of the room by the maestro himself, who had just arrived. Quat's attempt at humor was awkward and it was a relief when he introduced "field marshal" Donald Cox, who described the Black Panthers' ten-point political program, "handed down" by its "minister of defense," Huey P. Newton. Cox's presentation soft-pedaled violence and ended with a quote from the Declaration of Independence. Then the Panthers' chief counsel, Gerald Lefcourt, a white man, compared the situation in the United States to prewar events in Germany when the Nazis used the burning down of the Reichstag as the pretext for eliminating opposition parties. When pledges were requested, the grand total of contributions raised from guests, who included Otto Preminger, Sheldon Harnick, Burton Lane and Mrs. Harry Belafonte, was nearly ten thousand dollars. "As the guest of my wife," Bernstein called out, "I'll give my fee for the next performance of *Cavalleria Rusticana*. I hope that will be four figures." [It was actually two thousand dollars.]

The meeting might have passed off as just another *New York Times* "Chronicle" story about caring New Yorkers doing something to help the less fortunate had Felicia not made two miscalculations in her arrangements. She had welcomed members of the press, including Tom Wolfe, and she had not kept her husband away. Charlotte Curtis, the social editor, covered the event for the *New York Times*. Among other choice tidbits, Curtis heard Henry Mitchell, a "Harlem Panther defense captain," swapping complaints about the New York telephone service with Cynthia Phipps, one of the richest women in America. Mitchell's problem, he said, was that his line was tapped by the FBI.

Bernstein stood at the back of the proceedings until the pledges were in place. He had described himself as a guest but he could not resist taking over the questions. He moved forward close to Donald Cox and suddenly Charlotte Curtis had a scoop for next morning's *New York Times*.

> Leonard Bernstein and a Black Panther leader argued the merits of the Black Panther party's philosophy before nearly 90 guests at a cocktail party last night in the Bernsteins' elegant Park Avenue duplex.
>
> The conductor laureate of the New York Philharmonic did most of the questioning. Donald Cox, the Panther field-marshal and a member of

the party's central committee, did most of the answering, and there were even moments when both men were not talking at the same time.

"Now about your goals," Mr. Bernstein said from the depths of an armchair. "I'm not sure I understand how you're going to achieve them. I mean what are your tactics?"

Mr. Cox, a tall, handsome man in a black turtleneck sweater and gray pants, nodded his head.

"If business won't give us full employment," he said slowly, "then we must take the means of production and put them in the hands of the people."

"I dig absolutely," Mr. Bernstein said.

The phrase "I dig absolutely" was quoted out of context, according to a memorandum Bernstein prepared a week later. The word "dig," he said, was not part of his vocabulary. "The much less spicy truth is that the Panther Cox, in reply to a provocative question I had put to him, had ended his exposition with the question, 'You dig?' I, having dug little if anything of his non-philosophy, echoed somewhat impatiently, 'Yes, I dig absolutely. Go on.' " But Bernstein's explanation was never circulated to the press. Felicia had already written a strong letter to the *Times* but so much damage had been done in the intervening days that it was presumably deemed best to say nothing more.

Charlotte Curtis's report, a full page in the city edition, set tongues wagging gleefully all over Manhattan. To add to the embarrassment, the *Times*'s wire service relayed the story abroad. It appeared that Leonard Bernstein, the man who was said to have operated a color bar at the Philharmonic and allowed himself to be photographed in his underpants for a coffee table book, was now revealed as a naive bumbler who hobnobbed with terrorists.

Bernstein conducted the first of four performances of *Fidelio* on the evening of the Charlotte Curtis bombshell. He awoke next day to read not only Harold Schonberg's bad review but a hostile *Times* editorial as well:

FALSE NOTE ON BLACK PANTHERS

Emergence of the Black Panthers as the romanticized darlings of the politico-cultural jet set is an affront to the majority of black Americans. This so-called party, with its confusion of Mao-Marxist ideology and Fascist para-militarism, is fully entitled to protection of its members' constitutional rights. . . . [But] the group therapy plus fund-raising soirée at the home of Leonard Bernstein, as reported in this newspaper yesterday, represents the sort of elegant slumming that degrades patrons and patronized alike. It might be dismissed as guilt-relieving fun spiked with social consciousness, except for its impact on those blacks and whites seriously working for complete equality and social justice. It mocked the memory of Martin Luther King, Jr., whose birthday was solemnly observed throughout the nation yesterday.

Black Panthers on a Park Avenue pedestal create one more distortion of the Negro image. Responsible black leadership is not likely to cheer as the Beautiful People create a new myth that Black Panther Is Beautiful.

The irony was that until Charlotte Curtis's article came out, the Bernsteins thought they had done well. Their daughter Jamie, then seventeen, remembers they were "relieved it was over, and happy, and my mother was sitting in my father's lap. They felt they had done something worthwhile. And then all this terrible shit happened." Jews all across America—and in Israel, too—were stunned by what they saw as Bernstein's endorsement of the Black Panthers' anti-Semitism. The right-wing Jewish Defense League picketed the Bernsteins' Park Avenue apartment, and the Bernsteins received hate letters through the mail. Jewish subscribers booed Bernstein at the Philharmonic.

To the genuine anger felt by some was added the malevolent and destabilizing influence of the FBI director, J. Edgar Hoover, who gave instructions that guests who had attended the party should be traced and then sent anonymous letters outlining "the Black Panthers' anti-Semitic policy." In 1980, when this directive was revealed, Bernstein issued a memorandum to the press stating that FBI harassment included "floods of hate letters sent to me over what are now clearly fictitious signatures, thinly-veiled threats, couched in anonymous letters to magazines and newspapers . . . attempts to influence my long-standing relationship with the people of the State of Israel, plus innumerable other Dirty Tricks. None of these machinations has adversely affected my life or my work," he added, "but they did cause a great deal of unpleasantness to my wife who was more vulnerable than I to smear tactics."

Burton Bernstein had refused to attend the meeting. He blamed Felicia for the debacle and says that his friendship with his sister-in-law never recovered. Bernstein himself was heard privately agreeing that it was Felicia's fault though he loyally supported her in public and wrote angry letters of justification to the press. But although Bernstein did not organize the meeting, he had hogged the limelight too much not to assume some responsibility for it. He might have perceived that publicity was of dubious value on such a delicate issue, and could have instructed the freelance photographer to stop taking photographs and Charlotte Curtis to stop taking notes.

The most damning criticism came to the Bernsteins privately a month later in a letter from his old friend Rabbi Judah Cahn. It points to a basic flaw in Bernstein's stated position: he cannot have been fully aware that the Black Panthers were anti-Zionist. "As one who loves you deeply," wrote Cahn, "I needed no letter explaining why you called a meeting. . . . I knew that you were motivated by the highest ethical imperatives. . . . We should continue to support the American Civil Liberties Union, whose purpose it is to defend the rights of those who exercise unpopular causes. . . . I will fight for the right of the Panthers to a just trial . . . [but] frankly I would not open my home and ask my friends to make special contributions to their cause."

Bernstein suffered considerable loss of face. Within days of the event William F. Buckley, Jr., was having fun at his expense. "HAVE A PANTHER TO LUNCH," his column in the *Post* was headed. "A dialogue with a Black Panther is every bit as difficult to perform as a symphony by Schoenberg." James A. Wechsler, another *Post* columnist, fought back on Bernstein's behalf. "If that party on Park Avenue gave some of [the Panthers] a sense that we are not all in a massive search-and-destroy operation, it was not a frivolous exercise regardless of who said what to whom." Meanwhile, the journalist Tom Wolfe was working away at a twenty-five-thousand-word article for *New York* magazine: it would explode like a time bomb at the beginning of June.

Through all the furor Bernstein continued his five-week season with the Philharmonic, conducting two world premieres, *In Praise of Shahn* by William Schuman and Elliott Carter's *Concerto for Orchestra*. For his annual Wagner evening he conducted excerpts from *Götterdämmerung*. As he made his way into Philharmonic Hall through hostile pickets he must have breathed a sigh of relief that his father was not alive to see Leonard Bernstein being attacked for his alleged anti-Semitism—and while conducting the anti-Semitic Wagner of all composers. After one of the concerts he braved the picket lines (on which B'nai B'rith, CORE and the NAACP were all represented) to take his new conductor friend, Michael Tilson Thomas, to supper at Trader Vic's. When the meal was over, Tilson Thomas recalls, Bernstein opened a fortune cookie. It read, "It takes brains to be a real fool."

WHEN Bernstein arrived in London on February 18 he gave no hint to his British colleagues and friends of the pressures to which he had recently been subjected. His batteries were recharged merely by exposure to a new group of musicians, and his phenomenal energy was if anything increased as he plunged into a series of concerts that took him to five capitals in five weeks. "It's really an insane schedule but what I need is blessed overwork. It gives me the lift I most need and I need it now."

In 1969 Bernstein had adopted a suggestion of his agent, Robbie Lantz, and formed a new company, Amberson Productions, to make videotapes and films of his performances. Schuyler Chapin left Lincoln Center to become the company's executive producer, and a video of Verdi's *Requiem* performed at St. Paul's Cathedral was the first performance recorded. Nobody knew whether music videos would have a commercial future, but London Weekend Television negotiated a co-production deal with Amberson and the British Musicians Union. Oliver Smith supervised the lighting for the telecast and designed the royal blue dais upon which Bernstein and the soloists stood.

The setting was breathtaking, but the project was enormously risky since only one performance could be scheduled and many things could go wrong. Sir Christopher Wren's imposing architecture was famous for its whispering gallery but the eight-second echo presented a technical nightmare. There were casting problems, too. Plácido Domingo flew in to substitute for the ailing Franco Corelli. "He asked me for a 'mixed' voice," Domingo remembers of Bernstein, rehearsing the tenor's "Hostias" solo. "It was difficult to find something half way between full voice and *falsetto* but he knew what he wanted. He encouraged me to make a crescendo and broaden the tempo on the trill. In the performance it came out like a five-four bar. Afterwards he told me I owed him a quarter."

There was time for only a brief sound check but the performance was an inspiring one, marred only momentarily by the awesome boom of the cathedral chimes striking ten as the soprano Martina Arroyo sang the "Libera Me." Bernstein was his customary drained self when it was all over. "I'd give anything for a cigarette," he groaned as he planned the retakes. Smoking was strictly forbidden on the cathedral precincts, but invoking "the unbelievable beauty" Bernstein had just given them, the dean made an exception and reached into his clerical pants to produce a cigarette lighter.

Retakes—impossible for a "live" telecast—are essential for a video. It's an agonizing procedure in which the mistakes of the performance—large and small—are redone with such precision that the viewer and listener are unable to detect editing splices in the final product. Perfection came slowly; the fifteen-minute overtime segments mounted up. The amateur chorus dwindled to half its size as singers had to slip off to catch the last train home. But the end result was handsome enough to confirm Amberson's decision to invest in music videos. "Much of the splendor of a very special occasion was conveyed," reported the *Times* after the Good Friday telecast.

Bernstein's next stop was Paris, followed by Rome, Tel Aviv and Vienna. Because Felicia had to rush back to New York to look after Jamie, who was having boyfriend trouble, Bernstein invited the young composer Phillip Ramey to act as his assistant. Ramey, then thirty, has mixed memories of the assignment. He had often done the same sort of job for Aaron Copland, whom he adored, but he found Bernstein less sympathetic. At a Zeffirelli party in Rome, at which Ramey was discussing a composition by Ottorino Respighi with the composer's widow, Bernstein leaned across and said, "Elsa, don't believe a word he says; he's just my assistant." But performing *Fidelio* in Rome put Bernstein into a radiant mood, and he had a new king and queen with whom to socialize: Constantine, the recently exiled Greek monarch, came to the rehearsals with his wife, Queen Anna Maria, the Danish-born princess whom Bernstein had met in Copenhagen two years earlier. Bernstein also made friends with the English actor Edmund Purdom—a fanatic music buff—and his photographer wife, Vivianne. Purdom complained to Ramey that Vivianne was pursuing Bernstein, but it was Ramey's impression that Bernstein was more attracted to Purdom. Without Felicia to watch over him, Bernstein was gravitating toward the "perverty" Roman world she had half-jokingly warned him against fifteen years earlier when he first went to stay with Luchino Visconti. Ramey recalls talk of a Roman orgy which Bernstein eventually called off.

In Israel, Bernstein described the reading of Beethoven's *Eroica* Symphony that he gave with the Israel Philharmonic (to mark the twenty-fifth anniversary of the founding of the Weizmann Institute) as "the most perfect performance of my life. The orchestra was simply marvelous and I wept from the excitement." When he flew to Vienna on March 29 he was even more ebullient: "I directed the *Eroica* as if for the first time," he told the reporters. "The whole orchestra was crying." Beethoven was uppermost in his mind. Before launching his Viennese *Fidelio* production he had set himself a labor of Hercules: to conduct, in a two-week period, two performances of the Ninth Symphony in Vienna, and another set of performances, with the Boston Symphony Orchestra, in Boston. The Vienna production was mounted especially for Amberson's next video venture, a ninety-minute special for CBS called *Beethoven's Birthday,* and the Viennese press did not take kindly to what it called the dictatorship of the cameras at the Konzerthaus. The flimsy light blue drapes Oliver Smith hung between the Corinthian columns behind the choir suggested a Hollywood back-drop. A special rostrum was built for the soloists, jutting out high over the orchestra like the bridge of a boat. A cheap plaster bust of Beethoven, ridicu-lously small, looked down with blank expression from the organ loft. But Bernstein's interpretation of Beethoven's Ninth disarmed the carpers. The critic Rudolf Klein claimed that "the perfection of this presentation will remain a standard even in Vienna." The strong international quartet consisted of Gwyneth Jones (Bernstein's Octavian), Shirley Verrett, Plácido Domingo and Martti Talvela. Jones recalls how difficult it was to sustain the long soprano line in the unaccompanied quartet at the end of the "Ode to Joy." Bernstein insisted on an unearthly mysterious quality and a very deliberate tempo. "You had to hang on like grim death because you didn't want to disappoint him." Jones sang the Ninth several times with Bernstein: when they did it in Salzburg (in 1979) the performance was so intense, she remembers, that at the great choral climax on the words *"Vor Gott!,"* "I felt that the roof of the Festspielhaus would fly away and we would see God and all his angels." When she later expressed this feeling to Bernstein in his dressing room he commented, "Yes, and then comes Beethoven's fart!"—the double bassoon note that begins the ensuing "March."

After his performances in Boston a week later, Bernstein wrote an article for the Vienna newspaper *Die Presse* in the form of a letter to its music critic, Franz Endler. After more than twenty years of performing the Ninth he had found, he said, what was for him an entirely new element: "I discovered that Beethoven's music has *charm*. . . . To play Beethoven's music is to give oneself over completely to the child-spirit that lived in that grim, awkward, violent man. It is to be seduced by a ravishing innocence. . . . That is why we of this cynical world are still charmed by that quaint, old-fashioned notion of all men together as children of God—when we hear it articulated by Beethoven. It is the irresistible charm of Beethoven's belief that makes the idea and the music imperishable."

In May the Amberson film team, working for CBS Television, documented the opera *Fidelio* being brought to the stage in Vienna at the historic Theater an der Wien. Bernstein stood on the very spot where Beethoven had conducted the opera's premiere in 1805. *Fidelio*'s director was Otto Schenk, with whom Bernstein had collaborated on *Der Rosenkavalier*. Schenk recalls that Bernstein liked to air his ideas for the production in front of a posse of adulatory Viennese princesses and duchesses. For the final scene of *Fidelio* he outlined what Schenk called a Radio City vision in which the scenery would disappear into the flies (shades of *West Side Story*!) and the reunited husband and wife would be left in a cosmic limbo. Don Fernando, the Minister, was then to descend from the sky like an archangel. Schenk told Bernstein he had never met an archangel but he was certain Karl Ridderbusch, singing the role, did not look like one. In Günther Schneider-Siemssen's actual design, a mighty drawbridge was slowly lowered from the fortress at the back of the stage as the choral finale began. The light grew ever brighter, the crowds multiplied, and the closing pages of the opera were conducted by Bernstein in a frenzied trance which left everybody in the theater trembling—cast, orchestra, stagehands, public, even the film crew.

*Fidelio* was Bernstein's most successful venture into opera. "The sweep and conviction and underlying musical planning of Bernstein's overall conception carried the day," reported the *International Herald Tribune*'s David Stevens. The cast, led by Gwyneth Jones and James King, was splendid. Schenk worked hard to make the domestic comedy of the opening scenes realistic, so that at the miraculous gear-changing moment when the canon quartet "Mir ist so wunderbar!" begins, the whole theater seemed to hold its breath. For once, wrote Alan Blyth in *The Times* (London), "you really did believe that Marzelline is in love with Fidelio, that Pizarro is a monstrous incarnation of evil, that Florestan is at his last gasp, that he and Fernando are old friends." Reviews in the world press were uniformly positive.

Into the Viennese euphoria dropped Tom Wolfe's time bomb, the June 8 edition of *New York* magazine. On the cover was a mocking photograph depicting three generations of well-to-do Manhattan women in cocktail dresses, each with her right fist in a black leather glove raised in the clenched-fist Black Panther salute. The cover line read "FREE LEONARD BERNSTEIN!" Inside was Tom Wolfe's piece, "Radical Chic: That Party at Lenny's." Clay Felker's editorial introduction claimed that "beyond the surface incongruity of radical militants being entertained in the homes of the elite, this concern of the very high for the very low is an important phenomenon of our times."

Wolfe described the recent wave of sympathy for the plight of the under-privileged as a *nostalgie de la boue* and linked it to earlier periods in history, among them Regency London, when the nouveaux riches had sought to roman-ticize and emulate the demagogues and underworld hucksters among the poor and disadvantaged. He reported that there had been at least three Panther parties in New York before the Bernsteins' affair. His article ran for thirty pages with many photographs—the most damaging of which showed Bernstein seated and solemn on a chintz-covered armchair with an elegant Felicia perched to one side and the Panthers' "field marshal," Donald Cox, standing a touch deferentially behind Bernstein on the other, his handsome wide-set eyes looking quizzically (as well they might) into the camera.

Wolfe went into microscopic detail about the fixtures and furnishings of the apartment. He made fun of the Chilean servants hired from the "Spic and Span Employment Agency" and mocked Otto Preminger's accent and Barbara Walters's earnestness. But his description of Leonard Bernstein at the moment he took over the meeting was the unkindest cut of all: "Lenny is on the move. As more than one person in this room knows, Lenny treasures 'the art of conversation.' He treasures it, monopolizes it, conglomerates it, like a Jay Gould, an Onassis, a Cornfeld of Conversation. Anyone who has spent a three-day weekend with Lenny in the country, by the shore, or captive on some lonesome cay in the Windward Islands knows that feeling—the alternating spells of adrenal stimulation and insulin coma as the Great Interrupter, the Village Explainer, the champion of Mental Jotto, the Free Analyst, Mr. Let's Find Out, leads the troops on a 72-hour forced march through the lateral geniculate and the pyramids of Betz, no breathers allowed, until every human brain is reduced finally to a clump of seaweed inside a burnt-out husk and collapses, implodes, in one last crunch of terminal boredom."

Wolfe's lampoon, published later in book form, perpetuated the damage done to Bernstein's reputation earlier in the year. This time Bernstein did not attempt to fight back in the press. (But it should not be forgotten that when the Panthers at last came to trial in 1971 the prosecution's ludicrously flimsy case collapsed and the "twenty-one" were all set free.)

Within days of each other, Bernstein read the article and wrote the peroration to the Beethoven portrait he was filming for American television. His work, dignified and useful, was the most powerful response he could make to his critics. The "Ode to Joy," he said, "succeeds even with those for whom organized religion fails because it conveys a spirit of godhead and sublimity in the freest and least doctrinaire way. . . . It has a purity and directness of communication which never becomes banal. It's accessible without being ordinary. This is the magic that no amount of talk can explain."

Bernstein spent nearly six weeks in Vienna. Felicia came for only a few days around the premiere of *Fidelio*. She was told about Tom Wolfe's article but swore she would never read it. She left for a holiday in Venice with Lili Schönburg, to whom she confided that she wished to make a new start with her husband. Bernstein, meanwhile, held sometimes rowdy court out at Anita von Karajan's house in Grinzing. Gwyneth Jones remembers a postperformance party where Bernstein danced a strenuous *pas de deux* with the ballerina wife of the Vienna Philharmonic's principal horn player. The climax came when he jumped into the swimming pool.

On June 9 Herbert von Karajan brought the Berlin Philharmonic to the 1970 Vienna Festival. It was his first appearance for six years in the city whose musical life he had dominated for a decade. He conducted two Beethoven symphonies at the Musikverein on the same evening that *Fidelio* transferred to the State Opera. The critic Karl Löbl attended the concert, then caught the second act of the opera; he offered readers of *Die Presse* a comparison of the world's most famous conductors: "Karajan heats the music up, Bernstein sets it on fire. Bernstein is always spontaneous, Karajan performs what he has rehearsed. Karajan conducts Beethoven, Bernstein feels himself to *be* Beethoven. Bernstein shows his feelings. Karajan would never divulge them. Both are musicians: how wonderful to have them both here at the same time!"

In the wake of the triumph of *Fidelio,* the Austrian *Wochenpresse* suggested Bernstein as the key figure in a triumvirate with Marcel Prawy and Peter Weiser to run the Vienna State Opera. But Bernstein, who also turned down the Met when it approached him as a possible successor to Rudolf Bing, still wanted his freedom. His concept of a Mass for the Kennedy Center was at last catching fire in his mind. He told a Viennese reporter that he had found a theme and only needed time to write what would be a new musical—in the style of *West Side Story*. Some of the music was already in place. As a thank-you present for Susann Baumgärtel, the young wife of his Austrian assistant, he wrote out the melody of what was to become the closing ensemble in *Mass,* "Lauda, Lauda Laudé," changing her name to Susanna so that it would rhyme with Hosanna. (Bernstein called Susann his blue-eyed Alice in Wonderland; she became another of his lifelong friends.)

I N the summer of 1970 Bernstein returned to Tanglewood, as artistic adviser. He was the senior member of a directorial "troika" that included Seiji Ozawa as head of the festival and the composer Gunther Schuller as head of the school. Bernstein's opening-day speech was later reprinted by the *New York Times,* as if to make amends for the paper's one-sided treatment of the Bernsteins during the Black Panther incident back in January. First Bernstein evoked the spirit of Koussevitzky and what he called his central line, "the line leading to perpetual discovery, a mystical line to truth as it is revealed in the musical art." Then he talked of how the world had changed, how youth had become disillusioned since the atom bomb. From today's students, he went on, he heard only "tales of despair and hopelessness." His Tanglewood sermon was intended to send the young musicians off with high hopes:

> . . . It's the artists of the world, the feelers and the thinkers, who will ultimately save us, who can articulate, educate, defy, insist, sing and shout the big dreams. Only the artists can turn the "Not-Yet" into reality. All right, how do you do it? Like this: find out what you can do well, uniquely well—that's what studying is for, to find out what you can do particularly well. You. Unique. And then do it for all you're worth. And I don't mean "Do your own thing," in the hip sense. That's passivity, that's dropping out, that's not doing anything. I'm talking about *doing,* which

means (another old-fashioned phrase) serving your community, whether that community is a tiny town or six continents. And there's no time to lose, which makes your position twice as difficult, because you're caught in a paradox. You see, you've got to work fast, but not be in a hurry. You've got to be patient, but not passive. You've got to recognize the hope that exists in you, but not let impatience turn it into despair. Does that sound like double-talk? Well, it is, because the paradox exists. And out of this paradox *you* have to produce the brilliant synthesis. We'll help you as much as we can—that's why we're here—but it is you who must produce it, with your new atomic minds, your flaming, angry hope, and your secret weapon of art.

Jamie Bernstein, almost eighteen, was a guide at Tanglewood that summer, helping with visitors, running messages for the office, guarding the back entrance during concerts. "It was the worst summer of my life," she recalls. Not because of the Tom Wolfe article or her stormy love affair with a teenage contemporary. The problem was her father. For a school assignment on autobiography she had written about how much she took after her father's side of the family. "I was also gregarious and interested in being in the spotlight and loving attention and being full of leadership qualities." ("So what am I?" Felicia had asked her, "chopped liver?") But in the summer of 1970, Jamie remembers she was angry with her father for having missed her triumphant performance in a school production of *Guys and Dolls* the previous February, and for having been in Europe when she graduated. Then at Tanglewood she heard ugly rumors about his homosexual past. Deeply shocked, she wrote a long letter to her mother asking about "daddy's wild youth." Felicia summoned her back to Fairfield for a weekend family conference. After dinner father and daughter walked up to his studio. They sat side by side on the swing out on the porch. He told her everything she'd heard was a lie. "There are malicious people in the world who are jealous of me and they make up stories about me to make me look bad." He cited the Charlie Roth episode from the fifties as an example. Her father's denial left Jamie confused, but it was "all I had to go on for years."

At the end of the summer Bernstein and the New York Philharmonic went to Japan. His tour programs, for Osaka's Expo 70, were less adventurous than in 1961: Mahler's Ninth Symphony, the Berlioz *Symphonie Fantastique* (preceded by Copland's clarinet concerto) and an all-Beethoven evening. Seiji Ozawa shared the conducting and his program contained the only Japanese work, *November Steps* by Tōru Takemitsu. The two conductors were photographed in colorful sporting outfits at a baseball match between the Japan Philharmonic Symphony Orchestra and the New York Philharmonic, but Bernstein's participation in the game was limited to vocal support from the bleachers.

Kazuko Amano remembers that the Japanese public was more openly enthusiastic than on Bernstein's first visit, too much so at the end of the Mahler symphony. "The audience started to applaud before Lenny had finished conducting; his arms were still coming down slowly, slowly, still conducting a silent but alive music. . . . I was crying silently in my seat."

For Bernstein the most grotesque episode of the tour was his encounter in Tokyo with the novelist Yukio Mishima. Mishima was also a filmmaker of considerable reputation so it is possible that Bernstein was considering the possibility of a Japanese collaboration to take the place of his abandoned St. Francis project. The omens were not promising, however. When they met at Bernstein's hotel, Mishima was dressed like a Roman gladiator. Leather straps crisscrossed his bare chest and he wore body-hugging, metal-studded leather pants. The two men did indeed discuss the movies. Two days later three shaven-headed members of Mishima's private army accompanied Bernstein and Schuyler Chapin to a cinema where Mishima, dressed now in white uniform and with ceremonial sword at his side, was waiting to show them a feature film. "I think it's one of my best," he told Bernstein with a bow. It was the true story of a 1936 scandal in which a member of the imperial household eventually committed hara-kiri. Uncharacteristically Bernstein said nothing during the screening. He sat bolt upright until the bitter end, doubtless because the music used to accompany the long drawn-out process of disembowelment was the "Liebestod" ("Love Death") from *Tristan und Isolde,* the Wagner score Bernstein loved best of all. In his memoirs, Chapin tells how Bernstein rushed back to his hotel and was sick in the toilet. "No more of this, no more," was his only comment as he poured himself a large scotch. Yukio Mishima took himself out of the running as a potential collaborator two months later when he himself committed suicide, Japanese style, in front of his private army.

Back in New York from Japan, Bernstein was told that Roger Stevens, the director of the Kennedy Center, had suffered a serious heart attack. "Is there anything I can do to help?" Bernstein asked, having illegally penetrated the hospital's intensive care ward. Later Stevens recalled the reply he gave: "Lenny, one thing I'd like to have you do for me is finish *Mass."* The opening of the center, several times postponed, was twelve months away, and the injunction was expressed with such force that Bernstein worked on *Mass* thereafter with an almost missionary zeal, although he still had many conducting irons in the fire.

After five weeks with the New York Philharmonic he escaped, on December 6, to the MacDowell Colony. Much of the music for *Mass* was composed— or adapted from existing bottom-drawer compositions—during this period. In January he discussed the staging with a potential director Frank Corsaro. Jerome Robbins had already said no, pleading sickness, and Corsaro withdrew, too, commenting that there was enough material for nine masses. When Bernstein left for Europe in February 1971 the situation was similar to that in 1955 when he had gone to La Scala, Milan, leaving his producer, Ethel Reiner, with a half-finished *Candide,* no stage director and no lyricist. It was, however, a very Viennese quandary: desperate, but not serious. Bernstein knew by now the way he worked best. Musicals—and *Mass* is a musical in terms of its resources—are often put together at the last moment by many gifted people operating in a creative panic.

While Roger Stevens waited anxiously in Washington, Bernstein embarked on one of his most protracted European seasons. It began with a week in Paris, continued with a month of concerts with the Vienna Philharmonic on tour, followed by three more performances and a recording of *Der Rosenkavalier* in Vienna, and finally, in Israel, four performances of Mahler's Third Symphony. And into an already crowded schedule was inserted the first filming engagement under a contract Schuyler Chapin and Abe Friedman had negotiated whereby Bernstein's video projects were to be taken over by Unitel, a German film company based in Munich. All the symphonies of Mahler were to be captured over the next six years on the expensive 35-mm cinematic film gauge, wherever feasible with the Vienna Philharmonic Orchestra. Mahler's Ninth was already scheduled for the tour and it was filmed in Berlin. There was a symbolic value for Unitel's chief, Dr. Leo Kirch, in the decision to inaugurate the cycle on Karajan's home ground. (Karajan had been making his own music films with Kirch since the sixties.) Uppermost in Bernstein's mind, however, was not this latest skirmish in the conductors' war but his nervousness at signing a long-term contract with a German company. He was reassured by the information that none of the key figures at Unitel was old enough to have been a Nazi.

The Viennese musicians did not have Mahler's music in their bones. Their most recent performances had been of the Ninth under Otto Klemperer in 1968 and the Second, under Bernstein himself, in 1967. But five of the symphonies had been performed only once in the previous forty years. Bernstein wanted to document his relationship with the orchestra as they worked their way through the cycle of symphonies. The first documentary, built around rehearsals for Mahler's valedictory Ninth Symphony, was narrated by Bernstein himself under the title *Four Ways to Say Farewell*. Using British filmmakers and German equipment and finance, Bernstein had found a new way to create the stimulating music programs for adults that he had first made back in the 1950s for American television.

Filming at a public concert was an unusual experience for Unitel. Karajan and Böhm, the principal conductors with whom the company had previously worked, always made their music films under controlled conditions in a studio, movement by movement, with no public to disturb them. Bernstein had conducted hundreds of recording sessions for CBS in the same way. But he wanted his video productions to be documents of actual performances and he insisted on preserving the "live" atmosphere of a concert given in front of an audience. He agreed that there should be at least two performances for the editor to choose from, together with a retake session. Filming "live" with 35-mm film magazines containing only ten minutes of film stock meant cameras often had to be reloaded while the music was going on. Bernstein detested such interruptions when he became aware of them but he knew they were justified by the superior technical quality of the end result. Unitel's films could be exhibited in cinemas and reissued as television tapes and video cassettes. Bernstein was not the first conductor to build up an archive of film performances but by the end of his life he had by far the largest catalogue.

TOURING Europe with the Vienna Philharmonic in 1971 resembled the treadmill Bernstein used to complain about in Israel. He conducted twelve concerts in fifteen days: Munich, Zurich, Rome, Milan, Florence (twice), Munich (again), Düsseldorf, Berlin (twice), Hamburg, Vienna. When the orchestra appeared in London, he went to a postconcert party held at 10 Downing Street. On a day of violence, strikes and financial crisis Bernstein greeted Edward Heath by asking, "And how is your tottering government tonight, Prime Minister?" The Queen Mother was a guest of honor at the party, as was Princess Margaret. "Lenny tried to kiss my mother," she remembers, with the ghost of a smile; "Mummy doesn't like being kissed."

Settling in Vienna for three weeks, Bernstein remounted his 1968 *Rosenkavalier* and committed his interpretation to disc. CBS did not want to record *Der Rosenkavalier*. Goddard Lieberson had been promoted within the company's hierarchy and his successor, Clive Davis, believed opera was both too expensive to produce and not what the public wanted. Bernstein still had nine years to run on his contract, however, and he insisted, persuading CBS to hire Decca's former chief John Culshaw to be in charge of the recording. There was trouble with the singers from their first piano run-through, which began at five in the afternoon and did not finish until after one next morning. Most opera stars dislike having to give performances on successive days, but the Culshaw timetable envisaged thirteen recording sessions between the three Staatsoper performances, all packed into less than a fortnight. To add to the pressure, Otto Schenk was absent, directing a play in Munich, and Bernstein found himself involved with the stage rehearsals as well as working with an orchestra whose principal players seemed to change from rehearsal to rehearsal. ["They all want to play with you, Maestro!"] The premiere was underrehearsed—Walter Berry missed an entrance in the second act—and illnesses dogged the CBS sessions. News of the death of Stravinsky cast a further pall. Bernstein called the period a nightmare, but there is no sign of the tension on the sumptuous recording eventually released by CBS.

Jennie Bernstein, then seventy-three, was with her son in Vienna for the first time. Leonard wrote to Burton that she was "saying all the wrong things, talking Yiddish which she thinks is German, adding to all my problems by having wrong flight-tickets, losing her bag in the airport, etc. But she is apparently enjoying it all." As for himself, he said, "I can't wait to get out of Vienna at last and head for mad gay Israel."

Bernstein finally returned to New York on May 3. The next day he addressed his various ailments with visits to dentist, eye doctor, regular doctor, scalp popper and analyst. The real problem, however, was with *Mass*. In Bernstein's composition, a setting of the Latin text of the Catholic Mass is interwoven with songs and choruses in English expressing Bernstein's familiar theme concerning the difficulty of finding and sustaining faith in God at a time of recurring wars and countless instances of man's inhumanity to his fellow men. Bernstein was experiencing writer's block: he did not know how to finish *Mass*. He decided to consult Father Philip Berrigan, the Catholic priest who, with his brother and other peace workers, had been arrested for allegedly plotting the kidnapping of the presidential adviser Henry Kissinger. A week after Bernstein's return, Felicia had organized an evening in support of the Berrigans that raised thirty-five thousand dollars to help pay for legal support. On May 25 Bernstein drove to the Danbury Federal Correction Institute to consult with him. It was not an entirely successful visit. Bernstein took an hour to explain the plot of his *Mass,* and before Berrigan could offer much advice the guards said his time was up. The meeting provided the FBI with food for thought, however. J. Edgar Hoover sent a message to John Mitchell, the Attorney General, warning that the suspect Berrigan had been invited by Bernstein to supply a subversive text for his *Mass*. "Important government officials," wrote Hoover, "perhaps even the President, are expected to attend this ceremony [the Kennedy Center opening] and it is anticipated that they will applaud the composition without recognizing the true meaning of the words." But the prayer "Dona Nobis Pacem" (Give Us Peace) was hardly open to misinterpretation at the height of the Vietnam War.

In June, three months before the scheduled opening night, Shirley Bernstein, now an agent for playwrights, found her brother "terribly depressed and searching desperately for a collaborator to work on the lyrics for the songs." She proposed her own client, the young composer and lyricist Stephen Schwartz, whose musical, *Godspell,* had recently opened at the Cherry Lane Theater. "Lenny was almost docile," Shirley remembers; "I took him by the hand and led him into the show." *Godspell* is an adaptation of the Gospel according to St. Matthew. Bernstein enjoyed it and invited the gifted youngster (later he called him a genius) to look through his *Mass* sketches at his Park Avenue studio. After the meeting Bernstein called his sister in euphoria. "Oh my God, this is it. Now I can finish *Mass."* Bernstein believed the parallels between Schwartz and Stephen Sondheim to be uncanny: they shared a first name, initials, and youth; they were both composer lyricists and they both arrived at the optimum moment.

Schwartz's participation did indeed work wonders. Within two weeks the show was virtually completed. The production team was swiftly assembled. Gordon Davidson would direct. Alvin Ailey was named choreographer, and his troupe of dancers, led by Judith Jamison, were to provide the core of the dancing. Oliver Smith was to do the designs, and Maurice Peress was chosen as conductor since Bernstein would be busy writing and rewriting up to the last moment. As orchestrators Bernstein selected his Curtis contemporary Hershy Kay, who had done *Candide* with him, and Jonathan Tunick, who had just finished *Follies* for Stephen Sondheim. Sid Ramin gave advice about rock guitars and electronic keyboards.

"I feel young again," exclaimed Bernstein, "twenty-five years old, and as I was when I was doing *On the Town.*" The difference was that *Mass,* subtitled *A Theatre Piece for Singers, Players and Dancers,* was being prepared for a Washington run of eleven performances. No after-life was contemplated for it. Nobody, not even Roger Stevens, was prepared to take the risk of setting up a New York production to follow. Stevens had been nursing the Kennedy Center into life for fifteen years: what he wanted, and what he could pay for just this once with congressional funds, was the Show of the Century, something that would set the world talking and stretch the new opera house to the limit, technically and artistically, before it settled down to its regular work of providing conventional musical and dramatic entertainment for the nation's capital.

The cast of *Mass* numbered over two hundred. Alvin Ailey's dance company was twenty strong. There were twenty boys from the Berkshire Boys Choir, ten child dancers from Washington and thirty-two instrumentalists cast as street musicians. The Norman Scribner Chorus, amateurs recruited from the Washington neighborhood, numbered sixty more. There was a rock band, a brass band, and an orchestra in the pit. "It is much bigger than a Broadway musical," observed Gordon Davidson proudly.

With the dimensions of the show finally prescribed, but not all the music written, Bernstein made the astonishing decision to leave for California. In Los Angeles the Civic Light Opera company was in rehearsal with a full-scale stage production of *Candide* to which he had contributed the brand-new "Laughing Song" for the character of Martin, Dr. Pangloss's alter ego. Bernstein's personal attendance did not save *Candide* from receiving another set of mixed reviews, but the trip had an important repercussion on his personal life. Soon after he arrived on the West Coast, Bernstein telephoned an old friend in San Francisco and invited himself to stay during the run of *Candide* in that city. At a party in his honor he met Tom Cothran, the music director of KKHI, a local radio station. He fell in love instantly. Before dinner they discussed philosophy over cocktails, prompted no doubt by Voltaire's disdain for Leibnitz. Later they listened to the test tapes of *Der Rosenkavalier,* with Cothran perched on Bernstein's knee. Bernstein never failed to call Felicia each evening, but he and Cothran slept together for the rest of his stay.

Bernstein was almost fifty-three. In the photographs taken in Vienna during the *Rosenkavalier* sessions he looks even older. His hair was now gray through and through and the vertical lines on his cheeks were deepening by the month as his facial flesh slowly sagged. But falling in love with Tommy Cothran, like the fun of staging *Mass,* seems to have restored to him his sense of youth. Harry

Kraut, at that time still with the Boston Symphony, remembers the moment, three weeks later, when Bernstein told him about Cothran. "He was driving home after conducting the *Missa Solemnis* at Tanglewood and he got more and more excited about this boy he had met in San Francisco with whom he was madly in love, and the car went slower and slower until it stopped moving altogether, right in the middle of Route Seven."

So as Bernstein went into the final preparations for *Mass,* outwardly ebullient as ever, his personal life was in disarray. During the twenty years of his marriage (the anniversary fell on the day after the *Mass* premiere) he had had homosexual encounters, but he had never entered into a loving relationship with a man. Cothran, "a wonderful, twinkly, bright, endearing person," according to Bernstein's recording producer John McClure, was twenty-four when they met. Of Irish descent, he had studied English literature at Berkeley but dropped out before the final exams. He was musically erudite, played the piano well, loved literature and enjoyed word games. Bernstein brought him to Washington and Schuyler Chapin put him on the Amberson payroll to work on *Mass.* Jamie Bernstein, only five years his junior, described him as "very cute, goofy, and quick on the trigger. . . . We were so amazed because he bought an ancient VW for a hundred dollars and then rebuilt the engine himself with one of those little manuals." Cothran became part of the inner circle, swiftly slipping into the role of jester to Bernstein's king. Whether they also enjoyed an ongoing sexual relationship over the next five years is a matter for conjecture. It seems likely that Bernstein's passion moderated but not his affection. At all events Felicia and her children accepted Cothran unquestioningly as both family friend and Leonard's new professional associate. (Jack Gottlieb had left Bernstein's service when he quit the New York Philharmonic.) In the preface to the printed piano vocal edition of *Mass,* published that winter, Bernstein wrote, "I am particularly grateful to Thomas Cothran for his special assistance in preparing this score." Cothran proofread the entire thing.

Faced in July 1971 with a potentially destructive emotional conflict, Bernstein took evasive action by immersing himself in rehearsals and production conferences for *Mass.* Quadraphonic recordings of the "Kyrie," the "Alleluia" and the "Credo"—vital elements in Bernstein's novel sound concept, in which live action was to be mixed with prerecorded tape—were made in CBS's New York studio early in August. The entire caravan moved to Washington on August 24 with the leading character's final aria, a full-blown mad scene, still not complete. The show opened two weeks later.

At the final preview, on September 7, senators and congressmen got their first look inside the Kennedy Center, the building whose expense they had fought over for fifteen years. "Less than half the cost of Lincoln Center," Senator Fulbright boasted, "and less than the cost of one day of the Vietnam War in 1966." For this last dress rehearsal Bernstein agreed to drop the second of the three orchestral "Meditations" that punctuate *Mass:* everybody except the composer felt that the show was running too long at over one hundred minutes without an intermission. But afterward he was adamant: the cut must be restored for the premiere. Felicia tried overnight to dissuade him, to no avail: he knew what he wanted.

President Nixon disliked Bernstein's liberal politics and ducked out of attending the first night, offering his box to JFK's widow, now Mrs. Aristotle Onassis. The former First Lady announced she would attend, and then decided against it "for strong private reasons." The evening belonged to the Kennedy clan and to JFK's New Frontier cabinet colleagues. The late President's mother, Mrs. Rose Kennedy, became the guest of honor; with her in the presidential box were her surviving son, Senator Edward Kennedy, and his wife, the mayor of Washington and his wife, Aaron Copland, and Felicia and Leonard Bernstein. Many Republicans were also present in the audience of 2,200, among them Henry Kissinger. In socio-political terms the premiere of *Mass,* attended by the world's ambassadors and a cause for national pride, was the peak moment of Bernstein's life.

Curtain time was scheduled for 7:30 P.M. but it was nearly eight before Roger Stevens walked on the stage to shouts of "Bravo." "President Kennedy, more than any of his predecessors, lent dignity to the role of the arts in America," he said. "We have tried to do justice to his memory." Then the lights faded to a complete blackout and Betty Allen's prerecorded mezzosoprano voice singing "Kyrie Eleison" was heard from a loudspeaker downstage right, joined by a bass soloist on the left, then other solo voices mingling from the four corners of the theater. *Mass* had begun. Roger Stevens, who had been a supporter of Bernstein's since *Peter Pan* in 1950, remembers it as "the most thrilling night I have ever spent in the theater. The production lasted one hour and forty-five minutes. There was not a sound from the audience. At the end there were about three minutes of silence and none of us knew whether we had a failure or a hit on our hands. Then everyone rose to their feet and cheered for half an hour."

Bernstein, sporting a velvet tuxedo, was crying at the end. He gave President Kennedy's eighty-year-old mother an enormous bear hug, then kissed Joan Kennedy, Aaron Copland and Felicia, before proceeding to the stage to embrace every performer within grabbing distance. Rose Kennedy told waiting reporters she was overwhelmed. "It's stupendous. Jack would have loved it; it's what he was interested in: culture, art, joy, and pleasure in the arts." Many professional critics were equally ecstatic. "A magnificent work, masterfully contrived, marvelously performed" (Herbert Kupferberg); "the greatest music Bernstein has ever written" (Paul Hume); "It shook, exalted and moved me as have few new statements in recent years" (John Ardoin). The most influential review, however, was Harold Schonberg's in the *New York Times.* His first dispatch, carried next morning, contained some praise: "The best sections . . . are the Broadway-like numbers—the jazzy, super-rhythmic sections. . . .

About two-thirds of the Mass is gay and lighthearted." But Schonberg had no admiration for Bernstein's serious music. He thought it "pretentious and thin. . . . It is a pseudo-serious effort at re-thinking the Mass that basically is, I think, cheap and vulgar. It is a show-biz Mass, the work of a composer who desperately wants to be with it." For his second review, on Sunday, Schonberg got out the sledgehammer. *Mass* was, he wrote, "a combination of superficiality and pretentiousness, and the greatest mélange of styles since the ladies' magazine recipe for steak fried in peanut butter and marshmallow sauce."

N o w that the incense has cleared, *Mass* can be seen to be at the very center of Bernstein's creative work and the closest he ever came to achieving a synthesis between Broadway and the concert hall. The mixture of styles about which Schonberg made such a fuss is actually the guiding principle of the composition. The full title, however, is another example of Bernstein's difficulty finding satisfactory descriptions for his works. *Mass: A Theatre Piece for Singers, Players and Dancers* does not begin to convey the sweep of the work or its ambition. On the other hand, *Mass,* with no qualifying description, would be misleading. Robert Craft, in a deeply hostile review, proposed *Mass: The Musical.* Surprisingly, Wagner's description of *Parsifal*—a "sacred festival drama"—comes closest to an accurate description. Bernstein's *Mass* is similarly concerned with the meaning of Communion and needs festive circumstances if it is to receive an adequate production.

The text of the Catholic liturgy provides the spine of *Mass.* Bernstein set to music the same words he had conducted so often in Beethoven's *Missa Solemnis.* The action takes place not in a church but in limbo. In the first of the work's many culture shocks the opening hubbub of four solo voices singing the "Kyrie" is suddenly stilled and to the accompaniment of an electric guitar the Celebrant (the central character) sings, in English, the hymn "A Simple Song," followed by the psalm "I Will Sing the Lord a New Song." After dancing acolytes have dressed the Celebrant in ceremonial robes to the sound of a six-part "Alleluia" (pretaped), the auditorium is flooded with light and a brass band marches through the audience to the stage (an idea adopted, music included, from *The Skin of Our Teeth*), accompanied by what Bernstein labels the Street Chorus. They are joined by the boys chorus and the large mixed chorus. Brief but pungent solos are taken by rock singers, blues singers, and a preacher whose infectious gospel-sermon suggests that he is the son of Gershwin's Sportin' Life. There are thirty-one numbers in all.

Formally, *Mass* is Bernstein's most original work. He called it "an entirely new concept. It has all the qualities of a dramatic work, catastrophe and climax . . . all those terms out of Aristotle." Bernstein analyzed its underlying meaning in a program note he wrote the following year: "The ritual is conducted by a young man of mysterious simplicity (called the Celebrant) who throughout the drama is invested by his acolytes with increasingly ornate robes and symbols which connote both an increase in the superficial formalism of his obligation and of the burden that he bears. There is a parallel increase in the resistance of his Congregants—in the sharpness and bitterness of their reactions—and in the deterioration of his own faith. As the climax of Communion, all ceremony breaks down and the Mass is shattered. It then remains for each individual on the stage to find a new seed of faith within himself through painful Meditation, enabling each individual to pass on the embrace of peace (Pax) to his neighbor. The chain of embrace grows and threads through the entire stage, ultimately with the audience and hopefully into the world outside."

Bernstein's ambition was to create something that was, to use his own phrase about Beethoven, accessible without being ordinary. "I feel it's a work I've been writing all my life," he told Peter Davis, but its origins may well go back only to 1968 and the terrible morning in St. Patrick's Cathedral when he conducted the slow movement of Mahler's Fifth Symphony and saw the bereaved children of Robert Kennedy, all dressed in white, walking in procession to the altar with the Communion vessels. To this image can be added his preoccupation in 1969 with St. Francis: Franco Zeffirelli's outline film treatment involved time-traveling between the thirteenth century and today; musically, medieval polyphony was to be contrasted with modern rock. "A Simple Song" was to have been St. Francis's "Credo" before it became the Celebrant's hymn.

Bernstein intended *Mass* to be ecumenical in a musical as well as a religious sense. He wanted to appeal to young listeners, and to do so without making compromises. But by moving into religious territory, and by choosing Stephen Schwartz of *Godspell* fame as his co-librettist, he appeared to be challenging the authors of *Hair* and *Jesus Christ Superstar. Mass* became, like it or not, an expression of the post-Woodstock zeitgeist, its stage filled with young people, its lyrics peppered with jaunty internal rhymes.

At the heart of *Mass,* more than any social or religious concern, was Bernstein's passion for peace. In his extended setting of the prayer "Dona Nobis Pacem" the Celebrant is driven to desperation by the violence of the crowd and by his inability to command their love. On the word "pacem" he hurls the monstrance, the container holding the sacraments, to the floor. Bernstein identified himself with the Celebrant figure. *"Mass* follows three years of despair," he told an interviewer, "since Russian tanks invaded Prague [in August 1968]. When I'm writing, my first impulse is to communicate. So I stand for the audience. So the Celebrant is an extension of my thought."

The originality and durability of *Mass* have become clearer with the years. Like *West Side Story,* the work has proved practical, popular and suitable for entire communities to undertake. The musical idioms of the sixties now have a period flavor but the prayers for peace and the quest for renewed faith are as relevant as ever, and most of the singing parts can be assumed by reasonably gifted amateurs. But the role of the Celebrant will never be easy, either technically or spiritually. When he sings "A Simple Song" he must be not only St. Francis, and the Celebrant, but also an incarnation of Bernstein himself—the child inside the man who, like his image of Beethoven, "never grew up and to the end of his life remained a creature of grace and innocence and trust."

# PROFESSOR BERNSTEIN

*The Charles Eliot Norton Professor of*
*Music at Harvard University, 1973.*
PHOTO: PAUL DE HUECK, COURTESY OF THE ESTATE OF
LEONARD BERNSTEIN

*He was desperate to get something across, far beyond*
*the musical terms of the lectureship he assumed.*

—PRESIDENT DEREK BOK of Harvard
after Bernstein delivered the first of his
Charles Eliot Norton Lectures

THERE was a moment in the fall of 1971 when it seemed possible that
Leonard Bernstein might soon have three shows running on Broadway. "I
spent the summer," he told John Gruen, "lovingly tending to my faltering
children as they made their way to New York." Bernstein was referring to *Mass,*
to the West Coast *Candide* (which got only as far as Washington) and also to a
new production of *On the Town,* which previewed in Boston early in October
1971. The auguries were good. The spitfire Bernadette Peters sang the Nancy
Walker part of Hildy; Phyllis Newman, the ebullient wife of Adolph Green,
took the role Betty Comden had created, and Donna McKechnie, recently the
knockout dance soloist in *Company,* played Miss Turnstiles. But the indifferent
direction and choreography of Ron Field sank a $450,000 investment within
two months of the New York opening. Meanwhile a plan to run *Mass* twice

daily at Radio City Music Hall was dropped because the sheer size of the six-thousand-seat theater made it too impersonal for a work in which physical contact between performers and audience was essential. (At the end the boys' choir is directed to move into the audience, bringing the touch of peace.) So while Broadway was dominated by shows that possessed little musical originality, Bernstein was left with nothing for his hopes. Aaron Copland failed to persuade his fellow jurors on the Pulitzer Prize Committee to give the 1971 music award to *Mass*. In the classical field, meanwhile, Michael Steinberg dismissed the earlier *Kaddish* Symphony as "such junk."

The times seemed out of joint to Bernstein—and then he got the lift he needed. Dr. Harry Levin extended the formal invitation from Harvard for him to serve as Charles Eliot Norton Professor of Poetry for the following academic year, 1972–73. The appointment involved living at the college for two semesters, taking seminars and holding consultations with students, as well as delivering six lectures. The composers Copland, Hindemith and Stravinsky had delivered the Norton Lectures in earlier years as had the poets Eliot, Auden and Cummings. Bernstein considered the appointment to be the greatest academic honor ever bestowed upon him, and it gave him a new sense of purpose. "Everything I do is in one way or another teaching," he told an interviewer. "I even think of my conducting as teaching, in the sense that one is teaching one's vision of a piece to an orchestra, and through them to an audience. Anything which derives from the compulsion to share . . . comes in the category of teaching . . . I don't really possess my own feelings until I've shared them." The notion of teaching so obsessed him that he started to believe that everything he conducted should be preserved for posterity. "There has to be some didactic or pedagogical reason for my conducting—either that it is being recorded or filmed or is accompanied by an explanatory lecture. I don't simply go and conduct concerts any more." There was more than a whiff of hubris about such an assertion. He seems to have succumbed temporarily to the Great Man syndrome. The reality was that in America his concerts were rarely televised, union rates being prohibitively high. But elsewhere his conducting work was often filmed by Unitel (or by national broadcasters such as the BBC in the U.K. and NHK in Japan).

The next two years were to be dominated by preparations for the Harvard lectures, but Bernstein simultaneously began work on two composing projects. His collaborators were to be Jerome Robbins, with whom he was planning a dance drama based on *The Dybbuk*, and Alan Jay Lerner, who suggested a serious musical which would express their concern at the damage being inflicted on America by President Nixon's policies.

In the summer of 1971, Schuyler Chapin was wooed away to become deputy general manager at the Metropolitan Opera. (He remained close to Bernstein personally as a trustee of his business affairs.) To replace him, Bernstein turned to Harry Kraut, a music-loving Harvard man (1954) with a shrewd business-trained eye who had worked at the Boston Symphony for thirteen years, most recently as manager of Tanglewood. Kraut was to devise long-term plans—so many months assigned to conducting, so many to composing—according to Bernstein's sometimes capricious wishes. Helen Coates would continue to look after Bernstein's personal and family correspondence. When Abe Friedman died suddenly in February 1972, another lawyer took over his legal functions but Kraut became executive vice president of Amberson and his supervisory brief was extended to cover Bernstein's entire professional life—with an overlap into personal affairs. It was he who arranged for Tom Cothran to return to the Amberson payroll as a researcher for the Norton Lectures.

Bernstein's first conducting season under Kraut's aegis came in the spring of 1972. He began in London, where he had yielded to impassioned pleas by Lina Lalandi to succeed Igor Stravinsky as president of her English Bach Festival. At the Royal Albert Hall he conducted a Stravinsky memorial concert for London Weekend Television. In his new didactic spirit, Bernstein first narrated a cele-bratory film about the composer's significance which was projected on a big screen above the London Symphony Orchestra.

Then he tackled three Mahler symphonies in quick succession with the Vienna Philharmonic, beginning with the Fifth, which, like the Third the following week, had not been performed by the Philharmonic in Vienna since the *Anschluss* in 1938. As the *Wochenpresse* tartly observed, "until now the Philharmonic did Mahler only in extreme emergency cases." Despite their success with the Ninth the previous year, Bernstein felt a wave of hostility from the orchestra toward Mahler's music. "They didn't know Mahler. They were prejudiced against it. They thought it was long and blustering and needlessly complicated and over-emotional. In the rehearsals they resisted and resisted to a point where I did finally lose my temper because in God's name this was their composer as much as Mozart was, or Beethoven, who came from much further away." As if Bernstein's anger were not enough, the gods themselves sent the Viennese musicians a warning. In rehearsal Bernstein had called for a veritable earthquake of a climax to the Fifth's first movement. *("An dieser Stelle, meine Herren, will ich ein Erdbeben spüren.")* When the same point was reached at the Sunday morning subscription concert the double basses redoubled their efforts and the entire concert platform seemed to vibrate in sympathy with Mahler's anguish and Bernstein's passionate conducting. An onlooker glanced up to discover the magnificent chandeliers of the Golden Hall swaying to and fro above Bernstein's head. In the body of the hall panicking members of the public rose from their chairs and ran to the doors. The tremors of a genuine earth-quake were being felt all over eastern Austria. Bernstein kept conducting until the musicians let him know what had happened; then he spoke calmly to the audience, urging them to take their seats so the music could resume. "I actually didn't feel a thing," he said afterward. "Not a tremor. I was too involved in the music."

Two weeks later Bernstein's reading of Mahler's Fourth Symphony was

PROFESSOR BERNSTEIN ✑ 413

hailed by Karl Löbl as "heavenly chamber music." The orchestra had come to terms with Mahler. "They suddenly realized," Bernstein said later, "that they had become the vessel for something holy: Mahler's music was as sacred a bunch of notes as Brahms's symphonies."

Bernstein's Mahler cycle for Unitel continued in Israel with *Das Lied von der Erde*. The Israel Philharmonic accompanied two German soloists: the young Wagnerian tenor René Kollo and Bernstein's dear friend Christa Ludwig. While in Tel Aviv, Ludwig and Bernstein repeated a Brahms *Liederabend* they had already given at Town Hall in New York. In order to have enough raw footage to cover the recital, Unitel had decided not to film one of the many performances of *Das Lied*. Inevitably it was, according to Bernstein, the best performance of the week, and he held the director personally responsible for missing it. At the farewell party the director assured Bernstein that with three performances recorded the concert was already well covered. Scotch in hand, Bernstein insisted that every minute of every performance should have been filmed. The director told him he was unrealistic and self-indulgent. They glowered at each other. Bernstein said, "Well, if that's what you think you can just fuck off." Matching expletive for expletive, the director turned on his heel to leave the Israel Philharmonic guest house. In his blind rage he marched straight into a plate glass window and knocked himself out. Bernstein was the first at his side. Next morning, friends again, they went surfing together in Tel Aviv harbor.

While Bernstein was filming Mahler, Maurice Peress was conducting *Mass* at the Cincinnati May Festival. A week before the opening Archbishop Paul F. Leibold issued a pastoral letter forbidding Catholics to attend the work (which he had not seen) on grounds that it was blasphemous. The scandal stimulated the public curiosity, and a hastily arranged extra performance was quickly sold out. Ten days later the fifty-seven-year-old archbishop suffered a stroke and died. "I hope he had time to repent," was Bernstein's private comment when he was given the news.

In June *Mass* reopened for a second season in Washington and Jacqueline Kennedy Onassis finally saw the work she had instigated. The evening was interrupted by a woman who shouted "sacrilege" when at the height of his passion the Celebrant threw the monstrance to the floor. Bernstein was observed in his box beating his head with his fist. Bernstein told the *New York Times* that Mrs. Onassis made no comment backstage after the performance. "I think she was speechless. She still hasn't said anything." Later she sent him a signed photograph in which her hand tenderly touches Bernstein's cheek. The inscription reads:

*Lenny—"I loved it, yes I did"*
*and I love you too—*
*Thank you for making Mass so beautiful.*

Attending the same performance of *Mass* was the Protestant Episcopal Bishop of New York, Paul Moore. "It's the story of my life," he wrote Bernstein. "I could deeply identify with the inordinate demands people make upon the church and the priest and the deep revulsion one sometimes feels toward the role."

After Washington, Sol Hurok presented *Mass* for a month at the 3,800-seat Metropolitan Opera in New York. Hurok's marketing line was straightforward. "If you love *West Side Story* and great theater, you will love Leonard Bernstein's *Mass.*" The cast was scaled down to one hundred and seventy-five; Bernstein dubbed it a "dinky" version. Critical opinions still fluctuated wildly but the public voted with its pocketbook. In July *Mass* was No. 1 on *Billboard*'s classical chart and CBS Records announced that sales had reached over two hundred thousand copies.

In the summer of 1972, with the Norton Lectures still unwritten, Bernstein revised his priorities and canceled plans to conduct *La Bohème* (with Gordon Davidson as director) at Covent Garden and *Tristan* (with Visconti) in Vienna. The British were disappointed, the Austrians furious. But Bernstein said he felt restored to compositional health after *Mass.* He had started composing *Dybbuk:* the new Jerome Robbins ballet was intended for the twenty-fifth anniversary of the founding of the state of Israel, in the spring of 1973. And he and Alan Jay Lerner were far enough advanced with their concept of a political musical for its producer, Arnold Saint-Subber, to make a preliminary announcement in the *New York Times.* But before he could devote himself to composition and lecture-writing, Bernstein had agreed to conduct the opening production of Göran Gentele's first season as general manager of the Metropolitan Opera. Gentele was a charming man and a superb opera director. Bernstein enjoyed his wit and his European sophistication (they were the same age) and looked forward to a creative collaboration similar to his recent work with Otto Schenk. The opera chosen was Bernstein's schoolboy favorite, *Carmen,* and they had decided to revert to Bizet's original version with spoken French dialogue, a revolution for the "Met." Marilyn Horne and James McCracken were to head the cast.

Bernstein was in Tanglewood when Schuyler Chapin called him just before midnight on July 18 with the dreadful news that Göran Gentele had been killed in a car crash while on holiday in Sardinia. There was no question of canceling *Carmen.* Bernstein assured Chapin, who had been promoted to acting general manager, that he would lead the Metropolitan Opera in an act of homage. But on such short notice it was not possible to find a director of Gentele's stature to replace him, and the choice fell on Bodo Igesz, Gentele's assistant. The costume designer, David Walker, thought Bernstein "with all his 'charisma' should have brought it all together. . . . In this respect he has not been generous." But Walker was doing his first opera and could have had little idea of the magnitude of Bernstein's musical task. Publicly Bernstein behaved as the leader everybody needed. Privately, he was downcast. "Maybe this is a doomed production," he said. "Every time I hear the fate motive I think of Gentele." Helen Coates noted that her boss was "not happy through the rehearsals as so many of the ideas that he and Mr. Gentele had agreed on were not carried out by the young director who took over."

The first-night reviews were excellent, however, Harold Schonberg calling *Carmen* "a thoroughly absorbing experience." ("BEAUCOUP FRENCH ADDED TO CARMEN" was *Variety*'s headline.) All six performances were sold out. Yet Bernstein never returned to the Metropolitan Opera and probably the most lasting result of the *Carmen* was the signing of his first contract with Deutsche Grammophon. Relations between CBS and Amberson were in a bad way. CBS had had so little faith in the selling power of Bernstein's own music that they had insisted he contribute to the costs of recording *Mass*. Amberson, meanwhile, had queried CBS's accounting practices over recording royalties; CBS eventually made back payments of nearly a million dollars to Bernstein and the New York Philharmonic. The arrears stretched back to 1959.

In 1972 CBS dragged its feet about recording *Carmen*. *Der Rosenkavalier* had not sold well, despite the hype. Kraut opened negotiations with Deutsche Grammophon, which was searching for ways to expand internationally and counter Karajan's domination of the company: his recordings accounted for 30 percent of their turnover. Bernstein signed with DG after CBS reluctantly agreed to release him from his exclusivity. The Boston Symphony, under contract to DG, was allowed in return to record Stravinsky's *Oedipus Rex* with Bernstein for CBS. The *Carmen* contract almost collapsed when the Met chorus stood out for higher payments than the basic "scale" they and the orchestra had been offered. Schuyler Chapin trumped them by bringing in a freelance chorus for the studio recording. The Met got its splendid *Carmen* on disc, but at no small cost in terms of labor relations.

The *Carmen* recording—the first opera to be recorded in America for seven years—won a Grammy in 1973 and sold over one hundred thousand copies. But the stage production and the recording sessions left Bernstein physically drained and curiously disappointed: the drawbacks to opera, the inevitable accidents, the casting flaws and the performance compromises apparently outweighed the fun quotient, and Bernstein felt he did not need to do anything if there was no fun involved. Although he held discussions with many opera companies thereafter, the sad fact is that apart from his own work, and a revival of *Fidelio* in Vienna, he never again conducted an opera in an opera house.

I N the fall of 1972 Bernstein took up residence at Harvard. He had a pleasant suite of rooms in Eliot House overlooking the Charles River, where once he had rowed his skiff and talked with Marc Blitzstein. His lectures were set for the spring of 1973. Their subject would be transformational grammar. He intended to take Noam Chomsky's theories about the way different spoken languages derived from common laws of structure and apply them to the language of music. He would film all the orchestral examples in advance, and they would be projected on a cinema screen during the lectures. Harry Kraut worked out an all-embracing distribution concept which involved a second performance of each lecture in a television studio and the eventual sale of discs and videocassettes as well as a book.

It was in no sense a modest venture, but it was not a commercial one, either. Bernstein had to use his own money to set up the television production. His only supporter was Klaus Hallig, the enthusiastic American chief of Unitel. Robert Saudek, the guiding spirit of "Omnibus" in the 1950s, was hired by Amberson as the producer, and Boston's WGBH, a respected if somewhat impoverished educational television station, became a facilities partner. Bernstein mapped out six subjects and decided what orchestral examples he required; in December the Boston Symphony went to WGBH to record the illustrations. A prodigious amount of music was taped and converted into film to be projected at the lectures, including a semidramatized studio performance of Stravinsky's *Oedipus Rex* in which Bernstein's actor friend Michael Wager—a specialist in television commercial voice-overs—was the Speaker. "You will hear the drama of Thebes narrated by the voice of Drano," was Bernstein's cruel introduction to Wager at rehearsal, but after the performance he gave Wager a sculpted silver hand to celebrate their first collaboration. Tatiana Troyanos's stunning performance as Jocasta earned her the role of Anita when Bernstein made his 1984 recording of *West Side Story*. Jamie Bernstein's future husband, David Thomas, then a Harvard undergraduate, remembers Bernstein's first rehearsal with the Harvard Glee Club.

> Suddenly the door swung open and into the room walked Lenny, wearing cowboy boots and a red Apache neckerchief. He urged us to sing for him, to let him hear what we could do. Trembling, F. John Adams, the Glee Club's music director, began to lead us through the opening bars of *Oedipus*. He hadn't got far before Lenny signaled him to stop. "Obviously you have been listening carefully to Stravinsky's own record of this piece." "F" smiled and nodded, in an agony of pleasure and nerves. "Stravinsky was a great composer, one of the greatest," said Lenny, "but he was a *terrible conductor*. You're galloping through this as if it were a waltz, the way it is on his record, but we should attend to what Stravinsky wrote, not what he recorded. Look at the tempo marking! This opening section should be taken at half your speed, not even half. Now, allow me." So "F" was dismissed, and we began to relearn the piece, and for the first time to understand it, under LB's guidance.

Bernstein spent six weeks of Harvard's fall semester playing the part of a visiting professor to perfection, attending and giving seminars, meeting students individually, being guest of honor at a concert of his own music, playing squash with his daughter Jamie (a Radcliffe junior), dining with Harvard's president. He caused such a stir that the *Harvard Crimson* named him Man of the Year. "I can't tell you how exciting my Harvard experience is turning out to be," he told John Gruen. "I'm surrounded by youth. I'm in touch with life. . . . These kids are so incredibly brilliant."

There was only one problem. He had been having such a good time that even with the help of Mary Ahern and Thomas Cothran, who had been granted special student status at Harvard, he had not completed his six lectures. And in the winter they had to be put on hold for a few months while he resumed his regular life as composer and conductor.

At the New Year he flew to Los Angeles to give his blessing to the scaled-down version of *Mass* that Gordon Davidson had mounted at the Mark Taper Forum. (The California critics were no kinder than Harold Schonberg had been.) Two weeks later he went to Washington to make his strongest gesture yet against the newly reelected Nixon administration and the war it was pursuing in Vietnam. (Forty-six thousand Americans had been killed in Southeast Asia. The cost of the fighting was put at $110 billion.) With help from Senator Eugene McCarthy and Martin Peretz (an assistant professor at Harvard), Bernstein and Harry Kraut organized a concert called "A Plea for Peace" at the National Cathedral in Washington. It was timed to begin at the same hour as the official Inaugural Concert across town at the Kennedy Center. The final work on the Inaugural program, performed at President Nixon's express request, was Tchaikovsky's *1812 Overture,* complete with cannon effects, a perverse choice for a country at war. Bernstein programmed Haydn's *Missa Pro Tempore Belli*—his "Mass in the Time of War"—using a choir of one hundred twenty-five, many of whom had sung in his own *Mass.* Volunteers from the National Symphony played for minimum union fees. Three thousand people crowded into the cathedral. Another twelve thousand stood outside in the wind and rain listening to the music over loudspeakers. Liberals all over the country thrilled at this widely reported demonstration of antiwar feeling. A Southeast Asian armistice was signed in Paris a few days later.

In March Bernstein conceded that he would not be ready to deliver his Norton Lectures in the spring. This was no problem for Harvard: he could return in April for his seminars and deliver his lectures in the fall. Reprieved for the moment, he took a holiday on Gran Canaria in the Canary Islands at the suggestion of Harry Kraut, staying at the house of Kraut's pianist friend Christoph Eschenbach.

Eschenbach has a vivid memory of Bernstein's arrival:

> The first time he visited the house it was still rather new, a bit uncomfortable (Felicia later gave me precious advice about how to make improvements), though spacious. But the moment he arrived it was filled with that unique comfort of soul, with his resounding, deep voice, and his aura, which of course replaced all the furniture in the world. . . . A tradition there was to have the first invited guests plant a tree. He planted a palm tree on the edge of the 1200 foot canyon-like abyss. The moment

the tree was standing and waving its fans in the air, he intoned in Hebrew a psalm of David. His mighty voice resounded from the other side of the mountains. . . . He turned the landscape into a mixture of music and mythology. . . . That moment . . . gave me the clue to everything he did. Whether on a human level, or a daily, musical, theoretical or philosophical one, he opened himself always to the widest possible angle of the horizon, while embracing the center of heaven and the center of earth.

Eschenbach shared his house with another rising star among German musicians, Justus Frantz. Bernstein's meeting with Frantz had repercussions for his elder daughter as well as for himself. "My father," Jamie remembers, "fell in love with both of them, especially Justus. 'Jamie, you would love him, he's so cute, he's so beautiful, he's so funny, he's so smart, and you must meet him. . . .' Justus came to dinner and he seemed sort of square in a European way. . . . I never thought about it again until the summer when I was working for Amberson and my assignment was to do a feasibility report for a world-class music festival in the Canary Islands. . . . I met Justus Frantz again . . . and we fell madly in love and had this big affair, in the course of which Justus denied up and down that he had ever had an affair with my father. So people were always denying things to me."

In the spring of 1973 Bernstein set about the completion of his Norton Lectures; a further postponement would be too embarrassing. Back at Harvard, extra staff were recruited to type and retype his countless drafts. Editorial meetings resembled network television script conferences. The music performances were embellished with pages from the full orchestral scores. The use of printed music type on the screen gave the excerpts more cohesion. By the end of May only the finishing touches to the lectures themselves were still awaited.

In June the entire Bernstein family went to Rome, where Bernstein was to conduct a papal concert, taking with them their Chilean housekeeper Julia Vega, the only practicing Catholic in the group. Helen Coates, Harry Kraut and the publicist Margaret Carson completed the Bernstein delegation. All the women wore mantillas; they looked like extras in an amateur production of *Cavalleria Rusticana*. Bernstein presented the Pope with his recordings of music by Bach, Beethoven and Mahler. (Kraut had already made sure the Vatican had its copy of Bernstein's *Mass*. The Pope's welcome was no small compensation for all the sniping he had endured about *Mass* in America.) The eleven-year-old Nina was most impressed with the Pope's tiny red shoes. Getting to see Pope Paul VI (then seventy-five and celebrating the tenth year of his pontificate) had involved a lot of waiting around in antechambers—it was, she thought, like visiting the Wizard of Oz. The meeting ran way over schedule, forty minutes instead of the allotted fifteen.

At the concert, seen all over Europe on television, Bernstein conducted Bach's *Magnificat* and his own *Chichester Psalms*. It was a major ecumenical occasion. On the platform with the Italian Radio Orchestra stood the Harvard

Glee Club and the Newark Boys Chorus. A camera observed the Pope smiling benignly as two choirboys, one white, the other black, floated up to the high A flat of the final "Amen" in *Chichester Psalms*. Then His Holiness blessed the musicians and thanked the maestro: *"Ecco un Americano che vien a dare lezione musicale a noi della vecchia Europa"* (Behold an American who has come to give music lessons to us of the old Europe). Much embracing followed. If Bernstein could get away with kissing the wife of the U.S. President, then the Holy Father was an obvious target. That very morning he had received a cable from his old friend and laughing partner, Mike Mindlin. It was brief and to the point: "REMEMBER: THE RING NOT THE LIPS."

EARLY in 1973, when the Vienna State Opera, under new management, decided to shelve its proud plan to mount *Mass,* Peter Weiser offered to provide a stage at the Konzerthaus for a student production that Bernstein had seen and liked at Yale. The conductor, John Mauceri, had worked as Bernstein's assistant the previous fall when he was doing *Carmen* at the Metropolitan. Harry Kraut organized the financing of Yale's Vienna trip by putting together a co-production with the BBC, Austrian Television and WNET in New York, where it would be shown on the newly launched cultural series, "Great Performances." Bernstein flew in from Rome and received an almost papal welcome from the Viennese. Though the production toned down the alleged sacrilege contained in Bernstein's drama, its showing on British television the following month still sparked off a protest from an official Catholic body claiming to represent sixteen hundred English priests. The BBC promptly arranged a repeat showing.

Bernstein skipped Tanglewood in 1973 in order to work on the Norton Lectures and *Dybbuk,* prior to another spell of music-making in Europe. At the end of July he conducted two Brahms symphonies in Israel for Unitel, then vacationed in Gran Canaria before leading a sophisticated and visually witty studio production of *Trouble in Tahiti* for London Weekend Television. He proceeded to Scotland to conduct Mahler's *Resurrection* Symphony with Sheila Armstrong and Janet Baker as soloists, the Edinburgh Festival Chorus and the London Symphony Orchestra. He wanted his performance for the Unitel Mahler cycle to be filmed in a setting appropriate to the music's grandeur and religious theme and he settled on Ely Cathedral in England with its breathtaking blend of Norman and decorative styles. It had been one of the buildings he studied at Harvard in David Prall's aesthetics course. At considerable expense the enormous forces involved in the symphony reassembled at Ely for what turned into a traumatic weekend of filming. A camera crane collapsed. A bomb scare ruined the dress rehearsal. The sound track was invaded by squeaking bats flying high in the magnificent octagon tower and crashing into the film lights. But the performance itself had an epic power that Bernstein never surpassed.

The Ely filming had been a trial of strength for Harry Kraut. Unitel and the Vienna Philharmonic had wanted to maintain the continuity of a Viennese Mahler cycle. But Bernstein had not been happy, Kraut remembers, with the orchestra's resistance during the rehearsals for Mahler's Fifth the previous year, and he objected to the way leading players sometimes sent deputies from one rehearsal to the next. Kraut had prevailed because of a clause in the contract with Unitel stipulating that the Vienna Philharmonic was to be used only when "feasible."

On the way home Bernstein made his fourth visit of the year to Gran Canaria, this time with his family. Nina remembers that she had to share a bedroom with her mother, on the face of it an odd arrangement. Her father had only recently absorbed the news that Jamie was his rival for the affections of Justus Frantz. Perhaps the stress made him snore more than usual when he finally got to sleep.


ON October 9 Bernstein delivered the first of his six Norton Lectures at the Harvard Square Theater, a cinema seating fifteen hundred, the largest capacity in Cambridge. Seventy-five minutes after the lecture began, and a few minutes into the first substantial musical example—Mozart's G minor Symphony—a telephoned bomb threat was received (Bernstein's second within a few weeks) and fifteen hundred people had to retreat to the street. Two-thirds did not return, a bitter disappointment to Bernstein. But the much-postponed series was launched. Next day he moved to WGBH and recorded the same talk for television.

Physically he was well prepared for the repetitive effort involved in the six-week pattern of rehearsal, lecture, telecast. He had built up his stamina over the years by conducting the same arduous concert program—a Mahler symphony, say, or a *Missa Solemnis*—on three or four successive evenings. He had given television lectures by the dozen. But not on subjects of this density or at this length. Each lecture was like a full evening's one-man show in which he talked, played the piano and sang. His text was typed out on a teleprompter but it was not enough for him simply to read it: he had to know every word by heart and every inflection, every pause, so that the delivery was accurate yet sounded spontaneous and made a connection with his listeners. When he stroked his nose or stumbled on a word it was to give the impression that he was searching for his next illustration, but not a word had been left to chance.

Bernstein's professionalism did not extend to the duration of the lectures, which were hopelessly long for television and tough going even for Harvard students. Including an intermission the final program ran for four hours. But he took the line that he was going to be Norton Professor only once in his lifetime, and he would say everything he wanted to say while he had the chance. He had been excited since childhood by words, poetry and languages and in 1969 Chomsky's *Language and Mind* brought him into contact with the academic discipline of linguistics. He told his listeners that he had long been haunted by the notion that there was a worldwide, inborn musical grammar comparable to Chomsky's idea of an inborn set of rules for creating and responding to language. In his first three lectures, dedicated to musical phonology, syntax and grammar, he explored the way classical music since Mozart could be interpreted in terms of linguistic theory. In the later lectures he studied developments in nineteenth- and twentieth-century music—with decreasing reference to semantics and with more reliance on good old-fashioned music appreciation. The last three titles were "The Delights and Danger of Ambiguity" (following a musical development from Berlioz through Wagner to Debussy), "The Twentieth Century Crisis" (Ravel, Schoenberg, Mahler) and, quoting Keats, "The Poetry of Earth" (Stravinsky's *Oedipus Rex*). Not surprisingly, Stravinsky emerged the top man in Bernstein's pantheon. Animating all the lectures was Bernstein's belief that tonality is a natural law. The overall title of the series, *The Unanswered Question,* was borrowed from the harmonically ambiguous Charles Ives tone poem he particularly liked. "I'm no longer sure what the question is," he said in conclusion, "but I do know the answer is 'Yes.' "

Bernstein devoted more than a year of his life to the Norton Lectures. He was proud of them and of the stir they made in university circles, since he was flying in the face of entrenched positions across the Western world. Many distinguished academics had helped him, but his first acknowledgment was to Tom Cothran, "whose musical sensibilities and poetic insights fertilized my every idea." Despite their awkward lengths the lectures were transmitted by PBS in America and the BBC in Britain. Harvard University published them as a book, and in the 1990s they were reissued as videocassettes. The lectures were attacked at the time by several writers, notably Michael Steinberg in the *New York Times,* who characterized Bernstein's thinking as "sloppy and tendentious" and derided what he called Bernstein's "fatal gift of projecting himself rather than the topic at hand." But the Norton Lectures have proved to be among the most valuable and stimulating contributions ever made to musical education: in the brief history of television they stand on a par with Kenneth Clark's essays on civilization. Other universities certainly thought well of them: both Yale and MIT granted Bernstein five-year visiting fellowships. Had he wished he could have become a regular academic.

Instead he turned his attention to new works and old for the New York theater. While he had been preoccupied with transformational grammar, Harold Prince had assembled a team to transform *Candide.* Fresh from his success directing *A Little Night Music,* Prince conceived *Candide* as something closer to a circus than an operetta. He described his scheme to Lillian Hellman, Prince recalled, "and she said that was what she had always wanted, but *Candide?* Never again! She gave permission for Hugh Wheeler to write a new book, with the proviso . . . that none of her original dialogue be retained in the new version." It was Bernstein, Prince added, who suggested the reorchestration by Hershy Kay for a small band, with thirteen musicians, under John Mauceri's alert direction, distributed in four separate areas of the theater, mostly behind the audience. But Bernstein had no more appetite than Lillian Hellman to return personally to *Candide*. Neither had Richard Wilbur. So Prince invited Stephen Sondheim, one of his closest friends, to write new lyrics. The obliging Sondheim stipulated only that there should be no interference from Hellman or Bernstein.

On November 29, fresh from his Harvard triumph, Bernstein attended a piano run-through with no sets or costumes. He sat all alone on a sort of throne; afterward his only reaction was to ask Harold Prince (unsuccessfully) to restore the Act I syphilis song "Dear Boy." "This version of *Candide* was exactly what I wanted it to be," he said bravely in an interview. "It's exciting, swift, pungent, funny, and touching and it looks just like sideshows at a fair." As a bitter afterthought he added, "About half the score went in the process, I'm sorry to say." The superbly physical production, which Prince himself (echoing Voltaire) later described as a "schoolboy romp," could never do justice to the operatic parodies or the musical witticisms of Bernstein's original score. The new version ran without intermission for an hour and three-quarters. Wheeler's book was as coarse as the pantomime frolics of the cast, but the opening night was a sensational success. *Candide* played to sold-out houses for seven weeks at the tiny Chelsea Theater Center in Brooklyn, and in March transferred to the specially rebuilt Broadway Theater, where it ran for more than seven hundred performances. According to Clive Barnes, drama critic of the *New York Times,* *Candide* was "the most brilliant work Mr. Bernstein has ever composed." "You can't argue with success," Bernstein said.

Throughout the spring of 1974 Bernstein worked with Jerome Robbins on *Dybbuk*. "Lenny is depressed," Helen Coates noted, "because Jerry can't make up his mind how the ballet should go. So Lenny is at a standstill with it. Jerry is the most difficult person in the world with whom to collaborate." But also the most gifted, she might have added. Since the abandonment of *The Exception and the Rule* in 1969, Robbins had created a steady stream of dance masterpieces for the New York City Ballet, among them *Dances at a Gathering* and *The Goldberg Variations*. Bernstein had enormous respect for Robbins, and expectations for *Dybbuk* were high.

It was based on S. Ansky's 1920 Yiddish drama *The Dybbuk*. Bernstein and Robbins had been intrigued by its theme for nearly thirty years. In the folklore of the Ukraine, the land of their fathers, the dybbuk is a ghost who invades the spirit of a living person. Ansky's play describes how in loving friendship two young men swear an oath that if one should have a son and the other a daughter, the two offspring will marry. In a program note Bernstein went on to sketch the story:

> The friends separate and go out into the world, where each marries and has a child, girl and boy. The children, Chanon and Leah, meet when grown, and unaware of their parents' vow, fall deeply in love. However, their love remains undeclared for she is from a wealthy family and Cha-

non is a poor but devoutly orthodox theological student, a wanderer and seeker of secret truths.

When Leah's father arranges a more suitable marriage for her, Chanon desperately turns to the Kabbalah to help him win Leah for himself, and as a last resort he invokes the powerful but dangerous other-worldly formulae of ancient usage. At the supreme moment of discovering the secret words that unleash the dark forces, he is overwhelmed by the fierce ecstasy of the enlightenment and dies. At Leah's wedding, Chanon returns to her as a dybbuk and claiming her as his rightful bride, clings ferociously to his beloved. Finally, through counter-rituals instituted by the elders of the religious community, anathema is declared and the dybbuk is expelled. Leah, unable to exist without her predestined bridegroom, leaves her life to join him in oblivion. Throughout the play a supernatural being called "The Messenger" is an omniscient and prophetic witness to each evolving phase of the drama.

"Our ballet might be described as an *abstract* of the Ansky play," Bernstein added. "Emphasis is laid much less on narrative than on certain episodic peaks of the interior action."

The ballet was divided into eleven sections and lasted fifty minutes. The first performance was May 16, 1974. *Newsweek* called it "the loving handiwork of inspired men" and praised its "magical stage craft" and a "spine-tingling climax." Bernstein's music was well liked: Irving Kolodin thought it the most carefully considered and successfully crafted of his mature scores, "delicately scored, lyrically alive, rhythmically varied." But the public response was respectfully muted. Robbins was never entirely satisfied with his work. He modified it in 1975 and in 1980 he produced a virtually new ballet to the same music, called, plainly, *Suite of Dances,* which is for male dancers only and was put together without consultation with Bernstein. Neither ballet was in the New York City Ballet's repertoire in the early 1990s.

By way of introduction to the music Bernstein laid down his customary smokescreen. In a long interview in the *Times* before the premiere he tried to show how the Kabbalah, the eleventh-century Jewish system of theology and metaphysics, had dominated his musical thinking. In a program note for the New York Philharmonic the following year he spoke further about his numerological and verbal manipulations in composing *Dybbuk.* ". . . It was the integer 2 that particularly fascinated me, since Ansky's *Dybbuk* is really a drama about dualisms—Good and Evil, Ends and Means, Male and Female, Justice and Necessity, Self and Society, etc., with all their problematic intercombinations, and especially the duality of the so-called True World as opposed to *this* world in which we seem to reside." He was still thinking about dualism when, following his practice with *Fancy Free* and *Facsimile,* he fashioned purely orchestral music out of *Dybbuk.* The first suite is composed of "the music of this world (the Russian-Polish ghetto), which has a consistent ethnic quality, a

'Jewish' sound." The second suite consists of "the music of the True World (of God, Satan, and the Angels), which is Kabbalistic in nature, investigatory, experimental, aphoristic and far less ethnic in character." The first suite has cantor-like parts for two male singers. Suite No. 2 contains some of Bernstein's most original writing, using a serial technique which he worked out by translating Kabbalah symbols into numbers and relating those numbers to notes in the scale.

Bernstein made a convincing case on paper for dividing the *Dybbuk* music, but in public performance in successive weeks in New York in April 1975, the two concert suites fell flat. Fortunately he also recorded the full ballet score for CBS with the original performers, the New York City Ballet Orchestra. *Dybbuk* is one of his most considered orchestral scores, composed (or "manipulated" as he chose to describe it) over many months. It is the purest statement he made of his specifically Ukraine-Jewish heritage, yet despite the detailed program relating to Ansky's play, *Dybbuk* also holds its own as abstract music.

I N the spring of 1974 an era came to an end for the Bernsteins; they moved from 895 Park Avenue to the Dakota on West Seventy-second Street, overlooking Central Park. The Dakota was the oldest luxury apartment building in New York. It had become a fashionable place for rich Bohemian actors and writers, many of them friends of the Bernsteins. Michael Wager had an apartment there, as did Lauren Bacall and John Lennon and Yoko Ono. Felicia finally made up her mind to move when their friend Christoph Eschenbach turned up in jeans and a leather jacket at 895 and was sent to the service entrance. (Alexander's black schoolmates had been directed to the same route for years.)

Bernstein also bought a small apartment on the top floor for his studio. He was sad about moving, or so he told Helen Coates. "He says it is Felicia's 'ball' and so he must let her do it if it makes her happy." To move to the West Side was to make a statement: the Bernsteins were turning their back on the Establishment, quitting an apartment that had become, with the publication of Tom Wolfe's article, altogether too well known. The new apartment was smaller than the one at 895 Park Avenue, but the rooms were high-ceilinged and handsome, with a fine double space for music room and library. Only Nina of the three children was still living at home full time. Felicia fitted out the servant's room at the top of the building for her elder daughter.

In June, Jamie Bernstein completed her four years at Harvard. Her graduation was, she remembers, "a less-than-wonderful occasion. My parents were really uptight and I didn't know why." After the grand ceremony at Harvard Yard the graduating students returned to their individual houses to receive their diplomas and shake hands with the house master. "My parents missed that part, my individual moment in the sun, because they were still busy hugging and kissing Rostropovich, who had just escaped from Russia and was getting an honorary degree at Harvard that day. I was pretty ticked off about that." Back at Fairfield the next day Jamie discovered the reason for the tension. Felicia was about to enter the hospital for surgery. Nina, who was only twelve, remembers being told that her mother "had to have another thing taken off her nose. Mummy called from the hospital and I said, 'How are you doing?' And she said, 'Well you know, the funniest thing happened. They thought that the cancer was on my nose but it turned out to be in my breast.' That's the way Mummy worked. She wouldn't be straight about anything."

Felicia Bernstein was only fifty-two. "Oh Phyllis, what a thing," was how she broke the wretched news to her friend Phyllis Newman. Increasingly isolated from her husband's conducting work abroad and from his inner life, she was determined to regain her strength and see her younger daughter through her teens. She made a good recovery from her mastectomy, and soon looked as elegant and beautiful as ever. But Phyllis was not the only friend who saw her from that summer on as a doomed woman.

# CRISES AND CATASTROPHE

*The Bernsteins' last holiday-greeting card
together, fall 1977.*
PHOTO © HENRY GROSSMAN, COURTESY OF THE ESTATE OF LEONARD BERNSTEIN

*You would think I might want to give up. On the
contrary it makes me only want to do more.*

—LEONARD BERNSTEIN,
*New York Times* interview,
December 11, 1977

FELICIA'S illness remained a family secret. But only a month after her operation Leonard was also in the hospital, complaining of shortness of breath after eating lobster at Fairfield. The local doctor had been summoned and having heard ectopic beats in Bernstein's heart rhythm was taking no chances. Rumors of a heart attack flooded the musical grapevine and anxious inquiries flowed into Tanglewood, where he was due to conduct the Koussevitzky Centenary concert: a Vienna newspaper reported him on his deathbed. But it was a false alarm. He returned to Fairfield dressed in doctor's whites, with a stethoscope around his neck, and arrived in Tanglewood displaying countless needle pricks in his forearm. Despite the warning of his wife's illness, he had left Bridgeport General Hospital smoking a cigarette. (Felicia hadn't given up either.)

Bernstein's Sunday afternoon Boston Symphony Orchestra concert in the Shed attracted an audience of 16,688—one of the largest in Tanglewood's history. At the end of the ten-minute "Adagietto" from Mahler's Fifth Symphony he silently gestured the audience to stand for a minute in Koussevitzky's memory. Bernstein's sense of ritual never deserted him. Public observance of grief and sadness was easier to handle than the gnawing uncertainties of his personal life. His continuing friendship with Cothran and his burst of affection for Justus Frantz were perhaps only the tips of the iceberg that threatened the equilibrium of his marriage.

At Tanglewood he lived much of his life in the public eye. When he lunched with his brother's family and friends at the nearby Alice's Restaurant, Adolph Green and he sang the songs and performed the party tricks of their youth while other diners smiled tolerantly at the foibles of the famous.

In the late summer of 1974, after conducting Mahler's Fifth Symphony in New York's Central Park for an audience of a hundred thousand, Bernstein took the New York Philharmonic on a Pacific concert tour. His son Alexander went with him. In New Zealand they skiied and sailed and soaked in hot mineral baths between concerts of Mozart and Mahler. He wrote to Felicia, "We miss you terribly; it seems incredible that ten days ago I had a last glimpse of you standing in the airport being abandoned by your males. I hope you're not too lonely, that there are all kinds of cheery *visitas* and chums. . . . Well the siren blows for Australia and we're off, as Shirley would say, across the Straits of Magellan."

In Japan, where Pierre Boulez arrived to share the orchestra's fortnight-long visit, Bernstein was greeted with more hysteria than before. At one concert fifty fans rushed to the front to touch hands and throw him flowers as he left the platform. Others wept disconsolately backstage when they could not find the right staircase to get to see the maestro for an autograph. But he found Japan less charming than on previous visits: he lamented the disappearance of the kimono from the streets and expressed his fear about the extremism he observed in Japanese audiences. "They are younger and they care and they are infinitely more intense in their listening . . . but they are just insane about Western music." To American journalists he spoke about the new musical he was writing with Alan Jay Lerner, *1600 Pennsylvania Avenue* (i.e., the White House): "We are trying to tell the story of the little white lie, by which I mean the big black lie." In the wake of President Nixon's resignation (to avoid impeachment) he felt a cloud lifting: "We have come out of the muddy, murky and treacherous period that has been going on since Kennedy's murder."

Always on the move, it seemed, Bernstein was not an easy man with whom to collaborate. When he returned to New York in mid-September he had less than a fortnight to spend working with Lerner before he was off again, this time to Europe. In Vienna he continued his Mahler cycle at the opening concert of the newly refurbished Konzerthaus. For the sake of completeness he included the opening adagio movement of Mahler's unfinished Tenth Symphony, which he had hitherto resisted. His brief annual visits had become almost routine business for the Austrian press. One columnist was reduced to publishing details of Bernstein's favorite meal at the Israeli-owned Stadtkrug restaurant, where he liked to dine off the golden plates that had once belonged to Hermann Goering: *Frische Gänsegrieben* (fresh goose crackling), *Orientalischer Hummus* (hummus) and *Wiener Tafelspitz* (boiled beef—often served with dumplings and apple cream sauce). He had only himself to blame for his spreading waistline.

At Warwick, in England, Bernstein received his first (and only) honorary degree from a British university. In London he met up again with Lerner, who was talent-spotting for *1600* (he found the actress Patricia Routledge) and on the point of marrying his seventh wife. They hoped to have *1600 Pennsylvania Avenue* in rehearsal early in 1975. Back in New York they worked on the show through the late fall and into the winter. Bernstein talked at different times with John Dexter and Francis Ford Coppola about directing it; a strong hand would be needed to sort out the conflicting demands in Lerner's book of political comment and Broadway entertainment. By January Bernstein realized that another postponement was inevitable, and he flew to Antigua for a vacation. He was having a difficult time with Lerner, who became despondent every time he reached an impasse, yet did not want to seek help from a director.

In contrast to the previous year, Bernstein spent most of 1975 working on *1600 Pennsylvania Avenue,* but in the spring came a brief interruption to conduct the New York Philharmonic. The ovation he received on April 24 after a performance of Tchaikovsky's Fourth Symphony apparently went to his head. "I have just made a decision," he told the audience. "I don't know how, I don't know when, but I'm going to come back to this orchestra." Troublemakers interpreted the speech as a veiled criticism of his successor—who announced soon afterward that he would not renew his contract after 1977—and a bid to return to power. But Carlos Moseley, now president of the Philharmonic, was his usual diplomatic self about Bernstein's offer: "There will be great joy if he can give us more time." Bernstein had no intention of applying for a second term as music director. Conducting was like a drug to him: he had simply been carried away by the euphoria of the moment.

On May 1, on a working holiday with Alan Lerner in the Canary Islands, Bernstein made his most serious attempt yet to give up smoking. Before he went, Alexander and Felicia agreed to stop smoking with him. The effort was short-lived. "I'm a dope, I'm an idiot, I spoil it all with smoking," Bernstein observed pathetically in the summer. But the work was coming along. "Yesterday," Helen Coates noted loyally at the end of May, "I heard about ten of Lenny's songs for the new musical. . . . I think it's going to be marvelous." After one of his briefest-ever sojourns in Tanglewood, he bought himself more composing time by canceling a performance of *Chichester Psalms* the BBC was planning for him to conduct at Chichester Cathedral. He had vain hopes of finishing the Alan Lerner show before leaving for Salzburg in early August.

The Salzburg Festival was Herbert von Karajan's empire, and virtually the last European cultural citadel for Bernstein to conquer. His first appearance there since he and the New York Philharmonic had passed through on tour in

1959 was supervised by a powerful triple alliance—the Vienna Philharmonic, Deutsche Grammophon and Harry Kraut. His other record company, CBS, swamped the shop windows of Salzburg with portraits of Bernstein. They seemed particularly prominent on the road Karajan took every morning when he drove into the city from his home in Anif. When Bernstein attended Karajan's production of the opera *Don Carlos*, he made a conspicuous entry, leaning over the balustrade to greet his friends in the orchestra—the Vienna Philharmonic—just before Karajan entered to conduct. The open rivalry continued when Bernstein broke tradition by insisting on throwing open his dress rehearsal to students and other young people who could not afford Salzburg ticket prices.

The first of Bernstein's two concert appearances was in the middle of the month, with the resident London Symphony Orchestra. His program was one of his favorite triple-role, triple-bills: *Chichester Psalms,* Mozart's G major Piano Concerto (K. 453) and the Sibelius Fifth Symphony. Then he took a week's holiday with friends of Justus Frantz to work on *1600 Pennsylvania Avenue* on the exclusive island of Sylt in the North Sea. There is no road transport on Sylt, so his piano was brought in by train. The island was fog-bound the entire week and communication by telephone was cut off after sheep ate the cable.

Back in Salzburg his entire family assembled for a spectacular fifty-seventh birthday party hosted by the Austrian Chancellor, Bruno Kreisky. During a week of glittering Salzburg social life Bernstein heard *Cosi Fan Tutte* conducted by Böhm, after which Bernstein exclaimed, "I'd give my balls to have written four bars of that music." At Mozart's birthplace he needed no encouragement to be photographed playing Mozart's newly restored 1780 fortepiano. He told the attendant journalists that to play a Mozart piano concerto in Salzburg had been one of the great experiences of his life.

Every morning he rehearsed Mahler's Eighth Symphony with the Vienna Philharmonic. There had been only one previous performance of the "Symphony of a Thousand" in Austria since the 1930s—conducted by Dimitri Mitropoulos in 1960 shortly before his death. Bernstein inspired the soloists, among them Margaret Price, Agnes Baltsa, Hermann Prey and José van Dam, to work together like members of a permanent ensemble. Vienna's leading choirs, professional and amateur, were forged into a powerful instrument. Despite the preceding weeks of exhausting festival, the Vienna Philharmonic played like men possessed. "It was," wrote Karl Löbl, "an incomparable event. The recreation of music could never be more demanding, more exciting, more thrilling or more beautiful."

The two parts of Mahler's Eighth Symphony are performed without an intermission, but it is customary for the conductor to make a five-minute pause after the half-hour first movement. A spellbound young conductor named Charles Bornstein, who had been permitted to listen from the wings, noted the silent ritual which took place when Bernstein came off the platform during the Salzburg performance. He stood, seemingly exhausted, in front of a semicircle of four assistants. They went to work on him swiftly and silently like seconds at a boxing match. The first young man gingerly removed Bernstein's sopping wet conducting suit (tailored as ever by Otto Perl) and his piqué shirt and tie. Everything was drenched in sweat. Simultaneously the second assistant lit an L&M cigarette, took several puffs himself to get it going, and thrust it between Bernstein's lips. A third assistant offered him water from an elegant silver tumbler. The fourth man dried Bernstein's hair and gently slapped water from another tumbler onto his face. Then he toweled Bernstein all over with one hand, combing and patting his hair with the other. When Bernstein's ablutions were completed, the first attendant slipped on a clean white shirt. As Bernstein tied his own tie, he occasionally consulted the little hand mirror held up for him by the third assistant. A new tail suit was proffered for him to step into. The second assistant lit another cigarette, puffed on it and exchanged it for the one in Bernstein's mouth. More sips from the goblet were offered. A whispered, "Are you all right, Mr. Bernstein?" were the only words spoken during the entire ceremony. He said nothing, but interwoven with the deep inhalations of the second cigarette the worrying wheeze of his fast and erratic breathing could be heard yards away.

The five minutes were nearly up. Cologne was splashed on Bernstein's new pocket handkerchief. He flattened out the lock of hair above his right eyebrow with his cigarette hand and moved toward the stage manager's corner. Standing immediately next to a No Smoking sign he dropped his cigarette to the floor and squashed it with his shoe. Then he reverently kissed each of his Koussevitzky cuff links, squared his shoulders, took a deep breath and walked back on stage. He had never left the exalted sound world of Gustav Mahler.

A F T E R Salzburg Bernstein conducted the LSO and the Orchestre Nationale at the 1975 Edinburgh Festival. Then, in Paris, he mounted another of the spectacular but hazardous "on location" conducting events that distinguished his final decades. The challenge was to perform the *Requiem* by Hector Berlioz in the location for which it had been composed, the imposing seventeenth-century church of St-Louis des Invalides where Napoleon is buried. The *Requiem,* a royal commission honoring a slain French general, calls for four brass bands placed in the galleries running high up around the chapel. French Radio's two Paris orchestras and the 140 members of the Radio France Chorus were joined by the Welsh tenor Stuart Burrows. Eight timpani played by four musicians added to the spectacle.

Bernstein was in his element controlling the huge forces on this sacred ground, and for a fleeting moment in Les Invalides he imagined himself as Hector Berlioz (who never conducted there), conjuring up the natural quadrophony of the brass bands and the incredible sound combinations (such as the blending of a single flute with three trombones) in which the *Requiem* abounds. But the rehearsals needed iron concentration since the church was an acoustical death trap: the musicians had difficulty hearing each other and the concealed pitch pipes of an electronic organ were of limited success in helping the chorus to stay in tune.

The performances brought out *le tout Paris,* headed by the music-loving President Giscard d'Estaing. Protocol required that Giscard be the last to enter. Not to be outdone, Bernstein first entered the chapel as part of the procession and then doubled back so that he could come up the aisle again behind the President and leap to the podium to give the downbeat for the "Marseillaise." When Bernstein decided on instant retakes after the performance, the presidential party stayed to hear a second "Lacrymosa" even more ravishing than the first. But Fritz Buttenstedt, Unitel's co-producer of the French telecast, emerged visibly distressed after watching the performance on a monitor screen. The walls of the Invalides are draped with regimental flags acquired in battle by victorious French armies. Unfortunately, all that could be made out behind Bernstein in his frequent close-ups was a Nazi flag with a swastika, acquired by General Leclerc's forces in a rare victory in North Africa during the Second World War. Bernstein's telecast of the Berlioz *Requiem* did not receive wide distribution in Germany.

LATE in September Bernstein returned to New York intent on finishing *1600 Pennsylvania Avenue.* The first producer, Arnold Saint-Subber, had pulled out in June. "I loathed it," he said afterwards. "I tried desperately to get everyone to abandon it." Harry Kraut remembers Saint-Subber facing up to Lerner shouting, "it stinks, it stinks, it stinks." Bernstein and Lerner, the "two rich old Jews," as they were to call themselves later, had ignored the warning. Where other angels feared to tread, Roger Stevens could be relied upon to back his undying admiration for Bernstein's music. But even Stevens and his partner, Robert Whitehead, had declined to go out and raise money until they were satisfied that the problem with the book had been resolved. Lerner undercut their objections when he persuaded the Coca-Cola company (whose chairman had been a friend since schooldays) to become the sole backer with an initial investment of nine hundred thousand dollars. Coca-Cola would be seen doing something imaginative for the swiftly approaching bicentennial year and at the same time making money for its shareholders. There was not even a backers' run-through: the names of Bernstein and Lerner were thought to be a guarantee of success.

From the moment the Coca-Cola deal was announced in mid-September *1600 Pennsylvania Avenue* was doomed. With the money in place, the natural desire to get the show on the road stifled the producers' more prudent instincts. After all, which Broadway musical had been completely finished before it went into production? And every can of Coke sold in the bicentennial year could publicize the show.

Rehearsals for *1600 Pennsylvania Avenue* began in late January for a Broadway premiere in May. It opened in Philadelphia (after two postponements) on February 26. When Bernstein finally completed his score, two weeks into rehearsal, he wrote "Deo Gracias" on the last page, in the manner of Joseph Haydn; then he surrounded the inscription with amulets to ward off the evil eye, so perhaps he knew already that something was amiss. But when he spoke to reporters in Philadelphia before the show opened he was in an ebullient mood: "I've never been so confident, so thrilled, about a show while I was doing it," he said.

Bernstein and Lerner had been at Harvard at the same time (Lerner was two weeks younger), but they hadn't become friends until the late 1940s and had worked together only once, in 1957, when they wrote two spoof commencement choruses as a fund-raising gimmick for their alma mater. Lerner had amassed a huge fortune in partnership with composer Frederick Loewe, writing *Brigadoon, Camelot* and, most successful of all, *My Fair Lady.* Since Loewe's retirement Lerner had had a string of flops (apart from *Coco,* in which Katharine Hepburn had starred) and he seemed to have lost his magic. He smoked incessantly and bit his nails so voraciously that they bled. As a consequence, he always wore white cotton gloves, and bloodstained discards were sometimes discovered in the men's room of the offices he visited. As a friend and colleague he was said to be intensely agreeable and devastatingly persuasive. Felicia liked him and had encouraged her husband to work with him.

When Lerner first approached Bernstein in the summer of 1972 he was depressed by Nixon's electoral strength and the inability of the Democrats to dislodge him. Bernstein was sympathetic, just as he had been when Lillian Hellman had suggested a satirical response to the excesses of McCarthyism back in 1953. They decided to make their points about the power of the presidency and the nation's treatment of its black people inside a musical which would tell the story of the first hundred years of the White House. The same leading actor and actress were to play eight different presidents and first ladies. (Inexplicably, Andrew Jackson and Abraham Lincoln were left out.) The same leading black actor and actress were to play the three generations of servants who worked at the White House during the century. This musico-historical pageant would take place within the framework of a rehearsal. The actors, white and black, would argue about the meaning of the history they were enacting, and some of these discussions would also be set to music. A musical within a play with music: it was a cumbersome formula; small wonder that Saint-Subber had rebelled against its pretentiousness.

Bernstein was very clear that "the subject is not the presidency but the house. . . . Both the house and the play become metaphors for the country." Ignoring Sam Goldwyn's dictum that messages should be left to Western Union, Lerner asserted at the same press briefing that he was not preaching: "We're just telling what we feel. I hope we achieved it without being dogmatic, pedantic or sermonizing."

It was a pious hope but the public was not impressed. Foiled in his attempt to get his money back, one man kicked through a glass door in his haste to leave the theater as the first night in Philadelphia dragged on for close to four hours. Roger Stevens, who had earlier described the show as "the musical of the decade" ("Why not the century?" Bernstein had asked) was soon in charge of damage control following a sheaf of awful reviews. *Variety* called the book "stultifyingly ponderous and repetitious." Bernstein's music was well liked, particularly by Irving Kolodin, who praised a delightful pastiche of various nineteenth-century styles to match the presidential pageant. Three or four numbers were even picked out as potential hits. But drastic action was needed to cure the book problem. Jerome Robbins looked and turned away. "Only two titans could have a failure like this," he said later. Other close friends and colleagues, among them Mike Nichols, Arthur Laurents and Shirley Bernstein, urged Bernstein to close immediately. Lerner, perpetual optimist, refused. Besides, the Coca-Cola cash deal required a Broadway opening. The director Frank Corsaro left the show and Roger Stevens hired Gilbert Moses and George Faison, who had recently worked together on the direction and choreography of *The Wiz,* a successful black version of *The Wizard of Oz.* Moses stripped out the moralizing rehearsal scenes but had no convincing new concept to propose. It was like changing chairs on the *Titanic,* said one of the actors.

In the midst of rehearsals Bernstein had flown to Butler University in Indianapolis in February for a five-day festival of his music. On George Washington's birthday, Indiana's Republican governor declared a Leonard Bernstein Day. In March he returned to New York for his spring season with the Philharmonic. But he canceled several concerts in order to do more work on *1600 Pennsylvania Avenue* in Washington. Tom Cothran flew down with him and predicted in his diary that it would be "a sure flop due to college production incompetence and speedfreak twitching A.J. Lerner—a musical in itself." The show opened on Broadway on May 4 and closed after seven performances. The notices were abysmal. "Tedious and simplistic," "school pageant," "bicentennial bore," "a crummy idea"—there was no bottom to the pit of humiliation into which Bernstein fell. It was the worst failure of his professional life.

After putting in an appearance at the opening night party at Sardi's Bernstein joined his commiserating family and friends at the Dakota. There, Harry Kraut remembers, he lashed out at Felicia, blaming her for encouraging him to collaborate with Lerner. Felicia rushed away in tears. Next day the Bernsteins flew to San Miguel de Allende in Mexico for a holiday in a borrowed villa. Leonard was in the blackest of moods and sometimes stayed in bed all day. The house was overfurnished, there were mosquitoes, and the pool was in the shade by the time Bernstein wanted to swim.

It is too easy to lay the blame for the musical's failure at Alan Jay Lerner's door. His lyrics are often apt and witty, and several of his scenes—the selection of the Potomac River site, the British invasion of 1812, the bedtime dialogue between President and Mrs. Monroe—are cleverly constructed. For his part Bernstein was only intermittently working at the highest level of invention and he was surprisingly self-indulgent. He wrote brilliantly for the chorus, but he wrote too much; his original score was longer, he confessed, than Wagner's *Rheingold.* To judge from the way the book developed from its early draft, Lerner seems to have been a little overwhelmed by Bernstein's passionate didacticism, which was all very well in a personal statement like *Mass* but hardly appropriate for a Broadway musical. Patricia Routledge, the brilliant British actress who played the First Lady, and for whom Bernstein wrote the show-stopping "Duet for One," a dialogue between two presidential wives, thought Lerner wanted to write a musical comedy and Bernstein an opera. She described the show as "a diamond-studded dinosaur."

The upshot is that a major Leonard Bernstein score has been lost. There is not even a cast recording: Bernstein vetoed it. He salvaged some of the numbers for use in later compositions, and one of the songs, "Take Care of This House," has achieved independent life as a blessing on new ventures of all kinds: Frederica von Stade sang it at President Carter's Inauguration Gala in January 1977. But for the third time in his life, following *The Skin of Our Teeth* in 1964 and *The Exception and the Rule* in 1968, Bernstein faced the agonizing experience of having to write off a musical—in this case one he had worked on intermittently for more than three years. Responsibility must in the end be pinned on both Lerner and Bernstein for not having listened to the advice of their colleagues. In his tongue-in-cheek lyrics for the 1957 Harvard songs, Lerner anatomized the arrogance of their university attitude:

> We're the lonely men of Harvard,
> Alone, alas, alack are we!
> And that's the curse we share,
> It's the cross we've got to bear
> For our irrefutable superiority.

IT is clear from interviews he gave in 1975 and 1976 that Bernstein suddenly became aware of his mortality. "I wonder how to divide the time I have left," he told Paul Hume. The exaggerated enthusiasm with which he had earlier praised *1600 Pennsylvania Avenue*—"I've never been so confident, so thrilled"— perhaps concealed some insecurity about his composing talents and certainly raised questions about his theatrical judgment. But his uncertainty went deeper. He was facing a crisis about his sexuality. Close friends had assumed for some time that his marriage was based on friendship rather than physical attraction, but Harry Kraut remembers him bursting into tears when he confided that he had lost his sexual appetite for his wife since her mastectomy. Meanwhile he was finding his craving for the love of young men more and more difficult to suppress, even on home territory. Felicia had had disagreeable intimations that her husband was abandoning the discretion that was part of their unspoken covenant. She opened a love letter to Leonard from a man. She received a phone call in Spanish from another man who told her Leonard and his assistant were having a homosexual affair. She insisted that the assistant be removed, and he was transferred to an office job with Amberson. When she arrived at a party the same evening she saw him in the room. She turned on her heel and rushed out of the restaurant, pleading sudden illness. It was becoming more difficult by the day to sweep problem issues under the carpet.

Bernstein did not want to hurt his wife, and yet he had already revealed the extent of his frustration by attacking her in front of friends, ostensibly about *1600 Pennsylvania Avenue*. Away from home and among his intimates he made no secret of his affection for Tom Cothran nor of a new friendship he began in 1976 with Chris Barnes, a black airline steward he met in Washington and later helped to earn a lawyer's degree. He was torn between his innate conservativism, reflected in his deep affection for his wife and family, and his longing to "come out" while he still had time to live a different life. In May 1976, when he set off on a six-week bicentennial tour of the United States and Europe with the New York Philharmonic, Tom Cothran went with him, listed as his traveling secretary.

Although his programs of American music were triumphs in many cities, the telecast of a New York Philharmonic concert in London that June revealed in close-up an astonishingly downcast Bernstein. He took *An American in Paris* at a funereal pace, while the *Rhapsody in Blue* was marred by flurries of wrong notes and more lugubrious tempi. His private sadness was showing through the public mask. Earlier in the orchestra's tour, in Sarasota, Florida, he had made so many mistakes in the Gershwin that he felt obliged to write an apology in the visitors' book. Back in New York for Bicentennial Day, July 4, he joined the mayoral party in Battery Park, where he had the honor of reading from the Declaration of Independence. Then the Bernstein family adjourned to the Riverside Drive apartment of their photographer friend Henry Grossman to watch the great review of the tall sailing ships. Harry Kraut remembers witnessing another semipublic falling out between Leonard and Felicia at the party before Bernstein left to prepare for his New York Philharmonic concert that evening in Central Park.

Storm clouds gathered. Bernstein wanted to resume work on *Songfest,* his new song cycle, originally commissioned for the bicentennial by the Philadelphia Orchestra. He had shelved it to finish *1600 Pennsylvania Avenue* and now intended it for the National Symphony in Washington. He loved reading through anthologies of American poetry with Tom Cothran, looking for poems to set, and he talked of taking a summer place on Long Island where they would work together. Felicia had meanwhile rented a house in Martha's Vineyard for a family holiday—without Cothran, whose intimate presence she was beginning openly to resent. But the rupture, when it came, was probably triggered by something much more trivial, even casual. On Sunday July 11 the Bernsteins had a big party at Fairfield to celebrate Alexander's twenty-first birthday. Harry Kraut remembers thinking that Bernstein was behaving foolishly, brazenly flirting with one of the waiters brought in by the caterer. Perhaps he had been repossessed by the "automatic little demon" he had described to his sister in 1950, the urge to seduce that made him careless of the consequences, "blind to the inner knowledge of the certain ensuing meaninglessness." It's even possible that Felicia stumbled across her husband in a compromising situation. At all events, she stayed in her room long after the festivities had begun. When she did join the party, Jamie remembers, her still-puffy eyes were concealed behind dark glasses. Leonard had hired a plane to fly over the Fairfield house trailing the message, "Happy Birthday, Alexander." But when the plane made its first pass Alexander was nowhere to be found. His father eventually discovered him indoors quietly smoking a joint with some friends, and flew into a rage, Alexander remembers, out of all proportion to the alleged misdemeanor.

The children did not know yet that Felicia had given Leonard an ultimatum. If he persevered with his plan to spend time alone with Tom Cothran she did not want him to come back home. Michael Wager remembers being dumbfounded. Why, he asked Bernstein, had he forced the issue? Bernstein said he felt compelled to bring the subject into the open. He might have added that over the previous weeks he had seen his analyst, Dr. Milton Horowitz, almost daily. A year later, shifting the blame, Bernstein told Jamie that Horowitz had encouraged his relationship with Cothran—"it was largely his fault."

BERNSTEIN called Harry Kraut at eight that Monday morning. "Well it's over," he said. Sometime in the night he had made his decision to leave home. He was now at his Dakota apartment; the staff were away at Fairfield and he did not know how to fix himself a cup of coffee, let alone his life. As a first step, Kraut persuaded him to reduce the inevitable gossip by renting a house in California rather than the Hamptons for the working holiday with Cothran. While arrangements for the summer were being made, Bernstein fulfilled conducting engagements at Robin Hood Dell and Tanglewood. His remarkable performance of Liszt's *Faust* Symphony with the Boston Symphony Orchestra was filmed and recorded at Symphony Hall in Boston. Professional colleagues were given no hint that his personal life was in disarray.

In August and September 1976 he and Cothran spent six weeks together in Carmel, on the Pacific Ocean between Los Angeles and San Francisco. While they sang and swam and read poetry, in Bernstein's mind gingerly testing the possibility of making a permanent life together, Felicia was going through hell at Martha's Vineyard. She could not come to terms with her husband's defection. She told friends he had gone to California to work with Arthur Laurents. Ellen Ball, who was in the process of divorcing Burton Bernstein, remembers that Felicia was "so unhappy she couldn't sleep. . . . She was up all night, just reading and smoking. She said, 'I'm smoking this much until it hurts, physically.' " Kenneth Ehrman saw Bernstein in California. "He was torturing himself asking what to do about his personal life, and I think he felt a lot of guilt about Felicia." Yet the pain seemed to spark his creativity: in the space of a week in September he wrote four songs destined for his *Songfest* cycle.

In mid-September Bernstein returned to New York and rented a suite in the Novarro Hotel (since renamed the Ritz Carlton). Cothran was installed in an adjacent room. It was as if the maestro were visiting a foreign city with his assistant close at hand. But this was Manhattan, and he was making calls from a hotel less than a mile from his own apartment to arrange dinners with his children and even his estranged wife. He and Felicia dined early at the fashionable Côte Basque one evening in October. It had to be early because Felicia had gone back to work. She had a good supporting part (as a seductress of sorts) in Pavel Kohout's *Poor Murderer,* a new Broadway play starring Maria Schell, directed by her old teacher Herbert Berghof. Bernstein saw a preview a few days later. Nothing had been publicly announced about the separation but anyone who saw Bernstein knew that something out of the ordinary was going on. He had returned from California sporting a mustache and a beard. He looked like an Old Testament prophet. "I hate it!!! and have told him in no uncertain terms," noted Helen Coates. "It makes him look older and he said he knew it but at the same time it makes him feel ten years younger!"

Bernstein had already left for Europe when a publicist working on Felicia's play tipped off the *New York Daily News* about the separation. On October 28, the much syndicated column by "Suzy" had the headline "WEST SIDE STORY '76: BERNSTEIN AND WIFE SPLIT." "Their break-up comes as a shock to all," the report continued. The unsuspecting fourteen-year-old Nina Bernstein read about it over somebody's shoulder on a bus on her way to school. She had been told almost nothing, she complained later; she never was. The rupture was an international story. *Newsweek* reported "it is a trial separation, with no divorce planned." *People* magazine a week later carried an optimistic quote from Felicia: "We hope to reconcile."

In Munich the bearded Bernstein conducted the Chilean pianist Claudio Arrau and the Bavarian Radio Orchestra in a fund-raising concert to help Amnesty International in its protests against human rights abuses, specifically in Chile. It was the beginning of an important new orchestral relationship with the Bavarians. In Vienna he conducted Mahler's Sixth Symphony, which made a fine (but bearded) conclusion to Unitel's Mahler cycle. With Tom Cothran at his side he moved on to Paris, where he could fantasize about being Oscar Wilde to Cothran's Lord Alfred Douglas. With the French Radio orchestra he recorded two more Berlioz masterpieces for disc and video—the *Symphonie Fantastique* and *Harold en Italie.* In a second concert he worked with Mstislav Rostropovich, who was so bowled over by the depth of feeling Bernstein released in his interpretations of *Schelomo* by Bloch and the Schumann cello concerto that he resolved never to record either of the works again.

But Bernstein's almost casual approach to the choice of "takes" from his Berlioz recording for EMI shocked the recording producer John Mordler.

"When I asked him to repeat a passage in order to rectify some untidy ensemble he refused to believe that anything was wrong," Mordler recalls. "However I did manage to persuade him to come to the Control Room to hear the passage in question, at which he exclaimed 'The trombones are so untogether—I just love it!' and he dashed off to the airport." Jamie Bernstein remembers the tension of the bleak November days when her father returned to New York. Felicia asked Jamie and Alexander to promise that they would not have supper with their father after his concerts if it meant seeing Tom Cothran as well. Jamie risked her mother's fury and refused.

Helen Coates saw in the separation a chance to reassert some influence over Bernstein. "I really doubt that they will again live together," she wrote to Alan Fluck in England. "People are quite shocked about it. I was not too surprised myself." Felicia was furious when she discovered that Helen Coates was giving similar signals to Manhattan friends who phoned to inquire.

Bernstein soon shaved off his beard but he went public about his decision to leave his wife when he conducted the New York Philharmonic in December 1976. He prefaced his performances of Shostakovich's Fourteenth Symphony with a fifteen-minute talk. The composer was facing death when he composed the work, he said, and also hurling defiance at Soviet tyranny and authoritarianism. "Studying this work," he went on, "I came to realize that as death approaches [he was fifty-eight] an artist must cast off everything that may be restraining him and create in complete freedom. I decided that I had to do this for myself, to live the rest of my life as I want." George Plimpton's mother remembers returning home from the concert still startled from having heard Leonard Bernstein come out in this flamboyant way.

Ellen Ball said that what "destroyed" Felicia was Bernstein telling people that young Tommy Cothran was his best friend, the one who understood his music. "Felicia had understood him a long time before that. She was very musical and she had been his best friend. . . . Whatever way Bernstein went public would have been just as hurtful to Felicia because they obviously had a pact never to do that. She was very loyal. He had been very loyal until then."

In December Tom Cothran went back to Paris for two weeks by himself to look for an apartment where he and Bernstein could start a new life in the new year. They were reunited on Christmas Eve for a holiday in Barbados. Cothran was privately bitter. New York, he wrote to a friend, was "a jungle wilderness of hostilities," in which all Bernstein's friends took Felicia's side. Though he had a lively and well-stocked mind, there was a heartless side to Cothran. He was not sympathetic to Bernstein's predicament. "It seems I have a great gift for the Matrimonial Squabble," he wrote to another friend. "All is well, generally speaking, twixt us twain—gets bedder and bedder ev'ry day—but there is a problem. Madame, it seems, is going slightly bananas—in a fury."

Back in New York a fortnight later, Bernstein described himself (in a letter to his old friend Ken Ehrman) as "caught in a depressed turmoil of drives and choices. As of this minute, I don't know what to do." When he took his three children to Washington to meet President Carter at his inauguration, he wanted to take Cothran, too. Harry Kraut warned him it would be like lighting a Roman candle for the press. "Tell him he can wear one of my dresses," said Felicia. At the Inaugural Concert he conducted the first performance of his setting of "To My Dear and Loving Husband," a seventeenth-century text by one of America's first woman poets, Anne Bradstreet, intended for *Songfest*. The poem, sung by a trio of women, extols the sense of fulfillment a wife feels within the state of marriage. He dedicated the song to Rosalynn Carter. Some of the audience must have found it somewhat tactless toward Felicia.

He hated making his wife unhappy and missed the order and creature comforts of family life. Nevertheless he flew off to spend the winter in Palm Springs with Tom Cothran. His plan was to complete his song cycle, work on a historical music series for BBC-TV (with Cothran as the co-writer) and start thinking about an opera based on *Lolita*. But living together was a nightmare. Cothran liked to be up early, play piano four or five hours a day, write up his journals, read serious books rather than do puzzles. Bernstein tended to stay in bed all day when he was not motivated by a rehearsal schedule or a concert tour.

Once he settled on a composing project such as *Songfest,* however, Bernstein worked with speed and application. He was the Rock of Gibraltar itself compared to the flaky Cothran, who in his myriad attempts at writing left behind nothing more substantial than a series of wonderfully funny and illuminating travel letters. Even in their physical tastes the two men were not very compatible. Cothran tripped on acid and had a voracious sexual appetite. Bernstein may have taken part in an occasional orgy (and talked about doing so more frequently) but sex for him was usually an adjunct to the game of conquest as well as an end in itself. As for drugs, he tried pot from time to time but said that it made him cough too much. He claimed to be allergic to hashish. His worst addiction was to nicotine.

In mid-February Bernstein returned precipitately to New York. He told Harry Kraut it was impossible for him to live with Cothran and he wanted a reconciliation with Felicia. For his part, Cothran may well have become tired of his friend's incessant "guiltburgers," as Bernstein called them. The two men parted without rancor and remained close.

Persuading Felicia to take him back was not easy. She was a proud woman and she had been humiliated. "The son of a bitch, he beat me to it," she had said to their mutual friend Michael Wager when Leonard walked out on her. But in March Leonard and Felicia took the first step: they appeared together in public at a benefit concert in the new Alice Tully Hall. Felicia and Wager recited the witty Edith Sitwell poems set to music by William Walton in *Façade,* with Bernstein conducting. The *Daily News* photo caption read "Marriages may stand or fall but art is forever." The next evening Bernstein dined at the Dakota with his family and then he set off for Europe. For the English Bach Festival in London, he conducted Bach's *Magnificat* and two works by Stravinsky, *Les*

*Noces* and *Mass,* a program of such austerity that even with Bernstein's advocacy it failed to sell out the Royal Festival Hall. It was a different story in Israel, where the Israel Philharmonic had organized a Leonard Bernstein festival to mark the thirtieth anniversary of his debut in Palestine. His mother, sister and three children all joined him. John Mauceri and Lukas Foss shared the conducting. Bernstein himself led a revised version of his *Kaddish* Symphony, in which, for the first time, the Speaker's part was taken by a man. Michael Wager worked with Bernstein to remove the most extreme of the narration's overwrought passages. He proposed lines from the Old Testament as an alternative, but Bernstein eventually decided to stick with his own prose. Watching her father drive away after one of the performances Jamie noted in her diary how closely he had come to resemble the Jehovah figure of the Speaker's text: "O my Father: ancient, hallowed, lonely disappointed Father. Rejected Ruler of the Universe, Angry wrinkled Old Majesty . . ."

Next Bernstein flew to Vienna to record the Prologue from Boito's *Mefistofele* with Nicolai Ghiaurov. (Deutsche Grammophon needed a short work to couple with Liszt's *Faust* for a double LP.) Then he and Tom Cothran spent ten days in Morocco. Cothran and Bernstein had terrible fights, Harry Kraut recalls; Bernstein was in a wretched mood and rarely left his room. Paul Bowles, on whom they called in Tangier, thought that Bernstein had changed for the worse since the forties. He had become "smarmy" and "false"; "a small crumb of what he once had been." His success had been "painfully destructive" of his personality. It was a chilling assessment.

From North Africa Bernstein flew to Paris to give a benefit concert for cancer research, with Montserrat Caballé as his soloist in the closing scene from *Salome.* Uniquely for Bernstein, the entire program consisted of music by Richard Strauss. While in Paris he met Felicia, who was on her way to Greece for a vacation on the island of Patmos with her friend Richard Avedon. When he returned to New York he slept in his studio at the top of the Dakota. Jamie noted in her diary that her father was "depressed," her mother "remote." Every ten days or so, the Bernsteins had dinner together. They met on sadder occasions, too, such as the funeral of Goddard Lieberson at the end of May. Lieberson, who produced the famous original-cast recordings of *Candide, West Side Story* and *On the Town,* had been Bernstein's earliest supporter at Columbia Records. The day after Lieberson's death Bernstein canceled an important concert in Strasbourg, France, with only two weeks' notice. French newspapers reported that he was sick but did not specify his illness. The skeptical Pierre Vozlinsky, manager of the French Radio orchestra, sent him a cactus plant instead of get-well flowers. Bernstein responded with a pot of Moroccan honey. The truth was that in his depressed state he had neither the energy nor the time to learn two hours of music. On the night when he should have been conducting Berlioz's *La Damnation de Faust* in front of the French President and the German Chancellor, Bernstein was at a New York theater with Felicia seeing *The Importance of Being Earnest.* The previous day, June 15, the *Daily*

*News* columnist "Suzy" had announced "the Leonard Bernsteins are together and everyone is hoping it will stick."

The reconciled couple told their children they had decided to spend a month's vacation together later in the summer at a country castle in southern Austria, close to Villach, where a Bernstein Festival was to be held. They then planned to visit the Bayreuth Festival before Bernstein went on tour with the Israel Philharmonic in Germany. Asked her opinion by her father, Jamie said she was rather shocked that her mother had agreed to the plan: it seemed like jumping into the eye of the hurricane.

Early in July the Bernstein family moved up to Tanglewood for a week, and Bernstein's mother came across from Boston to join them. To judge from the photographs in the local gossip columns, everybody was cheerful. But appearances were deceptive. Felicia had lunch with Phyllis Newman Green at the Red Lion Inn, Stockbridge. "Felicia told me that she had some back pain that probably came from a pinched nerve, but that there *was* some little shadow on the X-ray," Newman recalls. "She didn't want to frighten the children, but had really come up to tell her youngest daughter, Nina, what was going on in case she had to go back into the hospital. I told her I knew she was fine. She agreed. End of conversation. Her choice."

Felicia had said nothing about X-rays to her husband. Harry Kraut drove her to Philadelphia to hear Bernstein conducting Ingrid Bjoner and James King in *Tristan und Isolde* at the Dell. On the ride down she coughed a lot in the car but said it was bronchitis, nothing serious. Next day she postponed her flight to Europe, explaining that her doctor had ordered her not to fly for a few days. Leonard went on ahead to settle in.

But Felicia did not arrive. "Black Friday (Bronchoscopy)," Bernstein wrote in his date book on July 22. On the brink of renewing their married life— Bernstein told Harry Kraut that he and his wife had begun sleeping together again—Felicia had been diagnosed with lung cancer. Bernstein flew straight back to New York, moved into the family apartment, and mobilized the best care available for his stricken wife. "I'm afraid it's going to be pretty grim," the specialist warned. When Felicia returned from the hospital on August 2, Jamie wrote about her father in her diary. "As the FMB crisis recedes, his nervous energy and obsessiveness and despair take up their rightful old places, and the depression is creeping back. For awhile there, it was all channeled into Mummy. And a frightening concentration of negative energy it was, too. He brought Mummy this angel from an Austrian church—a little plaster angel, painted gold and pastels—very *gemütlich* and sweet. Mummy placed it on a stand to the left of her bed, so it perches over her shoulder. All I could think of, looking at that angel, was that it was the visual manifestation of LB's concept that every day of FMB's life from now on must be about death."

Felicia began daily radiation treatments at Memorial Hospital in New York. After days of agonizing, Bernstein resolved to maintain his European festival plans: canceling them would have put an unwelcome spotlight on Felicia's struggle. The Israel Philharmonic played Bernstein's own three symphonies in Villach and then in Berlin and Mainz, with Christa Ludwig, Lukas Foss and Montserrat Caballé as soloists. While he was touring Bernstein spoke to Felicia every day on the telephone. Deutsche Grammophon recorded *Kaddish* with Caballé as part of a new long-term contract that also committed Bernstein to conduct the Vienna Philharmonic in a cycle of Beethoven symphonies. Jewish conservatives who criticized him for forming close ties with a German company had to acknowledge that Bernstein had also persuaded Deutsche Grammophon to undertake many recordings with the Israel Philharmonic.

Like a circus stuntman, he leaped from one galloping orchestra to the other at the end of August. He left the Israel Philharmonic in Mainz on the evening of the twenty-sixth and began rehearsing the Vienna Philharmonic on the afternoon of the twenty-seventh in Salzburg. He launched his new Beethoven cycle with a typically unorthodox move. The Fifth Symphony was coupled with the C sharp minor Quartet, op. 131, played in the Mitropoulos edition by the strings of the Vienna Philharmonic. Many of the musicians were suspicious of what seemed like a gimmick. "Trust me," said Bernstein. After a sticky first half-hour the rehearsal developed into one of the most exalted work sessions of his life. Beethoven's profoundly spiritual music gave Bernstein an outlet to express his own troubled feelings.

After a powerful concert at the Salzburg Festival, he flew home to New York to be with Felicia for three days. In the performance of the C sharp minor Quartet filmed the following week at the Konzerthaus in Vienna, Bernstein's grief and fury are plain for all to see. He said later that if he were allowed to nominate for posterity only one of his hundreds of recordings, the Opus 131 would be his choice. He dedicated it to Felicia.

Before the reconciliation, Felicia had already decided she wanted to move from Fairfield. In the fall of 1977 she found a house in East Hampton, Long Island. Bernstein had no desire to give up his Connecticut base but would do anything to make Felicia happy, so he bought the house in East Hampton as well. Every three weeks that fall Felicia had to endure chemotherapy sessions that left her retching and exhausted. Nevertheless she joined her husband in Washington in October when President and Mrs. Carter came to hear the National Symphony Orchestra in an all-Bernstein program that was Rostropovich's inaugural concert as the orchestra's music director. The concert included three premieres: the first two honored Rostropovich and Washington: a witty five-minute overture called *Slava!* that reworks two numbers from *1600 Pennsylvania Avenue,* and the *Three Meditations,* for cello and orchestra, based on music heard in *Mass.* In between, Rostropovich conducted the *On the Waterfront* Suite with a fervor appropriate to a Tchaikovsky tone poem. When Bernstein took a bow with him, the spectacle of their musical friendship warmed everybody's hearts: they were the two most demonstrative huggers and kissers in the music world.

In the second half Bernstein conducted the premiere of *Songfest: A Cycle of American Poems for Six Singers and Orchestra*—a blessedly straightforward title. Paul Hume described the work as "a glowing testimonial to the richness and variety of vigorous and beautiful new ideas that are now pouring out of this remarkable man."

Bernstein had a special feeling for the genre of concert songs with orchestra —he loved to conduct Mahler's song cycles and symphonies with songs and he had composed song movements in his own *Jeremiah* and *Kaddish* symphonies. Britten's *Spring* Symphony (which he knew) was his closest model; in fact he had begun work on *Songfest* with a symphonic grouping in mind, planning four movements and as many as eight singers. The final structure, consisting of twelve songs for six singers, is simpler: an opening sextet is followed by three solos; next come three ensembles—duet, trio, duet; a second sextet is followed by solos for the other three singers, so that each singer has had one moment in the sun before the work is rounded off by a third sextet. The poems celebrate America's cultural diversity, executed in as many musical styles as there are songs in the cycle. Blacks, gays, exploited women, contented wives, belly dancers, teenagers and expatriates all have their say.

In order of appearance, the poets chosen were Frank O'Hara, Lawrence Ferlinghetti, Julia De Burgos, Walt Whitman, Langston Hughes and June Jordan (two poems were combined in a duet), Anne Bradstreet, Gertrude Stein, Conrad Aiken, Gregory Corso, Edna St. Vincent Millay and Edgar Allan Poe. With due respect to Bernstein's Broadway lyricists, *Songfest*'s poems were probably the best texts Bernstein ever set. He responded to them with good humor, wit and passion, making the cycle his most openheartedly and unpretentious American work, in the contradictory, laid-back spirit of Frank O'Hara's bidding poem:

> Let us do something grand
> Just this once    something
> small and important and
> UnAmerican . . .
> Not needing a military band.

Echoing another line of Frank O'Hara, the critic Andrew Porter called *Songfest* "a real right thing." If there is a flaw, it is that the words do not always cut through Bernstein's elaborate orchestration. Bernstein himself was to lead performances in half a dozen countries in which the poems were spoken by actors (sometimes his own children Nina and Alexander) before the songs were sung. In theory an admission of failure, the practice makes an effective hour of words and music.

Felicia Bernstein must have had mixed feelings about *Songfest*. The work was the result of Tom Cothran's collaboration with her husband and the choice of Gertrude Stein's deadpan prose poem "Storyette H.M." ("H.M." was Henri Matisse) must have seemed all too relevant to her marriage.

She: One was married to someone.
He: That one was going away to have a good time.
She: The one that was married to that one did not like it very well that the one to whom that one was married then was going off alone to have a good time and was leaving that one to stay at home then.

But Felicia could hardly have remained unmoved by the beauty of Bernstein's setting of the Walt Whitman poem "To What You Said." The words express with uncloying simplicity the tender feeling that one man can have for another: the meltingly beautiful melody, first heard on a solo cello and then hummed by the other five soloists as the solo baritone intones the poem to a descant, had been heard the previous year as the opening chorus of *1600 Pennsylvania Avenue*.

Bernstein's own favorite was a setting of Edna St. Vincent Millay's sonnet "What lips my lips have kissed." Were its closing lines an epitaph for Bernstein's middle years?

> *I cannot say what loves have come and gone,*
> *I only know that summer sang in me*
> *A little while, that in me sings no more.*

Bernstein himself refused to accept such an autobiographical interpretation. "Summer still sings in me," he told Mike Wallace in 1979. "Not so often as it used to but it sure does. Otherwise I would have jumped in the lake long ago. . . . If nothing sings in you, you can't make music."

The success of *Songfest* rekindled Bernstein's desire to compose. Daydreaming in an interview with Paul Hume, he said he would like "during the rest of his life to write a real American kind of opera, perhaps with the same singers as *Songfest*. We could all go off somewhere for a month and talk for ten hours a day and out of that would evolve the scenario for an opera." It was announced soon afterward that he was writing a full-length work destined for production by the Houston Grand Opera.

IN November Felicia had an operation to remove the pericardium, the membranous sac around the heart; in December the heart itself began causing anxiety. Nevertheless, with Michael Wager supporting her, she made the arduous journey to Vienna to join her husband when he led a revival of *Fidelio* in January 1978. Her hair had fallen out as a result of the chemotherapy and she wore an elegant Russian fur hat over her bald head. When a concert-goer sitting behind her at the Musikverein asked her to remove the hat she was forced to decline. On February 5, the eve of Felicia's fifty-sixth birthday and the thirty-second anniversary of their meeting, Leonard gave a defiantly cheerful party for her in the marble dining room at the Hotel Sacher.

She traveled with him to Milan, where he conducted two performances of *Fidelio* with the Vienna State Opera at La Scala. Then, exhausted, she flew back to New York to resume her chemotherapy. Deeply troubled, Bernstein took the Vienna Philharmonic to London and Paris—where he received the ribbon of *officier* of the Légion d'Honneur from ninety-year-old Nadia Boulanger. He spent six weeks in all with the Viennese musicians, then a fortnight in Amsterdam conducting the *Missa Solemnis* with the Concertgebouw Orchestra. He arrived back in New York tired and dejected.

Felicia's lung cancer had been deemed inoperable: her only hope lay in more chemotherapy, and the aftereffects of the treatment were ghastly. As the spring approached she decided she wanted to move into her East Hampton house right away. It was hastily fitted up for her by her designer friend Gail Jacobs with furniture taken from the Dakota apartment and the Fairfield house. Ellen Ball went out to East Hampton with Felicia before she moved in: they both slept in the guest room at Phyllis and Adolph Green's house nearby. Felicia coughed all night. "It was an awful cough, so much pain. And I remember saying to her, 'Felicia, you can get through this if anybody can!' She said, 'I know. I'm trying.'"

Phyllis Newman Green remembers shopping with Felicia, buying "cotton sheets, cotton nightgowns, imported, fine, everything for the bed." When she finally left New York City, Felicia was driven out to East Hampton by ambulance. Her bed was installed upstairs so that she could look out at the sea. Bernstein canceled everything to be with her, returning to the city only for weekly sessions of antismoking therapy. Martha Gellhorn visited. So did Felicia's younger sister Nancy and her husband. Her elder sister, Madeleine, came to stay, and Jamie Bernstein moved in to help run the house. Bernstein's niece Karen remembers a look of despair in Felicia's face, "but also determination that she was going to beat something." "I'll be better next week," she told Gail Jacobs, "and then you can come and we'll get the furniture right downstairs." Jamie bought a white wicker wheelchair to help Felicia move around the house. To Jamie her mother looked, "all sunken and gray and withered and ashen."

While still living at the Dakota, Felicia had returned to the Catholic Church. Monsignor Puma, who had instructed her in New York, drove out to East Hampton one Sunday to hold a Mass in her bedroom. He said he had never known anybody to generate so much spiritual energy.

Burton Bernstein had hopes of effecting a reconciliation with Felicia after the coldness which had developed in the wake of the Black Panther meeting and her support for Ellen in his painful divorce. But Felicia did not recognize him when he came to her bedside.

Toward the end, Shirley Bernstein remembers, Felicia was given what were called "Brompton cocktails—a mad mixture of drugs and alcohol which had reportedly been developed at the Brompton Road cancer hospital [the Royal Marsden] in London during the war to alleviate the pain of the terminally ill." For a few days the drugs induced a state of euphoria; then her brain became addled. Ellen Bernstein remembers Felicia waking up one night and exclaiming at the beauty of her expensive Porthault sheets. "I came and sat next to her and took her in my arms. She said to me, 'You are so beautiful. Don't belittle yourself. Have strength.' And she started talking in rhymes. It was so weird." She told her husband she had seen death sitting on the bedpost at the foot of her bed. Her eyes grew huge. They seemed to be full of intelligence, pleading with her visitors, yet often what she said made no sense.

On her deathbed Felicia was a tiny figure. With her wizened face and her crew-cut hair she looked, to Ellen Ball, like Christ on the cross. The priest came to give her the last rites but, sustained by drugs, an oxygen machine and her own fierce willpower, she lived on for days longer than the doctors believed possible. Every few hours her nurse gave her another injection of Demarol to ease her pain. Bernstein seemed helpless in his paralyzed grief. "She's meant to live," Ellen Ball remembers him saying, "otherwise she would be dead. So let's stop the medicine." He phoned the doctor and said, "I don't want her to have any more. I want her, I love her. I don't care if she's half paralyzed, she's my Felicia. I'll keep her warm." It was decided to continue the Demarol injections for another day. Felicia fought them ferociously, believing the nurse was trying to harm her. In the evening Jamie helped the nurse administer the routine injection. Felicia was reassured by her daughter's presence; Jamie cradled her mother in her arms as she drifted in and out of consciousness. Later that night, while Michael Wager was keeping watch, he heard her screaming, "I don't want to die, I don't want to die."

She died early the following morning, on June 16, 1978, four years to the day since she had entered New York Hospital for her mastectomy operation.


PEOPLE who habitually repress their anger are thought by some doctors to be particularly vulnerable to cancer, although no precise physical link has been identified. For thirty years Felicia had kept her feelings reined in—with rare exceptions, like the day she threw her paintings into the Mediterranean. Her frustration mounted in the 1970s with Bernstein's increasingly flamboyant homosexual behavior until the humiliating trauma of their separation caused her feelings to burst out uncontrollably. She had screamed with rage over the telephone at Bernstein when he was in California with Tom Cothran, and again when he was back in New York. Bernstein told Cothran that he thought his wife was going mad.

A more likely cause for her fatal disease was the fact that Felicia had been a heavy smoker for more than thirty years. But neither the timing nor the actual cause of Felicia's illness is the real issue. The crushing impact on Leonard Bernstein was that he believed himself responsible for his wife's death, and his sense of guilt never left him. Felicia was the greatest love of his life. He never recovered from her loss, and he never forgot the curse she uttered when he told her he was leaving her for Cothran. She had pointed her finger at him in fury and predicted, in a harsh whisper: "You're going to die a bitter and lonely old man."

# PART SIX

*With Nina in Houston before the premiere of
his opera* A Quiet Place.

# 1978 – 1990

# ANYTHING BUT TWILIGHT

# TOWARD A QUIET PLACE

*Private grief in a public spotlight. Bernstein's*
*sixtieth-birthday celebration, 1978.*
PHOTO CHRISTINA BURTON, COURTESY OF THE ESTATE OF LEONARD BERNSTEIN

*There love will teach us*
*Harmony and grace.*
*Then love will lead us*
*To a quiet place.*
—*Trouble in Tahiti,*
   lyric by Leonard Bernstein

A requiem Mass was spoken for Felicia in the living room at East Hampton. She also received a Jewish service to satisfy Bernstein's own sense of propri- ety. She was buried in Green Wood, a nonsectarian cemetery in Brooklyn. The simple stone is marked "Felicia Montealegre Bernstein 1922–1978." At the shivah held in the Dakota, the first mourner to arrive, on the dot of the appointed hour, was Jacqueline Onassis.

"As her last weeks were very sad and agonizing for Lenny and all who were with her, Felicia's end was a blessing," Helen Coates noted. "Nevertheless it has been a very hard blow for Lenny. I am sure that time and music will heal his grief, but this is a terribly hard period of adjustment." She was mistaken: neither time nor music healed Bernstein's grief. "There's not a minute in my life when I don't think of her," he told a friend in 1985. This was an exaggera- tion, certainly, but the sense of her presence never left him. After he had conducted an Amnesty International benefit concert in New York in 1987, attended by his three children, he told the audience that Felicia had been in his thoughts while performing Mahler's *Resurrection* Symphony. She is "the person I love most in the whole world."

After Felicia died Bernstein never slept again in the house at East Hampton. (It was sold that same year.) He moved back to the Dakota and two weeks later he went to Greece, where Leo Kirch had offered him a cruise on the Unitel company yacht *Silver Cross.* Shirley and Burton went with him. Shirley remembers how he would sit by himself for hours alone at the yacht's prow. "We tried everything but standing on our head and spitting nickels," Burton recalls. By the week's end Burton had at least persuaded him to laugh once or twice.

Soon after returning to America, still in a grim frame of mind, Bernstein went down to Washington to attend a gala sixtieth birthday party—thrown in his honor. With his wife barely two months dead, the world would have respected his decision had he asked for the celebration to be canceled. But the birthday event at Wolf Trap on August 25 was to be a major fund-raiser for the National Symphony Orchestra, then almost three quarters of a million dollars in debt. Lucrative television coverage in America and Europe had been arranged, so Bernstein agreed to allow the elaborate program to go ahead. Six thousand five hundred people attended on one of the swelteringly hot and muggy evenings that are Washington's summer specialty. Before the concert Bernstein was guest of honor with his eighty-year-old mother at a party attended by the rest of his family and several hundred of his friends, among them Elizabeth Taylor.

The orchestra played excerpts from Bernstein's concert hall scores, Aaron Copland and Mstislav Rostropovich conducting, and Lauren Bacall hosted a medley of songs from his Broadway shows. The concert concluded with Bernstein himself conducting the last two movements of Beethoven's Triple Concerto with Menuhin, Rostropovich and Previn as soloists. (Backstage, it was affectionately described as "four conductors in search of a concerto.") Lillian Hellman's speech of appreciation after the second intermission threw a pall over the already damp proceedings; she paid tribute not to Bernstein but to his late wife, Felicia. "Leonard Bernstein will have to live with the memories of their many good times and also with those of the last horrible months," Hellman said, shocking some of Bernstein's friends in the audience. "Perhaps he will become the wiser for it, and these memories will lead him to create even greater things."

Bernstein later called the Wolf Trap party "the most horrible night of my life." As for his next creative project, the search for a theme that would inspire him went on for two years. In the end he settled on an opera about a family as hung up by its emotionally overwrought past as anything in Hellman's *Little Foxes.* The writing of this opera, *A Quiet Place,* then occupied him on and off from October 1980 to June 1983. Throughout those years he was conscious, he said, of his life force ebbing away. "I don't mind that I'm aged," he said on the eve of his sixtieth birthday, "that my hair is white, that there are lines in my face. What I mind is the terrible sense that there isn't much time." Yet he abandoned his attempts to give up smoking, and with Felicia gone as his anchor he did nothing to curb his other self-indulgences. The act of conducting was his lifeline, and in September he renewed his activities. In Vienna he conducted five Beethoven symphonies for his new Unitel cycle; in Munich he introduced German audiences to his *Songfest.*

For a while Tom Cothran returned to his role as Bernstein's comforter and jester, and there was renewed talk of a collaboration between them on an operatic version of *Lolita,* in which Dietrich Fischer-Dieskau was to be cast in the role of Humbert Humbert. But there was no way the twelve-year-old Lolita could be adequately portrayed in operatic terms, and the project was dropped.

When President Carter inaugurated the Kennedy Center awards for achievement in the performing arts in December 1978, the classical music honoree was Arthur Rubinstein, then ninety-one. Bernstein made the introductory speech, as his was the first music to have been played at the center. The link was underlined by the choice of repertoire. John Rubinstein, the pianist's son, sang "A Simple Song" from Bernstein's *Mass.* Soon afterward the White House invited Bernstein to participate in a diplomatic and economic mission to Mexico by conducting the Mexico City Philharmonic Orchestra. Nina Bernstein, then almost seventeen, remembers the visit as one in which her father rose to new heights of social impossibility. The Bernsteins, father and daughter, joined the presidents, their ambassadors and their wives for a state dinner. Bernstein broke the ice by singing Mexican folk songs with President López Portillo for Jimmy Carter's pleasure. Then he mortified Nina by insisting she show everybody how beautiful she looked with her hair in a bun. ". . . and they of course all said, 'Oh, just lovely.' 'Look at that neck,' says Daddy; 'so like her mother.' Well, what are you going to do with the man? I wanted to kill him!"

Bernstein's dinner table talk with President Carter added to Nina's sense of embarrassment. "He had a solution for everything. I remember thinking, all seventeen years of me, 'How naive! God, Daddy.' This was Daddy's politics: 'Just feed them, okay? Don't bother me any more with this hunger thing. Just fix it!'" But after they had spoken, Carter wrote on Bernstein's place card, "Please come and see me any time." "Daddy was so pleased he framed it. But he never did go to see him."

Vacationing in Puerto Vallarta after his Mexico City concert, Bernstein fell in with Richard Burton and his beautiful new wife, Susan. The two men discussed *King Lear,* which the Welsh actor was planning to produce and perform in New York. Bernstein returned home full of Shakespeare. Nina was thrilled because she was studying *Lear* at school. "We sat there . . . talking about this play together, and it was very exciting. . . . Daddy had a psychological theory about Lear's mid-life crisis . . . and we rediscovered each other, and after that came what he used to call 'the great love affair between Leonard Bernstein and his daughter Nina.' I became his date to everything. He preferred to have me around more than anyone. We had endless private jokes. We just loved each other so much. And a good thing, too, because he was home and I was home and there weren't nobody else home.

"I started becoming protective of Daddy because he didn't have a wife any more. . . . I'd say, 'Now don't stay out too late, and don't misbehave, whatever you do.' And sure enough the next day in the New York *Post* there would be a picture of him dancing on the tables at Studio 54 and I'd say, 'Oh dear, I'm going to have to talk to him again.' It was a complete reversal." Jack Gottlieb remembers hearing Bernstein ask Nina if he might invite Tommy Cothran for dinner: Nina refused.

The comforting friendship lasted into the summer, when Nina accompanied her father on his fourth tour of Japan with the New York Philharmonic. Bernstein left the United States despondent after the first anniversary of Felicia's death on June 16. Matters worsened in Tokyo when Kazuko Amano called on him at the Okura Hotel. She had brought him red roses, she remembers. "I took a certain time before recognizing him: white hair, pale and like a shadow. I rushed to him. 'Lenny!' I gave him the flowers. As usual he asked 'The family is well?' 'No,' I had to say. 'No? Why, what happened?' Remembering Helen's advice 'never to mention Felicia or cancer,' I just said: 'Lenny, I am facing the same tragedy as you had last year. . . .' Lenny took me firmly in his arms shouting, 'Oh no!' His voice was so big that everyone at the lobby looked at us. Harry and the others stood silent. Then Lenny started to ask me questions. 'Is he having injections? He is suffering! Poor Reiji! Oh my dearest!' "

After two months' intensive conducting during which he had worked on the same program—Haydn's *Theresien Mass* and Shostakovich's Fifth Symphony—with the London Symphony and the Vienna Philharmonic in quick succession, and then undertaken an exhausting Far East tour with the New York Philharmonic, Bernstein finally understood that unless he cleared the decks he had no hope of satisfying what he dramatically called his "last chance" to compose an opera. While he was in Japan he decided to cancel all his conducting engagements for 1980 and make it a "sabbatical year"—an odd concept for somebody who officially had no binding ties with any organization. But Bernstein used "sabbatical" to mean that he would concentrate on composing, thus implying that his conducting life was the norm from which he was departing. He had still not decided on a composing project, and in any case, until November 1979 he was on a conducting marathon: Tanglewood, the Robin Hood Dell, Israel, Salzburg, a break in Positano to discuss a film of *Aida* with Zeffirelli, Hamburg (to sing his blues song "Big Stuff" for his new *Fancy Free* recording with the Israel Philharmonic), Vienna (where he concluded his Beethoven cycle for Unitel with an exceptionally fine Ninth Symphony on the stage of the State Opera), Paris and back to Zeffirelli again in Positano. Finally, he made a triumphal visit to Berlin, where with help from a management keen to prove its independence, he had overcome Karajan's resistance and was invited to conduct the Berlin Philharmonic in a pair of Amnesty International benefit performances of Mahler's ever-alluring Ninth Symphony. It took a while for the Berlin players to respond to his extrovert style at rehearsal. Their trouble, he told them, was that they'd forgotten music-making was supposed to be fun. The recorded performance, released posthumously, won a Grammy in 1993.

Bernstein was at his most capricious during these hectic fall weeks. A photo-call at the Hôtel Crillon in Paris, intended to produce a striking cover portrait for Deutsche Grammophon's Beethoven symphony set, was turned into an embarrassing charade. He arrived in his white tie and tails with half a dozen young men in tow, like Alcibiades at the banquet for Socrates, and proceeded to show off shamelessly, lunging at the camera with his Koussevitzky cape like some latter-day Count Dracula. Yet this was the same Leonard Bernstein who a few afternoons earlier had said farewell to Nadia Boulanger on her deathbed and left an imperishable account of his visit:

> I was ushered into her bedchamber by the angelic and anxiety-ridden Mlle. Dieudonné, who, with forefinger to lips, and seconded by an attending nurse, whispered a sharp order: *Ten minutes only.* As it turned out, the visit lasted closer to one hour.
>
> Nadia was beautifully dressed and groomed, as if for the coffin. Her crucifix gleamed at her throat; her eyes and mouth were closed; her whole face seemed closed in coma. I knelt by the bed in silent communion. Suddenly there was the shock of her voice, deep and strong as always (how? her lips did not seem to move; how?) *"Qui est là?"* I could not respond for shock. The Dieudonné forefinger whipped to the lips. Finally I dared speak: "Lenny. Léonard. . . ." Silence. Did she hear, did she know? *"Chèr Lenny . . ."* She *knew;* a miracle. Encouraging signal from Dieudonné. I persevered: "My dear friend, how do you feel?" Pause. Then that *basso profundo* (through unmoving lips!): *"Tellement forte."* I drew a deep breath. *"Vous voulez dire . . . intérieurement?"* *". . . Oui. Mais le corps—"* *"Je comprends bien,"* I said hastily, to shorten her efforts. *"Je pars. Vous devez être très fatiguée."* *"Pas de fatigue. Non. Point. . . ."* A protracted pause, and I realized she had drifted back into sleep.
>
> Signals from the astonished attending ladies suggested my departure, but I was held there, unable to rise from my knees. I knew there was more to come, and in a few minutes it did come: *"Ne partez pas* [Do not leave]." Not a plea, but a command. I searched my mind anxiously for the right thing to say, knowing that anything would be wrong. Then I heard myself asking: *"Vous entendez la musique dans la tête?"* Instant reply: *"Tout le temps. Tout le temps."* This so encouraged me that I continued, as if in quotidian conversation: *"Et qu'est-ce que vous entendez ce moment-ci?"* I thought of her preferred loves. *"Mozart? Monteverdi? Bach, Stravinsky, Ravel?"* Long pause. *"Une musique . . .* [very long pause] *. . . ni commencement ni fin. . . ."*
>
> She was already there, on the other side.

In October 1979 Bernstein took part in a three-week season in Washington with the Vienna Philharmonic and the Vienna State Opera, conducting two concerts and five performances of *Fidelio*. Other operas were in the hands of Zubin Mehta and Karl Böhm. After attending *Così Fan Tutte,* Bernstein went down on his knees to Böhm in his dressing room. "You have taught me how to conduct Mozart tonight," he said. "Good," replied the aging Austrian. "Then maybe you'll stop waving your arms about like *this!*" And he gesticulated furiously in an imitation of Bernstein at the rostrum.

In New York Bernstein's concert performance of *Fidelio* at Avery Fisher Hall (as Philharmonic Hall had been renamed in 1975) caused a stir. Several music critics felt they were being patronized by the inclusion of a lengthy narration to replace the opera's spoken dialogue, but Bernstein was unrepentant: "Judging by the thrilling and grateful reaction, I can only conclude that it succeeded." The speaker, Michael Wager, nevertheless remembers hisses and boos from a claque in the audience, most audibly when Bernstein joined the end of the dungeon scene to the first bar of the *Leonore* Overture No. 3.

There was one more public engagement before Bernstein could think of turning himself back into a composer—his speech of appreciation of the seventy-nine-year-old Aaron Copland at the Kennedy Center Honors on December 2. Copland's music, Bernstein said, "can have an extraordinary grandeur, an exquisite delicacy, a prophetic severity, a ferocious rage, a sharp bite, a prickly snap, a mystical suspension, a wounding stab, an agonized howl—none of which corresponds with the Aaron we loving friends know; it comes from some deep mysterious place he never reveals to us except in his music. . . . I have only once seen him in anger . . . and [only once] seen him weep, when at a Bette Davis movie that caused me to ooh and ah and marvel and groan 'No no no!' at the unbearable climax—I am always very vocal at Bette Davis movies— he turned to me, his cheeks awash with tears, and sobbed, 'Can't you shut up?' "

On December 3, 1979, Bernstein had thirteen months ahead of him with no conducting engagements and several options for composition. He had already announced that he and Arthur Laurents were working on an opera, but wouldn't reveal the details. And for a few weeks he was simultaneously considering an original musical film under the aegis of the director Francis Ford Coppola about Preston Tucker, a visionary of the postwar automobile industry. In a bizarre episode, Coppola invited Bernstein, Betty Comden and Adolph Green to California, put them up in a motel near his home and gave them a room with a piano to work in. "Lenny composed and we wrote lyrics and we kind of had a good time," Comden remembers. "Then suddenly we left and not one cent changed hands—if you can picture it—and we never heard from him again."

Nina Bernstein remembers the demise of her father's more substantial collaboration with Arthur Laurents, on a musical set in Renaissance times with the working title *Alarums and Flourishes.* "It was all about how we need structure in our lives to be free. . . . As he talked about it, this sense of foreboding came upon me; I finally had to tell him, 'Daddy, do you know what? This has been done. It was called *Pippin.*' He was so distressed he just dropped it there and then." Bernstein described his decision not to proceed with Arthur Laurents, taken on July 4, as a personal declaration of independence—the work was becoming, he said, "more and more Broadway-ish"—but six months of a composing sabbatical were gone, involving many drafts of book, lyrics and music, and he had nothing to show for them. It was a familiar complaint.

Once again he was able to pull something out of the fire, however, thanks to three timely commissions. He had agreed in April 1980 to write a divertimento for the Boston Symphony Orchestra's centenary season. Now that he had extra composing time on his hands he expanded the commission into a fifteen-minute autobiographical suite—"a fun piece"—of eight brief movements. "It reflects my youthful experiences here where I heard my first orchestral music," he told the *Boston Globe* on the eve of the September premiere. "I nearly fell out of my chair I was so excited."

The material in *Divertimento* is wildly varied in character but musical unity of a sort is provided by the presence and repetition in every number of the notes B and C, standing for Boston Centennial. The finale, "The BSO Forever," is a pastiche of the swaggering "Radetzky March," which was a regular feature of Arthur Fiedler's Pops concerts. Bernstein adds to the fun by instructing first the two piccolo players and later the entire brass section to stand up for their solos—a joyful effect borrowed from traditional renditions of J. P. Sousa marches. Other dance movements such as the "Samba" and the "Turkey Trot" are in the Pops spirit (the cheerfully strutting "Turkey Trot" was rescued from the abandoned film score of *Tucker*). The "Blues" is a reference to Bernstein's boyhood visits to Boston nightclubs. In the plaintive "Mazurka" movement Bernstein quotes the oboe cadenza which occurs before the reprise of the first movement of Beethoven's Fifth Symphony as a tribute to the BSO symphony concerts he attended as a teenager. A solemn canon for three flutes—Bernstein's own favorite section in the work—was intended to evoke memories of Koussevitzky, Munch and other BSO personalities who had passed away. The most successful movement in the *Divertimento* is a devastatingly charming waltz in 7/8 time for strings alone, which is Bernstein's homage to Tchaikovsky in general and to the 5/4 waltz of the Sixth Symphony—a Koussevitzky favorite—in particular. Its simple tune also served as the melody for a defiantly tasteless twenty-eighth birthday song for Jamie Bernstein, which began: "Shit-a-brick, time is running out on me:/I must get moving fast undoubtedly." As a good father, Bernstein was both gently upbraiding his elder daughter for her use of unseemly language and reminding her that it was time either to be launching a career or thinking of marriage.

In the summer of 1980 Bernstein composed *Touches,* for solo piano, subtitled

*Chorale, Eight Variations and Coda,* as a test piece for the 1981 Van Cliburn International Piano Competition. Nine minutes in duration, this is Bernstein's longest movement for solo piano—but he avoided extended musical argument, offering instead a series of variations which, despite their brevity, tax to the utmost the technical and intellectual skills of the interpreter. In October he dashed off another composition, a lightweight, two-minute orchestral overture to honor the memory of André Kostelanetz.

During the fall of 1980 Bernstein gave disturbing signals that he was struggling with a compulsion to step outside the bounds of conventional good behavior. Without Felicia to keep him in check he seemed no longer to care what he said or whom he shocked. When he conducted a Carnegie Hall performance of Copland's *A Lincoln Portrait* in November, with the composer himself narrating, a reporter noted at rehearsal that Bernstein not only gave Copland notes in front of the orchestra about how to speak the lines but also chose tempos that made Copland "look askance at him once or twice and then gesture in mild frustration." At another Copland celebration (at Symphony Space in New York) Bernstein infuriated some members of the audience by quipping cheerfully "he went to pee" in order to explain Copland's nonappearance on the platform after Bernstein had spoken a eulogistic introduction.

Earlier that night Bernstein had been one of the speakers at a publisher's party given by Macmillan in the presence of the former British Prime Minister Harold Macmillan, to launch their new twenty-volume edition of Grove's Dictionary of Music and Musicians. The date, November 22, was the name day of St. Cecilia, the patron saint of music. But it was also the seventeenth anniversary of the assassination of President Kennedy. Instead of praising the musical encyclopedia, Bernstein's speech—as reported in the *New York Post*—was devoted to what he ironically labeled "irrelevancies."

### BERNSTEIN SHOCKS A GALA AUDIENCE

Lenny Bernstein has done it again. The emotional maestro—given to frequent sobbing public outbursts—launched into a blistering attack on the American people at a black-tie gala Saturday night at the Waldorf. . . . Bernstein launched his bizarre diatribe by saying he hadn't wanted to come at all. He rambled on: the long, fringed scarf he was wearing over his tuxedo wasn't the latest in evening wear, he said. It was simply his way of hiding several unruly shirt buttons. Then he noted mournfully that it was Nov. 22, and everyone, including the *New York Times* was ignoring JFK's death. Americans "are not willing to confront" national traumas, he said—unlike the British, who always pull themselves up by the bootstraps after a terrible scandal. Whereupon Bernstein brought up the Profumo scandal, the one involving notorious call girl Christine Keeler that led to the downfall of Sir Harold's government in 1963. Some 450 shocked guests, including writer Lillian Hellman and composer Virgil Thomson, had taken just about enough of Bernstein's incredible tactlessness when

Eric Lloyd of the *Wall Street Journal* stood up and said "You're talking rubbish." . . . Undaunted, Bernstein insisted that every one stand up for a mournful two minutes in tribute to JFK before he would stop.

Bernstein's version of the event was that he had had drinks with Sir Harold Macmillan before the party started and had obtained his approval to speak about their mutual friend Jack Kennedy. ". . . and I was heckled all the way through. . . . With that kind of national attitude it's no wonder that the current rages of the musical theater are things like *Grease* and *Sugar Babies*. But I pray that we'll get back our souls and our sense of intellectual adventure and curiosity."

The *Post*'s reference to his "frequent sobbing public outbursts" was an example, Bernstein felt, of the conservative hostility surfacing in the aftermath of Ronald Reagan's recent victory in the presidential election. Bernstein soon used a supposedly nonpolitical ceremony—where he received an award "for distinguished achievement"—at the Third Street Music School Settlement in New York—to lash out at the incoming administration for its evident lack of interest in the arts. Republicans at the gathering were reported to be shocked, but Bernstein's gloomy forecast proved accurate enough.

In December of 1980, in the dying days of the Democratic presidency, he made his final visit to a friendly White House. The occasion was the third Kennedy Center Honors and this time Bernstein himself was one of the honorees, protesting only halfheartedly that he was too young to qualify for a lifetime achievement award. He took his entire family to Washington for the weekend, including his mother and her sisters, Bertha and Dorothy. The eighty-one-year-old Helen Coates was also in the party, thrilled to meet the President. After the reception Bernstein and his family were invited to rest in the historic bedroom where Lincoln had signed the Emancipation Proclamation. Left on their own, the Bernsteins placed a menorah on the mantelpiece and lit their Hanukkah candles before leaving for the ceremony. "We were really proud of our little act of solidarity with the Jews everywhere," Nina Bernstein remembered. Alexander prudently moved the flaming menorah to the bathroom.

THAT Bernstein was still traumatized by the death of Felicia can be deduced from the letters he received in the fall of 1980 from Tom Cothran. In 1979 Cothran had decided to drop out of American life. He went first to Italy and then on to what he called the "Mysterious East," where he considered studying Hindu philosophy in India or Zen in Japan. Cothran's response to a letter from Bernstein, his first communication in more than a year, gives an idea of the kind of outspoken friendship Bernstein had lost when Cothran headed for Shangri-La. ". . . As for Depressions (severe; less severe; other), this must stop—A *second* Mourning Period!! How many shall we expect?! Birth and re-death—

you're free, dear, you must get out and *live*—shuck off all that nonsense at the grave. Now that Nina is off to Harvard . . . you can get out of that mausoleum and move into a nice comfy place of your *own*—don't let anyone else decorate it for you, do it yourself—*You* decide what chairs you want and what table and what goes where. . . . and don't shirk it because you have *other more important things to do*—make hideous mistakes—it'll be *all yours. D'y'hear?"*

Cothran was ribbing Bernstein about his workplaces. When the Bernsteins moved into the Dakota, Felicia had fitted out his study on the top floor in a relatively modest style: he confessed to the designer Gail Jacobs (and presumably to Cothran as well) that he would have preferred something more sumptuous. After Felicia's death, Gail Jacobs created a studio for him in what had been Felicia's bedroom, replacing everything pink and feminine with taupe paper, Pompeian red velvet draperies at the window and deep brown carpets. "It looks like the studio of a rich composer!" Bernstein exclaimed when he first saw it. "You *are* a rich composer," Michael Wager had observed. "No," Bernstein corrected him, "a rich *conductor* but a *poor* composer."

A week later Cothran made another attempt to jolt Bernstein out of his *"second* Mourning," this time by questioning the value of his frequent consultations with the psychiatrist Dr. Milton Horowitz. "Will psychoanalysis ever get to the bottom of things if the matter is—moral? . . . To me it seems that you are mourning not just for Felicia, but for that life you don't feel you gave her, the deep sexual love which was the only thing she really wanted. If you suspected from the beginning that that were true, should you have allowed her to marry you at all? And if you did, wouldn't you think that you might feel some qualms, justifiably? Fame, career, Amberson—life is a hard bargainer. I think the price you paid was too high. But I'm not sure that you think so. Or else you would have turned them in for something better."

While he was in Japan Cothran fell seriously ill: he flew home to his parents in Chicago where lymphoma was diagnosed. He responded positively to the radiation treatment he received, but a spark had been destroyed; where he had been brightest among the bright he became slow and ordinary. Subsequently his lymphoma B was revealed to be an early manifestation of AIDS.

In Cothran Bernstein lost an intimate collaborator, ironically the only person who might have filled the void left by Felicia. A taste of what he missed can be gleaned from two of Cothran's dispatches in late 1980. The first was his reaction of disbelief to the news that Bernstein planned to shelve his new composing project in order to conduct in Europe. "For Heaven's sake DON'T STOP!" Cothran wrote; "i.e. *cancel 1981* . . . Do you really at this point propose to go *back* to conducting?" The second was a critique of Bernstein's operatic ambitions. "It's clear to one and all, and should be clear to you as well, that you should be writing first-class quick musical comedy that borrows from everywhere (including Wagner, if you want) but that throws out the heavy plush. . . . Your way is to play one thing against another, and when you are able to glide along just above the edge of irony, the result is good. You get so *serious*. It's the knell."

Despite Cothran's warnings, Bernstein's next opera was to be very serious indeed.


IN October 1980 he finally met somebody with whom he felt he could collaborate. Stephen Wadsworth Zinsser, who had been at Harvard with Jamie Bernstein, had been commissioned to write a feature article about Bernstein for the *Saturday Review*. His first request for a meeting was turned down, and he wrote to Bernstein, hoping to change his mind. "The only truly guileless sentence in the letter—for the letter was a very calculated attempt to get the story—was the last one. 'P.S.,' it said, 'Interested in librettos?' He telephoned me the next day. . . . 'If you bring me the scenario for a sequel to *Trouble in Tahiti* by Tuesday at four o'clock,' he told me (it was Friday), 'I will give you your interview. Fair trade?' "

Wadsworth (he dropped Zinsser for his creative work) never wrote the interview and only the opening funeral parlor location was retained from his draft scenario. But the fact that the two men had independently thought of a death as the starting point for a sequel to *Tahiti* convinced Bernstein that he had found his man. Here was another Stephen to follow Sondheim and Schwartz, and one who like Bernstein had recently suffered a family bereavement—the death of a beloved sister in a car crash. Wadsworth was only twenty-seven and he had written only one libretto, but he was culturally ambitious and fascinated by the challenge of setting the American vernacular to music. He saw himself as the enabler, the one who got the maestro to work. It was not his place, he felt, to question the wisdom of Bernstein's wish to attempt a sequel to a work he had written almost thirty years earlier. (Bernstein had occasionally talked about a follow-up for decades, most recently with two potential librettists, the New York satirical duo Monteith and Rand.)

Wadsworth's first task had been to create flesh-and-blood characters from Bernstein's original concept. It was Bernstein's own idea that Junior, the son of Dinah and Sam, mentioned but never seen in *Trouble in Tahiti,* would have grown up to be a psychotic homosexual with incest fantasies about his sister. Where Bernstein felt vaguely the presence in the drama of a French-Canadian, Wadsworth developed the ambiguous character of François, who has been and perhaps still is the lover of Junior. Recently François has married Junior's younger sister Dede, who was probably conceived by Sam and Dinah in a last-ditch attempt to save their marriage. Dinah has just died, in a car crash she probably caused by her drunken driving. For Dinah's chief mourners, Wadsworth extrapolated from the text of *Tahiti* her adoring brother Bill and Bill's wife, Susie. The other characters are a doctor; the doctor's wife, who was in love with Dinah; the family psychoanalyst; and the funeral director. With suicide, homosexuality and incest-fantasy all prominent, the story line resembled popular television drama: Why has Sam not spoken to his son for twenty years? From beyond the grave, how can Dinah help the warring factions in her family to be reconciled, to forgive, to learn to love one another?

Once he had found a collaborator, Bernstein perversely put his operatic work on hold while he resumed his conducting career. No matter what he said to the contrary—"writing music is the most important thing I can do," he had claimed in his television interview with Mike Wallace—Bernstein remained as hooked on the baton as he was on nicotine. In 1981 he was on the road for almost half the year. With the New York Philharmonic he premiered new works by Foss and Rorem, and offered a retrospective for Copland's eightieth birthday. In Israel he premiered what is in effect his flute concerto, *Halil*. In Rome he performed his *Kaddish* at the Vatican: the Pope, who was recuperating from an assassination attempt, listened on a specially installed closed circuit audio system in his bedroom. But Bernstein considered his most important conducting activity of the year to be the recording of *Tristan und Isolde* he made in Munich with the Bavarian Radio Orchestra. For Bernstein, *Tristan* was "the central work of all music history, the hub of the wheel. . . . I have spent my life since I first read it, trying to solve it. It is incredibly prophetic, full of pre-Freudian insights." His experience of the work went back thirty-five years. He had done scenes and acts and bleeding chunks on television and in concert halls; he had even planned a Bayreuth production with Wieland Wagner. In Munich's Hercules Hall he could finally come to grips with the complete opera in a production where the music would not be compromised. The opera would be performed in concert version with live telecasts, one act at a time, in January, April and November. With only one act to perform the singers would not run out of steam, as they so often did in the opera house. So the reasoning went, but Bernstein himself had such a bad spring cold that he conducted Act I with a baton in one hand and a handkerchief in the other, while the Tristan, Peter Hofmann, missed the entire dress rehearsal of Act III in November because of sickness.

Since Bernstein himself was at the front of the concert platform and the singers, in stylized costumes reminiscent of "Star Trek," were on a narrow strip of acting space behind the orchestra, the conductor inevitably dominated the proceedings. There were no props—not even a goblet from which the lovers could drink the love potion. But Bernstein was not worried by the visual incongruities. As a German newspaper observed after Act I, the staging was neither fish nor fowl but the evening was pure *Tristan*. And a great *Tristan* interpreter, Karl Böhm, gave Bernstein's sometimes agonizingly slow reading his personal blessing. "For the first time," he said to Bernstein after attending the dress rehearsal, "someone dares to perform this music as Wagner wrote it." His own performance of the Prelude, recorded at Bayreuth, was four minutes faster than Bernstein's.

Bernstein's partnership with Hildegard Behrens, his exceptionally gifted

Isolde, was one of the most thrilling sights ever witnessed on a concert platform. After the third-act dress rehearsal Bernstein left the stage in a daze and walked to his dressing room in tears. But Behrens fell ill before the performance. Because she was nursing her two-month-old baby she could not take antibiotics, and the live performance of Act III became a sorry anticlimax as she coughed her way through the "Liebestod": the Philips recording had to be patched together from the rehearsals. Bernstein was undeterred: "My life is complete," he exclaimed extravagantly when the project was finished (he was only sixty-three); "I don't care what happens after this. It is the finest thing I've ever done."

Naturally there were contrary opinions from those who found the tempos intolerably deliberate and the singing too variable, but the English critic Edward Greenfield described Bernstein's reading as "the most spacious recording ever put on disc. His rhythmic sharpness goes with warmly expressive but unexaggerated concentration and deep commitment."

*Tristan* was the last opera recording he made for a company other than Deutsche Grammophon, with whom in October 1981 he signed a six-year exclusive contract. It was still his goal to compose an American opera, but as a recording artist Bernstein had become thoroughly European.

I N the summer of 1981 Bernstein and Wadsworth mapped out a game plan for the new opera, working first in a farmhouse near Tanglewood and then in Fairfield, where Wadsworth drafted the text at the house while Bernstein composed in his studio. Wadsworth worked on evolving an American vernacular language for the libretto that would reflect the nervous, repetitive, disjointed way people communicate and fail to communicate in "real" life. Sometimes they worked side by side. "We turned one quartet I had written into a trio," Wadsworth recalled, "changing almost every line, and I sat by the piano as he set it to music. He wouldn't let me leave. He was scared, of course. I was, too, especially when I had to tell him I didn't like something he had written—an at-first daunting task that I came to love. We hammered away in this manner until we were *both* satisfied with the music. Meanwhile we ate huge midsummer tomatoes and steaks and listened to every note of American music we could find. He wanted to see and hear my reactions. We told each other about our lives, played anagrams . . . and decided to seek a commission for our opera."

Out of this idyllic collaboration emerged a proposal lucid enough to enable Harry Kraut to persuade three opera houses—Houston Grand Opera, the Kennedy Center and La Scala, Milan—to agree to share the costs of commissioning the work and mounting the production, beginning in Houston in the summer of 1983. In a long memorandum prepared for Kraut to send to the opera managers Bernstein noted that the new opera, still known only as *TinT II*, would be at least twice as long as *Trouble in Tahiti*, thus approximately the length of Strauss's *Salome*. The idea was for *Tahiti* to play before the intermission and for the new opera to follow; there would be three scenes played without a break. *TinT II,* Bernstein continued,

> . . . will be in totally other style, *TinT I* having been a deeply serious (even tragic) theme clothed in the lightest of disguises; jazzy, tuneful (in a pop sense), etc. for reasons of caricature, irony, satire, etc. The characters *were* cardboard. *TinT II,* au contraire, goes deeply into each character, plus a good number of new ones. The music no longer avails itself of strophic or stanzaic song-forms (as did *TinT I*); it is anything but "pop"; musical styles range from dodecaphonic, strictly serial, to diatonic chorales. It is very romantic, very cool, very passionate. The libretto is "heavy" (in the kids' sense); strong, sad, even depressing, and deeply investigatory of interpersonal pain. Except for special purposes, it avoids obvious rhyme and sequential forms, as in pop music, but plays subtly with vernacular elements (as does the music) in a way that LB believes takes that famous "next step" toward whatever LB once hoped "American Opera" could one day be.

Once the groundwork of the new opera was laid Bernstein disappeared for three months to conduct Brahms in Vienna and Wagner in Munich; he scheduled his first sustained composing time for January 1982, in Bloomington, Indiana. "Before actually setting pen to paper," Wadsworth recalls, "Lenny went to bed for nine days, terrified. We hadn't written very much up to then and both knew that if we didn't produce now we probably never would. Eventually, and suddenly, he awakened and composed most of what is now Act I." Bernstein wrote fast. Some of the music was fresh, like Dede's *Valse Manique.* From *1600 Pennsylvania Avenue* he took the song "Me," and expanded it into Old Sam's aria of anger, "You're late, you shouldn't have come." For Junior's outburst in front of the coffin of his mother, "Hey, Big Daddy, you're driving me batty," he built from an aria sketched for Humbert Humbert in the abandoned *Lolita.*

Bernstein was at Indiana University as the first fellow of a new Institute for Advanced Study. He gave three conducting classes and rehearsed some of his new opera at workshops with student singers, but he lived a twenty-minute drive away from the campus. There were social diversions nonetheless, and many parties, since everybody wanted to play with the maestro. He also had dinner twice with Charles Webb, the dean of Indiana University's School of Music, and became instant friends with the entire family.

After only a few weeks of frantic work in Bloomington, Bernstein was obliged to shelve the opera again, leaving it "ragged and bleeding in the middle of Act I," while he took up the baton for his spring conducting season. In Washington he conducted the National Symphony in his *Halil,* for flute and orchestra, first performed the previous year by Jean-Pierre Rampal with the Israel Philharmonic. It was composed in the winter of 1980–81 and based partly on music he had written earlier for a fiftieth-anniversary salute to CBS Television. It was inspired by the story of Yadin, a promising Israeli flute student killed in his tank close to the Suez Canal during the 1973 war. (*Halil* is the Hebrew word for flute). The work is similar in weight to Bernstein's *Serenade;* it is written for string orchestra, harp and a wealth of percussion requiring two players. There are also parts for piccolo and alto flute, which ideally should be played offstage. The sixteen-minute work is in a single rhapsodic movement, alternating moments of lyricism and violence, and Bernstein set great store by it. It is "formally unlike any other work I have written, but it is like much of my music in its struggle betwccn tonal and non-tonal forces. . . . It is a kind of night music which from its opening twelve-tone row to its ambiguously diatonic final cadence is an on-going conflict of nocturnal images: wish-dreams, nightmares, repose, sleeplessness, night terrors—and sleep itself, *Death's twin brother.*"

In the final section—the sleep after the terror of an unmistakable night battle—the solo flute falls silent as if to suggest Yadin's wasteful death, and a hidden alto flute is heard as a touching metaphor for the spirit departing from Yadin. In the Washington performance given by the flautist Ransom Wilson, the *Tribune* critic was impressed by "a brooding, terrific element which whispers of nightmares and nameless horrors." But the tranquil blessing of peace with which *Halil* ends—the duet between dark-toned alto flute and solo viola is particularly effective—makes this one of Bernstein's most positive statements among his abstract compositions.

LATER in the spring of 1982 Bernstein locked horns with the BBC Symphony Orchestra over a concert which paired *Songfest* with Edward Elgar's *Enigma Variations.* He arrived for his first rehearsal unforgivably late and antagonized the already frustrated players by immediately talking for a good ten minutes about his love for "Eddie" Elgar and the passion they shared, across the grave, for puzzles, word games and enigmas. The atmosphere was reminiscent of his first *Falstaff* rehearsal in Vienna in 1966. But when Bernstein began to make music with the British musicians, a new orchestral love affair did not materialize. Many of the players felt the opening theme dragged interminably under his direction. Accustomed to the stiff-upper-lip interpretations of British conductors, they found Bernstein's approach intolerably mannered and overconducted. Worse, he appeared condescending both to the orchestra and to Elgar—in living memory nobody had called him "Eddie." One of the brass players offered a critical comment. Bernstein was momentarily thrown off balance, but when the same player muffed an important phrase Bernstein called out, "You talk big, but you don't deliver." The player blushed scarlet, the orchestra laughed, and Bernstein began to win them over. The *Enigma* performance at the Royal Festival Hall was almost ten minutes longer than was customary and many critics' eyebrows were raised at what they thought to be Bernstein's act of self-indulgence. But he heard Elgar through European ears, emphasizing his links to the music of Schumann and Tchaikovsky. When the DG recording was issued, Yehudi Menuhin, who half a century previously had worked with Elgar, wrote to say he had never heard anything more beautiful.

Despite their vastly different backgrounds, Elgar and Bernstein had something in common as composers. Both were inveterate raiders of the bottom drawer and both worked outward from their short sketches to assemble complete movements.

For the next two months Bernstein hopped across oceans and continents as if he were a professional tennis player driven on by the demands of the circuit rather than a composer with an opera to finish. In Israel he conducted Stravinsky concerts (1982 was Stravinsky's centennial year) and continued rerecording his own compositions with Deutsche Grammophon. Then he took the Israeli Orchestra on tour, to West Germany, Mexico and Texas. At the final Mexico City concert his new assistant, Charlie Harmon, discovered during the intermission that Bernstein had inadvertently left the score of *Le Sacre du Printemps* in his hotel room. The audience was kept waiting for an hour while Harry Kraut raced back to the city in a taxi at ninety mph. When the performance eventually got under way the score remained unopened on the stand: Bernstein knew the work by heart. In Houston the podium was covered with plastic carpet. During an especially vigorous performance of Tchaikovsky's *Francesca da Rimini* he slipped in his own sweat and fell off the rostrum with a thud. "I'm all right," he muttered to the two violinists who picked him up, still conducting; the music continued without missing a beat. (He was to fall once again in Chicago in 1984, this time at the end of a concert. Stepping off the podium after taking a bow he tripped and plunged headlong to the floor, where he lay "for what seemed like an eternity." He was lifted to a chair, his face beet-red, and eventually helped offstage. A hospital checkup indicated that his only injury was a chest bruise caused by the impact of Mitropoulos's medallion, which he wore around his neck.)

Bernstein was in New York in May 1982 just long enough to take his seat in the American Academy (he occupied the chair left vacant by the death of Samuel Barber) before returning to Europe to conduct more Stravinsky, in Milan and Venice. Only five days later he was sharing a Stravinsky celebration concert with Michael Tilson Thomas in Washington Cathedral. Then at the beginning of July, turning his back on Tanglewood, he flew to California to inaugurate a new teaching institute organized by the Los Angeles Philharmonic. The previous summer he had taken umbrage publicly against Tanglewood's administrators for "trying to be too many things to too many people." The Boston Symphony musicians had grumbled about the all-Bernstein program they performed for a July 4 concert. They were, a journalist reported, impatient with rehearsing his "show tunes," unimpressed by his new music and furious with his loquacious, digressive rehearsal style. The management had prevented him from recording *Rhapsody in Blue,* as he had wanted. He was quoted in a small-circulation New York paper, the *Soho Weekly News,* as being "sick of that lousy, fucking orchestra." He canceled his winter conducting engagement for the Boston Symphony's centennial season and plans already in the pipeline to create a West Coast Tanglewood were rushed through.

Based on the UCLA Westwood campus, the institute was to concentrate on orchestral and conducting training and give occasional Sunday concerts at the Hollywood Bowl. As artistic director, a title he shared with Daniel Lewis, Bernstein coached the student orchestra and divided his programs with young conductors, exactly as at Tanglewood. The atmosphere was more laid back, however, and his own dress code and lifestyle were bewilderingly casual: everything hung out, including his potbelly. "One minute he could look like the most paternal of rabbis; the next like the most outrageously ribald rock star."

His programs with the professionals of the Los Angeles Philharmonic included *Rhapsody in Blue* and the West Coast premiere of *Songfest.* But Californians wanted to hear his popular compositions rather than his settings of arty poems whose words often could not be heard above the orchestra: when the Los Angeles Philharmonic played at the open-air theater in Concord near San Francisco the audience left in droves during *Songfest* and some of those who stayed were heard to boo.

In Los Angeles the orchestra rented a house for Bernstein (chosen by his song-writing daughter Jamie, who lived in L.A. for several years) on Moraga Drive in a remote area of Bel Air. There was a pool and a floodlit tennis court, and he had a small staff—valet, cook, and temporary chauffeur—to look after him. He enjoyed teaching and the company of the conducting students, but Los Angeles could never replace Tanglewood in his affections. He was depressed that summer and occasionally he was lonely. Ernest Fleischmann's son, Martin, then eighteen and working as Bernstein's driver, remembers an evening on the cook's night off when the two of them were alone at the house. Martin prepared a succulent meal of crab's legs—one of Bernstein's favorite dishes. After dinner, Martin remembered, "He took my hand and he led me through Beethoven's Ninth."

Bernstein left California in mid-August, intending to spend two weeks working on his opera with Stephen Wadsworth in Santa Fe. He promptly fell ill with bronchial flu and had to fly home. In September he commenced a filmed cycle of Brahms concertos and symphonies with the Vienna Philharmonic. After that, the only diversion from his new opera was the premiere in mid-October of the "opera house version" of *Candide,* at the State Theater in Lincoln Center. Hugh Wheeler expanded his off-Broadway book, Harold Prince directed, and John Mauceri conducted a two-act version to which half an hour of music had been lovingly restored—although not always to its original place. Bernstein wanted a *Candide* played more for ideas and for feeling, whereas Prince and Wheeler's version still went for belly-laughs. Nevertheless, this *Candide* became the City Opera's most successful production of a modern work. Twenty-six years after its Broadway premiere, the operetta had at last found a welcoming home in New York.

When work resumed on the new opera, it had acquired its title *A Quiet Place,* a phrase from Dinah's yearning aria in *Trouble in Tahiti.* The opera's premiere had been fixed for June 1983, so once again Bernstein would be faced with a hectic race to finish a major work. The well-organized Wadsworth, who initially had been appalled by Bernstein's waywardness and his talent for digression, was now dedicated to the job of getting the composer to the finish line. Like others before him, he found Bernstein receptive to ideas and always generous, but not an easy man with whom to collaborate: suffering regularly from insomnia, he would work at night and then sleep through the day. (When Charlie Harmon became his personal assistant early in 1982, one of his first jobs, he remembers, was to play loud piano arrangements of *The Mikado* all afternoon in order to wake the maestro up.) Wadsworth kept Bernstein at his desk all through the winter. "I haven't water-skied," Bernstein complained, "I haven't played squash, didn't go south in the winter. I would eat, cough, compose and get fat." In the spring of 1983 student workshop performances were organized, scene by scene, at his Dakota studio and at the Juilliard School. Irwin Kostal and Sid Ramin were brought in to work on the orchestration. Against their protests, Bernstein insisted on writing for electric guitar and for a synthesizer. "This is a modern story," he said; "the synthesizer will be just wonderful." Kostal recalled that Bernstein "lined up the most awful sounds for it; at the first orchestral rehearsal it blew the fuses." (The use of amplified sound in the pit will always create balance problems. Such problems were intensified in Houston, where the voices were also amplified.)

When Gordon Davidson was approached about directing the opera he declined. He was uncertain, he confided later, "whether Lenny was ready to wrestle with that highly charged landscape so soon after Felicia's death and in the midst of sorting out his own life." But Bernstein was committed; there was no turning back. Stephen Wadsworth, who wanted to direct, was deemed too inexperienced by Houston's manager, David Gockley, and Peter Mark Schifter was put in charge. Houston's music director, John De Main, a pupil of Bernstein's at Tanglewood in 1971, was the conductor: he had the temperament to cope with a noisy composer at his back. Bernstein attended the last three weeks of rehearsals, often flaunting the ten-gallon hat he had been given on his arrival in what he later, with almost sublime tactlessness, called Cow Town. (Doubtless he would have preferred the premiere to be at La Scala.)

Family and friends from around the world attended the opening, which was picketed by right-wing demonstrators objecting to the reportedly gay content of the new work. Bernstein received a seven-minute ovation at the end, but critics found much to dislike. Donal Henahan, then the senior music critic of the *New York Times,* was the most deeply hostile. "It continually rings false. It occasionally shudders on the edge of sounding more than cosmetic, but more frequently its portentous and epic tone is wildly inappropriate. The score smoothly blends tonality and atonality while ranging from lyrically contemplative commonplaces to strident outcries of the sort employed to let a soap opera audience know something seemingly significant is happening. . . . *A Quiet Place* is as hollow and faddish as *Mass*." Alan Rich in *Newsweek* talked of "four hopelessly uninteresting people" slogging through "a dreary psychological quagmire" toward an unenlightening reconciliation that any soap opera buff could have predicted: "The spectacle of a prodigious talent in decline, or at least in eclipse, is never a heartening one."

But *A Quiet Place* was far from being universally panned. Leighton Kerner in *The Village Voice* wrote of "the birth of a powerful new opera." Andrew Porter told his *New Yorker* readers that the score was "one of the richest Bernstein has composed. . . . The melodic lines are as sharp-eared as Janacek's in their transformation of speech rhythms and speech inflections into music. . . . the double bill [*Trouble in Tahiti* was placed before the interval] can be likened to an American 'Ring' played out not with Aristotelian magnitude but in a Great Neck home."

Wadsworth says that he and Bernstein were not panicked by the bad reviews but they nevertheless told their production partners at La Scala and the Kennedy Center that they wanted to make extensive revisions. The performances scheduled for Washington in October 1983 were postponed so that they could follow the June 1984 production at La Scala, Milan. Three major problems had to be addressed: the evening was too long, the intermission came too soon, and the stylistic chasm between the two operas was too wide: the *Tahiti* prologue did not prepare the audience for the emotional rigors of what was to come—or so the argument ran. The solution, devised by John Mauceri, who was music adviser to Roger Stevens at the Kennedy Center, was to create a single three-act opera where before there had been two separate works. The long opening scene of *A Quiet Place* became the new Act I. Scene 2 became Act II, with the first half of *Tahiti* inserted near the beginning as a flashback and the second half "interleaved," as Bernstein called it, halfway through. Scenes 3 and 4 of *A Quiet Place* were combined into Act III. The interlude at the start of Scene 3 was dropped altogether—Wadsworth felt the public did not want to know about grumpy old Mrs. Doc's lesbian feelings for Dinah.

Radically revised, *A Quiet Place* took on the formal quality of a Jean-Luc Godard film: there was a beginning, a middle and an end, but not necessarily in that order. The work was still lopsided but in a different way, now that the subsidiary characters disappeared after the overlong first act. The structural problems had been shuffled rather than solved. But there was merit in having the flashbacks set to a different, slicker style of composition and in a lighter scoring, and the Italian critics gave the revised premiere at La Scala in June 1984 a positive reception. Stephen Wadsworth directed and John Mauceri conducted, as he did the following month at the Kennedy Center in Washington. When Bernstein finally took over the baton in 1986 for the Vienna State Opera production, from which recordings and a telecast were also to be made, he grumbled at how difficult he had made things for the singers. But with more imaginative settings (by Thomas P. Lynch) and Bernstein's own conducting authority behind it, the Vienna production was inevitably the most satisfying, even though *A Quiet Place* is too intimate to be an ideal choice for a big stage such as Vienna and the orchestra of Austrian Radio was not of the first rank.

Wadsworth felt that the warmth of the response in two major European opera houses confirmed the universality of Bernstein's music and placed the opera, despite its Americanness, in the European tradition. Bernstein himself made no broad claims. He said his opera was an attempt to make people recognize the violence and rage contained within themselves and to pacify these emotions by reaching out with affection to each other, in the same spirit in which the choirboys at the end of *Mass* go out into the audience spreading the gospel of love. Such gestures may verge on what H. L. Mencken once called "the swamp of uplift," but as Bernstein's *Village Voice* champion Leighton Kerner put it, "the emotional tension of the words and the abrasive theatricality of the music make hard participatory listening well worth your while."

*"If I can write one real moving American opera that any American can understand (and one that is, notwithstanding, a serious musical work) I shall be a very happy man."* It had taken him thirty-five years, but with *A Quiet Place,* Leonard Bernstein finally achieved the ambition he had first voiced in 1948. Whether he was a happy man was another question.

# ROYAL PROGRESS

*"Do you do this sort of thing often, Mr. Bernstein?"*
*Barbican Centre, London, May 6, 1986.*
PHOTO CLIVE N. TOTMAN

*Grow old along with me!*
*The best is yet to be,*
*The last of life, for which the first was made.*
—ROBERT BROWNING,
Rabbi Ben Ezra

ON August 25, 1983, Leonard Bernstein celebrated his sixty-fifth birthday in his birthplace, Lawrence, Massachusetts. He had actually lived
in the town for only a few weeks as a newborn baby, and had last
visited it forty-nine years previously, in 1934, to get the name on his birth
certificate altered from Louis to Leonard. But the citizens of Lawrence proposed to dedicate an outdoor theater to him in their heritage park and to
provide not one but two local orchestras—the Merrimack Valley Philharmonic
to play excerpts from his own compositions and the Greater Boston Youth
Symphony and Chorus to perform the "Ode to Joy" and accompany Bernstein
himself reading (for the only time in his life) the text of *A Lincoln Portrait*. So
Bernstein turned down birthday invitations from Tanglewood and Central
Park, New York, and the Hollywood Bowl and drove through the cheering if
slightly bewildered crowds lining the streets of Lawrence in an open-topped
1928 Ford roadster, looking as homespun as James Stewart in Frank Capra's
classic, *It's a Wonderful Life*. Lawrence was known as Immigrant City and

parading schoolchildren dressed in Latvian, Irish and Spanish costumes were led by a girl with a banner marked "Chile," in honor of Felicia. At the park Bernstein wrote "Peace, Paz, Pace, Shalom" in clay for a plaque to be affixed to the stage bearing his name. He picnicked on the banks of the Merrimack, not far from the mills where his mother had worked as a girl (more than seventy years previously) and visited the Resnick family's three-decker house on Juniper Street, where he had lived as a baby.

Wherever he went that day he made speeches in favor of nuclear disarmament. "I am dead serious about solving the most deadly and self-perpetuating of problems the world has ever had—its own suicide." Months earlier he had decided to turn his birthday into a demonstration by wearing a sky-blue armband and inviting musicians all around the world to do the same. On his behalf Harry Kraut lobbied every musician and friend on the Amberson mailing list and distributed thousands of strips of blue cloth provided by mills at Lawrence and cut to size by a bevy of famous actors and actresses working for the disarmament cause. Supporters in the United States, Western Europe, Russia, Japan, Israel and South America pledged to wear them. The response in Germany was especially strong. In Hungary, the Prime Minister, János Kádár, wore one.

At the free concert in Lawrence (conducted by a new Japanese protégé from Tanglewood named Eiji Oue) Bernstein was flanked by his whole family: mother, aunts, brother, sister, cousins, children, nieces, nephews. An unseasonable wind prevented the announced fireworks display but Bernstein put on one of his own when he was persuaded (without much difficulty) to conduct the *Candide* overture as an encore. At a fund-raising dinner he entertained the guests—who between them had contributed thirty thousand dollars for music scholarships—by jiving with his daughter Jamie and jitterbugging with his sister Shirley. The day was refreshingly free from the media-inspired exaggerations of the sixtieth birthday at Wolf Trap. Lawrence was having a hard time economically. Bernstein helped the town to project a positive message about itself, while Lawrence gave Bernstein a platform to get across his plea for a nuclear freeze.

On days like that he was still fun to be with. But by the mid-1980s his family and friends were having to live through times when his behavior was less attractive. As his daughter Jamie remembers, "He was getting much harder to be around: he was doing more Scotch and relying more heavily on his Dexedrine." When he mixed the drug and the alcohol he "would have a personality change . . . he would get vituperative and irritable and snap at people and say awful things and bang the table and throw lit cigarettes at us. . . . It got to the point that Daddy being a pain in the ass was the norm and when he was fun to be around became a nice, special exception. After my mother was gone . . . there was no one to check him except us and there were limits for us because we didn't live with him. So after that it was just Maestro City all the way."

With Nina at Harvard, the only other person who still lived at the Dakota apartment was the housekeeper, Julia Vega. "The moralistic input of my mother," Jamie remembers, "was transferred onto Julia, who in a funny way took on a lot of those wifely roles. She was the one who would carp at him for smoking too many cigarettes and staying up too late." When Bernstein invited a man to stay overnight, a bed was made up for the guest in the spare room and he would ruffle the sheets in order not to shock Julia. But she knew perfectly well what was happening.

Bernstein had returned to the primarily homosexual life he had lived in the years before before his marriage, becoming noisily aggressive about the need to declare one's sexuality, despite all the pain he himself had caused by his public statement in 1976. At the Tanglewood cafeteria, surrounded by students, he shocked a journalist by singing "Ev'rybody out of the closet" to a tune from Tchaikovsky's Fifth Symphony. Phillip Ramey remembers Aaron Copland, in his eighties, giving a dusty answer when Bernstein urged him to "come out": "I think I'll leave that to you, boy."

Nobody ever took Tom Cothran's place in Bernstein's affections but in the late 1970s he formed a close friendship with Robert Lee Kirkland III, a young journalist working at that time for *Newsweek International.* And early in the 1980s he began a complex relationship with Aaron Stern, then in his early thirties, who was dean of the American Conservatory of Music in Chicago. Stern's progressive if somewhat hazy ideas about the way the arts should be used to influence general education fascinated Bernstein and led him to advance Stern substantial cash sums over the decade for field experiments in teaching. The uncanny power Stern wielded over Bernstein baffled and infuriated members of Bernstein's permanent staff. Bernstein confided to a family friend that although he did not like him very much, "Stern turned him on." According to Stern, Bernstein set out to seduce him: Stern says he was a companion, not a lover. The durability of their friendship was based more on a shared interest in music and education and on a sympathy for Eastern mysticism unexplored in Bernstein's other relationships.

In addition to Stern and Kirkland, Bernstein formed friendships with literally dozens of other men during the eighties. He was especially vulnerable to the charms and musical talents of the young male conductors with whom he worked each year. No doubt he wanted to seduce and possess them, but he loved teaching them even more.

It would in any case be wrong to assume that Bernstein was now moving predominantly in a homosexual milieu. His intimate circle was as eclectic as his music. It included his family (his brother Burton married a *New Yorker* colleague, Jane Anderson, in 1984), many of his old Broadway friends and younger artists whose company he enjoyed, among them the handsome Italian film director Franco Amurri and his girlfriend at that time, the actress Susan Sarandon (for whose child Bernstein wrote a birth day poem); the conductor and pianist Michael Barrett and his future wife, the violist Leslie Tomkins;

Barrett's violinist friend Paul Woodiel, who was a brilliant anagrammist; and Jamie's friend David Thomas, a film distribution executive in Chicago (he moved later to Channel 13, WNET, in New York), who one day in the summer of 1984 made an old-fashioned gesture and formally asked Bernstein for Jamie's hand in marriage.

The wedding was to be the first happy family event since Bernstein's sixty-fifth birthday. At the first meeting of the future in-laws, David Thomas remembers, "Lenny was hugely relieved to learn that my mother had a Jewish brother-in-law, that my parents were interested in music, and that these people from Ohio were not, as he had feared, something out of *American Gothic.* After dinner the . . . 'grown-ups' walked arm in arm down the street away from the restaurant singing, 'Why, oh why, oh why-oh? Why did we ever leave Ohio?' in harmony and Lenny kissed both my parents goodnight, on the lips. Before I said my own goodnight, Lenny made me cap the evening by exchanging neckties with him. Good theater."

Bernstein paid a king's ransom to give his daughter a wedding reception in the Starlight Roof of the Waldorf-Astoria. He embarrassed not a few of the four hundred guests when his congratulatory toast enumerating his son-in-law's virtues ended with the boast: "and he's *straight.*"

Thomas found he had not only married a high-spirited and gifted rock singer, poet and composer: he had also entered a closely knit clan that took its tone from the patriarchal figure of Leonard Bernstein. Communication within Thomas's own family was, he says, deliberate and guarded. "Jamie's family could hardly bear more than forty-eight hours without phone calls from one another, always greeted each other effusively after absences, and tried to have dinner together as often as possible. Dinners were about talk—loud, animated talk. . . . Periodically Lenny would shout that we should all be silent and listen to *him,* for a change, and we would, for a minute or two until, inevitably, parenthetical contributions from the sidelines accumulated into the familiar roar. . . . Upon leaving the table Lenny might sidle over to the piano, more frequently than not to play something silly. . . . He might play one composer in the manner of another, or improvise together a chain of musically-related nonsequiturs. . . ."

Jamie's marriage had a stabilizing effect on her father. There was a sense in which the laid-back Thomas replaced the courteous and elegant Felicia in the family circle. The centrifugal force of family love had pulled Bernstein back from the brink of divorce in 1977 and it kept what had become a monstrous ego in some kind of check for the rest of his life.

Bernstein's indifferent state of health was the biggest threat to his well-being. When he contracted amoebic dysentery during the state visit to Mexico in 1979 he consulted Dr. Kevin Cahill, one of New York's leading specialists in tropical diseases. He would never place himself completely under doctor's orders but Cahill became a good personal friend as well as personal physician and medical adviser and for a decade he kept Bernstein's insatiable demand for prescription drugs within reasonable bounds. Bernstein's most dangerous habit was smoking. Since he hadn't been able to give it up, he tried to reduce the risk by using Aquafilters. When his television director forbade him to smoke during a long interview for the BBC, he was reduced to sucking an empty filter on screen like a baby with a pacifier.

Bernstein continued to work for noble causes such as world peace, racial harmony and nuclear disarmament. He supported Amnesty International, cancer research, the Save the Children Fund and, from as early as 1983, AIDS research. But at the heart of his life, day in and day out, was music. He spent part of each winter in Fairfield, Connecticut, and New York, making side trips to Key West, where the low pollen climate had always been friendly to his asthma and the sympathetic intellectual community included his favorite poet, James Merrill, and the writer John Malcolm Brinnin, with whom he enjoyed long evenings of anagrams. For the rest of the year he was never in the same city for more than a few weeks. He traveled from one concert hall to the next like a visiting potentate. His secret was to keep moving; he was continually refreshed by the renewal of old friendships and the making of great music with great orchestras. Forty years after his first guest engagements he was still crisscrossing the American continent but now it was on grand tours—with the New York Philharmonic, the Vienna Philharmonic, the Israel Philharmonic and, on one occasion, the less prestigious French National Orchestra, with which he'd had connections since 1947. Once he had reconciled his differences with its Boston-based management, he also set great store by his annual teaching visits and conducting engagements at Tanglewood. But the center of gravity of his concert-giving had shifted to Europe. From 1983 to 1990 he worked every year with the Vienna Philharmonic, six years out of eight with the Bavarian Radio Orchestra in Munich and five with the Santa Cecilia Orchestra in Rome, whose presidency he assumed in 1985. He continued his long association with the Israel Philharmonic and renewed his links with the London Symphony, of which he was named president in 1986. In 1985 he opened a fruitful new period with the Concertgebouw in Amsterdam.

Wherever he went in Europe he was made welcome by monarchs, presidents and prime ministers. Nearly every evening when he was not conducting there would be public receptions or private parties in his honor. He held press conferences and received prestigious awards (he gave away the $150,000 of his Siemens Prize to music colleges around the world). From London he made a trip to Epsom Downs to watch the Derby; at the Vatican a private viewing of the Sistine Chapel ceiling was arranged so that he could inspect "his" Jeremiah on Michelangelo's newly restored fresco.

There were always at least three people in his traveling team. His manager, Harry Kraut, took care of business matters and long-term planning. He was particularly strong at organizing special events with extra-musical significance and putting into practice Bernstein's desire to help gifted students or Jewish Russian émigré musicians.

His musical assistant doubled on personal matters. In 1986 Charlie Harmon moved to Bernstein's archive, to be succeeded in the assistant's post by Craig Urquhart, who went with Bernstein on his travels, and by Phillip Allen, who looked after him when he was at home. The assistant got Bernstein up in the morning, took care of his copious wardrobe and his concert clothes, assembled the traveling library of study scores for the next engagement, installed the audio equipment to study test balances of new recordings while on the road—not forgetting medicines, inhalers, Tums, Aquafilters, scotch (Ballantine's) and cigarettes. When Urquhart started touring with Bernstein in 1986 he remembers packing twenty-two suitcases. By forward planning and living off the land he reduced the number to twelve.

The third member of the touring team was the assistant conductor, who at each port of call made sure the orchestra's individual parts were correctly marked with Bernstein's indications of expression and his bowings for the strings. The conducting assistant sometimes conducted preliminary read-through rehearsals, prepared choruses, conducted offstage bands, and even took over when Bernstein was sick. He was also Bernstein's liaison with his regular Deutsche Grammophon producer, Hans Weber. Working for Bernstein was a useful stage of apprenticeship for conductors of the caliber of Jacques Delacôte, Guido Ajmone-Marsan and David Shallon.

To the team was added the entourage. Often Bernstein would take with him a member of his family or invite old friends like Adolph Green or Betty Comden to join him. He would also invite a personal traveling companion, often Aaron Stern. Within hours of Bernstein's arrival in a new city the atmosphere of a royal progress would develop in his suite as friends came to make dates for dinner or deliver gifts of favorite delicacies while supplicants pleaded for auditions for gifted youngsters, sittings for sculptors, sessions for television interviews, photo-calls and record signings.

Bernstein had a favorite hotel in each city, and in each hotel he had a favorite suite. His personal assistant traveled ahead to ensure that everything was as it had been on the previous visit. When the Sacher in Vienna redecorated his rooms without consulting him he switched to the Bristol, which offered round-the-clock room service and a personal headwaiter for the maestro. In London he always stayed at the Savoy in a suite with a view of the Thames. He especially adored the hotel's afternoon teas with scones, clotted cream and cucumber sandwiches. In Munich his suite at the Vier Jahreszeiten was adjacent to the rooftop swimming pool and his postconcert parties at the hotel included a midnight swim—in the buff, if so desired. His favorite cities were Paris, Rome and Jerusalem. At the Hôtel Crillon his penthouse living room had a terrace overlooking the Place de la Concorde. In Rome his suite at the Hotel de la Ville had an equally breathtaking view of the eternal city's rooftops and hills. His suite at the King David looked out over the majestic Old City; in the Tel Aviv Hilton he always occupied the Presidential Suite.

It would be easy to snipe at this expensive display had it not been accompanied by first-rate music-making. And often Bernstein bore much of the cost himself. In Israel he gave his fee back to the Philharmonic. In London he was paid only half his regular international fee, in Vienna even less and nothing toward the hotel. In other countries orchestras were happy to pay hotel bills and expenses in addition to hefty performance fees because Bernstein's concerts were guaranteed to be among the highlights of their season. And while he undoubtedly lived well, he had also become music's spokesman to the world, giving himself generously to musical projects too numerous to describe individually.

DURING the 1980s Bernstein revived his interest in making television programs. The first, in September 1984, was a fly-on-the-wall-style documentary about the Deutsche Grammophon recording sessions for *West Side Story,* which he conducted with a controversial cast. The gamble was with the principal singers. Kurt Ollmann as Riff and Tatiana Troyanos as Anita were as American as apple pie, but Kiri Te Kanawa, a lyric soprano of great fame and distinction, could not entirely conceal her operatic breeding or her oratorio-English. Cast at the last minute as Tony, the leader of the Jets, the equally renowned tenor José Carreras worked heroically but with less than total success to eradicate his Spanish accent. But the lapse in verisimilitude was more than compensated for, to Bernstein's mind, by the opportunity to have his only romantic love music sung by two of the world's most sumptuous voices, accompanied by a larger, more virtuosic orchestra than could ever be squeezed into a theater pit.

Bernstein was more involved behind the scenes in this film, produced jointly by the BBC and Unitel, than in anything he had done since his Beethoven and Mahler documentaries of 1970 and 1971. He was interviewed daily and spoke the commentary himself. No attempt was made to soften what was in places a surprisingly harsh picture of the tensions generated behind the scenes. He had never conducted his musical before and he worried away at details every night, raising public hell with his copyists next day for not transferring all his last-minute markings into the musicians' parts. "I was up until four o'clock in the fucking morning," he complained, conveniently forgetting that he should have had the whole thing ready before the sessions began and had quite likely not started his work until after midnight. "You didn't do your homework," he called out offensively more than once to the producer John McClure and his German colleagues in the control room when they requested retakes, and he slumped over the conductor's desk in deep depression when at the very end of a long session José Carreras balked at singing the sustained top B flat in the song "Maria," asking that the passage be taken in a later session when his voice was fresh. Carreras was as angry as Bernstein—a camera caught him swearing in Spanish. But when work resumed the next day, all was well: the top note poured out gloriously.

Despite the occasional display of tetchiness, Bernstein was on a high all week. As with *Tristan,* he had plunged into a major project with singers he did not know, and much to his relief the gamble paid off. The film shows him falling in love with his own music. It's already a classic of a kind, he said, "so funky—yet it sounds as if I just wrote it yesterday."

In the same year, 1984, Bernstein labored long on another BBC television program called *The Little Drummer Boy,* a musical and psychological study of Gustav Mahler as the Jewish boy who had made good in the Christian world. He set out to define what he argued was the essential Jewishness in all Mahler's music. His thesis did not find universal approval. His friend the opera director Otto Schenk, a good Viennese social historian, thought Bernstein was mistaken in his claim that an assimilated Jew like Mahler would have felt guilty about abandoning his faith. But *The Little Drummer Boy* showed Bernstein once more asserting his own religious roots. "Judaism is the hardest of all religions because there are no ultimate rewards except on earth—no promises about the Hereafter, no guaranteed Kingdom of Heaven—only the conviction that God will love you if you do his work." Death was often in Bernstein's thoughts in the years leading up to his seventieth birthday. One of the most striking sequences in his Mahler film was a demonstration that all nine of Mahler's symphonies included a funeral march.

In Bernstein's next BBC television project, *The Love of Three Orchestras,* he sketched in his conducting career and used excerpts from performances by the orchestras of New York, Israel and Vienna to explain why these three institutions were his favorites. The Vienna Philharmonic emerged as the outright winner because, he claimed, the players' love of music-making always guided their decisions. "They are so proud to have this great tradition, they are so loving of what they do and of who they are. This is something I catch like a disease—it's so contagious for me because I operate in terms of love."

Another slice of autobiography appeared several years later in the Unitel production, *Teachers and Teaching.* Bernstein reminisced with Lukas Foss about their piano teacher Isabelle Vengerova and showed how Koussevitzky had taught him to conduct the space between the beats. Michael Tilson Thomas described a coaching session with Bernstein in which they made up rhymes to match the energy of the big theme in Schumann's *Rhenish* Symphony.

Bernstein's other autobiographical projects for television were never completed. In May 1985 he returned to the subject of being Jewish. He had just been conducting scenes from Wagner's music dramas at a concert at the Vienna State Opera. How was it possible, he mused aloud, for a Jew to feel such deep love as he did for the music of a composer as anti-Semitic as Richard Wagner? To explore the paradox of his position, Bernstein took a Viennese film crew to the shrine of psychoanalysis, the Freud Museum at 19 Berggasse. He spoke fifty minutes of carefully scripted self-examination in Dr. Freud's consulting room. But he ran out of steam once he had sketched in the background and posed the question: "What's a nice Jewish boy like you doing here playing racist music?" In fact Jews had been conducting Wagner for a hundred years. Bernstein had been doing so himself since 1941. He had vague hopes of using the film to persuade the Israelis to permit Wagner performances by the Israel Philharmonic but could never devise a satisfactory conclusion. The unfinished rough-cut remains on the shelf in the Unitel film library, as does a rambling, three-hour interview about his childhood and musical education which he taped in 1987.

Bernstein probably saw more than a little of himself in Wagner. Not, of course, the anti-Semitism—although he relished the Jewish brand of self-depre-catory humor that led him to call the Israel Philharmonic "the Jew Orchestra" —but the love of luxury, the loving and dynamic relationships with singers and theater people of both sexes, the profound affection for his children, and above all the creative personality, the ego. "Some of us grow up more successfully than others," Bernstein declared in 1985. "I have the feeling that Wagner never grew up in this sense, that he retained all his life that infantile feeling of being the center of the universe." There is surely an echo here of Bernstein's 1970 asser-tion that an unexpected element in Beethoven's creative makeup was to be found in his childlike charm.

Earlier in 1985 he had opened his heart to an unusual degree when he preached a sermon at the Unitarian Church of All Souls in Manhattan. He chose as his theme Albert Schweitzer's phrase "the Will to Love." He took it very seriously, he said, "because it is almost a definition of the meaning of my life. Not out of principle, reason or conviction, but mysteriously, genetically, psychobiologically—I don't know—the Will to Love guides my living from day to day, always has, and always has messed it up to a remarkable degree, and still does. . . .

"The Will to Love is exhausting. It causes one to love far too many people, and to love them deeply, with commitment. It is obviously very difficult, if not impossible, to honor so many commitments simultaneously, or even one at a time, over a considerable geographic expanse. It is unfair to those I love, espe-cially to those who love me in return, and it therefore causes suffering, which is the opposite of what the Will to Love intends. This is true not only of beloved individuals but of whole families, including my own, and including my orches-tra-families around the world, for in conducting one I can obviously not be conducting all the others. Moreover, because love is so demanding of time and energy, it causes my work to suffer, compositions to remain uncomposed, old and new scores to remain unlearned. . . .

"Probably the best I can have done today," he concluded, "is to remind you of what you surely knew already, of the life-or-death importance of living out the Will to Love; to remind you by my personal confession of success or failure in my own struggle to make love a practiced reality; to remind you by nudging your awareness—*and* my own—of the profound moral imperative we share to make our lives a moment-by-moment, uninterrupted action of bearing witness."

Bearing witness took many forms. In February 1985 he flew to Rio with Aaron Stern to experience Carnival in the company of the young Brazilian conductor Flavio Chamis. After watching a samba competition for twenty-four hours, Stern remembers, Bernstein ventured onto the crowded Ipanema beach wearing nothing but a string bikini and his gold shekel necklace and Mitropoulos cross. Somewhat to his chagrin nobody recognized him. It was a different story when he flew to Los Angeles. Cindy Lauper, a hugely popular rock singer, went down on her knees to him when he attended the 1985 Grammy ceremonies to receive a Lifetime Achievement Award for his work as a recording artist; the composer Quincy Jones made the presentation. On July 4, 1985, he conducted his *Songfest* at a televised concert on the lawn behind Washington's Capitol; Nina and Alexander, who had both studied acting at the Herbert Berghof studio, read the poems. (They had also performed Maria and Tony's spoken dialogue for the *West Side Story* recording the previous September.)

LATER in the summer of 1985 Bernstein made a significant political gesture with what he called a Journey for Peace, giving two concerts in Hiroshima with the European Community Youth Orchestra to mark the fortieth anniversary of the dropping of the first atomic bomb. It was, he said, "an act of prayer, personal and profound," and he insisted on programming his *Kaddish* Symphony as the main work, with Barbara Hendricks as soloist and a youth choir from Vienna. The ECYO would have preferred something more conventional such as the Verdi *Requiem,* which might have attracted an international telecast. Two works on the program—a Mozart violin concerto played by the fourteen-year-old Japanese-American prodigy Midori and a new *Hiroshima Requiem* by a Japanese woman composer, Tomiko Kōjiba—were conducted by Eiji Oue, who, like Ms. Kōjiba, had been born in Hiroshima.

The orchestra assembled and gave its first concert in Athens (Greece had just joined the European Community) before making the sixteen-hour journey to Japan. By sunrise on the anniversary day, August 6, Hiroshima's Peace Park was crowded and the air was pungent with the smell of incense burning at the monuments and shrines dotted about the area. At one of the shrines Leonard Bernstein joined a delegation of musicians led by Seiji Ozawa and his brother Mikio, who laid wreaths of flowers and sang a newly composed *Requiem* chorus as well as Japanese and German folk songs. (Ozawa remembers that a Nazi song crept embarrassingly into the selection.) It was probably the earliest hour Bernstein had ever risen, and he looked appropriately somber. The memorial ceremony, attended by fifty-five thousand people, began at eight-fifteen, the precise moment of the bomb's explosion, with the ringing of the Peace Bell. Its sound was echoed by more than three hundred temple bells across the city of Hiroshima, where sixty thousand citizens had instantly perished and three times as many had since died as a direct result of the bomb. The mayor of Hiroshima and the Japanese Prime Minister both made speeches calling for abolition of nuclear arms.

With his customary lack of concern for the diplomatic proprieties Bernstein had used a press conference to criticize his hosts, attacking the conflict between Japan's rival antinuclear groups. The American embassy went out of its way to emphasize that Bernstein had no official status in Hiroshima and plans for a live telecast of his concert to America collapsed. But Bernstein's sense of timing was never better demonstrated than by the decision to go to Hiroshima. The second Strategic Arms Limitations Treaty—a major step toward disarmament —was signed in Helsinki in the fall of 1985; the musicians in Hiroshima— young and old—could justifiably feel that they had helped to influence world public opinion. Bernstein complained that the U.S. press was ignoring his mission, but he spoke up for peace on CBS's "Morning News" and, interviewed live on ABC's "Good Morning America" at the end of the evening's concert in Hiroshima, he said, "I hope it does some good to grant us the wisdom that war is obsolete and that we should stop all this nonsense once and for all."

The ultratheatrical *Kaddish* was a difficult work to present to the undemonstrative Japanese, but the concert confirmed Bernstein's power to make a big audience feel it had been involved in a profound ceremony. The applause ran on for ten minutes. Stories of his wild behavior away from the concert hall reinforced his mystique; earlier on the tour, in Athens, he had mounted the pillion of a police escort's motorbike and was delivered from his hotel not just to the hall but right up to the platform where the orchestra was growing impatient at his late arrival for the rehearsal. "Lenny" was incorrigible.

After a second Hiroshima concert the following day, the same program was repeated by the travel-weary players in Budapest and then Vienna. Bernstein's physical resilience proved astonishing that summer. First he flew from Vienna to Hamburg to be interviewed by Helmut Schmidt, the former German Chancellor. Bernstein was helping his old friend Justus Frantz to establish a new festival in Schleswig-Holstein. From Hamburg he flew to Tel Aviv and with the Israel Philharmonic embarked on his second tour to Japan in a month, preceded by two concerts in Munich and followed by four more in the United States. A reporter in San Francisco was shocked to find Bernstein looking drawn and vulnerable. "His eyes, remembered as so alive and expressive, are empty. His speech, so beguilingly sophisticated and eloquently decorated, is slow, unfocused. Hours of flying have made him stiff. Two or more double scotches have added their toll. . . . 'There are all these important things to do,' he whispers. 'God, the number of things I have not done.' "

In the same interview Bernstein spoke publicly for the first time about his desire to compose another opera. "I have a lot of music to write and this next opera is a terribly important one. I just hope I last until it's done." Bernstein had been thinking about this work as early as 1980 when he wrote himself a note headed "multi-language opera." He envisaged interlocking scenes in French, English, German and Italian, and defined the piece as an operatic *Decline of the West*. "What is the point of mixing languages?" he asked himself in his note. "Babel," he answered. "Confusion: our society is carrying on as if unaware of certain doom."

Stephen Wadsworth had been to Fairfield for his first meeting about this new multilingual opera in July 1984, just after the successful Washington performances of *A Quiet Place*. "He gave me a little scenario: a couple of guys, in Florence, buying an antique in a shop." Wadsworth was baffled. He developed a set of characters anyway, but could see he wasn't addressing what Bernstein needed to write about.

On a page of manuscript paper dated January 1985 Bernstein scribbled another note to himself about the larger meaning he was looking for: "The sense of starting the ghastly cycle again. . . . But we have not yet found ways, short of murder, to act out our suppressed rages, hostilities, xenophobias, provincialisms, parochialisms, mistrust and need for superiority. We still need some kind of lower class as slaves, prisoners, enemies, scapegoats. Can it again come to the ugly equation: Reds = Jews?"

One reads on with an increasing sense of gloom. Plagued by the idea that he must write something significant, Bernstein was showing little interest in characters and no flair for a story. Wadsworth developed a plan for a three-act opera in twenty-one brief scenes, treating half a century of history since the Holocaust in locations as far apart as a Soviet psychiatric hospital (Raoul Wallenberg was to figure in the opera) and a Washington war memorial. Russian and Yiddish were added to the languages. "The key story (which ultimately unifies all the others) must be a story of *faith*," wrote Bernstein. In May 1985 Wadsworth's revised synopsis was received cautiously but on the whole positively by Carl Helmut Drese, the new director at the Vienna State Opera, which was considering a commission. It was the week of Bernstein's Wagner concerts (in Vienna) and his unfinished analysis session with Sigmund Freud. There was clearly some link in his mind between anti-Semitism and his own "suppressed rage," but he never succeeded in articulating it.

Wadsworth and Bernstein discussed characters and casting in Rome the following month. But Bernstein was not inspired by Wadsworth's concepts as he had been by *A Quiet Place*. He took months to respond to the draft libretto of the first scene and when he did he was highly critical: "too historical, heavy, realistic." A week later Wadsworth told Bernstein he could not continue. He had a life and a career of his own to pursue as an opera director and teacher. Bernstein may have been uneasy about Wadsworth's outline but he was devastated by his withdrawal. He hauled himself up from the dinner table at the Dakota, Wadsworth remembers, suddenly an old man. "I'm very tired," he said. "I think I have to go to sleep now." And he trudged out of the room. Four years were to pass before he returned to his opera. Meanwhile the composing period assigned to early 1986 was "shot to hell." He went into a deep depression.

Even when Bernstein was in seemingly terminal gloom, there was nothing, as Jamie Bernstein Thomas later observed, that "a little Viennese adulation couldn't turn around." In the fall of 1985 he concluded the filming of a Schumann symphony cycle and launched a new survey of Shostakovich symphonies. In the spring of 1986 he returned to Vienna to conduct *A Quiet Place* at the State Opera. There was more adulation in May, when the London Symphony Orchestra mounted a Bernstein festival at the Barbican Centre, directed by John Mauceri, that put all previous efforts in the shade. There were free concerts of songs and chamber music in the foyer, cinema screenings of television programs and of *West Side Story* and *On the Waterfront,* a brilliant student production of *Mass* at the Guildhall School, and in the concert hall four programs of music by Bernstein and by the composers who had influenced him, including Gershwin, Mahler and Blitzstein.

The climax of the festival was a concert of his own music that Bernstein conducted for the Queen and the Duke of Edinburgh. Neither could be described as passionate devotees of twentieth-century music, but in the international glamour league they ranked with the Pope and the American President. The royal presence guaranteed a sold-out hall for the concert and brought in its train a massive display of British protocol. The Queen was to make a grand entrance down the Grand Tier. When she and her party reached their places in the first row (but not before) Bernstein would receive a sign, relayed from the stage manager to the orchestra's concertmaster, to conduct the British national anthem. Bernstein made his own entrance, received his ovation and waited— for once in his life upstaged at a symphony concert. When the Queen arrived, things went hilariously wrong. The audience rose and the royal party began its descent, but Bernstein, who claimed afterward that he had been given the signal, launched the orchestra into "God Save the Queen" when Her Majesty was only halfway down the stairs. She froze immediately, and the courtiers and officials behind her narrowly escaped toppling like dominoes in her wake.

Bernstein's conversation with the Queen after the concert went immediately into the family's anecdote collection. "Do you do this sort of thing often?" she asked him. Nina Bernstein was near her father. "He stood there with a look on his face. 'What could she mean?' I saw the ideas going through his head. . . . 'Do I meet royalty often? No. Do I . . . wear black often?' And he actually said, 'Well if you mean, do I conduct often, why yes I do. Do I conduct my own music often? Yes, I do.' And the Queen looked utterly nonplussed." When she reached Nina, the Queen inquired whether she had come all the way from America "just for this."

The festival enhanced Bernstein's British reputation. In the *Sunday Times,*

David Cairns called him "the genius with the common touch. . . . His populist concern is something to be respected and honored in an age not notable for serious music's close contact with the common man."

The round of European honors continued in Paris, where President Mitterrand conferred on Bernstein the rank of Commander in the Légion d'Honneur. In Munich he received the Hartmann medal. He had overtaken Karajan (now seventy-eight and ailing) as the leading conductor in the German-speaking world. From Munich he flew north to open the first Schleswig-Holstein Festival in Kiel with a performance of Haydn's *The Creation,* making a timely statement before the performance (in the wake of the Chernobyl nuclear plant disaster) that linked Haydn's joyful evocation of nature with the need to protect the environment. While in Kiel he inaugurated his first European teaching course for young conductors, giving four conductors forty minutes each with the Bavarian Radio Orchestra. In September he gave three young Americans a chance to share his program and conduct the New York Philharmonic.

At the memorial service for Alan Jay Lerner, who died of lung cancer in June 1986 aged sixty-seven, people in the crowd held up signs saying, "We love you, Lenny. Please stop smoking." But Bernstein positively flaunted his bad habits. "I was diagnosed as having emphysema in my mid-20s, and to be dead by the age of 35. Then they said I'd be dead by the age of 45. And 55. Well, I beat the rap. I smoke. I drink. I stay up all night. I screw around. I'm overcommitted on all fronts." The notorious quote appeared in *USA Today,* as a prelude to a national tour with the New York Philharmonic in August 1986.

There were emotional fireworks behind the scenes that summer. Days before the Philharmonic tour began, Harry Kraut resigned, fed up, as he put it later, with Bernstein's capriciousness and "the impossibility of getting a word in edgeways." He agreed to withhold a public announcement until a successor had been appointed. Schuyler Chapin came in to hold the fort at Amberson and the publicist Margaret Carson went out on the tour with Bernstein. Her main concern was to keep him from talking to the press about the forthcoming allegedly "tell-all" biography by Joan Peyser. Publication was not due until April 1987 but Bernstein had already confided to the *New York Times* that he was dreading it, despite initial enthusiasm for the project. He talked about writing his own candid autobiography, for publication after his death, but got no further than videotaping an interview with Stephen Wadsworth.

Harry Kraut's resignation was of brief duration; Bernstein realized he could not do without him, and Kraut was swiftly persuaded to return to the Amberson fold. As Stephen Wadsworth saw it, Bernstein "had abdicated responsibility for his own life—Amberson had become too big a machine to stop and start." This opinion was widely shared, although Bernstein in fact had the power to cancel or to reschedule and did so with sufficient frequency to be described as a man with a whim of iron.

While the New York Philharmonic was playing in Los Angeles, Jamie's musician friend David Pack asked Bernstein what he would like for his birthday later in the month. Bernstein, who was intrigued with Michael Jackson's androgynous beauty, said he wanted Jackson at his concert. Through his producer, the composer Quincy Jones, Jackson said he would not be able to attend. Pack remembers Bernstein's reaction: "You tell Michael Jackson that I *command* him to come to Royce Hall tomorrow." Jackson came, saw and was conquered. According to Pack, "Michael was overwhelmed. At one point, Leonard actually jumped probably three feet in the air and Quincy leaned towards me and rolled his eyes, because here was Leonard showing some fancy footwork to Michael Jackson." Backstage at the concert intermission, Bernstein wrapped both his arms around Jackson, picked him up and kissed him on the lips. "Do you always use the same baton?" Jackson asked when he got his breath back. (The answer was "no.")

Michael Barrett was Bernstein's conducting assistant on the tour. He recalls that at the supper party that night he was with Bernstein and Jackson when they adjourned together to the men's room. Behind closed doors Bernstein put his hand to Jackson's be-rouged face and asked him point-blank if he was wearing makeup. "I have a pimple," Jackson shyly confessed in his boyish voice; "didn't you used to have pimples when you were young, Mr. Bernstein?" For Bernstein, who recounted the story of his encounter a dozen times, this was a fantastic breakthrough. "We found common ground; we were talking about zits."

In the fall of 1986 the Israel Philharmonic celebrated its fiftieth anniversary with a high-profile two-continent tour. On the program was *Jubilee Games,* a new work in two movements that Bernstein had composed the previous summer specifically for the Israel Philharmonic Orchestra, with help on its orchestration—because of time pressure—from Jack Gottlieb and Sid Ramin. Bernstein said at the premiere that he hoped "one day soon to add another movement or two." *Opening Prayer* for baritone solo and orchestra, which he wrote for the gala reopening of Carnegie Hall in December 1986, was duly attached to *Jubilee Games* as the middle movement, but after conducting the three-movement version with the New York Philharmonic in November 1988, he was still not satisfied. In January 1989 he composed *Seven Variations on an Octatonic Theme,* and in April 1989, in Tel Aviv, he conducted the world premiere of what had become a new work in four movements which he called, in the tradition of Bartók's great display piece, *Concerto for Orchestra.* The *Opening Prayer* became the final movement and the theme and variations were incorporated as the concerto's second movement.

The first movement, entitled "Free-Style Events," incorporates more innovations than any other Bernstein composition. The orchestral players are asked to shout the number seven, *sheva* in Hebrew, seven times and follow that with fifty—*hamishim*—to symbolize the jubilee, or fiftieth birthday, achieved after seven seven-year cycles. The musicians are invited to perform three different types of musical improvisation, some of it to prerecorded tapes. Bernstein had become fascinated with group improvisation while doing warm-up exercises with student orchestras at the Juilliard School, at Tanglewood and in Schleswig-Holstein. Now he was experimenting with freewheeling improvisatory techniques thirty years after everybody else. He described the movement as "musical athletics, with cheers and all. It is also charades, anagrams and children's counting-out games. But mainly it is celebratory, therefore spontaneous, therefore aleatoric, ranging from structured improvisation to totally free orchestral invention." In her *New York Post* review, Harriett Johnson wrote of this music: "We hear a bolder Bernstein . . . more rough in his use of dissonance, a more virile uninhibited composer."

Bernstein sometimes miscalculates the sheer ugliness produced by group improvisation in an infinite variety of pitches; the other three movements in the concerto are more accessible, if less adventurous. Coming after the raucous excitement of the first movement, the slow-movement theme and variations have an almost oriental spareness and simplicity. The music was originally composed as a duet (for recorder and cello) at the request of an English recorder player, Helena Burton. As orchestrated, the first three variations demonstrate contrasting instrumental tone colors: flute with horn, trumpet with double bass, clarinet with trombone. Each of the other four variations is scored for instruments of the same family. The movement's title, "Mixed Doubles," mirrors the equivalent movement, "Play of the Couples," in Bela Bartók's *Concerto for Orchestra*.

The third movement, "Diaspora Dances," is a celebration of the joyous Hasidic spirit ranging, according to Bernstein's own program note, "from the Middle East back to Central European ghettos and forward again to a New Yorkish kind of jazz." Bernstein again used the voices of the orchestral musicians, this time to whisper in unison the words *Hai* (Hebrew for "alive") and *Hayim* (*Le'hayim* is the Hebrew toast to life itself).

Bernstein was happy for the final movement to be performed separately on appropriate occasions as an "Opening Prayer." But this peaceful "Benediction" —the movement's alternative title—makes an effective conclusion to the concerto after the hurly-burly of the previous movement. The melody, heard first on the oboe and then, considerably slower, on the violins, is an exact transcription of the piano "Anniversary" Bernstein dedicated to his friend Aaron Stern. Bernstein compared the two verses, the second slower than the first, to the development of a friendship in which, as feelings deepen, every aspect of the relationship is reexamined under a microscope. The movement closes with the blessing, a brief baritone solo—three verses, sung in Hebrew, from the Book of Numbers:

*May the Lord bless you and keep you.*
*May the Lord make his face to shine upon you and be gracious unto you.*
*May the Lord lift up his countenance upon you and give you peace.*

When one looks for recurring themes over the entire range of Bernstein's creative output, one is struck by how deeply the interior life of this worldly man was influenced by his Jewish heritage, by the Hebrew texts he learned as a child (at his father's behest) and by the synagogue music he heard sung in Temple Mishkan Tefila every Friday evening. His first major composition, the *Jeremiah* Symphony, was a setting of beautiful Hebrew words about desolation and despair, taken from the Book of Lamentations. His big choral works, the *Kaddish* Symphony (a Jewish requiem in all but name), the *Chichester Psalms* and *Mass,* all include settings of Hebrew or Aramaic religious texts, while the *Dybbuk* ballet score is the most obvious demonstration of his concern for the mystic aspect of his Jewish blood and faith.

Bernstein's creative achievement is, however, not only the most significant body of specifically Jewish work achieved by a Jewish composer working in the field of classical music (Ernest Bloch and Darius Milhaud are his only rivals) but also a substantial contribution to the mainstream of twentieth-century composition. He was much less prolific (and less facile) than Felix Mendelssohn, to whom he was sometimes compared in his youth, or than Franz Liszt, with whom he shared both a flamboyance of character and an obsessional urge to teach, but he resembled both those illustrious predecessors in the fact that despite his equal fluency as a performer and interpreter, his compositions have survived. His symphonies, concertos, operas, ballets and choral works (not to mention his shows) have proved their durability because they are imbued with expressive power couched in accessible musical language. In the 1960s Bernstein was widely dismissed as a reactionary, an involuntary eclectic whose borrowings from such diverse sources as Bartók, Copland, Gershwin, Hindemith, Mahler, Shostakovich and Stravinsky ruled him out of contention for serious consideration as a composer. But as the pendulum of taste swung back toward tonality, the essential musicality which underpins Bernstein's harmonic conservatism was there for all to hear and respond to. Despite his acknowledged eclecticism, his scores declare themselves, like Francis Poulenc's, within a few bars. His individuality was expressed in his rhythmic vitality, his wide-leaping melodies, his method of composing by thematic metamorphosis, his choice of subject matter (frequently theatrical in its dramatic impact) and his radical formal innovations in such works as the threefold *Kaddish,* the "crossover" *Mass* and the improvisational *Concerto for Orchestra.*

In short, one may confidently contradict his statement to young people that music was essentially not about the "Lone Ranger" but was concerned only with notes and rhythms and modulations. His compositions, seen as a body, offer a powerful expression of the human spirit in many manifestations—from comic high spirits in *Wonderful Town* to tragic uncertainties in the haunting F sharp in the double basses with which *West Side Story* concludes, from the seraphic, unworldly beauty of Agathon's music in the *Serenade* to the unhappy family groping toward mutual understanding which makes the final scene of *A Quiet Place* so touching.

Duality is of Bernstein's essence: he was Whitmanesque in his ability to contain contradictions and triumphantly survive. Alongside the theme of faith lost and faith renewed which he expressed in many compositions, one discerns another recurring theme, his love for the City of Sin, that "helluva town," New York. No composer sang of an urban landscape in so many moods or with such intensity: *Fancy Free, On the Town, The Age of Anxiety, Wonderful Town, On the Waterfront, West Side Story* and, to a lesser extent, *Trouble in Tahiti* and *Songfest* all have New York settings, affectionate, harsh, nerve-tingling and anxious. But by the 1980s, New York was a song that sang in him no more.

THE Israel Philharmonic tour in the fall of 1986 was followed by projects that were to keep Bernstein busy conducting and recording past his seventieth birthday and into the 1990s. In Vienna he began a Sibelius cycle for Deutsche Grammophon. In Rome he recorded a spirited *La Bohème,* also for Deutsche Grammophon, using a cast of young American singers. For a multi-orchestra Mahler symphony cycle he conducted five Mahler symphonies in seven months in 1987—an astonishing feat of emotional and physical endurance—numbers one and four with the Concertgebouw in Amsterdam, numbers two and three with the New York Philharmonic and number five with the Vienna Philharmonic.

His relationship with the Vienna Philharmonic flourished. In 1987 he returned with them to the Salzburg Festival, where Bruno Kreisky's successor, Franz Vranitzky, gave him a birthday gift of a handsome gray *Wetterfleck* raincoat. (When Bernstein thanked him with a slobbering kiss, the chancellor ostentatiously took out a large handkerchief to mop himself dry.) Under his leadership the orchestra made its first visit to Israel in 1988. On their return to Vienna, the musicians gave a benefit concert for the Jerusalem Foundation.

While in the United States Bernstein cut down his concert appearances, Germany, and especially Berlin, became increasingly important to him. He played in East and West Berlin with the Concertgebouw in 1987, with the LSO in 1988 and with the Schleswig-Holstein student orchestra in 1989. He spent as long each year in Schleswig-Holstein as he did in Tanglewood. The atmosphere at Salzau, where he taught for three festival seasons, beginning in 1987, was similar to Tanglewood in the early days, with Bernstein himself playing Socrates to scores of aspiring musicians. After morning rehearsals he would lead a dozen sturdy young men on preprandial swimming excursions in one of the countryside's many lakes. He lodged with friends of Justus Frantz, the Reventlow family, in their grand *Herrenhaus* a few miles from Salzau; for a few weeks each summer he was almost childishly happy with the simple life.

In 1987 he took the student orchestra on a tour of the Schleswig-Holstein region; the entire orchestra paid an impromptu visit to the bedside of their principal supporter, Minister-President Uwe Barschel, who had been hospitalized following an airplane crash. (Barschel died in mysterious circumstances later the same year.) In 1988 the students went on tour to the Soviet Union. *Songfest* was performed in Gorky Park and Bernstein introduced his daughter Nina to her Russian relatives from Siberia and the Ukraine. At the end of a side trip to Leningrad, Nina remembers, Bernstein stayed up all night before an early flight and made a midnight visit to the graves of Pushkin and Tchaikovsky in the Alexander Nevsky Cemetery.

While perestroika was taking hold in Russia, the homosexual community of New York was being decimated by AIDS. Bernstein had many friends who were struck down, none closer than Thomas Cothran, whose photograph he kept on a music stand in his Fairfield studio. Bernstein made a painful visit to Cothran's sickbed in November 1986. Cothran babbled about his desire to die in Katmandu, prompting Bernstein to ask Charlie Harmon, who was with him, to check out the cost of an ambulance flight to Nepal. But the nurse looking after Cothran dressed him in a T-shirt from Katmandu and said he was there already. (Cothran died four months later.) The day after the visit, Bernstein and Harry Kraut resolved to organize a benefit concert at the Public Theater for the American Foundation for AIDS Research. "We did it in ten days," Bernstein told the *Times*. "Everybody I called said yes." Among the performers were Isaac Stern, Michael Tilson Thomas and three of Bernstein's finest leading ladies, Hildegard Behrens, Eileen Farrell and Marilyn Horne. "The evening ended," remembers Dr. Mathilde Krim (one of the research fund's founders) "with a standing and swaying audience joining the performers in singing 'Somewhere.' There wasn't a dry eye in the house." It raised nearly three hundred thousand dollars for unfunded AIDS projects.

In 1987 Bernstein and Kraut helped organize the first "Music for Life" AIDS benefit, at Carnegie Hall. It raised $1.7 million for patient care. His work as a fund-raiser went back to 1983. Bernstein himself did not have AIDS. As a routine matter for insurance policies he was tested several times and found to be HIV negative. Yet, as David Patrick Stearns observed tartly in an article for the since-defunct *Ovation* arts magazine, Bernstein seemed to be intent on killing himself in his exuberance for living. "His composing life is littered with unfinished and abandoned projects. . . . He has promised pieces for trumpeter Wynton Marsalis and skater-dancer John Curry. . . . He vows to revive his disastrous Bicentennial musical *1600 Pennsylvania Avenue* but [says] 'it's the Holocaust opera that's tearing at me to be written. . . . It's too important to drop.' "

Instead of finding a new librettist, Bernstein was persuaded by Jerome Robbins to look again at *The Exception and the Rule*. Stephen Sondheim declined to return to the project, but John Guare, now a renowned playwright, was enthusiastic and for three months in the spring of 1987 there were planning meetings nearly every day; the producer Gregory Mosher wanted to mount the show, now retitled *The Race to Urga,* at Lincoln Center. After three weeks of discussions, Bernstein drafted a long memorandum to his creative colleagues. The new story line, he wrote, is "straight and strong and funny and hard-hitting, especially with its Prologue and Epilogue and the few message songs in between; but apparently that's not enough to justify our efforts morally; we are ethically bound to reach an affluent public at all costs and by all means." Once again he seemed to be tying the millstone of significance around their collective necks.

According to Michael Barrett, who was brought in to prepare the musical numbers, the Bernstein score was full of potential: songs from the abandoned *Caucasian Chalk Circle* project were used to amplify the selection. A gifted cast was recruited, and Robbins staged a fortnight of open rehearsals at the Mitzi Newhouse Theater in May. But at an early rehearsal Bernstein had whispered to Barrett, "It's not going to work," and sadly he was right: *The Race to Urga* sank, virtually without trace, for the second time. Robbins felt that Bernstein had given him only "grudging" support.

In the midst of disappointment there was a new life: Bernstein's first grand-child, Francisca Ann Maria Thomas, was born on March 4, 1987. Jamie had enjoyed her father's reaction to her pregnancy. "I was big and he loved that I was big and I have a funny photograph of the two of us comparing bellies to see who had the bigger one." Jamie and David—Bernstein called them, collectively, "Jave"—had a second child, their son Evan, in October 1989. "It was," Jamie said, "the biggest *nachas* of my life to be able to give him grandchildren."

Hard on the heels of the cancellation of *The Race to Urga* came another cause for depression: the publication of Joan Peyser's biography of Bernstein. Peyser had spent a day with Bernstein in Tanglewood four years previously when she was preparing the entry on him for The New Grove Dictionary of American Music. She had been editor of the *Musical Quarterly,* published by Schirmer, and her writing pedigree included a life of Pierre Boulez as well as a study of twentieth-century music. On the day they met, Bernstein had been ready to offer Peyser instant confidences. Charlie Harmon, his assistant at the time, remembers him pointing out the house on Lake Makheenac he had rented in 1947 and cheerfully discussing the tension that built up there between Shirley and Felicia. When Peyser announced her intention of writing his biography, Bernstein's first response, passed on to friends and colleagues in a note from Harry Kraut, was to deny her the status of an authorized biography, since he wanted to write his own memoirs, but to cooperate with her research. At a reception inaugurating the Museum of Broadcasting's 1985 Leonard Bernstein exhibition, Peyser introduced herself to Jamie, who accepted an invitation to go to Peyser's apartment for drinks and snacks. Nina, Alexander and Jamie's husband, David, were also included. There the siblings were wooed, as Jamie put it, like Hansel and Gretel being trapped by the wicked witch. Eventually Peyser led the conversation around to questions about their father's sexuality. Alerted to her sensationalist (and homophobic) approach, the official Amberson position shifted to an attitude of armed neutrality, but not before Peyser had spoken to many of Bernstein's openly homosexual friends. Despite extensive factual research, the biography is marred by many inaccuracies, a biased approach and inane psycho-babble. On publication the book was widely reviewed, sometimes favorably, and was briefly on the best-seller list. In an exercise of damage limitation, Schuyler Chapin was prompted by Alexander Bernstein to persuade Bernstein not to talk about the book in public. In fact he never read it. "I made a solemn promise to my children on my knees"—and as with the Tom Wolfe "radical chic" scandal in June 1970, he missed the publication furor because of engagements abroad. From mid-May to the end of July he was in Europe, teaching, and receiving such international honors as the Royal Philharmonic Society's Gold Medal in London and the Siemens Prize in Munich.

When he returned to America, the MacDowell Colony presented Bernstein with its Gold Medal. Ned Rorem spoke a generous and perceptive tribute, which for the Bernstein camp made amends for his revelation to Joan Peyser that he and Bernstein once slept together in 1943. However, David Diamond's arguably overzealous cooperation with Peyser was too much for Bernstein to take. His response to an August 1988 birthday greeting from Diamond bristled with antagonism:

> Dear DD:
> Thanks for the birthday wishes, but how dare you talk of no communication from me when the last I've seen or heard from you was after I'd lost five years of my life learning and teaching and performing your 9th Symphony [in 1985] and you walked off with your 75,000 bucks and little or no thanks and remained unheard from except via certain people who read your weighty input to a Peyser book which I have promised my children on my honor never to read. . . . I think that after decades of saving you from suicide, mental collapse, poverty, public fantasizing, and generally spoiling other people's lives you may owe me a bit more than a green posterity-oriented birthday greeting, but never mind . . .
> . . . (as always, ungenerous to my colleagues)
> Goodbye and good luck.

David Diamond remembers being wounded to tears by what he felt to be the unfairness of the attack. His prize for the symphony had been fifty thousand dollars, not seventy-five. And Bernstein had had the score for five months, not five years. Worse, Bernstein was spitting on their shared past. He defended himself in an eight-page letter to which Bernstein did not reply until October, when it was clear there could be no reconciliation:

> Dear old David:
> I've just returned from Europe and discovered your letter of two months ago. I don't want to discuss details, but I do want to say that I'm sorry I wrote you in the way I did. I should never have sent that letter in

such a burst of anger (I can't remember ever having written such a letter to anyone, and besides, the anger was probably related to something else and only triggered by you).

So, I'm sorry; but I must say I meant every word of it.

Shalom uv'rachah [Peace and Greetings]

In April 1988 Bernstein composed a song suite for a fund-raising concert dedicated to Jack Romann, of the Baldwin Piano Company, who had died of AIDS. Michael Tilson Thomas played the piano duet accompaniment with Bernstein at the premiere. He remembers that the rehearsals were like a game. Bernstein was in his sportive mood at his Dakota studio: improvising, experimenting, virtually falling off the music bench in his exuberance, creating a musical tribe out of his four singers, his copyists and his reserve pianists, Michael Barrett and Stephen Blier. He had finally achieved the atmosphere he had dreamed of ten years earlier when he had talked to Paul Hume about improvising an entire opera with his *Songfest* cast.

The suite's title, *Arias and Barcarolles,* came from the remark President Eisenhower had made in 1960 after Bernstein played *Rhapsody in Blue* at the White House. ("I like music with a theme," Ike had said to Lenny, "not all them [*sic*] arias and barcarolles.") Bernstein's cycle can be seen as a sketch for a musical and lyric self-portrait: seven ages of man are depicted in the seven songs for soprano and baritone. The "Prelude," derived from a song Bernstein wrote for Jamie's wedding, states the first of many aspects of love the work explores. The soloists sing love lyrics while the spiky and discordant piano duet accompaniment sets up a contradictory, questioning mood. Bernstein directs that the words are to be sung without expression, plunging the listener into a world of ambivalence and irony.

The "Love Duet" that follows mixes commonplace questions of married life —"What shall we name the baby?/Why can't I give up smoking?/Why are the nations raging?/Am I aging?"—with a witty debate on the structure of the very song that is being sung.

The third song, "Little Smary," for soprano, evokes musical contrasts between the upbeat story-telling tone of a mother—relating one of Bernstein's favorite bedtime stories—and the Alban Berg–like anguish of a child faced with the tragic loss of her rabbit ("wuddit"). Bernstein credited his mother with the text, and she was made a member of ASCAP.

In "The Love of My Life," for solo baritone, Bernstein returns to the vernacular style of *A Quiet Place;* the dedication, "To Stephen Wadsworth for Kurt Ollmann," underlines the link with the opera. (Ollmann had sung workshops for the opera in 1983.) The lyric is an essay on the impermanence of love.

*The love of my life may still arrive tonight*
*Or maybe not;*
*Maybe* did *arrive once when I wasn't aware.*

The fifth song, "Greeting," for solo soprano, was originally composed in 1955 after the birth of Bernstein's son Alexander. The text is without an ounce of irony: only its innocence saves it from sentimentality.

The sixth song is a setting of a poem by a modern Yiddish poet whom Bernstein greatly admired, Yankev-Yitskhok Segal. The story tells of a klezmer fiddler invited to play at a wedding, who not only gets the better of the village elders but transforms their opposition into ecstatic participation. Bernstein might have become such a klezmer musician had his parents stayed in Russia.

In a swift change of mood that is technically difficult for the baritone to accomplish, Bernstein followed wild Yiddish with American satire. "Mr. and Mrs. Webb Say Goodnight," named for Dean Charles Webb of Indiana University, begins and ends with the Webbs' noisy teenage sons Malcolm and Kent keeping their parents awake—as Bernstein himself had done as a boy—by singing a jesting, game-playing dialogue. The middle section of the song contains two contrasting strands. Mrs. Webb picks a bone with her husband—to lyrics Betty Comden had drafted for *Tucker*—and Mr. Webb replies in the dulcet tones of a cabaret crooner, soothing his wife with a happy shared memory.

Bernstein completed his autobiographical suite with a concealed reference to his mother. For her eighty-eighth birthday he had sent her a song in slow waltz tempo entitled "First Love (for My Mother, March 1986)." The lyric revolved around a happy numerical coincidence, between his mother's age and the number of keys—eighty-eight—on the piano, his own first love. In *Arias and Barcarolles,* Bernstein left out the words and called the movement "Nachspiel"—"Epilogue." He instructed the two singers to hum along with the simple Satie-like melody on the piano, an unworldly and touching effect.

Four singers shared the songs in the first version, which Bernstein announced as a work in progress. The revision for two singers only, soprano and baritone, had its world premiere when Bernstein was in Israel in April 1989. "A's and B's" is Bernstein's last contribution to his musical autobiography; it is intimate, at times wryly self-mocking and bewilderingly eclectic, always unpretentious and blessedly free of guilt, breast-beating and all aspects of faith lost or retrieved.


ON May 11, Bernstein took part in the Carnegie Hall celebration of Irving Berlin's 100th birthday. His downbeat contribution "My Twelve-Tone Melody," went down badly with the Berlin family. Two days later he left for Glasgow to attend *Candide* at Scottish Opera. John Mauceri, the music director, had brought in an English director, Jonathan Miller, and an English writer, John Wells, who were both acknowledged satirists. Mauceri restored a further half hour of musical numbers, while Wells and Miller revised the dialogue and added several new scenes based directly on incidents in the original novel. The effect was to push the show away from the broad farce of the Hugh Wheeler version toward the skeptical satire of Voltaire's original.

Bernstein arrived for the last two days of rehearsal and stayed for the opening gala performance at which he sat next to the Duchess of Gloucester, the royal patron of Scottish Opera. During the performance the duchess looked on impassively. In the interval she asked Bernstein whether he was responsible for the story. "No ma'am," he replied, wise by now to regal questionnaires. "It was written by Voltaire." Under John Mauceri's devoted leadership the performance was a triumph. At last Bernstein had seen a *Candide* that made no compromises, and in a relatively intimate opera house perfectly scaled to *Candide*'s operetta proportions.

The production was televised in Britain by the BBC (but nowhere else, because of copyright problems) and later in the year Jonathan Miller remounted it at London's Old Vic for a Christmas run, demonstrating that *Candide* could be scheduled nightly like a musical yet produced to opera house standards of singing. It won the Olivier Award for best musical of the year.

O N August 25, 1988, the Boston Symphony Orchestra began a four-day "birthday bash" at Tanglewood in honor of Bernstein's seventieth birthday. Bernstein did what he did every year: he taught conducting students, coached the Tanglewood Music Center orchestra, "hung out" with the composition students assembled under the genial eye of the English composer Oliver Knussen and conducted the Boston Symphony in Haydn and Tchaikovsky symphonies for the annual Koussevitzky Memorial Concert. But around these musical activities was woven the most elaborate celebration ever devised for a living American composer. At the Sunday afternoon concert—the final event in the four-day-long marathon—Seiji Ozawa conducted *A Bernstein Birthday Bouquet, Eight Variations on a Theme by Leonard Bernstein.* The theme was "New York, New York" from *On the Town.* The variations were composed by Luciano Berio, Leon Kirchner, Jacob Druckman, Lukas Foss, John Corigliano, John Williams, Tōru Takemitsu and William Schuman. For Bernstein it was a heartwarming demonstration of the affection in which he was held by his peers. He had been equally touched on Friday by a "Prelude" event (in the Shed) of songs commissioned in his honor by a dozen other composers: David del Tredici, George Perle, Ned Rorem, Peter Schat, Stephen Schwartz, Harold Shapero, Bright Sheng, Alvin Singleton, Stephen Sondheim, Michael Tilson Thomas, Yehudi Wyner and his daughter Jamie.

Saturday was given up to tributes from young people. In the morning, an orchestra of high school students from the Boston University Tanglewood Institute gave a stirring performance of the *Jeremiah* Symphony, conducted by Eiji Oue. In the evening a new production of *Mass* was presented by students of the Opera Theater of Indiana University. By an extraordinary feat of preplanning and rehearsal back home, the show was built, lit and rehearsed in a single day: Dean Webb had been determined to have Bloomington represented at the party.

Three conductors—Seiji Ozawa, Michael Tilson Thomas and Leon Fleisher—shared the Tanglewood student orchestra's Friday evening concert of music especially loved by Bernstein: the Brahms Double Concerto with Midori and Yo-Yo Ma, Stravinsky's *Capriccio* with Peter Serkin, Ives's choral *Thanksgiving* and the choral movement from Mahler's *Resurrection* Symphony with Roberta Alexander and Christa Ludwig as the soloists. The choice of young Midori was appropriate: not only had she traveled with Bernstein to Hiroshima, she had made front-page news the following year when she twice broke a violin string while performing his *Serenade* at Tanglewood. Yo-Yo Ma also had special reason to be indebted to Bernstein: part of his Harvard education had been paid for with a Bernstein scholarship. (Bernstein stopped adding to the scholarship's endowment in 1985 in a much-publicized dispute with President Bok concerning the university's policy toward nuclear disarmament. He renewed his funding in 1989.)

Bernstein wandered through the events and the parties held in his honor in something of a daze. There was no way in which he relished being seventy but neither could he turn his back on the expression of so much love. The most difficult day for him was August 25, the birthday itself, a gala intended to top all birthday galas. In true American-enterprise style, the Boston Symphony's management obtained Bernstein's blessing to turn the birthday into a massive fund-raising event for Tanglewood Music Center. At the pre-gala cocktail party the guest of honor was Jennie Bernstein, ninety years old and still going strong. She was accompanied by her younger sisters Dorothy and Bertha. A poem extolling the maestro was recited by a trio whose membership encapsulated the show business glamour and wealth of the occasion: Kitty Carlisle Hart, Ann Getty and James Wolfensohn, president of Carnegie Hall.

> He is *the Joy of Music* [trilled Ann Getty]
> *The title of his book.*
> *If music be the food of love*
> *He is our master cook.*

An audience of eight thousand gathered for the birthday concert. Beverly Sills was a genial moderator: the entertainment she introduced had been devised to reflect every aspect of Bernstein's musical life, interspersed with videotaped greetings from Bernstein's orchestras in Israel, Bavaria, Schleswig-Holstein, Vienna, London and New York, and from friends unable to be present such as Jerome Robbins and Barbara Cook. Michael Tilson Thomas, John Mauceri and John Williams shared the conducting with Seiji Ozawa. From the opera world Gwyneth Jones flew in from Canada to sing Leonora's great aria from *Fidelio* and Christa Ludwig launched a new career in operetta, singing "The Old Lady's Tango" from *Candide* with much hip-swaying and the clatter of castanets.

"Slava" Rostropovich had been in Sicily early that same morning: by a combination of private jet and Concorde he arrived in time to play the epilogue from Strauss's *Don Quixote* in memory of Bernstein's 1943 debut with the New York Philharmonic. Afterward he strode into the audience to greet his friend with a giant hug. Lukas Foss accompanied Dawn Upshaw in *I Hate Music,* first sung in public down the road at Lenox exactly forty-five years earlier. Yo-Yo Ma played the cello obbligato in "To What you Said" from *Songfest*—sung by Robert Osborne—and Barbara Hendricks, Jennie Tourel's favorite pupil, sang the lullaby from *Kaddish* with a chorus of schoolgirls from Boston. Stephen Sondheim wrote biting new lyrics for Kurt Weill's "Poor Jenny" retitled "Poor Lenny"—the man who could never make up his mind what he wanted to be. "Keep it that way" was Sondheim's conclusion. Perched on a bar stool to deliver the song, the raspingly elegant Lauren Bacall brought the house down. The camera showed Bernstein, seated next to his mother, gamely laughing his head off at Sondheim's digs. Jamie, Nina, Alexander and David Thomas kept up the family tradition of gentle mockery with an *a cappella* song called "The Seven-Oh Stomp." Jamie and David were also in the backing group when Phyllis Newman did the "Swing" number from *Wonderful Town.* Patti Austin, Victor Borge, Betty Comden, Quincy Jones, Bobby McFerrin and Frederica von Stade were among the other stars: Frank Sinatra sent a telegram. After four hours the gala concluded with a greeting from Seiji Ozawa. "Tanglewood was your legacy," he said, addressing Bernstein in his box across a sea of faces. "We love you Lenny: you helped to make our Tanglewood garden glow." Then the entire company came on stage to sing the closing number from *Candide.*

When Bernstein came on stage to hug and kiss his friends, few people knew that he had not been in his seat for long sections of the show. He was being treated for a prostate condition and had somehow misunderstood the prescription instructions: the upshot was that he needed desperately to urinate every hour—not an easy matter on a gala evening when one is guest of honor.

What gave Bernstein the greatest satisfaction that night was the evident happiness of his mother. At the party at Blantyre after the show, Jennie was still holding court and watching her grandchildren dance when Bernstein himself left for bed. He had a Boston Symphony Orchestra rehearsal next morning. It was a measure of the geographical shift in his status that his Sunday afternoon concert with the BSO, interspersed with highlights of the birthday gala, was televised "live" to Europe, but not to viewers in America.

On the Sunday before his birthday, the *New York Times* published a long poem by Bernstein in the tradition of his 1965 account of his sabbatical year. It was a playful piece, extolling the virtue of love, in which he ended by urging his readers to grow up and acknowledge who they were; men and women, "who can take the Four-letter word [Love] and make it live / By learning to give, to give, to give, to give."

A month later, the Viennese laid on their own birthday celebration at the State Opera. At another party, Bernstein's friends at Deutsche Grammophon presented him with a golden gramophone. When he got home to his hotel after the festivities, he wrote a poem for his friend John Malcolm Brinnin that revealed a darker, uncomfortably harsh Leonard Bernstein, by no means at peace with himself or the world:

*(The Birthday Continues . . .)*

*I am celebrated beyond bearing.*
*The adjectives become intolerable*
*As they hump one upon another, Two-Dogs-Fucking;*

*Double-descriptives, à la* Time:
*Masterful/loving, peacemaker/igniter,*
        und so weiter,
*Ass-licking, ego-rimming, soul-sucking.*

*On the other hand, what right have I to complain?*
*How dare I envy the young, so driven, confused,*
*Ambitious up the hall? And yet I do.*
*They lust, they penetrate, they get it up.*
*They flock about me, linger in my arms;*
*But I withdraw (if they've not done so first)*
*And I am left to write these lines, alone,*
*Alone, and safe from ultimate exposure,*
*Or foolish rash commitment. (That was a close one.)*

*The contrasts out-sonata Beethoven:*
*Bright gala! (empty bed); The blare! (The blues)*
*Encomia! (sinusitis, prostatism,*
*And all the spooks of swift-advancing age.)*

*Today is my free day; What shall I do?*
*I do not want another thousand kisses.*
Na, Ja, Vielleicht fahre ich in den Prater
*And kiss at length one pure and total stranger.*

It is the Marschallin in *Der Rosenkavalier* who goes riding in the Prater after sending her lover away. The next day the real Leonard Bernstein was made an honorary citizen of the State of Austria and the day after that he was leading the normally staid Vienna Philharmonic in his jazzy *Prelude, Fugue and Riffs*. It was impossible to pin him down to one personality. "I feel that I have lived five lives or so already," he said in his *Times* poem. His continuing ebullience made a striking contrast to the frailty of the eighty-year-old Herbert von Karajan, who came to Vienna early in October 1988 with the Berlin Philharmonic. After hearing Karajan conduct *Verklärte Nacht* at the Musikverein, Bernstein called on him in the conductor's room they both knew so well. Karajan reiterated an invitation for Bernstein to conduct his orchestra again. The two men retreated to the inner dressing room, where Bernstein helped Karajan, who was crippled with arthritis, to use the washbasin. It was their last meeting.

# THE LIVING LEGEND

*Last concert, Tanglewood, August 19, 1990.*
PHOTO WALTER H. SCOTT

*I want to devote most of the remaining energy and
time the Lord grants me to education.*

—LEONARD BERNSTEIN at the
Pacific Music Festival, June 1990

I N the fall of 1988, as he entered his eighth decade, Bernstein's composing
work was at a standstill. He had found nobody rash enough to want to replace
Stephen Wadsworth as the librettist for his new opera project; the prospect of
a dance collaboration with the great Martha Graham had faded after promising
discussions (and a few lines of music) in the spring; *Jubilee Games* remained an
unfinished work for symphony orchestra and *Arias and Barcarolles* had had only
one workshop performance. But as a teacher of young conductors and student
musicians his activity was undiminished. His plans included an ambitious proposal to establish a music festival in the Far East with Michael Tilson Thomas
and the London Symphony Orchestra. The original venue was to have been
Beijing, but after the repression of Tiananmen Square in June 1989, the project
was switched to Sapporo in Japan and retitled the Pacific Music Festival. Nor
did his conducting and recording activities slacken. During the 1988–89 season
he worked with the New York Philharmonic, the London Symphony, the Santa
Cecilia of Rome, the Israel Philharmonic, the students of Schleswig-Holstein
and the Vienna Philharmonic. After Karajan's death in July 1989, Bernstein
finally ventured into Bruckner territory with the Viennese. (He had previously
said that Karajan's interpretations could not be bettered.)

His emotional life was also flourishing. In the fall of 1988 he became captivated by Mark Stringer, a tall twenty-four-year-old conducting student from Georgia. Stringer's reaction was similar to that of other young musicians who fell under Bernstein's spell. "He was the most important man in my life, intellectually and emotionally. . . . He would read poetry to me until two and three in the morning. . . . He was an incredible intellectual stimulus. . . . No other human being had ever given me total trust, looking past all my emotional immaturities. . . . No one believed in me more. . . . So I poured every ounce of dedication into my work for him." Stringer became Bernstein's musical assistant, and for a time he rekindled a physical passion on Bernstein's part. Bernstein confided to his assistant Phillip Allen that he felt like a virgin again.

I N the fall of 1988 Bernstein kept up his tradition of championing American music when he worked with the New York Philharmonic, tackling a group of short works by Charles Ives and David del Tredici and introducing New Yorkers to the extended three-movement version of his own *Jubilee Games*. He also programmed Ned Rorem's recent violin concerto, with his friend Gidon Kremer as soloist. He tinkered with the work, as he had talked of doing thirty years earlier when he premiered one of Rorem's symphonies, but Kremer insisted on restoring the original version before the DG recording was made.

Between his dates with the Philharmonic and his winter retreat to balmy Florida, he made a flying visit to Cambridge University to see the first British production of *A Quiet Place*. His affection for James Kelleher, a gifted student conductor of twenty who had spent a summer at Tanglewood, overrode any qualms he and his publisher might have had about entrusting the opera to a group of undergraduates with no production experience, no publicity machine and no theater: the Corn Exchange in Cambridge, which has no pit, was hopelessly inadequate. Moreover, the national music critics had misguidedly been allowed to attend a dress rehearsal after illness and cash-flow problems forced a delay in preparations.

The production was much better than its unattractive, steel-scaffolding setting. Kelleher conducted astonishingly well, and as the critic Malcolm Hayes observed, the performance given by young professionals "brimmed with musical and acting talent." It was curious, Hayes continued, that while public money was being lavished on a Philip Glass opera at the English National Opera, "a totally superior American opera" was being mounted in Cambridge under less favorable conditions. Hayes praised *A Quiet Place*'s "seasoned intelligence, bitter-sweet affection and dazzling musical flair." Bernstein made a postperformance curtain speech describing Kelleher's achievement as "a miracle" and after supper in a Cambridge restaurant sat down at a piano and regaled his friends with songs from *Candide*. The next evening he was at the rousing London opening of Scottish Opera's *Candide* production. John Wells described Bernstein's presence as being like "a magnum shot of Dr. Hansniesandbumpsideisi's Rejuvenator."

AARON Stern was among the houseguests for the first week of Bernstein's winter sojourn in Key West. Soon after his departure Bernstein sent Stern a poem that gives a hint of the metaphysical ground they covered in their conversations. He had been watching the sunset from his balcony.

> *For Aaron*
> *—Because Ay is forever*
> *—Because Ay is Yes*
> *—Because Ay is a cry of joy*
> *—Because Ay is a cry of surprise*
>
> _____
>
> *—Because Ay is the Eye that sees light*
> *—Because Ay is I, my self, my seeing*
>  *My surprise, my joy*
>   *my pain, my yes*
>    *my Forever*
>     *LB Key West 4 Jan '89 (Sunset*
>     *meditation in which Forever was*
>     *experienced for some months)*

In February 1989 Helen Coates died, at the age of eighty-nine. At the memorial he organized at the Dakota, Bernstein read a poem he'd written for her. In death as in life she brought out the sentimental in him:

> *"Goodness," you would say, "goodness gracious!"*
> *And you departed with grace as you were meant to.*
> *You remain, all the same, just as you were meant to;*
> *In a million mysterious, graceful ways.*

In April 1989 Bernstein made a brief visit to Israel to conduct three unfashionable but major symphonic scores by Paul Hindemith and the premiere of the final version of his *Jubilee Games,* retitled *Concerto for Orchestra.* With Michael Barrett in support he also coached two Israeli singers for the premiere of the definitive version of *Arias and Barcarolles.* Standing in as tour manager while Harry Kraut was in China, Schuyler Chapin was shocked by the deterioration he observed in Bernstein's health. But it was almost twenty years since Chapin had accompanied his friend on a trip abroad; to Bernstein's assistant, Craig Urquhart, the worrying symptoms—severe coughing and shortness of breath—were everyday occurrences that gave no special cause for concern.

Bernstein was deeply depressed by the political mood in Israel. In Jerusalem he and Chapin went with Mayor Teddy Kollek and Bernstein's painter friend Yossi Stern to a ceremony at Israel's Holocaust Memorial. The Israeli Prime Minister of the day, Yitzhak Shamir, gave an inflammatory address, predicting that Arab conduct toward the Jews would be worse than that of the Nazis. Chapin recalled watching Kollek—"the man who had rebuilt the city of Jerusalem by amassing private funds and bringing together Jew and Arab in common cause—slide down in his seat. He covered his eyes, shaking his head, and muttered something to Lenny, who reached over and hugged him." Kollek joined Bernstein that evening in a restaurant (in the Arab quarter) and tried to persuade him that his next opera should be on the subject of King David. Bernstein was still fascinated but the Holocaust theme took priority: the need which it embodied to warn the world against repeating its mistakes was all the more urgent in Shamir's Israel. "They are burning books again," he told Mark Stringer when he got back to America. "What has happened to my Israel? For the first time I feel old."

In June 1989, only a month after his visit to Israel, Bernstein returned to Europe for two more months of conducting. At the beginning of August he was back at Fairfield, working with John Wells on a new approach to the Holocaust opera. Wells had several opera librettos to his credit before bravely accepting Bernstein's invitation to collaborate. He took a hint from the note Bernstein had appended to Stephen Wadsworth's 1985 outline—"needs more surrealism, less logic in the *stories;* the real logic should be in the interaction of them"—and came up with a proposal for a first act made up of "a sequence of apparently unconnected and slightly unhinged anecdotes, set vaguely in the present day, but all, as we probably won't discover till Act Two, having their roots in the Holocaust." The multilanguage concept remained intact: the opera's working title was *Babel.*

Yet Bernstein cannot have been entirely convinced that he was on the right track because he was still exploring alternatives. He described one of them as "Saul, David, Jonathan Triangle Opera," for bass, baritone and tenor. According to his two-page synopsis, Saul and David were to sing a "Hate-love duet with harp (suggestions, lightly-done, of sexual attraction to D.)." Bernstein even drafted the dialogue for a full-blown love scene between David and Jonathan.

In February 1990 he documented a project for a double bill in which the one-act "Triangle Opera" would be followed by what he described as "Dybbuk Cycle," in two acts and several languages—English, German, Hebrew and Yiddish. His scribbled notes suggest that David and Jonathan would become the Two Ghetto Fathers whose solemn oath binds their children Leah and Channon. The story of the star-crossed lovers and the breaking of their marriage promise would be yoked to the Holocaust, which as Bernstein put it in his notes, "happens in the interval." The second act was a post-Holocaust story exploring, with the same characters, what Bernstein saw as the ambiguous position of the Jews in the world, hated as both money-lending capitalist elite and perennial victims.

Despite many months of intermittent but arduous work with John Wells, the prospects of a breakthrough seemed bleak indeed, so long as Bernstein remained obsessed with the Holocaust theme. When he broached the idea of a collaboration with Peter Shaffer, his playwright friend told him the idea was "narrow and foolish" adding that if he was depressed he should write a comedy. (John Guare was another playwright who declined the invitation to work together.)

In contrast, Bernstein's conducting plans involved grand projects stretching well into the 1990s: they included Mendelssohn's *Elijah* in New York in December 1990, the Mozart *Requiem* in Vienna for Mozart's bicentenary in December 1991, *Peter Grimes* at Tanglewood the following summer. In the twelve months from September 1989 to August 1990 he gave some of the most memorable concert hall performances of his entire conducting career. But his luck with his health, which had held for fifty years, was finally to run out in the spring of 1990. The great occasions of this season were also the last of his long musical life.

T A N G L E W O O D in August 1989 was a quiet affair for Bernstein compared to his seventieth-birthday celebrations. He conducted the students in Tchaikovsky's Fourth Symphony and the Boston Symphony in the Shostakovich Fifth; both were works he planned to rerecord soon with Deutsche Grammophon. His seventy-first birthday was celebrated with a modest picnic in a tent for a mere one hundred guests; Leon Fleisher serenaded him with "The Man I Love."

Three days later he was in Poland preparing for the first of the season's big adventures, a mixed media event held in Warsaw's Grand Opera House on September 1 to mark the fiftieth anniversary of the outbreak of World War II. Cameramen from the BBC worked side by side with Polish Television technicians; the satellite relay went to Russia, Japan, and the United States—but not to Germany. The orchestra and choruses were Polish, the soloists—Barbara Hendricks, Hermann Prey and Marek Drewnowski—came from Germany, Poland, and the United States. Krzysztof Penderecki conducted movements from his *Polish Requiem*. Lukas Foss, by birth a Jew from Berlin, conducted *A Survivor from Warsaw,* narrated by the Norwegian actress Liv Ullmann, whose grandfather had died in Dachau. Each musical work served as a point of reflection in a film documentary that told the story of the wartime childhood, in ghetto and concentration camp, of another Warsaw survivor, the lawyer Samuel Pisar, who had become an American citizen. Bernstein introduced the program and conducted the last two works, Beethoven's *Leonore* Overture No. 3 and his own *Chichester Psalms*. His plea for peace and unity never had a more poignant context.

After the concert the Communist Polish President, General Wojciech Jaruzelski, and the newly elected Prime Minister Tadeusz Mazowiecki, former adviser to the Solidarity movement, greeted Bernstein and his fellow artists at a typically formal East European reception in the conductor's loge. It was exactly thirty years since Bernstein's first visit to Warsaw. Poland had since won its freedom: these were the men who were leading the breakaway from the exhausted Soviet Union. An elated Bernstein insisted on taking them to the crowded cast party in the opera canteen, where he toasted the beauty of the President's wife and hung a boar's tooth around the Prime Minister's neck, accompanying the gesture with "three big kisses."

His next engagement was with the Vienna Philharmonic. Working on the last three Beethoven piano concertos with Krystian Zimerman and on an orchestral version of Beethoven's F major Quartet, op. 135, Bernstein was in tremendously good spirits. "I've never conducted better in my life," he told Mark Stringer. "Remind me of this if I ever get depressed in the spring." Bernstein had earlier declared that only the C sharp minor Quartet, op. 131, was suitable for performance by string orchestra, but in practice the F major, op. 135, was if anything even more powerful. Bernstein conducted the slow movement at the impressive memorial concert for Herbert von Karajan on September 16.

Craig Urquhart remembers Bernstein's routine in Vienna. "He could never get enough study time. So many mornings I would find Lenny slumped over a score, a 'reddy-blue' pencil in hand [instructions in red were to be transferred to the orchestral parts; blue indicated notes for himself], an ashtray full of cigarettes, an empty box of chocolates, half-eaten crackers, cold coffee in his cup, asleep yet still wanting to work. But it was time to get up and go to rehearsal and he would wake up with a start and say, 'Oh no, not yet. I don't know this piece yet. How can I do this rehearsal?' He would continue to search for new meanings in the notes, never hurried, as if time would wait for him, and somehow it always did. Then would come the waiter with breakfast, a pleasant intrusion but still an intrusion: the eggs would sit, the coffee would cool and the maestro would continue his search for truth. 'Lenny, don't you think it's time to shower?' 'Don't rush me. I know. We have time.' That was always his line about half an hour before we went to the Vienna Philharmonic. He would proceed with his shower-bath after endless delays—he couldn't figure out the simplest sort of bath tap—and endless discussions about wardrobe. 'Oh, I had this poem last night. Did I write it down?' . . . Then came the debate of what to wear in scarves, and which of the many glasses to choose and we were off, except 'Good Morning, Maestro' greeted him in the lobby and he had to know all about this hotel porter's night off and that one's family, as we got in the car. He studied the score all the way to the Musikverein, where there were more greetings from the porter and then the handshake with Beethoven [one of his rituals in Vienna was to salute the statue in the passageway]. . . . On the podium, I placed his half-moon glasses, the baton, the reddy-blues and the towel to let the gentlemen of the orchestra know he had arrived. He still needed a few more minutes with the score and then the rehearsal would begin."

During his stay Bernstein attended two performances of Mozart's *Figaro* on successive nights. He enjoyed every bar of the traditional Jean-Pierre Ponnelle production at the Staatsoper (Ivan Fischer conducting) but next night departed at the interval from the postmodern Peter Sellars production being recorded at the Austrian TV studios. He had an excuse: he needed time to study for his performances at a three-week festival in Bonn dedicated to Beethoven and Bernstein. Craig Urquhart remembers Bernstein's performance there of Beethoven's Seventh Symphony (on only one rehearsal) as the strongest interpretation he ever heard. A visit to play the piano at Beethoven's birthplace was part of his inspiration.

Back home Bernstein conducted the New York Philharmonic in two weeks of concerts. The first program was devoted entirely to Copland's music, ranging from the early *Music for the Theatre* (1925) to the sinewy twelve-tone score *Connotations*. *Newsday*'s critic, Tim Page, called it a "lost masterpiece" and wrote that Bernstein's New York appearances were "eagerly anticipated, savored fondly, reflected upon with gratitude: the *wunderkind* has become the grand old man." In the second half of the program Bernstein conducted Copland's clarinet concerto and *El Salón México*. "The finale was thrilling, as Bernstein let Copland's snatches of mariachi, violent rhythms and earthquake tympanies hurtle, unfettered, to an apocalyptic close." With the last chord he literally jumped off the podium, laughing out loud. Aaron Copland was too frail to attend Bernstein's tribute. "Some day," Page wrote, "the idea of a Copland concert conducted by Leonard Bernstein will tantalize our grandchildren in the same way that we are tantalized by tales of Caruso and Stokowski."

An all-Tchaikovsky program the following week—in what proved to be his last appearance at Avery Fisher Hall—inspired equal enthusiasm from critics. His interpretation of the Fourth Symphony was said to be "rivetingly, definitively manic-depressive." Bernstein's tempos in Tchaikovsky seemed to be becoming slow to the point of stasis: cynics suggested that his recording company paid by the minute. The Philharmonic Archive's records reveal that on this occasion he added only four minutes to his 1960 timing of the Fourth Symphony; *Francesca da Rimini,* however, had stretched from nineteen minutes to twenty-seven. Bernstein came to identify as closely with Tchaikovsky as he did with Mahler, giving searingly intense interpretations of both composers. Jack Gottlieb remembers him coming off the podium after a performance of the *Pathétique* white of face and seemingly in a trance: "I have been on the brink," he murmured.

In November 1989 Bernstein was due to go to the White House as one of twelve recipients of the National Medal of the Arts, presented annually by the U.S. President to arts patrons and creative artists. Bernstein had not set foot in the White House since the night of the Hanukkah candles in December 1980. "I haven't gone there because it's had such sloppy housekeepers and caretakers." This time he accepted; the medal would please his mother for one thing, and although the honor was finally the President's gift the recommendation for it came from a worthy body, the National Endowment for the Arts. But a week before the ceremony, the Endowment withdrew a grant of ten thousand dollars from a New York Artists Space exhibition entitled "Witnesses: Against Our Vanishing," about the ravages of AIDS, on the grounds that it violated recent congressional legislation, initiated by Senator Jesse Helms, against government funding of obscene or openly political art. The exhibition included controversial works by Robert Mapplethorpe and Andres Serrano, but the endowment's new chairman, John Frohnmayer, was reacting to David Wojnarowicz's explosive catalogue article, in which he described Jesse Helms as "a repulsive senator from Zombieland." Never slow to support freedom of expression, Bernstein let it be known that he would neither accept the medal at the White House nor attend a dinner given by the NEA. "I cannot risk that coming to Washington to be officially honored during your administration might imply that I am an 'official' artist content to collect a medal in kind and gentle silence while hoping for less stifling days ahead," he wrote to President and Mrs. Bush. When the hapless Frohnmayer discovered that the exhibition's catalogue (he had not seen the show itself) had been privately funded, he reinstated the grant, but Bernstein had by then been withdrawn.

The affair coincided with the last days of the 1988 presidential election campaign between George Bush and Michael Dukakis. On October 30 the *New York Times* published a pro-Dukakis piece by Bernstein headed "I'M A LIBERAL AND PROUD OF IT." Rightwing journalists mocked him. "People like William Buckley, Jr., William Safire and George Will think of me as a kind of 'liberal fool,' " he told the writer Jonathan Cott. "Basically a liberal is a progressive who wants to see the world change and not just stick in the *status quo*. So yes, I'm a liberal, but one who believes in people, not in some 'thing.' And I've never felt more strength and confidence."

Mrs. Jennie Bernstein was not amused by the public fracas surrounding her son. She telephoned to remonstrate: "You're on the front page of the New York *Times!*" "Hold your water, baby," Bernstein replied—or so he told Cott—"I was also on the front page of the Washington *Post* . . . some of my most conservative Midwestern friends sent me congratulatory messages."

IN mid-October 1989 Bernstein met an amiable young giant of a man, almost six feet five and twenty-eight years old, who was to be the last love of his life. Mark Adams Taylor was an aspiring novelist from Alabama who wrote speeches for the president of New York University. Harry Kraut invited him to a party at the Dakota after one of Bernstein's Aaron Copland concerts. Taylor remembers that at that first meeting Bernstein, "wanted us to connect. He held on to every word I said, treating me as if I were a puzzle he would eventually solve." When Taylor, a courteous Southerner, wrote a formal note of thanks after the Dakota party, Bernstein called him up, ostensibly to edit the letter: Taylor had misspelled Copland with an "e" and misplaced an "only." And, greatest error, he had not given a telephone number, obliging the maestro to look it up. But in the same call he asked Taylor back to the Dakota for dinner. "His children came over later and ate Chinese carry-out in the library. We sat around and watched one of his concerts on PBS. His little granddaughter stood at the TV set and conducted along. I burped his grandson."

Bernstein hated the word "seduce," Taylor recalls, "but he was notorious for the scores of young men he had had. . . . I was beyond belief seduced but it was not merely sex. Although there was that. But no sleaze. . . . Sheer poetry were the words of love he professed for me. He took the letters of my name and made puzzles and poems out of them. . . . He renamed me . . . not my name but a monogram, M.A.T., 'Mat.' " (There was a good reason for avoiding the name Mark. Mark Stringer was still working as Bernstein's musical assistant.)

Bernstein drove Taylor out to Fairfield with his own *Serenade* playing on the car stereo. "Do you know this piece?" Bernstein asked. "I was never one of your fans," Taylor coolly replied, adding nonetheless that the music sounded "like voices you hear when you're in love, but alone." Bernstein enjoyed the analogy and reveled once again in the opportunity to play Socrates. He took to telephoning Taylor's psychotherapist (of whom, according to Taylor, he was jealous) and left poetic love messages on Taylor's answering machine. "If I declined his invitations," Taylor recalls, "or stayed at home to work, I would be besieged with phone calls and faxes."

On Bernstein's side there were no holds barred in the intimacy of their friendship: he told Taylor that he had murdered his wife, torturing her to death by leaving her for a man. "You loved her?" Taylor asked. "More than I love myself," Bernstein replied. "Passionately?" "Every one I love, I love passionately."

The friendship rejuvenated Bernstein. He even felt well enough to start playing squash again with his old friend Louis d'Almeida. Initially d'Almeida was worried: "He can't play at his age, he's going to die on the court. Well, so, let him; it would be a wonderful way to go!" Bernstein got his breath back by holding long analyses between each point, and in his vain desperation to win would announce a change of rules in mid-game.

EARLY in December 1989, Bernstein left for London to perform and record with the London Symphony what was intended to be the best of all possible concert versions of *Candide,* a work he had never conducted himself. As with *West Side Story,* the luxury casting (Deutsche Grammophon was recording the project) emphasized the operatic nature of Bernstein's musical satire. The cast was led by Jerry Hadley as Candide and June Anderson as Cunegonde, and also included Kurt Ollmann, Della Jones and two opera house veterans, Nicolai Gedda and Christa Ludwig. None had sung in *Candide* on stage, though Ludwig's "Old Lady's Tango" had been a big success at Tanglewood's seventieth birthday party. The most controversial casting was of Adolph Green as Dr. Pangloss. Although he had never learned to read a score, Green had a phenomenal musical memory as well as a satirical humor second to none, which made him the ideal person to speak the witty narration the composer had written with John Wells. Bernstein guided him affectionately through his musical performance.

The *Candide* project almost came to grief because of an influenza bug that crippled London in the opening weeks of December. Not even Buckingham Palace was exempt from its ravages, which led Bernstein to dub it the "royal" flu. All the principals succumbed in turn, and both Candide and Cunegonde had to be replaced (by Donald George and Constance Hauman) for the second concert at the Barbican. Bernstein was suffering himself but he soldiered on heroically, sustained by the sheer joy and sense of triumph at hearing his operetta performed by fine singers and chorus and a great orchestra.

THE fall of 1989 was an extraordinary period in world affairs, with Communist regimes challenged and crumbling in almost every East European state, most notably in Germany where the frontier between East and West was opened on November 9. Bernstein felt especially close to Berlin, and after the *Candide* recording he flew to Germany to rehearse for an extraordinary manifestation of support. On Christmas Day he was to lead an international orchestra in Beethoven's Ninth Symphony at the Schauspielhaus in East Berlin, having done the same at the Philharmonie Hall in West Berlin two days earlier. The Bavarian Radio Chorus and Symphony Orchestra formed the performing nucleus and there were to be other musicians from East Germany and from the four occupying states who had waged war against Germany: France, Great Britain, the Soviet Union and the United States. The four soloists were June Anderson from the United States, Sarah Walker from the United Kingdom, Klaus König from East Germany and Jan-Hendrik Rootering from West Germany.

When the musicians arrived, the most characteristic sound in a Berlin seething with excitement was the gentle tapping of the hammers, picks and chisels chipping away at the hated Berlin Wall. Bernstein himself carved out a chunk to take home to his family. He also lit Hanukkah candles at Berlin's oldest synagogue and was filmed with Justus Frantz (at that time head of Bavarian Radio's Music Department) inspecting the newly opened Brandenburg Gate, where on December 24, the first day of complete freedom, almost a quarter of a million West Berliners were to pour into the old East Berlin to stroll with their families down the broad and almost empty avenues, while East Berliners in similar numbers went through to the West.

The entire world was watching Berlin's euphoria and Leonard Bernstein was at the heart of the celebrations: because of his past endeavors it seemed quite natural for an American Jew to be in charge of Germany's reunification celebration. And his sense of showmanship did not desert him: he decided upon a change of words in Schiller's "Ode to Joy." Instead of *"Freude"* (joy), the chorus would sing *"Freiheit"* (freedom), making it the "Ode to Freedom." Although traditionalists resented the tampering with a revered German classic, the gesture made uncommonly good copy in newspapers around the world.

Physically still weak from the "royal" flu, Bernstein took all the rehearsals and conducted a preliminary performance before an enthusiastic audience in East Berlin on the afternoon of the twenty-third. The musicians were then driven to West Berlin for an evening performance. Gone were the tedious and humiliating restrictions of visa and passport control at Checkpoint Charlie. *"Alle Menschen werden Brüder"* (All men will be brothers), the choir sang out in West Berlin's principal concert hall, the Philharmonie; the concert was projected on two giant screens in the Kurfürstendamm, and watched in a drizzle by thousands of West Berliners.

December 24 was a feast day for Berliners and a rest day for Leonard Bernstein. He needed it. In the midst of so much heady public activity he had also stirred up emotional drama in his personal life. He persuaded Mark Taylor to join him by delivering a first-class air ticket to his New York doorstep. Taylor flew first to Munich, where the preliminary rehearsals took place; he found Bernstein surrounded by a veritable court of protégés past and present, and lavishing particular attention on two young Germans, a medical student and a conductor. Then the maestro spent much of the flight from Munich to Berlin kissing his assistant conductor, "a confessed heterosexual," as Taylor put it. Though Taylor was at first appalled by Bernstein's insatiable desire to seduce every willing young man in the world, he swiftly became reconciled; Bernstein, who always loved giving presents, took him to an expensive boutique and bought him a handsome silk suit and a green tuxedo shirt—"gigolo green," Taylor called it. When Bernstein emerged to acknowledge the tumultuous applause after the performance of Beethoven's Ninth in West Berlin, he caught Taylor's eye in the audience. Taylor sensed that "he was saying he loved me and asking me to forgive him."

Mark Taylor's view of Bernstein was very different from what the photographer Christina Burton saw as she waited in the wings to greet him. She was shocked by the contrast between the image of the conductor she and Harry Kraut had just been watching on the big screen outside in the city—the epitome of spiritual and physical energy—and the dazed, shrunken and ashen-faced person who came toward them as if in a trance. Two performances of Beethoven's Ninth in one day had left him totally drained: his hands were ice-cold and the flesh on his face had collapsed. When he took his customary cigarette and scotch, his assistant Craig Urquhart had to shake him hard with his hands on both shoulders. The fearful moment passed, and Bernstein was soon signing autographs as if nothing untoward had occurred, but friends took it as a warning.

Christmas morning was cold and sunny. The statue of Friedrich von Schiller outside the Schauspielhaus looked down benignly on the assembling crowds.

Soon his stirring words were to ring out via satellite and news broadcasts to millions of listeners in twenty countries around the world. When the bass soloist began his great narrative the thrill that ran round the hall was palpable. The chorus sopranos entering a few moments later were reinforced and transformed by the fresh voices of the eighty-strong Dresden Philharmonic girls' choir—a poignant reminder that it was the coming generation of Germans that stood to benefit most from the fruits of reunification and the end of political oppression.

This Christmas Day concert was the highest point in Leonard Bernstein's public life as a citizen of the world. After the concert, the East German government—in its dying days as a separate power—presented him with the Star of Friendship between Peoples. The mood of optimism engendered by the Freedom Concert, as it came to be called, quickly faded in the light of harsh political and economic realities. But for a few days Bernstein's gesture of brotherhood epitomized the hopes and aspirations of the Western world.


PAUSING in New York only to consult Dr. Cahill, the exhausted Bernstein retreated to Key West for a month to rest and to work on the Holocaust opera with John Wells. But the flood of visitors he had invited made it hard to concentrate. Aaron Stern was the first to arrive, insisting on "quality time" to discuss his educational projects. Nick Webster and Stephen Stamas flew down from New York to woo him to take on more conducting and teaching with the New York Philharmonic. John Guare and Louis Malle came to talk about a movie proposal. Jamie Bernstein Thomas stayed in a nearby house with her husband and two children for a week; Shirley Bernstein and Betty Comden passed through; Harry Kraut rented a house a few blocks away. Bernstein's Key West friends wanted him for dinner and anagram games.

Taking care to time his arrival for after Aaron Stern's departure, Mark Adams Taylor provided Bernstein with companionship, particularly in the insomniac hours. "We'd stay up all night long working on acrostic puzzles," Taylor recalls; "all at the expense of getting any real work done." For John Wells, gamely attempting to fashion a workable outline for the unwritten opera, it was a frustrating month. He had a table by the piano, and once or twice Bernstein donned a golden baseball cap and sat down to work with him on the lyrics and melody of a specific number. Inspiration was sluggish. Nevertheless Wells retains happy memories of Key West. Bernstein, he recalls with amazement, "was still diving into the pool; chuckling over a crystal train set he'd been sent by an admirer in Austria; shouting for more sushi in the local Japanese restaurant; clapping a sponge on his head on a deserted beach and quoting *Lear;* wondering operatically how he could be so deep in love; playing and singing the whole of the first act of *The Mikado,* every word and every cue accurate after fifty years; hugging everyone, kissing everyone; steering the boat back from the reef; wondering, operatically again, why he needed to share every experience, even looking at a sunset, and why he couldn't bear to look at it alone; doing insanely difficult crosswords until six o'clock in the morning, then coming down grumpy at lunchtime saying he hadn't written any music all night; reading Lewis Carroll's *Pig That Could Not Jump* with big sad tears running down his cheeks; dancing round the pool with his baby grandson in his arms, singing 'All I Do Is Dream of You.' "

But to closer friends Bernstein confessed that he did not "feel right"; he was not recovering his strength as he had always done in the past after winter weeks in Florida. Soon after his arrival he jotted down in his date book a checklist of ten minor ailments, presumably before discussing them on the telephone with Kevin Cahill in New York. He was in no mood to break his vacation, so he missed hearing what proved to be his last completed composition. On January 14, 1990, the Empire Brass Quintet gave the premiere at the Metropolitan Opera of *Dance Suite,* a set of five brief pieces—sketches from his bottom drawer—that Bernstein contributed to the fiftieth anniversary gala of American Ballet Theatre. When he did return to New York, in February, he was still unwell: a recurrence of the influenza bug obliged him to cancel a conducting appearance at the Curtis Institute. Then his aunt Bertha died and he flew to Boston to comfort his mother. In mid-February he left for Vienna and two weeks with the Vienna Philharmonic. The music-making was as intense as ever, but the lifestyle was changing. Deutsche Grammophon invited music critics to Vienna from all over Europe to sit in on rehearsals of the Bruckner and celebrate the signing of their new long-term contract with Bernstein, but Craig Urquhart successfully persuaded him to leave the postconcert dinner early and go home to rest.

Back in New York for three weeks Bernstein consulted his doctors, dined with his friends and led the Vienna Philharmonic through three concerts at Carnegie Hall. Then he returned to Europe to conduct Mozart's C minor Mass with the Bavarian Radio Symphony Orchestra and Chorus. Before the rehearsals he attended a party thrown by Amberson to mark its twenty-year partnership with Unitel. Unitel's boss Leo Kirch had become one of Europe's most powerful media czars, and although their politics were very different he and Bernstein had great personal sympathy for each other: Kirch always supported Bernstein's artistic projects to the hilt, even when, as in the case of the films of Sibelius symphonies in Vienna or of Debussy tone poems in Rome, there was little prospect of commercial viability. Yet Bernstein was feeling so weary that he would have skipped the evening if Craig Urquhart hadn't persuaded him that he owed it to Kirch and Harry Kraut to attend.

For the recording of the Mozart Mass, which Bernstein had never conducted before, Bavarian Television chose the spectacular eighteenth-century church, part of a much older abbey, in the small town of Waldsassen in Oberpfalz, one hundred and fifty miles north of Munich. It was the latest in a series of religious choral works by Haydn and Mozart that Bernstein had done with the Bavarians in settings of rococo splendor. Waldsassen's situation was significant to Bernstein: the small town lies at the very heart of Europe, halfway to Berlin and close to the Czechoslovak border. Warring armies had been passing through since the Middle Ages. "Here, in *mittel Mittel* Europa," Bernstein said in his filmed introduction to the Mass, "one gets a sense of how utterly old-fashioned war is. . . . More and more forbidden borders are opening, one after another, all over this exciting, historic and vastly complicated continent. Miracles are in the air; it is the time and the place for Mozart, that he may strengthen us, bless us, and help us—at long last—to achieve peace on earth."

Bernstein, his staff and the television team all lodged in a modest hotel, which was presided over by a genial Bavarian who had never experienced such an invasion. President Václav Havel, whom Bernstein was due to meet in June, sent his personal pastry cook from his *dacha,* not far across the border. Beneath the amused gaze of the Waldsassen locals, the invaders consumed huge meals at long tables in a Tanglewood spirit of comradeship. The customary paraphernalia of the Bernstein traveling circus was absent. There were few English-language newspapers, television sets or fax machines. Even telephoning was difficult. Gone, too, were the hangers-on. In Berlin at Christmas 1989 eight young admirers from Cologne had slept on the floor in Bernstein's hotel suite: here there was no room at the inn for anybody without a job to do. The hotel's *Stube* was the venue for an entertainment provided by a local family with some exceptionally gifted children (by an astonishing coincidence, the eldest had studied at Tanglewood and Salzau), who one evening performed their accordion-accompanied version of *West Side Story* for its enchanted composer.

But all through the week Bernstein complained privately of a new disability. "Every time I take an inhaling breath there is a sharp jabbing pain in my lower left lung," he told Mark Stringer. Craig Urquhart was nervous: his grandmother had complained of a similar pain before she was diagnosed with cancer. Bernstein's doctor friend from Munich, Jutta Mauermann, gave him electrotherapy, a treatment in which she specialized. He told her it made him feel better, but when she was gone he would say, "It doesn't make a dent." He kept pain at bay with Tylenol and an occasional dose of a prescription painkiller. He told Stringer that the only time he did not feel pain was when he was conducting.

Outwardly, Bernstein was in surprisingly good spirits in Waldsassen. The second performance of the Mozart Mass was followed by a lengthy session of retakes for the video, and later that night Bernstein wrote a memorandum for Mark Stringer, passing on his thoughts, to one just beginning his career, about the mystical link between audience, performers and music.

> The key to the joy of conducting is simply knowledge—but of a special kind: that knowledge of a work that makes you belong to it, or to have authored it (not the kind that makes it belong to you) . . . You know how the verbal and musical texts mesh or just miss meshing; you know the problems, the sublimities, the highs and lows, and you have become its guardian, keeper of the flame. . . . Only tonight did I *begin*

to have this joy, the feeling of composing in performance (after enough rehearsals, a dress rehearsal and a first performance). It had something to do with not wearing glasses, with not turning pages, with being with the 150 performers, playing and singing *their* notes, together and separately, rather than the notes in the score before me. It had something to do with retakes: not only the increased security of instant re-play, but telling the public about which retakes we were to do, inviting them in to join us, to become part of the cosmos known as the C Minor Mass.

Instead of returning directly the next day to Munich, Bernstein accepted an invitation from Friedelind Wagner to make a detour and visit Richard Wagner's opera house in nearby Bayreuth. Friedelind, who bore an uncanny resemblance to her grandfather, was well known in the music world as an opera coach and teacher. Unlike her mother she was anti-Nazi. She had lived in America during the war, thanks to Toscanini's intervention, and had first met Bernstein in 1944. She had made the long journey to Waldsassen from her Lucerne home to hear Bernstein conduct and then to lead him to Bayreuth's famous Green Hill.

Bernstein had long since given up conducting in opera houses but he was deeply moved to be on the holy ground of the Festspielhaus. After contemplating the auditorium silently for some time, he descended into the pit. He stood at the podium where he would have conducted *Tristan* had Wieland Wagner not died prematurely, looking down on the steeply raked orchestral seating below him. Mark Stringer pretended to be the concertmaster to give Bernstein a better idea of the unique Bayreuth orchestral layout. Bernstein sang a little to test the acoustics and commented that he would have enjoyed conducting in his shirt-sleeves—the conductor cannot be seen by the audience.

The Bernstein group then drove over to Villa Wahnfried, the handsome house Wagner built for himself when he came to live in Bayreuth. Bernstein pretended for a moment to be Ludwig II of Bavaria, and Friedelind acted her own grandfather showing the royal patron over the property. She had grown up here and played games with Adolf Hitler when he came to visit the family. Wahnfried had been partially destroyed by American bombing in 1945, but the living room—restored and now part of the Wagner museum—still contained the beautiful rosewood Steinway piano upon which Wagner had rehearsed with his singers more than a century previously. Bernstein couldn't resist the temptation to play it. *"Das klingt wirklich wie eine Klarinette,"* he said; it really sounds like a clarinet. "You could create the sound of an entire orchestra on this piano." And that is what he did, playing first the Prelude to *Tristan* and then some of the love music from Act II.

At first he did not want to visit Wagner's grave in the garden outside the house, but in the end he relented, and for a few moments the group of visitors contemplated the simple stone slab. It was big enough, Bernstein observed, for them all to have danced on it. With Friedelind Wagner as his guide, he had finally made a sort of peace with the man he had hated for so long—but hated, as he put it, on bended knee.

BERNSTEIN conducted the Mozart C minor Mass at two concerts in Munich, then flew with one of his young German friends to Paris (in Unitel's private jet) to attend an evening of his concert films at the Louvre. From his rooftop suite at the Hôtel Crillon he telephoned "Mat" and made a date for dinner in New York two days later, on April 10. He was flying home via Boston in order to be with his mother for the Passover seder on the ninth. "Let's have a day of all days," he said to Taylor, "tennis and margaritas, reading fan letters. I'm going to live and love forever."

Back in New York, the twists and turns of Bernstein's emotional life became secondary to a new and overwhelming concern for his health. In Waldsassen he had told Mark Stringer that his stabbing pain was similar to the one Felicia had described at the beginning of her fatal illness. He had X-rays taken in New York but they revealed nothing. Kevin Cahill suggested that Bernstein's back pain might be coming from a pulled muscle caused by coughing, but nonetheless he called for a multiple CAT scan. Inspecting the body at a different angle from the X-ray machine, the scan revealed a tumor near the top of the left lung. Cahill invited Dr. Thomas Fahey to consult, and a needle biopsy was carried out a few days later. The process is somewhat less arduous than exploratory surgery: a hypodermic needle is inserted into the body and through it a small tissue sample is extracted. In Bernstein's case no cancerous cells were discovered by this limited exploration, but expert opinion nevertheless suspected him to be suffering from a type of malignant tumor known as mesothelioma, which attacks the membrane surrounding the lung. Mesothelioma has been statistically linked to exposure to asbestos, but not to cigarette smoking.

Bernstein was told that the cancer was curable, and an immediate course of radiation therapy was decided upon. Above all else, Bernstein wanted to keep the news secret from his mother; it was also important not to cause unnecessary worries in Sapporo, on the Japanese island of Hokkaido, where he was due to launch the first Pacific Music Festival in less than two months, or in Tanglewood, where plans were almost complete for the student orchestra's first-ever European tour. It was decided to administer daily radiation treatments at Memorial Hospital. Bernstein worked out a *modus vivendi* with Harry Kraut and his two personal assistants: he would attend under an assumed name, and describe the sessions in his date book under the code name of "poetry readings." He was driven to the hospital either by Urquhart or by Tricia Andryszewsky, the tough new personal secretary who had replaced Helen Coates. "It was bizarre," Urquhart remembers, "because nobody was supposed to know that he was having radiation yet after the treatments he would go into the doctor's office and have a scotch and eat cheese and crackers." His cover might well have been blown when he met the English journalist Ian Ball, who had married

Ellen Bernstein after her divorce from Bernstein's brother. "He asked me what I was doing in those sterile halls," Ball remembers, "and I put the same question to him. The reply, delivered with a dynamic upward thrust of the arm, was pure Bernstein: 'I'm involved in a new experiment with life.' " After one of these "poetry readings," the jewelry Bernstein had taken off for the treatment —his Mitropoulos medallion and the gold and silver shekel Felicia had given him—could not be found. He took the loss very badly; it was a sign, he said to Urquhart, that his luck was running out.

The treatment continued for two weeks. Not a whisper of it leaked out to the press. Pleading weakness after a severe attack of influenza, Bernstein canceled a conducting engagement at the American Spoleto Festival in Charleston but he was judged strong enough by his doctors to make another strenuous trip to Europe soon afterward, to conduct at the Prague Spring Festival. Knowing little or nothing of his recent ordeal, Bernstein's European friends noted his evident happiness to be back in Prague, the scene of his first European success in 1946. He praised the beauties of the city, fantasized about buying an apartment on the banks of the River Moldau and strolled over the Charles Bridge on a lovely spring day, basking in the attention of passers-by. The American ambassador, Shirley Temple Black, arranged a party in his honor.

Bernstein also had a long meeting with President Václav Havel, who had reason to be grateful to his guest: in 1977 Bernstein had pulled out of a planned visit to Prague to protest the Czech government's imprisonment of dissident writers. Now the American and British visitors in Bernstein's party urged Havel to continue support of Mikhail Gorbachev in his internal struggles with Boris Yeltsin. But from Havel's point of view Gorbachev's achievement was now a historical fact: his time, Havel hinted, was over. Bernstein, more romantic and less pragmatic, was shocked.

When Bernstein conducted Beethoven's Ninth to close the festival, the word *Freiheit* was again substituted for *Freude*. Four national soloists were led by one of Bernstein's favorite artists, the soprano Lucia Popp. Conducting a great orchestra in a stirring event worked wonders on Bernstein's spirits, but telltale signs revealed that all was not well. For the first time in his conducting life, his dressing room door was closed to well-wishers and even to colleagues "on doctor's orders to reduce stress"—actually because the radiation treatment had left distressing scars on his chest. Bernstein's devoted European lawyer, Fritz Willheim, brought tubes of oxygen from Vienna in case he had a recurrence of the breathing problem brought on by his emphysema. An Italian-born New York acupuncturist, Adriano Borgnia, had recently joined the entourage. In Prague, Borgnia's treatment, administered several times a day, brought Bernstein a measure of relief from pain.

But within days of his return from Prague to America on June 4, he was engulfed in a new physical crisis. The radiation treatment in May appeared to have greatly reduced the pleural mesothelioma, but a side effect of the radiation was causing a dangerous level of fluid to accumulate in the interstice between the pleural sac and the lung itself. Immediate remedial action was needed. In Lenox Hill Hospital a tube was inserted through Bernstein's ribs so that the fluid could be drained off. Despite his allergy, doctors then decided to take a calculated risk and inject tetracycline as a sclerosing agent into the interstice, with the intention of sealing it. Unfortunately, Bernstein's body reacted violently to the drug: painful herpes infections erupted on several areas of his body, including his eyes and his penis. Craig Urquhart remembers it as "an awful, awful day . . . a real turning point for him spiritually. . . . I found out, much to my amazement and disgust, that after I left he was visited by friends and they ordered up ravioli and there were empty bottles of scotch and vodka. His friends were unaware of the horrors he had undergone."

Shirley Bernstein had been keeping a loving eye on her brother since his illness began. She had accompanied him to Prague, and on June 16 she took him home to Fairfield to recuperate. The date was an inauspicious one for somebody who believed there were no coincidences in life: it was the twelfth anniversary of Felicia's death. Normally a patient emerging from radiation treatment and a minor operation would expect a period of rest and recuperation to follow, but in ten days' time the first Pacific Music Festival was due to begin. The budget for this new Tanglewood at the Art Park outside Sapporo was close to $5 million, and Bernstein was scheduled to conduct two concerts with the London Symphony Orchestra and one with the Pacific Music Festival student orchestra, whose players had been recruited from twenty-three countries. There were young conductors to be coached and speeches to be made; he was to be the guiding spirit, the Koussevitzky figure, of the entire festival.

Inevitably, Bernstein wanted to go to Japan. He loved conducting, he loved teaching, he loved the idea of sowing Tanglewood seeds in Japanese soil. Besides, the festival was to move to Tokyo and Osaka after two intensive weeks in Sapporo. The Emperor and Empress of Japan were due to attend his first Tokyo performance and he had never met an emperor. Michael Tilson Thomas and several young conductors would be with him at the festival to share the load. As always he was ready to gamble, not with his artistic reputation this time, but with his very life.

Dr. Cahill and his consultants warned Bernstein of the risks involved—but they allowed him to proceed. Privately his radiologist predicted that Bernstein would have to be flown back in an ambulance plane. Harry Kraut did everything possible to reduce the strain. Bernstein stayed at the Nidom, a brand-new (still unopened) Finnish-style hotel, set in lovely wooded country at Tomakomai, an hour's drive from Sapporo, and he was cared for by a devoted staff. His regular cook, Patty Pulliam, ran the household and ordered meals from the French and Japanese hotel chefs, supplemented by fresh vegetables she bought herself in the local market. No expense was too great for the Japanese, she remembers: among the wines was a copious supply of Château Latour 1961. Craig Urquhart looked after Bernstein's personal affairs. Robert Arbuckle, a seasoned campaigner after a year in the Amberson office, worked for Harry

Kraut. Margaret Carson's deputy, Robert Gallo, was there to handle the international press. Adriano Borgnia was flown in to continue the acupuncture treatments he had been administering since May.

Despite the precautions, Bernstein's last Japanese visit began like a nightmare. He had persuaded Mark Taylor to accompany him, and as they were leaving the Dakota a distraught Julia Vega pulled at Taylor's coat, pleading in vain with him not to let Bernstein travel. "He will listen to you, Mr. Taylor." Bernstein could not sleep on the flight and was in pain from shingles, probably a side effect of the tetracycline treatment. In mid-flight Taylor woke up to find him in the steward's galley, using a small mortar and pestle to grind up tablets of a prescription painkiller. He snorted the resultant powder like snuff and washed it down with scotch. He looked green. Taylor was desperately worried that he would wake up next to a corpse but after three recuperative days in Tomakomai, where the climate was pleasantly temperate, Bernstein emerged, elegantly dressed in a white cotton suit, for the festival's opening ceremonies.

He made his dedication speech in a wavering voice. He wanted, he said, "to devote most of the remaining energy and time the Lord grants me to education, sharing as much as I can with younger people—especially very much younger people—whatever I know not only about music but also art, and not only about the arts but also about the relation between art and life. And about being oneself, finding one's self, 'knowing who you are,' and doing the best possible job. If I can communicate some of this . . . I will be a very happy man." He spoke slowly, his forehead lined with tension. His physical deterioration was truly shocking to behold.

He picked up a little strength once rehearsals with the musicians began. When he coughed, or struggled for breath, the students looked understandably anxious: such suffering was not part of the joyful curriculum for which they had enlisted. The planned concert programs had been rescheduled to lessen Bernstein's load: instead of his own *Concerto for Orchestra,* which would have been particularly taxing because of the improvisatory sections, he taught the students the Second Symphony by Schumann. With the London Symphony Orchestra, he dropped Bruckner's arduous Ninth Symphony in favor of more familiar music: Beethoven's Seventh, Britten's *Sea Interludes,* and his own *Serenade* (with Midori). At the rehearsals with the students, flashes of the old Bernstein could be seen: in the Schumann symphony he ordered the entire first violin section to stand up and play the brilliantly virtuosic closing bars of the "Scherzo" movement as if they were all soloists. "So this has never been done before," he called out, which was probably true for Japan, although he had once asked the Vienna Philharmonic to do the same thing: "there's always a first time. I love you. You make old guys like me feel young again." But privately he was weak as a kitten. In a rehearsal break he put his head on Kazuko Amano's shoulder and whispered, "Kazuko, I am tired." He was sweating profusely as a result of the painkilling drugs he was taking. And it was becoming more and more difficult for him to breathe.

The English journalist Lesley Garner wrote a vivid account of Bernstein arriving for a rehearsal. "He is chewing gum. [Actually, Nicorettes, prescription gum spiked with nicotine.] He is swaggering along in a candy-striped anorak, jeans with 'LB' embroidered on the back pocket, and silver-toed Cuban-heeled cowboy boots. [He had given himself the boots as a seventieth-birthday present. The raised heels helped to compensate for his accelerated rate of shrinkage.] He renews himself by touch. As he walks along the front line of the orchestra he has a handclasp for a cellist, a hug for the diminutive [concertmaster], a kiss for 33-year old Marin Alsop, his conducting assistant. He ignores the steps which are three feet away and insists on scrambling up on to the platform unaided. It is a piece of bloody-minded defiance. Once on the podium, his diminutive, gnome-like figure grows visibly, charged by the unfailing power of passion for music."

Michael Tilson Thomas noted the same defiant spirit when Bernstein turned up for dinner wearing black jeans and a sailor's horizontally striped T-shirt with a red kerchief at his throat. He danced an impromptu apache dance, with Tilson Thomas accompanying him at the piano. But such elation was absent when Lesley Garner interviewed Bernstein for her newspaper. " 'Something has got to give in a man of my advanced years,' he says slowly, with an edge of gallows humor. 'I've had much more than my share of life's gifts . . . but I have not repaid the good Lord by taking care of my body. It starts with a force called gravity. Somehow things start falling and drooping that never did. And your fluids dry up, like your tears. I have to put drops in my eyes at night. To turn pages I must lick my fingers; that's an old man's habit. Other things dry up, other fluids.' . . . Bernstein is patently unrespectable. He likes to shock. He likes to flaunt his legendary sexuality. Even in his seventies, whatever he says about his failing juices, he is a powerfully sexy man. This combination of physical magnetism, emotional passion, intellectual depth and lightning responses is what keeps an orchestra on its toes."

Against the odds Bernstein seemed to be surviving in Japan. True, he complained of severe back pain when conducting Beethoven's Seventh Symphony, yet he hosted an Independence Day party on July 4 and not only turned up at Bob Gallo's sixty-fifth birthday party a few days earlier but played the piano for forty-five minutes—retrieving from the depth of his memory the songs that had been popular at the time of Gallo's birth. But for Craig Urquhart the happiest evening of the trip was the one Bernstein spent at home with Patty Pulliam, "Mat" Taylor and himself, when they all drank *sake* and took turns reading poems from Bernstein's paperback *Golden Treasury*.

Bernstein's condition worsened as soon as the caravan transferred to Tokyo. He was taking far too many drugs for his own good. The aftereffects of the tetracycline injection were still causing great discomfort. Dr. Borgnia's acupuncture treatments brought no relief and his rooms at the Tokyo Century Hyatt (the Imperial Suite, naturally) were so vast and impersonal that he preferred to stay in bed most of the day. Outside the temperature was 102 degrees and the humidity 100 percent (or so it seemed to Bernstein).

Somehow life went on. With "Mat" Taylor and other friends he attended the Kabuki Theater on July 9 and next day he conducted the LSO at Suntory Hall in a concert which ended in comic confusion. The plan was for the Emperor and Empress to take their leave after the conductor had left the platform but the Japanese royals appeared to have confused the word "concertmaster" with "conductor" and were patiently waiting for the LSO's orchestra leader, rather than its maestro, to make his departure. Meanwhile the orchestra had been instructed to remain on stage until the royal party left. It took several minutes for the impasse to be broken, by which time the exhausted Bernstein had taken rather more curtain calls than even he deemed appropriate. Between bows he could be spotted pointedly waving good-bye to their imperial highnesses through the stage door. The hint was finally conveyed to the emperor. Bernstein was in good spirits at the dinner that followed.

Yet the days in Tokyo were purgatorial for Craig Urquhart. He hated Bernstein's dependency on the painkilling drugs. "The real question is why he bothers at all," he wrote in his diary. "Here is a very sick man who knows he is doing his *danse macabre*." Mark Taylor was equally unhappy. He had willingly agreed to accompany Bernstein out of love and sympathy but he soon became "profoundly disturbed," as he put it, by Bernstein's deterioration, and he resented Bernstein's affection for Kunihiko Hashimoto, his Japanese liaison officer and friend. There were volatile episodes between them: when Taylor sensed he was more of a hindrance than a help he returned to New York earlier than planned. Bernstein pressed on with the second scheduled LSO concert on July 12. Still before him were a huge outdoor arena concert in Yokohama featuring the combined orchestras of the LSO and the Pacific Music Festival, and four regular concerts involving further travel to Kyoto and Osaka. But on the morning of the fourteenth, Urquhart walked into Bernstein's suite and found him collapsed on the floor, unable to crawl to his bed. Arrangements were made to fly the maestro home. A press announcement was hastily prepared: "Leonard Bernstein is suffering from exhaustion as a result of trying to fulfill his professional obligations while not having fully recovered from several ailments he suffered this spring." The ailments were identified as severe influenza, pleurisy and pneumonia. Michael Tilson Thomas and Eiji Oue took over the remaining concerts.

"How I wished he could have left under happier conditions," Kazuko Amano remembers. "There were many hostile comments in the press. . . ." Mrs. Amano went to Bernstein's hotel to make her farewells. *"Vous êtes le grand amour de ma vie,"* she remembers telling him. "Lenny had a nice shy smile as he replied with dignity, *'Il ne faut pas exagérer, Madame.'* To which I answered, trying to sing, *'Non, je n'exagère pas,* Leonar . . . do!' 'It sounds like an opera,' chipped in Michael Tilson Thomas, trying to make things happier, too. I mentioned Tanglewood. 'Tokyo is so polluted you got ill. You will be far better in Tanglewood after a good rest.' 'Yes, yes' murmured Lenny, and it was time to go down to the car. We all took the same elevator, trying to act joyfully like children. But everyone was crying in the depths of their hearts. . . . Lenny embraced everyone more tenderly but also more silently than usual. I was the last one to say *'Au revoir,* Lenny.' And before getting into the car, for the first time during our forty and more years of friendship, Lenny looked back and called me 'baby.' 'Thank you, Kazuko baby; give my love to the children.' "

Next evening, Bernstein met his worried family around the dinner table at the Dakota. And then he retreated to Fairfield. His strength and courage were to be tested as never before in the weeks that followed: in mid-August he was scheduled to appear at Tanglewood. A week with the student orchestra was to be followed first by the annual Koussevitzky Memorial Concert with the Boston Symphony and then, to honor the fiftieth anniversary of the founding of the Berkshire Music Center, by a week-long European tour for the student orchestra.

Naturally there were contrary opinions about the wisdom of pressing on with these projects. Most of all, Bernstein wanted to conceal the seriousness of his illness from his mother. He was stimulated by working with young people, he wanted to continue with his educational work, he enjoyed touring and he would be paying homage to two of his greatest masters, Serge Koussevitzky and Aaron Copland, whose Third Symphony would be played by the students. New medical examinations gave no cause for alarm. So despite Bernstein's collapse in Japan, Dr. Cahill did not seek to forbid the Tanglewood venture: he considered work to be the best therapy. But he continued to urge that Bernstein reduce his dependency on prescription painkillers and sleeping medications.

Less than a month after the ignominious retreat from Tokyo Bernstein was on the road again. He was feeling much better, but bad luck began immediately. The house usually rented for him in Great Barrington was not available in 1990 and the alternative, in Lenox, turned out to be so damp and smelly that it was instantly nicknamed the "Mildew Palace." The weather was unseasonably cold and wet. Bernstein contracted bronchitis again. (He was treated by Tanglewood's official doctor, Desmond Tivey.) The customary joy at being back in the Berkshires was replaced by depression. At the first rehearsal of Copland's Third Symphony many of the students were tired after a party the night before and unfamiliar with the Copland idiom. Bernstein became so testy that he asked Mark Stringer, who was attending Tanglewood as an auditor, to take over. During the next two days Stringer licked the symphony into shape. Bernstein resumed work after a three-day rest and it seemed as if he had turned the corner. He spent five hours with the orchestra on the Copland and then coached a student conductor for an hour in Beethoven's *Leonore* Overture No. 3, divulging several tricks of the conductor's trade; in a rapid scale passage for the cellos he recommended dividing the players to avoid smudginess, half of them playing *legato,* the other half giving each note a separate bow. When he rehearsed the Copland he said, "I want five different textures here," only to interrupt himself: "Who am I to say that *I* want it? *Aaron* wants it." "Stupido Maestro" he called himself, when he erroneously announced a metronome figure instead of a rehearsal number. (He was quoting Toscanini, referring to himself, back in 1949.) During a rehearsal break Lukas Foss, Tanglewood's guest professor of composition, asked Bernstein how he was doing. "I'm still upright," Bernstein said, with a wry smile. "You're better than a piano," Foss observed: "You're both upright and grand."

Backstage before the Copland performance Mark Stringer found Bernstein distracted. "How do they expect me to conduct when all I can think about is getting my next breath?" he complained, surveying the oxygen bottles that had been brought into the dressing room. But he had always said, "If they can prop me up, I will go on," and having kissed the Koussevitzky cuff links he was pushed out to conduct, an El Cid of the orchestra.

After ten minutes on the podium he began to show the effects of oxygen deprivation. "You would see his brain go click," Stringer remembers. "It was sad, because it made the Copland extremely dogged." The Boston critic Richard Dyer had a different reaction: "All of the charisma was there, the radiant dedication to the music. . . . The ailments drop away when Bernstein leaves the everyday world behind and enters into the life-enhancing element of music." Peter Schwenkow, the impresario for the student orchestra's forthcoming European tour, attended Tanglewood in person and decided that it was realistic to confirm the project for the following week.

Bernstein had planned a strong program for the BSO's Koussevitzky Memorial Concert on Sunday, August 19. Beethoven's Seventh Symphony was to be the major work, preceded by Britten's *Four Sea Interludes,* and the first performance under Bernstein's baton of *Arias and Barcarolles,* in an orchestration by the young Chinese composer Bright Sheng. He had spent part of his free day restudying his work with Sheng (and retouching some of the effects) but after half an hour of rehearsal he decided to entrust the performance to the Boston Symphony's resident assistant conductor, Carl St. Clair. Next day, he coached the singers Judy Kaye and Kurt Ollmann at the Mildew Palace; Mark Stringer remembers he was fuddled from medication and lack of oxygen: "He really wasn't thinking clearly." Jamie Bernstein Thomas had an equally depressing experience. She had written a poem in anticipation of her father's seventy-second birthday. "He couldn't concentrate long enough to see why it was cool."

His mother came to his Sunday afternoon concert at Tanglewood. So did every member of his family and many of his closest New York friends. Musicians he had known since 1940 were also there, celebrating Tanglewood's fiftieth anniversary as a music school. Though he could always rise to an occasion, his strength had ebbed away disastrously in the past few days. He began with Britten's *Four Sea Interludes;* the performance was, in Richard Dyer's words, "slow, spacious, colorful, atmospheric and majestic." *Arias and Barcarolles* followed. He heard his work from the radio control room. The voices required amplification to carry to the back of the Shed, and the songs made only a moderate impression on the public. He spent part of the interval stretched out on a table being massaged. Then came Beethoven's Seventh. He walked slowly and painfully on to the platform. The customary flamboyance was gone; when he conducted he could hardly lift his arms above the waist and much of the intensity at the rostrum was generated by his eyes. The "Allegretto" second movement was desperately slow, like a funeral march. In the third movement he was seized by a coughing fit. Like a boxer staggering after a heavy punch, he grabbed the rail behind him for support, coughing uncontrollably into his red silk handkerchief. In the audience his daughter Jamie and his friend Phyllis Green Newman clutched each other in terror. After what seemed like an eternity to the musicians he resumed contact with them, conducting with his eyes and his shoulders and his knees. Nina Bernstein imagined him collapsing at the podium, as Dimitri Mitropoulos had done; she would rush forward to cradle him in her arms, Cordelia to his Lear—but with the roles reversed.

The Boston players responded to the crisis magnificently. Under the leadership of their concertmaster, Malcolm Lowe, they kept playing, willing Bernstein back into action. The breathing crisis passed and he was able to resume conducting with his arms. He concluded the symphony with a finale of controlled but ferocious energy that left him completely shattered. The huge ovation that followed was as much for the man as it was for the music. When he trudged off the stage his shoulders were hunched, and according to Mark Stringer his face was absolutely slate gray. But he was proud of what he had done and immediately began analyzing the interpretation. His ninety-one-year-old mother met him: "I saw that he wouldn't be able to do much more after that," she said.

There was an enormous crush backstage, but only family and fellow musicians were allowed into the greenroom. Bernstein changed and was driven up to Koussevitzky's former residence, Seranak, in order to greet the Tanglewood veterans at the traditional postconcert reception. A well-wisher seriously advised him to have a heart transplant. When he met Tanglewood's administrators, Leon Fleisher and Dan Gustin, he said, "Who am I kidding? I can't do this." The students were told that night that their European tour must be canceled. Bernstein left the party early and instead of returning to Fairfield as planned he was driven to New York so that he could see his doctors in the morning.

# 40.
# FINAL DAYS
# AUGUST—OCTOBER 1990

*With his grandson Evan Thomas in Fairfield*
*two months before his death.*
PHOTO JAMIE BERNSTEIN THOMAS

*Afraid*
*Died in my vocabulary*
*Long ago—except of hurting*
*Someone I love, and then*
*Of not writing my Piece*
*Before my Not-To-Be*
> —from "Finalizing the Deal, I Believe You Call It,"
> Leonard Bernstein, May 1990

PHYLLIS Newman joined Bernstein and his sister for the limousine drive to New York. "They were both smoking," she remembers; "I had to plead with them for air. Leonard was exhausted and sweating terribly. We played a game of mental jotto, then I suggested he take a rest, and he laid his head on my lap. I created a story for him, an endless tale about human beings with animal bodies. He wanted to know all about them, how they looked, what language they talked, how they made love. It was very imaginative talk. He laughed a lot. Then he went to sleep."

When Craig Urquhart returned to the Dakota that evening he found Bernstein sitting at his desk with a scotch. "He had changed clothes, and showered, and he looked fabulous as only Lenny could. It was unbelievable. He was like a totally different person. He looked so relieved and so at ease with himself. [He said:] 'You know it's incredible how I did my first concert at Tanglewood and I did my last concert at Tanglewood. There's a real sense of closure.' "

Next morning Bernstein stayed in bed. He refused at first to visit Dr. Cahill but Harry Kraut insisted. Apart from his health there was a practical matter: a doctor's examination was needed in connection with the insurance claim on the canceled Tanglewood tour. Cahill told Bernstein, who had been doubling and trebling up on his prescriptions for months on end, that he was abusing himself with drugs. "You're supposed to take half a Valium, not six."

Three days after his return from Tanglewood the drugs ran out. He spent his seventy-second birthday, and several days each side of it, in Lenox Hill Hospital, being dried out from pills and alcohol. Officially he was "out of the city": Tricia Andryszewsky revealed his whereabouts to none of his friends. On his birthday he broke his cover: he telephoned Mark Taylor and asked him to the hospital. Taylor sat with his friend for an hour—visits were officially restricted to fifteen minutes—and gave him a pedicure as an impromptu birthday present.

When Bernstein returned to his apartment on August 28 he found it had been taken over by alien forces—white-coated registered nurses who guarded his medicine chest and watched him night and day. His medical advisers, joined now by Dr. Samuel Klagsbrun, a psychiatrist who specialized in problems of drug dependency, were taking no chances with a patient who was becoming obsessed with the idea that his death was imminent.

In fact a thorough investigation had found no sign of any malignancy: early in September Bernstein was told by Dr. Saul Farber, one of America's leading internists, that he had successfully survived a bout of cancer. But to have any hope of full recovery, given his by now rampaging emphysema, he would have to follow a strict medical regimen. Bernstein hated the intrusion at the Dakota; one of the nurses had even been lecturing him on godliness and urging him to pray. He persuaded Harry Kraut and Kevin Cahill to allow his assistant Phillip Allen and Cahill's son, Sean, an exercise coach, to take over, and nurse him full time at Fairfield. There Patricia Pulliam did the cooking and Julia Vega looked after the house: Julia had long been in charge of daily Bernstein rituals such as the squeezing of the orange juice, the parceling out of the vitamin pills and the making of the coffee according to Felicia's recipe.

Dr. Cahill issued typed instructions: "The purpose and orientation of this program is toward recovering fitness. . . . Visitors, even family, should be kept to a minimum so as not to interfere with LB's treatment." When Bernstein awoke each day he first inhaled through a nebulizing machine to break up the mucus in his lungs and get the oxygen flowing. His medications—he took six in the morning and seven at night—attempted to cope *inter alia* with chronic indigestion, breathing difficulties, viral infections, unsteady heartbeat, and irregular urine flow. Loss of appetite was another problem. He was supposed to take a fiber substitute and drink two cans of a high-protein liquid meal every day, but he hated the stuff. Insomnia continued to haunt him: attempting to beat it in the small hours, he would still double his prescriptions.

Sean Cahill persuaded Bernstein to do a few exercises and Patty Pulliam would gently massage his feet every day, but he remained in great pain. Allen remembers him being profoundly depressed. "We spent hours in conversation about what you put up with and when you decide that the infirmity and the pain become beyond bearing." He rarely went outdoors. Even though an invalid's inclinator was installed on the staircase, he spent more and more time in his upstairs bedroom. Without the drugs the pain would have been intolerable, but as a consequence of taking them his brain sometimes clouded over: "He couldn't concentrate," Allen recalls, "he couldn't read a book anymore, and he couldn't bear to listen to music." Much of the day passed in silence.

The public line was that Bernstein needed only rest and quiet to help him pull through: a conducting appearance at an AIDS benefit in New York at the end of October had already been announced; he was due to lead the Philharmonic in *Elijah* at Lincoln Center in December. And if it took him a while to regain the strength needed to conduct, the argument ran, he would still be able to compose, and teach, and write his memoirs, and meet people. Such talk was no consolation to Bernstein: he wanted life on his own terms or he did not want it at all. Despite the devoted nursing, the diet control, and the exercising, his condition did not improve. Breathing was becoming more and more difficult, the pain more intense.

Over the last weekend in September family and friends assembled at Fairfield to celebrate Shirley Bernstein's birthday and on October 1 Bernstein went back to New York for more tests. The new enemy was fibrosis, an affliction that develops in only 3 percent of patients who have undergone radiation, causing the lungs to become rigid and unable to inflate and deflate efficiently.

Phillip Allen fitted up an invalid's tray table in Bernstein's bedroom at the Dakota so that he could eat and read a little in bed. Music could be played in from the hi-fi equipment installed in the adjoining study. Walking became more and more difficult so Allen also bought an adjustable wheelchair to enable Bernstein to move around the apartment. He hated that wheelchair; it was a symbol of his impotence. Sometimes he would take meals in the morning room, but he was least uncomfortable reclining in his chair near the window of his bedroom. Oxygen tubes and an oxygen machine were close at hand. Michael Wager, who now lived two blocks from the Dakota, volunteered to share the nursing with Phillip Allen and Sean Cahill. From the beginning of October "Mendy" Wager rarely left the Dakota; he would doze in the adjacent studio during the long—and for Bernstein often sleepless—nights, while Allen slept upstairs in the studio apartment on the top floor.

Tricia, the secretary, came in daily to do the correspondence and keep visitors at bay. "He doesn't want to see anybody at present" was her stock reply, which inevitably upset old friends and relations. Ellen Ball came to the Dakota anyway, and was appalled by her former brother-in-law's deterioration. "Can you imagine," he said to her, "I can't even do the puzzle anymore!" When his neighbor and dear friend Lauren Bacall dropped by with a message (in response to the birthday card Bernstein had sent her on September 16) he called her into his room. He was sitting in his chair dressed in white pajamas, she remembers, with a drink in his hand. "It's all happened so fast," he said to her. To another visitor, Martha Gellhorn, he spoke openly of suicide. The eighty-two-year-old Gellhorn would have none of it. "I said, 'Come on, buck up, Lenny, just hang in there. . . . I'll be back in three weeks and we'll talk it over again.' " The optimistic Gellhorn suspected (as others did) that his physical weakness was partially caused by painkilling drugs, from which she felt he should swiftly be weaned. But Bernstein was convinced his death was not far off. At breakfast one morning Craig Urquhart found him looking out of the windows at the trees of Central Park, weeping silently. He told his son Alexander that he did not intend to allow himself and the family to go through the long-drawn-out agony to which Felicia had been subjected in 1978.

In the meantime he established a balance of medications that allowed him to retain his lucidity for reasonable stretches of time and he set about putting his house in order. As a first step he decided to withdraw completely from conducting. This meant a public statement and that in turn necessitated a telephone conversation with his mother in Boston to warn her. "He called me," Mrs. Jennie Bernstein remembered, "and I said to him, 'Let me come down. I want to give you a hug and a kiss. . . . He said: 'Wait awhile, Mother. I'm not feeling that well right now. . . . Come down when I feel a little better.' " She never forgot his last words to her: "Should have listened to you, Mother; I'm paying for it dearly."

Harry Kraut drafted a press statement which was to be simultaneously released by the orchestras and festivals with which Bernstein had announced plans for 1991 and beyond. Bernstein personally fussed over its phrasing and punctuation as if it were the script for a "Young People's Concert." "LEONARD BERNSTEIN WITHDRAWS FROM CONDUCTING" was the heading: in the final draft the word "withdraws" was crossed out and "retires" substituted. Henceforth, the announcement said, "he will devote his professional energies to composing, writing and education. He has been advised by his physician . . . that conducting and performing on the piano will likely be activities too strenuous for his *present* physical stamina to support." The word "present" was inserted in Bernstein's own hand: a touching testimony to his divided state of mind; he refused to let go in public. "As soon as his health allows," the statement went on, "Maestro Bernstein will continue his work on a new chamber piece to be performed next spring, a new musical theater piece he hopes to complete by next summer, several educational projects, several film and recording projects, as well as his memoirs. In addition, he hopes to be well enough to participate in the October 28th Carnegie Hall concert 'Music for Life.' "

Harry Kraut flew to Europe on October 6 to give Bernstein's principal collaborators in London, Hamburg, Munich and Vienna details of the announcement they were all to make. The shocking news took everyone by surprise except the officers of the London Symphony, who had witnessed Bernstein's suffering in Japan. The true state of his health had been such a well-kept secret that even the Amberson office staff had been in the dark. Newspapers published articles assessing Bernstein's conducting career. He read some of them and was reassured. They did not feel like obituaries; commentators accepted unquestioningly the proposition that there was work he could do away from the podium. If the miracle happened and his strength returned he could make a comeback: meanwhile he was spared the embarrassment of more last-minute cancellations. But the decision to announce a formal retirement from conducting appears in retrospect to have been a preliminary death sentence. Conducting had been the source of Bernstein's magic power, his wand of youth. Permanently to deny him conducting was to deny him life.

Bernstein's condition deteriorated rapidly. In the second week of October a swelling the size of a walnut appeared on the left side of his chest. Nina glimpsed it when she visited her father and was horrified. Dr. Cahill called Harry Kraut in Europe to say he feared that the cancer might be spreading to Bernstein's liver. He would have to be hospitalized the following week for further tests.

Bernstein resumed daily entries in his date book on October 3, after leaving September blank. Several of his visitors were professional: as well as Dr. Cahill's calls he had exercise sessions with Steve Glassman, a physiotherapist, and he saw the drug-dependency psychiatrist, Dr. Klagsbrun, four times a week. For nearly fifty years psychoanalysis had been more important to Bernstein as a key to self-knowledge than any form of organized religion: he told Craig Urquhart that there were things he could talk about with Klagsbrun and nobody else. Mostly they discussed Judaism from a psychiatrist's understanding.

Bernstein tried to console his friends as much as to seek solace for himself. With Aaron Stern he would talk education and mystic relationships; with Michael Barrett the subject was music; with "Mat," Taylor's plans for creative writing. He felt the most relaxed in Taylor's company: he gave instructions to Tricia and Phillip that "Mat" was to be allowed access at any time. On October 8 Taylor came to dinner and stayed the night in Bernstein's bedroom. Normally an exceptionally sound sleeper, he remembers being awakened by strange yellow lights moving on the ceiling, reflections of brightly lit buses driving past outside the apartment. The loud throb of a noise machine only partially screened out the honking taxis and the occasional raucous fire engine racing by on Central Park West. Bernstein was reclining in his wheelchair, half asleep. He was hallucinating, Taylor recalls, that he was on a cruise ship and obliged to meet some people at a reception. The boat, he said, was his prison and his punishment. Then he wanted to play the piano, though it was four in the morning. "There's a song in my head. More than one; a cacophony. Too many songs going at once."

He complained bitterly to Taylor that night about his insomnia. What kept him awake, he confided in a moment of clarity, was not guilt but fear, fear of not leaving anything behind. When Taylor, seeking to give reassurance, told him he was a living legend, he jumped on the word, "living," and said living was what made one a legend. "The obvious fear is that I'll be remembered—however vaguely—not as a composer but as a conductor. . . . I've lost God, you see, and I'm afraid of dying. . . . When you stop loving life, when death's burden takes over, oh there's no point and it's all so useless. Love brings on tears, and I can't cry."

Accustomed to his ill health in recent years, his family found it hard to grasp the gravity of his condition. In the days following the announcement of his retirement he saw Shirley and Burton (and Burton's wife, Jane, and daughter Karen), and his own children and grandchildren. Craig Urquhart, who was in attendance every day, remembers the look of shock on Burton Bernstein's face when he saw his brother in a wheelchair. Among the musicians who were alerted were two conductors to whom he felt close. John Mauceri spoke to him about the completion of Blitzstein's *Regina* and the future of his son Ben, who was Bernstein's godson. When Michael Tilson Thomas called he brought a macabre composing proposition for Bernstein to consider. Tilson Thomas and the choreographer John Neumeier were working on a ballet project for the 1991 Salzburg Festival; they wanted Bernstein to undertake for it the completion of the requiem Mozart had left unfinished at his death. For a moment Bernstein was genuinely intrigued, Tilson Thomas remembers. "Mozart? The *Requiem?* D'you really think . . . ?" Then he shrugged his shoulders. "I'm so sorry," he said. Tilson Thomas was on his knees beside the chair. He said, "I love you anyway, Lenny." "A fine time you chose to tell me," Bernstein replied, in his best Yiddische Mama imitation.

Other meetings were not so cheerful. Warned about Bernstein's condition by Craig Urquhart when they met at a Carnegie Hall recital, Adolph Green and Phyllis Newman made a date for dinner at the Dakota on October 12 with Betty Comden and the three Bernstein children. Bernstein never lost his determination to put on a good show; Allen or Urquhart shaved him every day and kept him looking spruce even in pajamas. But he was too weak to join his friends at the dinner table. Phyllis Newman was a levelheaded actress who had survived cancer herself and watched Felicia Bernstein die of it twelve years previously. She felt she could have sat at Bernstein's bedside all evening, but she could not bear eating dinner in the dining room without him. After half an hour she made an excuse and went home. Comden and Green soldiered on; there was, Patty Pulliam remembers, "an uneasy feeling in the house."

The next day, Saturday, October 13, Leslie Tomkins and Michael Barrett were due to call on Bernstein and play a transcription for viola of his clarinet sonata, which they were soon to perform at a public concert. Bernstein felt too unwell to meet them and called off the rehearsal, but he listened attentively to a tape Craig Urquhart had made at a run-through earlier in the week. Since there was no replay machine in the bedroom, Urquhart turned up the sound on the studio's player and they listened through the open door. The volume was so high it penetrated the kitchen, too, and when Urquhart went there for a moment the worried Julia Vega asked, "What, has Mr. Bernstein gone *deaf,* too?"

Later in the day Bernstein suggested to Michael Wager that they should read the book of Job. Wager looked at him in disbelief: Job is one of the Bible's grittiest characters. "Yes," Bernstein confirmed, "I think it's about time." After four chapters, though, he said, "We've had enough of *this.*" Instead he proposed a trilingual word game—adding a letter at each turn, in French, German or Italian. Wager began with the letter "M." The sequence developed well: M— Mi—Mie—Mise—Miser—Misere. Wager proposed *Meister* and felt sure he had won but Bernstein capped it with the Italian word for a profession or trade— *mestiere.* Later in the afternoon Bernstein asked Craig Urquhart to choose music from the library shelves—Beethoven sonatas, the *Goldberg Variations*— and arrange the scores on the piano on the off-chance that he might decide to get in his wheelchair and play. "It gave me hope," Urquhart remembered. "I sat with Lenny and held his hand. He was in his bed and that was the one thing I could do for him. . . . And when I went to say good-bye he said, 'Come back here and give me one more kiss,' and I knew that I would never see him again." When he reached home Urquhart wrote in his daily diary: "I loved holding Lenny's hand today, the slow peaceful process of passing on."

Aaron Stern came to supper that evening. Although Stern had no support- ers within the Amberson circle, Bernstein had always encouraged his educa- tional work; he went so far as to give Stern a public endorsement in an interview he did with Jonathan Cott in November 1989 for the magazine *Rolling Stone.* "I and a musical friend named Aaron Stern," he said, "have conceived of an institution called the Academy for the Love of Learning. We haven't done too much with the idea yet, but it's registered as a non-profit corporation, and besides the obvious attempts to get music and kids together, there will be the overriding goal of teaching teachers to discover their own love of learning." Nearly a year had passed since the interview. Cott's eight-thou- sand-word article had been read in proof by Bernstein, but *Rolling Stone,* which rarely did pieces on classical musicians, had twice postponed publication.

Bernstein's personal support for Stern had not waned: he had recently promised Stern the hundred-thousand-dollar check that accompanied the Praemium Imperiale he had been awarded in June by the Japan Art Associa- tion. During the summer Stern had been doing fieldwork with a dozen teachers in Nashville, using Bernstein's *Arias and Barcarolles* as a text for a series of workshops. Instead of analyzing the music the participants had been asked to explore their own inner feelings as they responded to Bernstein's songs. "You are the only person I can still learn from," Bernstein had told Stern: "What you did in Nashville this summer was 'it.' "

As Stern wheeled him down the corridor Bernstein defiantly grabbed an open pack of cigarettes from the table in the hall. They ate in the morning room with the oxygen machine as their only companion. Julia Vega had prepared one of their favorite dishes: matzoh ball soup. Bernstein's opening question shook Stern: "Is there anything else I can do to help prepare you for my death?" Stern was silent for a long time. He might have requested that he be formally placed in charge of all Bernstein's educational projects. Instead, what he said was, "I need to know that you know how much I love you." To which, Stern remembers, Bernstein replied after some reflection: "I can't say why or how, but yes I do know it. I believe it."

At the dinner table Stern read out loud a dozen poems by the thirteenth-century Persian mystic Jelaluddin Rumi, works dealing with death and the hereafter. He began with Rumi's last poem, in which the dying poet says good-bye to his son.

> *Go to your pillow and sleep, my son.*
> *Leave me alone in the passion*
> *of this death-night.*

Bernstein listened to Stern's mystic readings with eyes closed. Some of the time he was only half awake. Perhaps he was even a little bored. But occasionally he would open his eyes and say, as Aaron Copland had done fifty years previously when listening to one of Bernstein's early compositions, "Now that was fresh, that was good; let me hear that again."

They lingered over the meal and the readings for three hours. "Tell me the truth: do I look as if I'm getting better or worse?" Bernstein asked at one point. Stern said he appeared to be gaining strength. "I think about my life and there are so many stains," Bernstein said. Stern sensed his friend was troubled by the need to make some kind of confession. It emerged in a flurry: he had been relieved, even glad, he said, when Felicia died, because it gave him the freedom for which he had been longing. But ever since, he had felt guilty for having had such a feeling. Was he never to be rid of this guilt? Or of his other guilt, toward his fellow Jews? He was a fraud, he said, or he would have been able to write his Holocaust opera. "If I knew what I wanted to say I wouldn't be sitting here now."

When Stern wheeled Bernstein back to his study that evening, Mendy Wager took over watching him.

"I'm thinking about writing my eulogy," Bernstein had told Wager earlier in the week.

"What are you going to say?" Wager asked.

"Cut down in the prime of his youth . . ." came the sonorous reply.

"And after that?"

"That's up to you."

Wager helped Bernstein to take his many medications and later slipped into the studio to sleep himself. In the small hours of the night Phillip Allen was awakened in his attic bedroom at the top of the Dakota. A desperate Bernstein was on the telephone from his bed. "Help me," he gasped, "I can't breathe." Wager, asleep in the next room, had not heard his calls for help: perhaps Bernstein, in his semicomatose state, had not cried out but only thought he had. Allen raced down eight flights of stairs to find his master choking as he fought for breath. The canular tubes inserted into his nostrils had slipped out in his sleep and he had been too disoriented to replace them. Allen helped him to the bathroom and calmed him. "I don't want to die this way," Bernstein said as he prepared to sleep again.

A few hours later he had a second crisis of breathing. This time Wager was on hand to cope with it. He remembers Bernstein crying, "Please, please give me oblivion." In the morning Sean Cahill helped Bernstein to get his breath back after a third agonizing period of retching. Allen and Cahill wanted to get him into the hospital immediately but he was adamantly opposed to the idea. Soon he was feeling better, sitting up in bed, by turns smoking, gulping oxygen, and defiantly eating Patty Pulliam's homemade chocolate butter crunch.

Peace and quiet were essential after Bernstein's exceptionally disturbed night. Allen telephoned Mark Taylor and asked him to postpone his visit. All through the day Alexander Bernstein came in and out, keeping an eye on things. A game of chess was started and abandoned after ten minutes. Bernstein's sister Shirley visited, and he spoke to other members of his family at Fairfield, where his grandson was enjoying his first birthday. Charlie Harmon, Bernstein's devoted music editor, came by to see him. The composer Bright Sheng, who was busy revising his orchestration of *Arias and Barcarolles,* talked his way past the sentries and sat with Bernstein for part of the afternoon watching a "Live from Lincoln Center" telecast on Channel 13. Yo-Yo Ma was playing a Rachmaninov cello sonata with Jeffery Kahane. "Bernstein was humming along," Sheng reported; "he looked himself, was very much himself and we spoke about many things. He was lucid, even witty."

Betty Comden was another visitor. She sat on Bernstein's bed and they laughed together as they recalled "The Three Psychopaths," a Revuers' number about the famous movie villains of the 1930s. Bernstein was only a fan: he had never performed the song with the Revuers, but he remembered every line of the lyrics.

When he had examined Bernstein in the morning, Kevin Cahill had concluded that he was developing a bronchial infection. At around six o'clock in the afternoon he returned to Bernstein's bedside to give him an injection of antibiotics. Bernstein used the gadgetry of his chair to tilt himself into a nearly upright position. Then Michael Wager and Sean Cahill tried to lift him across to his bed. It was not easy to move him so Dr. Cahill told them he would administer the injection to Bernstein where he was, propped up between the two men at the side of the bed. He bared Bernstein's left flank and injected the needle. Before he could push the plunger home Bernstein's body suddenly stiffened. "What is this?" he asked, in an incredulous tone. Then he slumped in Wagner's arms, dead. It was 6:15 P.M. on Sunday, October 14.

Dr. Cahill gave the cause of death as a "heart attack brought on by progressive emphysema complicated by a pleural tumor and a series of pulmonary infections."

Alexander Bernstein was watching a ball game on television when Sean Cahill alerted him to his father's collapse. He rushed in and dropped to his knees. Phillip Allen, out shopping on Columbus Avenue when Tricia Andryszewsky beeped him to call in, ran back to the apartment and helped Sean Cahill to change his master's pajamas for the last time. Julia Vega picked out the pajamas from the drawer and, good Catholic that she was, spoke a blessing in Spanish. She also placed a small pillow under Bernstein's chin. Alexander and his aunt Shirley waited for the rest of the family to make their somber way to the Dakota from Evan's birthday party in Connecticut. Newly arrived from Europe, Harry Kraut was informed of the death when he called from his apartment to say that he was on his way over to visit. Cheated of the opportunity to say farewell to his beloved friend and chief, he began to break the sad news around the world. The men from the funeral home took the body away in a black bag, out through the kitchen and the Dakota's inconspicuous service entrance on Seventy-third Street.

Craig Urquhart had spent five years helping Bernstein choose clothes from his wardrobe. His last task, at Alexander Bernstein's request, was to decide on the clothes in which to bury him two days later. He laid out one of the formal dark suits Bernstein wore for the Vienna Philharmonic Sunday morning concerts, with his half-frame conducting glasses and a red silk handkerchief in the top pocket, and his Légion d'Honneur commander's insignia in the buttonhole. He chose Bernstein's favorite leather boots. A baton and the score of Mahler's Fifth Symphony were placed in the coffin alongside the body. In his pocket were a lucky penny and a piece of amber. The children added a copy of *Alice in Wonderland*. The funeral was held in his Dakota apartment. His grave is next to his wife's in the Green Wood cemetery in Brooklyn.

A tidal wave of emotion rocked the musical world following the announcement of his death. Press, radio, television, concert halls, schools, universities, synagogues, churches—all responded swiftly and significantly. Lincoln Center's flagpoles were draped in black. On Broadway the lights on the theater marquees were dimmed for a minute at eight o'clock on the evening of the sixteenth.

From the countless words written and spoken about Bernstein's creative life, perhaps those of his great collaborator Jerome Robbins best sum up the sense of grief: "Here in America, we have lost one of the most vital makers and shakers of the musical world. . . . The scope and dimension of all his interests and the diversity of all that musical energy is gigantic, almost superhuman, and it will be missed. . . . A hunk of our landscape has disappeared with Lenny's death."

Three memorial services took place in New York. The first, held exactly a month after Bernstein's death, was at Carnegie Hall on the forty-seventh anniversary of his debut there. Musicians from all "his" orchestras flew in to participate in the New York Philharmonic's tribute. The most poignant moment came when the international orchestra, led by Rainer Küchl of the Vienna Philharmonic, gave a conductorless performance of the *Candide* Overture. A month later, New York's theater community paid its own tribute, devised by Arthur Laurents, at the Majestic Theater. On New Year's Eve the annual peace concert at St. John the Divine was transformed into a third memorial, bringing together representatives of governments, universities and music festivals to celebrate Bernstein the teacher and humanist.

Leonard Bernstein wrote his own closing prayer in his *Kaddish* Symphony.

> *We have both grown older, You and I.*
> *And I am not sad, and You must not be sad.*
> *Unfurrow your brow; look tenderly again*
> *At me, at us, at all these children*
> *Of God here in this sacred house.*
> *And we shall look tenderly back to You.*
> *O my Father: Lord of Light:*
> *Beloved Majesty: my Image, my Self!*
> *We are one, after all, You and I;*
> *Together we suffer, together exist.*
> *And forever will recreate each other.*
> *Recreate, recreate each other!*
> *Suffer, and recreate each other!*

PHOTO DAN WEINER, COURTESY OF SONY CLASSICAL

# PRINCIPAL EVENTS IN THE
# LIFE OF LEONARD BERNSTEIN

1918   Born Lawrence, Massachusetts, August 25, first child of Samuel and Jennie Bernstein, both immigrants from czarist Russia. Childhood in Boston.

1928   First piano lessons, with Frieda Karp.

1929   Graduated William Lloyd Garrison Grammar School; entered Boston Latin School.

1930   Piano lessons with Susan Williams.

1931   Bar Mitzvah.

1932   First piano recital; piano studies with Helen Coates.

1934   First Sharon Players production, *Carmen.*

1935   Graduated from Boston Latin; freshman year at Harvard University; piano studies with Heinrich Gebhard.

1937   First professional appearance as a solo pianist with orchestra (Ravel piano concerto); first met Aaron Copland, Adolph Green and Dimitri Mitropoulos; conducted *The Pirates of Penzance* at Camp Onota, Pittsfield, Massachusetts.

1938   Music Editor, *Harvard Advocate.*

1939   Graduated from Harvard *cum laude* in music; composed and conducted score for *The Birds;* entered Curtis Institute, Philadelphia. Conducting studies under Fritz Reiner; piano studies with Isabelle Vengerova; orchestration with Randall Thompson; score-reading with Renée Longy Miquelle.

1940   Conducting studies under Serge Koussevitzky at Tanglewood summer school, known as the Berkshire Music Center.

1941   Graduated from Curtis Institute.

1942    Completed first published work, Sonata for Clarinet and Piano; assistant to Koussevitzky at Tanglewood; moved to New York; completed First Symphony, *Jeremiah*.

1943    Appointed assistant conductor New York Philharmonic by Artur Rodzinski; substituted for Bruno Walter at Carnegie Hall concert November 14.

1944    First performances of *Jeremiah, Fancy Free* and *On the Town;* guest-conducting engagements (Pittsburgh, Boston, Montreal, New York, Hollywood Bowl and elsewhere).

1945    Conducted ten major American orchestras; appointed music director, New York City Symphony Orchestra, 1945–47.

1946    First European conducting appearances in Prague and London; conducted U.S. premiere of Britten's *Peter Grimes;* first performance of *Facsimile;* first engagement to Felicia Montealegre Cohn (broken off in 1947).

1947    First visit to Israel; conducted in France, Belgium and Holland.

1948    Served as musical adviser, Israel Philharmonic Orchestra, 1948–49; conducted concert at Beersheba during War of Independence; first appearances as conductor in Munich, Budapest, Vienna, Milan and Rome.

1949    Piano soloist in first performance of his Second Symphony, *The Age of Anxiety,* conducted by Koussevitzky.

1950    Premiere of *Peter Pan.*

1951    Appointed head of conducting studies at Tanglewood, following the death of Koussevitzky; marriage to Felicia Montealegre Cohn.

1952    First performance of *Trouble in Tahiti;* birth of daughter Jamie; moved to the Osborne on West Fifty-seventh Street, New York City; artistic director, Festival of Creative Arts, Brandeis University.

1953    First performance of *Wonderful Town;* conducted *Medea* at La Scala, Milan.

1954    Scored the film *On the Waterfront;* first performance, in Venice, of *Serenade* (violin soloist, Isaac Stern); first television appearance on "Omnibus."

1955    Conducted Symphony of the Air season in New York; birth of son Alexander; first performance of *The Lark* in New York.

1956    Guest conductor, New York Philharmonic Orchestra; premiere of *Candide.*

1957    Joint principal conductor, New York Philharmonic, 1957–58; premiere of *West Side Story;* conducted inaugural concert of Frederic R. Mann Auditorium, Tel Aviv.

1958    Music director, New York Philharmonic, 1958–69; shared Latin-American tour with his predecessor, Dimitri Mitropoulos; conducted first of fourteen seasons of "Young People's Concerts."

1959    Toured Europe and Soviet Union with New York Philharmonic; first book, *The Joy of Music,* published; signed long-term contract with Columbia (later CBS) Records.

1960    Mounted Mahler centenary season with New York Philharmonic.

1961    Toured Japan with New York Philharmonic; film version of *West Side Story* released; moved to 895 Park Avenue, New York City.

1962    Birth of daughter Nina; conducted inaugural concert at Philharmonic Hall, Lincoln Center (later Avery Fisher Hall).

1963    Purchased "Springate," country residence at Fairfield, Connecticut; first performance of Third Symphony, *Kaddish,* in Tel Aviv.

1964    Sabbatical year from New York Philharmonic, 1964–65; conducted *Falstaff* at Metropolitan Opera.

1965    First performances of *Chichester Psalms* in New York and Chichester; commenced two-year survey of the twentieth-century symphonic music with New York Philharmonic.

1966    First engagements with the London Symphony Orchestra, the Vienna Philharmonic Orchestra and the Vienna State Opera (*Falstaff* ).

1967    Conducted concert on Mount Scopus to mark reunification of Jerusalem; completed Mahler symphony cycle for CBS.

1968    Conducted *Der Rosenkavalier* at Vienna State Opera; New York Philharmonic tour of Western Europe and Israel.

1969    Named lifetime Laureate Conductor on retirement from music directorship of New York Philharmonic Orchestra.

1970    Fund-raising meeting for Black Panthers held at Bernstein residence; conducted bicentennial production of Beethoven's *Fidelio* in Vienna; named artistic adviser, Tanglewood (1970–74).

1971    Signed first contract for music-performance films with Unitel; premiere *Mass,* inaugurating the Kennedy Center, Washington; conducted one thousandth performance with New York Philharmonic.

1972    Conducted *Carmen* at the Metropolitan Opera and recorded it for Deutsche Grammophon.

1973    Delivered six Charles Eliot Norton lectures, *The Unanswered Question,* at Harvard University; conducted for Pope Paul VI at the Vatican.

1974    First performance of *Dybbuk* ballet; led New York Philharmonic on tour of New Zealand, Australia and Japan; moved to the Dakota, New York City.

1975    First appearance with Vienna Philharmonic at the Salzburg Festival; first performance of *By Bernstein*—revue of hitherto unperformed Bernstein songs.

1976   Premiere of *1600 Pennsylvania Avenue;* trial separation from his wife; first fund-raising concert for Amnesty International.

1977   Leonard Bernstein festivals in Israel and Austria; reconciliation with Felicia Bernstein; first performance of *Songfest* and *Three Meditations from "Mass."*

1978   Death of Felicia Bernstein.

1979   Conducted Berlin Philharmonic Orchestra in Mahler's Ninth Symphony.

1980   First performance of *Divertimento,* commissioned by Boston Symphony Orchestra; received the Kennedy Center Honor for Lifetime of Contributions to American Culture Through the Performing Arts.

1981   Premiere of *Halil;* recorded *Tristan und Isolde* in Munich.

1982   Artistic director, Los Angeles Philharmonic Institute.

1983   Premiere of *A Quiet Place* at Houston Grand Opera.

1984   Revised *A Quiet Place* (incorporating *Trouble in Tahiti*) at La Scala, Milan; Deutsche Grammophon recording of *West Side Story;* marriage of daughter Jamie to David Evan Thomas.

1985   Journey for Peace to Hiroshima.

1986   Bernstein Festival at Barbican Centre, London, attended by Queen Elizabeth II; inaugurated Schleswig-Holstein Festival; first performance of *Jubilee Games,* commissioned by Israel Philharmonic Orchestra.

1987   Birth of granddaughter Francisca; inaugurated conducting classes at Salzau, Germany.

1988   First performance of *Arias and Barcarolles;* four-day seventieth-birthday celebration at Tanglewood.

1989   First performance of *Concerto for Orchestra* (expanded version of *Jubilee Games);* participated in "September 1, 1939," memorial concert in Warsaw; conducted and recorded *Candide* in London; led international celebrations in Berlin marking reunification of East and West Germany with Freedom Concert on Christmas Day.

1990   Inaugurated the Pacific Music Festival in Sapporo, Japan; last concert with Boston Symphony Orchestra at Tanglewood (August 19); died October 14 at 6:15 P.M. at his New York home.

# PRINCIPAL COMPOSITIONS
# OF LEONARD BERNSTEIN
## (WITH FIRST PERFORMANCE DATES)

1. ❧ WORKS FOR THE THEATER

*Fancy Free* (ballet), 1944

*On the Town* (musical), 1944

*Facsimile* (ballet), 1946

*Peter Pan* (songs, choruses, incidental music), 1950

*Trouble in Tahiti* (opera in one act), 1952

*Wonderful Town* (musical), 1953

*On the Waterfront* (film score), 1954

*Candide* (operetta), 1956

*West Side Story* (musical), 1957

*Mass: A Theatre Piece for Singers, Players and Dancers,* 1971

*Dybbuk* (ballet), 1974

*1600 Pennsylvania Avenue* (musical), 1976

*A Quiet Place* (opera in two acts), 1983 (the revised three-act version incorporating *Trouble in Tahiti,* 1984)

*The Race to Urga* (musical—workshop performances only), 1987

2. ❧ ORCHESTRAL WORKS FOR THE CONCERT HALL

*Jeremiah,* Symphony No. 1, 1944

*Fancy Free* and *Three Dance Variations from "Fancy Free,"* concert premiere 1946

*Three Dance Episodes from "On the Town,"* concert premiere 1946

*Facsimile,* concert premiere 1947

*The Age of Anxiety,* Symphony No. 2 (after W. H. Auden) for Piano and Orchestra, 1949, revised 1965

*Serenade* (after Plato's "Symposium") for Solo Violin, Strings, Harp and Percussion, 1954

*Prelude, Fugue and Riffs* for Solo Clarinet and Jazz Ensemble, completed 1949, premiere 1955

*Symphonic Suite from "On the Waterfront,"* 1955

*Symphonic Dances from "West Side Story"* 1961

*Kaddish,* Symphony No. 3, for Orchestra, Mixed Chorus, Boys' Choir, Speaker and Soprano Solo, 1963, revised 1977

*Chichester Psalms* for Mixed Choir, Boy Soloist and Orchestra 1965 [Bernstein preferred boys' voices for the soprano and alto lines]

*Dybbuk,* Suites No. 1 and No. 2 for Orchestra, concert premieres 1975

*Songfest: A Cycle of American Poems for Six Singers and Orchestra,* 1977

*Three Meditations from "Mass"* for Violoncello and Orchestra 1977

*Divertimento for Orchestra* 1980

*Halil,* Nocturne for Solo Flute, Piccolo, Alto Flute, Percussion, Harp and Strings, 1981

*Concerto for Orchestra,* 1989 (incorporates the two-movement *Jubilee Games* of 1986 the *Opening Prayer* of 1986 and the *Variations on an Octatonic Theme* of 1989)


3. ⟡ CHORAL MUSIC FOR CHURCH OR SYNAGOGUE

*Hashkiveinu* for Solo Tenor, Mixed Chorus and Organ 1945

*Missa Brevis* for Mixed Chorus and Countertenor Solo (or septet of solo voices), with percussion, including handbells, 1988; adapted from the incidental music to *The Lark,* 1955


4. ⟡ CHAMBER MUSIC

Sonata for Clarinet and Piano, 1942

Brass Music (five pieces for horn, trumpet, trombone, tuba and piano), 1959


5. ⟡ VOCAL MUSIC

*I Hate Music: A Cycle of Five Kid Songs for Soprano and Piano,* 1943

*La Bonne Cuisine: Four Recipes for Voice and Piano,* 1948

*Arias and Barcarolles* for Mezzo-Soprano, Baritone and Piano Four Hands, 1988

*A Song Album,* 1988 (includes individual songs not published elsewhere, as well as the two early cycles and single songs from *Peter Pan, Candide, Mass* and *1600 Pennsylvania Avenue)*

## 6. ∽ PIANO MUSIC

*Seven Anniversaries*, 1944

*Four Anniversaries*, 1948

*Five Anniversaries*, 1965

*Thirteen Anniversaries*, 1988

*Touches: Chorale, Eight Variations and Coda*, 1981 (test piece for the 1981 Van Cliburn International Piano Competition)

## 7. ∽ MISCELLANEOUS

Leonard Bernstein wrote numerous occasional works, including fanfares, choruses, songs and piano pieces. They served as birthday and wedding presents, and other forms of memorial and tribute.

## 8. ∽ BOOKS

*The Joy of Music*, 1959; now in print from Anchor Books, 1994

*Leonard Bernstein's Young People's Concerts*, 1962; now in print from Anchor Books, 1992

*The Infinite Variety of Music*, 1966; now in print from Anchor Books, 1993

*The Unanswered Question*, 1976; Harvard University Press

*Findings*, 1982; now in print from Anchor Books, 1993

# NOTES TO SOURCES

THE page number is followed by the first few words of the reference. Within the page, references are given in order.

Full details of books from which quotations are taken are included in the Selected Bibliography.

All letters quoted are from the Bernstein Archive unless otherwise stated.

Letters which are dated only by month were not dated by the correspondents and have been assigned a date by the author, based on other biographical information.

Quotations from the Bernstein Archive Oral History interviews are identified by the initials O.H. Other interviews and archives consulted are listed in the Additional Sources section of the Selected Bibliography.

Leonard Bernstein is identified throughout as LB. After her marriage, Felicia Montealegre becomes FMB.

PART ONE
CHAPTER 1—BEGINNINGS

3  she remembered the clock . . . Telephone conversation with Mrs. Jennie Bernstein.

4  "There was always music . . ." Jennie Bernstein, O.H.

5  *Family Matters* . . . Burton Bernstein, *Family Matters: Sam, Jennie and the Kids.* This portrait of the Bernstein family (essential reading) first appeared in *The New Yorker.*

6  "He always had a good story . . ." Jennie Bernstein, O.H.

6  Dorothy would spy . . . Dorothy Resnick, author's interview.

6  Pearl had forgotten . . . Shirley Bernstein, author's interview.

8  "by a glorious teacher . . ." BBC-TV/Unitel, *Childhood.*

8  "Everything they taught me . . ." Speech at fund-raiser for St. Augustine's School, New York, December 4, 1986.

8  "With any luck . . ." BBC-TV/Unitel, *Childhood.*

8  "We were of the Conservative persuasion . . ." Ibid.

10  "It all had to be ticketyboo . . ." Jennie Bernstein, O.H.

10  "The piano . . ." BBC-TV/Unitel, *Childhood.*

11  "They'd always have . . ." Jennie Bernstein, O.H.

12  "I loved all music . . ." BBC-TV/Unitel, *Childhood.*

## CHAPTER 2—FAMILY LIFE

13 "It was the biggest trip . . ." BBC-TV/ Unitel, *Childhood*.

14 "lapping up everything . . ." Letter, 1960, Philip Marson to LB.

14 "Mind if I try?" Sid Ramin, O.H.

15 The very approximate English . . . Burton Bernstein, *Family Matters*.

16 "We were all having breakfast . . ." Shirley Bernstein, O.H.

16 "He has one fault . . ." LB speech to Amer-

ica Israel Cultural Foundation, reprinted in *Findings*, "The Whole Megillah."

17 "His concept . . ." LB interview with Paul Hume for Kennedy Center Archive, 1981.

17 "I began giving lessons . . ." BBC-TV/ Unitel, *Childhood*.

17 "I guess . . ." Ibid.

18 best all-around camper . . . Refers to Camp Iona in New Hampshire.

## CHAPTER 3—THE PROVINCIAL BOY GROWS UP: 1932–1935

20 "I had never experienced . . ." BBC-TV/ Unitel, *Childhood*.

20 "He came after school . . ." Mildred Spiegel Zucker, O.H.

21 "There's enough noise . . ." Shirley Bernstein, O.H.

21 "He'd be all the guys . . ." Ibid.

21 On the weekends . . . Burton Bernstein, *Family Matters*.

21 "June 26 '33 I bought Bolero!!!" LB letter courtesy of Sid Ramin.

22 "inexpensive but rather satisfying" LB to Helen Coates, June 1933.

22 "Now even the pedal . . ." LB to Helen Coates, September 1933.

22 "Together we wrote . . ." BBC-TV/Unitel, *Childhood*.

23 "It all took place . . ." Ibid.

23 "My summer has so far . . ." LB to Helen Coates, July 13, 1935.

23 "always center . . ." Victor Alpert, O.H.

23 "Strewn around . . ." Shirley Bernstein, *Making Music: Leonard Bernstein*. Shirley Bernstein's entertaining biography of her brother was published in 1963.

24 "They all laughed . . ." Jennie Bernstein, O.H.

24 "For that seventy-five cents . . ." Shirley Bernstein, O.H.

24 "He had to find . . ." Shirley Bernstein, O.H.

25 Gebhard's fee . . . Mildred Spiegel Zucker, O.H.

25 "She taught me . . ." LB speech at Pine Manor College, 1987.

26 "I certainly do appreciate . . ." Sam Bernstein to Helen Coates, June 24, 1933.

26 "I can't seem to practice . . ." LB to Helen Coates, June 1933.

26 Burton remembers . . . Burton Bernstein, *Family Matters*.

27 . . . standing ovation . . . (for Koussevitzky), Mildred Spiegel Zucker. This reminiscence was first supplied in 1978 in connection with an LB sixtieth-birthday memoir. Apropos jealousy, LB scribbled on the margin of the document: "Doesn't sound like me." But Mrs. Zucker confirmed the anecdote in 1991.

27 "The neighbors . . ." Jennie Bernstein, O.H.

27 "Your letter of July 16th . . ." Sam Bernstein to Helen Coates, July 24, 1934.

28 "There stands ready . . ." School essay in the Bernstein Archive, n.d.

28 "Most people have experienced . . ." School essay in the Bernstein Archive, October 22, 1934.

29 "There were a couple of people . . ." Robert Lubell, O.H.

30 "Oh my lover—" Lines by LB, copy courtesy of Barbara Firger, niece of Beatrice Gordon.

30 "a dream of a girl . . ." Shirley Bernstein, O.H.

30 "I know how interested . . ." LB to Helen Coates, July 13, 1935.

30 "Great God . . ." LB to Mildred Spiegel, July 1935.

31  The class song . . ." BBC-TV/Unitel, *Childhood*.

31  "With the fine recommendations . . ." LB to Helen Coates, August 1935.

## CHAPTER 4—HARVARD

33  "You could not study . . ." BBC-TV/Unitel, *Childhood*. All Bernstein quotes in this chapter are from that source.

34  "We would sit . . ." LB's introduction to *The Art of Pedaling* by Heinrich Gebhard.

34  "Lenny had a natural inclination . . ." Mildred Spiegel Zucker, O.H.

35  ". . . hair-raising fairy story . . ." LB to Beatrice Gordon, January 30, 1937.

36  "had gone bananas" LB speech at Mitropoulos benefit, New York, December 2, 1979.

36  *The Occult* published in *Findings*.

38  "We had a great time . . ." Mildred Spiegel Zucker, O.H.

38  "A sallow, bloated . . ." Adolph Green to LB, August 1968, courtesy Adolph Green.

39  "When Lenny invited . . ." Burton Bernstein, *Family Matters*.

## CHAPTER 5—BROADER HORIZONS

40  "I envisaged the composer . . ." BBC-TV/Unitel, *Childhood*.

41  ". . . with an authority . . ." *Christian Science Monitor,* November 1, 1937.

41  ". . . assurance and a considerable technique . . ." *Boston Herald,* November 1, 1937.

41  *"Battleship Potemkin* rode at anchor . . ." Irving Fine, *Modern Music,* Vol. XXII, No. 4, 1945.

41  "A new world of music . . ." This account combines sentences from *Findings* and BBC-TV/Unitel, *Childhood*.

41  "We found ourselves . . ." Account taken largely from Vivian Perlis, *Aaron Copland: 1900–1942*.

42  ". . . by their very simplicity . . ." Virgil Thomson, *American Music Since 1910*.

43  "a young violinist . . ." Perlis, *Aaron Copland: 1900–1942*.

43  ". . . writing a violin sonata . . ." *Findings,* "Aaron Copland at 70."

43  "I remember we went back . . ." William Schuman, O.H.

44  ". . . opened brilliantly . . ." *Harvard Advocate,* March 1938.

45  "Dear Leonard . . ." Aaron Copland to LB, March 1938.

45  "He recalled sadly . . ." *Findings, The Occult.*

45  "My dear, dear boy . . ." Dimitri Mitropoulos to LB, February 5, 1938.

45  "I've always felt . . ." Dimitri Mitropoulos, *A Correspondence with Katy Katsoyanis.*

45  "All my life . . ." Dimitri Mitropoulos to LB, February 5, 1938.

46  "Yes, you are right . . ." Dimitri Mitropoulos to LB, May 4, 1938.

46  "Your picture is so good . . ." Dimitri Mitropoulos to LB, June 7, 1938.

46  "There is, behind the soul . . ." Dimitri Mitropoulos to LB, November 8, 1938.

46  "I am very happy . . ." Dimitri Mitropoulos to LB, February 8, 1939.

47  "I never graded students . . ." Arthur Tillman Merritt, O.H.

47  "Lenny didn't come . . ." Harold Shapero, O.H.

48  "a morose but willing widow . . ." Unpublished Bernstein essay, Bernstein Archive.

48  "California is all . . ." LB to Helen Coates, September 10, 1938.

48  "Lenny told the kid . . ." Letter to the author from Kenneth Ehrman.

49  "met a wonderful girl. . . ." LB to Kenneth Ehrman, April 10, 1939.

49  "It's getting to be hard . . ." LB to Aaron Copland, October 1938.

49  "Of course come to N.Y. . . ." Aaron Copland to LB, October 1938.

50  "not a first-rate genius . . ." BBC-TV/Unitel, *Childhood*.

50  "Faced with the impossibility . . ." Shirley Bernstein, *Making Music.* The opening sentence of the essay established her brother's knockabout style: "In 1848, the cat was out of the bag in Europe."

50  "The Absorption of Race Elements into American Music" published in *Findings*.

50  "The thesis tries to show . . ." LB to Aaron Copland, November 19, 1938.

51  Copland replied . . . Aaron Copland to LB, December 1938.

51  "I thoroughly disapprove . . ." Note on Bernstein thesis dated May 2, 1939.

51  "Maybe a job . . ." LB to Kenneth Ehrman, April 10, 1939.

52  "seduced my soul" *Findings*, "Tribute to Marc Blitzstein."

53  ". . . Without any highbrow premise . . ." Alistair Cooke, NBC Radio 12, January 1938.

53  ". . . operatic socialism . . ." Virgil Thomson in *Modern Music*. This and preceding review quoted in Eric Gordon, *Mark the Music*.

53  "I met his plane" *Findings*, "Tribute to Marc Blitzstein."

53  ". . . the most talented . . ." *Boston Post*, May 27, 1938.

54  "I made it fairly clear . . ." Marc Blitzstein to LB, June 2, 1939, Eric Gordon, *Mark the Music*.

CHAPTER 6—NEW YORK, NEW YORK!

56  ". . . But I'd much rather . . ." LB to Aaron Copland, April 1939.

56  "Aaron—Patiently . . ." LB to Aaron Copland, June 1939.

57  "I went to a party . . ." Adolph Green, O.H.

57  "violent complaints . . ." LB to Helen Coates, July 1939.

58  "all planned for me . . ." LB to Helen Coates, July 19, 1939.

58  "I really feel . . ." Helen Coates to LB, July 1939.

58  "very handsome and mercurial . . ." Betty Comden, O.H.

58  "Life on the world front . . ." LB to Helen Coates, July 19, 1939.

59  "Harris was very nice . . ." LB to Aaron Copland, August 1939.

59  "I can remember . . ." Vivian Perlis, *Aaron Copland, 1900–1942*.

60  "And there stood . . ." "Young People's Concert," quoted in *Findings*, "In Praise of Teachers," 1964.

60  "I've just finished my Hebrew song . . ." LB to Aaron Copland, August 29, 1939.

61  "It is the best thing . . ." Aaron Copland to LB, September 1939.

CHAPTER 7—THE CURTIS INSTITUTE: 1939–1940

64  "our little Jewish wonder" Author's interview with LB.

64  "It looks like . . ." LB to Helen Coates, October 17, 1939.

65  "accepted Mitropoulos's offer . . ." Ibid.

65  "I feel happy . . ." Dimitri Mitropoulos to LB, October 17, 1939.

65  "Speaking on Thursday . . ." LB to Helen Coates, October 17, 1939.

65  "She would have a heart attack . . ." Lukas Foss, O.H.

65  "She stopped me . . ." Unitel, *Teachers and Teaching*.

66  " 'Doesn't it say *piano*?' " Ibid.

66  "I was mistaken . . ." LB to Helen Coates, November 7, 1939.

66  "Give it up!" Lukas Foss, O.H.

67  "a Harvard smart aleck . . ." *Findings*, "Memories of the Curtis Institute."

67  "They got along famously" Phyllis Moss, O.H. After his retirement from Curtis, Stöhr fell on hard times. Bernstein sent him a check for five hundred dollars every year.

68  "refined" heterosexual love . . . Bernstein revealed this episode to his Austrian friend Peter Weiser.

68  "We called him Leonardo da Vinci . . ." Janice Levit, O.H.

68  "I remember taking walks . . ." Phyllis Moss, O.H.

68  Lukas Foss remembers . . . Lukas Foss, O.H.

69  "Don't be too hard . . ." LB to Helen Coates, February 15, 1940.

69  "Marc Blitzstein reports . . ." Aaron Copland to LB, March 1940.

69  "I must meet you . . ." Dimitri Mitropoulos to LB, December 22, 1939.

69 "Dear Folks . . ." LB to his parents, January 1940.

70 "Today has been horrible . . ." LB to David Diamond, April 23, 1940.

71 "He's no false promiser" LB to David Diamond, spring 1940.

71 "certainly the most glorious thing . . ." LB to Helen Coates, April 16, 1940.

72 "a clever musical satire . . ." Quoted on record sleeve, Bernstein Archive.

## CHAPTER 8—TANGLEWOOD: 1940

75 "So long as art and culture exist . . ." Quoted in Vivian Perlis, *Aaron Copland, 1900–1942.*

76 "Between one beat . . ." Unitel, *Teachers and Teaching.*

77 "Koussevitzky pleaded . . ." Ibid.

77 "Dearest Folks . . ." LB to his parents, July 11, 1940.

77 "He seems to like me . . ." LB to Helen Coates, July 26, 1940.

78 "I don't think we ever slept" *Findings,* "For S.A.K."

78 Seranak . . . The name was created from the letters SERge Alexandrovich NAtalie Koussevitzky.

79 "he taught the essence . . ." Ibid.

79 "possessed by music . . ." *Findings,* "On Tanglewood, Koussevitzky and Hope."

79 " 'The Central Line' . . ." Ibid.

79 *"The composer comes first" Findings,* "Varèse, Koussevitzky and New Music."

80 ". . . had his share of vanity . . ." Ibid.

80 "When Koussevitzky stepped out . . ." *Findings,* "Letter to Olga Koussevitzky."

80 "You must conduct your lives . . ." *Time,* August 18, 1941.

80 "Not forgetting the trombones" Moses Smith, *Koussevitzky.*

80 "This summer to me . . ." LB to Serge Koussevitzky, August 1940.

81 "Please don't think . . ." LB to Serge Koussevitzky, September 30, 1940.

81 "There has been a terrific tumult . . ." LB to Helen Coates, October 16, 1940.

82 "I've finished the Fiddle Sonata . . ." LB to Aaron Copland, September 1940.

82 "Not seeing you . . ." LB to Aaron Copland, n.d. 1940.

82 "We took the same girl . . ." Harold Shapero, O.H.

## CHAPTER 9—FINISHING TOUCHES

84 "Be archi-particular . . ." Aaron Copland to LB, November 1940.

84 "The piece came . . ." Aaron Copland to LB, December 1940.

85 "Look especially . . ." LB to Aaron Copland, December 10, 1940.

85 "Lenny was at the counter . . ." Shirley Gabis Perle, O.H. All Shirley Gabis quotes in this chapter are from the O.H.

87 "I was called in . . ." LB to Helen Coates, November 11, 1940.

87 "La vie est . . ." LB to Aaron Copland, Undated postcard December 1940.

88 "Mother and I . . ." Helen Coates to LB, December 8, 1940.

88 "Eat *sensibly* . . ." Helen Coates to LB, October 20, 1940.

88 "The phenomenon of music on the brain . . ." LB to Aaron Copland, December 1940.

89 "secret anti-Bernstein club . . ." *Findings,* "Memories of the Curtis Institute."

89 "What's that . . ." Theodor Uppman, author's interview.

89 "It would be a kind of paraphrase . . ." LB to Aaron Copland, March 1941.

89 "Has it ever occurred . . ." Aaron Copland to LB, March 1941.

89 "Judging by your remarks . . ." Benjamin Britten to LB, April 20, 1941.

90 *"Bravo!—a thousand times! . . ."* Helen Coates to LB, April 26, 1941.

91 "Life, dear one . . ." LB to Shirley Gabis, May 1941.

CHAPTER 10—TANGLEWOOD REVISITED: JUNE 1941–AUGUST 1942

92  "We all thought . . ." Harry Ellis Dickson, O.H.

93  "These two weeks . . ." LB to Mildred Spiegel, July 1941.

94  the story goes . . . Steven Ledbetter, ed., *Sennets and Tuckets,* "First Summer" by Andrew L. Pincus. Nineteen forty-one was in fact the second summer.

94  "I started playing . . ." Carlos Moseley, O.H.

94  "A vapse his bit me!" Barbara Erde Mandell, ed., *Tanglewood Remembered—1941.*

95  "Again it is my privilege . . ." LB to Serge Koussevitzky, August 1941.

95  "to get away from people . . ." LB to Aaron Copland, November 3, 1941.

95  "Key West for a rest . . ." LB to Shirley Gabis, August 28, 1941.

96  "I confessed all . . ." LB to Aaron Copland, November 1941.

96  "I don't mean this . . ." LB to Aaron Copland, March 1942.

97  "Lenny knew that symphony . . ." William Schuman, O.H.

97  "I remember the times . . ." Helen Coates to LB, December 1, 1940.

98  "Things progress apace . . ." LB to Aaron Copland, May 1942.

99  "You write 'em, kid, and I'll do 'em." An echo of a 1942 War Defense Bond slogan: "You buy 'em—we'll fly 'em."

99  "It was wonderful . . ." LB to Aaron Copland, June 20, 1942.

99  "It was marvellous . . ." Aaron Copland to LB, June 23, 1942.

99  "Both of us . . ." Mandell, ed., *Tanglewood Remembered—1942.*

100  "We have had . . ." LB to Aaron Copland, August 1942.

CHAPTER 11—THE NEW YORK BOHEMIAN

101  "I keep being . . ." Aaron Copland to LB, May 6, 1943.

102  "You're asthmatic . . ." Aaron Copland to LB, January 1943.

102  "Me voici in NYC" LB to Aaron Copland, August 31, 1942.

102  "I'm writing a piece called 'Victory Jive' . . ." LB to Aaron Copland, September 1, 1942.

102  "You sound so Newyorky" Aaron Copland to LB, September 2, 1942.

102  "His *forte* is conducting . . ." Aaron Copland to André Kostelanetz, September 1942.

103  "because he learned . . ." Harold Shapero, O.H.

103  "These are certainly . . ." LB to Olga Naumoff, Koussevitzky's secretary (the niece of Natalie Koussevitzky), November 1942. Olga married Koussevitzky after the war.

103  . . . were never lovers . . . Edys Merrill Hunter, O.H.

104  "a little on the Copland side" LB to Aaron Copland, March 14, 1943.

104  "I want," thundered Copland . . . Aaron Copland to LB, March 25, 1943.

104  "I came to New York . . ." Shirley Bernstein, *Making Music,* p. 60.

104  "great success" . . . LB to Helen Coates, enclosing reviews, February 19, 1943.

105  "It's all very nice . . ." Lukas Foss, O.H.

105  "get drunk . . ." Ned Rorem, O.H.

105  "I felt the need . . ." LB to Aaron Copland, March 14, 1943.

105  "It's still full . . ." Aaron Copland to LB, March 25, 1943.

105  "tender, sharp, singing . . ." *Herald Tribune,* March 15, 1943.

106  "superb and musicianly . . ." *Herald Tribune,* April 1, 1943.

106  Bowles "had a genuine gift . . ." LB to Lawrence Shifreen, University of Maryland, March 25, 1977.

106  "Please let me know . . ." Artur Rodzinski to LB, March 10, 1943.

106  "I am very glad . . ." Artur Rodzinski to LB, April 7, 1943. Both letters by courtesy of New York Philharmonic Archive and Richard Rodzinski.

107  "he wants to do my Symphony . . ." LB to Aaron Copland, June 1943.

107 "I know you want me . . ." Aaron Copland to LB, July 3, 1943.

107 "He asked me up . . ." LB to Aaron Copland, July 1943.

107 "Kouss. went *overboard* . . ." LB to Aaron Copland, August 2, 1943.

107 "I wish to draw . . ." Serge Koussevitzky to U.S. Army Medical Examiner, August 27, 1943.

108 "I don't usually go in . . ." LB to Aaron Copland, July 1943.

### CHAPTER 12—OVERNIGHT SENSATION

110 "I am going to need . . ." *Reflections,* USIA.

111 "Mexico in September . . ." LB to Aaron Copland, July 1943.

111 "In the evenings . . ." Halina Rodzinski, *Our Two Lives.*

111 "It's one of those . . ." Aaron Copland to LB, September 15, 1943.

112 "Dear Serge Alexandrovich . . ." LB to Koussevitzky, September 1943.

113 "It was a one-room affair . . ." LB unpublished interview about Carnegie Hall with Burton Bernstein, 1989, Bernstein Archive.

113 "This publicity business . . ." LB to Helen Coates, October 1943.

113 "Sometimes I had a chance . . ." Burton Bernstein interview, 1989, Bernstein Archive.

114 "Call Bernstein . . ." Rodzinski, *Our Two Lives.*

114 "The best recital . . ." *Herald Tribune,* November 15, 1943.

114 "Lenny and Jennie . . ." Friede Rothe, O.H.

115 "Well this is it" *Reflections.*

115 "He showed me . . ." Burton Bernstein interview, 1989, Bernstein Archive.

115 *"Oy gevalt"* Burton Bernstein, *Family Matters.*

115 "He gave me two little pills . . ." BBC-TV/ Unitel, *The Love of Three Orchestras.*

116 "I flung them . . ." Burton Bernstein interview, 1989.

116 "the house waved . . ." Burton Bernstein, *Family Matters.*

117 "LISTENING NOW . . ." Bernstein Archive.

117 "I feel completely exhausted . . ." *New York World-Telegram,* November 15, 1943.

117 "all aglow . . ." *Reflections,* USIA.

117 "YOUNG AIDE LEADS PHILHARMONIC" *New York Times,* November 15, 1943.

117 "some of the flares . . ." *New York Sun,* November 15, 1943.

117 "Mr. Bernstein had to have . . ." *New York Times,* November 16, 1943.

117 "an opportunity like a shoe-string catch . . ." *New York Daily News,* November 15, 1943.

### PART TWO
### CHAPTER 13—THE *JEREMIAH* SYMPHONY AND *FANCY FREE*

122 "occasionally slips out . . ." *New York Post,* November 16, 1943.

122 "Do you know the biggest paper . . ." *The New Yorker,* November 27, 1943.

122 "How could I know . . ." Burton Bernstein, *Family Matters.*

122 "Lenny dear . . ." Jennie Bernstein to LB, November 24, 1943.

122 "His rhythmic understanding . . ." *Herald Tribune,* December 14, 1943.

123 "How can I be blind . . ." *New York Journal-American,* November 20, 1943.

123 "I am excited . . ." LB to Serge Koussevitzky, January 27, 1944.

124 Mrs. Rodzinski conceded . . . Halina Rodzinski, O.H.

124 "It is not a masterpiece . . ." *Herald Tribune,* February 19, 1944.

124 "Congratulations . . ." Possibly this telegram was invented by Bernstein. He spoke about it to John Gruen in *The Private World of Leonard Bernstein,* but there is no copy in the Bernstein Archive. An interview in *Cue,* December 1943, mentions a plan for the Philharmonic to perform *Jeremiah* in February 1944. But the reporter may have mixed up the cities.

125 "It outranks . . ." *Herald Tribune,* March 30, 1944.

125 "As for programmatic meanings . . ." Program book, Pittsburgh Symphony Orchestra, January 28, 1944.

125 deriving from synagogue melodies *Musical Quarterly,* April 1980.

126 "Solid symphony" Reported in the *Boston Herald,* May 12, 1944.

126 "Funny you should ask that . . ." Burton Bernstein, Carnegie Hall interview, 1989.

127 "The curtain rises . . ." New York City Symphony Orchestra program note January 1946.

127 "improvised and composed . . ." Tobi To-

bias, "Bringing back Robbins's *Fancy Free"* *Dancemagazine,* January 1980.

127 "We got down . . ." Betty Comden, O.H.

128 "It was not planned . . ." *Christian Science Monitor,* May 13, 1954.

128 "Just exactly ten degrees . . ." *New York Times,* April 19, 1944.

128 "Besides being a smash hit . . ." *Herald Tribune,* April 19, 1947.

128 "Fast and fabulous . . ." *Cue,* May 1944.

128 "acrobatic, a specialty rhumba . . ." *Time,* May 23, 1944.

128 "Fun? I'll say!" LB to Aaron Copland, April 1944.

CHAPTER 14—*ON THE TOWN*

129 "Even in his earliest . . ." Oliver Smith, O.H.

130 "The main thing was . . ." *New York Times,* January 8, 1945.

131 On June 13 . . . "Lyon's Den," *New York Post.*

131 "The floor nurses . . ." Shirley Bernstein, *Making Music.*

131 ". . . God's gift . . ." "A Silhouette of Leonard Bernstein," by John Richmond, *Tomorrow,* March 19, 1945.

131 ". . . I'm Napoleon . . ." Shirley Bernstein, O.H.

131 "I noticed Lenny . . ." Halina Rodzinski, *Our Two Lives.*

131 "Hollywood is exactly . . ." LB to Aaron Copland, August 16, 1944.

132 "Just think . . ." Aaron Copland to LB, August 25, 1944.

132 "My birthday . . ." LB to Helen Coates, August 25, 1944. The *Hollywood Citizen* wrote (August 27) that Oscar Levant played with "the tinny superficiality of the average café pianist."

132 "semi-performances" *New York Times,* January 8, 1945.

132 "I like the smell . . ." Oliver Smith, O.H.

133 "The show is a wild monster . . ." LB to Aaron Copland, September 1944.

133 "He took my second act . . ." Quoted in Dramatists Guild Round Table Series, Landmark Hits, Summer 1981, *On the Town.*

133 "a little polka-like cowboy tune" Ibid.

133 "My name is Jerome Robbins . . ." Allyn Ann McLerie, O.H.

134 "Sit down and write . . ." *Parkersburg* (Virginia) *News,* November 1944.

134 "T. S. Eliot" Shirley Bernstein, O.H.

134 "potentially the first . . ." *Boston Herald,* November 25, 1944.

134 "Backstage . . ." Sono Osato, *Distant Dances.*

135 "an energetic blend . . ." *Christian Science Monitor,* December 16, 1944.

135 "A little ornate . . ." *Boston Post,* December 16, 1944.

135 "could develop . . ." *Variety,* December 20, 1944.

135 Two nights before . . . *New York Times,* January 8, 1945.

135 Associated Press . . . Reviews of *On the Town* in New York, December 29, 1944.

136 "an epoch-making score . . ." *Herald Tribune,* June 24, 1945.

136 "that dance should . . ." Program book, San Francisco Symphony Orchestra, February 12, 1946.

136 "In another important sense . . ." Dramatists Guild Round Table, 1981.

136 "He was furious with me . . ." *P.M.,* December 27, 1944.

## CHAPTER 15—THE FIRST AMERICAN CONDUCTOR GETS HIS FIRST ORCHESTRA

138 "I think of you . . ." LB to Serge Koussevitzky, February 1946.

139 "I'll play the Grieg . . ." Arthur Rubinstein, *My Many Years.*

140 "No other composer . . ." *Herald Tribune,* March 29, 1945.

140 "I have been collecting . . ." LB to Helen Coates, April 30, 1945.

141 "It looks as if . . ." LB to Helen Coates, June 1, 1945.

141 "Mexico ist schain!" LB to Aaron Copland, June 8, 1945.

141 "a pair of very effete . . ." Tennessee Williams, *Memoirs.*

142 "a lovely pool . . ." LB to his family ("Dearest folks"), June 1945. The original was pasted into Sam's 1945 scrapbook.

142 "a confused young man . . ." *San Francisco Sun,* June 1945.

142 "Most of the study time . . ." Shirley Bernstein, *Making Music.*

143 "We're getting together . . ." *P.M.,* September 26, 1945.

144 It was a fine achievement . . . A list of the New York City Symphony programs, 1945–47, is held in the Bernstein Archive.

144 "For vividness . . ." *New York Times,* October 9, 1945.

## CHAPTER 16—FINDING HIS WAY

147 "Felicia was built like a boy" Friede Rothe, O.H.

147 "This is a heavenly evening" LB to Helen Coates, February 9, 1946.

147 "The rehearsal today . . ." LB to Helen Coates, February 16, 1946.

148 "And are they celebrating . . ." LB to Helen Coates, May 9, 1946.

149 "Frankly speaking . . ." François Valéry to Charlie Harmon (former Bernstein archivist), March 18, 1991. "Lenny's royal generosity will never be forgotten," M. Valéry added in a letter to the author, October, 1993.

149 "miserable 'Ford-Hour' type . . ." LB to Aaron Copland, June 9, 1946.

149 "I have rarely felt . . ." LB to Shirley Bernstein, June 9, 1946.

150 "He gave vivid performances . . ." *The Times* (London), June 17, 1946. Bernstein appears to have conducted the first London concert of Wagner's music since the outbreak of World War II.

150 "I was one of the first . . ." USIA, *Reflections.*

150 "A great experience . . ." LB to Serge Koussevitzky, June 22, 1946. Koussevitzky had studied under Nikisch as a young man.

152 a Broadway play . . . *Swan Song* by Ben Hecht and Charles McArthur. It opened in May 1946 and Felicia Montealegre took over the leading role in June. Both Burton Bernstein and Eric Gordon (biographer of Marc Blitzstein) may be confusing 1946 with 1947, when Felicia was more frequently at Tanglewood.

152 The dashing Burtie . . . Author's interview with Burton Bernstein, February 20, 1992.

152 "There's no use pretending . . ." *Time,* August 19, 1946.

152 "a drain on the attention . . ." *New York Sun,* August 7, 1946.

152 "thrilled to death . . ." Phyllis Curtin, O.H.

152 "I hope you know . . ." Sarah Caldwell, O.H.

153 Aldeburgh Festival . . . Bernstein was, however, approached by Peter Pears in the mid 1970s, after Bernstein had conducted Britten's *A Time There Was* with the New York Philharmonic.

153 "The inspiration . . ." LB letter to Helen Coates, December 9, 1946, included this draft.

153 "To a frantic score . . ." *Time,* November 4, 1946.

153 ". . . four smash comedy hits . . ." *Fancy Free, Interplay, On the Town,* and *Billion Dollar Baby.* Robbins was involved in a creative struggle every bit as intense as Bernstein's.

154 "My last talk . . ." Serge Koussevitzky to LB, December 1946.

154 "Dear Serge Alexandrovich . . ." LB to Serge Koussevitzky, December 27, 1946.

155 "A real debut vehicle . . ." LB to Helen Coates, December 7, 1946.

156   "It involves score . . ." LB to Aaron Copland, December 1946.

156   "I'm intrigued . . ." Aaron Copland to LB, December 1946.

156   "Felicia is wonderful . . ." LB to Helen Coates, December 7, 1946.

156   "She's an angel . . ." LB to Helen Coates, December 12, 1946.

156   "I'm toying with the idea . . ." LB to Helen Coates, December 22, 1946.

156   "It was the most wonderful news . . ." Sam Bernstein to LB, December 1946.

157   "I tell you dear . . ." Jennie Bernstein to LB, December 1946.

157   "This is how Leonard Bernstein's engagement . . ." *New York Post,* January 6, 1947.

## CHAPTER 17—THE CONDUCTOR AS MESSIAH

158   "I have become engaged . . ." LB to Serge Koussevitzky, January 2, 1947.

159   "It was wonderful . . ." Felicia Montealegre to Helen Coates, January 22, 1947.

159   With Leonard Bernstein . . . *New York World-Telegram,* May 6, 1947.

159   "Somehow I really relax . . ." LB to Helen Coates, January 30, 1947.

159   "one of my top jobs . . ." LB to Helen Coates, February 3, 1947.

160   "The whole modern movement . . ." *Christian Science Monitor,* February 2, 1947.

160   "One felt that he loved . . ." *Herald Tribune,* February 14, 1947.

160   "He felt its whole structure . . ." *New York Times,* February 13, 1947.

160   "Boy Wonder . . ." *Newsweek,* March 8, 1947.

160   "no dress shirts . . ." LB to Helen Coates, January 30, 1947.

161   "He denies . . ." *Variety,* February 21, 1947.

161   ("we had to repeat . . ." Isaac Stern, O.H.

161   "The atmosphere was tense . . ." Shirley Bernstein, *Making Music.*

162   "There is a strength . . ." LB to Koussevitzky, April 25, 1947.

162   "Palestine opened . . ." LB to Helen Coates, April 25, 1947.

162   "The café sitters . . ." *New York Daily News,* May 8, 1947.

162   Not since Toscanini's opening . . . *New York Times,* quoted in Peter Gradenwitz, *Leonard Bernstein.*

162   "They rise with the crescendi . . ." *Palestine Post,* May 2, 1947.

163   "I was in tears . . ." *Time,* May 12, 1947.

163   bobby-soxer faction *New York Journal-American,* May 15, 1947.

163   Shirley Bernstein . . . Interview with author.

163   "The very worst . . ." Isaac Stern, O.H.

164   "The orchestra of Eretz-Israel . . ." LB to Felix Rosenbluth, Chairman Palestine Orchestra, May 9, 1947.

164   "Would you accept . . ." Telegram to LB from Palestine Orchestra, June 6, 1947.

164   Bruno Zirato . . . Bruno Zirato (Columbia Concerts) to Helen Coates, July 8, 1947.

165   "I'm awfully happy . . ." LB to Helen Coates, May 20, 1947.

165   "First, I must say . . ." LB to Aaron Copland, May 28, 1947.

165   "After the fourth performance . . ." LB to Aaron Copland, November 8, 1948.

165   "PARIS BRUSSELS . . ." LB cable to Helen Coates, June 12, 1947.

167   "I can take it alright . . ." Felicia Montealegre to LB, December 1947.

## CHAPTER 18—THE MAN FROM ANOTHER WORLD

168   "The most bumptious . . ." *New York Sun,* September 23, 1947.

169   "an altogether stimulating . . ." *The New Yorker,* December 6, 1947.

169   "more varied and progressive . . ." *New York Times,* December 28, 1947.

169   "Bernstein Audience" *Herald Tribune,* March 21, 1948.

169   "embraced a career . . ." *Herald Tribune,* October 9, 1947.

170   the writer Henry Simon . . . Interview published in November issue of *1947.*

170  "IN SPITE OF . . ." Eric Gordon, *Mark the Music*.

171  "labor's only victory . . ." *Theatre Arts,* March 1948.

171  "a forerunner . . ." *Houston Post,* January 4, 1948.

171  "Most of my scores . . ." *Findings,* "Me Composer—You Jane," dated January 14, 1948. No reference to original publication is provided and there is no manuscript in the Bernstein Archive.

171  "Being engaged this long . . ." Felicia Montealegre to LB, December 1947.

171  "I am being pressed . . ." LB to Menaham Mahler-Kalkstein, December 29, 1947.

172  "Please understand . . ." Cable, January 7, 1948.

172  "Your attitude . . ." Cable from Palestine Philharmonic, January 10, 1948.

172  "You must believe . . ." Cable, January 11, 1948.

172  "STEINBERG UNAVAILABLE" Cable from Palestine Philharmonic, January 20, 1948.

173  "I am proud and happy . . ." Printed in many newspapers, March 6, 1948.

173  "these things cannot be done . . ." Newbold Morris to LB, March 9, 1948.

174  "This announcement . . ." *Variety,* April 14, 1948.

174  "I want to tell you . . ." LB to Serge Koussevitzky, April 21, 1948.

175  "It will be an honor . . ." American Fund for Palestine Institution newsletter, April 1948.

175  "something to live for . . ." Yehudi Menuhin, *Unfinished Journey.*

175  "I had expected . . ." LB to Serge Koussevitzky, May 8, 1948.

175  "First, it's all ruins . . ." LB to Helen Coates, May 7, [5?] 1948.

176  cigarette packs Carlos Moseley, O.H.

176  "One violinist told me . . ." LB to Helen Coates, May 8, 1948.

176  "At the close . . ." *New York Times,* May 1948.

176  "a great crowd . . ." Carlos Moseley, O.H.

176  "The Munich concert . . ." LB to Helen Coates, dated "2:30 am 11 May 1948," Verona, Italy.

177  stench of Dachau . . . Jack Gottlieb, who began working for LB in 1958, recalls Helen Coates's remonstrance when Felicia Bernstein had the uniform removed, so it must have been treasured for at least ten years.

177  " 'the other Leonardo' . . ." LB to Helen Coates, May 16, 1948.

177  "We have witnessed . . ." *Magyar Radio* article by Tibor Polgar, May 28, 1948.

177  "This young genius . . ." *Szabadsdag,* May 23, 1948.

177  ". . . such a scene . . ." LB to Helen Coates, May 20, 1948.

178  Seefehlner made no bones . . . Egon Seefehlner, author's interview.

178  "It was the toughest . . ." LB to Helen Coates, May 29, 1948.

178  "They learned Jeremiah . . ." LB to Helen Coates, May 29, 1948.

178  "I had a bad moment . . ." LB to Helen Coates, June 10, 1948.

179  Adler was disappointed . . . Ellen Adler, author's interview.

179  "I may live April 1 . . ." LB to Helen Coates, June 10, 1948.

179  "It would be a pity . . ." *Herald Tribune,* October 19, 1947.

CHAPTER 19—HISTORY-MAKING DAYS

181  It was shelled . . . *The Times* (London), obituary of Menachem Begin, March 10, 1992.

181  "to repatriate . . ." Press statement, Bernstein Archive.

183  "How to begin? . . ." LB to Serge Koussevitzky, October 28, 1948.

184  "It's the works . . ." LB to Aaron Copland, November 8, 1948.

184  "returned to the piano . . ." *Palestine Post,* concert on October 21, 1948.

184  "A solitary minaret . . ." *Palestine Post,* November 28, 1948.

185  "MOZART IN THE DESERT" *Time,* December 6, 1948.

185  Egyptians were sure . . . *New York Post,* April 24, 1948.

185 "In the event . . ." Menahem Mahler-Kalkstein to LB, November 29, 1948.

185 "That broke my heart" *Pittsburgh Sun-Telegraph,* January 24, 1949.

185 "I can serve music . . ." LB to Menahem Mahler-Kalkstein, January 22, 1949.

185 Sam Bernstein . . . Dr. Uri Toeblitz, letter to author.

186 "The list of instances . . ." LB to Menahem Mahler-Kalkstein, July 9, 1949.

186 Bernstein's feat . . . Mike Mindlin, author's interview.

187 Montgomery Clift . . . Jerome Robbins, letter to author.

187 *"January 6, 1949 . . ." Findings,* "Excerpts from a *West Side Story* Log." Reproduced from *Playbill,* September 1957, the first edition of a new magazine distributed *gratis* in New York theaters.

187 "Prejudice will be the theme . . ." *Augusta Chronicle,* February 26, 1949.

187 a pressing love affair . . . Arthur Laurents, author's interview.

188 *Trouble in Tahiti* . . . He wrote *Peter Pan* songs and *Prelude, Fugue and Riffs* in 1949.

188 "fascinating and hair-raising . . ." Program note written by Leonard Bernstein for the Boston premiere, April 8, 1949.

189 "Rockabye Baby" *New York Times,* August 14, 1949. Taubman was reporting on the Tanglewood performance.

189 "the finest single movement . . ." *Boston Globe,* April 9, 1949.

190 "a kind of separation . . ." Program note, April 8, 1949.

190 derived from synagogue music . . . Jack Gottlieb, "Symbols of Faith," *The Musical Quarterly,* April 1980.

190 "started to sing to him" *Christian Science Monitor,* April 8, 1949.

191 "I am sending you . . ." LB to Serge Koussevitzky, July 26, 1944.

## CHAPTER 20—THE END OF THE FIRST CONDUCTING CAREER

192 "I loved it . . ." Gene Kelly, O.H.

193 "A happy film" *Variety,* December 6, 1949.

193 "the best musical . . ." *New York Daily Worker,* December 9, 1949.

193 "We had to shorten . . ." Gene Kelly, O.H.

193 "It was like Venus de Milo . . ." *Philadelphia Inquirer,* June 27, 1949.

193 "very eclectical" Letter, Samuel Adler to the author.

194 "I've been going . . ." LB to Burton Bernstein, November 1, 1949.

194 "I am forty-one . . ." Olivier Messiaen to LB, October 5, 1949.

194 "If Bostonians suffer . . ." *Christian Science Monitor,* December 9, 1949.

194 "a really arousing . . ." *New York Sun,* December 11, 1949.

194 "the trashiest Hollywood . . ." *Musical America,* January 1, 1950.

195 "an amazing performance" *Herald Tribune,* December 11, 1949.

195 "Your casual throwaway phrase . . ." Marc Blitzstein to LB, April 16, 1950.

195 "Don't be upset . . ." Marc Blitzstein to LB, May 19, 1950.

195 "Leonard Bernstein has taken time off . . ." *New York Times,* April 24, 1950.

196 "He was in rare form . . ." Quote and Toscanini letter from John Briggs, *Leonard Bernstein.*

196 "controlled and meaningful" *New York Post,* January 4, 1950.

196 "Lenny dear . . ." Marc Blitzstein to LB, January 4, 1950.

197 "tremendously distinguished" *New York Times,* February 27, 1950.

197 "a tiresomely sentimental . . ." *New York Daily News,* February 27, 1950.

197 "probably not equalled . . ." *Newsweek,* March 6, 1950.

197 a dual personality . . . *New York World-Telegram,* February 20, 1950.

197 "jammed Carnegie Hall . . ." *New York Post,* February 27, 1950.

197 "Maestro Leonard Bernstein . . ." Walter Winchell, January 12, 1950.

197 "Take heart again . . ." *Pittsburgh Press,* January 7, 1950.

198 "They lost my tails . . ." LB to Burton Bernstein, April 18, 1950.

198 "Bernstein approaches the piano . . ." *Ha'aretz,* June 25, 1950.

199 "How strange . . ." LB to Shirley Bernstein, April 26, 1950.

200 "I have been engaged . . ." LB to Shirley Bernstein, May 19, 1950.

201 "an overpowering revelation" *New York Times,* July 6, 1950.

201 "I love Mahler's music . . ." Ralph Degens article, Bernstein Archive.

202 "You have the right . . ." Helen Coates to LB, September 14, 1950.

203 "in a taxi . . ." Shirley Bernstein, *Making Music.* Burton Bernstein remembers the journey as being on the way *to* the airport at the end of their stay.

203 The deer-hunt . . . Burton Bernstein, author's interview.

204 "The concerts in Milan . . ." LB to Burton Bernstein, November 21, 1950.

204 "You'll never believe . . ." LB to Burton Bernstein, November 28, 1950.

205 "men and women . . ." *New York Times,* January 10, 1951.

205 "a pre-war German provincial orchestra" *New Leader,* February 1951.

205 "He cajoles, he grimaces . . ." *Toledo Times,* February 1, 1957.

205 "I find that conducting . . ." LB to Helen Coates, January 20, 1951.

205 "like going over Niagara Falls . . ." *Milwaukee Journal,* January 23, 1951.

205 "But the dark hints . . ." LB to Helen Coates, April 19, 1951.

206 "I regarded this . . ." Martha Gellhorn, author's interview.

206 "I will shortly . . ." LB to Helen Coates, April 19, 1951.

206 ". . . a really nice surprise . . ." LB to Helen Coates, April 30, 1951.

207 "wrestling delightedly" LB to Helen Coates, May 27, 1951.

## CHAPTER 21—RITES OF PASSAGE

208 "Good or bad . . ." Marc Blitzstein to Minna Curtiss, August 1951, quoted in Gordon, *Mark the Music.*

208 "Lenny dear . . ." Felicia Montealegre to LB (Thursday 27, no date).

209 "When are you . . ." Felicia Montealegre to LB, April 1951.

209 "I know now . . ." Felicia Montealegre to LB, April/May 1951.

209 "I think of you . . ." Felicia Montealegre to LB, May/June 1951.

209 "Who knows . . ." Ibid.

210 "We ate . . ." *Berkshire Eagle,* July 2, 1951.

210 "Where were you?" Shirley Bernstein, *Music Making.*

210 "Lenny and I . . ." Burton Bernstein, O.H.

210 the clincher . . . *Saturday Evening Post,* June 16, 1956.

210 "Engagements are horrible . . ." *Berkshire Evening Eagle,* August 5, 1952.

211 "She had more Yiddishisms . . ." Burton Bernstein, O.H.

211 ". . . making pastry . . ." Ibid.

212 "We were very nervous . . ." Ibid.

212 "Everybody was on edge" Ibid.

213 "I miss you . . ." LB to Burton Bernstein, September 10, 1951.

213 "We are truly happy . . ." LB to Helen Coates, September 16, 1951.

213 "So you remember . . ." Anecdote provided by Jamie Bernstein Thomas, author's interview.

213 "The tensions . . ." LB to Philip and Barbara Marcuse, October 9, 1951.

214 "I am not committing . . ." LB to Helen Coates, October 1951.

214 "I have written . . ." LB to Aaron Copland, October 18, 1951.

214 "She was very in awe of him . . ." Martha Gellhorn, author's interview, July 1991.

214 "She is a busy . . ." LB to Helen Coates, October 1951.

214 " 'Things' are going . . ." Felicia Montealegre Bernstein (hereinafter FMB) to Helen Coates, October 21, 1951.

215 "Maybe you can . . ." LB to Burton Bernstein, December 11, 1951.

215 "Nothing ever went slowly . . ." LB to Philip Marcuse, November 29, 1951.

215 "L. looked marvelous . . ." Alexis Weissenberg to Helen Coates, November 13, 1951.

216 "The apes . . ." LB to Burton Bernstein, January 29, 1952.

216 "WE ARE PREGNANT" LB to Helen Coates, January 9, 1952.

PART THREE
CHAPTER 22—RETURN TO SHOW BUSINESS

220 "It's hard . . ." LB to Irving Fine, March 8, 1952.

220 "the technical direction . . ." *Boston Advocate,* June 1952.

220 "librettist, lecturer . . ." *Time,* June 23, 1952.

220 "I don't know . . ." LB to Irving Fine, June 22, 1952.

221 "no conducting . . ." *Berkshire Evening Eagle,* April 5, 1952.

221 "It didn't make much difference . . ." Sarah Caldwell, O.H.

221 "Tahiti was 200% better . . ." LB to Philip Marcuse, August 18, 1952.

222 "Jamie is a raving beauty . . ." LB to Irving Fine, September 9, 1952.

222 "light-weight piece . . ." *Herald Tribune* articles on May 6 and May 11, 1952.

223 "It is lively musically . . ." quoted in Gordon, *Mark the Music.*

223 "Two emptier, duller . . ." *Saturday Review,* November 29, 1952.

223 "from a weak libretto . . ." *Herald Tribune,* June 14, 1952.

223 "The trio sings . . ." *Detroit Free Press,* November 17, 1952.

224 "Lenny ran . . ." Betty Comden, O.H.

225 "We were writing . . ." Adolph Green, O.H.

225 "acrobatic production . . ." *New York Times,* February 22, 1953.

225 "so bass it's viol" *New York World-Telegram,* February 21, 1953.

226 best musical . . . *New York Times,* February 26, 1953.

226 "wonderful score . . ." *New York Daily News,* February 26, 1953.

226 "It was light . . ." *Nation,* March 1953. Harold Clurman managed to write the entire review without mentioning Bernstein's name.

226 "This is an opera . . ." *New York Times,* May 10, 1953.

CHAPTER 23—DIVERSIONARY TACTICS

228 "Most of our time . . ." LB to Irving Fine, October 20, 1952.

229 "We discovered . . ." LB to Irving Fine, September 19, 1952.

229 "miserably revolting" Mark Blitzstein to Mina Curtiss, May 7, 1953. Quoted in Eric Gordon, *Mark the Music* (p. 343).

229 "It has finally dawned on me . . ." LB to Abram Sacher, July 12, 1953.

230 "Serious music . . ." *Boston Morning Globe,* February 1, 1953.

230 "singing them loud . . ." Uzi Weisel, quoted in Barbara Erde Mandell, ed., *Tanglewood Remembered—1953.*

231 "I finally went down to Washington . . ." LB to Burton Bernstein, August 12, 1953.

231 "communist front" FBI documents released in 1980 under the Freedom of Information Act confirm that Bernstein had been investigated and informed upon. In 1950, for example, the American Embassy in Paris had been told by Secretary of State Dean Rusk to have nothing to do with him.

231 "Don't you ever . . ." Robert Joseph, O.H.

231 "There was absolutely . . ." LB to Helen Coates, September 18, 1953.

231 "I have been steeped . . ." FMB to LB, September 1953.

232 "The music is saturated . . ." *Jerusalem Post,* November 4, 1953.

233 "Never heard of . . ." LB to Helen Coates, November 11, 1953.

233 "so that her fury . . ." John Ardoin, *The Callas Legacy.*

233 "the world of opera . . ." Franco Zeffirelli, *Zeffirelli.*

233 "benign classicism . . ." John Ardoin, *The Callas Legacy.*

234 "What I have to say . . ." FMB to LB, December 1953.

234 "Darling Goody . . ." LB to FMB, January 7, 1954.

235 "real good friends . . ." LB to FMB, Ibid.

235 "I have decided . . ." LB to FMB, January 7, 1954.

236 "having a fling" *Herald Tribune,* February 12, 1954.

237 elegant jazz piano playing . . . LB received a check for thirty-nine dollars—"scale" for piano playing—on May 12, 1954.

237 "I've made millions . . ." LB to Helen Coates, April 26, 1954.

237 ". . . I get energy" *Los Angeles Times,* May 9, 1954.

237 "dramatic universality" *Newsweek,* August 2, 1954.

237 "about the best . . ." *Score,* June 1955.

238 "My life is all Lillian Hellman . . ." LB to Philip Marcuse, May 21, 1954.

238 "the finest work . . ." Marc Blitzstein to LB, August 31, 1954.

238 "I miss my family . . ." FMB to LB, August 1954.

238 "Miss you terribly . . ." LB to FMB, September 9, 1954.

238 "Isaac plays the *Serenade* . . ." LB to FMB, September 11, 1954.

238 ". . . started to talk . . ." Isaac Stern, O.H.

240 "I believe in people" Leonard Bernstein, *Findings,* "This I Believe."

240 "A negligible contribution . . ." *Herald Tribune,* September 26, 1954.

240 . . . praised Bernstein's luminous . . . *New York Times,* October 3, 1954.

241 "Thus," Robert Saudek recalled . . . Robert Saudek to Karen Bernstein, archivist.

241 ". . . going to perform . . ." Leonard Bernstein, *The Joy of Music,* "Beethoven's Fifth Symphony."

241 "an absorbing and adult" *New York Times,* November 21, 1954.

241 "one of the more electrifying . . ." *San Francisco News,* November 15, 1954.

## CHAPTER 24—FROM LA SCALA TO BROADWAY

243 "I've gotten all steamed up . . ." LB to FMB, February 4, 1955.

244 "They pushed me . . ." FMB to LB, February 1955.

244 "don't feel too badly . . ." FMB to LB, February 1955.

244 "My darling . . ." LB to FMB, February 1, 1955.

245 "Piero Tosi designed . . ." Franco Zeffirelli, *Zeffirelli.*

245 "the black fairy" LB to FMB, February 1955.

245 "Crazy people . . ." LB to FMB, April 22, 1955.

245 "I have had terrible notices . . ." LB to Helen Coates, March 20, 1955.

245 "What do you want . . ." Marc Blitzstein to LB, March 15, 1955.

245 "I've had de Sabata's . . ." Marc Blitzstein to LB, April 5, 1955.

245 "I cannot understand . . ." LB to Helen Coates, April 17, 1955.

246 "Lennuhtt, my stay . . ." FMB to LB, April 1955.

246 "I feel I ought . . ." LB to FMB, April 22, 1955.

246 "an evening of superb theater art" *New York Times,* April 20, 1955.

246 "I sat through . . ." FMB to LB, April 1955.

246 "Why won't . . ." LB to FMB, May 6, 1955.

247 "Darling Bubbles . . ." LB to FMB, May 6, 1955.

247 "We really are so broke" FMB to Helen Coates, April 11, 1955.

247 "it was a job . . ." LB to FMB, May 27, 1955.

247 "what is discreetly . . ." FMB to LB, May 1955.

248 "It was a mistake . . ." LB to Philip Marcuse, May 18, 1955.

248 "I don't know why . . ." *Washington Guide to the Arts,* January 1980.

248 "Don't think it's easy . . ." Leonard Bernstein, *The Joy of Music,* "Whatever Happened to that Great American Symphony?"

249 "The parenthetical name . . ." LB to Philip and Barbara Marcuse, July 28, 1955.

249 "The main materials . . ." *Berkshire Evening Eagle,* August 10, 1955.

250 "This is to be . . ." LB to Martha Gellhorn, August 30, 1955.

250 ". . . Boston Symphony's 75th Anniversary . . ." Due in 1956 but deferred for

many years, this "big orchestral work" became *Kaddish,* Symphony No. 3.

250 *Missa Brevis*—first performed in Atlanta, conducted by Robert Shaw.

250 "I suppose it's a little crazy . . ." *New York Post,* November 13, 1955.

251 "splendidly lucid primer" *The New Yorker,* October 31, 1955.

251 "the real beginning . . ." Leonard Bernstein, *The Joy of Music,* "The World of Jazz." LB dropped all references to *Prelude, Fugue and Riffs* in the printed version of his script. A CBS recording derived from the program, entitled *What Is Jazz?,* was very popular in the late 1950s.

252 "You see . . ." Leonard Bernstein, *The Joy of Music,* "The Art of Conducting."

253 "the perfect teleshow" *Variety,* December 7, 1955.

255 "The piece seemed to have . . ." Vivian Perlis, *Aaron Copland, Since 1943.*

255 Jewish . . . "but very Park Avenue" Craig Zadan, *Sondheim & Co.*

255 "I can't do this . . ." Stephen Sondheim, author's interview.

255 ". . . Hammerstein convinced him . . ." Stephen Sondheim, author's interview.

255 "I could explain . . ." Craig Zadan, *Sondheim & Co.*

256 "off-beat musical . . ." *New York Post,* January 17, 1956.

## CHAPTER 25—*CANDIDE*

257 "Lenny never . . ." *Saturday Evening Post,* June 16, 1956.

258 "It doesn't do . . ." LB to Philip Marcuse, May 25, 1956.

258 "Here we are . . ." Ibid.

258 "attractive in places . . ." *New York Times,* April 19, 1956.

258 "as near an authentic . . ." *Chicago Daily Tribune,* July 27, 1956.

259 "every page takes . . ." Narration, LSO concert version of *Candide,* December 1989.

261 "It's a spectacular . . ." *Variety,* October 31, 1956.

261 "I was almost . . ." William Wright, *Lillian Hellman.*

262 "Let's do a vulgar . . ." Richard Wilbur, author's interview, 1992.

262 "Since Voltaire . . ." *New York Times,* December 3, 1956.

262 "work of genius . . ." *New York Daily News,* December 9, 1956.

262 "wonderfully enjoyable . . ." *New York Daily News,* December 9, 1956.

262 "the popular instincts . . ." *New York Times,* December 16, 1956.

262 "it was O.P.E.R.A." *New York Sunday News,* December 9, 1956.

263 "arbitrarily closed it" Oliver Smith, O.H.

263 "the effortless grace . . ." Tyrone Guthrie, *A Life in the Theatre.*

263 "shuts himself off . . ." William Wright, *Lillian Hellman.*

263 "if you catch . . ." Ibid.

263 "There was no single . . ." John Briggs, *Leonard Bernstein.*

263 "her most unpleasant . . ." William Wright, *Lillian Hellman.* In her autobiography, *Pentimento,* she calls it "a bad and wasteful time."

263 "You've sold out" Oliver Smith, O.H.

264 "an art that arises . . ." Leonard Bernstein, *The Joy of Music,* "The American Musical Comedy."

## CHAPTER 26—*WEST SIDE STORY*

266 "grotesquely unauthentic" *Herald Tribune,* December 28, 1956.

266 "one of the finest things . . ." *Saturday Review,* January 12, 1957.

266 "a smart sophisticated little piece" *New York Times,* January 28, 1957.

266 "Omnibus" lecture . . . Bernstein, *The Joy of Music,* "Introduction to Modern Music."

266 "padded out by formula" *Saturday Review,* December 15, 1957.

267 "very likely to quit . . ." *Time,* February 4, 1957.

268 "I don't know . . ." Craig Zadan, *Sondheim & Co.*

268 Sondheim remembers . . . Stephen Sondheim, author's interview.

268    "Sondheim and Bernstein . . ." Harold Prince, *Contradictions.*

269    Prince threatened to pull out . . . Harold Prince, author's interview.

270    "If he'd had the time . . ." Irwin Kostal, O.H.

273    "a uniquely cohesive . . ." *Washington Post,* August 20, 1957.

273    "a new field . . ." *Daily News,* August 20, 1957.

273    "perhaps the love story . . ." *Seattle Times,* August 20, 1957.

273    "It's only Washington . . ." LB to FMB, August 23, 1957.

274    "I can see . . ." Stephen Sondheim, author's interview.

274    "to bring the language . . ." Ibid.

274    "I had a dummy lyric" *New York Times,* October 21, 1990, "*West Side Story*: the Beginnings of Something Great," by Mel Gussow.

274    "took longer to write . . ." Ibid.

274    "We raped Arthur's play-writing" Leonard Bernstein, Dramatists Guild Round Table, Fall 1985.

275    "It cries out for music" Author's interview

with LB (during DG *West Side Story* recording, 1984).

275    "I know I'm difficult . . ." Sid Ramin, O.H.

275    was startled to see . . . Stephen Sondheim, author's interview.

275    "I remember all my collaborations . . ." Dramatists Guild Round Table, Fall 1985.

275    "the amount of fuel . . ." Jerome Robbins, BBC-TV Obituary Tribute, October 19, 1990.

275    "It's an American musical" Ibid.

275    "a tragic musical comedy" Author's interview with LB (re *Trouble in Tahiti,* 1973).

276    772 performances . . . Harold Prince, *Contradictions.*

276    "capitulated to respectability" Brooks Atkinson, *Broadway.*

276    "unique concatenation . . ." Stephen Sondheim, author's interview.

276    "a profoundly moving . . ." *New York Times,* September 27, 1957.

276    he called it a "phoney" . . . *Nation,* October 27, 1957.

277    "*West Side Story* means much more . . ." Stephen Sondheim to LB, September 26, 1957.

PART FOUR
CHAPTER 27—THE HEIR APPARENT TAKES COMMAND

282    "He found a suitable baton . . ." *New York Post,* January 5, 1958. Leonard Lyons lived in the same apartment building as the Bernsteins.

282    . . . relatively small baton . . . Bernstein's batons were made for him in later years by the timpanist of the Metropolitan Opera, Dick Horowitz.

282    "he plans the format . . ." Letters exchanged between New York Philharmonic and the Internal Revenue Service, July 28, 1961. Courtesy New York Philharmonic Archive.

283    "every time . . ." Dimitri Mitropoulos, Foreword to Olin Downes, *10 Operatic Masterpieces.*

283    "Opera," he told . . . *Chicago Tribune,* November 21, 1957.

283    Toscanini received $110,000 New York Philharmonic Archive.

283    "is . . . heartbreaking and set . . ." Quoted in Howard Shanet, *Philharmonic.*

283    "I am like . . ." *Chicago Tribune,* November 21, 1957.

284    "With concerts like this . . ." *New York Times,* January 4, 1958.

284    "a return to Broadway . . ." *New York Times,* November 24, 1957.

284    "We're getting old . . ." *Time,* November 25, 1957.

284    "I want to think . . ." *Newsweek,* November 25, 1957.

285    "to settle down . . ." *Harrisburg Patriot News,* March 9, 1958.

285    "He is like a child . . ." *Milwaukee Journal,* December 5, 1957.

286    "He dresses before dinner" *Boston Globe,* November 14, 1957.

286    "She looked exquisite . . ." *New York Times,* April 28, 1958.

286    "The whole thing . . ." Joel Friedman, O.H.

287 "It rained madly . . ." LB to FMB, April 28, 1958.

287 "the all-time smash" LB to FMB, May 2, 1958.

287 "a great beige linen . . ." LB to FMB, Ibid.

287 "It seems all wrong . . ." LB to FMB, May 6, 1958.

287 "We exchanged notes . . ." *Findings*, "Image of Chile."

288 "Lenny was hailed . . ." Carlos Moseley, O.H.

288 "I had never imagined . . ." *Newsday*, February 17, 1961, "Conductor's Wife Leads Hectic Life."

288 Bernstein had arranged . . . Letter from FMB to Helen Coates, June 3, 1958. Bernstein also took a week out in Buenos Aires, conducting the Wagnerian Orchestral Association in two Mozart programs.

288 "18,000 people listened . . ." New York Philharmonic Commemorative Brochure, July 8, 1958.

## CHAPTER 28—MUSIC DIRECTOR AT THE NEW YORK PHILHARMONIC

290 "My job . . ." *New York Times*, December 22, 1957.

291 The new arrangements . . . Statistics taken from *Philharmonic*, Howard Shanet's invaluable history of the New York Philharmonic.

292 "It was a big affair . . ." Ned Rorem, O.H.

292 "the greatest genius . . ." Robert Chesterman, ed., *Conversations with Conductors* (1967 interview).

293 "What a difference . . ." *New York Times*, May 3, 1959.

293 "I have been hurt . . ." Chesterman, ed., *Conversations with Conductors*.

294 "lurking didactic streak" LB writing in November 1966, quoted in *Prelude, Fugue and Riffs*, fall 1993.

296 "the Young People's Concerts . . ." Ibid.

296 "Roger! This is Lenny!" Roger Englander, "No Balloons or Tapdances" (unpublished manuscript). Courtesy of the author.

296 The first "Young People's Concert" . . . *Leonard Bernstein's Young People's Concerts, What Does Music Mean?*, January 18, 1958.

297 "Lenny was absolutely . . ." Carlos Moseley, O.H. *Who Is Gustav Mahler?* was televised in February 1960. Bernstein visited Denver in August.

297 "Bernstein is content . . ." Tim Page, ed., *A Glenn Gould Reader*. "Oh for heaven's sake, Cynthia, there must be something else on."

## CHAPTER 29—TO RUSSIA WITH LOVE

298 "the most socially important . . ." *New York Journal-American*, October 4, 1958.

298 "I'm all for snobbism . . ." *New York Times*, October 1, 1958.

299 "The sound was radiant . . ." *Herald Tribune*, October 3, 1958.

299 "whistle clean articulation" *Saturday Review*, October 11, 1958.

299 "shining morning face" *New York Times*, October 3, 1958.

299 "Attaboy, Sugar . . ." *Time*, October 13, 1958.

300 "a large dose" *The New Yorker*, October 25, 1958.

300 "It's cost me . . ." *Paris Herald Tribune*, November 1, 1958.

300 *"Vous jouez trop français . . ." Dimanche-Lundi*, November 3, 1958.

301 *"Après Bach" France Soir*, November 10, 1958.

301 "a success of this quality . . ." Bernard Gavoty ("Clarendon") of *Le Figaro*, quoted in *The New Yorker*, December 2, 1958.

301 *"vaines convulsions" Le Carrefour*, November 14, 1958.

301 "While away . . ." *New York Post*, November 26, 1958.

302 "used to having me . . ." *St. Louis Post Dispatch*, December 12, 1957, syndicated interview by Olga Curtis.

302 "superhuman job . . ." *New York Post*, October 20, 1958.

302 "The feeling is never . . ." *Look*, November 11, 1958.

302 "mostly I compose . . ." Leonard Bernstein, *The Infinite Variety of Music*, "An Informal Lecture."

303 "the composing part . . ." *New York World-Telegram,* November 18, 1958.

303 "When he performs . . ." Ned Rorem, speech given at the MacDowell Colony, August 9, 1987, reprinted in Jack Gottlieb, ed., *Leonard Bernstein: A Complete Catalogue of His Works.*

303 "quite without a distinctive . . ." *The Observer* (London), December 12, 1958.

303 "Miss Hellman has no irony . . ." *Sunday Times* (London), May 3, 1959.

303 "Wilson was angry . . ." Dennis Quilley, author's interview. Quilley played Candide; Mary Costa was Cunegonde.

304 "I'm extremely humble . . ." BBC-TV, May 10, 1959. (Memorable for the author as the day he met Leonard Bernstein for the first time.)

304 "conductors don't like . . ." *News Chronicle* (London), May 7, 1959.

304 "was to discover" *Daily Express* (London), May 8, 1959.

304 "It was an all-day . . ." Jamie Bernstein Thomas, O.H.

305 "In Salzburg a problem . . ." Carlos Moseley, O.H.

305 ". . . a great deal of merriment . . ." Carlos Moseley, O.H.

306 "The party broke up . . ." *Time,* September 7, 1959.

306 "But the enthusiasm . . ." *New York Times,* August 23, 1959.

306 "the finest interpretation . . ." Tass Agency, quoted by the *Philadelphia Bulletin,* August 23, 1959.

306 "Their ensemble is wonderful . . ." *Sovetskaya Kultura,* August 27, 1959, quoted in the *New York Times,* August 28, 1959.

306 "Bernstein's force and magnetism . . ." *Herald Tribune,* September 13, 1959.

307 ". . . and his theory of accidental music . . ." *New York Times,* August 26, 1958.

307 "Before the Ives . . ." *Sovetskaya Kultura,* August 27, 1959.

307 "an unforgivable lie . . ." United Press International dispatch, quoted in *Musical America,* September 1959.

308 "I want it to be possible . . ." *New York Times,* August 26, 1959.

308 "They want to touch . . ." *Newsweek,* September 7, 1959.

310 "Felicia rushed to Pasternak" John Briggs, *Leonard Bernstein.*

310 "both a saint . . ." *Paris Herald Tribune* interview with Art Buchwald, September 27, 1959.

310 "My conversations . . ." LB to Rabbi George B. Liberman, August 2, 1960.

310 "You have taken us . . ." *Herald Tribune,* September 12, 1959.

311 "What I remember most . . ." Burton Bernstein, *Family Matters.*

311 "I find myself . . ." LB to Helen Coates, September 1959.

311 "stunt performance . . ." *The Times* (London), October 12, 1959.

311 "He looked . . ." *Daily Express* (London), October 12, 1959.

311 "At times he conducts . . ." *The Spectator,* October 23, 1959.

312 "a responsiveness . . ." *Washington Post,* October 13, 1959.

312 "If military strength . . ." *New York Times,* October 14, 1959.

312 "I have no more energy . . ." Washington press conference, October 13, 1959.

### CHAPTER 30—LAST YEARS AT CARNEGIE HALL

313 "There is a secret relationship . . ." Karlheinz Stockhausen to LB, November 8, 1959.

314 "My dear great friend . . ." Alma Mahler to LB, February 9, 1960.

314 "He's a marvelous teacher . . ." *St. Louis Post Dispatch,* October 23, 1961.

315 Bernstein's contract was to run . . . Schuy-

ler Chapin's *Musical Chairs* and *Leonard Bernstein Notes from a Friend* both discuss the negotiations in detail.

316 "I had a collapse-o" *New York Post,* June 11, 1960.

316 "It's got a theme . . ." Quoted in the preface to the published score.

316 "How the hell . . ." Sid Ramin, O.H.

316 "lovely but utterly unproductive . . ." LB to David Diamond, August 26, 1960.

317 "back in steaming Manhattan . . ." John Briggs, *Leonard Bernstein.*

317 "Hawaii was paradise . . ." LB to David Diamond, August 26, 1960.

317 "sounded contented . . ." FMB to LB, August 1960.

317 "the top moment . . ." LB to Shirley Bernstein, September 7, 1960.

317 "It will never cease . . ." Burton Bernstein, *Esquire,* "Leonard Bernstein's Separate Peace with Berlin," October 1961.

318 "Isn't it amazing . . ." Ibid.

318 "because of the German . . ." *New York Times,* September 24, 1960.

318 "An earlier biographer's assertion . . ." Joan Peyser, *Leonard Bernstein,* p. 281

319 "Exhibit A . . ." Telegram Frank Sinatra to LB, January 12, 1961.

320 "Who's taking care . . ." LB, Interview with Nelson Aldrich for the John Fitzgerald Kennedy Library, Boston.

321 "relatively few thematic ideas . . ." New York Philharmonic Program Note, February 13, 1961.

321 "At all times . . ." *New York Times,* April 16, 1961.

321 "fencing, hula-dancing . . ." *The New Yorker,* April 17, 1961.

322 "Bernstein's gaudy podium antics" *Time,* May 8, 1961.

322 "Hearing such a wonderful performance . . ." *Osaka Shimbun,* April 27, 1961.

322 "Darling: How can I . . ." LB to FMB, April 30, 1961.

322 ". . . the sound of that silence . . ." Bernstein wrote a number of poems in English observing the prescribed seventeen-syllable structure of the Japanese haiku. Jack Gottlieb set some of them in *Haiku Souvenirs.*

323 "Lenny needed many rehearsals . . ." Kazuko Amano, letter to author.

323 "My mother went crazy . . ." Seiji Ozawa, O.H.

324 "with his own bags . . ." Jamie Bernstein Thomas, O.H.

324 "a Persephone-like creature . . ." Judith Braun, O.H.

324 "Ellen and my parents . . ." Burton Bernstein, O.H.

325 "wildly, immorally sentimental . . ." *Time,* October 20, 1961.

325 "Nothing short . . ." *New York Times,* October 16, 1961.

326 Academy Awards . . . The official category for all four was "Scoring of Musical Picture."

326 "What is a father . . ." *Findings,* "Tribute to SJB."

327 Boulanger never forgot . . . e.g., February 26, 1971.

327 Danilian's young companion . . . Charles Wellrich, author's interview.

328 "what Dimitri Mitropoulos . . ." *New York World-Telegram,* April 7, 1962.

329 *The Creative Performer* . . . Bernstein's "Ford Hour" and "Lincoln Hour" programs, televised by CBS, can be viewed at the New York Museum of Television.

329 "It's been grueling . . ." LB to David Diamond, February 28, 1962.

329 "Dearest Beebles and Ellen . . ." LB to Burton Bernstein, July 30, 1962.

330 "a big patchwork . . ." *New York Times,* September 20, 1962.

330 "the exuberant conductor . . ." *New York Post,* September 24, 1962.

331 ". . . failed to pick up her voice" Don Hewitt, author's interview.

## CHAPTER 31—A KADDISH FOR A PRESIDENT

332 Unfortunately, Rivers's various portraits . . . Bernstein was unlucky with his portraitists. The René Bouché portrait in America's National Portrait Gallery is particularly disappointing.

333 "If that guy . . ." Lauren Bacall, O.H.

333 *pasto de choclo* . . . Schuyler Chapin, *Leonard Bernstein.*

333 "Herman Shumlin Hostess . . ." Schuyler Chapin, *Musical Chairs.*

333 "It was such fun . . ." Prince Rainier to LB,

October 30, 1962. Bernstein had sent him some American squash balls.

334    "Dr. Gaylin believes . . ." Telephone conversation with the author's wife.

334    "marvelous" "The Sound of a Hall," Young People's Concert, November 21, 1962.

334    "O Lenny, what is . . ." Lukas Foss to LB, December 28, 1962.

335    "Here, kid . . ." André Watts interviewed in *Great Performances*, PBS, October 1992.

336    "She had put on . . ." FMB to LB, April 1963.

336    "Whenever Nat mentioned . . ." Mrs. Nat Prager to LB, May 6, 1963.

336    "On August 1st . . ." LB to Shirley Bernstein, August 10, 1963.

337    "I've finished it . . ." Jamie Bernstein Thomas, O.H.

337    "Why the 'Resurrection' . . ." *Findings*, "Tribute to John F. Kennedy."

338    "It was his unqualified opinion . . ." Bernstein Archive.

338    "grave and inspiring . . ." LB to David Diamond, May 19, 1958. "The whole orchestra was in tears," he added.

339    "Whenever she stood . . ." *Findings*, "Jennie Tourel 1910–1973."

339    "FANTASTIC SUCCESS WITH PUBLIC . . ." LB cable to Helen Coates, December 11, 1963.

340    "I intended no sacrilege . . ." *Variety* article by Azariah Rapoport, December 18, 1963.

340    "Unashamed vulgarity . . ." *Boston Globe*, February 1, 1964.

341    "Never has the word . . ." *Christian Science Monitor*, February 1, 1964.

341    "Marc is dead . . ." LB to Shirley Bernstein, January 25, 1964.

341    "The work was performed . . ." *Herald Tribune*, January 24, 1964.

341    "long chain of beautiful . . ." *Findings*, "Tribute to Marc Blitzstein."

342    "snugly fitted" *New York Times*, January 3, 1964.

342    "This is bad . . ." *New York Times*, January 12, 1964.

342    "He tried everything . . ." *Herald Tribune*, January 3, 1964.

342    "has enlivened . . ." *Herald Tribune*, February 7, 1964.

343    "Lenny and I speak . . ." Franco Zeffirelli, *Zeffirelli*.

344    "In glad compliance . . ." *New York Times*, October 24, 1965.

347    "a dreadful experience . . ." LB to David Diamond, January 25, 1965.

347    "The orchestra is splendid . . ." LB to Helen Coates, May 14, 1965.

347    "wild in its force . . ." *Politiken*, May 17, 1965.

347    "The string orchestra . . ." Dean Walter Hussey to LB, August 14, 1964.

348    "It is quite popular . . ." LB to Dean Walter Hussey, May 12, 1965.

349    "like sleeping on grapefruit . . ." Jamie Bernstein Thomas, O.H.

349    "All we can do now is pray . . ." LB to FMB, overheard by the author.

349    "The Psalms went off well . . ." LB to Helen Coates, August 3, 1965.

349    "especially excited . . ." Dean Walter Hussey to LB, August 1, 1965.

349    "shallow experience" *Jewish Chronicle* (London), August 2, 1965.

349    "of the kind Luther . . ." *Sunday Times* (London), August 8, 1965.

350    Charles Ives's Third . . . The performances were conducted by Edo de Waart.

350    "a high-powered, apocalyptic . . ." *New York Times*, November 26, 1965.

350    "Leonard Bernstein laid himself bare . . ." *Herald Tribune*, December 10, 1965.

350    "one of the towering moments . . ." *The Times* (London), December 13, 1965.

350    "Leonard Bernstein at home . . ." *New York Times*, November 22, 1965.

351    "than anything being written . . ." *Milwaukee Journal*, June 22, 1966.

351    "the greatest pianist . . ." *New York Times*, January 17, 1956.

351    "Drab, tawdry and derivative . . ." *Herald Tribune*, February 11, 1966.

351    "His own serious style . . ." *Herald Tribune*, March 6, 1966.

## CHAPTER 32—THE CONQUEST OF VIENNA

352 "Of course I would love . . ." Robert Lantz, O.H.

352 "He got up . . ." Ibid.

353 "I don't know . . ." LB to Helen Coates, March 8, 1966.

353 "We were off and flying . . ." BBC-TV-Unitel, *The Love of Three Orchestras*. Felicia would tease her husband's loquacity by calling him "Mr. Klemps," a reference to the story about Dr. Otto Klemperer, whose long-winded instructions to an impatient orchestral player elicited the immortal question: "Hey, Mr. Klemps, you want it loud or you want it soft?"

353 "I am really married . . ." *New York Times,* March 14, 1966.

353 "This is a wonderful orchestra . . ." *Express* (Vienna), March 4, 1966.

353 "the players didn't . . ." *Records and Recording,* May 1966, article by Charles Reid.

353 "They want me . . ." LB to Helen Coates, March 8, 1966.

353 "you have a feeling . . ." *Records and Recording,* May 1966.

354 "world class on the podium . . ." *Express* (Vienna), March 15, 1966.

354 "fiery musicianship . . ." *The Times* (London), April 1966.

354 "*That* is a conductor . . ." Brian Large, author's interview.

354 "I wear it . . ." *Records and Recording,* May 1966.

355 "I'm not from Vienna . . ." Peter Weiser, *Wien Stark Bewölkt,* author's translation.

355 "as sweet as anything . . ." *Records and Recording,* May 1966.

356 "This is your Mozart . . ." Austrian TV documentary, 1966.

356 "the atmosphere of a great artistic event" *Express* (Vienna), April 4, 1966.

356 "the favorite child . . ." *Salzburger Nachrichten,* April 4, 1966.

356 "it was clear . . ." *Arbeiter Zeitung,* April 4, 1960.

356 "I've got the opera bug . . ." *High Fidelity,* June 1966.

356 "What a joy . . ." LB to Helen Coates, April 1, 1966.

356 "He has aged visibly . . ." FMB to Helen Coates, April 8, 1966.

356 "We had a chorus . . ." *Daily Mirror* (London), February 25, 1970. Bernstein was reminiscing to the LSO chorus at the time.

357 "arms outstretched . . ." *London Evening Standard,* April 18, 1966.

357 "I've brought some friends . . ." Brian Large, author's interview.

357 "I don't think he will ever . . ." Helen Coates to Alan Fluck, May 11, 1966.

357 "is your absolute *best* . . ." LB to David Diamond, January 28, 1965.

357 "Maturity seems to be creeping in . . ." *New York Times,* May 22, 1966.

358 "I am very close . . ." Bernstein Archive.

358 "the highest honor . . ." *New York Times,* June 22, 1966.

358 "had an unpretentious . . ." Gordon Davidson, O.H.

359 "an immensely gratifying experience . . ." *Los Angeles Times,* July 14, 1966.

359 "partly because of the revisions . . ." Ibid.

359 "LB has been disclosing . . ." Oscar Levant, *The Memoirs of an Amnesiac.*

359 "August here has been . . ." LB to Helen Coates, September 4, 1966.

359 "I can't go on . . ." Frank Milburn, O.H.

360 "It is a wonderful thing . . ." *New York Times,* November 3, 1966.

361 "When LB arrived . . ." Herbert Chappell, letter to the author (who was also present).

## CHAPTER 33—END OF AN ERA

363 "I feel very young . . ." *Time,* August 1968.

363 "Golly, she can upstage . . ." *New York Times,* March 3, 1967.

364 "I don't understand . . ." Lukas Foss, author's interview.

364 "Pop music seems . . ." *The Infinite Variety of Music,* "An Open Letter."

364 "praising rock in one breath . . ." *Boston Herald,* April 26, 1967.

364 "intense struggle . . ." LB to Helen Coates, June 2, 1967.

364 "the undisputed major event . . ." *New York Times,* June 12, 1967.

365 "the idea of resurrection . . ." *Findings,* "Jerusalem."

365 "scores of men . . ." *New York Times,* July 10, 1967.

365 "Lenny conducts . . ." *New York Times,* "The Day They Made Music on Mt. Scopus," by Adolph Green, August 9, 1967.

365 "I'm amazed . . ." *New York Times,* July 10, 1967.

366 "the extraordinary warm . . ." *Jerusalem Post,* July 14, 1967.

366 "Teach *him* to do . . ." Mike Mindlin, author's interview.

366 "My back has been . . ." LB to Lukas Foss, August 8, 1967.

366 "Something weighed him down . . ." John Gruen, *The Private World of Leonard Bernstein.*

366 "Dear A, can't sleep . . ." LB to Aaron Copland, August 4, 1967.

367 "I am tortured . . ." LB to Lukas Foss, August 8, 1967.

367 "He becomes the young Chaplin . . ." John Gruen, *The Private World of Leonard Bernstein.*

367 "trying to be nice . . ." Ellen Ball, O.H.

367 "It has always been . . ." John Gruen, *The Private World of Leonard Bernstein.*

367 "We were so horrified . . ." Jamie Bernstein Thomas, O.H.

368 "There was a problem . . ." Ellen Ball, O.H.

368 ". . . I was actually more . . ." Nina Bernstein, O.H.

368 "I had a blast . . ." Alexander Bernstein, O.H.

368 "We were made . . ." Jamie Bernstein Thomas, O.H.

368 "It all ties up . . ." John Gruen, *The Private World of Leonard Bernstein.*

369 "ADORE INSCAPE BRAVO . . ." LB to Aaron Copland, August 30, 1967.

369 "Mahler: His Time Has Come" *High Fidelity,* September 1967.

369 "much more powerful . . ." *New York Times,* October 4, 1967.

369 "with diamonds twinkling sinfully . . ." *New York Daily News,* October 4, 1967.

370 "looked as if he might dance . . ." *Cincinnati Post* and *Times Star,* December 27, 1967.

370 "they emerge . . ." *Hi-Fi Stereo Review,* December 1967.

370 "When Aaron heard . . ." Phillip Ramey, author's interview.

370 "Aaron, it's amazing . . ." Vivian Perlis, *Copland Since 1943.*

370 "Dear A, It's two days . . ." LB to Aaron Copland, November 12, 1967.

371 "To conclude this evening . . ." *The New Yorker,* December 23, 1967.

371 "Hey, Lenny, wanna change . . ." Irma Lazarus, O.H.

371 "the natural growth and decline . . ." *Time,* December 15, 1967.

371 "In five years . . ." *Philadelphia Inquirer,* January 28, 1968.

372 "I took the score apart . . ." *New York Times,* August 1968.

372 "in part fascinating . . ." *New York Times,* April 15, 1968.

372 "She was so marvelous . . ." *Time,* April 26, 1968.

372 "He captured . . ." Ibid.

372 "It was the longest . . ." *Opera News,* July 1968.

372 "Music's insinuating grace . . ." *The Observer,* April 28, 1968.

372 "he peeled off his jacket . . ." *Newsweek,* April 28, 1968.

373 "I am through . . ." Ibid.

373 "The Karajan approach . . ." *New York Times,* May 24, 1968.

374 "Well how am I . . ." George Plimpton, ed., *American Journey,* source of all quotations concerning Robert Kennedy's funeral.

375 "Good morning, Daddy" Courtesy of Jamie Bernstein Thomas.

375 "As this horrifying birthday . . ." *Time,* August 23, 1988.

375 "The television glamor . . ." *New York Times,* August 18, 1968.

376 "Relax, friend" Reproduced by courtesy of Norman Rosten.

376 "For all his flaws . . ." *New York Times,* August 25, 1968.

376 "Lenny wanted me . . ." Ernest Fleischmann, O.H.

377 "All three . . . were in tears . . ." Evelyn Ames, *A Wind From The West.*

377 "They gave flowers . . ." *New York Times,* September 19, 1968. Lincer was correct. In *Family Matters* Burton Bernstein records that in Sam Bernstein's hometown, Korets, twenty-five Bernstein relatives were murdered by the Germans.

377 "frenzied proportions" *The Observer,* September 29, 1968.

377 "too high . . ." *Daily Mail* (London), September 27, 1968.

377 "too much brilliance . . ." *Daily Telegraph,* September 27, 1968.

377 "Look, it's Lenny . . ." *New York Times,* November 10, 1968.

377 all the judgment . . . Charles Duncan, *Atlanta Journal,* October 30, 1968.

378 "Lenny, you *said* those things . . ." John Gruen, O.H.

378 "There is much in the book . . ." Helen Coates to Alan Fluck, January 5, 1969.

378 "To have Bernstein behind you . . ." Dietrich Fischer-Dieskau, *Reverberations.*

379 "I have tried to exploit . . ." *New York Times,* January 12, 1969.

380 " 'My legs are drawing' " Burton Bernstein, *Family Matters.*

380 "This form of worship . . ." May 2, 1969, Archive, Temple Mishkan Tefila.

380 "with quiet, eloquent intensity . . ." *New York Post,* May 9, 1969.

380 "In the performance . . ." *Village Voice,* May 22, 1969.

381 "one of the very few . . ." *New York Times,* May 19, 1969.

381 "I just couldn't find . . ." Ibid.

381 "We leave Boulez *nothing* . . ." Mike Mindlin, author's interview.

PART FIVE
CHAPTER 34—RADICAL CHIC

386 "I wouldn't call it . . ." *The New Yorker,* May 22, 1969.

386 "He played a melody . . ." Paul Simon, O.H.

387 "I was immediately at the piano . . ." *New York Times,* January 25, 1970.

387 They never saw the light . . . Several songs were used in *The Race to Urga* in 1987.

387 "farcical had it not been . . ." *New York Times,* September 30, 1969.

387 "money, guidance, orientation . . ." Ibid.

388 "a celebration of human rights . . ." "Young People's Concert," recorded January 10, 1970.

388 "I've worked and written . . ." *New York Times,* December 23, 1969.

389 "dangerously towards self-indulgence . . ." Franco Zeffirelli, *Zeffirelli.*

389 "somewhat devitalized the score . . ." *New York Times,* January 9, 1970.

389 "They wrote a lot of nonsense . . ." *New York Times,* January 25, 1970.

390 "Harlem Panther . . ." *New York Times,* January 15, 1970.

390 "Leonard Bernstein and a Black Panther . . ." Ibid.

391 The word "dig" . . . was not part . . . But he had used the word in 1957 when writing to Felicia about *West Side Story:* "We're having our first runthru for people on Friday— Please may they dig it!" August 8, 1957.

391 "False note on Black Panthers . . ." *New York Times,* January 16, 1970.

392 "relieved it was over . . ." Jamie Bernstein Thomas, O.H.

392 "the Black Panthers' anti-Semitic policy" *New York Times,* October 19, 1980.

392 "floods of hate letters . . ." Ibid.

392 "As one who loves you . . ." Rabbi Judah Cahn to LB, February 28, 1970.

393 "Have a Panther to lunch . . ." *New York Post,* January 20, 1970. Bernstein had conducted Schoenberg's Chamber Symphony No. 2 in October 1966 and been obliged in one performance to stop and start again.

393   "If that party . . ." *New York Post,* January 22, 1970.

393   "It takes brains . . ." Michael Tilson Thomas, O.H.

393   "It's really an insane schedule . . ." *New York Times,* January 25, 1970.

394   "He asked me for a 'mixed' voice . . ." Plácido Domingo, author's interview.

394   "I'd give anything for a cigarette . . ." Schuyler Chapin, *Musical Chairs.* Chapin provides a detailed account of the Verdi *Requiem* production.

394   "Much of the splendor . . ." *The Times* (London), March 30, 1970.

394   "Elsa, don't believe a word . . ." Phillip Ramey, author's interview.

395   "the most perfect performance . . ." *Yediot Achrondt,* March 29, 1970.

395   "I directed the *Eroica* . . ." *Christian Science Monitor,* April 14, 1970.

395   "The perfection of this presentation . . ." Ibid.

395   "You had to hang on . . ." Dame Gwyneth Jones, author's interview.

395   "I discovered that Beethoven's music . . ." *Findings,* "Letter to Franz Endler: Beethoven's Ninth."

396   Schenk told Bernstein . . . Otto Schenk, author's interview.

396   "The sweep and conviction . . ." *International Herald Tribune,* May 27, 1970.

396   "you really did believe . . ." *The Times* (London), June 2, 1970.

397   "succeeds even with those . . ." *Beethoven's Birthday,* CBS-TV. Under its secondary title, *A Celebration in Vienna,* this bicentennial program is distributed as a video in the United States by Kultur International Films Ltd.

398   "Karajan heats the music . . ." *Die Presse,* June 10, 1970.

398   "It's the artists . . ." *Findings,* "Of Tanglewood, Koussevitzky and Hope."

399   "It was the worst summer . . ." Jamie Bernstein Thomas, O.H.

399   "There are malicious people . . ." Ibid.

399   "The audience started to applaud . . ." Kazuko Amano letter to author.

400   "I think it's one of my best . . ." Schuyler Chapin, *Leonard Bernstein.*

400   "Is there anything I can do . . ." Roger Stevens, O.H.

401   Using British filmmakers . . . Tony Palmer and this author were the documentary directors.

402   "Lenny tried to kiss . . ." Princess Margaret, author's interview.

402   "They all want to play . . ." Overheard by the author in Vienna.

402   a nightmare . . . LB to Burton Bernstein, April 7, 1971.

402   "saying all the wrong things . . ." Ibid.

403   "Important government officials . . ." Jack Anderson, *The Anderson Papers.*

403   "terribly depressed and searching desperately . . ." Shirley Bernstein, O.H.

404   "I feel young again . . ." *Women's Wear Daily,* August 26, 1974.

404   "It is much bigger . . ." *New York Times,* August 24, 1971.

404   "At a party in his honor . . ." Letter in Bernstein Archive.

405   "He was driving home . . ." Harry Kraut, author's interview.

405   "a wonderful, twinkly . . ." John McClure, O.H.

405   "very cute, goofy . . ." Jamie Bernstein Thomas, O.H.

406   "President Kennedy . . ." *Washington Post,* September 9, 1971.

406   "the most thrilling night . . ." Jack Gottlieb, ed., *Bernstein on Broadway.*

406   "It's stupendous . . ." *Washington Post,* September 9, 1971.

406   "The best sections . . ." *New York Times,* September 9, 1971.

407   "a combination of superficiality . . ." *New York Times,* September 12, 1971.

407   "an entirely new concept . . ." *Washington Evening Star,* July 27, 1971.

407   "the ritual is conducted . . ." Israel Philharmonic Concert Program, May 21, 1972.

408   "*Mass* follows three years of despair . . ." *Women's Wear Daily,* August 26, 1971.

409   "never grew up . . ." Text from *Beethoven's Birthday—A Celebration in Vienna,* CBS TV 1971 (See note on page 397.)

## CHAPTER 35—PROFESSOR BERNSTEIN

410 "I spent the summer . . ." *New York Times,* December 9, 1971.

411 "such junk . . ." *Boston Globe,* September 9, 1971.

411 "Everything I do . . ." *ASCAP Today* vol. 6, no. 1, July 1972, interview with Walter Wager. (Amplified from interview transcript held in Bernstein Archive.)

412 "until now the Philharmonic . . ." *Wochenpresse,* May 10, 1972.

412 "They didn't know Mahler . . ." BBC-TV/ Unitel, *The Love of Three Orchestras.*

412 *"An diesen Stelle . . ."* The author attended the rehearsal.

412 "I actually didn't feel . . ." *Newsweek,* May 1, 1972.

413 "heavenly chamber music . . ." *Express* (Vienna), May 8, 1972.

413 "They suddenly realized . . ." BBC-TV/ Unitel, *The Love of Three Orchestras.*

413 "I hope he had time . . ." Margaret Carson, O.H.

413 "I think she was speechless . . ." *New York Times,* June 7, 1972.

414 "It's the story . . ." Bishop Paul Moore to LB, July 11, 1972.

414 "dinky . . ." Gordon Davidson, O.H.

414 "with all his . . ." Harvey E. Phillips, *The Carmen Chronicle.*

414 "Maybe this is a doomed . . ." Ibid.

415 "not happy through the rehearsals . . ." Helen Coates to Alan Fluck, September 25, 1972.

415 "BEAUCOUP FRENCH . . ." *Variety,* September 27, 1972.

416 "Suddenly the door swung open . . ." David Thomas, Bernstein Archives.

416 "I can't tell you how exciting . . ." *Los Angeles Times,* December 31, 1972.

417 "The first time he visited . . ." Christoph Eschenbach, letter to the author. The palm tree Bernstein planted is now (1994) "big and healthy and wards off very well the storms that threaten from the West."

418 "My father . . . fell in love . . ." Jamie Bernstein Thomas, O.H.

421 "whose musical sensibilities . . ." Leonard Bernstein, *The Unanswered Question,* author's note.

421 "sloppy and tendentious . . ." *New York Times,* December 16, 1973.

421 "and she said that . . ." Harold Prince, *Contradictions.*

422 no interference from Hellman . . . Stephen Sondheim, author's interview.

422 "This version of *Candide* . . ." Craig Zadan, *Sondheim & Co.*

422 "the most brilliant work . . ." *New York Times,* March 6, 1974.

422 "Lenny is depressed . . ." Helen Coates to Alan Fluck, February 24, 1974.

422 "The friends separate . . ." Leonard Bernstein, Program Note, New York Philharmonic, New Zealand–Australia tour, August 1974.

423 "the loving handiwork . . ." *Newsweek,* May 27, 1974.

423 "It was the integer 2 . . ." New York Philharmonic, Program Note, April 3, 1975.

424 "He says it is Felicia's 'ball . . .' " Helen Coates to Alan Fluck, January 27, 1974.

424 "a less-than-wonderful occasion . . ." Jamie Bernstein Thomas, O.H.

425 "had to have another thing . . ." Nina Bernstein, O.H.

425 "Oh Phyllis, what a thing . . ." Phyllis Newman, *Just in Time.*

## CHAPTER 36—CRISES AND CATASTROPHE

427 "We miss you terribly . . ." LB to FMB, August 1974.

427 "They are younger . . ." *New York Times,* September 6, 1974.

427 "We are trying to tell . . ." *Washington Post,* September 6, 1974.

428 "I have just made a decision . . ." *New York Times,* April 25, 1975.

428 "There will be great joy . . ." *New York Times,* April 26, 1976.

428 "Yesterday," Helen Coates noted . . . Helen Coates to Alan Fluck, May 28, 1975.

429 "I'd give my balls . . ." *The Guardian* (London), August 17, 1975.

429 "It was," wrote Karl Löbl . . . *Kurier,* September 1, 1975.

429 He stood, seemingly exhausted . . . Charles Bornstein letter, Bernstein Archive. The author witnessed a similar scene in Vienna three days later.

430 he imagined himself as Hector Berlioz . . . LB conversation with the author, September 1975.

431 downbeat for the "Marseillaise" Serge Roux, author's interview.

431 "I loathed it . . ." Ken Mandelbaum, *Not Since Carrie.*

431 "it stinks . . ." Harry Kraut, author's interview.

432 "I've never been so confident . . ." *Philadelphia Inquirer,* February 22, 1976.

432 "the subject is not the presidency . . ." Ibid.

432 "We're just telling what we feel" Ibid.

433 "the musical of the decade . . ." Ibid.

433 "stultifyingly ponderous and repetitive . . ." *Variety,* February 27, 1976.

433 "Only two titans . . ." *New York Post,* May 10, 1976.

433 "a sure flop . . ." Tom Cothran diary, April 4, 1976.

434 "a diamond-studded dinosaur . . ." Patricia Routledge, O.H.

434 "We're the lonely men . . ." *Time,* March 25, 1957, lyric by Alan Jay Lerner & LB?

434 "I wonder how to divide . . ." *Washington Post,* January 7, 1946.

435 a new friendship . . . Chris Barnes died of AIDS in 1988.

436 "it was largely his fault . . ." Jamie Bernstein Thomas's diary, May 16, 1977.

436 "so unhappy she couldn't sleep . . ." Ellen Ball, O.H.

436 "He was torturing himself . . ." Kenneth Ehrman, letter to the author.

437 "I hate it!!! . . ." Helen Coates to Alan Fluck, October 2, 1976.

437 "it is a trial separation . . ." *Newsweek,* November 8, 1976.

437 "We hope to reconcile" *People,* November 15, 1976.

438 "When I asked him to repeat . . ." John Mordler, letter to the author.

438 "I really doubt . . ." Helen Coates to Alan Fluck, December 19, 1976.

438 Felicia was furious . . . Margaret Carson, author's interview.

438 "Felicia had understood him . . ." Ellen Ball, O.H.

438 "a jungle wilderness . . ." Tom Cothran to "Philip," December 27, 1976.

438 "caught in a depressed fury . . ." LB to Kenneth Ehrman, January 14, 1977.

439 "Tell him he can wear . . ." Harry Kraut, author's interview.

439 "The son of a bitch . . ." Michael Wager, author's interview.

439 "Marriages may stand . . ." *Daily News,* March 16, 1977.

440 "smarmy" and "false" Paul Bowles, author's interview.

440 Richard Strauss . . . The program was *Don Juan,* songs with orchestra, *Till Eulenspiegel* and the closing scene from *Salome.*

440 "depressed" . . . "remote" Jamie Bernstein Thomas, diary, July 9, 1977.

441 "Felicia told me . . ." Phyllis Newman, *Just in Time.*

441 "I'm afraid it's going . . ." Jamie Bernstein Thomas, August 2, 1977.

443 "a glowing testimonial . . ." *Washington Post,* October 12, 1977.

443 "Let us do something grand . . ." Frank O'Hara, *To the Poem* from *The Collected Poems of Frank O'Hara,* 1971.

443 "a real right thing" *The New Yorker,* January 2, 1978.

444 "One was married to someone . . ." Gertrude Stein, "Storyette H.M.," from *Quotations and Prayers,* 1934.

444 "I cannot say . . ." Edna St. Vincent Millay, *Collected Poems,* 1923, 1951.

444 "Summer still sings . . ." "Sixty Minutes," CBS-TV, February 7, 1980. Paul Shales (*Washington Post,* same date) described Bernstein's appearance as "terminally but somehow embraceably hammy."

444 "during the rest of his life . . ." *Washington Post,* October 16, 1977.

445 "It was an awful cough . . ." Ellen Ball, O.H.

445 "cotton sheets, cotton nightgowns . . ." Phyllis Newman, *Just in Time.*

445 "but also determination . . ." Karen Bernstein, author's interview.

445 "I'll be better next week . . ." Gail Jacobs, author's interview.

445 "all sunken and gray . . ." Jamie Bernstein Thomas, O.H.

445 Burton Bernstein had hopes . . . Burton Bernstein, O.H.

445 "Brompton cocktails" Shirley Bernstein, author's interview.

446 "She's meant to live . . ." Ellen Ball, O.H.

446 "I don't want to die . . ." Michael Wager, author's interview.

447 "You're going to die . . ." Jamie Bernstein Thomas, O.H.

PART SIX
CHAPTER 37—TOWARD *A QUIET PLACE*

451 "As her last weeks . . ." Helen Coates to Alan Fluck, 2 July 1978.

451 "There's not a minute . . ." Christina Burton, author's interview.

452 "the person I love . . ." *New York Daily News,* April 22, 1987.

452 "We tried everything . . ." Burton Bernstein, O.H.

452 "Leonard Bernstein will have to live . . ." *Prince George's Post,* September 7, 1978.

452 "the most horrible night . . ." *Dayton Daily News,* April 1, 1979.

452 "I don't mind . . ." *Miami Herald,* August 27, 1978.

453 "and they of course all said . . ." Nina Bernstein, O.H.

453 "We sat there . . ." Ibid.

454 "I took a certain time . . ." Kazuko Amano, letter to the author.

455 "I was ushered . . ." *Findings, "Ni commencement ni fin."*

456 "You taught me . . ." Harry Kraut, author's interview.

456 "Judging by . . ." LB handwritten draft letter (not sent) to New York *Post,* November 13, 1979.

456 "can have an extraordinary . . ." *Findings,* "Copland at 79."

456 "Lenny composed . . ." Betty Comden, O.H.

457 "It was all about . . ." Nina Bernstein, O.H.

457 "It reflects . . ." *Boston Globe,* September 24, 1980.

457 "The material in *Divertimento* . . ." Author's interview with LB for Unitel (not transmitted), October 1984.

458 "he went to pee . . ." Steve Richman, author's interview.

458 "BERNSTEIN SHOCKS . . ." *New York Post,* November 24, 1980.

459 "and I was heckled . . ." *Los Angeles Times,* January 11, 1981.

459 "We were really proud . . ." Nina Bernstein, O.H.

459 "As for Depressions . . ." Tom Cothran to LB, September 17, 1980.

460 "It looks like the studio . . ." Gail Jacobs, O.H.

460 "Will psychoanalysis . . ." Tom Cothran to LB, September 25, 1980.

460 "For Heaven's sake . . ." Tom Cothran to LB, October 8, 1980.

460 "It's clear to one and all . . ." Tom Cothran to LB, September 17, 1980.

461 "The only truly guileless . . ." Stephen Wadsworth article in Deutsche Grammophon program booklet for *A Quiet Place.*

462 "writing music . . ." "Sixty Minutes," February 9, 1980.

462 "the central work . . ." *International Herald Tribune,* November 27, 1981.

462 "For the first time . . ." *Opera News,* August 1983.

463 "My life is . . ." Ibid.

463 "We turned one quartet . . ." Deutsche Grammophon program booklet for *A Quiet Place.*

464 "will be in totally . . ." LB to Harry Kraut, handwritten memorandum, September 2, 1981, typed and corrected by Kraut (Bernstein Archive).

464 "Before actually setting . . ." Deutsche Grammophon program booklet for *A Quiet Place*.

464 "ragged and bleeding . . ." *Cincinnati Inquirer*, February 15, 1982.

465 "formally unlike any other work . . ." Deutsche Grammophon program booklet for *Halil*, introductory article by Peter Gradenwitz.

465 "a brooding, terrific element . . ." *Washington Tribune*, March 26, 1982.

466 "I'm all right . . ." Zvi Litwak, O.H.

466 "trying to be too many . . ." *Boston Globe*, July 12, 1981.

467 "sick of that lousy . . ." Helen Epstein, *Music Talks: Conversations with Musicians*, "Listening to Lenny."

467 "One minute he could look . . ." Ibid.

467 "He took my hand . . ." Martin Fleischmann, author's interview.

468 loud piano arrangements . . . Charlie Harmon, author's interview.

468 "lined up . . ." Irwin Kostal, O.H.

468 "whether Lenny was ready . . ." Gordon Davidson, O.H.

468 "It continually rings false . . ." *New York Times*, June 20, 1983.

469 "four hopelessly uninteresting people . . ." *Newsweek*, June 27, 1983.

469 "the birth of a powerful new . . ." *Village Voice*, July 5, 1983.

469 "one of the richest . . ." *The New Yorker*, July 11, 1983.

470 "the emotional tension . . ." Leighton Kerner, "Disquieting Drama," Kennedy Center Program Book, July 21, 1984.

## CHAPTER 38—ROYAL PROGRESS

472 "I am dead serious . . ." *Lawrence Eagle Tribune*, August 26, 1983.

472 "He was getting much harder . . ." Jamie Bernstein Thomas, O.H.

473 "Ev'rybody out . . ." Helen Epstein, *Music Talks: Conversations with Musicians*, "Listening to Lenny."

473 "I think I'll leave . . ." Phillip Ramey, author's interview.

474 "Lenny was hugely relieved . . ." David Thomas, Bernstein Archive.

474 "Jamie's family . . ." Ibid.

480 "an act of prayer . . ." Press Release, May 1985.

481 "His eyes, remembered . . ." *Israel Today*, October 18, 1985.

482 "What is the point . . ." Bernstein Archive.

482 "He gave me a little scenario . . ." Stephen Wadsworth, O.H.

482 "The key story . . ." Bernstein Archive.

482 "I'm very tired . . ." Stephen Wadsworth, O.H.

483 "shot to hell" D. P. Stearns, "Bernstein Con Brio," *Ovation*, December 1986.

483 "a little Viennese adulation . . ." Jamie Bernstein Thomas, October 16, 1990.

483 "He stood there . . ." Nina Bernstein, O.H.

484 "the genius with . . ." *Sunday Times* (London), May 11, 1986.

484 "I was diagnosed . . ." *USA Today*, August 6, 1986.

484 "the impossibility of getting . . ." Harry Kraut, author's interview.

484 "had abdicated responsibility . . ." Stephen Wadsworth, O.H.

485 "You tell Michael Jackson . . ." David Pack, O.H.

486 "musical athletics . . ." Composer's Program Note, Deutsche Grammophon Booklet accompanying the *Concerto for Orchestra*.

486 "We hear a bolder Bernstein . . ." *New York Post*, September 15, 1986.

486 "from the Middle East . . ." Ibid.

489 "We did it in ten days . . ." *New York Times*, December 12, 1986.

489 "with a standing . . ." *Prelude, Fugue & Riffs*, published by the Leonard Bernstein Society, Fall 1992.

489 "His composing life . . ." *Ovation*, December 1986.

489 "straight and strong . . ." Bernstein Archive, "LB's List"—a note on "A Pray by Blecht," November 6, 1986.

490 "It's not going to work . . ." Michael Barrett, author's interview.

490 "grudging" Jerome Robbins, letter to the author.

490 "I was big . . ." Jamie Bernstein Thomas, O.H.

491 "I made a solemn promise . . ." Tanglewood Press Conference Transcript, August 1988.

491 "Dear DD . . ." LB to David Diamond, August 8, 1988.

491 "Dear old David . . ." LB to David Diamond, October 20, 1988.

495 "He *is* the Joy . . ." Text courtesy of Al Berr.

## CHAPTER 39 — THE LIVING LEGEND

500 "He was the most important . . ." Mark Stringer, O.H.

500 "brimmed with musical talent . . ." *Sunday Telegraph* (London), December 11, 1988.

501 "a magnum shot . . ." "John Wells to LB . . ." February 11, 1989.

501 " 'Goodness,' you would say . . ." Bernstein Archive.

502 "the man who had rebuilt . . ." Schuyler Chapin, *Leonard Bernstein*.

502 "They are burning books . . ." Mark Stringer, O.H.

502 "needs more surrealism . . ." "John Wells File," Bernstein Archive.

502 "a sequence of apparently . . ." John Wells to LB, September 2, 1989.

502 "Saul, David, Jonathan Triangle Opera" "John Wells File," Bernstein Archive.

503 "narrow and foolish" Peter Shaffer, author's interview.

504 "three big kisses" *The Independent* (London), September 4, 1989.

504 "I've never conducted better . . ." Mark Stringer, O.H.

504 "He could never get . . ." Craig Urquhart, O.H.

505 "lost masterpiece . . ." *New York Newsday,* October 24, 1989.

505 "rivetingly, definitively . . ." *New York Daily News,* October 30, 1989.

505 "I have been on the brink" Jack Gottlieb, author's interview.

505 "I haven't gone there . . ." *Rolling Stone,* November 29, 1990, the posthumous publication of a November 1989 interview with Jonathan Cott.

506 "I cannot risk . . ." Quoted by Mark Taylor, author's interview.

506 "People like William Buckley . . ." *Rolling Stone,* November 29, 1990.

506 "wanted us to connect" Mark Taylor, author's interview.

507 "Do you know this piece?" Ibid.

507 "You loved her?" Ibid.

507 "He can't play . . ." Louis d'Almeida, author's interview.

510 "We'd stay up all night . . ." Mark Adams Taylor, author's interview.

510 "was still diving . . ." Leonard Bernstein obituary, *The Independent* (London), October 16, 1990.

511 "feel right" Leslie Tomkins, author's interview.

511 three concerts at Carnegie Hall . . . Sibelius's First Symphony, on March 11, 1990, was the last work Leonard Bernstein conducted in New York. In the same program, Thomas Hampson sang two song cycles by Mahler.

512 "Every time I take . . ." Mark Stringer, O.H.

512 "The key . . ." LB to Mark Stringer, April 5, 1990. In shortening the text, the author has reordered the paragraphs indicated by the ellipses.

514 on bended knee . . . Memories of Bernstein's Bayreuth visit from author's interviews with Thomas Gayda, Daniel Mauermann, Mark Stringer and Craig Urquhart.

514 "Let's have a day . . ." Mark Taylor, author's interview.

514 "It was bizarre . . ." Craig Urquhart, O.H.

515 "He asked me . . ." Leonard Bernstein obituary, *Daily Telegraph* (London), October 16, 1990.

516 "an awful, awful day . . ." Craig Urquhart, O.H.

517 "He will listen . . ." Mark Taylor, author's interview.

517 "to devote most . . ." Pacific Music Festival brochure 1990

517 "So this has never . . ." *Sunday Telegraph* (London), July 15, 1990.

517 "Kazuko, I am tired . . ." Kazuko Amano, letter to author.

518 "He is chewing gum . . ." *Sunday Telegraph* (London), July 15, 1990.

518 He danced . . . Michael Tilson Thomas, author's interview.

518 " 'Something has got . . .' " *Sunday Telegraph* (London), July 15, 1990.

519 "The real question . . ." Craig Urquhart, O.H.

519 "profoundly disturbed" Mark Taylor, author's interview.

519 "How I wished . . ." Kazuko Amano, letter to author.

521 "I want five . . ." *Boston Globe,* August 14, 1990.

521 asked Bernstein how . . . Ibid.

521 "How do they expect . . ." Mark Stringer, O.H.

521 "You would see . . ." Ibid.

521 "All of the charisma . . ." *Boston Globe,* August 16, 1990.

521 "he really wasn't . . ." Mark Stringer, O.H.

521 "slow, spacious . . ." *Boston Globe,* August 20, 1990.

522 absolutely slate gray . . . Mark Stringer, O.H.

522 "I saw that . . ." Mrs. Jennie Bernstein, O.H.

522 "Who am I kidding? . . ." Dan Gustin, O.H.

## CHAPTER 40—FINAL DAYS: AUGUST–OCTOBER 1990

523 "They were both smoking . . ." Phyllis Newman Green, author's interview.

523 "He had changed clothes . . ." Craig Urquhart, O.H.

524 "You're supposed to take . . ." Ibid.

524 "the purpose and orientation . . ." Bernstein Archive, 1990 date book.

524 Loss of appetite . . . Phillip Allen, O.H.

525 "We spent hours . . ." Ibid.

526 "Can you imagine . . ." Ellen Ball, O.H.

526 "It's all happened . . ." Lauren Bacall, author's interview.

526 "I said, 'Come on' . . ." Martha Gellhorn, author's interview.

526 He told his son . . . Alexander Bernstein, author's interview.

526 "He called me . . ." Mrs. Jennie Bernstein, O.H.

526 "LEONARD BERNSTEIN WITHDRAWS . . ." Bernstein Archive.

527 "There's a song . . ." Mark Taylor, author's interview.

528 "The obvious fear . . ." Ibid. (Taylor noted down Bernstein's remarks at the time.)

528 "Mozart? The *Requiem?* . . ." Michael Tilson Thomas, author's interview.

528 "an uneasy feeling . . ." Patricia Pulliam, O.H.

529 "Yes . . . I think it's about time" Michael Wager, author's interview.

529 "It gave me hope . . ." Craig Urquhart, O.H.

529 "I and a musical friend . . ." *Rolling Stone,* November 29, 1990.

529 "You are the only person . . ." Aaron Stern, author's interview.

530 "Is there anything else . . ." Ibid.

530 "Go to your pillow . . ." Jelaluddin Rumi (1207–73), *Like This,* English version by Coleman Barks.

530 "Tell me the truth . . ." Aaron Stern, author's interview (Stern noted down Bernstein's remarks the same evening).

530 "I'm thinking about writing . . ." Michael Wager, author's interview.

531 "Help me . . ." Phillip Allen, O.H.

531 "Please, please, give me oblivion" Michael Wager, author's interview.

531 "Bernstein was humming along . . ." *New York Times,* October 16, 1990.

532 "Here in America . . ." BBC-TV "Omnibus" obituary, October 19, 1990. See the Prologue for an account of Leonard Bernstein's funeral.

# SELECTED BIBLIOGRAPHY

BOOKS BY LEONARD BERNSTEIN

BERNSTEIN, LEONARD, *The Joy of Music*. New York: Simon and Schuster, 1959. Reprinted by Anchor Books, 1994.

———, *The Infinite Variety of Music*. New York: Simon and Schuster, 1966. Reprinted by Anchor Books, 1993.

———, *The Unanswered Question*. Cambridge, Mass.: Harvard University Press/Cambridge Press, 1976.

———, *Findings*. New York: Simon and Schuster, 1982. Reprinted by Anchor Books, 1993.

———, *Leonard Bernstein's Young People's Concerts,* Jack Gottlieb, ed. New York: Simon and Schuster, 1962. Revised and expanded, Anchor Books, 1992.


BOOKS ON LEONARD BERNSTEIN

BERNSTEIN, BURTON, *The Grove*. New York: McGraw-Hill, 1961.

———, *Family Matters: Sam, Jennie, and the Kids*. New York: Summit Books, 1982.

BERNSTEIN, SHIRLEY, *Making Music: Leonard Bernstein*. Chicago: Encyclopedia Britannica Press, 1963.

BRIGGS, JOHN, *Leonard Bernstein*. New York: World Publishing Company, 1961.

CHAPIN, SCHUYLER, *Leonard Bernstein: Notes from a Friend*. New York: Walker, 1992.

EWEN, DAVID, *Leonard Bernstein*. London: W. H. Allen, 1967.

FLUEGEL, JANE, ed. *Bernstein Remembered*. New York: Carroll & Graf Publishers, Inc., 1991.

FREEDLAND, MICHAEL, *Leonard Bernstein*. London: Harrap, 1987.

GOTTLIEB, JACK, ed., *Bernstein on Broadway*. Introductory articles by George Abbott, Harold Prince, Jerome Robbins, Stephen Sondheim, Betty Comden and Adolph Green. New York: Amberson, 1981.

————, ed., *Leonard Bernstein: A Complete Catalogue of His Works*. 2d ed. New York: Jalni Publications/Boosey and Hawkes, 1988.

GRADENWITZ, PETER, *Leonard Bernstein*. London: Berg Publishers, 1987.

GRUEN, JOHN, *The Private World of Leonard Bernstein*. New York: Ridge Press, Viking Press, 1968.

LEDBETTER, STEVEN, ed., *Sennets and Tuckets: A Bernstein Celebration*. Boston: Boston Symphony Orchestra in association with David R. Godine Publishers, 1988.

PEYSER, JOAN, *Bernstein: A Biography*. New York: Beech Tree Press, 1987.


## GENERAL BIBLIOGRAPHY

AMES, EVELYN, *A Wind from the West*. Boston: Houghton Mifflin Company, 1970.

AMRAM, DAVID, *Vibrations*. New York: Macmillan, 1968.

ANDERSON, JACK, *The Anderson Papers*. New York: Random House, 1973.

ARDOIN, JOHN, *The Callas Legacy*. New York: Scribner's, 1982.

ATKINSON, BROOKS, *Broadway*. Rev. ed. New York: Macmillan, 1974.

AUDEN, W. H., *Collected Longer Poems,* Edward Mendelson, ed. New York: Random House, 1969.

BOWLES, PAUL, *Without Stopping*. New York: Putnam, 1972.

CARPENTER, HUMPHREY, *Benjamin Britten*. New York: Scribner's, 1993.

CHAPIN, SCHUYLER, *Musical Chairs*. New York: Putnam, 1977.

CHESTERMAN, ROBERT, ed., *Conversations with Conductors*. London: Robson Books, 1976.

CULSHAW, JOHN, *Putting the Record Straight*. London: Secker and Warburg, 1982.

DOWNES, OLIN, *10 Operatic Masterpieces* (foreword by Dimitri Mitropoulos). New York: Broadcast Music, 1952.

EPSTEIN, HELEN, *Music Talks: Conversations with Musicians*. New York: McGraw-Hill, 1987.

FISCHER-DIESKAU, DIETRICH, *Reverberations* (original German title: *Nachklang*). New York: Fromm International, 1984.

FORDIN, HUGH, *The Movies' Greatest Musicals*. Frederick Unger Publishing Co. (pap.), 1984.

FRIEDRICH, OTTO, *Glenn Gould: A Life and Variations*. New York: Random House, 1989.

GEBHARD, HEINRICH, *The Art of Pedaling* (foreword by Leonard Bernstein). New York: Franco Colombo, 1963.

GORDON, ERIC, *Mark the Music: The Life of Marc Blitzstein*. New York, St. Martin's Press, 1989.

GUTHRIE, TYRONE, *A Life in the Theatre*. New York: McGraw-Hill, 1959.

HEINSHEIMER, HANS W., *Best Regards to Aida*. New York: Knopf, 1968.

HELLMAN, LILLIAN (lyrics by Leonard Bernstein, Richard Wilbur, John Latouche, Lillian Hellman and Dorothy Parker), *Candide: An Operetta Based on Voltaire's Satire*. New York: Random House, 1957.

————, *Pentimento*. Boston: Little, Brown, 1973.

————, *Scoundrel Time,* Boston: Little, Brown, 1976.

KAPLAN, J. D., ed., *The Dialogues of Plato,* Benjamin Jowett trans. New York: Washington Square Press, 1950.

LANG, KLAUS, *The Karajan Dossier*. London: Faber and Faber, 1991.

LEVANT, OSCAR, *The Memoirs of an Amnesiac*. New York: Putnam, 1965.

LIBMAN, LILIAN, *And Music at the Close*. New York: Norton, 1972.

MANCHESTER, WILLIAM, *The Glory and the Dream*. Boston: Little, Brown, 1974.

MANDELBAUM, KEN, *Not Since Carrie: Forty Years of Broadway Musical Flops*. New York: St. Martin's, 1991.

MATHEOPOULOS, HELEN, *Maestro*. London: Hutchinson, 1982.

MENEGHINI, G. B., *My Wife, Maria Callas,* Henry Wisneski, trans. New York: Farrar, Straus & Giroux, 1982.

MENUHIN, YEHUDI, *Unfinished Journey*. New York: Knopf, 1976.

MITROPOULOS, DIMITRI, *A Correspondence with Katy Katsoyanis 1930–1960*. New York: Martin Dale, 1963.

MORDDEN, ETHAN, *Broadway Babies*. New York: Oxford University Press, 1983.

NAVASKY, VICTOR, *Naming Names*. New York: Viking Press, 1980.

NEWMAN, PHYLLIS, *Just in Time: Notes from My Life*. New York: Simon and Schuster, 1988.

OSATO, SONO, *Distant Dances*. New York: Knopf, 1980.

PAGE, TIM, ed., *The Glenn Gould Reader*. New York: Knopf, 1984.

PERLIS, VIVIAN, *Aaron Copland, 1900–1942*. New York: St. Martin's, 1984.

————, *Copland Since 1943*. New York, St. Martin's, 1989.

PHILLIPS, HARVEY E., *The Carmen Chronicle*. New York: Stein and Day, 1973.

PLIMPTON, GEORGE, ed., *American Journey: The Times of Robert Kennedy*. New York: Harcourt Brace Jovanovich, 1970.

PRINCE, HAROLD, *Contradictions*. New York: Dodd, Mead and Co., 1974.

RODZINSKI, HALINA, *Our Two Lives*. New York: Scribner's, 1976.

ROLLYSON, CARL, *Nothing Ever Happens to the Brave: The Story of Martha Gellhorn*. New York: St. Martin's, 1990.

ROREM, NED, *The Paris Diaries*. New York: Braziller, 1966.

————, *The New York Diary*. New York: Braziller, 1967.

————, *Settling the Score*. San Diego: Harcourt Brace Jovanovich, 1988.

RUBINSTEIN, ARTHUR, *My Many Years*. New York: Knopf, 1980.

RUMI, JELALUDDIN, *Like This,* Coleman Barks, trans. Athens, Ga.: Maypop Books, N.D.

SCHONBERG, HAROLD, *The Great Conductors*. New York: 1967.

SHANET, HOWARD, *Philharmonic*. New York: Doubleday, 1975.

SHAPIRO, DORIS, *We Danced All Night: My Life Behind the Scenes with Alan Jay Lerner*. New York: Morrow, 1990.

SHARAFF, IRENE, *Broadway and Beyond*. New York: Van Nostrand Rhinehold, 1976.

SHICKEL, RICHARD, *The World of Carnegie Hall*. New York: Julian Messner, 1963.

SMITH, MOSES, *Koussevitzky*. New York: Allen, Towne & Heath, Inc., 1947.

SPENDER, STEPHEN, *Journals 1939–1983*. New York: Random House, 1986.

STORR, ANTHONY, *Music and the Mind*. New York: Macmillan, 1992.

THOMSON, VIRGIL, *American Music Since 1910*. New York: Holt Rinehart & Winston, 1971.

TOOBIN, JEROME, *Agitato*. New York: Viking Press, 1975.

VOLTAIRE, *Candide,* anon. English trans. New York: Dover Publications, 1991.

WEISER, PETER, *Wien Stark Bewölkt*. Vienna/Munich: Brandstaller Verlag, 1984.

WHEELER, HUGH. *Candide: The Musical* (foreword by Harold Prince). New York: Macmillan, 1976.

WILLIAMS, TENNESSEE, *Memoirs*. New York: Doubleday, 1972.

WRIGHT, WILLIAM, *Lillian Hellman: The Image, the Woman*. New York: Simon and Schuster, 1986.

ZADAN, CRAIG, *Sondheim & Co.,* New York: Macmillan, 1974.

ZEFFIRELLI, FRANCO, *Zeffirelli: The Autobiography of Franco Zeffirelli*. London: Weidenfeld & Nicholson, 1986.

## ADDITIONAL SOURCES

*1. Oral History Interviews*—deposited in the Leonard Bernstein Archive

*Family*
Jennie Bernstein (mother), Shirley Bernstein (sister), Burton Bernstein (brother), Jamie Bernstein Thomas (daughter), Alexander Bernstein (son), Nina Bernstein (daughter), Karen Bernstein (niece), Ellen Ball (formerly Mrs. Burton Bernstein), Jane Anderson (Mrs. Burton Bernstein), Dorothy Resnick (LB aunt)

*Staff*
Phillip Allen, Jack Gottlieb, Charlie Harmon, Patricia Pulliam, Craig Urquhart

*Others*
George Abbott, Louis d'Almeida, Victor Alpert, Lauren Bacall, Rosamund Bernier, Judith Braun, Leonard Burkat, Sarah Caldwell, Margaret Carson, Schuyler Chapin, Saul Chaplin, Marion Lazar Claff, Betty Comden, Frank Corsaro, Phyllis Curtin, Gordon Davidson, Judi Davidson, Harry Ellis Dickson, Stanley Drucker, Roger Englander, Ernest Fleischmann, Elliot Forbes, Lukas Foss, Joel Friedman, George Gaines, Sylvia Gassell, David Glazer, Morton Gould, Adolph Green, John Gruen, Dan Gustin, Erik Haagensen, Edys Merrill Hunter, Robert Joseph, Gene Kelly, Irwin Kostal, Robert Lantz, Irma Lazarus, Janice Levit, Robert Lubell, Elaine Lubell, John McClure, Roddy McDowall, Allyn Ann McLerie, John Mauceri, Diana Menuhin, Yehudi Menuhin, Arthur Tillman Merritt, Frank Milburn, Mike Mindlin, Carlos Moseley, Phyllis Moss, Arnold Newman, Richard Ortner, Seiji Ozawa, David Pack, Shirley

Gabis Perle, Tod Perry, Sid Ramin, Halina Rodzinski, Ned Rorem, Friede Rothe, Patricia Routledge, William Schuman, Howard Shanet, Harold Shapero, Paul Simon, Oliver Smith, Anna Sokolow, Isaac Stern, Roger Stevens, Mark Stringer, Michael Tilson Thomas, Stephen Wadsworth Zinsser, Mildred Spiegel Zucker

2. *Additional Interviews*—carried out by the author in person or by telephone
Claudio Abbado, Ellen Adler, Mary Ahern, Guido Ajmone-Marsan, Antonio de Almeida, Alison Ames, Robert Arbuckle, Michael Barrett, Patricia Birch, Martin Bookspan, Paul Bowles, Naneen Boyce, Gunther Breest, Michael Bronson, Justin Brown, Kirk Browning, Lionel Bryer, Christina Burton, Helena Burton, Robert Chesterman, Barbara Cook, Alistair Cooke, John Corigliano, Jr., Jonathan Cott, Eric Crozier, Ned Davies, Agnes de Mille, Peter Diamand, David Diamond, Clare Dibble, Plácido Domingo, William Draper, Louise Edeiken, Phillipe Entremont, Mia Farrow, Verna Fine, Robert Fizdale, Martin Fleischmann, Alan Fluck, Ellis Freedman, Rodney Friend, Bob Gallo, Thomas Gayda, Martha Gellhorn, Valery Gergiev, Clive Gillinson, Morris Golde, Phyllis Newman Green, Edward Greenfield, John Guare, Henry A. Grunwald, Louise Grunwald, Till Haberfeld, Jerry Hadley, Bobbie Hallig, Klaus Hallig, Kitty Carlisle Hart, Hans Heinsheimer, Don Hewitt, Raphael Hillyer, Horant H. Hohlfeld, Peter Hollander, Marilyn Horne, Joseph Horowitz, Sir Ian Hunter, Gail Jacobs, Dorle Jarmel, Albert Johnson, Dame Gwyneth Jones, Quincy Jones, Richard Kaye, Ardis Krainik, Harry Kraut, Lina Lalandi, Brian Large, Arthur Laurents, Carol Lawrence, Richard Leacock, Mary Jo Little, Zvi Litvak, Karl Löbl, Christa Ludwig, Princess Margaret, Erich Mauermann, Sir Peter Maxwell Davies, Gustav Meier, Bishop Paul Moore, Kurt Ollmann, David Oppenheim, George Plimpton, Norman Podhoretz, André Previn, Harold Prince, Dennis Quilley, Phillip Ramey, Jean-Pierre Rampal, Azariah Rapoport, Steven Richman, Mstislav Rostropovich, Serge Roux, Julius Rudel, Wilfried Scheib, Otto Schenk, Stephen Schwartz, Edward Seckerson, Leonard Slatkin, Nicolas Slonimsky, Erik Smith, Priscilla Smith, Sir Georg Solti, Valerie Solti, Stephen Sondheim, David Stahl, Aaron Stern, Vera Stern, Thomas Stewart, Mark Stringer, Robert Tear, Dame Kiri Te Kanawa, Leslie Tomkins, Sir John Tooley, Basil Tschaikov, Jean Uppman, Theodor Uppman, Members of the Vienna Philharmonic, Pierre Vozlinsky, Michael Wager, John Walker, Albert K. Webster, Elly Weiser, Peter Weiser, Hugo Weisgall, Alexis Weissenberg, Charles Wellrich, Richard Wilbur, Fritz Willheim, Sigrid Willheim, Marianne Zeitlin

3. *Personal Reminiscences*—submitted to the author directly or to the LB Archive
Samuel Adler, Kazuko Amano, Susann Baumgärtel, Till Baumgärtel, Charles Bornstein, Herbert Chappell, Kenneth Ehrman, Christoph Eschenbach, David Israel, Daniel Mauermann, John Mordler, Hanno Rinke, Jerome Robbins, Mark Adams Taylor, David Thomas, Uri Toeplitz, François Valéry

4. *The Leonard Bernstein Archive*
- Press cuttings preserved on microfilm by Helen Coates, 1932–88
- Magazines
- Originals of Leonard Bernstein letters presented to the archive by the recipients
- Copies of typed letters dispatched by Leonard Bernstein (business and private)
- Letters sent to Leonard Bernstein (business and private)
- Recordings, liner notes
- Concert programs
- Nonmusical manuscripts—articles, reviews, poems, television and radio scripts
- Photographs, many annotated by Helen Coates
- Memorabilia—awards, citations, diplomas, etc.
- Date books 1944–1990

*5. Other Archives*
Boston Symphony Orchestra, Carnegie Hall, Chicago Symphony Orchestra, Curtis Institute, E.M.I. (London), Granada Television, Israel Philharmonic Orchestra, The John F. Kennedy Center for the Performing Arts, Library of Congress, London Philharmonic, London Symphony Orchestra, The Metropolitan Opera, Museum of Television and Radio, New York City Opera, New York Philharmonic Orchestra, New York Public Library, The State University of Wisconsin (Blitzstein papers), Temple Mishkan Tefila (Roxbury, Mass.), The Tanglewood Music Center, *Tanglewood Remembered: The Music Center Yearbook* (Barbara Erde Mandell, ed.), Teatro alla Scala, Milan, Vienna Philharmonic Orchestra

*6. Bernstein Interviews*—printed or transcribed from radio, television, or archival projects

WGBH Boston, 1985, re: Boston Latin School

BBC-TV/Unitel, 1984, re: *West Side Story*

BBC-TV/Unitel, 1985: *The Love of Three Orchestras*

BBC-TV/Unitel, 1987: *Childhood*—uncompleted, never aired

LWT, London, 1973, re: *Trouble in Tahiti*

Unitel, 1985, re: Wagner—uncompleted, never aired

Unitel, 1987: *Teachers and Teaching*

USIA, 1978: *Reflections* (film)

Burton Bernstein, interview with LB (excerpts were published in *Town and Country* magazine, July 1990), re: Carnegie Hall, 1989.

Paul Hume, Oral History Project, Kennedy Center Archive, 1981

*7. Unpublished Theses*—only those consulted by the author are listed
GOTTLIEB, JACK, "The Music of Leonard Bernstein: A Study of Melodic Manipulations." Urbana: Graduate College of the University of Illinois, 1964.
LEHRMAN, LEONARD, "Leonard Bernstein's *Serenade (after Plato's Symposium)*: An Analysis." Ithaca: Graduate School of Cornell University, 1977.
LUTHER, SIGRID, "The *Anniversaries* for Solo Piano by Leonard Bernstein." Baton Rouge: Louisiana State University, 1986.
VON OPPENHEIM, ALEXANDRA, "*Candide* von Leonard Bernstein" [production history 1956–89]. Hamburg: University of Hamburg, 1993.
PEARLMUTTER, ALAN, "Leonard Bernstein's *Dybbuk*." Baltimore: The Johns Hopkins University, 1985.

*8. Miscellaneous*
Dramatists Guild Round Table Series, *Landmark Symposiums,* Summer 1981, *On the Town;* Autumn 1985, *West Side Story.* (Excerpts reproduced by permission)
FINE, IRVING, "Young Americans: Bernstein and Foss," *Modern Music,* vol. XXII, no. 4, 1945.
GOTTLIEB, JACK, "Symbols of Faith in the Music of Leonard Bernstein," *Musical Quarterly,* vol. 66, April 1980.
Museum of Broadcasting catalogue, *Leonard Bernstein: The Television Work,* 1985.
Museum of Television and Radio catalogue, *The New York Philharmonic: A Radio and Television Tradition,* 1992.
*Prelude, Fugue and Riffs,* quarterly newsletter published by the Leonard Bernstein Society.

In a sense I was preparing this book for thirty years, since I first met Leonard Bernstein in a television studio in 1959. When I ran music programs for BBC Television in the 1960s, Bernstein's "Omnibus" programs were the inspiration for the music workshop essays we launched on the BBC's second network. (When I left the BBC in 1967 for a spell at London Weekend Television, my successor John Culshaw maintained the BBC connection.) With Schuyler Chapin as my executive producer I directed Amberson's early video projects, notably the 1970 Beethoven bicentennial program made in Vienna. It was while editing that documentary (during an August heat wave in New York) that Leonard Bernstein played the organ at my marriage. The doors were shut for half an hour before the ceremony while he practiced the march from *The Marriage of Figaro*.

I became Bernstein's principal film and television director for the twenty years of his association with Unitel, working for a month or more each season. I watched Bernstein's children grow up, played tennis with him at Fairfield and word games everywhere from Tanglewood to Tel Aviv, organized the seventieth birthday party in 1988 and his last televised European concert, in Prague, in June 1990.

It was while I was organizing the Carnegie Hall tribute in November 1990 that the idea of writing a portrait of Bernstein began to form. My first notion had been to write only about Bernstein's music, but it became clear that a substantial biographical study would help to set this remarkable, multifaceted career into some kind of framework. Music was his life, but his life was even more than his music. Next I had to persuade the Bernstein family and the trustees of the Springate Corporation, the nonprofit organization which administered Bernstein's correspondence and memorabilia, that I was an appropriate person to be entrusted with such a task. I'd made a number of autobiographical programs with Bernstein—*The Love of Three Orchestras, Teachers and Teaching,* an interview about his childhood—and I'd filmed most of his concert hall compositions, but I'd never written anything longer than a ten-thousand-word essay about provincial concert life in eighteenth-century France for the *Revue de Musicologie* back in 1956. The treatment I prepared nevertheless enabled me to leap the hurdle of family approval and soon afterward my enterprising agent, Joy Harris, of the Robert Lantz-Joy Harris Literary Agency, persuaded my esteemed publisher Stephen Rubin of Doubleday (himself a former music writer who reviewed Bernstein concerts in his day) that I was a gamble worth backing. Fortunately, publishers in other countries took a similar optimistic position.

When I shelved my television work and my responsibilities as a festival director at the Barbican Centre in London (my thanks to understanding colleagues) and set out on this new adventure, the very first persons I interviewed were two indomitable old ladies, Bernstein's mother, Jennie, then ninety-three, and his aunt Dorothy. Both have since passed away. Systematic research and interviewing began early in the summer of 1991. From September of that year, I moved forward simultaneously on research and writing decade by decade, completing my first draft in the summer of 1993. My handwritten manuscript and many revisions thereto were faithfully typed by Kelly Briney, aided (for the treatment and the opening chapters) by my daughter Clare Dibble. (Kelly also typed up transcripts of more than a hundred Oral History interviews carried out for the Bernstein Archive.)

My first editor at Doubleday, Sallye Leventhal, offered many useful suggestions before leaving the firm in 1992, opting for motherhood in preference to serving as midwife to my baby. I then had the good fortune to have the New York-based novelist Maggie Paley as my sympathetic but stern editor. Finally, Roger Scholl, an indefatigable editor with Doubleday, saw the slimmed-down manuscript to the press, simultaneously exercising his own razor-sharp vigilance in the name of clarity and narrative propulsion. I cannot thank these professionals too warmly, nor Andrew Clements, until 1993 editor of music books at Faber and Faber in London.

My gratitude goes also to the archivists of the institutions listed elsewhere in these back pages, in particular to Barbara Haws, the enthusiastic historian of the New York Philharmonic, whose splendid research facilities must be the envy of many other artistic organizations. I want also to record the unflagging assistance provided by Barbara Erde Mandell, who has faithfully assembled papers and memories pertaining to each year in the history of the Tanglewood (formerly Berkshire) Music Center. Her personal help in New York with such mundane tasks as the photocopying of paper mountains of documents and photographs has been greatly appreciated.

For any student of Leonard Bernstein's life the principal resource is the archive created in his lifetime by his assistant Helen Coates, a substantial section of which has since my day been relocated at the Library of Congress in Washington. Amongst its treasures (detailed elsewhere) the archive contains over 120 scrapbooks of press cuttings, transferred for longevity to microfilm, which chronicle in exhaustive detail Bernstein's public activities from his first piano recital in 1932 to his final concert in Tanglewood in 1990. To the archivist during my two and a half years of research, Karen Bernstein (Leonard Bernstein's niece), I offer undying appreciation, coupled with a deep obeisance to Helen Coates, who started it all. Alan Fluck generously allowed me to browse through her letters to him. David Diamond and Mildred Spiegel Zucker shared their important collections of Leonard Bernstein letters with me.

Next I turn to the other members of Leonard Bernstein's family: his brother Burton, his sister Shirley, and his three children, Jamie, Alexander and Nina. "Relatives are the biographer's natural enemies," Janet Malcolm suggested in a 1993 *New Yorker* piece about Sylvia Plath's biographers. Not this family, not this biographer, is my response. My contract with the trust representing the Bernstein family makes our legal relationship clear: "Springate shall not have any right to control the content of the book." But members of the family have read it in full or in part and they have all been generous with their time and exceptionally helpful, even concerning episodes which remain painful to remember many years after the event. Jamie Bernstein Thomas in particular has contributed many memories and photographs and provided relevant quotations from her diary, which is not housed in the archive.

I have had the benefit of advice from many other friends to whom I submitted the manuscript, in part or in full, for perusal. They include Phillip Allen, Schuyler Chapin, Betty Comden, Morris Golde, Adolph Green, Dan Gustin, Harry Kraut, Robbie Lantz, Barbara Mandell, Helen Morris, Edward Seckerson, Robert Skidelsky, David Thomas and Craig Urquhart. To Jack Gottlieb, Bernstein's assistant for three decades and author of the invaluable catalogue of his works, I have a particular obligation. A composer himself and Bernstein's assistant for close on thirty years, Jack has a unique overview of Bernstein's music. He read every page of my original manuscript, correcting facts, disputing opinions, sharing enthusiasms.

While writing the book I have lived in New York. I will never forget the unfailing amiability of other staff at the Amberson office over the past three years, notably Marie Carter, Amanda Jacobs, Laura Klein, Rania Bratberg, Rob Lind, Michael Palma, Jonathan Uman and Gregory Waugh. Thanks also to Michael Bronson and Elaine Warner, to Rob Radick and Harold Grabau at Doubleday, to Klaus Hallig and Horant Hohlfeld at ITTC-Unitel, to Steven Paul, Katherine Howard and Josephine Mangiaracina at Sony Music (formerly CBS Records) and to Alison Ames and Albert Imperato at Deutsche Grammophon in New York.

In conclusion I pay tribute to my wife's devotion in assembling the photographs which grace this book's individual chapters and the two sections of illustrations. Christina was herself a frequent photographer of Leonard Bernstein and a friend of his since 1970, when Oliver Smith and he first started calling her "Chrissie" during the rehearsal for the Verdi *Requiem* at St. Paul's Cathedral. In 1990, when he was guest of honor at Christina's birthday party in Vienna, he brought with him this acrostic sonnet as what turned out to be his last gift to her. The best way I can thank her now is to reproduce it in full.

*Carissima Chrissie: here's a sonnet*
*Halfly rhyming, tetrametric,*
*Roughly hewn, no gems upon it*
*I submit a loving attempt:*
*Short as I am in time, erratic,*
*Short of poetic breath (asthmatic)*
Ich wünsch' dir wohl und ganz von Herzen
*Every joy,* niente Schmerzen.

*Be happy in your birthday cheer—*
*Until at least the one next year.*
*Repeat for years and years thereafter*
*The miracle of inner laughter.*
*Oh yes, one other little thing:*
*No more Swedish blues: it's Spring!*

# PERMISSIONS

## QUOTATIONS FROM OTHER COPYRIGHTED MATERIAL

Lyric from an unpublished musical version of *The Skin of Our Teeth* (1964) by permission of Betty Comden and Adolph Green.

Lines from the poetry of Jelaluddin Rudi, translated by Coleman Barks, © Maypop, 196 Westview Drive, Athens, GA 30606.

Lines on Leonard Bernstein's 50th Birthday by Norman Rosten, by permission.

Letters from Marc Blitzstein printed by permission of the copyright owners Stephen E. Davis and Christopher Davis.

The extract from Benjamin Britten's letter to Leonard Bernstein is © 1994 the Trustees of the Britten-Pears Foundation and may not be further reproduced without written permission.

Letters from Dean Walter Hussey by permission of the Dean and Chapter of Chichester Cathedral.

Letters from Helen Coates by permission.

Letters from Tom Cothran by permission.

Excerpts from the Dramatists Guild Landmark Symposiums on *On the Town* (Summer 1981) and on *West Side Story* (Autumn 1985) reprinted with permission from the Dramatists Guild, Inc.

Business letters and telegrams printed courtesy of the Israel Philharmonic Orchestra.

Letters from Aaron Copland, Serge Koussevitzky and Dimitri Mitropoulos printed by permission.

Letter from Olivier Messiaen by permission of Mme. Messiaen.

Letter from Boris Pasternak printed with the kind permission of the Pasternak Estate, the Pasternak Trust, 20 Park Town, Oxford OX2 68H, England.

Reminiscences of Leonard Bernstein by kind permission of Mildred Spiegel Zucker.

Letter from Karlheinz Stockhausen by permission.

Letter from Alexis Weissenberg by permission.

The photographs of Leonard Bernstein with his son Alexander Bernstein and Felicia Bernstein with her daughter Jamie are copyright Richard Avedon.

Other photographs are credited on the page on which the photographs appear.

# INDEX